HANDICAPPED CHILDREN

STRATEGIES FOR IMPROVING SERVICES

By Garry D. Brewer
and James S. Kakalik

In the United States today, there are over 9 million persons under 21 years of age who are mentally or physically impaired enough to need special services. What exactly are their needs? How are these needs being met now? What can and should be done to meet these needs more effectively, either immediately or in the future?

This book, the outgrowth of a large-scale technical study undertaken by The Rand Corporation at the request of the U.S. Department of Health, Education, and Welfare, presents the first truly comprehensive answers to those questions. By avoiding esoteric language and by not presenting dense masses of data, the authors have made their findings accessible to everyone involved in serving handicapped children. Parents, teachers, doctors, administrators, social workers, volunteers, legislators, policy makers, and concerned citizens will all find valuable, practical information here.

Currently, over fifty federal and hundreds of state and local programs provide services for handicapped children. This book surveys the entire scene, giving credit where it is due and identifying the many inequities and problems that now exist. It discusses the complex new special education legislation in plain, understandable terms—what the legislation is, how it should be implemented, and what it is likely to cost.

The book's realistic recommendations include, among other changes, several that require only reallocation of existing resources, not new funding.

GARRY D. BREWER & JAMES S. KAKALIK

HANDICAPPED CHILDREN

Strategies for Improving Services

McGRAW-HILL BOOK COMPANY

New York   St. Louis   San Francisco   Auckland   Bogotá
Düsseldorf   Johannesburg   London   Madrid   Mexico
Montreal   New Delhi   Panama   Paris   São Paulo
Singapore   Sydney   Tokyo   Toronto

Library of Congress Cataloging in Publication Data

Brewer, Garry D
Handicapped children.

Based on a study conducted for the U.S. Dept. of
Health, Education, and Welfare.
Includes index.
1. Handicapped children—United States. 2. Handicapped
services—United States. I. Kakalik, James S.,
joint author. II. Rand Corporation. III. Title.
HV888.5.B73   362.3'0973   78-2490
ISBN 0-07-007680-4

1234567890   KPKP   7865432109

The editors for this book were Robert A. Rosenbaum and
Virginia Fechtmann Blair, the designer was Elliot Epstein, and
the production supervisor was Frank P. Bellantoni. It was set
in Optima Elegante by KBC/Rocappi.

Printed and bound by
The Kingsport Press.

CONTENTS

PREFACE

In the spring of 1972, at the invitation of the Assistant Secretary for Planning and Evaluation of the U.S. Department of Health, Education, and Welfare, The Rand Corporation undertook a comprehensive two-year, cross-agency evaluation of federal and state programs for assistance to handicapped children and youth. The study, performed under Contract No. HEW–OS–72–101, was directed by the authors of this book. Two lengthy reports were published: *Services for Handicapped Youth: A Program Overview,* R–1220–HEW, May 1973, and *Improving Services to Handicapped Children,* R–1420–HEW, May 1974. With support from The Rand Corporation, we have generalized and updated much of the material in those reports, and rewritten and greatly condensed it.

The HEW study, intended for use by the Assistant Secretary and other federal officials, state agencies, associations representing handicapped children, families with handicapped children, and the general public, pursued two broad purposes. The first was to describe the federal and state programs for service to mentally and physically handicapped children in the United States, to estimate the resources devoted to various classes of handicapped children, and to identify major problems with the service system. The second purpose was to help HEW officials improve the delivery of services by evaluating current policies and by suggesting improved policies and programs for the future. (Neither the earlier reports nor the views and conclusions in this book necessarily reflect the opinions or policies of HEW.)

Despite its immediate importance, the preparation of reports for a client as potentially influential as the Office of the Secretary of the Department of Health, Education, and Welfare is merely the first step in the long and demanding process of dissemination of what has been learned and implementation of policy recommendations for improving services to handicapped children. Much of the service system is not controlled by HEW, but is specified by law, controlled by state or local agencies, or driven by the private sector.

Our first report dealt with all types of handicapped children, but the second—at the client's request—focused on services provided to hearing and vision handicapped children. It was our firm belief that many, if not most, of the recommendations formulated in the second report either were directly applicable to the needs of all handicapped children or could be easily modified to serve these needs. Subsequent to our work for HEW, our research has centered on generalizing our earlier results.

In our earlier reports, we did not elaborate on the methodological innovations we made to carry out this project, because HEW was less concerned with the "how" of the study than with results and recommendations specific to HEW's responsibilities and capabilities. In this book, however, we emphasize our techniques and methods in the hope that others might be encouraged to adopt, partially incorporate, or otherwise learn from our experiences. For instance, the concept of adopting multiple perspectives of the policy setting is not well understood or represented in the existing literature and practice of public policy evaluation. One of several perspectives we took was that of the family with a handicapped child. We created a consumer's list of services a child might need that was basically independent of the existing, formal service program structure but against which we matched the formal structure to determine gaps, redundancies, and inconsistencies in service provision and policy. Another perspective we took was that of someone trying to plan and manage the entire service system. For instance, we developed several models of governmental roles for providing services, and similarly categorized functional mechanisms and rationales and governmental involvement in service delivery. We strove to clarify the goals and objectives of both service providers and service recipients—and we considered an array of modest and ambitious objectives, which ranged from limiting current government expenditures to developing the maximum potential of every handicapped person. We learned a great deal from assuming different points of view on the world of services for handicapped children, and share the lessons we learned with readers of this book.

The book is intended for a much wider audience than we have addressed heretofore, including practitioners at all levels of government, researchers, and those more specifically concerned with handicapped children and youth. We present our findings as matters of interest to the general public, both to call public attention to the needs of handicapped children, and to specify courses of action that the families and friends of handicapped children might take to improve matters. We do so because, at the time we filed our formal reports, it was clear that much work remained to be done to improve services—more work than any one agency of government could be expected to carry out. And although we expended considerable effort to assist HEW in carrying out specific recommendations, it was apparent that many other important avenues were open for disseminating the results of our study and improving the service system.

In the Epilogue we present our best recollections of "What Happened After the Research Reports Were Filed." In it we reconstruct the events that occurred after the formal project concluded, and share with the reader a few of our successes and more than a few of our frustrations in trying to get someone to read, consider, and act on the results of our research efforts to improve services for handicapped children.

ACKNOWLEDGMENTS

We gratefully acknowledge the cooperation and assistance of many people and organizations. Foremost are our coauthors on the original Rand reports on this study: Laurence A. Dougharty, Patricia D. Fleischauer, Samuel M. Genensky, and Linda M. Wallen. Each participated in the research and contributed one or two chapters to the original draft reports. Their contributions were invaluable. Willard I. Harriss performed excellent editorial surgery on the two original reports, cutting out large sections and creatively merging them into a single coherent and comprehensible draft manuscript which we could then proceed to generalize and update.

Without the initiative of the following people, the original study on which this book is based would not have been conducted: Laurence E. Lynn, Jr., former Assistant Secretary for Planning and Evaluation of the U.S. Department of Health, Education, and Welfare; Edwin W. Martin, Associate Commissioner of Education, Bureau of Education for the Handicapped (BEH); and P. Michael Timpane, former Director for Education and Social Services in the Office of the Assistant Secretary for Planning and Evaluation. Corinne H. Rieder and Suzanne H. Woolsey, as project monitors for HEW, offered valuable guidance and assistance in obtaining federal data. Robert B. Herman, as Program Planning, Policy and Coordination Officer of BEH, contributed significantly to the early structuring of the research. In addition, we received excellent cooperation in our interviews with more than a hundred federal officials responsible for the many programs providing services for handicapped youth.

We also received assistance indirectly from the Max C. Fleischmann Foundation, which funded a two-year Rand Corporation study of services for Nevadans who are mentally retarded or have mental health disorders. We were principal investigators in that study, which enabled us to learn a great deal about programs and services for mentally handicapped people.

In addition, The Rand Corporation sponsored the converting, updating, and generalizing of our reports into this book.

We are also very grateful for the cooperation, data, and suggestions for program improvement we received in our interviews with each agency serving handicapped youth in the states of Arkansas, California, Illinois, Massachusetts, and Wyoming. Over 160 agencies in the remaining states contributed significantly by completing our mail survey questionnaires.

Several dozen families with handicapped children, organizations representing the handicapped population, and private service agencies have contributed their experiences and views, thereby adding a vital component to this research.

Several other Rand colleagues and consultants also provided valuable assistance. Roger E. Levien was responsible for the initial discussions with HEW and provided useful guidance throughout. John A. Pincus, manager of Rand's Education and Human Resources program, oversaw and helped guide the progress of the research. David M. de Ferranti, Susan A. Haggart, George R. Hall, Carole N. Johnson, Konrad Kellen, Hubert L. Moshin, Linda L. Prusoff, Marjorie L. Rapp, Bernard Rostker, and Edward Woodward all made valuable contributions to the research on which this book is based. Ethel N. Bowers, Marjorie Roach, and Ethel Sniderman provided excellent secretarial assistance during the conduct of the research and the typing of the manuscript. Gene H. Fisher, Paul Y. Hammond, and Edward S. Quade reviewed and made helpful comments concerning drafts of our Rand reports.

Garry D. Brewer

James S. Kakalik

I

SERVING HANDICAPPED CHILDREN: A "CRISIS OF PERFORMANCE AND CONTROL"

Part I presents an overview of the population of handicapped children, current service policies, programs, and service problems, discusses goals and performance, and describes a way to map the system serving handicapped youth. Recommendations for service improvement are presented, and priorities on those recommended improvements are discussed.

The problems we identify are not peculiar to the system of services for handicapped children; many of them afflict the entire human service sector of our society. In the words of a former Secretary of the U.S. Department of Health, Education, and Welfare:

There is, in my opinion, a developing crisis—still largely hidden—facing the human service sector of our society, a crisis which may challenge the fundamental capability of our society to govern itself.

It is a crisis of performance—our institutions are failing to live up to our expectations.

It is a crisis of control—in many fundamental respects the human service system is developing beyond the scope of Executive control . . . or of Congressional control . . . or of consumer control . . . or of public control.

> —Elliot L. Richardson, "Responsibility and Responsiveness (II)," *A Report on the HEW Potential for the Seventies,* U.S. Department of Health, Education, and Welfare, January 18, 1973.

Chapter 1

DESCRIPTION OF THE STUDY

INTRODUCTION

More than 9 million mentally or physically handicapped children and youth in the United States aged 0 to 21 are functionally impaired enough to need services that "normal" youth do not require. We describe below all major current federal and state programs for those handicapped youth, detail the more than $7 billion spent on them annually, and identify major problems impeding the present service system. We also evaluate current policies and suggest alternative policies for improving the delivery of services to handicapped children.

Currently, there are over 50 different major federal programs and hundreds of state and local programs, which together expended at least $7 billion for handicapped youth in FY 1976, up from less than $5 billion in FY 1971. Without question, most of the programs are worthwhile and services are improving; but the service system faces major problems, and with better organization and support it could do far better. Many of the handicapped children are not receiving services, or are receiving the wrong or inadequate services. Extreme inequities prevail in the delivery of services; there are serious gaps in services offered; information is insufficient, control is inadequate, and most important, the resources devoted to these youths' needs are insufficient. In approximate terms, something like half of the services needed by handicapped youth aged 0 to 21 years were not being received in 1971. Our findings contain much new information, have surprised some of those responsible for the service system, and confirm what many have long suspected.

Our recommendations range from termination of some programs to consolidation and expansion of others, and from improvements in the management and structure of service programs to shifts in the mix of services provided. Chapter 2 summarizes our findings and recommendations and discusses priorities and tradeoffs in meeting service needs.

The majority of our recommendations, if adopted, would yield benefits that exceed their costs even if the benefits are measured in cold dollars-and-cents terms; and the benefits certainly exceed costs from the humanitarian viewpoint of the great enhancement in the quality of life of handicapped people.

The two most important points we want to convey are that:

- The unmet and inadequately met service needs of handicapped children are great.
- Certain critical services are neglected and grossly underdeveloped, such as prevention, identification of handicapped children, and the early direction of those children to services to alleviate the effects of the handicapping condition; these services should be expanded as soon as possible.

THE HANDICAPPED YOUTH POPULATION

Handicapped youth are defined here as young people from 0 to 21 years of age who are physically or mentally impaired to the degree that they need services not required by "normal" youth. This study deals with people who are generally called hearing or vision impaired, speech impaired, emotionally disturbed, mentally retarded, crippled or otherwise health impaired, learning disabled, and multiply handicapped. It excludes youth whose problems are attributable more to social conditions than to physical or mental disabilities, such as "disadvantaged" youth.

Estimates of the number of handicapped youth vary widely, depending on the definitions used, the data the estimator accepts as valid, and the type of service needed. Service agencies are not consistent in their definitions of handicaps and sometimes do not define them at all; moreover, their definitions are almost never clearly stated. Consequently, reliable data on the prevalence of handicapping conditions in youth generally are not available.

Table 1.1 presents the estimates used in this study, derived from a variety of sources. Details are presented in Chap. 5. Although we are not fully satisfied with the reliability of these estimates, we believe they represent the correct order of magnitude of the numbers of youth who require at least some special services.

The gravity of the problem is clear: Of the 83.8 million youth aged 0 to 21 in the United States in 1970, more than 9 million were handicapped.

Table 1.1
ESTIMATED NUMBER OF HANDICAPPED YOUTH AGED 0 TO 21 IN 1970

Type of Handicap	Number of Youth
Visual impairment	193,000
Hearing impairment	490,000
Speech impairment	2,200,000
Crippling or other health impairment	1,676,000
Mental retardation	2,800,000
Emotional disturbance	1,500,000
Learning disability	740,000
Multiply handicapped	(50,000)
Total	9,550,000[a]

SOURCE: See Chap. 5.

[a] Total has been adjusted to compensate for double counting of multihandicapped children.

SCOPE OF THE STUDY

The scope of this study is necessarily large and comprehensive, because the service needs, programs, and problems of serving handicapped youth are also large and comprehensive. This study is concerned with:

- All types of mentally and physically handicapped children and youth aged 0 to 21 years.
- All types of services needed by these handicapped youth, including: prevention of handicapping conditions, identification of handicaps, direction to appropriate service providers, counseling, medical treatment, education, special training (e.g., mobility or speech), vocational training, job placement, equipment, recreation and social activity, personal care, income maintenance, training of personnel to supply the services, construction of service facilities, and research.
- All government programs that provide the above services for handicapped youth.

The results of the study are both descriptive and prescriptive. We describe the existing service system and its problems, and present information on such factors as who is providing what services to whom, at what cost, by what methods, and with what effects. We analyze the service system in relation to the service needs of the target population of handicapped children it is intended to serve. We offer recommendations for alternative future policies for alleviating problems and improving the delivery of services and for improving the institutional structure and functioning of the service system.

Throughout this study, we frequently illustrate our points by citing data or cases having to do with hearing or vision impairment, mental retardation, or emotional disturbance. This seeming emphasis on certain types of handicaps owes largely to the original sponsors of our research, and does not imply that other handicaps are any less important. The U.S. Department of Health, Education, and Welfare (HEW) funded us to provide descriptive information for services to all types of handicapped youth; however, primarily because of limitations on HEW's available funds, we were requested to provide recommendations for improving services only to hearing and vision handicapped youth. HEW selected this emphasis not because these youth are more numerous than others (they are not) or more deserving of attention. Rather, HEW requested this emphasis because hearing and visually handicapped youth are more readily identified and classified; their handicaps can severely affect every aspect of their lives; a wide range of services and programs of varying effectiveness has been developed to serve them; data appear more readily available for these handicaps than for some others; and the assessment of program objectives, effectiveness, and benefits may be easier than it is for other handicapping conditions, such as emotional disturbance.

During the conduct of our study for HEW, however, we repeatedly perceived that most of our recommendations were applicable to the service system for all types of handicapped youth. This is true because most current service problems, programs, and policies apply to all types of handicapped children. Subsequent to our work for HEW, we conducted an intensive two-year analysis of services provided to people with mental health disorders or mental retardation in one state. (This work was funded by the Max C. Fleischmann Foundation.) That study further confirmed that the majority of our original recommendations to HEW were generalizable. Consequently, in preparing this book, we have generalized many of our recommendations, *when justified by the results of our analysis,* to apply to the handicapped youth population as a whole.

RESEARCH APPROACH

We have taken a *policy-analytic, comprehensive view of the system serving handicapped youth* to assess the relation of the system's constituent parts to its whole. Such a view is not commonly taken by any single government unit. Admittedly, because we have chosen to be comprehensive, we may very well err in reporting or failing to report important details about the system's various components. We are aware of the problem and have worked diligently to minimize it.

We have also taken *a comprehensive, target-population view of the service needs of handicapped youth* to assess the relationships among service needs and to judge how well the current and proposed service system policies are delivering and will deliver the mix of services needed. Again because such a view is not commonly taken by government units, it is often difficult to make informed tradeoffs among services.

In looking at the needs of handicapped youth, we found it essential to *disaggregate our analysis of the population by type and degree of handicap and by age,* since both needs and accessibility to the service system depend strongly on these factors.

A series of questions that we posed and attempted to answer illustrate various facets of the research:

- What are the *service needs* of each major subpopulation of handicapped youth?
- What are the characteristics of the *current service programs* for meeting those needs?
- What are the *problems* in the present mix of services delivered and in the present institutional structure of programs for meeting the needs?
- What are the *objectives* of various participants in the system?
- What *criteria* are useful in evaluating and comparing policy options?
- What *service-policy options* exist for alleviating problems and improving services?
- What are the *implications, in terms of costs and effects,* of meeting individual service needs and adopting program changes?
- What *federal and other government roles* might be adopted in implementing promising service-policy options?

With the data at hand, we can answer these questions only partially. The data often occur in inappropriate formats, are unavailable, are unreliable, or are not easily analyzed with conventional data processing techniques. It is sometimes not possible to conduct definitive analyses and make definitive recommendations based on available data. We discuss the problems created by data deficiencies and try scrupulously to identify assumptions, limitations, and the extent of data quality and reliability.

For an evaluation as complex as this, no single methodological technique will suffice; we use a *multimethod approach,* with the specific method used in any given case being dependent on one's question and the available data. The comprehensive, problem-centered approach we have taken is also beyond the skill and endurance of any one person; it calls for *interdisciplinary* research. Our research group included people trained in operations research, political science, business administration, economics, applied mathematics, and public administration. Consultative specialists, primarily educators and physicians, have been called upon as needed.

INFORMATION SOURCES

To gain an overview of the system of government-provided services flowing to handicapped youth, it was necessary to collect and analyze a great deal of information. The service system we found was fragmented, which implied that information about it would also be fragmented and that great effort would be required to collect and synthesize the data into a coherent picture.

Our information came from six basic sources: a survey questionnaire mailed to several major service agencies in each state; interviews with officials in 60 federal and state agencies; federal and state reports and unpublished data on specific programs; consultation with professional service personnel; literature in the field; and an interview survey of handicapped service recipients and their families.

GUIDE TO SUBSEQUENT CHAPTERS

This book is divided into three parts and an epilogue. Part I considers all services and gives an overview of our findings and recommendations. It describes the scope and approach of the study (Chap. 1), summarizes our findings and recommendations for improving services to handicapped children (Chap. 2), discusses service goals (Chap. 3), considers various governmental roles and rationales for adapting those roles in striving toward service goals (Chap. 4), and summarizes the definitions and prevalence data on the various types of handicapping conditions (Chap. 5).

Part II contains our detailed findings for individual types of services, along with the rationales for our recommendations for improvement. Nine major types of service needs are covered: prevention (Chap. 6), identification of handicapped children (Chap. 7), direction to appropriate service providers (Chap. 8), medical services (Chap. 9), education (Chap. 10), equipment (Chap. 11), mental health and mental retardation services (Chap. 12), vocational services (Chap. 13), and income maintenance (Chap. 14).

Part III (Chap. 15) summarizes the results of our survey of families with handicapped children.

The Epilogue describes several post-research initiatives undertaken to disseminate our results and discusses what has happened with regard to implementation of our recommended policy changes.

Chapter 2

SUMMARY AND RECOMMENDATIONS

SERVICE NEEDS OF HANDICAPPED CHILDREN

This book describes over 50 major federal programs[1] that provide services to handicapped youth. Most are within the Department of Health, Education, and Welfare, but agencies as dissimilar as the Library of Congress and the Department of Defense also have such programs. Many other programs are not discussed here because they involve low expenditures, affect few handicapped children, or deliver the same volume and type of service to children whether or not they are handicapped. The selection of the proper set of programs to include depends upon the policy decision addressed. Since this study does not focus on a single policy question, we include programs that are now, or seem likely to be, strongly relevant to policy alternatives for assisting handicapped youth. For ease of presentation of summary information, we chose to group the programs into areas by the five different types of agencies that administer them: health, education, mental health and mental retardation, vocational rehabilitation, and welfare.

This chapter summarizes the findings of our cross-agency evaluation of programs for the more than 9 million mentally and physically handicapped children in the United States who are functionally impaired enough to need services that "normal" children do not require.

To develop our recommendations for improving services, we began with the following basic service needs; a particular youth may

---

[1]We use the term "program" in a generic sense to describe a set of interrelated activities with some common unifying concept such as delivery of a common service (e.g., a rubella vaccination program); administration by a separate bureaucratic entity (e.g., the Vocational Rehabilitation program); or possession of a common goal (e.g., a research program for preventing birth defects).

require anywhere from one to all of them, depending on his or her age, type and degree of handicap, etiology, previous services received, and other factors:

- Prevention of handicapping conditions
- Identification of youth who are handicapped
- Direction to appropriate providers of needed services
- Medical treatment to correct, alleviate, or stabilize the handicap
- Equipment
- Special assistance in obtaining an education
- Psychological services and counseling of both the youth and his or her family
- Special training in skills such as mobility and speech
- Vocational training and job placement
- Recreation and social activity
- Transportation
- Personal care
- Income maintenance

This chapter summarizes government program expenditures for these service needs; discusses problems with those programs from the viewpoint of the service system as a whole and from the viewpoint of the handicapped population needing service; summarizes our findings and recommendations; and, in the last section, discusses priorities among our recommendations. Our detailed findings and supporting evidence are presented in Chaps. 6 to 15.

GOVERNMENT EXPENDITURES TO MEET SERVICE NEEDS

Figures 2.1 and 2.2 show, by type of agency, a breakdown of the estimated total annual government expenditures of $4.7 billion for services to handicapped youth. Amounts shown are all for a single fiscal year, 1970, 1971, or 1972, depending on the data available. Note that special education agency programs alone account for more than half the expenditures, followed by mental health and retardation, and welfare agency programs. The federal expenditures, estimated at $1.1 billion annually, represent only about $1 for every $3 from nonfederal sources; however, federal financial involvement varies considerably among programs. The largest program area for federal funds is special education, followed by welfare and health. Also note that nonfederal funding predominates in education and mental health and retardation, whereas federal funding predominates for health and vocational services. Welfare is about evenly divided between federal and nonfederal funding.

Figure 2.3 shows the distribution of funds among handicapping conditions. The mentally retarded are receiving over $2 billion annu-

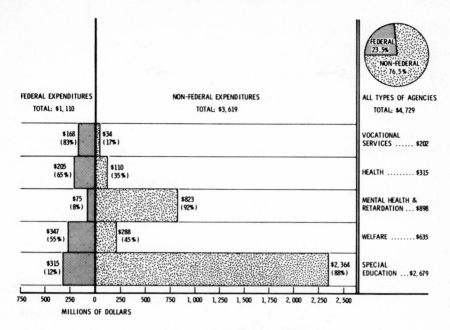

Fig. 2.1 Government expenditures for handicapped youth.

ally, by far the largest share (43 percent) going to any handicapped group. Much of this money is spent on special education ($1.2 billion) and residential institutions ($0.5 billion).

The emotionally disturbed receive the next largest share with 17 percent of all expenditures. The other handicaps (vision, hearing, speech impairments, crippling and other health impairments, and learning disabilities) each receive less than 13 percent of the total.

Total budgets, however, do not reveal much about the services a particular handicapped person receives. One way of examining per capita costs is to look at the average annual cost per handicapped youth aged 0 to 21 in the United States. As estimated earlier, this population is approximately 9.55 million, and hence the average annual government expenditure per handicapped youth is $495. But this does not mean that each youth receives $495 worth of government service; some obviously receive much more and many receive nothing. Fig. 2.4 shows the distribution of this average cost among service agencies by type of handicap.

Note that the expenditures per visually handicapped youth, at $793 annually, are higher than for any other handicap, and are followed closely by the expenditures per mentally retarded youth, at $726 annually. Expenditures per speech impaired youth are lowest, at $247 annually. On a per capita basis, no one type of handicap dominates expenditures, as the mentally retarded appear to do if one considers only the total expenditures without considering the relative sizes of the various segments of the handicapped population. Also note that expenditures in Fig. 2.4 are per handicapped youth, not per handicapped youth *served.* Funds expended per handicapped youth served are considerably higher, since many youth receive no service at all.

Since 1972 the most dramatic change undoubtedly has occurred in expenditures for special education; they have nearly doubled, from

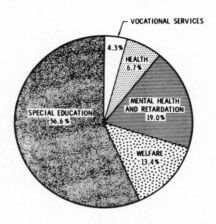

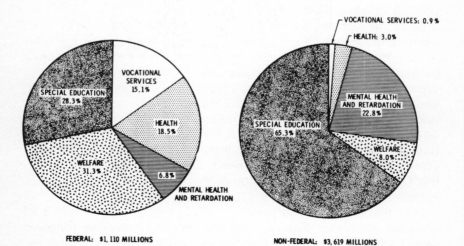

Fig. 2.2 Percentage of government expenditures for handicapped youth by type of agency.

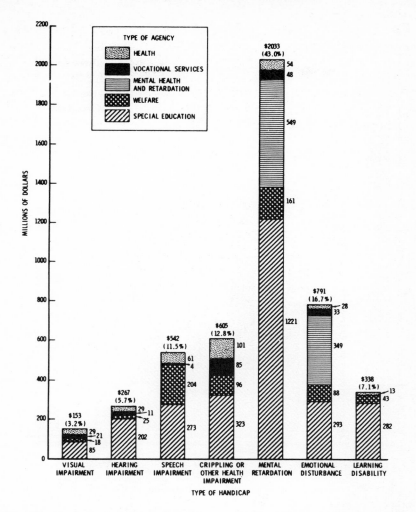

Fig. 2.3 Government expenditures by type of handicapped youth and type of agency.

$2.7 billion in FY 1971 to an estimated $4.7 billion in FY 1976. This implies that total annual government expenditures for all types of services grew to at least $7 billion in FY 1976.

PROBLEMS WITH THE PRESENT SERVICE SYSTEM

From the more than $7 billion expended by all levels of government annually, handicapped youth are receiving many needed and effective services. Humanitarian concerns are clearly evident in the expansion of programs and services in recent years. There is no question

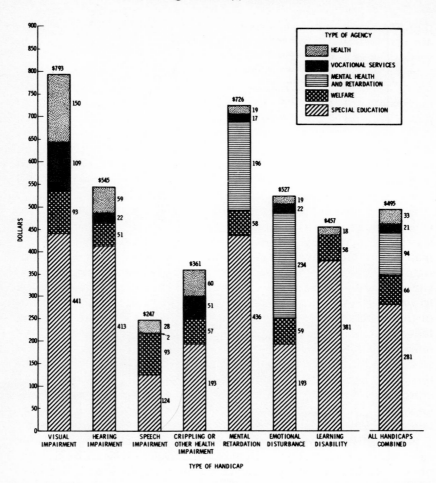

Fig. 2.4 Government expenditures per handicapped youth, by handicap and type of agency.

that these programs have very beneficial effects, but the service system still faces major problems.

Many children are still receiving no services, the wrong services, or inadequate services. The reason certainly is not a lack of programs. We have examined over 50 major federal programs, and the total number of programs rises into the hundreds when we add state, local, and private initiatives. Nor is the reason a lack of concern or effort on the part of service personnel, most of them dedicated people. Nor is it indifference in parents of the handicapped, many of whom make heroic efforts to secure needed services for their children. And no one can say that the quality of care that could be available is inferior, for the United States boasts some of the most advanced service techniques.

Perhaps it is easiest to blame inadequacy of funds, but that is too facile an answer. Insufficiency of resources is a major problem, but higher funding alone will not solve other basic problems that we find pervading nearly all aspects of the system: The complexity, lack of control, and disorganization of the system currently delivering services to handicapped youth defies efficient and effective operations; inequities and gaps in service delivery abound; and not enough information is available to manage the service system effectively and deliver the services needed.

To find out what the problems are, we interviewed officials responsible for major relevant federal programs and service agencies in five states; we tapped published material and agency data files; using a mail questionnaire we solicited views on problems from every major state agency serving handicapped youth in all 50 states; and we interviewed dozens of families with handicapped children. We also tried to view the system from a number of perspectives: that of the Office of the Secretary of Health, Education, and Welfare, of the state and federal operating agencies, and of the handicapped person and his family. We also looked at the service system disaggregated by type of service need, agency, type of handicap, severity of handicap, age of the youth, geographic location, program objectives, roles of the government, and the functional mechanism used to implement the program. Each view and disaggregation contributes different and important insights to the problems we discovered and tried to deal with.

In later chapters we summarize problems in meeting the needs for each type of service. In this section we survey and describe five generic types of problems we found: (1) inequity, (2) gaps in services, (3) insufficient information, (4) inadequate or deficient control, and (5) insufficient resources. Our discovery is not startling news; most of these problems are well known to professionals who work with handicapped persons. Nor are these problems unique to this system, but they are critical to it and demand full examination. To begin this task, we compiled most of the available data to document their existence and extent; to complete it, we analyze those and other data in later chapters to determine what might be done to resolve the problems.

Inequity

By any reasonable standard of fairness, a great deal of inequity prevails in the service system for handicapped youth. There is marked unevenness in accessibility to, and the level of, services. In each program area, large and often extreme variation occurs in per capita expenditures and services delivered across states and among handicaps. Eligibility rules differ sharply across the country. Within states, the service system short changes preschool children and rural youth.

One example of inequity is the favorable income tax treatment enjoyed by the legally blind but not other severely handicapped persons. For another, consider the cross-state variations in the vocational rehabilitation (VR) program: In 1970, the number of youth rehabilitated per 100,000 of the general population aged 14 to 21 ranged from less than 100 in some states to over 500 in others; and VR program expenditures per youth rehabilitated varied across the states from $800 to $4500. Next, consider special education programs: The estimated percentages of handicapped youth aged 5 to 17 being served in 1971 varied across the states from less than 20 percent to more than 90 percent; and the portion served varied among the types of handicaps from less than 25 percent of the hard of hearing or emotionally disturbed up to more than 75 percent of the speech impaired. Special education expenditures per youth served varied across the states for all handicaps from a minimum of $168 to a maximum of $2463. In other words, a child's chances of receiving special educational assistance, and the amount of that assistance, depend unmistakably on where his parents live. (To be fair, we should note that VR and special education are held up as examples here, not because they are worse than other programs, but because more data are available on them.)

Gaps in Services

Certain critical services are neglected and underdeveloped, particularly prevention, identification of those needing service, and direction or referral. It is especially tragic that prevention should be neglected, because for many types of disorders, high-quality preventive service is believed to completely forestall handicapping conditions in at least three-fourths of the cases of the particular type of disorder handled, and for some types of disorders, preventive service may forestall handicapping conditions in at least 99 percent of the cases. Yet of all government expenditures earmarked for handicapped children, only about 3 percent is spent on the vital services of prevention, identification, and direction. Only about 1 percent is targeted for prevention; 99 percent goes for service *after* the children are handicapped.

In many geographic areas, there are complete gaps in available services: no special education for partially sighted youth, for example, or no high-school-level special education for deaf youth in the entire region. To get the educational services needed, the whole family has to move, or the handicapped child must be sent away from home. Even if a full range of services is available, however, the absence of an effective local direction service may cause gaps in the mix of services a child needs and receives. Gaps may also result from the current institutional emphasis on single types of services. Many services, usually the "underdeveloped" ones, are not the prime responsibility of any one agency. Other gaps deprive particular age groups; for example, many preschool deaf children are not receiving services important for their language development, which may remain permanently impaired as a result. And gaps occur by state; for example, eligibility exclusions deny services to some types of children in one state, while a neighboring state imposes different exclusions in an identical type of program.

Insufficient Information

Efforts toward management improvement in most program areas are hampered by the total absence or severe lack of reliable data on program benefits and effectiveness. Usually, even if an agency collects management data, the data are limited to resource inputs and do not cover service outputs. (There are some notable exceptions; the VR program is a rare and commendable example.) There is also a problem of low-quality or nonexistent planning and evaluation, stemming partially from the root problem of poor or nonexistent data. In most programs, methods to obtain high-quality data on program effects have not been established. In some programs, *no one* really knows who is doing what for whom or with what effect. Looking across all programs at the federal level, for example, no one agency knows for sure how many handicapped children there are, what they need, what services are available, or how effective those services are.

Insufficient knowledge of who the handicapped children are is a common problem. Agencies generally do not serve a significant portion of the population in need, are generally unable to say how many unserved eligible handicapped youth there are and who they are, and with notable exceptions, generally make no major effort to find out.

Inadequate Control

There is no national policy for handicapped youth.

The service system is varied, fragmented, uncoordinated, and not particularly responsive to an individual's total needs. Partly because of the sheer number of institutions dispensing funds and services under many pieces of enabling legislation, no one person or group plans, monitors, or controls the handicapped service system in any comprehensive fashion. Policymaking, funding, and operating decisions are often made by entirely different groups of people, who have little or no data about program effectiveness to guide them; consequently, accountability is generally very weak.

Agencies responsible for a service sometimes do not even have control over the flow of funds for that service. For example, only about half of the federal funds for educational services for the handicapped flowed through the U.S. Bureau of Education for the Handicapped in 1971. Relations among agencies at the management level are often perfunctory at best, and their responsibilities sometimes overlap. For example, both the Crippled Children's Service and the Medicaid program fund medical services for financially needy handicapped youth, but they generally do so without benefit of effective coordination in the states; and the federal government provides substantial funds for preschool-age education through three separate programs (the preschool incentive grant portion of P.L. 94-142, the Early Childhood Education program, and the Headstart program).

The handicapped suffer the ill effects of lack of control most immediately in their dealings with direction or referral services, which are badly underdeveloped. One result is that children are sometimes placed in expensive special education programs—by default, as it were—because they were not directed to medical treatment or fitted with sensory aids at an early enough age so they could function adequately in a normal school setting. Without direction, handicapped children and their families are left to their own devices to thread their way through a bewildering maze of agencies, services, and programs. Parents go from one place to another seeking help for their children, and often unknowingly pass by needed services that are actually available.

Control over service providers also varies markedly. For example, there are great differences in state laws requiring or not requiring medical and audiological examinations before children are fitted with hearing aids. The result is that handicapped youth sometimes receive hearing aids when surgery may be far more effective.

Insufficient Resources

Providing full services to all handicapped children requires a financial commitment that our society has not been willing to make. A major fraction of all handicapped youth eligible for each type of needed service are not getting it. In approximate terms, something like half the services needed by handicapped youth aged 0 to 21 years were not being given in 1971. Insufficiency of resources still is the salient problem with today's handicapped youth service programs. Large unmet needs are common; for example, as noted in the federal "Education for All Handicapped Children Act of 1975":

> ... more than half of the handicapped children in the United States do not receive appropriate educational services. . . . One million of the handicapped children in the United States are excluded entirely from the public school system. . . .

Inadequacy of resources (dollars, personnel, and facilities) was the problem most often cited by the authors of previous studies and reports, by special commissions, by agency officials we interviewed, and in the responses to our mail survey. Still, resources are not the only problem; without major increases in current funding levels, a great deal could be done to improve the services themselves, the institutional structure, the matching of services with clients needing them, and data on the service programs.

Although the existing service system has many problems, many parts of it are excellent. The system as it is provides many needed services that greatly benefit the lives of handicapped children; but with better organization and support it could do far more.

SUMMARY OF RECOMMENDATIONS

We next summarize our recommendations for improving services for handicapped children. The recommendations are grouped by type of service need in the following order: prevention, identification, direction, medical services, education, equipment, vocational services, and income maintenance. We do not make recommendations in certain service areas, such as psychological services and recreational services, because we did not go into them deeply enough to justify our making recommendations.

Our detailed findings and recommendations, along with supporting rationales and evidence, are presented in the "Overview" and "Needed Improvements" sections of the relevant individual service chapters (Chaps. 6 to 14). To avoid redundancy and to equip readers with a brief summary of our recommendations, those details will not be repeated here. In the concluding section of this chapter, we discuss priorities among our recommendations.

Prevention

- Give a single federal agency prime responsibility and authority for prevention as a service.
- Revise and strengthen immunization programs, and provide funding for an open-ended period.

- Without deductibles, fully cover prenatal care, routine immunization services for children, examinations for youth up to age 21, and preventive medical treatment, in Medicaid and in any National Health Insurance program that may be established.
- Expand voluntary genetic testing and counseling services, accompanied by a high-risk registry for parents and potential parents of handicapped children.
- In the time period immediately following the birth of a child, provide family planning information to parents, and create a registry and follow-up for children born abnormal or at high risk of having some handicap.

Identification

- Evaluate and research various existing and proposed physical and mental impairment identification programs, for both school-age and preschool-age children, to learn details of their operation that contribute to effectiveness, and to assess their costs, benefits, and suitability for implementation throughout the country.
- When that evaluation is complete, institute a comprehensive mass screening program for physical and mental handicaps throughout the country, designed to reach every young school-age child. The screening programs we recommend would have two main components:
  — Parents of children beginning their first year of school, or entering a school for the first time, would be required as a condition for admission to present to the school either (1) the results of an approved health and developmental screening by a certified professional, or (2) a statement that the parents have decided not to have their child receive the screening services.
  — A screening program would be established in every local school district to identify all handicapped children who need special education and related services. This would reach all children of a specified age (perhaps 7, 8, or 9 years old) to identify any impairments that would not normally be detected by the preadmission health and developmental screening or that develop or become identifiable after the preschool screening.
- Expand and improve preschool identification programs:
  — Create new and improve existing high-risk registries, especially for children at risk in the 0 to 5 year age group not normally in contact with public service institutions. High-risk infants should be screened at birth, at least once between birth and age 5, and again upon entering school.
  — Sensitize people in contact with preschool children, such as parents, day care personnel, nursery school teachers, well-baby clinic personnel, social workers, pediatricians, and nurses, to the possible existence and effects of various phys-

ical and mental impairments, and inform them about simple tests for signs and symptoms of impairments.

— If detailed evaluation confirms their apparent desirability, give each child free checkups at various ages, with an age 2 medical checkup to include quality screening for various impairments. Reimbursement to pediatricians or other service personnel could be through National Health Insurance or some other program, and would follow their reporting the screening results to a health agency or other prescribed government agency.

• Create a follow-up component in every screening program, to see that the identified child receives diagnostic and other needed services.

• Adopt procedures (1) to assure that all Medicaid-eligible children and youth up to age 21 years receive early and periodic screening, unless such screening is formally refused, and (2) to assure that follow-up steps are taken to obtain diagnosis and treatment for those who need them.

• Collect all standards currently in operation for screening programs throughout the country, and summarize and analyze them with the end in view of developing a "model" code for screening.

• Encourage state certification and licensing boards to consider requiring general practitioners, family doctors, and pediatricians to demonstrate proficiency in the various screening and diagnostic procedures. Encourage such certification and licensing bodies to consider the need for improved and common standards for paraprofessionals and allied-skills professionals who conduct screening and diagnostic procedures, and for test instruments and procedures.

• Carefully design and establish a program requiring physicians and teachers to report all handicapping conditions to parents and the state Departments of Public Health and Education. We recognize the real possibility that privacy and service desirability norms may clash in this case, but we believe that careful design of the procedures ensuring legal and moral safeguards is possible and desirable.

Direction

• Undertake full-scale evaluations of the most promising existing partial models for providing direction service, to learn their strengths, weaknesses, and implications for an expanded, nationwide network of regional direction centers (RDCs) for handicapped children. Based on evaluation as noted above, conduct a thorough implementation analysis of five to ten pilot RDC projects in locations throughout the country. Such pilot operations should also be observed to facilitate subsequent rapid, efficient, and full-scale implementation.

• If the pilot projects confirm the soundness of the RDC concept, then incorporate improvements in the RDC design suggested by the pilot projects, and expand the effort as rapidly as possible into a nationwide network of Regional Direction Centers for Handicapped Youth.

Medical Services

- Conduct a full-scale evaluation of all Maternal and Child Health Service-supported programs with the end in view of concentrating future resources on the most critical needs and most effective programs. The remaining programs would be candidates for termination. Research studies on specific disorders should be transferred to the cognizant National Institute of Health.
- Pending resolution of difficulties experienced with the current Medicaid program, and pending the adoption of National Health Insurance or some other program to make high-quality, comprehensive medical care available to all youth, retain and expand the Crippled Children's Service (CCS) program.
- In the short run, pending the adoption of National Health Insurance or some other broad-based program, consider integrating CCS and Medicaid program operations in the states. The desirable comprehensive and financially open-ended nature of the Medicaid programs could benefit from some of the apparently better program administration features of CCS, which also provides for medical treatment for handicapped youth in financially needy families. A thorough evaluation of methods and effects of integration should precede implementation.
- Establish improved management procedures to yield much better Medicaid program management information; to cut delays; to improve the equity of eligibility standards; to ensure that mandatory provisions are implemented (e.g., screening); and to permit revision of medical payment schedules to reflect the realities of the medical marketplace.
- Establish National Health Insurance as a long-term solution. Make sure that it includes coverage for comprehensive medical services to all handicapped youth in need, and for the special needs of handicapped persons.

Special Education

- Increase the fraction of school-age handicapped youth receiving appropriate special educational assistance, and at the same time increase trained personnel and the comprehensiveness of special educational assistance available in each geographic area.
- Appropriate the substantial funds authorized by the federal "Education for All Handicapped Children Act of 1975" (P.L. 94-142).
- Expand the emphasis on the use of federal personnel preparation funds to include a major focus on inservice training for education of handicapped children, of regular educators, vocational

educators, and special educators, although appropriate preservice training of these three groups should not be slighted in the process.

- Improve evaluation and planning information on education of handicapped children.

Equipment

- Assure that all handicapped youth who can benefit from equipment have it.
- Coordinate and intensify efforts in support of research and development programs aimed at designing and testing new aids for the handicapped, and convert promising prototype devices into fully human-engineered production instruments.
- Assure that handicapped children are examined by a medical specialist before sensory aids are dispensed.

Vocational Services

- Expand the VR program to serve a larger fraction of the handicapped youth population.
- Establish clear guidelines on the categories of handicapped persons to be given priority in the receipt of VR services, and restructure existing incentives so that those categories are given priority, including abolition of the simplistic use and reporting of successful case closures.
- Conduct thorough evaluations of state programs that have significantly better than average gainful employment, occupation, and earnings results for handicapped youth, to determine desirable characteristics of those programs that may be exportable to other states.
- Increase the number and improve the geographic distribution of specialists in vocational services to specific types of handicapped persons.
- Increase the coordination between Vocational Education, Vocational Rehabilitation, and State Employment Service programs, and establish a mechanism for outreach to all handicapped youth in their latter school years, with follow-up after they leave school.
- Modify the State Employment Service (SES) program to provide more trained specialists in the placement of handicapped persons, and give those specialists a case load well below that of current SES personnel.

Income Maintenance

- Undertake research and evaluation to obtain much better planning information on the financial needs of handicapped persons.

- Limit direct cash transfers to handicapped youth and their families, in lieu of other mechanisms for making service available, to coverage of normal daily living expenses and to minor special service expenses.
- Either revise the income tax "extra personal exemption" program to include all severely handicapped persons with low incomes, not merely legally blind persons who file a tax return, or restructure the entire program concept.
- Exploit the opportunity provided by government contact with youth in families receiving income maintenance to identify handicapping conditions, to transfer youth from the Aid to Families with Dependent Children (AFDC) program to the higher-payment Supplemental Security Income (SSI) program, to diagnose and treat the youth under Medicaid or some other health program, and to direct the children to programs that can supply other needed services.

SETTING INTERSERVICE PRIORITIES

The answers to questions of who gets what, when and how, lie at the root of any government activity, form the basis for setting priorities among public service options, and determine the timing and means by which the various options are carried out.

To aid government officials in the formidable undertaking of answering these questions, several criteria have been developed that emphasize the salience of *resource consumption* at present and in the future, the *equity* of the distribution of current and recommended services, the *economic effects* of services to the handicapped, and the *quality of life* of handicapped people.

Priorities, Needs, and Objectives

To set priorities among services, one must consider how meeting the various needs of the handicapped population measures up against the criteria, and how well combinations of options further one's objectives. For instance, plausible objectives range all the way from developing the maximum potential of every handicapped person, to helping handicapped people be nondependent, to the control of long-run costs to the taxpayers incurred by serving the handicapped, and on down to the control or minimization of short-run costs. Other objectives exist or could be developed, but these are at least representative of some distinct and potentially conflicting ones.

To determine whether and to what extent these objectives have been met or could be achieved in the future, one needs measurement criteria such as those noted above. (Chapter 3 discusses objectives and criteria in detail.)

Setting priorities would be easy if a single goal were agreed upon by all and if progress toward the goal could be measured exclusively on one dimension for every recommendation. Unfortunately, that cannot be. Goals are numerous, and the costs and effects of recommendations for improving the service system must be measured along several dimensions. And with the scanty data available, it often is possible to know only the qualitative direction, not the quantitative amount, of the changes in the costs and effects on various dimensions. Consequently, setting priorities on recommendations such as ours necessarily must be a matter of judgment about the magnitude and nature of the costs and effects of the recommendations, and a matter of judgment about goals and tradeoffs among the types of costs and effects.

One can start from numerous points of departure. For example, if the assumed goal is to maximize the quality of life of the handicapped youth, one could develop a hierarchy of services and priorities that begin with prevention and progress as follows:

- Prevention
- Identification
- Direction
- Medical and Psychological Services
- Equipment
- Special Education
- Vocational Rehabilitation
- Income Maintenance and/or Personal Care

Prevention of the handicap not only would obviate the need for any other services, but would be a boon to the child. If prevention is unsuccessful, then the next most important services, from the child's standpoint, are early and correct identification and direction to prompt and proper medical or psychological services, because many potentially handicapping conditions can be cured or stabilized at a less debilitating level *if* they are detected early enough and treated correctly. If a handicapping condition occurs or persists nonetheless, the next most essential service is the provision of equipment, such as sensory aids, to minimize its effects. A significant number of impaired youth can *function* at reasonably high performance levels with appropriate aids, and consequently may need many other services less or not at all. But some fraction of the population will be functionally handicapped in spite of all efforts; achieving the best possible quality of life for these youth will hinge on the amount and quality of other supportive and remedial services available to them. Special education is clearly one of these, and logically precedes Vocational Rehabilitation—taken from the individual child's point of view as he or she matures—which in turn comes before the provision of income maintenance and personal care if VR is not feasible. Other services could be listed, but this represents a clear ordering of the minimum services intended to improve the person's well-being. The ordering in terms of quality of life can be summed up in two phases: Prevent the condition if at all possible; if it is not possible, then do what is needed to compensate for the handicap.

Another point of departure is society's perceived self-interests. For example, if our society is bent on maximizing the future economic benefits accruing to it, the list of priority services will be identical to that for improving the individual's quality of life, with the exception of income maintenance and personal care, which would not be high-priority services.

If society wishes to limit short-term costs but still achieve many long-term economic benefits, the basic list will be truncated even more by deleting relatively high-cost and low-benefit forms of each type of service.

When equity is the overriding criterion, a clear case can be made for maximizing effort in the identification and direction services. Fair and equitable treatment implies that people in similar circumstances with similar types or degrees of handicaps will be found and directed to appropriate and similar services. Whether and how fully those services are provided is related to other criteria and objectives, such as cost, quality of life, and economic benefits.

Priorities on Recommendations

Government officials' decisions on which of our recommendations to adopt, if any, will depend on the goals they choose and on the level of support the government is willing to provide.

To place our recommendations in perspective and to direct attention to some of the more general strategic possibilities, Table 2.1 outlines four scenarios of what government might do to improve services, depending on the level of effort it is willing to make: limited or no change in the level of effort, but significant management improvement; minimal change; modest change in the current effort, tied to major long-term benefits; and substantial increase in the level of effort to meet the full needs of handicapped children. We caution that each column heading applies to the aggregate of all recommendations in the column. Any single recommendation may require less than a modest effort. We also caution that cost does not necessarily reflect importance. A recommended step may be very inexpensive and yet be of highest priority in strategies other than the ones listed in the table.

Status Quo Level of Effort The status quo level of effort appeals especially to those interested in holding the line on, or even reducing, short-term expenditures. The wisdom of doing so, however, can be challenged on more than one basis, including both humanitarian grounds and society's long-term economic self-interest. For example, many disabling conditions are preventable, need not be handicapping if adequate and timely services are provided, and are, in terms of an individual's lifespan, considerably more expensive than short-term, often one-time, prevention service costs.

This is not to say that maintaining the status quo in terms of the level of fiscal effort also means maintaining the status quo in terms of management practices and institutional structures and functions. On the contrary, if one prefers to hold the line on costs, many changes can still be made in management practices and organizational structure that will enhance control over the system's operation and improve the quality and equity of services already provided. Even the quantity of services can be increased by improving efficiency and focusing on services that are cost-beneficial in both the short and long run. In fact, adopting all recommendations listed in the column labeled "Slight or No Change" in Table 2.1 should have these general effects. Included in this list are many information, management, and institutional improvements as well as a recommendation that could lead to trimming back one large program (Maternal and Child Health Service). Slight-change or no-cost recommendations are made for each of the eight major service needs. To begin to resolve most of the major problems, however, expenditures will have to expand.

Beginning to Face the Facts In this scenario, outlined in the "Minimal Increase" column in Table 2.1, it is assumed that at least a minimal increase in the level of effort is desired, in view of the large unmet needs of handicapped children and youth, inequities in service delivery, gaps in services, and lack of control of the service system. By "minimal" we mean no more than 5 percent above the current level of expenditures.

Identification and direction are vitally important, but underdeveloped, services that help resolve each of these problems. If one wanted to move slightly beyond the status quo level of effort, improving and creating identification and direction services according to the specific recommendations made for each would be a relatively

Table 2.1

SUMMARY OF RECOMMENDATIONS BY ALTERNATIVE DESIRED CHANGES IN LEVEL OF EFFORT

Service Need	Recommendations by Alternative Desired Changes in Level of Effort			
	Slight or No Change	Minimal Increase	Modest Increase	Substantial Increase
Prevention	Give a single agency prime responsibility for prevention.		Revise and strengthen immunization programs.	
			Cover prevention services (without deductible) under Medicaid and proposed National Health Insurance.	
			Expand voluntary genetic testing and counseling, accompanied by a high-risk registry.	
			Following a birth, provide family planning information, accompanied by a high-risk registry and follow-up.	
Identification	Increase program evaluation and applications research to discover suitability for widespread implementation.	Improve and expand preschool identification programs.		
	Require various types of service personnel to report handicaps.	Implement screening programs to reach every young school-age child.		
		Create a follow-up component in every identification program.		

	Develop a "model code" for screening. Encourage proficiency tests and certification standards for screening personnel.	Ensure that all Medicaid-eligible children are screened.	
Direction	Evaluate and pilot test Regional Direction Centers for Handicapped Youth.	After pilot testing, if desirable, create a national network of Regional Direction Centers.	
Medical treatment	Evaluate Maternal and Child Health Service programs; consolidate resources on a few programs, and terminate others. Consider consolidation of Medicaid and Crippled Children's Service programs. Improve Medicaid program operations.	Increase resources available to Crippled Children's Service program in the short term. Develop and implement a National Health Insurance program covering all handicapped youth, with special provisions for their needs.	
Special education	Improve evaluation and planning information.	Expand in-service training in education of handicapped children for regular, vocational, and special education teachers.	Increase the percentage of handicapped youth served; increase the number of specially trained teachers; increase the comprehensiveness of types of special education

Table 2.1

SUMMARY OF RECOMMENDATIONS BY ALTERNATIVE DESIRED CHANGES IN LEVEL OF EFFORT *(continued)*

Service Need	Recommendations by Alternative Desired Changes in Level of Effort			
	Slight or No Change	*Minimal Increase*	*Modest Increase*	*Substantial Increase*
				available in each geographic area. Appropriate funds authorized by the federal "Education For All Handicapped Children Act of 1975."
Equipment	Narrow the gap between research and application of equipment. Require medical exam prior to receipt of certain sensory aids.		Assure that all handicapped youth receive needed equipment.	
Vocational services	Fully implement Vocational Rehabilitation service priorities; adjust incentives and reporting. Increase program evaluation to discover suitability for widespread implementation. Coordinate VR, Voc. Educ., Spec. Educ., and State Employment Service Activities.		Expand the Vocation Rehabilitation program. Modify the State Employment Service Program to provide more trained specialists and lower caseloads.	

Income maintenance	Improve evaluation and planning information. Provide direct cash transfers to needy families for coverage of normal daily living expenses; use other mechanisms to provide other services.	Insure that all Aid to Families with Dependent Children (AFDC) child-recipients receive screening and treatment under Medicaid, and direction to other services.	Either revise the extra personal income tax exemption program for the legally blind to include all severely handicapped persons, or restructure the entire program concept. Transfer handicapped AFDC child-recipients to the Supplementary Security Income program.
Multiservice	Adopt all "Slight or No Change" in desired level of effort recommendations in each service need area.	Adopt all "Slight or No Change" and "Minimal Increase" in desired level of effort recommendations in each service need area.	Adopt all "Slight or No Change," "Minimal Increase," and "Modest Increase" in desired level of effort recommendations in each service need area.

inexpensive and, in our view, beneficial and efficient way to do it. All status quo "Slight or No Change" recommendations would also be implemented in this case.

"Facing the facts" implies that those responsible for the handicapped service system will make concerted efforts to find and then direct a maximum number of the handicapped to the services they require. The current level of government effort for other services could be maintained by setting priorities on who gets those services, and giving the others needed information so they can seek services privately. For those concerned with short-term economizing, this scenario should not be too hard to accept; identification and direction are both relatively low-cost services that yield many benefits to the individual and to the system. In Chap. 7 we present arguments why more identification is preferable to the status quo, even if the level of other services is not increased.

At some future time a fraction of currently unidentified and unserved handicapped youth will need other services. The exact fraction is not known, but it clearly will be higher than need be if they are not identified now, since improved early identification, direction, prevention, and treatment could eliminate or alleviate many handicapping conditions. Adequate identification and direction cannot spring into being overnight, but neither will a surge in the demand for services confront society suddenly or uniformly for all kinds and degrees of handicaps. There will be time to move beyond simple fact-facing, and there will be visible clues to which way public and private service programs can head to begin filling the gaps in available services.

A Modest Proposal with Long-Term Benefits   A "Modest Increase" in the level of effort could logically begin with a full-scale attempt to prevent as many handicaps as possible; would include good-quality services for those that cannot be prevented, to cure or stabilize the threatening condition and reduce the total amount and degree of handicapping in the population; would include the provision of equipment to those needing and able to benefit from it; and would include the administration of Vocational Rehabilitation to minimize the economic disadvantage of the handicapped individual. Adoption of all the recommendations listed in the column labeled "Modest Increase" in Table 2.1 would require an increase in annual government expenditures on the order of 50 percent above FY 1976 levels. We are confident that this figure is roughly correct, but we forgo detailed cost analyses here because the actual amount will depend on how recommendations are implemented.

For a long time and in various ways, responsible officials have promised much in the way of serving handicapped citizens and in reducing their dependence on public support. Delivering on those promises will certainly cost something in the short run, but the long-term payoffs in human, societal, *and* economic terms for implementing the recommendations associated with prevention, medical treatment, equipment, and VR, have all been shown to be positive—distinctly so, in most cases. The "Slight or No Change" and the "Minimal Increase" levels-of-effort recommendations would also be adopted in this scenario.

One might argue that "income maintenance" is important and should not be overlooked since it is necessary for some persons. We agree, but stress the development of all other, logically prior, services capable of reducing the future need for welfare payments.

A special educator may find fault with this scenario, arguing that, "After all, special education is a vital element in preparing these children for life, they have a right to special education, and you have already told us that a large fraction of those needing special education are not getting it." We strongly agree, and we recommend that substantial increases in special education expenditures be given high priority, but we point out that in this scenario it is assumed that *government officials do not want to substantially increase the level of effort.* Our primary special education recommendation requires a substantial increase in level of effort and hence could not be implemented in this hypothetical case of a modest increase in level of effort. The central point in this scenario is not that officials should ignore special education or cut current levels of special education programs, but that they should concentrate on *expanding* other services that do not require the hypothetically unavailable substantial increase in the level of government effort. Again, we are describing only one strategy that might be adopted in setting priorities among our recommendations; we could also develop others.

Meeting All the Needs To implement all of our recommended changes, one might add to the three previous scenarios the substantial resources required to furnish good-quality special education to all handicapped children, and to guarantee income levels at or above subsistence, as outlined in the last column of Table 2.1. We assign high value to these recommendations, and have deferred them to this scenario only because of their high cost. To implement all of our recommendations, we estimate that total annual expenditures, by all levels of government combined, would have to be approximately double the FY 1976 expenditures for handicapped children.

Chapter 3

THE ISSUE OF GOALS AND SYSTEM PERFORMANCE

To understand a system's purpose, one needs to understand its operating goals.[1] Where is the system heading? To measure its performance, one needs criteria.[2] Has the system arrived where it was meant to go, and if not, how far off the mark is it?

As we surveyed the myriad goals and objectives of the present system serving handicapped youth, we were struck by their multiplicity, their vagueness, the contradictions between operational and stated goals, and the idealistic and absolute nature which made some of the stated goals somewhat less than useful in the practical selection and operation of programs.

To specify evaluation criteria for handicapped youth (or other) programs, one must consider the goals of the overall system of services from several points of view, including those of the *affected population,* those of *officials responsible for formulating and executing individual policies and programs,* and those of *society as a*

---

[1]Goals are categories of preferred events, whether events desired in themselves or events desired because they are instrumental; e.g., health is desired in itself and is preferred to illness, and productive employment is desired as an instrumental event and is preferred to mass unemployment. See Daniel Lerner and H. D. Lasswell (eds.), *The Policy Sciences,* Stanford University Press, Stanford, California, 1951, pp. 9–10.

[2]As defined here, value refers to the worth or utility of an event rather than to the measures or criteria on whose scale such valuation is made. Furthermore, values and criteria can be distinguished from norms, which are rules governing behavior. Once criteria are established, the valuation of events on those criteria provides the grounds for rejecting or accepting particular norms as undesirable or desirable. In practice the major point is that values influence decisions in the selection of possible goal events to be considered (a program's "menu" of potential goals), and in the preference ordering of these goals. See "Concept of Value," *International Encyclopedia of the Social Sciences,* Macmillan, The Free Press, New York, 1968; and K. E. Boulding, "The Ethics of Rational Choice," *Management Science,* Vol. 12, February 1966, pp. 161–169.

whole.[3] Multiple, conflicting points of view surely will exist. It is less obvious, but nonetheless important, that programmatic evaluations should be likewise based on multiple performance criteria.

GOALS AS A MULTIFACETED PROBLEM

Let us first consider goals of *the affected population.* From discussions we have had with handicapped people, we surmise that if they were to set program service goals, such goals would be of the "greatest good for the greatest number" nature and would include concepts such as:

- Assurance that the needs of all handicapped persons for services such as housing, medical care, and education are adequately met; and
- Assurance that each handicapped person has the opportunity to develop functional capability to the maximum potential consistent with his physical or mental impairment.

This position is mediated somewhat in actuality. The objective of some members of this class of individuals would not necessarily be for the government to meet every need and to develop every potential of each handicapped person, but rather that *somehow* those needs must be met and the potential realized. This mediation of goal can occur because many of the handicapped simultaneously want to be as self-sufficient and self-reliant as possible.[4] Attaining the greatest good for the greatest number *and* developing social and economic independence for each handicapped person are in this case complementary and supportive goals. In fact, these goals have only been attainable for selected individuals because serving all handicapped persons has required a financial commitment that our society in general has not been willing to make. Because of resource limitations, other less costly objectives must be considered. The goals of *officials responsible for formulating and executing individual policies and*

[3]For a discussion of ways in which goal values are determined and justified, see, for example, Abraham Kaplan, *American Ethics and Public Policy,* Oxford University Press, New York, 1963; see also C. E. Lindblom, "The Handling of Norms in Policy Analysis," in Abramovitz et al., *The Allocation of Economic Resources: Essays in Honor of Bernard Frances Haley,* Stanford University Press, Stanford, California, 1959, pp. 160–179.

[4]At the root of this discussion is a basic concern for the quality of life led by the handicapped person. For good introductions to the scientific problems associated with the concept, see N. C. Dalkey, Ralph Lewis, and David Snyder, *Measurement and Analysis of the Quality of Life,* The Rand Corporation, RM-6228-DOT, August 1970, pp. 1–40; and Angus Campbell, Philip E. Converse, and Willard L. Rogers, *The Quality of American Life: Perceptions, Evaluations, and Satisfactions,* Russell Sage Foundation, New York, 1976, Chaps. 2–4.

programs are reflected in the services offered within particular programs designed to implement broad policy pronouncements. For example, one purpose of the Federal Vocational Rehabilitation Act is ". . . assisting States in rehabilitating handicapped individuals so that they may prepare for and engage in gainful employment to the extent of their capabilities. . . ." Subsequent sections discuss how these broad types of statements have been translated into actions for each pertinent class of services currently delivered to the handicapped population. Generally, service program goals may be consistent with the goals of an *individual* handicapped person but typically do not promise to meet the needs and develop the potentials of *all* handicapped persons. Furthermore, the phrase "subject to budget constraints" is the key implicit or explicit qualification of nearly every service program objective. We consider this constraint directly for each class of service.

The goals of *society as a whole* are fundamentally a collective ethical problem and hence not easily determined. One might hazard a guess as to what they are by considering governmental actions over a whole range of programs for the handicapped. Congress, the Office of the President, and the Department of Health, Education, and Welfare have responsibilities so broad that all in a sense represent society's goals by the actions actually taken; but having made this global observation, the analyst does not have much solid information to guide his detailed evaluation efforts. Certainly these overall societal objectives share humanitarian aspects and resource constraints with the objectives of the handicapped population and with those providing individual service programs. But unique and conflicting aspects of the actual goals tend to predominate, thereby making the determination of society's valuation of goal events nearly impossible.

Tradeoffs of services across populations must be made, and the basis on which tradeoffs are made may take extreme forms:

- Restrict current public expenditures—which implies low emphasis on expensive services such as education.
- Minimize total expected public expenditures over the lifetime of the handicapped—which implies high emphasis on vocational rehabilitation and preventive services and considerably less emphasis on welfare.
- Emphasize services provided primarily to the severely handicapped and the poor—which implies a conscious discrimination against the mildly handicapped and the non-poor.
- Emphasize services for the mildly handicapped when doing so achieves greater effectiveness per dollar expended—which implies discrimination of another extreme.

• Increase the number of people served for a given fixed budget to increase equity—which can imply that those having relatively greater needs may not be served or a large number of people may be served at an ineffective level or quality.

Of course, the above are usually not objectives in themselves, but factors that may influence the objectives actually stated or used. Other extreme possibilities may be described to indicate the basic dilemma of trying to determine societal, aggregate objectives with respect to the overall handicapped population or to the individuals who constitute it. In addition, there is a serious problem with the relevant time frames and perspectives operating for various participants. "The person or group with a time orientation toward the present [e.g., politicians] will have difficulty in seeing the value of inoculations against disease, a future occurrence."[5] But, in contrast, the handicapped individual's orientation may span his lifetime.

To begin working our way out of this thicket, we have concentrated on the stated objectives of individuals responsible for formulating and executing specific policies and programs and, for our immediate purposes, this has meant considering the President's public statements on the matter and reviewing various Department of Health, Education, and Welfare positions and adopted policies.

FEDERAL GOALS

Accounting for public positions and related policies is an important activity, for as Geoffrey Vickers points out:

> When we open our eyes to the scene around us, we find goals already set. Policies are being implemented, institutions are in action with all the historical momentum of buildings and establishments. Men are in mid-career. Budgets, even budget headings, have acquired prescriptive rights . . .[6]

The basic thrust of many of these extant events may be summarized in current trends: to increase the comprehensiveness of federal activities to ensure integrated rather than fragmented service; to increase participation possibilities in formulating policies and programs; to improve accountability procedures; to be aware of unintended consequences of individual policies and programs; to improve the structuring and functioning of service-providing institutions; and to reduce personal dependency on the government at all levels.

[5]S. H. King, *Perceptions of Illness and Medical Practice,* Russell Sage Foundation, New York, 1962, p. 53.

[6]Sir Geoffrey Vickers, "Who Sets the Goals of Public Health?" *The Lancet,* Vol. 1, March 1958, pp. 599f.

In 1973, at the time our original study was being conducted, the concepts behind the trends were generally laid out in the President's message on human resources in terms of "Four Principles," which may be summarized as follows:[7]

- Increase individual freedom of choice through government initiatives to give individuals a better opportunity in life.
- Supply incentives and opportunities instead of providing services directly.
- "Rather than stifling initiatives by trying to direct everything from Washington, federal efforts should encourage state and local governments to make those decisions and supply those services for which their closeness to the people best qualifies them."
- Ensure strict fiscal responsibility to avoid inflation, recession, or tax increases.

While these are suitable general statements of objectives, they do not go far enough in their detail or extent of coverage to give more than global insights into how programs should be structured.

A key specific source of insights into the actual, operating federal goals is contained in Elliot L. Richardson's remarkable report, "Responsibility and Responsiveness (II)," *Report on the HEW Potential for the Seventies,* January 18, 1973. It is remarkable in the sense that operating goals are clearly and concisely articulated, as are the policy changes needed to attain these goals.

- *Increasing comprehensiveness:* "In planning and programming, our perspective must be comprehensive. . . . Integration must replace fragmentation." And, the scope of HEW must expand "in the conceptual direction of the President's proposed Department of Human Resources, a direction of still greater comprehensiveness." (p. 10)
- *Increasing participation:* ". . . The effective management of HEW is crucially dependent upon: . . . the processes which define the relationships among people—the means openly and equitably to ensure the orderly and timely participation in the decisionmaking process by all affected parties." (p. 13)
- *Increasing accountability:* Improving HEW management means establishing and improving "clear and fair accountability." (p. 13)
- *Increase awareness of (un)intended consequences:* One presumes that this refers to the sensing of externalities, both positive and negative—disseminating and promoting the former and redressing and eliminating the latter. Improving HEW manage-

[7]As reported in *Education Daily,* Vol. 6, No. 42, March 2, 1973, pp. 1–2.

ment means developing "informed and sensitive appreciation of the consequences of intended actions." (p. 13)

• *Institutional reform:* "Institutional reform can . . . contribute to the conservation of limited resources. It can seek to assure that the agencies, organizations, and skills that are capable of making some contribution to the protection and development of human resources are properly deployed." (p. 21)

• *Foster non-dependency:* "The non-dependency goal would suggest that our objectives should be: 1. To create preventive mechanisms which identify the likelihood of people sliding down the scale of personal freedom of choice and reliance on others, and which remove the dangers that threaten the status of those people. 2. To create the conditions necessary to achieve earning capacity, self-care, and personal freedom of choice. 3. To assist those who are not self-supporting to progress to the highest position on the scale that is within their capability. And 4. To ensure the adequacy of income and services, qualitatively as well as quantitatively, and the preservation of human dignity, for those who are unable to progress up the scale."[8]

Because the "non-dependency" rubric subsumes so many more specific goals, it is worth reflecting on what it might mean for policymaking, institutional structure, and service provision. Specifically, what does it imply for clarifying objectives sufficiently well that more pointed evaluations of effectiveness might be carried out?[9]

One way of translating the non-dependency concept into operational terms would be to list succinctly a broad range of objectives potentially implied or embedded in the concept. These might take the following form:

• Assurance that the needs of each handicapped person are met, and that each has the opportunity to develop to his maximum vocational and social potential.
• Effective provision of individual services that foster independence subject to budget constraints.

[8]Secretary of Health, Education, and Welfare, "Planning Guidance Memorandum—1972," February 15, 1972.

[9]An important issue associated with the concept of "non-dependency" centers on the immutable fact that a proportion of the handicapped will never achieve anything like "normal" levels of non-dependence, indeed the permanent dependence of the severely handicapped is not to be treated casually. Leslie Gardner has treated this matter forthrightly. "[In the case of the severely handicapped] why continue to press for independence: would it not be preferable to accept severe disability gracefully and to come to terms with the inferior status (by current standards) and to work toward(s) . . . 'planned dependence'? In short, should we not educate for independence—indeed for inferior status—although this is against the grain of present-day ideas of citizenship for all, with its emphasis on work for gain?" Leslie Gardner, "Planning for Planned Dependence?" *Special Education,* Vol. 58, March 1969, pp. 27–30, at p. 28.

- Effective provision of closely related "packages" of services that foster independence, also subject to budget constraints.
- Minimization of current direct costs of providing services, subject to service obligation constraints.
- Minimization of total costs of providing services over the entire lifetimes of members of the handicapped population, subject to service obligation constraints.

It is important to distinguish between the ideas of *equity* and *adequacy*. *Equity* refers to social choices that distribute service fairly to the population. Increasing equity with a fixed level of resources implies providing lower levels of service to greater numbers of the population. *Adequacy* refers to the availability of enough service to meet the need; i.e., what portion of those in need receive quality services?

If the main concern is equity of service delivery, this implies certain functional emphases in the areas of research, development, demonstrations, and experiments to improve knowledge and to increase productivity which, in turn, make services available to more individuals at less cost. It also implies that we must create more comprehensive, responsive, and reliable reporting and statistical systems and more geographically disaggregated services to ensure fair distribution. It also means that provisions for planning and managing the services must be improved.

If service delivery is considered inadequate, then the problem is in some ways harder. Its resolution implies that attention should be focused on research and development to create services and "solutions" where none presently exist, and it furthermore implies that the level of service resources must be increased.

Although the federal objectives in various service areas will be discussed in subsequent chapters, for illustration we present the 1977 version of the federal objectives with respect to education of handicapped children:[10]

(a) The U.S. Office of Education is committed to assuring equal educational oportunities for all handicapped children. The efforts of the Office of Education in meeting this commitment are coordinated through the Bureau of Education for the Handicapped.

(b) Education of handicapped children has been adopted by the U.S. Office of Education as one of its major priorities. The six objectives designed to implement this priority are:

(1) To assure that every handicapped child is receiving an appropriately designed education;

[10]*Code of Federal Regulations,* Title 45, Public Welfare, Part 121, Definitions; General Provisions, Section 121.3.

(2) To assist the States in providing appropriate educational services to the handicapped;

(3) To assure that every handicapped child who leaves school has had career educational training that is relevant to the job market, meaningful to his career aspirations, and realistic to his fullest potential;

(4) To assure that all handicapped children served in the schools have a trained teacher or other resource person competent in the skills required to aid the child in reaching his full potential; and

(5) To secure the enrollment of preschool aged handicapped children in Federal, State, and local educational and day care programs.

(6) To encourage additional educational programming for severely handicapped children to enable them to become as independent as possible, thereby reducing their requirements for institutional care, and providing opportunities for self-development.

Similarly, the "Education for All Handicapped Children Act of 1975" (P.L. 94-142), stated the intention or objective of Congress is "to assure that all handicapped children have available to them, within the time periods specified . . . , a free appropriate public education. . . ."

Note in particular the words "equal educational opportunities," "handicapped," and "appropriate" education in the above statements of objectives. These words are subject to widely varying interpretations, as are the regulations and legislative details that attempt to define them.

We note the "equal educational opportunity" for handicapped children does not mean either equal resources or equal objectives for both handicapped and nonhandicapped children. In general, the educational resources and goals established for each handicapped child will be different and will be based on the child's needs and potential. For example, the Council for Exceptional Children personnel have defined equal opportunity in terms of "equal access to differing resources for differing objectives."[11]

CONTRADICTIONS AND OTHER PROBLEMS

There are at least five stated or observable contradictions in the objectives of the system serving handicapped youth. In addition, there are several related, primarily technical problems that do not appear to be easily resolved but that impede the realization of most of these objectives.

[11]F. J. Weintraub and A. Abeson, "Appropriate Education for All Handicapped Children: A Growing Issue," *Syracuse Law Review,* Vol. 23, 1973, p. 1056.

There is no national policy for handicapped children and youth. A large portion of the operational problem apparently occurs because there are basic contradictions embedded in the objectives established for institutional elements comprising the service delivery system.

Very few service programs that benefit handicapped children and youth are the *primary* responsibility of an operational agency. Programs serving handicapped youth exist everywhere in the federal government, but with the notable exception of the Bureau of Education for the Handicapped, hardly anywhere are these programs the main order of business.

The objective of increased participation in decisionmaking in fact does not appear to be realized. Someone must select a single choice from the array of those presented for a policymaker's attention, and this process inevitably results in a forced choice when resources are limited but demands on the resources are not. Resource choices are always being made, but apparently the number of persons participating in the budget allocations has not increased.

There is a contradiction between the increasing insistence on individual freedom and the parallel trend toward ever more complex forms of social intervention.[12]

The objective of ensuring equality of opportunity does not seem to be realized with respect to the handicapped, any more than it does for other disadvantaged groups in our society.[13] The "Education for All Handicapped Children Act of 1975" and Section 504 of the "Rehabilitation Act of 1973" hold out new and great promises of equal opportunity, but neither has been fully implemented; in fact, *regulations* for Section 504 were not even approved until 1977, and then only after widespread and widely publicized pressure was applied by handicapped people.

CRITERIA FOR MEASURING PERFORMANCE

Multiple measures and criteria are required for assessing system performance and measuring policy outcomes. Considering the variety of possible program effects, one must also use multiple criteria to evaluate policy alternatives, since the choices are so complex that it is both

[12]This is a major theme in Gunnar Myrdal, *Beyond the Welfare State,* Yale University Press, New Haven, Connecticut, 1959, pp. 99–102. It is considered in some detail in Jerald Hage and Michael Aiken, "Relationship of Centralization to Other Structural Properties," *Administrative Science Quarterly,* Vol. 2, 1967, pp. 72–92.

[13]The matter is not novel and has in fact been the source of unending reports, studies, books, and entreaties. See D. C. Marsh, *The Future of the Welfare State,* Penguin, Baltimore, 1964, for an overall view; and see J. S. Coleman et al., *Equality of Educational Opportunity,* U.S. Department of Health, Education, and Welfare, Office of Education, 1966, for a more detailed and well known statement.

inappropriate and misleading to consolidate a set of criteria into one overall effectiveness measure. More important, we need basic information before we can start to use those multiple measures.[14]

Because we are dealing with a variety of service objectives, it is useful to consider one set of simple dimensions along which several of the stated objectives might be measured, all the while taking the information deficiency into account. We have developed four dimensions and have created criteria to measure programs on each of them: (1) effects on the quality of life of the individual handicapped person, (2) future economic effects, (3) current resource consumption, and (4) equity. These dimensions permit one to make comparative judgments from several viewpoints without getting bogged down in arguments over which objective is "best."[15] Besides, it is quite conceivable that several analysts using different objectives will arrive at much the same policy recommendation—the so-called "dominant choice." Our study presents data on a spectrum of criteria, and the reader may assign his own weights to each criterion to suit his own objectives.

At any rate, as can be seen by reading this book, it is unwise for anyone working with the existing severely deficient data to expect great precision. Often, about all one can say with any confidence is that such-and-such a policy option would result in "major quality-of-life improvement" or "very low current cost relative to future economic benefits." Nonetheless, that may be enough. A sound policy choice can often be made if such general statements are known to be valid in the large.

Objectives are hard matters to understand and resolve. At a minimum, one should be made aware of what it means to pursue each of the stated objectives to something like its logical conclusion before deciding definitely on a particular allocation of resources. It may very

[14]On the information deficiency problem, see E. B. Sheldon and W. E. Moore (eds.), *Indicators of Social Change: Concepts and Measurements,* Russell Sage Foundation, New York, 1968; Judith Innes de Neufville, *Social Indicators and Public Policy: Interactive Processes of Design and Application,* Elsevier, New York, 1975, Chaps. 1–3, 5; and Daniel Bell, "A Social Report in Practice," *The Public Interest,* No. 15, Spring 1969, pp. 98–105, where this essential statement concludes the paper: "The nation must decide which objectives should have the higher priorities, and choose the most efficient programs for attaining these objectives. Social reporting cannot make the hard choices the nation must make any easier, but ultimately it can help to ensure that they are not made in ignorance of the nation's needs." (p.105)

[15]Two standard works detail what is involved in this issue: S. B. Chase (ed.), *Problems in Public Expenditure Analysis,* The Brookings Institution, Washington, D.C., 1968; and Robert Dorfman (ed.), *Measuring Benefits of Government Investments,* The Brookings Institution, Washington, D.C., 1965.

well turn out that the objective may not be attainable or it may cost a great deal in terms of other, more feasible objectives forgone in the bargain.

The evaluation criteria we intend to use are designed to show major policy effects, yet they are small enough in number to be manageable. Specific criteria should permit comprehensive evaluation, yet be as measurable as possible on each of four objective dimensions, discussed below: *current resource consumption, equity, future economic effects, and effects on the individual handicapped person.* These basic types of criteria are used to assess the implications of alternative policies on the service system, the handicapped population, and the public in general. To compare the different effects of various services and policies, we tried to select criteria that can be used as common denominators. Because the needs and ability to benefit from services differ for various handicapped subpopulations, these criteria must be applied separately for each subpopulation and for each service whenever feasible. Subpopulations are defined by such factors as age, degree and type of handicap, socio-economic status, and geography. Typical questions that might be raised are: How successful are alternative policies for meeting the needs of the handicapped? How many resources do various policies consume?

These criteria will be refined and supplemented as necessary in later chapters. The lack of data is, as usual, the greatest deterrent to evaluating programs for handicapped youth; consequently, it may not always be possible to use the criteria exactly as presented here, and in such cases, we shall attempt to construct and use indirect or proxy measures.

Criteria of Current Resource Consumption Although resource consumption could be measured strictly in *dollar terms,* we also consider *facilities* and *personnel* because of their long lead times. In analyzing finances, we attempt to specify both total annual expenditures for a program and the cost-per-youth served. Disaggregation of data by service and subpopulation is important to understand whose resources are being tapped (e.g., federal, state, the handicapped person, and his family) to serve which segments of the handicapped population, and to be able to weigh service effects against costs.

Criteria of Equity To measure how "fairly" a service is distributed among various subpopulations and to measure unmet needs, we consider *whether and how much of a needed service* the individuals in each subpopulation receive. Because each individual's needs and abilities to benefit from each service differ, equity does not mean that equivalent amounts of each service are necessarily provided each individual. Rather, equity involves two types of criteria: the percentage of the subpopulation needing service that actually receives it; and the variance among subpopulations in the quantity of services received.

If satisfactory data are not available on service effectiveness, service quantity measures are sometimes used as proxies for the more desirable output measures. For example, the effectiveness of prevention programs is commonly assessed by counting the number of people immunized against a potentially handicapping disease.

Criteria of Economic Effects We consider three criteria of economic effects (of service provision) on both the individual and various governmental levels by asking questions such as the following whenever possible: What is the expected net change in the present value of *expenditures for all future government assistance* to the handicapped person throughout his lifetime? For income maintenance? For all other services? What is the expected net change in the present value of the handicapped person's *future earnings*? And what is the expected net change in the present value of *future taxes* to be paid over the handicapped person's lifetime?

Criteria of Effects on the Handicapped Person In addition to economic effects, other important humanitarian service benefits are considered. Services may influence characteristics of the handicapped population in the following ways, which translate into four types of criteria:

1. Number of persons with various degrees of ability.[16]
2. Number of persons with various degrees of personal nondependence:[17]
   a. Self-care
   b. Family care—care within family
   c. Community-based care—care provided by agencies such as foster homes or halfway houses
   d. Confined care—care in institutions such as hospitals or long-term nursing homes
3. Number of persons with various degrees of economic nondependence
   a. Earnings and property income, including private insurance, investments and pensions

[16]More detailed scales of functional ability will be used where appropriate and feasible.

[17]Scales of nondependence used are those specified in Secretary of Health, Education, and Welfare, *Planning Guidance Memorandum—1972,* February 15, 1972.

  b. Work-related transfer payments, including social insurance
  c. Income-conditioned transfer payments
4. Attitude of handicapped youths' families on their post-service overall quality of life:
  a. Harmful effect on quality of life
  b. No effect
  c. Slightly beneficial effect
  d. Beneficial effect
  e. Very beneficial effect

Viewing all criteria for a single policy provides a good overview of the costs and effects of that policy; looking at a single criterion for several alternative policies enables one to compare and contrast al-

Table 3.1
SINGLE SERVICE EVALUATION CRITERIA

Type of Assistance/Service	Criteria
Prevention of handicapping conditions	Number of persons per 100,000 population initially acquiring each type handicap as compared with a base year.
Identification	Percentage of the handicapped population individually identified by the service system.
Direction	Percentage of those identified who are receiving a preferred mix of services.
Medical or surgical treatment	Probability of various changes in degree of handicap.
Income maintenance	Percentage of handicapped whose family income is above each of a set of specified levels.
Education	Average levels of various types of achievement.
Specialized training	Percentage of trainees achieving various levels of functional ability (e.g., in mobility, speech, activities of daily living).
Vocational training	Percentage of trainees continuously employed for at least 30 days following completion of training.
Job placement	Percentage of unemployed handicapped persons successfully placed.

ternative policies by that one measure. In general, however, the policy that is best by one measure will not necessarily be best by another. This highlights a difficult methodological problem: How is one criterion weighed against another in arriving at recommendations? Multidimensional preference theory is insufficiently developed to provide a general solution; consequently, trade-offs among alternative policies on various criteria must be made on a case-by-case basis. Still, the normal process of making value judgments in decisionmaking is enhanced by making objectives, criteria, and trade-offs as explicit as possible rather than by ignoring or considering them only implicitly. Data on some of these criteria are highly subjective; however, our approach is to try to incorporate all important factors explicitly rather than to include only those for which quantitative measures are available.

Criteria Relevant to Only One Type of Service   Until now we have discussed criteria which can be appropriately used to evaluate a variety of services. Criteria in Table 3.1 are each relevant to only one type of service, and because they are, they do not permit comprehensive service evaluation and hence shall be used in a supplementary fashion. For each criterion presented in Table 3.1 it is implicit that whenever possible a comparison would be made between data for persons receiving a service and those not receiving it.

Chapter 4

MAPPING THE SERVICE SYSTEM: ROLE MODELS, FUNCTIONS, RATIONALES, AND THE POLICY PROCESS

INTRODUCTION

Before delving into specific programs, it is useful to take a general view of how various government roles can be defined, what functions government programs may serve, and the rationales usually advanced for alternative roles and functions. This permits better understanding of specific individual programs in the broader context of other existing programs and of possible alternatives to existing programs.

This section presents the intellectual "map" we devised to locate and describe large pieces of the service system. First, we define coarse-grained, low-resolution *role models* of the operational institutions and the respective roles they perform. Next, we describe *functional mechanisms* by which those key institutions help produce services. To provide a sense of why the system functions as it does, we postulate *rationales,* both implicit and explicit, being advanced to justify the selection of broad classes of functional activities constituting policies and programs. And, finally, we lay out key *processes* by which the system appears to operate and change by way of detailing a general sequence of events through which policies and programs are created, implemented, and eventually ended.

MODELS OF FEDERAL INSTITUTIONAL ROLES

Several separate institutional roles (models) for the federal government are discernible in programs, and while we would not claim that a given operating institution conforms exactly to any of the four models described for illustrative purposes here, describing the pure models helps to locate specific governmental institutions within the context of the larger system.

There are essentially four dimensions for defining government roles: operations, policy and program control, dollars, and innovation/stimulation. Each dimension is a metric indicative of the degree and type of responsibility and authority vested in and exercised by any given government institution. The dimensions may be illustrated by posing the following operational questions:

- *Operations:* Is the government agency or institution directly providing services? Is it the delivery point for the affected population?
- *Policy and Program Control:* Is the agency mainly responsible for developing and monitoring policies and programs designed to produce specified services? Policy formulation and program regulation and evaluation are key examples.
- *Dollars:* Is the agency a primary source of funds supporting a given service or collection of services? Does it have the power to change the amount of those funds?
- *Innovation/Stimulation:* Is the agency primarily responsible for creating new ideas, programs, and policies and for encouraging operational agencies to adopt practices and procedures reflecting these ideas? Research, development, demonstrations, and so-called "social experiments" are all illustrative activities.

Each dimension will become clearer as we characterize our four illustrative role models. Specific, illustrative role models can be constructed by taking combinations of the above dimensions one or more at a time—for example, a "regulatory model" might involve policy control and innovation/stimulation but not direct operation or funding of service.

Model I: Direct Operation

If a single institution (or collection of institutions all related to the same service area, e.g., federal regional special education programs for the deaf-blind) is the primary locus for dollar support, policy and program formulation and monitoring, service delivery, and new developments, then that one institution or cluster of related institutions is playing a comprehensive role which we term "Direct Operation," because it is the direct service delivery that distinguishes this model from the following ones. The primary idea is that all responsibility and authority are concentrated in one or a few institutional entities. National defense is one such substantive area; the Bureau of Indian Affairs' responsibility for care and support of the Indian population is another; and certain selected aspects of federal participation in special education and Social Security activities provide yet other, more narrowly focused instances.

Given the size of the country's population, the diversity of its needs, and the complexity of programs that have sprung up to satisfy those needs, there is increasing awareness that universal rules and the Direct Operation modus operandi by the federal government may do more harm than good in some program areas.

> The detailed administrative approach does not work for clear enough reasons—which start with the impossibility of writing detailed rules to fit every case, and end with the lack of highly trained people to administer every case, assuming that an administrative solution is possible.[1]

The issue seems to boil down to the simple question, "Is it a good thing for the federal government to take on the direct responsibility for a certain service to a subpopulation?" If one is not convinced that the program will run better when Washington runs it, then there is a need to examine alternative structural models.

Model II: Controllership

"Controllership" reduces the extent of operation (direct service provision) but retains the remaining three dimensions. In this model actual service provision is delegated or otherwise turned over to some other institution (i.e., subordinate agencies such as the states and localities), but determinations of what to spend money on, how to spend it, and how to account for it are concentrated in one definable federal unit, as are the powers to allocate enabling resources and to create and generate new approaches to manage the underlying problems. The Community Mental Health Centers (CMHC) program of the National Institute of Mental Health has most characteristics of this model: it is funded primarily with federal dollars; Washington promulgates its policies and guidelines; innovations and new ideas evolve as a result of a separate provision of the basic federal legislation; the states and localities provide the services themselves. Many of the shortcomings, although not all, of the Controllership model are shared by the CMHC as well.

An inherent general problem with the Controllership model is its reliance on centralized financial coercion and its consequent lack of primary responsibility for those actually delivering the services. Often with this model, local officials, who know the most about the clients and their problems, are governed by complex and constricting rules handed down from higher bureaucratic levels. This causes clients who do not conform to the rules or qualify for fixed categories to be

---

[1]R. A. Levine, "Rethinking our Social Strategies," *Public Interest,* Winter 1968, pp. 88–92.

shunted from one agency to another; and it often makes it difficult to fix responsibility. Because those who actually deliver the services know they will be "blamed" for inadequate or poor performance, they tend to be unwilling to act in daring or creative ways.[2] It is a structural model and form of reasoning that has caused many organizations to limit themselves to administrative functions. When a hierarchy such as that implied in the Model II characterization prevails, leaders tend to impose what they consider rational guidelines on their subordinates without adequately considering the experiences of those who must put the policies into practice, a problem that is particularly severe, for example, in mental hospitals, but one that also exists in schools and in welfare systems.

Model III: Special Revenue Sharing, Plus

We use the term "special revenue sharing" in its *de facto* not its *de jure* sense.[3] Dimensions concentrated in this model are control over *broad* policy formulation and specific program evaluation and responsibility for innovative and stimulating activities. There is less direct service provision and drastic altering of the resource flow once initial allocations have been made. Broad policy formulation means that some intended recipient populations will be generally identified as likely beneficiaries of services, but more specific guidance than this will not be imposed; i.e., there will be no copious guidelines, no detailed programs, and minimal detailed concern for how resources actually are expended. The implicit idea is analogous to the private sector practice of leaving operational responsibility to a plant manager whose performance is then periodically assessed relative to other plant managers and to some absolute norm such as a profit and loss statement. The obvious difficulties involved in measuring public sector goods and services and the absence of any social balance sheet are not to be underestimated.[4]

[2]V. A. Thompson, *Modern Organizations,* Alfred A. Knopf, New York, 1965, pp. 129–137.

[3]While initiatives to institute special revenue sharing in the educational, health, and social service areas have all been proposed for adoption in recent years, *in fact* a number of identifiable programs already exist that share characteristics which could best be described as revenue sharing. See Richard P. Nathan et al., *Monitoring Revenue Sharing,* The Brookings Institution, Washington, D.C., 1975, for some interesting assessments of this experience.

[4]Worth Bateman, "Assessing Program Effectiveness," *Welfare in Review,* Vol. 6, January/February 1968, pp. 1–10; Peter Rossi, "Practice, Method, and Theory in Evaluating Social Action Programs," in J. L. Sundquist (ed.), *On Fighting Poverty: Perspectives from Experience,* Basic Books, New York, 1969, pp. 217–234; Jerome Rothenberg, *The Measurement of Social Welfare,* Prentice-Hall, Englewood Cliffs, New Jersey, 1961; and J. S. Wholey et al., *Federal Evaluation Policy: Analyzing the Effects of Public Programs,* The Brookings Institution, Washington, D.C., 1970.

We know that the federal government is able to collect taxes and to disburse funds efficiently; but some people are learning that it is less able to run large, detailed programs, or at least it does this far less effectively than taxing and disbursing. What this implies is an evolving trend to increased reliance on revenue sharing types of operations; however, it also implies that there are significant unrealized needs to account for performance.

The "Plus" in the Model III label elaborates the concept of "minimal federal concern" by developing the notion that the federal government has some right and obligation to evaluate the performance of service-providing agencies to whom it supplies special revenue sharing. Where are the significantly effective and ineffective programs, and what might be done to disseminate the former and discourage the latter? The underlying idea is to improve performance by rewarding those who are in fact "doing a good job," while not specifying in advance the mechanisms by which the job is to be done. When a "good job" is discovered, the reasons explaining why it is so are then liable to be scrutinized and perhaps implemented in other related areas where performance has not been as exemplary.[5]

To counter prevalent fears that transferred funds will be squandered in poorly conceived and operated state and local programs, the evaluation leverage must not be forgone and indeed must be developed to a considerably greater extent than it is at present. This requirement is primarily an informational one. Nowhere else in the system will there be an opportunity to view the "big" or comprehensive picture that is essential before one attempts to structure broad policies. This point is particularly true for our fourth or "Catalytic" model.

Model IV: Catalytic

Research, development, demonstration, and social experiments are all characteristics of the "Catalytic" model. Together they represent investments in intellectual and technical activities designed to improve services and productivity, thereby making scarce dollars go farther or be more effective; to improve operating systems, thereby en-

---

[5]This is not to say that special revenue sharing is a panacea, as evidenced in second thoughts that many state officials are having about the education aspect of it. See Karen De Witt, "Education Report/Handicapped Schoolchildren Enmeshed in Debate on Federal Role in Education," *National Journal,* February 10, 1973, pp. 199–205. The fundamental issue seems to be whether the amounts forthcoming from educational special revenue sharing will be adequate to meet the states' needs, particularly in light of recent court decisions interpreting the Constitution's 14th Amendment to include the right to an education for all handicapped children. The second thoughts are not about the structural concept of revenue sharing, per se, which has received many favorable initial reactions.

suring that services are delivered as efficiently as possible; and to improve the amount and quality of technical assistance available to those in the field, thereby improving the flow of newly created knowledge into the operating environment. The Catalytic model's primary medium of currency is information rather than money. If successfully carried out, its primary objective insures leadership based on the best knowledge about the system, its problems, and its possibilities. In operational terms, it aids in setting up program objectives and structure, rather than running the programs; it aids in selecting priorities based on solid analyses, rather than throwing money at problems; and it aids in controlling large, complex and hard-to-understand systems, rather than observing them as they plunge along out of control.

While the total Department of Health, Education, and Welfare budget is absolutely quite large, there is in fact very little discretionary or "controllable" latitude in it. Cash transfer programs, such as Medicaid and payment of Social Security benefits, are essentially open-ended; i.e., the dollar outflow cannot be reduced short of redefining eligible populations or, in the case of Medicaid, narrowing the range of coverage.[6] Because discretionary funds are limited, there is consequently a rather severe problem of allocating scarce resources and a need to create alternative bases to maintain power. In this case the new base is information. It is in part because of these demands that we observe considerable interest in the development of the Catalytic model on the part of certain Department of Health, Education, and Welfare officials.[7]

In his thoughtful discourse, *The Step to Man,* John Radar Platt has struck the key conceptual features of the Catalytic model in terms of organizations yet to be developed and functions yet to be performed.[8]

> But we have no . . . organizations that spend all of their time searching deliberately for new inventions and combinations for the solution of social problems. There is no General Electric, no national laboratory, with full-time research and development teams assigned to come up with ingenious ideas of improved social organization

[6]I. J. Lewis, "Government Investment in Health Care," *Scientific American,* Vol. 224, April 1971.

[7]The Bureau of Education for the Handicapped has adopted a "Catalytic" posture in recent years, and its efforts bear careful examination.

[8]J. R. Platt, *The Step to Man,* John Wiley, New York, 1966, pp. 132–133. Platt, in his capacity in the Mental Health Research Institute at the University of Michigan, has thought hard and well about many of the problems of large uncontrolled social systems and what might be done about them.

and communication and interaction. . . . The main reason why our solution of social problems lags so far behind our magnificent technology today may be that we have not yet organized the same deliberate search for ideas to deal with them. . . . Yet "social inventions" are possible, as we have seen, just as possible as technological ones, and might be searched for in the same way.

These abstractions will be illustrated concretely and, by doing so later, the possibilities of the Catalytic model will become clearer.

Mental retardation, which will be discussed later, is a pervasive and expensive handicapping condition in this country. One of the saddest facts about mental retardation is that many cases could be prevented or averted if present knowledge could be applied more widely. Unfortunately, this knowledge has not yet produced much practical "fallout" for the bulk of the present and future mentally retarded population. For example, we know how to recognize the chromosomal flaw that is responsible for mongolism (Down's Syndrome) and several other genetically related causes of retardation; we can, with amniocentesis, diagnose the problem in utero. But this knowledge, and the genetic counseling implied by its application, is not widely recognized and practiced. The Catalytic model would attend to this and many other mismatches of knowledge and practice as a first order of business, turning them to the collective advantage.[9]

To illustrate these structural models we have alluded to some general functional mechanisms that might characterize each, but we have not done so systematically. Let us turn now to that task.

FUNCTIONAL MECHANISMS

The models just considered lack specific detail. In concentrating on broad structural characteristics, they provide one with an approximate "sense" of the extraordinarily complex system we are describing. Understandably, embedded in the concept of model type are some basic ideas about the functional mechanisms that are used to produce certain fundamental services. For example, the Direct Operation model, by directly providing services, purchases, demonstrations, and so forth, employs practically every functional mechanism available and sometimes monopolizes a production of specific types of services for selected consumer subsets of the population. To gain more than a summary understanding of the system, one must be willing to go to a more finely resolved map to observe more system-

[9]See Peter Drucker, *The Age of Discontinuity,* Harper & Row, New York, 1969, especially Chap. 10, "The Sickness of Government," for some pertinent comments on this general issue.

atically and in greater detail these functional mechanisms, the services they produce or provide, and the rationales generally used to justify both mechanisms and services. The key point is that the models of federal roles represent only a coarse, general approximation of the system's actual detail and complexity. Better understanding demands finer resolution.

The general functional mechanisms with which federal agencies and programs in this system help produce a range of definable services or products include (1) the direct provision of services, (2) the purchase of services through funding of state or local government institutions, (3) the regulation of those providing services, (4) the investment in manpower and facilities that in time contributes to an adequate supply of services, and (5) the search for and dissemination of information both about the system, its problems, and its participants and about improved ways to provide services. After discussing the characteristic functions, we shall consider some rationales commonly employed to justify them.

These five mechanisms produce a variety of specific services that are the system's "products" as seen primarily from the perspective of the "consumer"—the handicapped child and his family.

Of the five functional mechanisms, the direct provision of services and the purchase of services through state and local government institutions, are plainly dominant in terms of federal dollars expended on them, their impact on the affected population, or any other suitable measures; however, the importance of the remaining mechanisms is not to be discounted, particularly since several of them appear to be underdeveloped and may represent strategic, exploitable opportunities.

Direct Provision of Services

Prime examples of services provided directly by the federal government are the Social Security Disability Insurance program; the Supplemental Security Income program providing aid to the aged, blind, and disabled; Gallaudet College; the Kendall and Model Secondary Schools for the Deaf; the National Technical Institute for the Deaf; St. Elizabeths Hospital; and the Indian Health Program. In each of these an agency of the federal government, rather than an agency of state or local government, provides services directly.

Purchase of Services

Prevention, medical treatment, vocational training, job placement, and identification are examples of services purchased with federal dollars through state and local agencies that provide the services directly. In most cases federal funds are matched by state or local funds according to formulas accounting for demographic and income differentials between states and locales. Immunization is a clear example of the prevention service, and mass screening for a variety of handicapping disorders illustrates the identification service. An example that does not depend exclusively on federal dollars for medical treatment is the Crippled Children's Service program. Vocational preparation and job placement are given in assorted Vocational Rehabilitation and State Employment Service programs with federal funds. As noted previously, the Department of Health, Education, and Welfare, except for a relatively few discretionary dollars, has relatively little control over the spending of its budget. Generally it is the scarcer discretionary funds that flow through the purchase of service programs cited above.

Another example of service purchase, in this case primarily the income maintenance service, is the Aid to Families with Dependent Children program which relies heavily on federal funds but is operated through state and local agencies. This is part of the larger "uncontrollable" segment of the Health, Education, and Welfare budget and hence has profound consequences for the orderly and effective operation of the overall system.

An important point with respect to income maintenance in general is that it provides an indirect means for the government to purchase other types of services, with the discretion of what other services are purchased for the handicapped youth left to the recipient of the income maintenance funds. In actuality, income maintenance is an intermediate or instrumental service that is subsequently convertible into medical treatment, personal care, recreation, and any number of other ultimately consumable services. However, this mechanism has inherent serious system deficiencies. Questions such as, "How many of what kinds of services does the population actually use?" and "What do those services really cost?" have been rendered virtually unanswerable because of the method by which income maintenance is delivered.[10] Also, given the poor quality of publicly available information on who supplies what services at what cost, with what benefit, how can a handicapped youth's family intelligently decide what

---

[10]When, for example, we discuss "Title XIX children" in the "Medical Services" chapter, the operational result of the functional problem manifests itself in terms of not knowing (1) how many recipients are handicapped, (2) what the handicapping conditions are for those who are afflicted, (3) what the total amount and cost of all services received are, and (4) generally, how well the services received are "doing the job." Program planning and operational control under such a situation are extremely difficult. Thus this problem is not unique to income maintenance.

services to purchase? Income maintenance is a notably large example of a service *not* provided by agencies primarily concerned with handicapped children. Therefore eventual demand for specific handicap-related services is known less well than it could be; consequently, control over the supply of those services diminishes.

Regulation of Those Providing Services

Regulation involves three conceptually different but related clusters of mechanisms, which depend heavily on the collection and analyses of information about the system: licensing, certification, regulation, and auditing may be considered as one such cluster; program coordination activities, through all levels of government, may be taken as another; and rulings by the courts or specialized agencies is the third.

Licensing, Certification, Regulation, and Auditing   The licensing of individuals and facilities who provide services is a prime direct means by which governments ensure the delivery of products with minimal standard quality. Contributing to the overall effectiveness of service are state and local licensing of special schools and homes used by children in the special education and personal care services; Food and Drug Administration licensing of drugs used in the medical treatment service; and local and national peer review boards that license and certify individuals who provide specialized training and education services.

Certification is ordinarily carried out on behalf of the government by tested and qualified members of professional skill groups, e.g., medical certification boards, education certifying bodies, and so forth. For example, the National Bureau of Standards has recently expanded its activities into the area of sensory aids and some prosthetics, assessing and implicitly certifying the quality, utility, and general "worth" of most commercially available hearing aids.

Auditing, taken narrowly to mean fiscal accountability, is ordinarily done by private firms and individuals who have at some prior time been "certified" to carry out this responsibility. It is also done on a larger scale and with a broader intent by representatives of the U.S. General Accounting Office, and personnel within federal departments.

Licensing, certifying, regulating, and auditing, taken together, represent a "high-leverage," low-cost functional mechanism for influencing the system serving handicapped children and youth.

Program Coordination Activities   Such is not the case, however, for program coordination activities, and data and information management deficiencies are at the root of the problem. Poorly coordinated or uncoordinated service provision is a common theme running throughout our study on the system serving handicapped children and youth. The problem is chronic and stems from program fragmentation and from the lack of information (about all services, programs, and activities affecting the lives of the handicapped) organized in comparable accounting formats to allow comparisons at various levels of comprehensiveness and aggregation. One operational implication of this functional deficiency is captured by Michael Marge:

> But when such information is not available, it is hoped we will be forgiven when we turn, as did the soothsayers of old, to our crystal ball to foretell the future.[11]

The problem is recognized and potential solutions have been offered;[12] but the problem persists, has not been satisfactorily resolved and, as a result, the effectiveness of delivery for a number of our identified services is diminished.

Court Rulings Court rulings can also have great significance vis-à-vis the operation of programs for handicapped youth. For example, landmark court rulings in Pennsylvania and other states have been aimed at guaranteeing each handicapped youth the right to an education.

Investment in Manpower and Facilities

Investment contributes generally to the supply of services, such as those identified, in terms of increasing the available stock of qualified

[11]When the article was written from which this citation is taken, Michael Marge was the Director, Program Planning and Evaluation, Bureau of Education for the Handicapped, U.S. Office of Education. Michael Marge, "Planning and Evaluation for the Future," *Exceptional Children,* Vol. 34, March 1968, pp. 505–508, quote at p. 508.

[12]Among these solutions, Program Planning and Budgeting Systems (PPBS), Program Planning And Evaluation, and Management Information Systems often play a major role. See, for example, David Novick (ed.), *Program Budgeting,* Harvard University Press, Cambridge, Massachusetts, 1965; and F. J. Lyden and E. G. Miller (eds.), *Planning Programming Budgeting: A Systems Approach to Management,* Markham, Chicago, 1967, especially Part IV, pp. 163–262, for general comments on the first "solution"; Edward Suchman, "A Model for Research and Evaluation on Rehabilitation," in M. B. Sussman (ed.), *Sociology and Rehabilitation,* American Sociological Association, New York, 1966, pp. 52–70; and A. J. Kahn, *Studies in Social Planning and Policy,* Russell Sage Foundation, New York, 1969, for pertinent comments on the second. The area of management information systems has a large literature and the new Medicaid Management Information System and several other less comprehensive, more special purpose systems are embryonic efforts to coordinate activities at the DHEW level.

humans[13] and suitable facilities.[14] Accounting for the impacts of these investments is hard enough,[15] and trying to link the investment function directly with each of our other handicapped youth services is even more challenging. Major service areas in which a more or less direct connection to investment may be made include medical treatment, education, special training, and sensory aids and other types of equipment. In the service area of education, for instance, there is a well developed empirically based literature that concentrates on that connection.[16] The impacts of investment on other services are not as well researched and known, although this represents one of those underdeveloped and exploitable areas we noted earlier.[17]

Research, Development, and the Dissemination of New Information

Another functional mechanism, whose impact on the specified services is hard to assess but which figures prominently as being both underdeveloped and exploitable, is the creation and dissemination of information. This is accomplished through research and development, but also includes the dissemination of information on the delivery of services to those operating direct service programs and to the consumer.

The connections between new knowledge and societal change have been considered extensively elsewhere,[18] and mainly involve the

[13]G. S. Becker, *Human Capital,* National Bureau of Economic Research, New York, 1964, pp. 94, 117–124, 128, is one standard source.

[14]Robert Dorfman (ed.), *Measuring Benefits of Government Investments,* The Brookings Institution, Washington, D.C., 1965, has a number of directly relevant pieces and is a generally good source of information on this matter.

[15]Bureau of the Budget, *Measuring Productivity of Federal Government Organizations,* 1964, gets at the issue of the assessment of investment in the public sector services. Political and economic discounting problems abound.

[16]Jerry Miner, *Social and Economic Factors in Spending for Public Education,* Syracuse University Press, Syracuse, New York, 1963; and O. A. Davis, "Empirical Evidence of Political Influence upon the Expenditure Policies of Public Schools," in Julius Margolis (ed.), *The Public Economy of Urban Communities,* Johns Hopkins University Press, Baltimore, 1965, are only two such examples.

[17]What are the operational time lags between periods at which investments in various human and supporting facilities are made and the points of return for each of the services of direct interest to those responsible for handicapped children? How do those time differentials compare with the time frames used by responsible authorities? What are the discount rates? These and a long list of related questions would serve as the basis of any concerted investigations in this area.

[18]J. L. Walker, "The Diffusion of Innovations Among the American States," *American Political Science Review,* Vol. 63, No. 3, September 1969, pp. 880–899; and G. D. Brewer, "On Innovation, Social Change and Reality," *Technological Forecasting and Social Change,* Vol. 5, No. 1, 1973.

development phases of the R&D function[19] and the coordinative aspects of the service regulation function.[20] James S. Coleman and several colleagues executed an empirical investigation of information brokerage done in the context of the creation and diffusion of new drugs among medical specialists.[21]

Unmet needs must be sensed, and that primarily concerns the information collection and processing aspect of the research and development and, to a lesser extent, the coordinative aspects of the regulative functions. However, that these functions are underdeveloped and have not worked well in the past is attested to by numerous demonstrations and disturbances carried out by those whose needs are apparently not being met.[22]

The research and development mechanism accounts for slightly more than 8 percent of the federal resources expended on handicapped children, and it operates both to create new knowledge, which in turn may improve individual services (either in their supply or their quality),[23] and to learn about the operation of the system, which may lead to improvements in system effectiveness and efficiency.[24] Besides activities recognized as research per se, this function includes demonstrations,[25] experiments,[26] and "seed money" projects

[19]Elihu Katz et al., "Traditions of Research in the Diffusion of Innovations," *American Sociological Review*, 1963, pp. 237–252; and G. F. Fairweather, *Methods for Experimental Social Innovation*, John Wiley, New York, 1968.

[20]Harold Wilensky, *Organizational Intelligence: Knowledge and Policy in Government and Industry*, Basic Books, New York, 1967.

[21]J. S. Coleman et al., "The Diffusion of an Innovation Among Physicians," *Sociometry*, Vol. 20, December 1957, pp. 253–270.

[22]Herbert Kaufman explains this well in his "Administrative Decentralization and Political Power," *Public Administration Review*, Vol. 29, January/February 1969, pp. 3–14. See also J. Q. Wilson, "The Strategy of Protest," *Journal of Conflict Resolution*, Vol. 3, September 1961, pp. 291–303, for a related assessment of the effectiveness with which unmet needs are being sensed and what specific groups of citizens are doing about it.

[23]For example, with respect to the income maintenance service, see L. L. Orr, R. G. Hollister, M. Lefcowitz, and K. Hester (eds.), *Income Maintenance: Interdisciplinary Approaches to Research*, Markham, Chicago, 1971.

[24]For the educational service, see C. H. Weiss (ed.), *Evaluation Action Programs*, Allyn and Bacon, Boston, 1972.

[25]J. W. Moss, "Research and Demonstrations," *Exceptional Children*, Vol. 34, March 1968, pp. 509–514, outlines the possibilities and experiences for special education services as applied directly to handicapped children.

[26]The commonly read piece by D. T. Campbell, "Reforms as Experiments," *American Psychologist*, Vol. 24, April 1969, pp. 409–429, provides a good general elaboration of the concept. A specific example of the connection between the R&D functional mechanism "experimentation" and the specific service "vocational training" is H. J. Meyer and E. F. Borgatta, *An Experiment in Mental Patient Rehabilitation*, Russell Sage Foundation, New York, 1959.

(i.e., one-time provision of resources designed to induce continuing support from third parties). Of these, experiments bear closer consideration.

Experiments allow different alternatives to be tested in a relative, realistic setting but at a small fraction of the cost of changing an entire ongoing system.[27] Such experiments have great obvious appeal, but only recently have any significant ones been carried out. Experimentation seems to have a strong "growth" potential within the relatively underdeveloped R&D functional mechanism.

RATIONALES

Rationales—the underlying reasons used to explain and justify the creation and existence of the functional mechanisms and the services they produce—vary widely in number, degree of ambiguity, and means of articulation. These rationales and their characteristic arguments may be simplified into at least five general types: (1) resource redistribution, (2) economies of scale, (3) internalization of externalities, (4) control and responsiveness, and (5) stimulation.

In short, we are considering questions such as, "What reasons are generally given for providing certain services in a location and not other services?" and "What general rationales are routinely employed to support what kinds of producing mechanisms?"

Redistribution of Resources

Redistributive rationales underlie many specific forms taken by the federal "purchase of service through state agencies." *Increasing the number and kinds of social goods and services,* such as those provided to handicapped children and youth, is tied by taxing strategies of several sorts to redistributive reasoning.[28] One rationale often offered for federal performance of a basic support function is that a major unmet need for services exists, and state and local agencies have not been able to fill that need because of budgetary problems under the current tax structure. Also encountered are appeals to increase the net productivity of human capital by upgrading the working potential of the handicapped segment of the population through

[27]For a discussion of the relationship between the experimentation mechanism and medical treatment, see W. J. Horvath, "The Systems Approach to the National Health Problem," *Management Science,* Vol. 12, 1966, pp. B391–B395.

[28]R. A. Musgrave, *The Theory of Public Finance,* McGraw-Hill, New York, 1958, Chap. 5, is a standard source detailing this point. For a more thorough technical discussion, see W. I. Gillespie, "Effect of Public Expenditures on the Distribution of Income," in R. A. Musgrave (ed.), *Essays in Fiscal Federalism,* The Brookings Institution, Washington, D.C., 1965.

direct purchases of services and investments in manpower and facilities.[29]

Redistributive rationales are intimately related to the functional mechanisms of purchase of services, regulation of service providers, and investment in means of producing services.

Rationales for redistributing resources reflect *equity or equality of opportunity* concerns in two distinct ways. For individuals, the concept of narrowing income differentials, as between the handicapped and the nonhandicapped, is easily understood and relates again mainly to purchase of service mechanisms. Redress of governmental-institutional service inequities, given variations in wealth among the states and localities, is a common rationalization for formulas in grant programs characteristic of many purchase of service mechanisms; e.g., grants are made to equalize educational opportunity, and in certain programs the funds for "designated poverty areas" are greater than for other areas. The net effect is redistributive, based on a consideration of equity or equality of opportunity.

Public services have long been determined and rationalized in terms of "effective demand," which roughly translates into the visible and pressing demands of those who know the service is available. As basically economic rationales have tended to give way to moral ones, however, the idea of unmet needs (resulting in lack of "equal opportunity") to justify redistributing resources has gained currency. The unmet needs concept may be defined in terms of *sensing* those who are in need and then *accommodating* those individuals, even if they cannot effectively demand service, both by broadening the scope and improving the quality of services provided them. Accommodating unmet needs is an underlying rationale used in many purchases of service arrangements and is basically redistributive in nature. Whereas effective demand was measurable in principle, unmet needs are far less so, with the result that assessing performance in satisfying unmet needs is extremely difficult.[30]

Financial assistance programs are related to the beneficiary's *needs* and *resources;* benefits flow rather automatically once categorical eligibility is established. Depending on who contributes and who receives benefits, income is redistributed. Wondering from whom to whom this income is in fact redistributed, Richard Musgrave has

[29]The relevant literature is voluminous but has been summarized in Jacob Mincer, "The Distribution of Labor Incomes: A Survey with Special Reference to the Human Capital Approach," *Journal of Economic Literature,* Vol. 8., March 1970, pp. 1–27.

[30]Points made in this discussion have been made well in another context by Heinz Eulau, "Skill Revolution and Consultative Commonwealth," *American Political Science Review,* Vol. 67, No. 1, March 1973, pp. 169–191, at p. 185.

speculated that it is from the middle and lower classes generally to special categories of the lower class.[31] Whatever the specific effect, financial assistance programs are rationalized primarily on redistributive grounds.

Economies of Scale

The basic idea of scale economies is related to the relative size of units of production, populations, and so forth.[32] While many explanations of scale economies have been advanced (including the use of nonhuman resources, the use of standardized parts, the breakdown of complex processes into simpler, repetitive ones, and the specialization of function), for our purposes we are primarily concerned with *specialization* considerations as viewed from two perspectives: those who provide services and those who receive them.

Providing specialized training for teachers of the small population of the deaf-blind is a manpower investment function rationalized by appeal to economy of scale arguments; it is just not as efficient nor as effective to train those few specialists in a variety of programs in every state as it is to bring them together in a very few locations for training. Constructing one or a few specialized schools for selected categories of very-low-incidence types of handicapped children could be likewise rationalized; e.g., it is more efficient and effective to have one school staffed by specially trained teachers providing college level education to the severely handicapped deaf than it is to provide facilities for them in every state. Having a few such facilities enhances regulation of service providers as well through mechanisms of licensure, certification, and the coordination of available resources. Critical masses of scarce and specialized research talent and equipment are also often assembled and supported with reference to scale economy arguments.

From the perspective of service recipients, this type of rationalization is often invoked in support of the direct provision of services—for instance, room and board expenses incurred by residents in a special school. The argument is that it would be more expensive to serve the individual as well in a nonspecialized setting. The argument depends on the presumption that the individual in question has

---

[31]R. A. Musgrave, *Fiscal Systems,* Yale University Press, New Haven, 1969, pp. 349–350.

[32]The literature on the general subject is extensive, but for two well known, representative efforts see, for example, W. Z. Hirsch, "Determination of Public Education Expenditures," *National Tax Journal,* Vol. 13, No. 1, March 1960; and H. E. Brazer, *City Expenditures in the United States,* National Bureau of Economic Research, New York, Occasional Paper #66, 1959.

some legitimate claim to be served at all, or as well.[33] Gallaudet College, the National Technical Institute for the Deaf, and other specialized schools for handicapped children are all to some degree rationalized on these grounds.

Internalization of Externalities

Many benefits of government programs are received beyond the bounds of political jurisdiction supporting the program. These benefits are termed "externalities" from the viewpoint of the supporting jurisdiction. When the externalities are large and of positive value, there typically will be less investment in the program than would be socially optimal. This can be made clear by way of example. Assume that a local school district could conduct a research program to develop a medical and educational treatment program for autistic children that was effective in bringing them back into normal society. If the cost were $1 million and there were very few autistic children in the local district, it is doubtful that the district would proceed with the program. The local benefits would be too small when compared with the cost. If the program were expanded nationwide, however, the research and development costs of $1 million would be small compared with the potential nationwide benefits. If the federal government were to fund the research program, the externalities as viewed by the local district would be internalized as viewed from the national level, and the proper incentives would exist for reaching the socially optimum level of investment in the program. This same rationale is also used in urging federal government support of training. Many states are hesitant to invest heavily in training professional personnel (e.g., physicians and lawyers) who then often migrate to another state. Again externalities exist that can be internalized by broadening the political jurisdiction from the local or state level to the federal level.

Control and Responsiveness

Arguments related to control and responsiveness rationales revolve around (1) the maintenance of standards of service quality, (2) fair

[33]However, counter-rationalizations are invoked in support of moves to reduce or do away with provision of service in the form of specialized schools. The argument in this case sometimes takes on the following form: Specialized schools are too expensive for the numbers they serve and hence should be abolished. Questioned implicitly in the process is the legitimacy of claimant demands for specialized services. Another major argument advanced against special schools for some types of children is that the children should be served in the least restrictive, most normal environment that is appropriate—that is, integration with non-handicapped children has effects that cannot be obtained in special schools.

provision of services, (3) the appropriate level of governmental responsibility associated with the production of services, and (4) accountability for use of funds.[34]

Quality control arguments are frequently offered in support of regulatory functions. Such arguments take the following representative form: It is the job of the federal government, and specifically the Food and Drug Administration, to ensure uniform minimal quality of some class of pharmaceuticals as a means of protecting the health and safety of all citizens; or the National Bureau of Standards must assess the relative performance characteristics of sensory aids. Often appeals to quality and uniformity of standards are offered in support of manpower and facilities investments as well. And, finally, the promulgation of guidelines is often couched in quality maintenance language.

Minorities and other special interest groups have long realized that their demands are more responsively met at some levels of government than at others, and hence a number of functions related to those demands are supported by responsiveness rationales. Perhaps the group needing services can exert pressure more effectively at the federal level than it can at the state or local level. These groups may represent small minorities at the lower levels of government, but through organization they may become a powerful lobby at the federal level. Handicapped persons and military veterans are examples of groups that may have more power at the federal level than at the local level because of powerful national organizations.

A variant of this responsiveness theme, and one that is more implicit than explicit, concerns the relative "visibility" of the service budget and the related *political* externalities it may create. Suppose that a particular service, such as comprehensive recreation programs for the mentally retarded, were proposed in the budget of some locality. As compared to the total budget, this proposed program may be a large enough proportion to gain visibility and hence be subject to extraordinary political scrutiny. Why should a local politician run the risk of paying a political cost for his promotion of such a program when he has little likelihood of reaping commensurate benefits—i.e., increased or at least undiminished political support? On the other hand, taken as a proportion of the total federal budget for the mentally retarded or, better still, for all the handicapped, the aggregate of all such recreation programs would probably be small enough that it

---

[34]Elliot L. Richardson, "Responsibility and Responsiveness (II)," *A Report on the HEW Potential for the Seventies,* HEW, Washington, D.C., January 18, 1973, Parts I and II are precisely on target.

would not attain "visibility," and hence would have a greater probability of being accommodated. The illustration is not as far fetched as it initially appears, and it goes part of the way toward answering our opening question about why some services are produced in certain places, while others are not.

Debates about the appropriate level of responsibility to conduct or produce a variety of services take a number of characteristic forms, many of which are essentially concerned with control and responsiveness. For instance, one such form might be as follows: It is the responsibility of the federal government to train doctors, researchers, or whomever, and to conduct research and development; if the federal government does not do it, then it will not get done in adequate quantity. Or this alternative form is sometimes encountered: It is the responsibility of the federal government to respond to those suffering from catastrophic problems, e.g., chronic renal failure and severe congenital heart disorder; if it does not respond, then no one will because the high cost per individual will result in lack of responsiveness by other levels of government. Counter-arguments exist, of course, and normally question either the premise which legitimates a claim to service or the one that sets the level at which the overall system should be responsive. Debate on decentralization-centralization is the standard medium for this latter issue.[35]

The accountability/control rationale for regulation is concerned with the responsibility of a government agency providing funds to oversee the use of those funds and establish accountability procedures to help assure the funds are spent effectively and as intended.

Innovation: Stimulation/Diffusion

This twofold rationale for providing seed money, initial construction and staffing funds, funding demonstration projects and disseminating information is basically that states and locales may desire to improve the service system but (1) because of lack of start-up funds or political inertia, they have difficulty in doing so, or (2) because of lack of available knowledge about improved ways of providing services, they cannot do so. The federal government may match state and local fiscal effort with federal grants. This lets the states buy more with their dollars and can increase the total amount spent on handicapped children. The federal government may also sponsor demonstration projects that permit state and local agencies to see a program in operation before deciding to fund it themselves. Demonstrations also

---

[35]Kaufman takes the matter up as does W. E. Moore, *The Professions: Roles and Rules,* Russell Sage Foundation, New York, 1970, pp. 167ff.

allow the federal government to pay initial investment costs; state and local governments then pay only annual operating costs. Demonstration projects thus lower both risk and cost to state and local governments of undertaking new projects. Theoretically, this leads to more state and local dollars flowing to services for handicapped children than there would be without the federal program.

Rationales, being as they are arguments or appeals to marshal support or to justify actions, take on numerous, seldom unambiguous, and often contradictory forms. For instance, every one of the control and responsiveness rationales commonly used could themselves be interpreted in terms of the rationales presented in earlier subsections. They are nevertheless commonly used, important, and must be taken systematically into account if our hopes are to comprehend a system as complex as that providing services to handicapped children and youth.

As with arguments pro and con for most policy issues, the strength of the individual argument usually varies on a continuum—e.g., the

Table 4.1
COMMON RATIONALES RELEVANT TO FUNCTIONAL MECHANISMS

Rationales	Direct Service Provision	Purchase of Services Through State and Local Agencies	Regulate Service Providers	Investment in Means of Producing Services	Research Development and Dissemination of Information
Redistribute resources					
Increase net productivity	M	M	M	M	L
Increase equity	M	H	H	H	L
Fill unmet needs, accommodation	L	H	H	H	L
Economies of scale/critical mass	H	—	L	H	H
Internalized externalities					
Total population benefits	L	L	—	H	H
Visibility	L	L	—	L	L
Control and responsiveness					
Quality control	—	—	H	L	—
Fair provision	L	M	M	M	L
Level of responsibility	L	—	M	M	H
Innovation: stimulation/diffusion	—	H	—	H	H

NOTE: Degree of relevance: H equals high, M equals medium, L equals low.

relative fiscal capacity of different levels of government varies continuously with time, and the timing and magnitude of the effects of a court order are not precisely known. In addition, the weight or value one assigns to various arguments depends on one's objectives. Consequently, one federal role or function may not be clearly preferable to another for all time and for all concerned parties. Table 4.1 summarizes the foregoing discussions. The table's basic message is that just as many or more rationales exist for regulation, investment, and research and development functional mechanisms (the relatively "underdeveloped" three) as exist for provision and purchase of services (the "well-developed" two).

THE POLICY PROCESS

A final way of visualizing the handicapped youth service system is to consider a general sequence of events through which its policies and programs flow from earliest initiation through ultimate termination.[36] This short subsection defines the policy process in a useful but not particularly novel way. It is included so that we may refer to steps in this process later when we describe current programs for handicapped youth, without having to stop there to define what we mean by the policy process. Describing parts of the service system in terms of this sequence of decisions has helped us understand the dynamics of the system and has contributed to suggestions for its improvement.[37]

Initiation/Invention

The earliest phase of the sequence begins when a given problem is initially sensed. Once a problem is recognized, many possible means to alleviate, mitigate, or resolve it may be explored. In this early creative phase, one comes to expect that numerous ill-resolved and inappropriate "solutions" will be advanced. Indeed, as much as casting about for answers, this phase concerns sharpened redefinition of the

[36]This process is not novel. It is basically the result of theoretical insights generated by H. D. Lasswell, most recently in his *A Pre-View of Policy Science,* Elsevier, New York, 1971, Chap. 5. Equivalent labels to those employed by Lasswell have been adopted for our more specific purposes. See also Garry D. Brewer, Ronald D. Brunner, and Harold D. Lasswell, "The Configurative Method," in Karl W. Deutsch (ed.), *Methods of Political Behavior Research: Handbook,* 1978, forthcoming.

[37]The process concept has been applied with some success in at least two specific instances to understand why large-scale and complex systems were not performing adequately. See Martin Shubik and G. D. Brewer, *Models, Simulations and Games: A Survey,* The Rand Corporation, R-1060-ARPA/RC, May 1972; and G. D. Brewer, *Politicians, Bureaucrats and the Consultant: A Critique of Urban Problem Solving,* Basic Books, New York, 1973.

problem. Invention refers to the fragile business of reconceptualizing a problem, laying out a range of possible solutions, and then beginning to locate potentially "best" choices within that range.

Estimation

Estimation concerns predetermining risks, costs, and benefits associated with each of the various policies or solutions that emerge from the initiation/invention phase. Calculation of the likelihoods that the various possible outcomes will occur is largely focused on empirical-scientific and projective issues, while the imputation of the desirability of those outcomes is more clearly biased toward normative concerns.[38] The objective of estimation is to narrow the range of plausible policy solutions, by excluding the unfeasible or the truly exploitive for instance, and to order remaining options according to well-defined scientific *and* normative criteria.[39] Resource analysis, Bayesian statistics, forecasting, model construction, and an assortment of other methodologies have evolved in response to the first requisite; market research, political opinion, and other survey techniques, benefit analyses, and rarely, *a priori* social-ethical assessment have been used for the second. An interesting combination of scientific and normative perspectives is inherent in efforts to conduct systematic social experiments, an activity held to be essential by, among others, Alice Rivlin. "[Social experimentation] must be an important federal activity, if we are to achieve breakthroughs in social service delivery."[40]

Selection

Ultimately, someone must select one or a few of the "invented" and "estimated" options, and that considerable task has traditionally been the responsibility and province of policymakers, however that role is characterized.[41] Narrowly circumscribed analysts seldom con-

[38]See Philip Morse and G. E. Kimball, *Methods of Operational Research,* John Wiley, New York, 1950, for a fuller explanation of these important differences. Frederick S. Hillier and Gerald J. Lieberman, *Operations Research,* Holden-Day, San Francisco, 1974 edition, is a good, representative technical source.

[39]A typical pitfall in the process is failure to examine a range of diverse interpretations, rationales, orderings, and calculations. This requirement is obvious, but in practice cannot be stressed enough.

[40]Alice Rivlin, *Systematic Thinking for Social Action,* The Brookings Institution, Washington, D.C., 1971, p. 120.

[41]Bernard Crick, *In Defense of Politics,* Penguin, Baltimore, 1964 (rev. ed.), captures the essence of selection. "So many problems are only resolvable politically that the politician has a special right to be defended against the pride of the engineer or the arrogance of the technologist. Let the cobbler stick to his last. We have a desperate need for good shoes—and too many bad dreams." (p. 110).

front the problem of striking a balance between the rational calculations done during the estimation phase and the multiple, changing, and conflicting goals operating throughout the entire sequence. It is a problem, among others, that is ultimately resolved by the politician, who

> ... has to balance the myriad forces as he sees best, and the citizens judge him only to a limited extent by his accordance with their preconceived ideas. Rather, a great political leader is judged like a great composer; one looks to see what he has created.[42]

And that brings us to implementation, the means for carrying out selected policies.

Implementation

Implementation refers to the execution of a selected option according to a plan. As witnessed by heightened interest and statements of concern about failures of public policy implementation,[43] however, it is a phase of the overall decision sequence that is little understood, not particularly appreciated, and not well developed, or as one distinguished group recently summarized it:

> We became increasingly bothered in the late 1960s by those aspects of the exercise of government authority bound up with implementation. Results achieved by the programs of that decade were widely recognized as inadequate. One clear source of failure emerged: political and bureaucratic aspects of the implementation process were, in great measure, left outside both the considerations of participants of government and the calculations of formal policy analysts who assisted them. Acting through governmental organizations existing in the midst of political cross-pressures is a necessary feature of modern public affairs. The art has been but little developed.[44]

It has become clear that to assess government performance, one must understand the implementation mechanisms operating to generate that performance, and one recommended approach has been to consider the incentive systems underlying individual, collective, and institutional behavior.[45] Improving governmental performance may de-

---

[42]W. A. Lewis, "Planning Public Expenditures," in M. F. Millikan (ed.), *National Economic Planning,* National Bureau of Economic Research, New York, 1967, pp. 201–227, quote at p. 207.

[43]Charles Schultze, *The Politics and Economics of Public Spending,* The Brookings Institution, Washington, D.C., 1968, pp. 104–105; and Eugene Bardach, *The Implementation Game,* The MIT Press, Cambridge, Massachusetts, 1977.

[44]The Research Seminar on Bureaucracy, Politics, and Policy, *A Report on Studies of Implementation in the Public Sector,* Harvard University, The John F. Kennedy School of Government, Cambridge, Massachusetts, March 1973, p. 1.

[45]J. S Berke and M. W. Kirst, *Federal Aid to Education: Who Benefits, Who Governs,* D. C. Heath, Lexington, Massachusetts, 1972.

pend on redesigning those underlying systems of incentives, if one concurs with Charles Schultze's observations:

> [The failure of federal programs is] positive failure—the failure to build into federal programs a positive set of incentives to channel the activities of decentralized administrators and program operators toward the program objectives.[46]

Evaluation

Initiation/invention and estimation are primarily forward-looking, anticipatory activities. Selection stresses the urgency of the present. Evaluation is backward-looking, concerned with inquiries about system performance and individual responsibility. Typical topics and questions that are reflected in the idea of evaluation include the following: What officials and what policies and programs were successful or unsuccessful? How can that performance be assessed and measured? Were any criteria established to make those measurements? Who did the assessment, and what were their purposes? To what ends was the valuation directed, and were they accomplished?

Evaluation is a necessary phase in the decision sequence, but the incidence of comprehensive and competent efforts in a wide variety of places is not great.[47] Institutionalization of evaluation can be either internalized (in-house) or externalized (such as by an auditing firm, a consultant, or an inspector general).[48] Evaluation is, or should be, a necessary input to the next and final phase of the decision sequence.

Termination

Termination refers to the adjustment of policies and programs that have become dysfunctional, redundant, outmoded, or unnecessary. From the conceptual and intellectual points of view, it is not a well-developed phase, but one whose importance in current affairs must not be underrated. How, for instance, can a policy be rationally adjusted or terminated without its having had a thorough evaluative assessment? Who will suffer from the termination? What provisions of redress have to be considered? What are the costs involved to the individuals affected by the termination? Can they be met from other sources? What might be learned in the termination process that will

[46]Schultze, op. cit.

[47]H. D. Lasswell, "Towards a Continuing Appraisal of the Impact of Law on Society," *Rutgers Law Review,* Vol. 21, No. 4, Summer 1967, pp. 645–677.

[48]The literature on the subject is not large, but it is growing rapidly. For an overview see F. G. Caro (ed.), *Readings in Evaluation Research,* Russell Sage Foundation, New York, 1971; and E. A. Suchman, *Evaluative Research,* Russell Sage Foundation, New York, 1967, Chaps. 1,2, 4–7, and 10.

inform the initiation and invention of new policies or programs in the same or related fields? The list of questions is long indeed,[49] but ignoring them or ignoring the fact that termination is linked intimately to the other steps in the decision sequence is both unnecessary and undesirable.

[49]The literature in this field is just developing. See the entire issue of the journal *Policy Sciences,* Vol. 7, No. 2, June 1976, which was devoted to this topic. See also, Garry D. Brewer, "Termination: Hard Questions—Harder Choices," *Public Administration Review,* No. 4, July/August 1978, for a more complete listing of the "hard questions," along with some of their more obvious and realistic implications. Herbert Kaufman, *Are Government Organizations Immortal?,* The Brookings Institution, Washington, D.C., 1976, asks perhaps the most pointed question in this regard.

Chapter 5

PREVALENCE ESTIMATES AND DEFINITIONS OF HANDICAPPING CONDITIONS

At the beginning of Chap. 1 we discussed the difficulties associated with prevalence estimates and definitions of handicapping conditions. This chapter discusses those difficulties in further detail, illustrates the varying prevalence estimates to be found in numerous sources, and gives our rationale for adopting the prevalence estimates used throughout this book.

DEFINITIONS

Recall that we broadly define handicapped youth as children and youth from 0 to 21 years of age who are mentally or physically impaired to the degree that they need services not required by "normal" youth. We make little effort here to find the "best" single specific definition of each handicapping condition, since we believe that the use of a single definition of a handicap to determine need for every type of service is inappropriate. From the standpoint of service policy, to establish eligibility for service the definition of a handicap should ideally be based on need or functional capability as well as ability to benefit from the service. Thus, the definition should depend on the type of service to be given. Operationally, this means that a set of definitions is needed for each type of handicap, not a single definition. A one-dimensional, purely binary definition—the child is either handicapped or he is not—is a blunt and inadequate instrument for measuring a handicapped child's service needs. Finally, the severity of effect of an impairment partly depends on the person's environment as a child and later as an adult. That is, the need for services depends on functional abilities. The loss of a leg may not be a significant handicap in the classroom, but is on many jobs calling for physical activity. Therefore, a child may not be handicapped in the eyes of the educator, but is in the eyes of the vocational rehabilitation counselor.

Every child is physically or mentally exceptional in some way. The definitional issue is one of degree; how exceptional and in what ways must a child be exceptional before society deems it desirable to provide special services not provided to "normal" children? No one would disagree with the premise that a severely retarded or a totally deaf child is exceptional, but when children have mild degrees of exceptionality the choice of whether or not to provide special services is more difficult. A fundamental truth is that sufficient funds are not available, and are not likely to be available in the near future, to provide every conceivable service to every individual child. So, decisions must be made on definitions of who will be provided special services. Hearing is a good example of an ability that varies in quality on a complex continuum from so-called "normal" to total deafness in both ears. At what points on the multidimensional continuum of hearing ability is the exceptionality such that society should deem it necessary to provide special services?

One can go a step beyond considering physical or mental impairment and define the exceptionality in terms of impaired functional capability or need for services resulting from the physical or mental exceptionality, e.g., the degree of difficulty the child has in understanding "normal" speech. But with limited funds, the same arbitrary cutoff problem exists for functional ability or need for service scales as for physical or mental impairment scales.

Obviously the definitions of exceptional children—the cutoff point or points that are chosen on whatever scale or scales of exceptionality—will affect the number of children eligible for special services and the funding level required to finance those services. Similarly, the funding levels reasonably likely to be available, and the likely costs and benefits from providing or refusing to provide special services, will affect society's definition of exceptional children. The federal definition of handicapped children in P.L. 94-142, the "Education for All Handicapped Children Act" passed in 1975, is

> . . . mentally retarded, hard of hearing, deaf, speech impaired, visually handicapped, seriously emotionally disturbed, orthopedically impaired, or other health impaired children, or children with specific learning disabilities who by reason thereof require special education and related services.

> The term "children with specific learning disabilities" means those children who have a disorder in one or more of the basic psychological processes involved in understanding or in using language, spoken or written, which disorder may manifest itself in imperfect ability to listen, think, speak, read, write, spell, or do mathematical calculations. Such disorders include such conditions as perceptual

handicaps, brain injury, minimal brain dysfunction, dyslexia, and developmental aphasia. Such term does not include children who have learning problems which are primarily the result of visual, hearing, or motor handicaps, of mental retardation, of emotional disturbance, or of environmental, cultural, or economic disadvantage.[1]

The definitions change with time and vary from one jurisdiction to another. For example, definitions of those children eligible for special education services in recent decades have shifted from exclusion to inclusion of: the more severely handicapped children, the very mildly handicapped children, and some children below the age of five years. Types of exceptionalities included have also expanded in recent years to include some children with "learning disabilities" not attributable to any specific physical or mental impairment, for example. As the definition of exceptionality is broadened over time, and as the use of such mechanisms as "individualized education programs" and "mainstreaming" for exceptional children expands, society is moving toward a system that provides a service program to match every individual child's needs. If the trend continues, the eventual result will be no need to label a child handicapped or disadvantaged or anything else in order to make him or her eligible for special services, since all children would be receiving services to match their individual needs. However, until such time as sufficient funds become available to provide all children with individualized services to match their needs, some categorization of children will be necessary to indicate those who are to receive special services.

In addition to changes and differences with time and place in the words used in definitions, nearly all definitions of exceptional children (including the federal definitions) are nonspecific in the sense that they permit a great deal of latitude on the part of local agencies and personnel to decide who actually are handicapped children. Because the interpretations of definitions are not necessarily comparable across jurisdictions, an individual child might be "handicapped" if he lived in one location but "normal" if he lived elsewhere. Or, he might be categorized as having one type of handicap in one location and another type in another location, even if both locations had the same set of possible categories of handicapping conditions. Especially nebulous terms in common use include "learning disabled," and "emotionally disturbed."

Just as the definitions of exceptional children differ with time and across jurisdictions, the definitions of service needs also differ with time and geographic location. The definition of service need for moderately retarded children in many jurisdictions used to be 24-hour-a-day residential care in a mental institution, with little attempt to provide specific educational services to help them develop toward their maximum potential. Today the prevailing notion is to provide special education and training services to develop the child's potential and allow him or her to function in the least restrictive environment possible, rather than providing interminable 24-hour-a-day custodial care.

A matter of controversy related to definitions is the "labeling" of children. Labels can have negative effects on individual children, which should be minimized to the extent feasible, but some forms of labels are unavoidable. The mere act of providing special services implies the child is different, and at least implicitly "labels" the child in his or her own mind and in other children's minds. The labels may be formal or informal, but they will exist in some form. The Hobbs' study[2] on the classification of children found that some form of labeling or categorization of children to receive special services is unavoidable and desirable. Categorization is desirable from the viewpoints of obtaining appropriate services for children in need, for planning and seeking support for programs, and for evaluation. Some sort of classification of groups of children, if not individuals, is unavoidable. The aim should be to retain its usefulness while striving always to minimize the sometimes negative effects of labels. One could, for example, label each child only as one having "exceptional needs," but use a more specific classification system *only* for data collection and reporting purposes.[3] For example, the individual child's file might contain data on various dimensions related to disability and special service needs, but no label beyond "exceptional." Counting of children in various other specific categories for federal or other reporting could still be done from the detailed data, but such categorical reporting would only be for a group of children.

Resolution of the definition issue is primarily a matter of making a value judgment and being precise in articulating that judgment. Most existing definitions appear to be purposefully vague, perhaps as a result of compromise to achieve a consensus or perhaps as a result of unwillingness to say precisely and unequivocally to any organization or group of lobbying parents that their children's needs are of low priority and will not be met. Resolution of the definition issue is also

[2]N. Hobbs, *The Futures of Children: Categories, Labels, and Their Consequences,* Jossey-Bass, San Francisco, 1975.

[3]See California State Board of Education, "California Master Plan for Special Education," Sacramento, California, January 10, 1974.

a matter for research, however. As will be shown later in this book, the dearth of data available on the costs and effects of serving or not serving exceptional children with various characteristics makes it difficult to make rational value judgments on the definition issue.

PREVALENCE ESTIMATES

To adequately plan services for exceptional children, the number of such children and their service needs must be estimated. If definitions of exceptionalities were in terms that indicated service needs, and if the incidence of the exceptionalities in the population were known, then estimating the magnitude and distribution of the exceptional-child population and its service needs would be relatively easy and would not be a major issue. Unfortunately, current definitions are not closely related to service needs (for example, knowing someone is mentally retarded or learning disabled or partially sighted tells you very little about what special education is required for them). And data on incidence rates of exceptionalities in the general child population are appallingly lacking. In some cases, vague and differing definitions such as for "learning disabled" children result in wide variations in incidence estimates (e.g., from 1 percent to 20 percent and more for learning disabilities in the school age population).[4] In some cases, it is difficult to measure and evaluate a potential exceptionality in a child (e.g., is a particular child seriously emotionally disturbed or not?). In some cases, available incidence data are based on nongeneralizable or poor-quality data (e.g., data from a very limited geographic area, or from merely asking parents if their child is handicapped).

Available data on incidence rates for handicaps in children have been reviewed in numerous reports.[5] The estimates of the total prevalence of exceptionalities among children and youth are typically in the 9 to 12 percent range or above.

[4]M. Fleischmann et al., *Report of the New York State Commission on the Quality, Cost, and Financing of Elementary and Secondary Education,* Vol. 2, New York, 1972.

[5]See, for example, Richard A. Rossmiller et al., *Educational Programs for Exceptional Children: Resource Configurations and Costs,* Department of Educational Administration, University of Wisconsin, Madison, August 1970; Patricia A. Craig, "Counting Handicapped Children: A Federal Imperative," *Journal of Education Finance,* Vol. 1, No. 3, Winter 1976; and P. Craig and N. McEachron, "The Development and Analysis of Base Line Data for the Estimation of Incidence of the Handicapped School Age Population," Research Note EPRC 2158-19, Stanford Research Institute, Menlo Park, California, January 3, 1975; Office for Handicapped Individuals, *Handicapping Conditions: A Resource Book—1975,* U.S. Department of Health, Education, and Welfare, Washington, D.C., 1975; and the sources cited in Table 5.2.

Table 5.1
ESTIMATED NUMBER OF HANDICAPPED YOUTH AGED 0–21 IN 1970

Type of Handicap		Number of Youth
Visual impairment		193,000
Partially sighted	180,000	
Legally blind[a]	45,000	
Hearing impairment		490,000
Deaf	50,000	
Hard of hearing	440,000	
Speech impairment		2,200,000
Crippling or other health impairment		1,676,000
Mental retardation		2,800,000
Emotional disturbance		1,500,000
Learning disability		740,000
Multihandicapped		50,000
Total		9,550,000[b]

SOURCE: See Table 5.2 and accompanying text.
[a] Including 32,000 partially sighted.
[b] Total has been adjusted to compensate for doublecounting of multihandicapped children.

Our estimate shown in Table 5.1, that about 9½ million of the 83.8 million youth aged 0 to 21 in the United States (1970 Census) were handicapped, is based on the best available data. However, we are not fully satisfied with its reliability. Nonetheless, we believe that it represents the correct order of magnitude of the numbers of youth who need at least some special services, by current societal standards of need.

Because of these definitional and data difficulties, later in this chapter we delineate our assumptions about each handicapping condition and its prevalence so that those who disagree can alter our estimates to arrive at their own conclusions. Table 5.2 presents an array of estimates of the prevalence of various handicapping conditions in youth. The most noticeable characteristic of these estimates is the wide variation among sources; the high estimate differs from the low by a factor of 6. The differences noted are partially due to varying definitions used. Those differences, and breakdowns within the categories of impairment (e.g., hard of hearing versus deaf), will be discussed in following subsections. Note that two of the estimates indicate a very small fraction are multiple handicapped, implying a small amount of double counting in some of the other estimates.

In interpreting estimates of the percentage of the handicapped population served by various government programs, one should keep in mind the uncertain size of that population. It was not within the scope of this study to analyze the relative merits of each set of esti-

Table 5.2
ESTIMATES OF THE PREVALENCE OF HANDICAPPING CONDITIONS IN YOUTH
(In percent of total youth population)

Handicap	Estimate										
	(a)	(b)	(c)	(d)	(e)	(f)	(g)	(h)	(i)	(j)	(k)
Mentally retarded	2.300	2.300	1.480	2.25	6.30	7.000	—	—	1.54	—	—
Hearing impairment	0.575	0.575	0.080	2.10	1.00	0.203	0.95	—	0.10	—	0.585
Speech impairment	3.500	3.500	2.400	5.00	4.50	1.300	1.30	—	3.60	—	5.000
Visual impairment	0.090	0.100	0.020	0.08	0.35	0.200	0.06	0.057	0.05	0.054	—
Emotionally disturbed	2.000	2.000	0.050	3.00	5.00	2.600	—	—	2.00	—	—
Crippled	1.000	0.500	0.028	0.50	0.35	0.180	—	—	0.21	—	—
Learning disabled	—	1.000	0.026	5.00	7.00	2.200	—	—	1.12	—	—
Other health impairment	1.000	(l)	—	0.50	—	0.050	—	—	(l)	—	—
Multihandicapped	—	0.060	—	—	—	—	—	—	0.07	—	—
Total	10.465	10.035	4.080	18.43	24.50	13.730	—	—	8.69	—	—

[a] R. P. Mackie, H. Williams, and P. P. Hunter, *Statistics of Special Education for Exceptional Children and Youth, 1957-1958*, USOE Bulletin No. OE-35048-58, 1963, as reported in R. A. Rossmiller, J. A. Hale, and L. E. Frohreich, *Educational Programs for Exceptional Children: Resource Configurations and Costs*, National Educational Finance Project, Special Study No. 2, Department of Educational Administration, University of Wisconsin, Madison, Wisconsin, August 1970.

[b] Estimated for age 5-19 youth in 1969. U.S. Department of Health, Education, and Welfare, *Handicapped Children in the U.S. and Special Education Personnel Required—1968-1969 (est.)*, Bureau of Education for the Handicapped, August 1970.

[c] Estimate developed from information contained in *1969-70 Summary of Special Education Services of Bureau for Special Education, Division for Handicapped Children, Wisconsin Department of Public Instruction, 1970* (mimeo) as reported in Rossmiller, op. cit., p. 122.

[d] Estimates developed by the North Dakota State Department of Public Instruction as reported in *Description of Special Education Program 1972-1973*, submitted to the Bureau of Education for the Handicapped.

[e] Estimates developed by the Nebraska State Department of Education as reported in *Description of Special Education Program 1972-1973*, submitted to the Bureau of Education for the Handicapped.

[f] Actual number of children in Alabama identified as needing special education service through teacher referral divided by the number of children 5-17 according to the 1970 U.S. Census. The number of identified children is taken from *Alabama Five-Year Plan Program for Exceptional Children and Youth*, State Department of Education, Montgomery, Alabama, August 8, 1972. Note that the number reportedly identified is often higher than other

Service, p. 9.

[h] Kenneth Trouern-Trend, *Blindness in the United States*, Travelers Research Center, Hartford, Conn., 1968.

[i] Rossmiller, op. cit., p. 121. This is the estimate used in the Rossmiller study after a review of other prevalence data.

[j] *Estimated Statistics on Blindness and Vision Problems*, National Society for the Prevention of Blindness, Inc., New York, New York, 1966.

[k] Derived from estimates in *Human Communications and Its Disorders—An Overview*. A report of the National Advisory Neurological Diseases and Stroke Council of the National Institute of Neurological Diseases and Stroke, National Institutes of Health, U.S. Department of Health, Education, and Welfare, Bethesda, Maryland, 1969.

[l] Included with crippled.

mates. We do note that the relatively recent (1970) estimates of prevalence used by the Bureau of Education for the Handicapped (column b) are comprehensive, were made after a review of multiple studies of incidence, and have been widely used.

In virtually all types of exceptionality, data usually are not available disaggregated by characteristics of the population that may be correlated with the incidence of exceptionalities (such as age, sex, race, and family income) so that one cannot discuss with high confidence the differences in prevalence rates in different age ranges or geographic areas. For example, the prevalence of certain handicapping conditions is thought to be strongly age dependent;[6] e.g., speech disorders are much more prevalent among elementary school age children than among those of high school age.

What is really needed in order to be definitive on incidence rates is a national survey of the general population with in-depth evaluation of the characteristics of each child submitted by professional evaluators. These evaluations should not merely conclude that a child is or is not handicapped, but rather should make data available on the child's abilities on a variety of dimensions. This would enable one to assess incidence on a range of different definitions and in terms of service needs. The 1964 data from the National Health Examination Survey[7] of noninstitutionalized youth are useful but deficient in that the data are not available on certain types of handicapped children (e.g., learning-disabled children) and the data on impairments and the definitions used in that survey were not always adequate to establish whether or not the child needed particular types of services.

The main problem with a national population survey with in-depth professional evaluation of each child contacted is its high cost. We did not estimate the cost of such a survey in detail, and any estimate would depend on how large a survey is conducted and how in-depth the evaluation of each child would be. However, such a definitive general population survey on incidence is clearly a multimillion dollar research effort. Just to do an in-person survey costs at least $80 per interviewee, and in-depth evaluation of the children by professionals would bring the cost to at least $200 per child.[8]

The new federal "Education for All Handicapped Children Act" deals with incidence by saying payment will flow in proportion to the number of children served, but not to exceed 12 percent of the children ages 5 through 17 in any state. That 12 percent represents a

---

[6]See Craig and McEachron, op. cit.

[7]National Center for Health Statistics, Report Series 11, U.S. Department of Health, Education, and Welfare, Washington, D.C.

[8]According to D. Hensler, a Rand Corporation survey expert, 1977.

somewhat liberal estimate of the number of exceptional children, based on the best available, but very deficient, data. A lower "cap" of one-sixth of the number of identified handicapped children is set for "learning-disabled" children.[9] The 12 percent cap is in part an attempt to inhibit overcounting of children as handicapped in order to qualify for more federal funds, and it is in part an inherent aspect of the definition of how exceptional a child must be to be considered handicapped under the federal definition.

We now proceed with discussions of definitions and prevalence for various commonly used categories of handicapping conditions.

VISUALLY IMPAIRED

Data on the incidence of visual impairment in youth are probably the best among the various disabilities. The reasons are several: visual impairment is relatively easy to detect; there is a standard measure of "legal blindness," and more widespread screening is done for it than for most other handicaps. The dichotomous definition of legal blindness does not allow the separation of the various functional capabilities among the visually impaired, and it stands to reason that services should not be the same for all those categorized as "blind." In fact, many of the legally blind are not and do not consider themselves blind, and services that are directed at the totally blind will not train the person who has residual vision to use that vision to best advantage. Therefore, a definition such as that for legal blindness gives some indication of who needs service, but is not sufficiently refined to indicate the type of service required, and does not include all those needing service.

The usual definition of legal blindness is that a person's visual acuity for distant vision does not exceed 20/200 in the better eye, with best correction; or his visual acuity is more than 20/200 but the widest diameter of his field of vision subtends an angle of no greater than 20°. That particular test does not measure vision over all ranges of distance, however. Many legally blind people are able to see close-up objects, such as books in small print, and hence are not really "blind" for many of the important functions of everyday life.

After considering many data sources, the National Society for the Prevention of Blindness (NSPB) indicated that the best data available suggest about 1 child in 4 of school age in the United States needs eye care; about 1 in 500 is partially sighted (i.e., uses sight as a chief

---

[9]That cap on learning disabilities will be removed after regulations are established which define specific learning disabilities and diagnostic procedures for identifying them.

channel of learning, including 42 percent of legally blind children and those with acuity after correction of better than 20/200 but less than 20/70—the approximate acuity with correction at which it becomes possible for the person to read ordinary newsprint); and about 1 in 2000 (0.054 in 100) is legally blind.[10]

Other estimates were shown in Table 5.2. The data indicate that the education agencies in the states are reporting a higher incidence of visual impairments than given in the National Health Survey and the Model Reporting Areas for Blindness Statistics. This is primarily due to differences in definition. One need not be legally blind to be visually handicapped in terms of the education process. North Dakota, for example, classified children with only 20/70 vision in the better eye after correction as partially sighted. As we indicated earlier, the definition of the handicap should depend on how vision relates to the service, e.g., the education process. It is easy to see that the sole use of the classification of legal blindness is misleading in terms of prescriptive action that the schools or other service agencies must take.

Table 5.3 presents estimates of the percentages of the legally blind with various degrees of vision. Only 16 percent are totally blind.

Using the NSPB prevalence estimates, and the fact that there were 83.8 million youth aged 0 to 21 in the United States in 1970, implies

[10]National Society for the Prevention of Blindness, *Estimated Statistics on Blindness and Vision Problems,* New York, 1966. For other detailed discussions of definitions and incidence rates, see Kenneth Trouern-Trend, *Blindness in the United States: Review of the Available Statistics with Estimates of the Prevalence of Blindness and Its Economic Impact,* Travelers Research Center, Inc., Hartford, Connecticut, 1968, p. 5; and Organization for Social and Technical Innovation, Inc., *Blindness and Services to the Blind in the United States,* OSTI Press, Cambridge, Massachusetts, 1971.

Table 5.3
DEGREE OF VISION: AGES 5–19

	Percent
Absolute blindness	16
Light perception	14
Light projection	1
Less than 5/200	8
5/200 but less than 10/200	6
10/200 but less than 20/200	12
20/200	26
Field restriction	1
Unknown	16

SOURCE: Kenneth Trouern-Trend, *Blindness in the United States,* 1968. These figures represent the degree of vision of those registered in the Model Reporting Areas in 1965.

that in 1970 there were about 21 million youth who required eye care; 45,000 legally blind youth; and 168,000 partially sighted youth, of whom perhaps 20,000 were legally blind. If one defines partially sighted to include measurable acuity less than 20/70 with correction, then there are perhaps 180,000 partially sighted youth, of whom 32,000 are legally blind.

For details on the prevalence of visual impairment by etiology, see the chapter on medical services.

HEARING IMPAIRED

Hearing losses may be grouped into two broad categories: deafness, or sense of hearing that is nonfunctional for the ordinary purposes of life; and hard of hearing, or a sense of hearing that causes difficulty with such things as understanding speech, but which is at least partially functional. For a more detailed discussion of definitions and sources of prevalence data than we present here, refer to the NINDS report.[11] According to that report, "Deafness has never been defined to the satisfaction of all authorities," and ". . . the task of ascertaining how many deaf persons there are in this country has never been accurately performed." We would add that the quality of the statistics on the hard of hearing is considerably worse than that for the deaf. The NINDS report suggests that the most widely accepted definition of deafness is as follows:

> Those in whom the sense of hearing is nonfunctional for the ordinary purposes of life. This general group is made up of two distinct classes based entirely on the time of the loss of hearing. (a) The congenitally deaf: those who are born deaf. (b) The adventitiously deaf: those who were born with normal hearing but in whom the sense of hearing becomes nonfunctional later through illness or accident.[12]

A more detailed and specific classification was used in the 1960–1962 U.S. Public Health Service Health Examination Survey. The breakdown of hearing loss is based on the decibels (dB) of sound loss in the 500 to 2000 Hertz range, which covers most of the speech range. The average hearing level in the better ear is divided into four ranges, with the associated functional interpretation:

[11]National Advisory Neurological Diseases and Stroke Council of the National Institute of Neurological Diseases and Stroke (NINDS), *Human Communication and Its Disorders—An Overview*, National Institutes of Health, U.S. Department of Health, Education, and Welfare, Bethesda, Maryland, 1969.

[12]The distinction is made because in the former case language development could not occur with the aid of the sense of hearing.

- 41 to 55 dB: Frequent difficulty with normal speech
- 56 to 70 dB: Frequent difficulty with loud speech
- 71 to 90 dB: Understands only shouted or amplified speech
- 91+ dB: Usually cannot understand even amplified speech

Other breakdowns use more categories, slightly different decibel breakpoints, or slightly different functional interpretations, but are generically the same. For example, Rossmiller uses a classification wherein a hearing loss of 20 to 45 dB in at least two frequencies in the speech range is classified as mildly hard of hearing.[13] Deaf or severely hard of hearing are those with a hearing loss of between 75 to 80 dB or greater across the speech range without the use of hearing aids.[14] The National Health Interview Survey takes a less scientific approach when it asks respondents if they feel they have deafness or serious trouble hearing with one or both ears. A different type of hearing disorder, on which very little data are available, is one in which the level of sound heard may or may not be normal, but there are dysacusic disturbances primarily symptomized by garbled hearing.

The NINDS report estimates there were 236,000 deaf persons of all ages in the United States in 1970. Using their same data source,[15] we note a prevalence of deafness in persons under age 15 of about 53 per 100,000 and 76 per 100,000 aged 15-24. Using these rates, we estimate the 1970 aged 0-21 deaf population is approximately 50,000 (impairment of 91 dB or more). The NINDS report estimates that "about 8,500,000 Americans (in 1970) have auditory problems of one type or another [impairment of about 15 dB or more] which are less severe than deafness but which impair communication . . . about 4.5 percent (circa 360,000) are under 17 years."[16] If we extrapolate at the same rate to the 0-21 age range, about 440,000, or 0.525 percent of those in that age range, are hard of hearing (impairment of about 41 to 90 dB). Prevalence estimates from various sources are shown in Table 5.4. We caution that children should not be termed hearing or vision handicapped simply on the basis of physical impairment, such as precisely 41 dB or more hearing loss, since many children with less loss, say 25 to 40 dB, may be functionally handicapped and in need of special services (e.g., a very young child with less than 41 dB of loss may have an education or language development problem).

---

[13]R. A. Rossmiller, J. A. Hale, and L. E Frohreich, *Educational Programs for Exceptional Children: Resource Configurations and Costs,* National Educational Finance Project, Special Study No. 2, Department of Educational Administration, University of Wisconsin, Madison, August 1970, p. 72.

[14]Ibid., p. 73.

[15]"Statistical Information Concerning the Deaf and Hard of Hearing in the United States," *American Annals of the Deaf,* Vol. 104, 1959, pp. 265-270.

[16]*Human Communication and Its Disorders—An Overview,* p. 13.

Table 5.4
PREVALENCE OF HEARING IMPAIRMENTS, BY DEGREE OF IMPAIRMENT
(Percent of total youth population)

Degree of Impairment	Estimate								
	(a)	(b)	(c)	(d)	(e)	(f)	(g)	(i)	(k)
Hard of hearing	0.500	0.500	0.08[1]	2.0	0.85	0.200	0.95[1]	0.11[1]	0.525
Deaf	0.075	0.075		0.1	0.15	0.003			0.060

SOURCES: Same as for Table 5.2.
[1] Combined.

Of the approximately 683,000 youth in the United States who have either a hearing or a vision handicap, some not reliably known fraction are multiple handicapped, i.e., are also retarded, emotionally disturbed, learning disabled, crippled or other health impaired, or have more than one sensory handicap. A very few thousand are both hearing and vision handicapped; although commonly labeled "deaf-blind," a great diversity of sensory ability exists in that small population, few of whom are both profoundly deaf and totally blind.

For details on the prevalence of hearing impairment by etiology, see the chapter on medical services.

SPEECH IMPAIRED

Speech impairment includes absence of a larynx, stammering, stuttering, poor articulation, and other ill-defined troubles with speech. Since there is no precise definition of speech impairment, it would seem reasonable that there might be no reasonable consensus about the prevalence of this impairment. This tends to be confirmed by the data in Table 5.2. For a discussion of various prevalence data, see the NINDS report.[17] In 1970 there were about 63 million youth aged 5 to 21, which leads to an estimated 2.2 million speech impaired youth if a 3.5 percent rate is used, or to an estimated 3.14 million if a 5 percent rate is used.

The National Health Survey (NHS) gives by far the lowest estimate. It was based upon the response to the question about whether there were any speech defects in the family. One cause could be that most people do not think their speech difficulties are as significant as a speech therapist would. Another cause is that cases of cleft palate and deafness were classified in categories other than speech impaired in the NHS, though they might benefit from speech therapy.

[17] Ibid., pp. 16-19.

CRIPPLED AND OTHER HEALTH IMPAIRED

Crippled and other health impaired includes physical handicaps not characterized as speech, hearing, or visual handicaps. Crippled includes orthopedic or muscular impairments such as the absence, paralysis, or other impairment of the limbs, back, or trunk. This category also includes children with chronic disease or other relatively long-term physical impairment such as problems involving the heart, blood, respiratory, or digestive systems.

Estimates of the prevalence of a crippling or health condition will differ from estimates of a "handicapping" crippling or health condition. That is, a loss of a finger may not interfere with the educational process, and hence the child would not be considered handicapped with respect to that service. From an aesthetic or medical viewpoint, however, the child could be considered crippled. The estimates for the prevalence rates shown in Table 5.2 are mainly from education sources and hence may underestimate those actually crippled or other health impaired. This is suggested in Table 5.2, where the National Health Survey found 2.6 percent of the population physically handicapped, which is well above any of the estimates from the other sources.

Using the Mackie, Williams, and Hunter[18] rate, which is consistent with the rates observed in various service programs, would result in an estimated 1,676,000 youth aged 0-21 with these types of handicaps.

MENTALLY RETARDED

Reacting to a variety of descriptors of mental retardation (e.g., age at onset, IQ, mental age, educability), the American Association on Mental Deficiency (AAMD) has combined the concepts of functional proficiency and measured intelligence and has gained wide acceptance for the following definition.[19]

> Mental retardation refers to substantially subaverage general intellectual functioning existing concurrently with deficits in adaptive behavior, and manifested during the developmental period.[20]

[18]*Statistics of Special Education for Exceptional Children and Youth, 1957–1958,* USOE Bulletin No. OE-35048-58, 1963.

[19]The definition problem is thorny, to say the least. We refrain from trying to resolve it here, but recommend that the interested reader consult the following representative works: R. Heber, "Mental Retardation: Concept and Classification," in E. R. Trapp and Paul Himelstein (eds.), *Readings on the Exceptional Child,* Appleton-Century-Crofts, New York, 1962, pp. 69–81; and American Association on Mental Deficiency (AAMD), *A Manual on Terminology and Classification in Mental Retardation,* Monograph Supplement to the *American Journal of Mental Deficiency,* 3d ed., Washington, D.C., 1973.

[20]AAMD, *A Manual on Terminology.*

Under AAMD definitions, the developmental period extends up to age 18, and substantially subaverage means an IQ test score of at least two standard deviations below average (i.e., approximately 70 or below). The definition of mental retardation adopted by the American Psychiatric Association (APA) is basically the same as the AAMD definition.[21]

Mental retardation is sometimes divided into levels indicating severity: mild (Stanford-Binet test IQ of 52-68); moderate, (IQ 36-51); severe (IQ of 20 to 35); and profound (IQ below 20).[22] Other categorizations, such as "educable" and "trainable," are often used by educators to indicate the type of special educational assistance needed; they are related to IQ only loosely, since the child's functional proficiency is a major factor in determining need for service. The AAMD relates the special education classification to IQ as follows:

> Mild retardation is roughly equivalent to the educational term *educable;* moderate retardation includes those individuals who are likely to fall into the educational category of *trainable;* the severe group includes individuals sometimes known as *dependent retarded;* individuals in the profound retardation level are among those sometimes called "life-support" level. These terms are, of course, not absolute nor static. A child classified as mildly retarded may be better served in a "trainable" class than an "educable" one; some children at the severe retardation level may function successfully in a "trainable" group; children may move up or down between categories. The level does not necessarily dictate the particular service needed, but may be helpful as one criterion in planning.[23]

The term "developmental disability" includes several disabilities, of which mental retardation is the most prevalent. Specifically, a developmental disability is a substantially handicapping condition which: (1) is attributable to mental retardation, cerebral palsy, epilepsy, or to other neurological conditions found by the Secretary of the U.S. Department of Health, Education, and Welfare to be closely related to mental retardation or to require treatment similar to that required for mentally retarded individuals; (2) originated before the individual reached age 18 and can be expected to continue indefinitely.[24]

Mental retardation is a flexible concept, a fact reflected in the experience of the so-called "disappearing retardate," i.e., a person who

[21]American Psychiatric Association, *Diagnostic and Statistical Manual of Mental Disorders,* 2d ed., Washington, D.C., 1968.
[22]AAMD, *A Manual on Terminology.*
[23]Ibid.
[24]*Federal Register,* Vol. 39, No. 235, December 5, 1974.

as a child was identified and treated as retarded but who lost that identification in later life through integration into the society. This is possible since the parameters used to identify one as mentally retarded relate both to assessments of subnormal intelligence *and* to adaptive behavior (which can be modified throughout the person's lifespan).[25]

Considering national sources of information, the National Association for Retarded Citizens (NARC) uses a prevalence rate of about 3 percent for all ages.[26] Of the 3 percent of the population that is retarded, the NARC provides the following breakdown: 89 percent mild, 6 percent moderate, 3.5 percent severe, and 1.5 percent profound retardation.[27] Those percentages are based on IQ alone; not all people with an IQ below 70 meet the second part of the mental retardation definition—deficits in adaptive behavior—and hence not all are functionally mentally retarded. R. Conley has conducted what is probably the most thorough recent analysis of the large number of limited studies that have been done throughout the years around the nation on the prevalence of mental retardation. Those studies show a wide range of prevalence; reported rates ranged from 1.2 to 18.4 percent. His best estimate is that, nationwide, IQs less than about 70 prevail among 3 percent of the population, and that the prevalence varies by age as follows: about 4 percent for age 0 to 4 years, 3.3 percent for age 5 to 19 years, 2.7 percent for age 20 to 64 years, and 2 percent for 65 years of age and over.[28] Again, not all of these people are functionally mentally retarded. The U.S. Bureau of Education for the Handicapped (BEH), in its 1970 estimate of the number of handicapped children aged 5 to 19 years in the United States who need special education, used a prevalence rate of 2.3 percent.[29] Conley uses a rate of nearly 4 percent in his work on the costs and benefits of mental retardation programs. While this is close in absolute terms to the 2.3 percent used by BEH, the relative difference in percentage terms is 74 percent. Extrapolating Conley's estimates to the entire 0-21 age range yields a population estimate of about 2.8 million.

[25]George Tarjan et al., "Natural History of Mental Retardation: Some Aspects of Epidemiology," *American Journal of Mental Deficiency,* Vol. 77, 1973, pp. 369–379, contend that as many as two-thirds of the mildly retarded adolescents and young adults lose their identification as retarded simply through aging and adaptation and/or through retesting with more sensitive instruments.

[26]*Facts on Mental Retardation,* NARC, 2709 Ave. "E" East, Arlington, Texas 76011, 1973.

[27]Ibid.

[28]R. Conley, *The Economics of Mental Retardation,* The Johns Hopkins University Press, Baltimore, Maryland, 1973, p. 39.

[29]U.S. Department of Health, Education, and Welfare, *Handicapped Children in the United States and Special Education Personnel Required—1968-1969 Est.,* Bureau of Education for the Handicapped, August 1970.

EMOTIONALLY DISTURBED

The difficulties of defining and measuring the prevalence of mental retardation pale in comparison with those associated with defining and measuring mental health disorders. When professional mental health personnel agree upon what constitutes mental health, and reliable methods of measuring it are available, then high-quality data can be collected on the prevalence of mental health problems.

Current definitions leave a great deal to judgment about whether a child is emotionally disturbed or not. For example, emotionally disturbed children have been defined as those demonstrating one or more of the following characteristics:

1. An inability to learn that cannot be explained by intellectual, sensory, or health factors.
2. An inability to build or maintain satisfactory interpersonal relationships with peers and teachers.
3. Inappropriate types of behavior or feelings under normal conditions.
4. A general, pervasive mood of unhappiness or depression.
5. A tendency to develop physical symptoms, pains, or fears associated with personal or school problems.[30]

Just what is considered "inappropriate" behavior under "normal" conditions will vary by individual assessor. Since teachers are a principal source in identifying handicaps and are usually not trained to identify the emotionally disturbed population, a large margin for error is introduced. A tendency may prevail to classify those who are difficult to handle in the classroom as emotionally disturbed. One would expect a relatively large variance in the estimates of the prevalence of emotionally disturbed youth. Table 5.2 tends to bear this out. If one applies the BEH rate to the aged 3-21 population, one estimate would be about 1.5 million youth.

Since mental health can be described on many different dimensions, since a child's current mental condition can fall anywhere on the continuum of each of those dimensions, and since society's views on what is "normal" change with time and circumstance, one is necessarily being arbitrary when one draws lines between "normal" and "not normal" on combinations of those dimensions. For practical reasons, society itself must arbitrarily cut through this Gordian Knot; there are children and youth who, in the judgment of the majority of today's society, have mental health problems and need substantial psychological or psychiatric services.

The American Psychiatric Association (APA) has published a man-

[30]Rossmiller, Hale, and Frohreich, op. cit., p. 95.

ual of approved diagnostic terms for "mental disorders."[31] It places diagnosed mental disorders into ten categories: (1) mental retardation, (2) organic brain syndromes (psychotic and nonpsychotic), (3) psychoses not attributed to physical conditions listed under organic brain syndromes, (4) neuroses, (5) personality disorders and certain other nonpsychotic mental disorders, (6) psychophysiologic disorders, (7) special symptoms, (8) transient situational disturbances, (9) behavior disorders of childhood and adolescence, and (10) conditions without manifest psychiatric disorders and nonspecific conditions.

A psychosis is by definition a severe mental disorder and falls within the scope of this study. Other types of mental disorders can be classified by severity as "mild," "moderate," or "severe," and hence may include people who do not have a substantial need for special services and therefore do not fall within the scope of this study. However, the APA manual makes no attempt to define what constitutes the three levels of severity; as a result, statistics sorted among those levels are not fully meaningful.

In this study, the term "mental health disorders" will include primarily the problems in six of the APA categories: virtually all psychotics, and children and youth with more severe disorders within the categories of organic brain syndrome, neurosis, personality disorder (not due to alcohol or drug abuse), transient situational disturbances, and behavior disorders of childhood and adolescence.

Organic brain syndromes[32] are defined in brief by APA as

> Disorders caused by or associated with impairment of brain tissue function. These disorders are manifested by the following symptoms:
> (a) Impairment of orientation
> (b) Impairment of memory
> (c) Impairment of all intellectual functions such as comprehension, calculation, knowledge, learning, etc.
> (d) Impairment of judgment
> (e) Lability and shallowness of affect
>
> The organic brain syndrome is a basic mental condition characteristically resulting from diffuse impairment of brain tissue function from whatever cause. Most of the basic symptoms are generally present to some degree regardless of whether the syndrome is mild, moderate, or severe.

---

[31]*Diagnostic and Statistical Manual.* A new edition of the APA "Psychiatric Glossary" was not yet available at the time of this writing.

[32]Ibid., p. 22. In addition to the brief definitions given, the APA Manual presents more extensive definitions of most disorders in the course of discussing subcategories of major types of disorders.

People with organic brain syndrome may or may not be psychotic. Psychosis is defined in brief as follows:

Patients are described as psychotic when their mental functioning is sufficiently impaired to interfere grossly with their capacity to meet the ordinary demands of life. The impairment may result from a serious distortion in their capacity to recognize reality. Hallucinations and delusions, for example, may distort their perceptions. Alterations of mood may be so profound that the patient's capacity to respond appropriately is grossly impaired. Deficits in perception, language and memory may be so severe that the patient's capacity for mental grasp of his situation is effectively lost.[33]

Psychoses may occur with or without organic brain syndrome. A frequently used diagnosis in the latter case would be schizophrenia, which is defined in brief as:

A group of disorders manifested by characteristic disturbances of thinking, mood and behavior. Disturbances in thinking are marked by alterations of concept formation which may lead to misinterpretation of reality and sometimes to delusions and hallucinations, which frequently appear psychologically self-protective. Corollary mood changes include ambivalent, constricted and inappropriate emotional responsiveness and loss of empathy with others. Behavior may be withdrawn, regressive and bizarre.[34]

Schizophrenia eludes precise definition; the manual's foreword contains the admission that "Even if it had tried, the Committee could not establish agreement about what this disorder is; it could only agree on what to call it."[35]

Neuroses are briefly defined in the following terms:

Anxiety is the chief characteristic of the neuroses. It may be felt and expressed directly, or it may be controlled unconsciously and automatically by conversion, displacement and various other psychological mechanisms. Generally, these mechanisms produce symptoms experienced as subjective distress from which the patient desires relief. The neuroses, as contrasted to the psychoses, manifest neither gross distortion or misinterpretation of external reality, nor gross personality disorganization. A possible exception to this is hysterical neurosis, which some believe may occasionally be accompanied by hallucinations and other symptoms encountered in psychoses. Traditionally, neurotic patients, however severely handicapped by their symptoms, are not classified as psychotic because they are aware that their mental functioning is disturbed.[36]

33 Ibid., p. 23.
34 Ibid., p. 33.
35 Ibid., p. ix.
36 Ibid., p. 39.

The APA manual characterizes "personality disorders and certain other nonpsychotic mental disorders" in brief as (1) disorders of personality marked by "deeply ingrained maladaptive patterns of behavior that are perceptibly different in quality from psychotic and neurotic symptoms. Generally, these are life-long patterns, often recognizable by the time of adolescence or earlier"[37] (e.g., paranoid, obsessive-compulsive, antisocial); (2) sexual deviations; (3) alcoholism, defined as occurring when "patients whose alcohol intake is great enough to damage their physical health, or their personal or social functioning, or when it has become a prerequisite to normal functioning;"[38] and (4) drug dependence, afflicting "patients who are addicted to or dependent on drugs other than alcohol, tobacco, and ordinary caffeine-containing beverages. Dependence on medically prescribed drugs is also excluded so long as the drug is medically indicated and the intake is proportionate to the medical need. The diagnosis requires evidence of habitual use or a clear sense of need for the drug."[39]

Psychophysiologic disorders are "characterized by physical symptoms that are caused by emotional factors and involve a single organ system, usually under autonomic nervous system innervation."[40]

The "special symptoms" category includes people whose special symptoms (e.g., disturbance of speech, learning, sleep, feeding, or several other aspects of life) are not the result of an organic illness or defect or other mental disorder.[41]

The "transient situational disturbances" category

> . . . is reserved for more or less transient disorders of any severity (including those of psychotic proportions) that occur in individuals without any apparent underlying mental disorders and that represent an acute reaction to overwhelming environmental stress. . . . If the patient has good adaptive capacity his symptoms usually recede as the stress diminishes.[42]

"Behavior disorders of childhood and adolescence" is a term:

> . . . reserved for disorders occurring in childhood and adolescence that are more stable, internalized, and resistant to treatment than *Transient situational disturbances* but less so than *Psychoses, Neuroses, and Personality disorders*. . . .Characteristic manifestations include such symptoms as overactivity, inattentiveness, shyness, feeling of rejection, over-aggressiveness, timidity, and delinquency.[43]

[37]Ibid., p. 41.
[38]Ibid., p. 45.
[39]Ibid., p. 46.
[40]Ibid.
[41]Ibid., p. 48.
[42]Ibid., pp. 48–49.
[43]Ibid., p. 50.

Comprehensive epidemiologic data in the mental health area barely exist nationally. Not only are there few consistent definitional criteria, but identification of those whose behavior is disordered or deviant is severely underdeveloped. At best, the occasional survey of people being served in a location gives one a crude idea about these matters, but mainly about how many are being served, not how many need service. Nationally, in 1971, there were reportedly 847 patients of all ages per 100,000 population receiving inpatient psychiatric services, and 1134 per 100,000 population receiving outpatient services at state, county, private, general with psychiatric service, and Veterans Administration hospitals.[44] In addition, 305 people per 100,000 population received inpatient, outpatient, and day treatment services at federally funded community mental health centers. The above numbers include those people who were active clients at the beginning of 1971, plus those admitted to the program during the year. There is some unknown amount of duplication of counting because of people who were admitted more than once per year and/or were served by more than one program in 1971. Adding the total clients served by the different programs nationally, including the duplications, yields a total of 2286 per 100,000 population, or about 2.3 percent; eliminating duplications would probably bring the number of *different* people receiving some psychiatric service nationally to somewhat under 2 percent.

In an often-cited survey conducted in Manhattan in 1955, it was *believed* that about 10 percent of the population suffered from a "definite psychiatric disorder."[45] It has become clear, however, from accumulating experience with community mental health centers across the country, that the mere opening of such a center may be enough to "surface" those in need.[46] One wonders how many of these new clients were mentally ill all along, but were hidden away by protective and frightened friends and relatives.[47] It strains the credulity to think that people generally become more prone to mental illness at about the same time new programs are developed. A further

[44]U.S. National Institute of Mental Health, *Utilization of Mental Health Facilities, 1971,* Series B, No. 5, Washington, D.C.

[45]Leo Srole et al., *Mental Health in the Metropolis: The Midtown Manhattan Study,* McGraw-Hill, New York, Vol. 1, 1962, p. 230.

[46]David Mechanic, *Mental Health and Social Policy,* Prentice-Hall, Englewood Cliffs, N.J., 1969, has considered this eventuality.

[47]Muriel Hammer, "Influence of Small Social Networks as Factors in Mental Hospital Admissions," *Human Organizations,* Vol. 22, Winter 1963–64, pp. 243–251, thinks that because of the disconnected nature of the identification and referral processes— mainly as they relate to geographic separation from primary care facilities—this may be a possible explanation for the sudden overloading of newly opened community facilities. The evidence presented is not conclusive.

question is whether these high levels of untreated mentally ill are actually "sick," i.e., whether in fact they would be better served under other auspices than the community mental health centers. Creating community *mental health* centers, rather than community *health* centers or community *social service* centers, may encourage definition, labeling, and treatment of problems solely as mental health problems. Given the poor quality of available information, no one really knows the answers to these questions.

In 1970 the President's Task Force on the Mentally Handicapped concluded that 20 million Americans (about 10 percent of the population) could benefit from mental health services.[48] The National Joint Commission on Mental Health of Children cited a figure of 1.4 million youngsters under age 18 in need of immediate psychiatric care (2 percent of the young population), and further opined that this estimate by the National Institute of Mental Health was "considered by that institute and most mental health professionals to be a conservative figure."[49] The report goes on to estimate that "an additional 8 to 10 percent of our young people are afflicted with emotional problems (neuroses and the like) and are in need of specialized services."[50]

The U.S. Bureau of Education for the Handicapped uses a figure of 2 percent for the national prevalence of children with "emotional disturbance" severe enough to require special education services.[51] The best we can say is that the prevalence is on the order of 2 to 10 percent of the population based on national data and that 2 percent is probably a conservatively low estimate.

LEARNING DISABLED

Learning disabled children have been defined as follows:

> Children are said to have special learning disabilities when they have a disorder in one or more of the basic psychological processes involved in understanding or in using language, spoken or written, which may manifest itself in imperfect function in listening, speaking, writing, reading, spelling, or doing mathematical calculations. Such disorders include conditions described as perceptual handi-

[48]*Action Against Mental Disability,* The Report of the President's Task Force on the Mentally Handicapped, Government Printing Office, Washington, D.C., September 1970.

[49]*Crisis in Child Mental Health: Challenge for the 1970's,* Report of the Joint Commission on Mental Health of Children, Harper and Row, New York, 1969, p. 250.

[50]Estimated for youth aged 5 to 19 in 1969; U.S. Department of Health, Education, and Welfare, *Handicapped Children in the United States and Special Education Personnel Required—1968-69 (Est.),* Bureau of Education for the Handicapped, August 1970.

[51]Ibid., p. 254.

caps, brain injury, minimal brain dysfunction, dyslexia, and developmental aphasia but do not include those with learning problems primarily the result of visual, hearing, or motor handicaps or mental retardation.[52]

This definition is not very precise. Many responsible for identifying learning disorders have not been trained for such work, and, as a result, many of the classifications are basically educated guesses unsupported by research evidence.[53]

Estimates of the prevalence of the learning disabled cover a wide range. The Fleischmann Report quoted one figure as high as 20 percent.[54] Again, however, we have a problem in determining where the cutoff should be made in the continuum of learning disorders. Unless that cutoff is standardized (or various levels of severity are standardized) at an educationally meaningful point, the estimates of prevalence cannot be very helpful as a basis for policy development.

Table 5.2 contains various estimates of the prevalence of a learning handicap. The Wisconsin study found this disorder to be rare. Only 26 out of 100,000 children would be affected with this type of learning disorder if the Wisconsin estimate were correct. More dramatically, only one out of eight elementary schools with an enrollment of 600 each would be expected to have a learning disabled child. If the Nebraska estimate were correct, then each of these same schools would have 42 learning disabled children. The discrepancy is obvious, but at this point, without more precise definition and data, it is irreconcilable. Applying BEH prevalence rates to the population aged 3 to 21 leads to an estimate of 740,000 learning disabled in that age range in 1970.

[52]*Minimal Brain Dysfunction in Children,* Public Health Service Publication No. 20015, 1969, p. 2.

[53]E. C. Frierson and Walter Barbe, *Educating Children With Learning Disabilities: Selected Readings,* Appleton-Century-Crofts, New York, 1967, p. 3.

[54]M. Fleischmann, *Report of the New York State Commission on the Quality, Cost and Financing of Elementary and Secondary Education,* Vol. 2, Albany, New York, 1972.

II

NEEDS OF HANDICAPPED CHILDREN

Part II details our findings on current policies, programs, and service problems, and presents our recommendations for improving services to handicapped children, with a chapter devoted to each of nine major service needs: prevention, identification, direction, medical services, special education, equipment, mental health and mental retardation services, vocational services, and income maintenance.

"The blessing is not in living, but in living well."
Lucius Annaeus Seneca
Epistolae ad Lucilium, 63 A.D.

Chapter 6

PREVENTION

OVERVIEW

Prevention is a neglected and seriously underused service. This neglect is costly both to society and to handicapped youth and their families, not only in money but in the tragic fact that a large fraction of the handicaps occurring in youth could be prevented. That fraction may be as high as one-third or one-half; given the poor state of the data, no one really knows for sure. Prevention can be achieved as the direct result of improved services (such as timely identification of the disorder and proper medical treatment); as the direct result of immunization efforts; and indirectly as a result of improved prenatal care, family planning, genetic counseling, abortion, and other practices.[1] Each of these strategies is discussed below.

In contrast to the nearly $5 billion expended annually in FY 1971 by all levels of government for service to all types of handicapped children, we are able to identify only some $50 million specifically targeted for prevention activities for children; in other words, about 1 percent is targeted for prevention and 99 percent for service after the child is handicapped. The precise level of funds targeted for prevention is a matter of definition, but the inescapable conclusion is that the level is very low (see Chap. 2).

In early 1977, HEW Secretary Joseph A. Califano noted that 20 million of the 52 million U.S. children under the age of 15 are inadequately immunized against major diseases for which vaccines are available.[2] He has proposed extending and upgrading childhood immunization efforts, a concept we endorse.

[1] For an overview of prevention of handicapping conditions and prevention strategies, see "Prevention," *Handicapping Conditions, A Resource Book,* Office for Handicapped Individuals, U.S. Department of Health, Education, and Welfare, Washington, D.C. 20024, 1975.

[2] *The New York Times,* April 6, 1977, p. 1.

Prevention is one of the more neglected services, and the up-and-down fortunes of prevention programs sometimes resemble "The Perils of Pauline." Crisis or the threat of impending crisis is often necessary to galvanize official government attention to the prevention service, with the result that prevention programs have been heavily oriented to specific diseases and often limited in duration and total funds expended.

If one-in-ten existing handicaps in youth had been prevented, the future savings to the government might have been about $500 million per year for all handicapped youth. This represents, for each handicap prevented, over $6000 in the cost of future government services (discounted at 8 percent) over only the first 21 years the youth has the handicap. The total value of the youth's increased quality of life due to not being handicapped is much more important, and may be worth at least 10 times that amount, or much more, depending on one's value judgment.

Traditionally, two classes of prevention have been distinguished: primary and secondary. Primary prevention tries to forestall some harmful process or event. Primary refers to those activities done for the entire "population at large," not specifically the handicapped population. Secondary prevention concentrates on early identification and treatment, so that the consequences of the potentially debilitating process or event either do not appear or are rendered less harmful. Secondary is done for the limited population of "identified vulnerable, high-risk groups." Standard public health doctrine also considers the possibility of tertiary prevention, efforts to reduce the duration of negative effects through a course of treatment and rehabilitation of handicapped people.

Prevention of handicaps is so self-evidently a "good" objective that no one can dispute its usefulness or desirability, but only its costs, methods, and feasibility. Politicians have occasionally turned prevention into a rallying cry, as President Kennedy did in 1963:

> First, we must seek out the causes of mental illness and of mental retardation and eradicate them. . . . For prevention is far more desirable for all concerned. It is far more economical and it is far more likely to be successful. Prevention will require both selected specific programs directed especially at known causes, and the general strengthening of the fundamental community, social welfare, and educational programs which can do much to eliminate or correct the harsh environmental conditions which often are associated with mental retardation and mental illness.[3]

[3] John F. Kennedy, "Message from the President of the United States Relative to Mental Illness and Mental Retardation," *House Document No. 58,* 88th Cong., 1st Sess., Government Printing Office, Washington, D.C., 1963.

Prevention is far harder to practice than to preach, however. Experience has shown that prevention not only is difficult to define, it is even more troublesome to put into action.

The following sections of this chapter deal with existing prevention programs and, for illustrative purposes, with the prevention of hearing and vision disorders, mental health disorders, and mental retardation. The chapter concludes with a discussion of needed improvement in prevention programs. The discussions are limited wherever possible to primary and secondary prevention. Subsequent chapters that describe treatment services deal more fully with tertiary prevention through treatment of people with handicaps (e.g., special education so that a mentally retarded child is not functionally retarded as an adult).

PREVENTION PROGRAMS

This section first discusses operational prevention service programs and then those oriented toward prevention research. Before discussing specific programs, however, it is useful to examine program goals as they relate to prevention activities.

Personal "nondependency" as a goal to which prevention relates has been formulated in the following terms by Elliot L. Richardson, former Secretary of Health, Education, and, Welfare:

> . . . the non-dependency goal would suggest that our objectives should be: 1. to create prevention mechanisms which identify the likelihood of people sliding down the scale of personal freedom of choice and reliance on others, and which remove the dangers which threaten the status of those people.[4]

The "likelihood" idea is related to prevention research activities, and the "removal of danger" idea with operational prevention service programs.

Another objective to which a prevention program can relate is to reduce expected public expenditure and quality-of-life disbenefits over the lifetime of persons in the total handicapped population. Prevention can reduce future public expenditure by reducing the absolute number of those entering the handicapped population and by providing a full range of remedial and restorative services to those already in that population. Handicap prevention is not done well in the United States, as attested to by the persistent prevalence of handicapped persons with preventable etiologies and by the simple and persistent statistic that the United States ranks fifteenth among

---

[4]"Planning Guidance Memorandum—1972," February 15, 1972.

nations in infant mortality.[5] The provision of remedial and restorative services is not done very well either, as attested to by other chapters of this book.

If so many disorders are demonstrably preventable, why do so many handicapped children still enter the population because of them? If so many other disorders are suspected of being to blame for handicaps, why is research directed at the resolution of these disorders so poorly orchestrated? Several explanations are possible for the stunted growth of prevention programs.

S. H. King has advanced an explanation for the undervaluation of inoculation programs that may be applicable to prevention programs in general: "The person or group with a time orientation toward the present (e.g., politicians) will have difficulty in seeing the value of inoculations against disease, a future occurrence."[6] Undervaluation may occur for the full range of prevention programs for the same reason. Conserving today's prevention funds may make good short-term economic sense to a hard-pressed public official; in the long run, such a policy may be penny-wise and pound-foolish. What appear to be savings—even small savings—may inflict prolonged and expensive consequences when one considers the high human and economic costs of an impaired individual over the years, both to the person and to society.[7]

Underinvestment in prevention services may also occur because those agencies currently administering prevention programs, usually health agencies or personnel, do not benefit from the future reduced costs of service such as special education, vocational services, and welfare, which are administered elsewhere. Thus, from the narrow viewpoint of the administering agency, rather than the viewpoint of

[5]The 1972 rate was 19.2 deaths before the age of 1 year per 1000 live births. On this measure, the United States is ranked behind Sweden (11.1/1000), Japan (12.4), France (14.4), the United Kingdom (18.0), Canada (18.8), East Germany (18.8), and others. *Scientific American,* Vol. 229, No. 3, September 1973, pp. 64–66. The contribution of adequate prenatal care (a preventive practice) was underscored in that report. A 1968 health survey found that the then-prevailing infant mortality rate of 21.9 for all of New York City could have been reduced to an estimated 14.7 if all the mothers surveyed had received a *modal* amount of prenatal care. For those in New York City judged to have received "adequate" prenatal care, the rate was 13.3, for "intermediate" care it was 18.5, and for "no" or "inadequate" prenatal care it was 35.8. It was concluded that there existed "a gross misallocation of services by ethnic groups when the risks of the women are taken into account."

[6]*Perceptions of Illness and Medical Practice,* Russell Sage Foundation, New York, 1962, p. 53.

[7]This is precisely the conclusion of Ronald W. Conley, *The Economics of Mental Retardation,* The Johns Hopkins University Press, Baltimore, Maryland, 1973, a sophisticated and convincing analysis of service programs for the retarded.

all government agencies as a whole, prevention may be a net long-term as well as a short-term cost.

Seriously inadequate information also hampers and misdirects prevention services and research. Foggy information on the prevalence of various etiologies can produce only foggy estimates of the extent to which the individual disorders contribute to the handicapped population, and how these prevalences are changing over time. One result is that research attention focuses somewhat indiscriminately on both rare and commonplace diseases and disorders.[8] Another result is that erratic information makes it hard to marshal compelling arguments for prevention.

Still other explanations may be: few theories relate prevention costs to other service costs (partly, no doubt, because of the paucity and imprecision of the basic information); known data on all other service costs are not routinely related to the immediate costs of conducting research into disorder causes and processes or to the operational costs of carrying out a prevention program; no one has direct and comprehensive responsibility for prevention; and insufficient attention is being given to the applications of research findings to prevention program operations and to dissemination of those findings to practicing physicians, who are a major source of prevention through proper medical treatment of handicap-causing disorders.

Operational Prevention Service Programs[9]

Immunization is a clear instance of preventive service, for which there is a number of programs. Communicable Disease Prevention and Control has been legislated through the basic "Public Health Services Act" and updated periodically by amendments.[10] It includes the epidemiological program of the National Center for Disease Control, which had $1.709 million in FY 1972 for consultation, technical assistance, and training for state health agencies, among other responsibilities; a communicable disease control program, funded at

[8]Jacob Feldman, *The Dissemination of Health Information,* Aldine, Chicago, 1966, has addressed the general question of data as it relates to rational decision making on research expenditures and for prevention has concluded that the poor available information on the time of onset and etiology has inhibited concerted attention and remediation.

[9]A grand total of $153 million for *all* federal "Preventive Health Services" is listed in U.S. Department of Health, Education, and Welfare, *Justifications of Appropriation Estimates for Committee on Appropriations, FY 1973,* Vol. II, pp. 1–63.

[10]Public Health Service Act, Secs. 301, 314, 317, 361–369. Bio-Dynamics, Inc., *Evaluation of the Rubella Immunization Program,* DHEW/ASPE, Contract No. HEW-OS-70-153, Washington, D.C., 1972, pp. 7–18, presents a thorough legislative digest.

$7.213 million in FY 1971, that offers a variety of immunization activities to children; and Health Service Development Project Grants to the states, which have supported, among other activities, the rubella immunization project at a rate of $14.5 million and which allocated some $500,000 for a modest but expanding program for Rh desensitization in FY 1973.[11] Additionally, some number of immunization services and activities are conducted through the Maternal and Child Health Service.

Venereal disease, an etiology linked to congenital disorders, is also a preventive responsibility of the National Center for Disease Control. It was funded at a $16.0 million level in 1972.[12]

General prevention along a broad but not very deep front is provided under Maternal and Child Health and Crippled Children's Services programs.[13] A 1969 survey indicated that, for *all* services for *all* conditions, there were some 190 MCHS and 19 CCS supported program activities in the states that could be directly labeled "preventive." Of this total, no single type of prevention service was provided in all the states.

Medicaid has an operational prevention component inherent in its early and periodic screening, diagnosis, and treatment provisions. (See the discussion of Medicaid in Chap. 9.)

The "Health Maintenance Act of 1973" is popularly regarded as a prevention initiative,[14] but it cannot be reliably estimated how much the $375 million total to be expended over the five years of its existence will reduce handicapping in the young.

Finally, many other governmental programs include prevention as a secondary activity, but with unknown effects. In this class would be improved prenatal care; family planning; identification and direction, where they exist; and a few operational genetics counseling programs. While precise numbers cannot be estimated, the sum total of all such activities is relatively small.

Prevention Research Programs

Preventive research programs are a main responsibility of several institutes within the National Institutes of Health, but it is often difficult to say what portion of a research program on impairment in general

---

[11]*Justifications of Appropriation Estimates,* p. 17.

[12]*Update to the 1972 Catalog of Federal Domestic Assistance,* Office of Management and Budget (OMB), Washington, D.C., November 1972, p. 186.1.

[13]A narrative is contained in Edwin M. Gold et al., "Total Maternal and Infant Care: An Evaluation," *American Journal of Public Health,* Vol. 59, No. 101, October 1969, pp. 1851–1856.

[14]See, e.g., "Nixon Preventive Health Bill," *The New York Times,* December 30, 1973, pp. 1, 13.

should be evaluated as a benefit to the young in particular. For example, research to promote the understanding, treatment, and prevention of glaucoma is universally beneficial, but one cannot say how much of the current glaucoma research budget of the National Eye Institute should be counted as a benefit for handicapped children.

The National Institute for Child Health and Human Development (NICHD), primarily through its perinatal biology and infant mortality program, and to a lesser extent through its growth and development and population and reproduction programs, is conducting research contributing to the prevention of many types of handicapping. Perinatal biology and infant mortality represented a total expenditure of $10.8 million in FY 1972 for research in 318 grants and contracts.[15] Studies on maternal complications in pregnancy, toxemia and diabetes, malnutrition affecting the fetus, respiratory distress, Rh sensitivity, hypoglycemia, and erythroblastosis fetalis, all added to prevention.

The National Institute for Neurological Diseases and Stroke (NINDS) contributes to prevention research, e.g., through its communication disorders prenatal and perinatal programs.[16]

The National Eye Institute (NEI) had a budget of $24.95 million in FY 1973, broken down according to disease classes as follows: retina and choroid, $6.2 million; sensory motor, $3.7 million; corneal, $3.0 million; glaucoma, $2.7 million; and congenital and developmental, $530,000.

The National Institute of Dental Research (NIDR) conducts a cleft lip and palate research program, which was funded at $2.0 million in FY 1970.

The National Institute of Allergy and Infectious Diseases (NIAID) supports research into methods of control of allergic, immunological, and infectious diseases, which contain many etiologies related to handicaps.

The National Institute of General Medical Sciences (NIGMS) supported genetic research with $33.5 million in FY 1973, some portion of which aids prevention of handicapping; the same is true for its programs on general clinical service and trauma.

Private research activities exist, but their total contribution to research in this area is not known.

[15]NICHD, Program Statistics and Analysis Branch, Interview, June 7, 1973.

[16]The perinatal program has over the years been conducting an extensive study of neurologically and sensorially handicapped children, resulting in a rich source of unique data. A great deal of potential knowledge is contained in this file, but much analytic work remains to be done to realize the full benefits from it.

We now proceed to more specific discussions of prevention, using various types of handicapping conditions for illustrative purposes.

PREVENTION OF HEARING AND VISION DISORDERS

A number of hearing and vision disorders can be prevented. Table 6.1 is a partial listing of those disorders in which disabling sensory handicaps appear to be relatively more preventable, given the current state of the medical art. The disorders themselves are described in some detail in the "Medical Services" chapter of this book.

Rubella is preventable; an effective vaccine has been in widespread use since 1969, but implementation and scientific problems still impede full prevention (they are discussed below).

Ototoxic deafness is known to result from the use of certain drugs, and others are suspected. For those known to cause hearing loss, prevention should be a near certainty, but is not. For those antibiotics suspected to be related to hearing loss, a clear case can be made for additional prevention research. We know how to prevent handicapping from inappropriate drug use, but drug-deafened children still enter the population.

Any number of disorders exemplified by various forms of otitis media are liable to cause sensory deficits *if* they are improperly treated, left untreated, or treated late because of faulty identification, direction, and treatment services.

Retrolental fibroplasia can be devastating, but it is generally known that excessive oxygen is responsible for the blindness it causes. Even at the current state of knowledge, a majority of the people entering the population blinded by RLF should not be. With additional prevention research into oxygen dosages and the mechanisms by which oxygen "poisons" the eye, better techniques of monitoring oxygen administered to infants, better incubators, and improved understanding by physicians (especially pediatricians and obstetricians), the disease is probably about 95 percent or more preventable. The remaining 5 percent would occur in those stark and critical situations where blindness may reluctantly be chosen as the lesser undesirable outcome in a life-threatening situation. Better prenatal care, to cite a more general prevention strategy, could furthermore lessen the prevalence of prematurity (a proven relationship exists between prenatal care and the likelihood of a premature birth) and hence the need for oxygen therapy.

A number of disorders can be corrected or contained and need not cause handicaps; however, success in nearly all of these depends on the earliest possible identification (before the age of 5 in most cases) and correct medical treatment.

Table 6.1
SOME SENSORY DISORDERS AND DISEASES WITH HIGH
PROBABILITY OF PREVENTION

| *Disorder or Disease* | Handicap | | *Method* |
	Vision	*Hearing*	
Rubella	X	X	Immunization
Ototoxic deafness		X	Proper medical treatment
Noise deafness		X	Remove offending source; institute hearing conservation measures; keep children away from explosive sounds
Otosclerosis		X	Diagnosis and surgical treatment
Otitis media		X	Identify, diagnose, and treat correctly. Persistent care
Mumps		X	Immunization
Measles		X	Immunization
Meningitis		X	Prompt, proper medical treatment
Rh sensitivity		X	Proper identification and sound care
Retrolental fibroplasia	X		Proper medical treatment (specific case); prenatal care (general case)
Amblyopia, strabismus, myopia	X		Prompt identification, diagnosis and treatment
Cataract	X		Early detection and treatment
Glaucoma	X		Detection before irreparable damage is done; proper treatment
Retinoblastoma	X		Treatment of affected child. I.D. for parents-to-be suspected of being trait carriers, genetic counseling, and family planning

NOTE: For each disorder, high-quality preventive or medical treatment service is thought to result in no handicapping condition in at least three-fourths of the cases, and for some disorders, in at least 99 percent.

Several disorders are detectable with *in utero* assessment techniques, even at the relatively underdeveloped state of the practice,[17] but the degree of preventive potential depends on the accessibility of an up-to-date identification and preventive care program, genetic counseling, and the choice by parents on whether or not to terminate the pregnancy when a major handicapping disorder is actually detected.

We now turn to the question of strategies for prevention of hearing and vision disorders and discuss prenatal care; immunization; timely

[17]Dr. John Hobbins and his associates at Yale have, as of 1978, made dramatic progress in the sampling of fetal blood, as early as the eighteenth week of gestation, and relating this to an assortment of genetically (and other) related disorders. Something on the order of 10 research hospitals worldwide are able to do this kind of work.

identification, direction and proper medical treatment; family planning; genetic counseling; and abortion and other practices.

Prevention Strategies and Tradeoffs

In deciding whether to implement any of the prevention strategies to be described, or in deciding on modification of existing prevention programs, one must confront the question of the tradeoff between current costs of a prevention program, future costs in terms of the reduced quality of life of persons whose handicaps are not prevented, and future costs of service to those persons. While the logic is clear, it is extremely difficult to make a tradeoff in practice. Not only are data lacking, but dollar estimates attached to decreases in quality of life are bound to be somewhat arbitrary. For example, suppose one desires to determine the level of preventive activity that results in a minimum total of prevention costs plus "disamenity" costs associated with reduced quality of life and with later service needs due to handicaps not prevented. For illustration, a simplistic version of the problem is presented in Fig. 6.1, which plots hypothetical costs of prevention, "disamenity" costs of handicaps not prevented, and total costs.[18]

The purpose of a mathematical analysis of data plotted in such a figure could be to assess relative prevention strategies to determine how far a strategy could be used before the returns become marginally disadvantageous—i.e., the cost of one more prevention exceeds the "disamenity" cost of not preventing one more handicap. To perform this type of analysis, data must be available for each prevention strategy and each disorder, and one must be able to arrive at a way of expressing quality of life in money or commensurate terms.

In practice, the type of analysis implicit in Fig. 6.1 has little direct relevance.[19] The available data make it difficult enough to account with any accuracy for all factors contributing to prevention costs, e.g., research, training, operations; and no one can reliably estimate the costs or benefits of as yet unrealized technological breakthroughs as

[18]A related discussion is contained in Charles D. Scott, "Health Care Delivery and Advanced Technology," *Science,* Vol. 180, June 29, 1973, pp. 1339–1342. The topic has also been treated in D. P. Rice, *Estimating the Costs of Illness,* Public Health Service, Publication No. 947-6, Washington, D.C., 1966; and Chauncey Starr, "Social Benefit Versus Technological Risks," *Science,* Vol. 165, 1969, p. 1232.

[19]We are not saying that conducting such analyses is not without value; rather, we are facing the immediate practicality issue. An otherwise elegant and thorough analysis ran into difficulty on precisely this point: see S. Fanshel and J. W. Bush, "A Health-Status Index and Its Application to Health-Services Outcomes," *Operations Research,* Vol. 18, No. 6, November-December 1970, pp. 1021–1066. This article contains an excellent bibliography describing the state of the field.

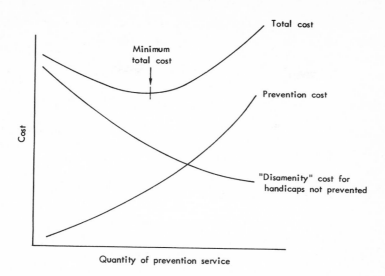

Fig. 6.1 Hypothetical prevention cost relationships.

they may contribute to an improved prevention service. Data to provide a clear understanding of factors causing a specific disorder, and the contributions of a given preventive strategy to reduced prevalence and to reduced future service cost, are not fully available either. And finally, this style of analysis necessarily overlooks some difficult but important problems, including the "cost" and "worth" of human life, individual variations in preferences, thresholds of pain or suffering, and other bearable or perhaps unbearable costs of "disamenity."

What is left to us, then, to help decide whether increased prevention activity is desirable? For the Vocational Rehabilitation program, where data are relatively good, we are able to perform a fairly sophisticated benefit-cost analysis (see Chap. 13); the basic point made there is that program-costs to society, to the taxpayers, and to the handicapped individual are all less than the program's corresponding future economic benefits; and increased quality of life adds even more benefits. We use a similar line of argument, for example, in a rubella immunization program analysis made later in this section. We show that the costs of the rubella prevention program are far less than the future discounted incremental costs of special education for persons whose handicaps the program could have prevented. (And added quality-of-life benefits and reduced future costs of other services would justify this program still further.)

Another approach is to consider the service costs for hearing and vision handicapped children, asking how expensive a prevention program can be and still fall below the service costs for handicaps not prevented. For example, assume that the FY 1971 annual government expenditure of $420 million for services for the 683,000 hearing and vision handicapped youth, or $615 per handicapped youth, is representative of the average annual incremental cost for the handicap to be prevented by a proposed program.[20] The present value of 21 years of expenditures for the handicapped youth is approximately $6150 at an 8 percent discount rate. In this example, the prevention program would be justified, on grounds of reduced future service costs alone, if the prevention cost per handicap prevented is less than about $6150. If one further assumes, not unreasonably, that the humanitarian quality-of-life benefits of not being handicapped are worth at least 10 times this reduced service cost, then the program would be justified on humanitarian grounds alone if prevention cost is less than about $60,000 per handicap prevented. In other words, the program would be justified on humanitarian grounds if costs are $60 per youth and only 1 in 1000 youth receiving the service had a handicap prevented as a result (or $6 and 1 in 10,000, or $600 and 1 in 100).

We now turn to a summarization of individual types of prevention strategies.

Prenatal Care as a Prevention Strategy

Partly because of the leadership along a broad research front provided by the National Institute of Child Health and Human Development, more is being learned about the critical importance of prenatal care as a general preventive strategy. Specific relationships between a number of prenatal conditions and subsequent sensory disorders are known; and many other suspected conditions, given the prevalence of "unknown prenatal influence" as an etiologic class for sensory handicaps, have become fitting research topics.

In an informative summary of "dos and don'ts" for a pregnant woman, Jane Brody[21] has made the following observations—all of

---

[20]The $615 figure is not the true value of the incremental cost, of course, but it is probably of the correct order of magnitude. Estimation of the actual incremental cost is considerably more complex; it involves such factors as determining what amount of current expenditures would not be reduced, such as a portion of Medicaid for families that might be needy even without a handicapped child, and such as various program "overhead" costs; and predicting what would be the particular government program organizational reactions to a smaller handicapped population, such as more outreach to find clients, or providing a higher level of service to individual clients. It would also be necessary to estimate the incremental cost savings and increased benefits for the particular mix of types and degrees of handicaps to be prevented.

[21]*How a Mother Affects Her Unborn Baby,* National Institute of Child Health and Human Development, Washington, D.C., 1971 (reprint).

which contribute generally to reduced chances of producing an abnormal baby.

- Most important is the early and periodic prenatal examination by a competent physician. All adverse indicators, e.g., low birth weight, prevalence of defects, fetal misadventure, are positively related to poor or nonexistent prenatal care.
- Drug intake, including common nonprescription, prescription, and "dangerous" drugs should be sharply curtailed or eliminated altogether. If drugs must be taken, it should be done *only* with the guidance and prescription of a physician, preferably the obstetrician responsible for the prenatal course of treatment. In this regard, no drug—no matter how "harmless" it is— is to be considered above reproach. Definitive research has just not been done in sufficient quantity to rule out the potentially damaging effects of *any* drug or foreign chemical substance, and this includes aspirin, nicotine, caffeine, and vitamins taken in excessive amounts, as well as prescription medications, e.g., steroids, progesterone, antibiotics, diuretics, antihistaminics, anti-depressants.[22]
- Proper nutrition is important as a part of sound prenatal care; protein deficiencies, for instance, are known to be related to decreased cerebral development.[23]
- Abdominal x-rays should be avoided, especially in the first weeks of pregnancy.
- Live virus vaccines should not be administered if pregnancy is suspected; included on this list are smallpox, measles, rubella, mumps, and yellow fever.

Good general prenatal care will also detect syphilis in routine serologic workups. Congenital syphilis is apparently on the increase, and has been suspected in congenital sensorineural hearing loss, keratitis, and cataract.

The relationship between prenatal drug intake and subsequent hearing loss in the infant has been established for antibiotics in the mycin group, is suspected with other antibiotics, and is known to exist in the case of quinine. Various hearing disorders linked to drug intake include congenital malformation of the Organ of Corti and irreversible damage to the auditory nerve. Congenital cataract and drug intake are suspected to be related. The general caution noted for prenatal drug use pertains.

---

[22]NICHD supports a modest program in Prenatal Pharmacology that addresses many of these issues.

[23]See also *Nutrition and Human Development: A Special Report Prepared for the National Advisory Child Health and Human Development Council,* NICHD, Washington, D.C., November 17, 1969.

X-rays in the early stages of pregnancy are suspected in cases of congenital cataracts and other malformations of the eye.

Finally, vaccination of a pregnant female against mumps, rubella, and measles with a live-virus vaccine is capable of infecting and causing harm to the fetal sensory organs.

Immunization

A major strategy for prevention of sensory handicaps is to immunize to prevent diseases and disorders that can cause handicapping, such as measles, mumps, and especially rubella and Rh sensitivity. While the probability of handicapping from measles and mumps is relatively low, there is great danger with Rh sensitivity and rubella (especially if a woman contracts it during the first trimester of her pregnancy). And, as we will illustrate for rubella, the cost of an immunization program can be low compared with the costs of handicapping.

A problem is that many persons are not receiving this obvious type of prevention service. For example, reports from the National Center for Disease Control in Atlanta have registered concern that not enough children in rural and central city areas are being vaccinated against polio and measles. Especially significant was the finding that about one-half of central city children surveyed were *not* protected against measles or polio. More than 75,000 cases of measles were reported in 1971, an increase of 28,000 over the previous year.[24] It is a persistent problem, reflecting both the fragmented nature of the health system generally and the particularly limited interest given to preventive activities as contrasted with most other services.[25] It apparently takes an epidemic, or the threat of one, to force preventive immunization into the forefront.

[24]See *Education Daily,* May 5, 1972, p. 6, which also notes that both measles and diphtheria have risen sharply since 1970, a finding alleged to be linked to certain federal government officials' "reluctance to support special vaccination programs," whereby preventive activities have been "lumped into a generalized program which gives local and state governments freedom to choose how the money will be spent." This condition persists and by 1977 had reached near-crisis proportions. For example, measles had reached epidemic proportions in several sections of the country by early 1977 (*Time,* February 20, 1977).

[25]Former Secretary of Health, Education, and Welfare Abraham Ribicoff is quoted as saying that the vaccination programs existing then had two major weaknesses: "First, they have been so closely related to school admissions that they have provided poor coverage for preschool children. Second, they have been least effective in reaching families in low-income neighborhoods." *Proceedings,* 2d Annual Immunization Conference, May 1965, p. 5, as cited in Bio-Dynamics, Inc., *Evaluation of the Rubella Immunization Program,* Department of Health, Education, and Welfare, Office of the Assistant Secretary for the Planning and Evaluation, Contract No. HEW-OS-70-153, Washington, D.C., 1972, p. 8.

No one government agency is primarily responsible for coordinating immunization programs (including research, assuring production and quality of the vaccine or serum, delivery of the service, and then evaluation of program effectiveness). And government costs for immunization are not borne by the same agencies that reap future benefits—these benefits being "successful" prevention, cases of diseases that did *not* occur and did *not* cause handicapping, and hence service costs that were *not* incurred later.

While the National Center for Disease Control has been a leader in promoting immunization programs, implementation has been delegated to state and local health authorities, who are left for the most part to their own devices. The results have been mixed, as documented in a definitive rubella evaluation study conducted for the Office of the Secretary, Department of Health, Education, and Welfare by Bio-Dynamics, Inc.[26]

Rubella It took a major epidemic in the early 1960s to galvanize official attention in the case of rubella, but in the absence of subsequent catastrophes, maintenance of this attention and activity has waned. Specific details of what this entails for the rubella prevention program include the following:

- There is marked unevenness in the quality of community-run programs and slight provision available to correct the more deficient ones.
- Identification of people in at-risk groups is not uniformly well done, with the result that coverage is uneven.
- School-based programs miss many preschoolers.
- Maintenance and surveillance are crudely developed and "the probability of satisfactory maintenance after federal funding ends is poor."
- Private physicians are not included in the reporting procedures of the program; program effectiveness studies are thereby biased.
- The Center for Disease Control needs considerable strengthening to carry out its responsibilities.

And finally, the most significant finding of all:

At this time there is substantial evidence that seven years of the Vaccination Assistance Act did not provide all states with the means to continue high levels of immunization. The Federal grants mechanism did not provide adequate incentive to build this at the local level nor the technical assistance to show how it can be done. The established public health structure demonstrated capability to carry out the attack phase but not the maintenance phase.[27]

[26]Bio-Dynamics, Inc., op. cit., pp. 75–81.

[27]Ibid., pp. 6–9. Nothing seems to have happened in the last six years to alter this finding.

The importance of long-term maintenance of preventive activities may be stressed in a simple cost exercise designed to relate prevention costs to service costs for handicaps resulting from inadequate prevention.

The rubella epidemic of 1963–1965 left an estimated 20,000 to 30,000 handicapped children in its wake, a tragedy that society will be paying for in many significant ways for years to come.[28] In his analysis, Donald Calvert estimated the special educational costs alone associated with the impaired subset of the epidemic population.[29] We have made our own more conservative estimates based on special education expenditure data presented in Chap. 10 of this report for the *discounted incremental costs* above the cost of regular education. Further, we have omitted educational costs for what Calvert has termed "mild to moderate" handicaps, biasing our special education cost figures down even more. As can be seen in Table 6.2, Calvert's and our estimated special educational costs differ significantly; however, even taking our intentionally conservative estimate as a basis of comparison, there is a striking difference between the $202 million increased special educational costs due to that one rubella epidemic and the $41.6 million total authorized under the Rubella Immunization Program.[30] And we have not even considered increased costs of

[28] J. L. Sever et al., "Epidemiological Observations of Rubella in the Collaborative Perinatal Research Study," *Proceedings, International Conference on Rubella Immunization,* Stockholm, Sweden, February 18–20, 1969.

[29] Donald R. Calvert, *Report on Rubella and Handicapped Children,* Department of Health, Education, and Welfare, Bureau of Education for the Handicapped, Washington, D.C., May 1969.

[30] P.L. 89-749, Section 314(e).

Table 6.2
ESTIMATED COSTS FOR 13 YEARS OF SPECIAL EDUCATION OF HANDICAPPED CHILDREN RESULTING FROM THE RUBELLA EPIDEMIC OF 1963–1965

Handicap	Number	Undiscounted Total Cost: Calvert Estimate	Discounted Total Incremental Cost: Rand Estimate
Visually impaired	5,500	$250,250,000	$ 35,500,000
Hearing impaired	12,000	468,000,000	77,400,000
Deaf-blind	1,250	227,500,000	81,000,000
Retarded/crippled	1,250	48,750,000	8,100,000
Total	20,000	$994,500,000	$202,000,000

SOURCE: Donald R. Calvert, *Report on Rubella and Handicapped Children,* Department of Health, Education, and Welfare, Bureau of Education for the Handicapped, Washington, D.C., May 1969.

NOTE: Rand estimates are based on expenditure data presented in Chap. 10. Thirteen-year costs are discounted at 8 percent to time of birth.

services other than special education in the calculation, not to mention the degradation of quality of life inflicted by the handicaps.

The urgency of such preventive programs is manifest if we look only at the high annual cost associated with the special education of deaf-blind children: from \$12,000 to \$14,000 per child.[31] For the estimated 1250 deaf-blind children resulting from the 1963–1965 rubella epidemic, this represents an annual outlay of \$15 million (using the low estimate)—but in 1972 only \$7.5 million was expended for establishing and supporting Deaf-Blind Centers for *all* of the 4728 identified deaf-blind children in the United States as of January 1, 1972.[32]

The messages from this example and discussion are clear:

- Rubella can be prevented.
- Rubella-caused handicaps are expensive.
- Prevention is decidedly cost-effective.

But,

- Attention to the rubella immunization program has flagged, with potentially tragic and costly results.

It would be easy to conclude summarily with the recommendations that renewed vigilance be applied to rubella immunization efforts; but several confounding facts must be taken into consideration before making such an appeal.

There was evidence that rubella may have been controlled as a result of the mass immunization program. The Center for Disease Control noted only 21,424 cases of rubella in the first 39 weeks of 1972, a 44 percent decline over a comparable period in 1971.[33] While the trend was downward since the 1969 initiation of rubella immunization efforts, one must caution that rubella occurs periodically. From all indications, 1977 would appear to have been at the leading edge of one of these periods. Control of the disease is not accomplished "once and for all," and eradication is probably out of the question given its worldwide prevalence.

There is also evidence that the "herd immunity" approach adopted in the original rubella program does not work as well as it was ex-

---

[31]The low estimate is that used by California's School for the Blind in their Deaf-Blind program, and the high figure is that reported by Calvert for Massachusetts' Perkins School for the Blind's program in 1969.

[32]U.S. Congress, House, Subcommittee of the Committee on Appropriations, *Hearings, Part 2, Office of Education and Special Institutions,* 92d Cong., 2d Sess., 1972 (hereafter cited as *Hearings*), p. 403.

[33]Reported in *Education Daily,* Vol. 5, December 20, 1972, pp. 1–2. Estimates vary, but somewhere between 30 and 40 million children have been immunized in the program.

pected to.[34] For instance, Klock and Rachelefsky, in reporting on an epidemic localized to Casper, Wyoming, in early 1971,[35] found that while 83 percent of the elementary school and 52 percent of the preschool population had been immunized (and for these groups protection was excellent), older youth had not been immunized while young, and some 1000 cases of rubella occurred in a population of some 40,000. Eighty-four percent of those afflicted were teen-agers, and 27 cases occurred in women, 7 of whom were pregnant. While others have used these findings to argue for the repeal of some 22 state laws mandating rubella immunization as a requirement for school admission, the following are the conclusions drawn by the investigators from the Casper case:

> Although the vaccination of prepubertal children in Casper did not prevent an epidemic, this effort undoubtedly did prevent infection of a number of pregnant women after the epidemic began. If youn-ger children had not been immunized, the outbreak would have been more extensive, and the number of exposed, susceptible women would have been much higher. Thus, childhood rubella im-munization remains an important method of rubella prevention; however, because of the potential for outbreaks in older children this procedure should be supplemented by other methods of ru-bella control. The most important of these is the identification and vaccination of susceptible, non-pregnant women in the child-bear-ing age.[36]

Other specialized literature on the rubella immunization issue gen-erally supports these findings and conclusions.[37] Among other partial results contained in this body of literature, the following summary points stand out:

[34] J. P. Fox et al., "Herd Immunity: Basic Concept and Relevance to Public Health Immunization Practices," *American Journal of Epidemiology,* Vol. 94, 1971, pp. 179–189. The concept is that, if a sufficiently large fraction of the population is im-mune, transmission of the disease is inhibited and the potential for an epidemic re-duced.

[35] Lawrence E. Klock and Gary S. Rachelefsky, "Failure of Rubella Herd Immunity During an Epidemic," *New England Journal of Medicine,* January 11, 1973, pp. 69–72.

[36] Ibid., p. 72.

[37] National Center for Disease Control, "Rubella Virus Vaccine: Recommendation of the Public Health Service Advisory Committee on Immunization Practices," *Annals of Internal Medicine,* Vol. 75, 1971, pp. 757–759; D. M. Horstman, "Rubella and the Ru-bella Syndrome: New Epidemiologic Virologic Observations," *California Medicine,* Vol. 102, 1965, pp. 397–401; S. A. Plotkin, "Virologic Assistance in the Management of German Measles in Pregnancy," *Journal of the American Medical Association,* Vol. 109, 1964, pp. 105–108; J. J. Witte et al., "Epidemiology of Rubella," *American Journal of Disabled Children,* Vol. 118, 1969, pp. 107–111; S. A. Wyll and M. G. Grand, "Rubella in Adolescents: Serologic Assessments of Immunity Levels," *Journal of the American Medical Association,* Vol. 220, 1972, pp. 1573–1575; H. M. Meyer, Jr., and P. D. Parkman,

(footnote continued on next page)

- As contrasted with selective vaccination programs directed at the at-risk population of women of child-bearing age, the herd immunity concept does not appear to be completely reliable.
- More than 95 percent of those vaccinated develop serum antibodies and appear in the short term to demonstrate protection. (Reinfection rates among naturally immunized and vaccinated populations have not been established but should be given careful surveillance.)[38]
- The chances of a previously immunized female becoming reinfected and, if reinfected, transmitting the disease to the fetus, are not known.[39]
- It is known that the vaccination is capable of producing unpleasant side effects, both in children and particularly in postpubescent females.[40]

A conservative recommendation, based on these findings, has been offered by Vincent Fulginiti, a virologist, in the following terms:

> The author feels there is sufficient uncertainty about the effectiveness of mass rubella immunization, sufficient question concerning pharyngeal virus growth in the vaccinee, and sufficient doubt about the significance of side effects to question the wisdom of utilizing rubella vaccine routinely in childhood. A preferable alternative at present would be to immunize all prepubescent females, to test all women in the child-bearing age group for rubella antibody, and to immunize those who are susceptible (approximately 15%). It is necessary to make absolutely certain that pregnancy is avoided for at least 2 months following such immunization.[41]

However, this recommendation is somewhat at odds with a recent Public Health Service Advisory Committee opinion that all children between the ages of 1 year and puberty should receive a rubella vaccination.[42]

(footnote continued from previous page)

"Rubella Vaccination: A Review of Practical Experience," *Journal of the American Medical Association,* Vol. 215, 1971, pp. 613–619; A. D. Heggie and F. C. Robbins, "Natural Rubella Acquired after Birth," *American Journal of Disabled Children,* Vol. 118, 1969, pp. 12–17; and R. H. Green et al., "Rubella: Studies in its Etiology, Epidemiology, Clinical Course, and Prevention," *Transactions of the Association of American Physicians,* Vol. 77, 1964, pp. 420–427.

[38]D. M. Horstman et al., "Rubella: Reinfection of Vaccinated and Naturally Immune Persons Exposed in an Epidemic," *New England Journal of Medicine,* October 1970, pp. 771–778.

[39]Plotkin, op. cit., pp. 105–107.

[40]L. Z. Cooper et al., "Rubella: Clinical Manifestions and Management," *American Journal of Disabled Children,* Vol. 118, 1969, pp. 18–29.

[41]Vincent A. Fulginiti, "Immunization," in C. Henry Kempe et al., *Current Pediatric Diagnosis and Treatment,* Lange Medical Publications, Los Altos, California, 1972, pp. 107–122, at pp. 117–118.

[42]National Center for Disease Control, "Rubella Virus Vaccine: Recommendation."

A basis for reconciliation of the views is contained in our following recommendations for an improved rubella immunization program:

- Mandate vaccination for all prepubescent females through a school-based program conducted under the auspices of the National Center for Disease Control.
- Create a model code for state marriage license serologic screening practices with the objective of including an additional test for the presence of rubella antibodies.
- Conduct an appeal through the mass media and professional medical publications to encourage all childbearing females to obtain such tests from their private physicians. The decision to proceed with vaccination, in the estimated 15 percent thought not to be naturally immune, then becomes a uniquely determined one between doctor and patient.
- Conduct periodic studies of reinfection rates among vaccinated and naturally immunized populations to determine whether the efficacy of the initial, massive rubella immunization program is sustaining or not.

The first recommendation represents a reduced but more tightly focused extension of the national rubella immunization program. With continuous application, all of the at-risk population will be protected in the long term. Prepubescent restrictions for administration of the vaccine minimize the danger of arthritic complications, and not selecting male children confronts the breakdown in herd immunity noted by Klock and Rachelefsky; for males, contracting the disease may present fewer and less severe risks than possible complications of adverse reactions to the vaccine.

Given that on the order of 4 million live births per year were recorded in the decade between 1960 and 1970,[43] about 2 million vaccinations per year would be needed to reach the entire at-risk population on an annual cohort basis. At costs of $0.47 per dose,[44] total vaccine costs would be around $1 million per year in the long run. Even at $5.00 per dose, the costs of $10 million per year would be small relative to savings in later service costs for handicaps not prevented.

The second recommendation is more an identification plus prevention service than a purely preventive one. Blood tests for syphilis are required in most states already, and the test for rubella antibodies is rather easily and inexpensively done at the same time. Provision to

---

[43]U.S. Bureau of the Census, *Statistical Abstract of the United States, 1972,* Washington, D.C., p. 50.

[44]Bio-Dynamics, Inc., op. cit., p. 39.

test women for the rubella antibodies has been enacted into law in California in the form of Senate Bill 1002, approved in August 1972.[45] Briefly, the law requires, with several exceptions, a physician's certification that in addition to being free from syphilis, all female marriage license applicants have been tested for an immunological response to rubella. Nothing beyond informing the woman is contained in the law, but presumably positive identification could result in advice to consult a private physician about the possibility of obtaining a vaccination.[46] The law itself represents a "natural" social experiment, involving a state with 10 percent of the nation's population, and deserves to be evaluated as such, to assist other states considering following suit with versions of the same legal provision. The possible damage in an unsuspected pregnancy by administration of the rubella vaccine is known to be great. It is also known that the virus is often long-lived, which means that any childbearing female *should not* become pregnant for *at least* two months after receiving the vaccine.

Our third recommendation stresses the private physician's role, as opposed to a direct governmental one, in reaching childbearing women who are either unmarried or already married and hence would be missed in a screening of marriage license applicants.

The issue of reinfection rates is not settled but warrants careful surveillance. The rubella vaccine has been in widespread, albeit sporadic, use in the United States less than 15 years, certainly insufficient time to establish its long-term persistence with great reliability.

Rh Sensitivity Immunization   Development and use of the Rh desensitizing gamma globulin has resulted in a reduction of newborn jaundice, and with it a reduction in the associated hearing disorder of erythroblastosis fetalis. However, to prevent sensitization and subsequent threat to children born later, the RhoGAM must be administered within 72 hours after the Rh-negative mother has terminated pregnancy of an Rh-positive child. Blood-typing and antibody screening are considered an important part of effective prenatal care,

---

[45]*Deering's Code of Civil Procedure,* Vol. I, Pamphlet No. 5, 1972, Chapter 714, pp. 22–23; and *Civil Code of the State of California,* Sections 4300 and 4302, as amended by S.B. 1002, 1972. Implementation was delayed until January 1, 1974.

[46]The California blood test law also contains a reference to possible use of the serologic specimen for identification of "carriers of genetic diseases, including, but not limited to, sickle cell anemia and Tay-Sachs disease, and that such tests may be performed at the same time as those tests required in Section 4300." *Deering's Code,* p. 23. The implications of this law are potentially far-reaching, a point discussed in a following section on genetic counseling.

and based on the bilirubin levels obtained in amniocentesis (when indicated), specific management procedures of mother and unborn child may be required.[47] Immunization, typing, screening, evaluation, and management are all elements of responsible preventive care. The extent of reduction in handicapping resulting from having this kind of care widely available is not known, but is clearly significant.

Routine Immunization Modern standards of pediatric practice call for a routinized immunization program such as the representative schedule approved by the Committee on Infectious Diseases of the American Academy of Pediatrics (Table 6.3). Exact timing and sequencing are matters left to the physician's discretion.

Following such a schedule increases protection against a number of formerly devastating diseases. Of the group, measles, mumps, and rubella have all been implicated in sensory handicapping, and faithful adherence to a basic immunization program should ensure prevention at a relatively high level.

[47]A. G. Charles and E. A. Friedman, *Rh Isoimmunization and Erythroblastosis Fetalis,* Appleton-Century-Crofts, New York, 1969; and J. T. Queenan, *Modern Management of the Rh Problem,* Harper Medical Division, Hagerstown, Maryland, 1967.

Table 6.3
REPRESENTATIVE IMMUNIZATION SCHEDULE

Age	Immunization
2 months	1. Diphtheria, tetanus (toxoids), and pertussis (antigen) combination injection (DTP) 2. Trivalent oral polio vaccine (TVOP)
4 months	1. DTP 2. TVOP
6 months	1. DTP 2. TVOP
1 year	1. Measles 2. Tuberculin test
1 to 12 years	1. Rubella vaccine[a] 2. Mumps vaccine
1½ years	1. DTP 2. TVOP
4 to 6 years	1. DTP 2. TVOP
14 to 16 years	1. Tetanus and diphtheria toxoids (adult form). At this age and every ten years thereafter.

SOURCE: Committee on Infectious Diseases of American Academy of Pediatrics, as summarized in C. Henry Kempe et al., *Current Pediatric Diagnosis and Treatment,* Lange Medical Publications, Los Altos, California, 1972 ed., p. 111.

[a] See comments in above section on rubella.

However, as noted earlier in this chapter, evidence indicates that general and proper adherence to such a schedule is not always forthcoming, especially for rural and central-city children. The long-term benefits achievable under preventive programs, such as those contained in the "Vaccination Assistance Act of 1962" and recent extensions and amendments to that act, should not be forgone in the interests of short-term economies. Public Law 91-464 in particular has some creative and interesting possibilities for comprehensive and significant prevention of many sensory handicaps, e.g., those associated with rubella, measles, venereal disease, mumps, and Rh sensitivity, among others.[48]

Identification, Direction, and Medical Treatment

Other chapters stress the need for early identification, appropriate direction to servers with requisite skills, and skillful medical treatment of the underlying disorder. Details of those discussions will not be repeated here; however, adequate provision of these services has a distinct preventive component.

While one cannot precisely estimate the reductions in handicapping that improvements in these services bring about, the effects are certainly positive. In principle, such improvements could reduce the handicaps attributable to the *majority* of the different types of sensory disorders. From a preventive viewpoint, the problem is not inadequacy of technical knowledge and skill, but a problem of promptly identifying children in need and putting them in touch with the considerable medical-technical expertise that already exists. To the extent that society can solve that problem, a remarkable number of lifelong sensory disorders are, in the strictest sense of the word, *preventable.*

To realize some of these benefits, we urge the adoption of all our recommendations made with respect to identification, direction, and medical treatment services (see Chaps. 7, 8, and 9).

Early and correct identification of potentially handicapping conditions is perhaps the single most important and underrated service in the array of potential prevention strategies. It is the keystone in a truly comprehensive and effective program for the handicapped. Early identification also has a distinct, but ill-appreciated, preventive component: it increases the likelihood that cause and outcome will be known and properly associated, and that early warning will be given of changes in causes of handicapping in the total population. The implications for improved prevention research and operations are clear.

---

[48]P.L. 91-464, 91st Cong., S.2264, October 16, 1970.

A related prevention strategy is to avoid providing types of medical treatment that can cause or exacerbate handicaps. We have already discussed two types of treatment to be either avoided when possible or used judiciously otherwise: administration of ototoxic drugs, such as quinine and certain antibiotics in the mycin group, possibly resulting in damage to the auditory nerve; and administration of excessive oxygen to premature infants, possibly resulting in retrolental fibroplasia (see Chap. 9).

Family Planning

Family planning is another general preventive strategy that can reduce handicapping. While relationships between the likelihood of mental impairment in the infant, the age of the mother, and the total number of children produced have been established,[49] similar demographic analyses have not been carried out for the sensorially handicapped, as far as we can determine. One may only surmise that family planning practices, such as having only two children and only at maternal ages between 20 and 34, could have some positive, but inestimable, effect on the prevalence of sensory handicaps in the overall population.

Genetic Counseling

Hereditary factors are known to be important determinants of the number of hearing and vision handicapped children in the total population. Chung and his associates have estimated, for example, that about half the cases of profound hearing impairment can be traced to genetic origins.[50] And over one-half of the cases added to the Model Reporting Area "legal blindness" registers in 1969 and 1970 for youth aged 19 and under were listed as owing to "prenatal influence," indicating the hereditary importance of many visual disorders.[51] Some 50 defined syndromes have been associated with hereditary hearing loss,[52] and numerous visual disorders are similarly characterizable.

Such factors generally indicate that more attention should be given to genetic screening and research into the hereditary hearing and

[49]*American Journal of Mental Deficiency,* Vol. 60, January 1956, pp. 557–569.

[50]C. S. Chung, O. W. Robison, and N. E. Morton, "A Note on Deaf Mutism," *Annals of Human Genetics,* Vol. 23, 1969, pp. 357–366.

[51]Harold A. Kahn and Helen B. Moorhead, *Statistics on Blindness in the Model Reporting Area, 1969-1970,* National Eye Institute, DHEW Publication (NIH) 73-427, Washington, D.C., 1973, p. 75, Table 17d.

[52]B. W. Konigsmark, "Hereditary Deafness in Man," *New England Journal of Medicine,* Vol. 281, 1969, pp. 713–720, 774–778, 827–832.

vision handicaps. The establishment of an accurate genetic diagnosis, according to W. E. Nance,

> is a prerequisite for rational counseling, which in turn can prevent the tragedy of a second affected child. Because of the extensive heterogeneity that exists among the various types of hereditary deafness, the risk of affected children for deaf couples is often quite low, but again, reliable prediction depends upon an accurate diagnosis. Specific remediation is possible for some forms of hereditary deafness, and future research will undoubtedly bring to light new types for which effective treatment and even prevention or cure is possible.[53]

While the future trend may include increased genetic counseling, including the taking of blood and tissue cultures for chromosome morphology, many significant difficulties must first be surmounted before this form of preventive service can realize its potential in widespread use.[54]

Experience with a national genetic screening program to detect sickle cell anemia, perhaps the largest-scale genetic screening and counseling program in existence, has shown that the underlying intentions of those running the program are not necessarily shared by those being screened and that the unanticipated, and frequently negative, consequences of the program bear some serious consideration.[55]

- Mass screening has indicated that the issues related to public education, community relations, and the private lives of the identified trait-carriers are in need of resolution.
- The identified individual's reactions are not always positive and favorable.
- Community resistance is more common and far greater than any of those responsible for the program had expected.
- There is a real danger that those identified as carrying the trait will suffer from the stigma associated with that finding. (See Chap. 7 on problems of identification.)
- The eugenic implications of the entire program loom large and are far from being resolved.

Other reports on genetic screening programs have similar messages. For example, Leonard and associates report that for a study

[53]W. E. Nance, "Genetic Counseling for the Hearing Impaired," *Audiology,* Vol. 10, 1971, pp. 222–233, at p. 223.

[54]*The International Directory, Genetic Services,* The National Foundation—March of Dimes, White Plains, New York, 1971 ed., lists some 680 genetic service units throughout the United States and Canada. This represents a fourfold increase in five years.

[55]Barbara J. Culliton, "Sickle Cell Anemia: National Program Raises Problems as Well as Hopes," *Science,* Vol. 178, October 20, 1972, pp. 283–286.

sample of parents having had children with cystic fibrosis, phenylke-tonuria, and Down's Syndrome, only about one-half had "a good grasp of the information given, one-quarter gained something, and one-quarter learned very little,"[56] as a result of genetic counseling. The problem appeared, in this case, to be related to the skills of the physicians who participated in the counseling program, among other reasons. The information level attained by parents is critical in deter-mining whether and how such knowledge will be used in making decisions about having additional children. Exacerbating the deci-sion-making process are religious concerns, emotional conflicts be-tween the parents, and a general lack of understanding of genetics and the probabilities associated with subsequently producing handi-capped offspring.

The general issue of genetic screening and counseling represents a clear instance of technology's having outpaced society's ability to use, accept, and cope with the technology. Many persons, fortu-nately, are becoming concerned with some of these implications, although the day when effective, widespread prevention of handi-capping through genetic screening and counseling practices over-takes us still seems remote. Ethical, societal, and practical political questions are at least discernible.

On the ethical and social dimensions, a distinguished group under the leadership of Marc Lappé, of the Institute of Society, Ethics, and the Life Sciences, has mapped the roughest contours of the hazard-ous terrain confronting society in the general area of genetic screen-ing.[57] Among the many thorny issues raised in this report, the follow-ing appear especially salient with respect to the longer term prospects for preventive practice.

- Does information obtained by genetic screening fall outside the normal confidentiality provisions enjoyed in the traditional doc-tor-patient relationship?
- What is the relationship between adverse genetic information and the remedial actions implied in such information? This issue is at the heart of the unresolved debate on the legality and moral-ity of abortion, among other things.
- What are the deep scientific *and* human implications of program-matic objectives of any genetic program?

[56]Claire O. Leonard, Gary A. Chase, and Barton Childs, "Genetic Counseling: A Con-sumer's View," *The New England Journal of Medicine,* Vol. 287, No. 9, August 31, 1972, pp. 433–439, at p. 433.

[57]Marc Lappé et al., "Ethical and Social Issues in Screening for Genetic Disease: A Report from the Research Group on Ethical, Social and Legal Issues in Genetic Coun-seling and Genetic Engineering of the Institute of Society, Ethics, and the Life Sci-ences," *New England Journal of Medicine,* Vol. 286, May 25, 1972, pp. 1129–1132.

- How can the quality of test and screening instruments be assured to avoid the multiple pitfalls and human costs associated with misidentification?
- What compulsory measures are implied in the true positive identification of a parent pair likely to produce "defective" offspring? The Lappé group states unequivocally: "As a general principle, we strongly urge that no screening programs have policies that would in any way impose constraints on childbearing by individuals of any special genetic constitution, or would stigmatize couples who, with full knowledge of the genetic risks, still desire children of their own."[58]
- What provisions can be adopted to ensure informed consent of the participants in any screening program?
- How can participants be adequately apprised of the risks involved in possible psychic and social injury?
- Should the purpose and objectives of the screening program be made publicly available?
- Have competent counseling provisions been developed in advance of the screening activity to provide follow-up information and service to those thought to have a potential for parenting genetically handicapped offspring?
- How can rights of privacy be ensured?

The general tone of the report and the guidelines promulgated are ones of cautioning about the extreme potential risks and costs involved in a genetic screening program.

> We are concerned about the dangers of societal misinterpretation of similar conditions and the possibility of widespread and undesirable labeling of individuals on a genetic basis . . . protecting the confidentiality of test results will not shield all such subjects from a felt sense of stigmatization nor from personal anxieties stemming from their own misinterpretation of their carrier status. Extreme caution should therefore be exercised before steps that lend themselves to stigmatization are taken.[59]

The cautionary theme is carried several steps further in a paper by Breyer and Zeckhauser.[60] They argue not only that there should be no federal control of genetic programs, but that such involvement might force issues and decisions to the surface that are better left submerged. For instance, popular belief holds that it is the physician's role to preserve life, while at the same time, as individuals, we are

[58]Ibid., p. 1130.
[59]Ibid., p. 1132.
[60]Stephen Breyer and Richard Zeckhauser, "The Regulation of Genetic Engineering," paper presented to the American Academy for the Advancement of Science session on Genetics, Man, and Society, December 1972.

vaguely aware that in given situations a doctor may allow a newborn child to die. While most doctors probably would not engage in questionable practices, and those few who do are undoubtedly under great stress, the authors ask whether it would be wise to force a legislature to set rules and regulations for such situations. In the words of those authors, "Can we not in some individual cases permit ethical decisions to kill, although we would forbid them were they to become elevated into the general consciousness through formulation of a legal principle?"[61]

In the absence of any simple answer to this and other disturbing questions, Breyer and Zeckhauser counsel for caution on the part of the federal government, advice which seems appropriate under the current circumstances.

> At this time, the outline of genetic engineering problems can be seen only dimly, if at all. Proposals to institute formal regulatory procedures in this area, for example to license or forbid varieties of genetic research, must be viewed with suspicion. On the other hand, it would surely seem appropriate for the federal government to stimulate increased study of, discussion of, and concern about, the problems of social and genetic engineering. But this would seem to be the present limit of prudent . . . government control.[62]

[61]Ibid., p. 8.

[62]Ibid., pp. 10–11. The general subject is as important as it is complex. Representative literature on the topic of genetic screening and counseling, and on the genetic origins of many hearing disorders, is summarized in the following: J. R. Sorenson, *Social Aspects of Applied Human Genetics,* Russell Sage Foundation, New York, 1971; E. Mendelsohn et al. (eds.), *Human Aspects of Biomedical Innovation,* Harvard University Press, Cambridge, Massachusetts, 1971; F. C. Fraser, "Genetic Counseling and the Physician," *Canadian Medical Association Journal,* Vol. 99, 1968, pp. 927--934; WHO Expert Committee, *Genetic Counseling,* World Health Organization, Technical Report No. 416, New York, 1969; E. Beutler et al., "Hazards of Indiscriminate Screening for Sickling," *New England Journal of Medicine,* Vol. 285, 1971, pp. 1485–1486; C. O. Carter et al., "Genetic Clinic: A Follow-Up," *Lancet,* No. 1, 1971, pp. 281–285; B. W. Konigsmark, "Hereditary Deafness in Man," *New England Journal of Medicine,* Vol. 281, September 25, October 2, and October 9, 1969, pp. 713–720, 774–778, and 827–832; K. S. Brown, "The Genetics of Childhood Deafness," in F. McConnell and P. H. Ward (eds.), *Deafness in Childhood,* Vanderbilt University Press, Nashville, Tennessee, 1967, pp. 177–202; J. H. Allen et al., "Dominantly Inherited Low-Frequency Hearing Loss," *Archives of Otolaryngology,* Vol. 8, 1968, pp. 242–250; B. Martensson, "Dominant Hereditary Nerve Deafness," *Acta Otolaryngolica,* Vol. 52, 1960, pp. 270–274; G. R. Fraser, "Profound Childhood Deafness," *Journal of Medical Genetics,* Vol. 1, 1964, pp. 118–151; C. S. Chung et al., "A Note on Deaf Mutism," *Annals of Human Genetics,* Vol. 23, 1957, pp. 357–366; W. F. Edwards, "Congenital Middle-Ear Deafness with Anomalies of the Face," *Journal of Laryngology,* Vol. 78, 1964, pp. 152–170; and P. J. Waardenburg, "A New Syndrome Combining Developmental Anomalies of the Eyelids, Eyebrows and Nose Root with Pigmentary Defects of the Iris and Head Hair and with Congenital Deafness," *American Journal of Human Genetics,* Vol. 3, 1951, pp. 195–253.

Abortion and Other Practices

Abortion is a difficult topic related to genetic counseling. Were a genetic screening, counseling, and diagnosis service to exist, abortion would be an obvious option following true positive identifications through amniocentesis or *in utero* assessment techniques yet to be developed and perfected.

With respect to rubella detection, one preventive technique reported by Ruben as being practiced in Scandinavia is that

> the expectant mother has a blood titre drawn at the beginning of her pregnancy and again at the end of the third month of the pregnancy. If the rubella titre has become elevated during that time, she is advised of the possibility that she may have had a sub-clinical infection of rubella. A decision can be made at that time as to whether or not the pregnancy should be continued.[63]

While recent court decisions have helped clarify abortion as a medical practice, the case is far from closed. In an assessment of the practice made in 1969, Beck and her associates stressed many important research issues, several of which had clear policy implications.[64] The discussion and the research issues appear to have continuing validity.

Prevention of handicapping via sterilization as a family planning practice is, if anything, an even more controversial subject—a point underscored in recent revisions and clarifications of Department of Health, Education, and Welfare guidelines on the practice in federally funded programs.[65]

Sensational revelations to the effect that pediatricians in charge of an infant intensive care unit at the Yale-New Haven Hospital had given some 43 seriously deformed and impaired infants the "right to die," deserve mention as perhaps a logical-moral limit in preventive strategies.[66] The magnificent lifesaving technologies that have greatly improved medicine in the last decade or so have brought with them

---

[63]Robert J. Ruben, "Prevention of Deafness," in Doin Hicks (ed.), *Medical Aspects of Deafness,* Council of Organizations Serving the Deaf, National Forum Number IV, Atlantic City, New Jersey, March 3–5, 1971, pp. 35–45, at p. 35.

[64]Mildred B. Beck et al., "Abortion: A National Public and Mental Health Problem—Past, Present, and Proposed Research," *American Journal of Public Health,* Vol. 59, December 1969, pp. 2131–2143. One-half of the article is devoted to a recitation of research questions. The plea for research is repeated in somewhat different form in S. H. Newman, M. B. Beck, and S. Lewit, "Abortion, Obtained and Denied: Research Approaches," *Studies in Family Planning,* Vol. 53, May 1970, pp. 1–8.

[65]"Doctors Scored on Sterilization," *The New York Times,* October 31, 1973.

[66]The disclosure has attracted widespread public attention. See, for example, "43 Deformed Infants Given 'Right to Die'," *Los Angeles Times,* October 27, 1973.

moral and ethical questions that demand full and humane inquiry. Should a severely impaired infant be allowed to die? Bound up in this chilling question are other imponderable issues: What constitutes "severely impaired"—that is, whose definition is to prevail? Will improved technology force this definition to change over the years to the point where a relatively "minor" impairment by 1977 standards, such as a hearing or vision defect, becomes a "severe impairment" by the standards of a few decades hence? Who decides if and when the child should be allowed to die? How is one able to certify that the infant's "right to die" has been guaranteed, in the argot of the current euphemism?

It is not at all clear how these issues will be resolved, or even if they will be resolved, but they are demanding increased humane attention. As with genetic counseling, if there is to be a governmental role at all outside the courts, prudence seems to dictate that it be confined to research—not allowed to intervene in control or operations.

PREVENTION OF MENTAL HEALTH DISORDERS[67]

So little is known about the specific causes and prevention of mental health disorders that preventive measures lack precision and it is difficult to evaluate their effects. Prevention of mental illness is not a new idea; but it is seldom made into an operational program. Even successful prevention is hard to prove. The central predicament is dramatized in the following commentary on the causes of manic-depressive behavior disorders, thought to account for as many as three to four mentally ill persons per 100,000 population (so afflicted as to require inpatient care):

> Although etiological theories are many, our knowledge of the caus-
> ative factors is scanty, and we must view affective behavior disor-
> ders as of unknown and exceedingly complex etiology. Statements
> about etiology in the literature do not differentiate between severe
> and mild disorders, between single depressive or manic attacks and
> recurrent and cyclic disorders. In general, it is assumed that in se-
> vere and cyclic disorders, organic factors, and in milder and spo-
> radic reactions, psychological events are more likely to be contribu-
> tory. This clearly is a gross oversimplification.[68]

[67]As primary sources we use information obtained from our medical consultants; for textual documentation we use Frederick C. Redlich and Daniel X. Freedman, *The Theory and Practice of Psychiatry*, Basic Books, New York, 1966, esp. Chap. 10. While our topical focus is on children, the nature of the subject—and the discourse related to it— are more general.

[68]Ibid., p. 539.

Other disorders of mental health are similarly opaque to reliable and consistent etiologic discrimination.

Table 6.4 provides some crude suggestions about conditions that account for mental disorders and compares age cohorts according to primary diagnoses. The large percentage of the total devoted to "Other"—25 percent—again reflects the crudity of etiologic knowledge.

Because available data are so poor, it is a matter for debate whether biology or environment is the greater force in mental health disorders (although there are those who believe otherwise).[69] It appears that "major disorders are, indeed, distributed more or less equally through space and time," and that "all major disorders seem to occur in all cultures,"[70] but then again, no one really has adequate evidence about the prevalence and causes of mental health disorders.

How does one "prevent," in the crudest sense, disorders whose causes are so poorly understood?

Genetic control programs are of no significance in practice today. In the absence of etiologic data, genetic counseling for mental health problems has yet to pass from the realm of academic inquiry into application. If and when it does, the questions we raised earlier concerning genetic counseling in the hearing and vision disorders area will have to be addressed. Researchers have explored schizophrenic families and occasionally deduced that the children of such families tend to be socially and psychologically maladjusted.[71] But are they so because of their genes or because they are reared in an unstable environment? (In either case, some people argue that psychotic parents should not attempt to rear children at all.)[72] In a massive compilation of family data spanning four generations, Sheldon Reed and his associates have done a great service in terms of basic data collec-

---

[69]In a much-heralded work, M. Harvey Brenner divined a consistent relationship between economic cycles and mental hospital admissions.

> First, it is clear that instabilities in the national economy have been the single most important source of fluctuation in mental-hospital admissions or admissions rates. Second, this relation is so consistent for certain segments of the society that virtually no major factor other than economic instability appears to influence variation in their mental hospital rates. Third, the relation has been basically stable for at least 127 years and there is considerable evidence that it has had greater impact in the last two decades. *Mental Illness and the Economy,* Harvard University Press, Cambridge, Massachusetts, 1973, p. ix.

[70]Redlich and Freedman, *The Theory and Practice of Psychiatry,* p. 5.

[71]See for example, Ronald O. Rieder, "The Offspring of Schizophrenic Parents: A Review," *Journal of Nervous and Mental Disease,* Vol. 157, No. 3, 1973, pp. 179–190. Most of the ongoing work in this area as of 1973 is noted in his review.

[72]Michael Rutter, *Children of Sick Parents,* Oxford University Press, New York, 1966, examines many aspects of this question.

Table 6.4

ESTIMATED NUMBER OF TOTAL TERMINATIONS FROM OUTPATIENT PSYCHIATRIC
CLINICS IN THE UNITED STATES BY MENTAL DISORDER AND AGE, 1969

Diagnosis	All Ages	<5	5-9	10-14	15-17	18-19	20-24	25-34	35-44	45-54	55-64	65-74	75+
Total	818,865	15,426	80,049	113,751	79,959	37,220	95,307	153,142	115,843	70,567	34,786	14,635	8,180
Mental retardation	29,879	2,900	8,180	7,931	3,183	1,186	1,755	2,042	1,211	836	451	113	91
Organic brain syndromes associated with alcoholism	4,833	—	—	13	35	45	227	726	1,186	1,352	890	278	81
Organic brain syndromes associated with syphilis	552	—	13	82	20	7	13	53	57	84	138	52	33
Organic brain syndromes associated with drug or poison intoxication	2,770	2	20	94	371	357	765	486	283	182	123	52	35
Organic brain syndromes associated with cerebral arteriosclerosis and senile brain disease	5,388	—	3	5	4	2	5	35	61	229	1,002	2,165	1,877
Other organic brain syndromes	16,746	904	3,598	2,552	981	474	1,141	1,664	1,488	1,386	1,234	762	562

Schizophrenia	100,784	480	1,717	2,897	3,880	4,331	14,333	27,158	23,381	14,189	6,000	1,777	641
Major affective disorders	12,519	7	13	25	69	70	443	1,045	2,043	3,834	3,466	1,218	286
Psychotic depressive reaction	5,470	6	23	85	141	128	477	1,021	1,185	1,001	847	390	166
Other psychoses	3,371	17	47	85	90	112	352	575	636	657	520	217	63
Depressive neuroses	70,340	89	507	1,967	2,584	2,854	10,626	19,504	14,682	9,467	5,410	1,983	667
Other neuroses	56,060	218	2,679	4,581	2,685	2,562	9,108	15,865	10,056	4,892	2,237	694	483
Personality disorders	124,455	420	4,914	13,769	12,996	7,281	22,192	31,441	18,980	8,608	2,477	840	537
Alcohol addiction	17,188	3	2	22	64	91	566	3,373	5,696	4,861	2,074	347	89
Drug dependence	7,558	—	2	122	648	867	2,127	2,134	1,013	401	152	65	27
Psychophysiologic disorders	5,319	35	317	502	372	207	616	1,126	1,018	614	345	128	39
Transient situational disturbance and adjustment reaction to infancy	144,089	3,115	27,610	41,326	29,822	7,924	9,262	11,154	7,337	3,545	1,453	833	708
Other	211,544	7,230	30,404	37,693	22,014	8,722	21,299	33,740	25,530	14,429	5,967	2,721	1,795

SOURCE: Unpublished data from the National Institute of Mental Health, HSMHA, as reported in the *Mental Retardation Sourcebook of the Department of Health, Education, and Welfare,* DHEW publication No. (OS) 73-81, September 1972, p. 91.

tion, but nonetheless, they are able only to "suggest" the possibility of hereditary factors in psychosis.[73]

A large literature on neurotic etiologies has amassed over the years, but hard knowledge remains in short supply. David Cohen has recently summarized work in this field; however, his concluding comment about needed further research speaks for itself:[74]

> This kind of research would be worth the enormous time, expense, and effort required. It would facilitate the development of true theories capable of predicting onset, duration, intensity, and type of reaction.

Providing a stable and stimulating living environment is a preventive "good,"[75] but then, so are many similar activities. Teaching people how to know themselves, to perceive and understand reality, to make realistic plans, to relate to others, to care and be cared for, to accept and deal with change, to accept responsibilities, and to practice effective birth control are all potential preventive approaches. Each has proponents and detractors, and each has some claim to legitimacy. For all of these approaches there exist related intervention practices, but for all of them—approaches and practices alike—the preventive aspect of reducing mental health disorder is still open to question. There is less doubt about the need to increase public awareness of mental health problems (most books on the issue recite that need like a litany), but even here there are few clear prescriptions,[76] many all-too-clear problems,[77] and not many notable successes.

It is hard to disagree with those who urge more research and more attempts at primary prevention.[78] Knowledge is what we need; we are still far from being able to make confident recommendations about preventive activities done for the "population at large."

[73]Sheldon C. Reed et al., *The Psychoses: Family Studies,* W. B. Saunders, Philadelphia, Pennsylvania, 1973.

[74]David B. Cohen, "On the Etiology of Neurosis," *Journal of Abnormal Psychology,* Vol. 83, No. 5, 1974, pp. 473–479, at p. 478.

[75]Gerald Caplan (ed.), *Emotional Problems of Early Childhood,* Basic Books, New York, 1955, is a standard although dated source.

[76]S. Richard Sauber, *Preventive Educational Intervention for Mental Health,* Ballinger, Cambridge, Massachusetts, 1973, has detailed a thorough, logical plan for public education, and this work warrants attention. The results are not in yet, however. Gerald Caplan, a prominent spokesman for prevention, has laid out some of the requisites in his *Support Systems and Community Mental Health,* Behavioral Publications, New York, 1974.

[77]Elaine Cumming and John H. Cumming, *Closed Ranks,* The Commonwealth Fund, Cambridge, Massachusetts, 1957.

[78]The optimistic note resounds in Gerald Caplan, *Principles of Preventive Psychiatry,* Basic Books, New York, 1964. The pessimistic echo is that the federal government in 1974 was spending only about $3 million a year on the problem. The near-term prognosis is not roseate.

Society is somewhat better equipped to provide secondary prevention to help "identified vulnerable, high-risk groups," but there are problems here, too. A person with a high risk of developing a mental disorder is too seldom in touch with skilled mental health providers to be identified early so that secondary preventive measures can be taken. More often than not the disorder develops and advances over an extended period of time as the person becomes a subject of concern and perhaps hostility to family, friends, co-workers, physicians, ministers, teachers, and so on. Ultimately, if fortunate, the person is taken on by a competent psychologist or psychiatrist, by which time the object is treatment, not prevention. Procedures should be designed to make the mental health service system and its prospective clients more readily accessible to each other.[79]

While the Community Mental Health Center (CMHC) movement, often hailed as a "third revolution" in mental health,[80] was intended to tackle both prevention *and* treatment, it is clear from the record that prevention has remained more promise than actuality.[81]

Mandating prevention in the CMHC program nationwide did not facilitate matters—it merely raised legislative and public expectations and heaped yet another service responsibility on the fledgling CMHCs. Trying to satisfy the mandate, consultation and education units were ordered by the National Institute of Mental Health (NIMH) to prevent mental disorders.[82] The order is all the more mystifying when one considers the persistent paucity of NIMH research programs specifically focused on preventive issues. Despite the fact that the study of prevention is a part of NIMH's legal mandate,

> There is an obvious need for coordination of activities and effective communication between the different components of the Institute. Research is unevenly distributed amongst the range of possible preventive techniques.

[79]Redlich and Freedman note one actual case, in Amsterdam, where procedures appear to be working reasonably well: Paul V. Lemkau and Guido M. Crocetti, "The Amsterdam Municipal Psychiatric Service," *American Journal of Psychiatry*, Vol. 117, 1961, pp. 779–786.

Collaborative efforts between Vancouver's public health nurses and psychiatrists were found effective in reducing the lag time. See M. Albert Menzies, "Preventive Psychiatry: The Psychiatric Team as Consultant to the Public Health Nurse," *Canadian Medical Association Journal*, Vol. 93, October 2, 1965, pp. 743–747.

[80]M. B. Smith, "The Revolution in Mental Health—A Bold New Approach?" *Transaction*, Vol. 5, 1968, pp. 19–23.

[81]According to Felice Perlmutter, reporting on her investigation of this matter in 1974, "The practice of prevention activity in community mental health centers appears to be inadequately and inconsistently developed on an unplanned, crises-oriented basis." "Prevention and Treatment: A Strategy for Survival," *Community Mental Health Journal*, Vol. 10, No. 3, 1974, pp. 276–281, at p. 276.

[82]*Consultation and Education: A Service of the Community Mental Health Center*, National Institute of Mental Health, Washington, D.C., 1966.

> There is a lack of hard conceptualization and no evaluation of decisionmaking in regard to where research might be most useful.
>
> There are only a relatively few staff members who are interested in prevention and have any understanding of the nature of preventive techniques.
>
> A prime need is for research to investigate whether it is possible to establish some of the claims in regard to prevention.[83]

The point is that a national leadership is absent. It is no wonder that, nationally, the preventive dimension of the consultation and education units of CMHCs has floundered.[84]

Characteristic practices identified as secondary prevention include counseling for people who are grappling with one of life's many crises, such as death of a family member, serious illness, handicaps, accidents, and economic deprivation; helping people resolve problems of interpersonal relations (husbands and wives, parents and children, bosses and workers, and so on); and identifying "developmental" and "situational" conflicts early enough that appropriate treatment can be pursued (the distinction between *treatment* and *prevention* blurs at this point).

The problem from a policymaker's viewpoint, with all of these possible secondary prevention practices, is exceedingly complex. Which practices are the more effective? Which ones even work? The lack of data poses fundamental difficulties not to be resolved in this or any other analysis. All that can be responsibly said is that any or all of these practices may contribute to a reduction in the incidence and prevalence of mental health disorders.

Allocating scarce resources, the practical matter at hand, is of course related to one's priorities and objectives. We believe there are more demonstrably effective ways to spend money than on additional primary and secondary prevention of mental health disorders, important though that is. Consequently, we have no recommendations for additional expenditures in this area.

Because tertiary prevention is directed toward "treatment and rehabilitation," there is no practical difference between it and services discussed in other chapters.

---

[83]NIMH Research Task Force, Study Group on Treatment Techniques, *Report to the Director,* National Institute of Mental Health, Vol. 8, Washington, D.C., 1973, p. 103 (mimeograph). According to the same source, NIMH expends no more than $3 million per year on prevention, and these funds are not concentrated in the programs of the Institute, but spread throughout (p. 90).

[84]A. I. Levinson and S. R. Reff, "Community Mental Health Center Staffing Patterns," *Community Mental Health Journal,* Vol. 6, 1970, pp. 118–125.

PREVENTION OF MENTAL RETARDATION

The parameters used to identify a person as mentally retarded relate to assessments of subnormal intelligence *and* the person's adaptive behavior at each state of the lifespan. Evidence indicates that one's IQ is somewhat modifiable, considerations of testing fidelity and even reliability aside; one's adaptive behavior or level of functioning in society is even more subject to adjustment by the provision of services such as special education and training (a form of tertiary prevention).[85]

There are some data on the more than 200 identified specific causes of mental retardation, but these are far from complete, either as to prevalence for any specific disorder or for comprehensiveness among disorders. Metabolic errors, genetic anomalies, drug abuse, environmental pollution, radiation of pregnant women, infections, accidents, improper nutrition, and even the accelerating capacities of the medical system to sustain life have all at one time or another been implicated as causative elements in mental retardation. Societal conditions affecting behavioral adaptation are also related to mental retardation, but the data on the nature and extent of the relationships are poor.

The data presented in Table 6.5, however, are at least suggestive of proportionate distributions among causative etiologies. As noted in the table, 32.2 percent of the new patients were diagnosed as "Uncertain cause—functional reaction alone manifest"; and an additional 16.9 percent were diagnosed as "Unknown cause—structural reactions manifest". In other words, the retardation of 49.1 percent of the new patients in mental retardation clinics who were medically classified had *uncertain* or *unknown causes.* It appears that research is needed into possible ways of improving basic data collection on the reasons for patients' mental retardation and in time into the basic causes of retardation itself.

When the generic categories of causation are further broken down into the specific medical classifications, we find that the largest group ("Uncertain causes—functional reaction alone manifest") breaks down principally into the vague and unilluminating categories of "Other," 13.3 percent, and "Cultural familial," 8.78 percent. For the second most prevalent generic classification, "Prenatal influence,"

---

[85]George Tarjan et al., "Natural History of Mental Retardation: Some Aspects of Epidemiology," *American Journal of Mental Deficiency,* Vol. 77, 1973, pp. 369–379, contend that as many as two-thirds of the mildly retarded adolescents and young adults lose their identification as retarded people through adaptation or retesting, or both.

congenital cerebral defects were the most often reported, at a total of 9.76 percent, and mongolism (Down's Syndrome) was second at 8.15 percent. The "Other" category, which is the most prevalent under "Unknown cause--structural," is also unilluminating. In the "Trauma" category the most frequently reported cause, at 5.76 percent, was anoxemia at birth (subnormal oxygenation of the arterial blood).

Putting aside the difficulties in counting the exact extent of retardation due to specific causes, one may still gain insight about preven-

Table 6.5
NUMBER AND PERCENT OF MENTALLY RETARDED NEW PATIENTS IN MENTAL RETARDATION CLINICS IN THE UNITED STATES BY MEDICAL CLASSIFICATION AND SUBGROUP, FY 1971

Primary Medical Diagnosis of Condition Causing or Associated with Mental Retardation	*Patients*	
	Number	*Percent*
Total mentally retarded	13,744	100.00
Infection	851	6.19
Prenatal infection	372	2.71
Postnatal cerebral infection	479	3.49
Intoxication	440	3.20
Toxemia of pregnancy	163	1.19
Other maternal intoxications	51	0.37
Bilirubin encephalopathy (Kernicterus)	120	0.87
Post-immunization encephalopathy	14	0.10
Other	92	0.67
Trauma or physical agent	1,611	11.72
Prenatal injury	192	1.40
Mechanical injury at birth	291	2.12
Anoxemia at birth	792	5.76
Postnatal injury	336	2.44
Metabolism, growth, or nutrition	517	3.76
Cerebral lipoidosis, infantile	18	0.13
Other disorders of lipoid metabolism	24	0.17
Phenylketonuria	142	1.03
Other disorders of protein metabolism	33	0.24
Galactosemia	16	0.12
Other disorders of carbohydrate metabolism	27	0.20
Arachnodactyly	6	0.04
Hypothyroidism	73	0.53
Gargoylism (Lipochondrodystrophy)	31	0.23
Other	147	1.07
New growths	182	1.32
Neurofibromatosis	85	0.62
Trigeminal cerebral angiomatosis	10	0.07
Tuberous sclerosis	59	0.43
Intracranial neoplasm, other	28	0.20

SOURCE: U.S. Department of Health, Education, and Welfare, *Mental Retardation Clinic Services, 1971*, Maternal and Child Health Service, 1972.

Table 6.5 (continued)

Primary Medical Diagnosis of Condition Causing or Associated with Mental Retardation	Patients	
	Number	Percent
Prenatal influence	3,397	24.72
Cerebral defect, congenital	989	7.20
Cerebral defect, congenital associated with primary cranial anomaly	352	2.56
Laurence-Moon-Biedl syndrome	9	0.07
Mongolism	1,120	8.15
Other	927	6.74
Unknown cause—structural reactions manifest	2,316	16.85
Diffuse sclerosis of brain	40	0.29
Cerebral degeneration	39	0.28
Prematurity	866	6.30
Other	1,371	9.98
Uncertain cause—functional reaction alone manifest	4,430	32.23
Cultural-familial	1,207	8.78
Psychogenic, associated with environmental deprivation	585	4.26
Psychogenic, associated with emotional disturbance	554	4.03
Psychotic (or major personality) disorder	279	2.03
Other	1,805	13.13

tive initiatives by considering certain disorders or biological processes that do in fact cause retardation. However, since no one knows conclusively exactly how much retardation is "caused" by various classes of disorders, we do not have much guidance to inform decisions about the allocation of preventive resources among disorder classes.

The President's Committee on Mental Retardation has estimated that overall the incidence of biological mental retardation can be cut in half by the year 2000 if current knowledge is applied. However, that Committee indicated that the prevention of socio-cultural, "mild" mental retardation is more uncertain.[86]

The literature repeatedly cites four major causative factors of mental retardation, around which the following discussion is organized:[87]

- Genetic disorders
- Maternal and child health factors
- Malnutrition and undernutrition
- Societal-environmental influences

[86]President's Committee on Mental Retardation, *Mental Retardation: Century of Decision,* Department of Health, Education, and Welfare, Publication No. (OHD) 76-21013, Washington, D.C., 1976.

[87]Our discussion is adapted from Michael J. Begab, "The Major Dilemma of Mental Retardation," *American Journal of Mental Deficiency,* Vol. 78, No. 5, 1974, pp. 519–529. It is an excellent, thoughtful, and concise treatment of the major issues.

Genetic Disorders

Genetic diseases and disorders account for a significant but imprecisely known share of the mentally retarded population. Many exciting preventive therapies are being devised, stemming largely from major discoveries about the nature of genetic structure and process,[88] but direct and widespread application of this knowledge is still years away. Cystinosis, Wilson's Disease, Tay-Sachs Disease, and many others may one day be conquered through careful modification of the afflicted person's enzymatic processes or through sophisticated transplant procedures; however, the state of knowledge and related technology are such as to counsel against premature attempts. It is important for those providing mental retardation care to keep abreast of developments in these rapidly changing and improving fields.

The following discussion takes up three major activities in the prevention of genetic disorders: genetic counseling and associated practices; Rh immunization; and phenylketonuria (PKU) screening and treatment.

Genetic Counseling   Carriers of genetic disorders comprise a small but significant proportion of the general population.[89] For example, the genes for PKU and other "in-born errors of metabolism" are carried by some 3 percent of the population.[90] Genetic knowledge has been translated into both primary and secondary preventive methods for parts of this group, although difficulties remain with applications of these methods.

Genetic counseling is a potentially important form of prevention in mental retardation, but will demand much careful thought and both human and capital investment.[91] Counseling includes informing prospective parents of the probable odds that they will have an abnormal child. A problem is that such counseling can be given realistically only to potential parents in families that already have a history of

[88]James Watson, *Molecular Biology of the Gene,* W. A. Benjamin, New York, 1965; and idem, *The Double Helix,* Atheneum, New York, 1968.

[89]W. Roy Breg, "Genetic Aspects of Mental Retardation," *Quarterly Review of Pediatrics,* Vol. 17, 1962, pp. 9–23.

[90]Robert Guthrie and Steward Whitney, *Phenylketonuria: Detection in the Newborn Infant as a Routine Hospital Procedure,* U.S. Department of Health, Education, and Welfare, Children's Bureau Publication No. 419, Washington, D.C., 1964; and V. Elving Anderson, "Genetics in Mental Retardation," in Harvey A. Stevens and Rick Heber (eds.), *Mental Retardation: A Review of Research,* University of Chicago Press, Chicago, Illinois, 1964, pp. 348–394.

[91]Robert W. Day, "Genetic Counseling and Eugenics," in Irving Philips (ed.), *Prevention and Treatment of Mental Retardation,* Basic Books, New York, 1966, pp. 192–195.

abnormal children. The counseling can occur before pregnancy and hence influence the decision to conceive the child, or after pregnancy has begun, when diagnostic procedures can provide specific information about certain types of genetic disorders. For a few disorders, e.g., Tay-Sachs and galactosemia, there are straightforward diagnostic procedures; others demand very sophisticated equipment and personnel. It nearly goes without saying that screening and counseling of possible carriers of genetic disorders must be simple, inexpensive, and reliable to warrant large-scale application efforts. "To the extent that groups of women vulnerable to genetic disease can be identified, screening becomes feasible and prevention possible."[92]

Several disorders are detectable in the unborn fetus with *in utero* assessment techniques, but as we indicated earlier, realizing the full preventive potential depends upon the accessibility of an up-to-date preventive diagnosis and care program, genetic counseling, and the decision on the part of the parents regarding the desirability of terminating a pregnancy when a genetic disorder is actually detected.

Down's Syndrome is an important causative category in mental retardation, occurring in about one in every 600 babies.[93] Its prevention through family planning and *in utero* assessment (amniocentesis) is within the limits of available knowledge. We know certain characteristics of the population most likely to have Down's Syndrome or mongoloid children. Table 6.6 shows the relationships between the age of the mother, birth order, and the likelihood of a pregnancy resulting in mental impairment.

H. A. Lubs and F. H. Riddle have conducted a detailed epidemiological study which indicates that some 1 to 2 percent of the children born to women over 35 years of age will have chromosomal malformations, and Down's Syndrome is predominant among these.[94] Women over 35 account for only about 13 percent of all pregnancies, and yet they have nearly half of all Down's Syndrome children.[95] Women under 20 also produce a disproportionately large number of Down's-related mentally retarded children.[96] The use of prenatal diagnostic procedures, such as amniocentesis, for these two at-risk

[92]Begab, "The Major Dilemma," p. 523.

[93]National Association for Retarded Citizens, *Facts on Mental Retardation,* Arlington, Texas, 1973.

[94]"Chromosomal Abnormalities in the Human Population: Estimates of Rates Based on New Haven Newborn Study," *Science,* Vol. 169, 1970, p. 495.

[95]Begab, "The Major Dilemma," p. 523.

[96]Robert W. Day and Stanley W. Wright, "Down's Syndrome at Young Maternal Ages: Chromosomal and Family Studies," *Journal of Pediatrics,* Vol. 66, 1965, pp. 764–771.

Table 6.6
BIRTH ORDER AND MATERNAL AGE AS FACTORS IN MENTAL DEFICIENCY

Birth Order	Ratio of Observed to Expected (Percent)	Maternal Age	Ratio of Observed to Expected (Percent)
1	52	Under 20	121
2	92	20-24	95
3	135	25-29	88
4	145	30-34	95
5	268	35 and over	146

SOURCE: *American Journal of Mental Deficiency,* Vol. 60, January 1956, pp. 557-569.

groups would allow the parents to make informed decisions concerning therapeutic abortion and, depending on those parental decisions, could reduce the incidence of mongolism significantly.[97] We stress again that we are not taking a stand for or against abortion, which is a matter for parental and legal decision.

Detecting chromosomal abnormalities *in utero,* and other revolutionary advances in diagnostic procedures, demand sophisticated laboratory facilities most likely to be provided in modern medical centers. Genetic counseling is highly useful today in preventing mental retardation; it will become even more useful as new diagnostic techniques are developed, including the taking of fetal blood and tissue cultures for chromosome morphology.

Physician screening for genetic disorders (such as Down's Syndrome) using amniocentesis is occurring, but we are unaware of the exact extent of it. There are reasons for less than optimal employment of this important technique; they include basically technical matters; e.g., some physicians are untrained in the technique, inadequate equipment and facilities in some areas, and moral issues underlying much of the debate on therapeutic abortion.[98]

Were a genetic screening, counseling, and diagnosis service to exist, the need for decisions on therapeutic abortion would be an obvious consequence of true positive identifications through amnio-

[97]One of the more authoritative sources on these issues is Aubrey Milunsky, *The Prenatal Diagnosis of Hereditary Disorders,* Charles C Thomas, Springfield, Illinois, 1973.

[98]Amitzi Etzioni, a sociologist and an authority on genetic issues, announced at the 1975 annual meeting of the American Association for the Advancement of Science (New York, January 1975) that results of a national survey of obstetricians/gynecologists indicated that over half would *not* use these techniques, even with pregnant patients over age 40. He stated that the primary reasons were related to medical conservatism about adopting new practices and techniques.

centesis, chromosomal morphology, or other assessment techniques yet to be developed and perfected. This and related issues were discussed earlier in the section on hearing and vision disorders.

Rh Immunization Development and use of the Rh desensitizing gamma globulin has reduced jaundice in the newborn and thus has also reduced incidence of the associated mental disorder, kernicterus. To prevent sensitization and subsequent threat to additional children, however, the RhoGAM must be administered within 72 hours after the Rh-negative mother has terminated pregnancy of an Rh-positive child. Blood-typing and antibody screening are considered important parts of effective prenatal care; and depending on the bilirubin levels obtained in amniocentesis (when indicated), specific management procedures of mother and unborn child may be required.[99] Immunization, typing, screening, evaluation, and management are all elements of responsible preventive care. The extent of the reduction in handicapping conditions resulting from this kind of care is not known, but is clearly positive.

Phenylketonuria (PKU) Screening and Treatment An example of a retardation-causing etiology that has yielded somewhat to secondary preventive measures is phenylketonuria (PKU).[100] Prevention in this case is pointed toward early detection; infants are screened by means of urine tests[101] and by a newer and more satisfactory test (the Guthrie Inhibition Assay) for elevated serum phenylalanine.[102] The latter test has been found superior for the following reasons:[103]

- More reliable test results, i.e., fewer false negative results.
- Earlier diagnosis (within the first three days of life) than with urine tests.
- Better chances that all children will be tested than with urine test (which may miss symptoms in children who do not manifest them in urine for as long as several weeks after birth, when they have gone home).

[99]J. T. Queenan, *Modern Management of the RH Problem,* Harper Medical Division, Hagerstown, Maryland, 1967.

[100]S. I. Goodman, "Some Advances in the Prevention of Mental Retardation," in Irving Schulman (ed.), *Advances in Pediatrics,* Vol. 2, Year Book Medical Publications, Chicago, Illinois, 1972.

[101]Including the ferric chloride test, the diaper test, the filter paper test, the Phenistix test, and the chromatographic test.

[102]Described in Guthrie and Whitney, *Phenylketonuria.*

[103]David Hsia et al., "Screening Newborn Infants for Phenylketonuria," *Journal of the American Medical Association,* Vol. 188, 1964, pp. 203–206; a standard, but thorough, summary is contained in F. L. Lyman (ed.), *Phenylketonuria,* Charles C Thomas, Springfield, Illinois, 1963, Chap. 7.

Such screening has been shown to be decidedly cost-effective, despite the low incidence of the disorder.[104]

The disease is hereditarily transmitted—an error of metabolism—and may be treated and "prevented," if detected early enough, through a carefully controlled dietary regime. Untreated, PKU almost without exception results in mild to severe retardation, including a predisposition to seizures and assorted medical anomalies.

Even here, however, prevention is not a certainty. Opinions differ, ranging all the way from those who claim that the disease can be eradicated with adequate screening, diagnosis, and early treatment, to those who question both screening procedures and the efficacy of the treatment.[105]

Evidence has been presented suggesting that there may be some preventive potential, easily overlooked, to be gained by testing older children. Dietary treatment has significantly increased the IQ of children as old as 8 who were found to suffer from PKU.[106]

Finally, because it is genetic in origin, and both parents must carry the gene, a number of primary preventive measures could be considered. They include establishing local PKU registers for use in genetic counseling programs and testing mothers of retarded children during subsequent pregnancies for elevated serum phenylalanine levels.[107]

Newborn screening for a number of other extremely low-incidence metabolic disorders leading to mental retardation is within the realm of technical feasibility. However, there are a large number of known, possible causative etiologies,[108] as well as "uncertain causes"; most are of extremely low incidence; and aside from Down's Syndrome,

[104]Massachusetts and Delaware, to cite only two states where analyses of PKU programs have been published, have had important and positive experiences. Massachusetts Department of Public Health, "Cost-Benefit Analysis of Newborn Screening for Metabolic Disorders," *New England Journal of Medicine*, Vol. 291, No. 26, December 26, 1974, pp. 1414–1416. The Delaware experience is reported in "State-Federal Spotlight," *Insight*, April 1975, p. 2, where the following claim is made: "To date [since 1962] 118,000 babies have been tested, and eight infants who were found to have the rare condition were placed on special diets . . . The tests cost about $6000 per year [and it was noted] if the eight babies had gone untested and spent their lives in institutions for the mentally retarded, the cost to the state would have been $500,000 for each child."

[105]E. Daren et al., "Statement on Treatment of Phenylketonuria," *Pediatrics*, Vol. 35, No. 3, 1965, pp. 501–503.

[106]A. Moncrief, "Testing for Phenylketonuria After Infancy," *British Medical Journal*, Vol. 1, No. 5441, 1965, pp. 1065–1066.

[107]R. W. Coffelt, "Unsuspected Findings From a PKU Newborn Screening Program," *Pediatrics*, Vol. 34, No. 6, 1964, pp. 889–890.

[108]Milunsky, *Prenatal Diagnosis*, contains a comprehensive listing of the possibilities.

PKU, and Rh sensitization, most others are not the subject of widespread screening by physicians. In fact, many are as yet outside the capability of all but the best-equipped and staffed medical research centers.[109] Cautions about expanding screening programs to other disorders have been stressed by Efron (and others) in the following terms:

> Screening programs have thus enormously increased both our knowledge and our awareness of our ignorance. The experience with massive PKU screening in particular has indicated that we know very little about inborn errors of metabolism. Certainly, the simple concepts which were the basis of the compulsory legislation for PKU are open to question. It is hoped that we can pursue our course of investigation of the other inborn errors of metabolism without imposition of compulsory screening programs which necessarily lead to treatment by inexperienced persons and which necessarily imply that there is an effective "tried and true" therapy which must be administered as soon as the diagnosis is made. Our state of knowledge about the best treatment for these disorders is as primitive as that about the pathophysiology of the diseases.[110]

Maternal and Child Health Factors

Prematurity and low birth weight are known to be highly associated with mental retardation and other disorders. As medical technology has advanced and newborn survival rates have risen, the incidence of mental retardation associated with those factors has risen.[111] As with nearly all aspects of retardation, the evidence is not uniformly consistent and there is disagreement over precise causal connections and incidence rates. For instance, the observed fact that low birth weight is correlated with race, socioeconomic status, and complications of pregnancy adds confusion to the inquiry into the true causal connection between weight and retardation. However, according to one knowledgeable researcher, "From the data it could be deduced that prematurity is hazardous because the immature central nervous system is more subject to damage [than the full-term one]."[112] That view

[109]It should be noted, however, that the Massachusetts screening program routinely detected very-low-incidence metabolic disorders in addition to PKU; adaptation and adoption of that program in other settings could have similarly advantageous effects. Our general cautions on the need for high-quality staff and equipment remain.

[110]Mary L. Efron, "Metabolic Factors in the Prevention of Mental Retardation: Compulsory Screening Legislation Open to Question," *Rhode Island Medical Journal,* April 1967, pp. 255–257, at p. 257.

[111]Lulu O. Lubchenco et al., "Sequelae of Premature Birth: Evaluation of Premature Infants of Low Birth Weights at Ten Years of Age," *American Journal of Diseases of Children,* Vol. 106, 1963, pp. 101–115, assert that IQ is directly related to birth weight.

[112]Harry A. Waisman, "Recent Advances in Mental Retardation," in Phillips, *Prevention and Treatment,* pp. 125–144, at p. 127.

is plainly supported in the literature.[113] A number of factors have been implicated as responsible for prematurity and low birth weight, and hence primary preventive efforts logically focus on them.

Infectious diseases, anemias in pregnancy, toxemia in pregnancy, viral diseases, toxoplasmosis, mechanical injury at birth, and anoxia have all been singled out for research attention, and success in understanding each represents a hopeful source of reduction in the incidence of retardation.

From the above and related lists of causative agents, it appears that several generalized preventive strategies afford some potential respite. Included are improved prenatal and perinatal health care, family planning, and immunization.

Prenatal and Perinatal Health Care   More is being learned regularly about the critical importance of maternal and child care before, during, and soon after birth as a general preventive strategy. Specific relationships between prenatal conditions and subsequent mental disorders are known,[114] while many others are suspected and, given the prevalence of "Unknown prenatal influence" as an etiologic class, have become fitting research topics. The discussion in the previous section on prenatal and perinatal care as it relates to hearing and vision disorders applies here also.

Family Planning   A combination of better family planning and reduced family size is a preventive strategy that is relevant to both mental health problems and mental retardation. Its effects on the overall reduction of handicapping conditions in the population are not to be underestimated, for it has been demonstrated that smaller family size is positively associated with lower fetal, neonatal, and postnatal mortality and morbidity rates; with lower prematurity rates and consequently lower incidence of handicaps such as seizures and cerebral palsy; with more adequate prenatal care and better education for children; with lower incidence of infectious disease in parents and children; with better growth, in both height and weight, among preschool and school children; and with higher IQ scores.[115] As we noted earlier, relationships between the likelihood of mental

[113]A representative review and sampling of which is contained in D. V. Caputo and W. Mandell, "Consequences of Low Birth Weight," *Developmental Psychology,* Vol. 3, 1970, pp. 363-383.

[114]A. Zitrin et al., "Pre- and Paranatal Factors in Mental Disorders of Children," *Journal of Nervous and Mental Diseases,* Vol. 139, 1964, pp. 357-361.

[115]*Lengthening Shadows: A Report of the Council on Pediatric Practice of the American Academy of Pediatrics on the Delivery of Health Care to Children,* 1970, American Academy of Pediatrics, Evanston, Illinois, 1971, p. 55.

impairment in the infant, the age of the mother, and the total number of children in the family have been established. Family planning in this case has to do with learning in advance the odds of producing a defective child. One may surmise that wider adoption of family planning practices, such as completing the family before the mother reaches age 40, will somewhat reduce mental retardation in the overall population.

Immunization   Immunization is another general strategy to prevent infection-caused mental retardation. Both the National Center for Disease Control and consistent findings of the U.S. General Accounting Office indicate that significant fractions of children in both central city and rural areas are not being vaccinated against preventable diseases. Of central city children surveyed, for example, it was found that about one-half were *not* protected against measles or polio. In 1971, more than 75,000 cases of measles (a causative factor in mental retardation) were reported, an increase of 28,000 from the previous year.[116] It is a persistent problem,[117] reflecting both the fragmented nature of the health system generally and the particularly limited interest given to preventive measures as contrasted with most other services.

Rubella is a major causative factor in mental retardation and a host of other disorders. We discussed the cost-effectiveness and details of rubella immunization in a previous section of this chapter.

Measles is another infectious disease that can cause mental retardation but against which immunization is effective. In about one in every 1000 cases of measles, encephalitis occurs; when it does, it results in death in 10 to 20 percent of the cases and a long lasting central nervous system defect in 33 to 50 percent. About one in 3000 children who have measles will become retarded as a result.[118]

Other retardation-causing diseases may one day yield to preven-

[116]Reported in *Education Daily,* May 5, 1972, p. 6, where it was noted that both measles and diphtheria have risen sharply since 1970, a finding alleged to be linked to government reluctance to support vaccination programs.

[117]In June 1974 the General Accounting Office again warned of the likelihood of epidemics because immunization rates had been allowed to fall far below acceptable rates nationally. Specific states were singled out for criticism. *Education Daily,* June 25, 1974, p. 2. From preliminary, 1977, accounts, these forecasts were prescient and tragic.

[118]C. Kennedy and T. F. M. Scott, "The Management of Acute Febrile Encephalopathies," in *The Prevention of Mental Retardation Through the Control of Infectious Diseases,* as reported in R. Conley, *The Economics of Mental Retardation,* The Johns Hopkins Press, Baltimore, Maryland, 1973.

tion through immunization,[119] but, at the moment, measles and rubella are positively controllable etiologies.

Malnutrition and Undernutrition

There is little doubt concerning the general ill effects of malnutrition and undernutrition, both to pregnant women and to developing children.[120] Malnutrition studies have concentrated on animals, on follow-ups to starved wartime populations,[121] and on a few "underdeveloped" countries.[122] The research results tend to confirm that there is a relationship between malnutrition, socioenvironmental factors, and mental competency. The precise relationships and links are not yet known; as with many other preventive strategies, all that can be said is that an undernourished mother and her child, all other things being equal, are more likely to have mental handicaps than are well-nourished ones.

Care is needed to ensure that economically underprivileged and potentially undernourished segments of the population have adequate food.[123]

In at least one federal government project, strong assertions about these matters have been presented:

> It has been estimated that 75–85 percent of all mentally defective children are born in a poverty environment. All the statistical data available reaffirm the connection between poverty and malnutrition,

[119]Two English physicians, Elek and Stern, have developed a vaccine for cytomegalic inclusion disease, thought to be responsible for as many as one mentally retarded individual per 2000 live births. This viral disease is believed to cause damage to the fetus by transmission through the placenta. The vaccine is new, has been tested on humans, and is presently undergoing final experimental testing. *The New York Times,* August 17, 1973.

[120]*Nutrition and Human Development;* and M. B. Stoch and P. M. Smythe, "Does Undernutrition During Infancy Inhibit Brain Growth and Subsequent Intellectual Development?" *Archives of the Disabled Child,* Vol. 38, 1963, pp. 546–552.

[121]Z. Stein et al., "Nutrition and Mental Performance," *Science,* Vol. 178, 1972, pp. 708–713; and A. N. Antonov's classic, "Children Born During the Siege of Leningrad in 1942," *Journal of Pediatrics,* Vol. 30, 1947, pp. 250ff.

[122]S. A. Richardson et al., "The Behavior of Children in School Who Were Severely Malnourished in the First Two Years of Life," *Journal of Health and Social Behavior,* Vol. 13, 1972, pp. 276–284 (Jamaica); and J. Hoorweg and Paul Stanfeld, "The Influence of Malnutrition on Psychological and Neurological Development," in *Nutrition, the Nervous System, and Behavior,* Panamerican Health Organization, Washington, D.C., 1972 (Uganda).

[123]R. V. Rider, M. Taybeck, and Hilda Knoblock, "Associations between Premature Birth and Socioeconomic Status," *American Journal of Public Health,* Vol. 145, 1955, pp. 1022–1028.

between malnutrition and disease. Malnutrition appears to be the common denominator of each of the problems—low birth weight, infant mortality, mental retardation, and intellectual malfunction. Any attempt to break the cycle of poverty characterized by these phenomena must include nutritional intervention, or this wastage of human life will continue unabated.[124]

The report concludes with appeals for nutritional intervention, and does so on cost-effectiveness as well as other grounds. "The total cost of a city's supplemental feeding program—$100,000-$500,000—is less than the estimates of lifetime expenses of a few retarded infants."[125]

Societal-Environmental Influence

Disputes regarding biologic relationships to mental retardation pale in comparison with those attending societal-cultural-environmental relationships to mental retardation. The debate has gone on long enough to have won the handy label of the "nature-nurture" controversy.

On the one hand, the extreme "naturalist" view is summarized in an oft-cited but timeworn passage of Sarason:

Despite the well-nigh perfect correlation between the garden variety of mental deficiency and unfavorable social conditions, the consensus among workers in the field is that cultural factors are relatively unimportant.[126]

Few would accept this at face value today; but equally few are willing, on the other hand, to accept so extreme a "nurturist" view as that postulated by Perry:

. . . to prevent the greatest number of cases from ever happening, . . . (clinicians) must become concerned with radical changes in our social order . . . This order produces mental deficiency by poverty; racial discrimination; tax protection of the advantaged classes.[127]

We are confronted with a practical problem in deciding where one can responsibly focus attention with an end in view of lessening the incidence of mental retardation through societal-environmental initiatives.

[124]Select Committee on Nutrition and Human Needs, U.S. Senate, *To Save the Children: Nutritional Intervention Through Supplementive Feeding,* 93d Cong., 2d Sess., Government Printing Office, Washington, D.C., 1974, p. 47.

[125]Ibid.

[126]Seymour R. Sarason, *Psychological Problems in Mental Deficiency,* Harper & Row, New York, 1953 ed., p. 134, reproduced in the 1959 ed.

[127]Steward E. Perry, "Notes for a Sociology of Prevention in Mental Retardation," in Philips, *Prevention and Treatment of Mental Retardation,* pp. 145–176, at p. 173.

The societal-environmental setting does make some difference, particularly in the lives of the mildly retarded where central nervous system pathologies are not evident.[128] The unresolved controversy centers on the nature and degree of the societal-environmental contribution to the extent of retardation and the amount of remediation, i.e., prevention, that can be effected on society and the environment and hence on retardation. Improvement in health, education, welfare, housing, nutrition, vocational programs, and other programs for the general population, would contribute in some positive but not reliably known degree to the prevention of mental retardation. Conley has calculated that "if all groups in society had the same percentage of persons with IQs below 50 as middle- and upper-class white children, the prevalence of this level of mental retardation would decrease by almost 80%."[129]

Aside from improving these types of programs for the general population, a would-be preventive interventionist has only a few strategic options.[130]

- *Effective family planning* appears to be a worthwhile undertaking, particularly for intellectually subnormal parents, among whose offspring data confirm that retardation *does* occur with far greater frequency than would be expected purely from chance.[131]
- *Early intervention,* based on the best current knowledge, can improve sensory, language, and problem-solving skills, and aid the full development of basic adaptive behavior.

We described the former strategy earlier with respect to biologic disorders, but the basic functional requisites are similar in this case. What appears to be lacking at present is a coordinating and guiding institution to implement a needed family planning education and operations program--and *to sustain it.*

The latter strategy is less well developed in specific relation to the prevention of mental retardation. We are aware of at least one scientifically designed and executed experiment in which intervention of

---

[128]Frank Riessman, *The Culturally Deprived Child,* Harper & Row, New York, 1972, is a standard source.

[129]R. Conley, *The Economics of Mental Retardation,* The Johns Hopkins University Press, Baltimore, Maryland, 1973, p. 323.

[130]See Begab, "The Major Dilemma," pp. 526–529.

[131]Rick F. Heber et al., "The Influence of Environmental and Genetic Variables on Intellectual Development," in H. J. Prelun et al., (eds.), *Behavioral Research in Mental Retardation,* University of Oregon, Eugene, Oregon, 1968, p. 8.

several varieties has been attempted in a controlled setting.[132] The referenced work is complete with training guides, teaching materials, and several helpful, how-to-do-it appendixes.

NEEDED IMPROVEMENT IN PREVENTION PROGRAMS

Our recommendations for improved prevention services follow.

Give a single federal agency prime responsibility and authority for prevention as a service. Studies should be conducted to collect much better information on prevention and to evaluate alternative prevention strategies for specific disorders to enable more informed policies. The few federal prevention research and operational programs that exist provide spotty coverage of the population, at best, and are scattered through various agencies. No single agency is primarily responsible for looking at prevention as a service. Not only would it be desirable to rationalize research expenditures based on the needs of the population (particularly as it changes) and to exploit research findings with evaluations and demonstrations if called for, but basic cost-benefit analyses are needed to inform future resource debates about research versus treatment and about prevention versus service after handicapping. The present lack of information and evaluation of prevention activities is extreme.

Revise and strengthen immunization programs and provide funding for an open-ended period. The messages here are very clear: several potentially handicapping diseases can be prevented; many youth are not immunized; communicable-disease-caused handicaps are prevalent; and prevention of certain diseases (such as measles, polio, and rubella) are decidedly cost-effective in terms of reduced future service costs, not to mention the extremely important reduced quality-of-life effects of the handicaps. We analyzed rubella in great detail, for example, and recommend mandating rubella vaccination for all prepubescent females through a school-based program conducted under auspices of a federal program; creating a model code for state marriage license serologic screening practices with the objective of including an additional test for the presence of rubella antibodies; and appealing through the mass media and professional medical publications to encourage all childbearing females to obtain such tests from their private physicians.

Without deductibles, fully cover prenatal care, routine immunization services for children, examinations for youth up to age 21, and

---

[132]Rick F. Heber et al., *Rehabilitation of Families at Risk for Mental Retardation,* University of Wisconsin, Rehabilitation Research and Training Center in Mental Retardation, Madison, Wisconsin, 1972.

preventive medical treatment in Medicaid and in any National Health Insurance program that may be implemented. Adoption of this recommendation and those made in other chapters for early identification, direction, and service is perhaps the most important means of preventing handicaps.

We recommend expanded voluntary genetic testing and counseling capabilities, accompanied by the creation of a high-risk registry, for parents and potential parents of handicapped children. We stress that genetic testing and counseling would be provided on a voluntary basis; the intention is not to tell families what to do, or to offer value judgments on a family's decisions, but to provide them with information they can use in arriving at their own decisions to conceive and bear children. The creation of a high-risk registry (with information and direction-like referral built in) would help make genetic counseling available to those most likely to benefit from it. The registry could include, among others, pregnant women over 35 and under 17 and families with a history of a handicap-causing genetic disorder.

For example, Conley has conducted a detailed economic benefit-cost analysis of amniocentesis for the detection of Down's Syndrome children, comparing the cost of testing and prevention with the lifetime service costs. He found that screening the entire population is not justified on an economic basis alone, but that testing of high-risk groups yields economic benefits that clearly outweigh the economic costs.[133]

In the time period immediately following birth of a child, we recommend the provision of family planning information to parents, plus creation of a registry and follow-up for children born abnormal or at high risk of having some handicap. The registry and follow-up for high-risk children would be especially valuable in permitting early detection of handicaps, so that preschool special education and training and other services (tertiary prevention) could begin at an early age.

[133]Conley, *The Economics of Mental Retardation, pp. 312–315.*

Chapter 7

IDENTIFICATION

OVERVIEW

Broadly speaking, identification is the recognition and correct follow-up assessment of both a child's abilities and disabilities. While the bulk of the literature on the subject is concerned with recognition, follow-up assessment is at least as important in the service of the handicapped person.[1] Questions like the following illustrate the nature, importance, and utility of thorough identification:

- At what age is service intervention timely, and hence identification needed?
- How and by what institutional mechanism can the child's handicap be identified, and errors of identification minimized?
- What pathological condition underlies the disability?
- How seriously does the disability limit current and future functional capability?
- Are secondary disabilities likely to be "caused" by the basic condition, e.g., speech impairment because of hearing problems?
- Can the condition and disability be corrected, reduced, or prevented through timely intervention?
- How can a handicapped child be assured of proceeding beyond the stage of identification and into the stage of receiving needed services?
- Where can an appropriate range of services be obtained to minimize the handicapping effect of the disability?

In general terms, children who are handicapped become identified to the service system primarily through one of three mechanisms: (1) personnel in some segment of the service system (e.g., private physicians or teachers) notice symptoms of a disorder, (2) the individual or his or her family seeks assistance, or (3) a testing and screening pro-

[1]This distinction has been made well in Society of Medical Officers of Health, "The Needs of Handicapped Children," *Public Health* (London), Vol. 83, 1969, pp. 136–147.

gram may detect them (e.g., an I.Q. and adaptive behavior testing program to detect mental retardation in school age children). However, even if a handicapped child is identified by one part of the service system, the mechanism of making referrals to all other appropriate service programs is often not used; therefore the child is often unidentified to and unserved by some or all of those other programs.

While parents are usually the first to suspect impairment in those handicapped children that are identified, formal identification programs screen at least part of the child population for certain handicaps in many states. For example, programs supported with funds from the U.S. Maternal and Child Health Service and Crippled Children's Service screened an estimated 10 million children for vision impairment and 6.25 million children for hearing impairment in 1973. Children in states with comprehensive screening programs usually are tested at more than one age, and so the above figures do not represent children receiving their *first* screening. Coverage of the population is far from universal. A 1969 survey of State Plans for the Maternal and Child Health Service and Crippled Children's Service showed that: 12 states reported having some type of a general vision testing program, 20 reported some preschool vision testing, 19 reported school vision testing, and 2 reported glaucoma vision testing; 15 states reported some type of a general hearing test program, 11 reported some infants' hearing testing, 22 reported some preschool hearing testing, and 23 states reported school hearing test programs.

Some additional screening for many different types of handicaps is done under the state-operated but federally funded and regulated Medicaid program, which requires early and periodic screening, diagnosis, and treatment of Medicaid-eligible children. It has been difficult, however, to elicit compliance and full implementation of these provisions from the states. Data accounting for total numbers of people screened, referral rates, disease incidence, and follow-up measures undertaken are beginning to be collected, but the results are incomplete. To the basic question, "How many children were screened under this program?" asked by the U.S. Medical Services Administration in January 1973, 26 states either did not reply or did not have implemented programs.[2] Thus, the present federal role with respect to identification programs is one of funding and research but not operation or strong control.

Without proper and universal identification programs, no clear picture of the overall needs of the handicapped population can be drawn, and large known gaps in delivery of services to the handi-

---

[2]See the chapter on medical services.

capped population cannot be filled. Without adequately trained, certified, and funded screening personnel, misidentification (errors of both omission and commission) can be distressingly frequent. Lacking better informational connections between those specialists providing identification and other service providers, follow-up of individuals and their direction to an appropriate mix of needed services is often not done, or not done very well. Follow-up and adjustment of the total supply of services at the system level, to reflect changes in the number, kind, and distribution of the overall population, are, for similar reasons, not done very well either.

Identification is one of the more neglected services. Even the best of the formal identification programs—the vision and hearing screening of children—is far from universal for school-age children, is often poorly implemented, and is often nonexistent for preschoolers. This is unfortunate, for early identification is especially important in some cases, notably for deaf youth who need early language development assistance and for any youth with a treatable etiology causing degradation of functional ability. Much of the identification that does occur is done informally by parents, schoolteachers, and others not specially trained to recognize handicaps.

As important as the identification service is, why is it so underdeveloped? Several explanations are possible. One plausible argument is that since all available service resources are being used already, it is pointless to go looking for more people. But that argument may be answered in at least three ways. An equity-related answer is that not all the people with the most need or the greatest ability to benefit are among those known to the service system. An adequacy-related answer is that if we were to identify more of those in need, the system might eventually respond with a more adequate level of resources. And an information-related answer is that even if the government chooses not to serve a handicapped person, he or she at least could be identified and armed with information about the exact mix of services needed—information helpful in seeking nongovernment-supported services.

In the remainder of this chapter we review problems with current identification programs, summarize the state of the art in identification techniques for children of various ages, and make several recommendations for improving the identification service. Since we did not have the resources to analyze identification in detail for every type of handicapping condition, and since the original study on which this book is based focused primarily on identification of hearing and vision disorders, we will use those two sensorial disorders as case studies in this chapter. In the chapter on prevention of handicapping conditions we use mental retardation as a case study and discuss identification programs in detail as they relate to prevention of the handicap.[3] However, as will be seen throughout this chapter, most of the identification concepts and difficulties apply more generally to all types of handicaps.

PROCESS AND PROBLEMS OF IDENTIFICATION

The specific problems related to identification as a distinct service may be summarized in the following terms: (1) failure to detect handicapped children, (2) misidentification, (3) labeling and stigmatization, (4) inadequate follow-up procedures, (5) insufficient personnel training and certification, and (6) failure to create, use, and exploit technology. Each of these topics forms the basis for a subsection below.

We first characterize the "Identification Process" (see Fig. 7.1) to facilitate pinpointing several deficiencies in the current situation. This characterization was suggested by the Illinois Commission on Children, whose 1972 report we recommend as a creative and constructive approach to many of the problems noted in our book.[4]

At the preawareness stage, the child is thought to be and is treated as "normal." No one has any inkling that the child is impaired. For a severely and obviously impaired child, this period may be as brief as the time between delivery and the first examination in the newborn nursery. For others, this stage may persist well into the school years, when learning or developmental problems should at last set the identification process into motion. The basic objectives of identification are to minimize the time lapse from preawareness to the delivery of

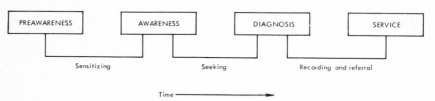

SOURCE: Illinois Commission on Children.

Fig. 7.1   Identification Process.

[3]For a summary of identification of mentally retarded children, see John Meier, *Screening and Assessment of Young Children at Developmental Risk,* The President's Committee on Mental Retardation, DHEW Publication (OS) 73-90, Washington, D.C., March 1973. For a summary of identification of emotionally disturbed children, see E. M. Bower, *Early Identification of Emotionally Handicapped Children in School,* Charles C Thomas, Springfield, Illinois, 1969.

[4]Illinois Commission on Children, *Report of a Committee on Early Location and Care of Children with Handicapping Conditions,* State of Illinois, January 1972, pp. 13-14.

needed services and to minimize the chance that those services will *never* be delivered. Methods to attain those objectives form the bulk of the remaining discussion and underlie most screening and diagnosis procedures.

Sensitizing occurs when some person—a parent, neighbor, physician, relative, teacher—suspects that the child is "different" in some significant way. The process occasionally breaks down here because of what we might call "background noise" in communications between mothers (usually) and physicians. Physicians are all too familiar with the "anxious mother syndrome," wherein parents fall prey to the conviction that all sorts of things—usually illusory or exaggerated—are wrong with their children. The unfortunate result is that the physician, his alertness dulled from hearing so many false alarms, often fails to heed the mother whose fears are well founded.[5] Sensitizing is the attempt to alert people in contact with children into being more careful observers, careful enough that the possibility of a handicap is not dismissed out of hand when a clue is presented that the child may not be "normal."

Awareness is the partially confirmed realization that the child's behavior or performance is abnormal for his age, plus perception of the ways and extent to which his performance differs. The awareness phase is where most mass screening programs are concentrated. All they generally seek to accomplish is to identify children who are not behaving or performing up to some normal levels expected for children of similar demographic and developmental characteristics. Awareness is *not* the same as complete diagnosis, although it is an important preliminary step to diagnosis.

Seeking is one form of follow-up. It is the critical step that sees the child through to more detailed and competent examination, usually by specialists in the *suspected* disorder. Since awareness is not diagnosis, the critical importance of competent and thorough confirmation and measurement of the disorder cannot be stressed enough.[6]

---

[5]Some surprising statistics on identification are offered in G. Fellendorf and I. Harrow, "Parent Counseling, 1961–1968," *Volta Review,* Vol. 72, January 1970, pp. 51–57. The authors state that for children in the 0 to 6 age range, initial identification of hearing impairment is made by the parents in 70 percent of the cases, followed by grandparents and relatives at 16 percent, then physicians at 7 percent, friends at 6 percent, and teachers at 2 percent. The implications of this empirical finding are many and include the need for rudimentary education of the newborn's parents to warn them of behavioral signs that may call for professional evaluation, and the need for physicians to take the parent's concern seriously.

[6]The consistent reference made by parents in our family survey to this phase of the identification process must be noted here. It is addressed primarily in the chapter expressing our concern for developing and implementing better direction services, although its relationship to identification is also strong.

Failing a screening test merely indicates that a child did not perform as normal children do in the test; it does not indicate why the child failed. For example, the child may have been distracted, may have had a cold, or may have been frightened by the test or the testing personnel. Nor does the test indicate what the child's unique residual capabilities may be, or whether intervention may improve or correct the condition. It takes competent, specialized assistance to begin making such determinations. Parents, as we have noted, are not always fully knowledgeable consumers; they probably require directional assistance during the seeking phase to get their children to the proper specialists for examination, and to help plan for obtaining the full set of services the child may need if diagnosis indicates a handicap.

Diagnosis is the *thorough* evaluation of the disability. Thoroughness in this sense comprises a full and forthright assessment of the disability, the services required, and the most likely and desirable futures for the child. Besides the critical information a physical or mental health specialist will bring to the diagnosis, the need for a full needs and service assessment should be stressed at this point.

Recording and referral, a frequently missing element in the identification process, pertains to the follow-up of the awareness and diagnosis. The most elegant and technically sophisticated diagnosis in the world is of little or no value if nothing is done as a result of it. If the child needs surgery, does he get it? Are the parents told what is needed and where to get it? If hearing aids or glasses are required, are the appropriate aids designated, are the parents told where to get them, are they taught how to use and maintain them, and is the child trained in the use and importance of the aid?[7]

Service is the actual delivery of those services found to be needed in the diagnostic and referral stages. Did the child get needed professional service, and does the parent have some idea of what should be done in the home to help the child? Have teachers been informed about the child's problem so they can arrange appropriate special education? Have follow-up visits been arranged, if needed, to check that the delivery service is accomplishing what it is supposed to? Problems occur at each of these phases in the identification process. We consider only a few of the more general ones in the following discussion.

Failure to Detect Handicapped Children

There is no formal institutional mechanism to screen and identify handicapped children after they leave the newborn nursery until they

[7]Once again, our family survey had very little that is positive to say about this aspect of the current identification programs.

enter elementary school, usually at age five. Screening of school-age children occurs in many locales, but is far from comprehensive.

In later chapters of this book, we document the large fractions of the population of handicapped youth that are not receiving needed services. The question then becomes: do the service programs typically know who the unserved youth are? That is, have these youth usually been identified but not served? The answer is clearly no. In our interviews with personnel in over 30 different state agencies in Arkansas, California, Illinois, Massachusetts, and Wyoming, we routinely asked if the service agency knew who the unserved youth were. Aside from an occasional official who mentioned a short waiting list, the response to our question was that no, the agency did not know who the unserved were by name. Usually, these officials could do no better than to say they assumed the unserved children were more predominant in rural or inner-city areas. The lack of identification is not surprising since comprehensive identification programs do not generally exist.

Failure to identify handicapped children may be related to a general inadequacy of resources to treat and care for more children than are already being served. If there were better and more complete identification of disabled children, there would be some undeniable obligation to do something for those who are discovered. The prospects of a thorough identification program, particularly with respect to the "missed cohort" aged 0 to 5 years,[8] present several logical, strategic options for service provision, as summarized in Fig. 7.2.

Under option "a," existing levels of identification effort would be reduced or, at the limit, eliminated altogether. At the same time, the reduction in service demand that this would probably generate would be translated into a reduced total bill for all types of services. For the national context, this would represent a "get out of the business" strategy; for less inclusive contexts, such as a local area or even a state, it would be a strategy of "transfer the problem elsewhere."

Reducing identification efforts while maintaining the current level of service expenditures, option "b," could have several outcomes; it might mean that service levels to those already in the system or fortunate enough to get in "naturally" would be maintained or improved, or it could mean that services would be concentrated on those who are severely impaired. Such a strategy is plausible in the case of hyperinflation of medical costs, for example.

---

[8]Even in relatively affluent and sophisticated local settings and programs, the number of children who *do not see a physician* in the 0 to 5 years of age period may be as high as 25 to 30 percent of the total population in the cohort (interview, Dr. Frederick A. Frye, Department of Pediatrics, Children's Hospital, San Diego, California, February 1972). This in itself is a point worthy of additional empirical investigation.

Identification Resources	Treatment and Follow-up Resources		
	Decreased	Maintained	Increased
Decreased	a	b	c
Maintained	d	e	f
Increased	g	h	i

Fig. 7.2 Possible strategic options: levels of identification versus levels of treatment and follow-up.

If one decreased identification resources while increasing other system resources, option "c," services might improve for those fortunate enough to receive them, or the variety of services might be expanded. This strategy fosters the illusion that "excellent" services are provided, but the illusion is created at the expense of some number of the population in need.

Maintenance of the status quo in identification also could have three accompanying levels of other service expenditures; that is, other service provision may decrease, remain the same, or increase. When the total capacity of the service system is reduced (option "d"), we arrive at a fair representation of some of the current government service programs, faced as they are with rapidly expanding and inflating medical and other service costs (which result in a net real loss in total buying power). The status quo is represented in option "e." The system's other-service capacity may be increased while the present level of identification is maintained (option "f"); the line of thought behind this option can be roughly expressed as, "We have more than we can take care of adequately now, so let's just serve those we know about better."

Options "g" and "h" call for increased identification efforts, but with either reduced or steady levels of total service provision—two variants of the attitude, "Let society take care of the children, but find as many of them as possible."

Finally, there is the possibility that both identification and total service provision will increase, as indicated in option "i". This option would realize many of the stated objectives of those responsible for the service system, and it is certainly the option that would generally satisfy handicapped individuals and their families to the greatest extent.

This exercise summarizes a number of extremely difficult choices confronting this or any other society when faced with the problems of lack of identification and services. The choices bristle with thorny moral, economic, and ultimately political considerations. On the one hand, it is in the clearest interest of the disabled child to be made aware of his problem and to be diagnosed (and the earlier the better, if remedial services are to have greatest possible efficacy). On the other hand, at a total societal level, more and better identification may impose costs. The tacit recognition of some of these costs may underlie many poor identification programs or explain the absence of any programs at all. Which course is the more prudent for our society: minimal identification and "acceptable" services to those identified—approximately the current national situation; or maximal identification and either inadequate or more costly services? We estimated earlier that in approximate terms, if all handicapped youth between the ages of 0 to 21 were to receive all needed services, then the 1976 annual governmental expenditure for services to handicapped youth would have to be at least doubled. Is society willing to face this prospect squarely, a willingness at least partially implied in an honest commitment to find as many handicapped children as possible?[9]

When one turns from the contemplation of society's goals, one bumps headlong into a host of more prosaic reasons why many handicapped children are not identified.

The unavailability of reliable, timely, and comprehensive information about the overall handicapped population means that service agencies do not really know very well what to be looking for in the general population and when to look for it. Furthermore, there are other reasons that many children are overlooked: (1) Lower socioeconomic groups consistently do not share in society's goods and services, and identification services are no different from others in this respect. (2) Many "high risk" children—those born prematurely, or to mothers who have had little or no prenatal care, or born under great stress, or to parents with abnormal clinical or genetic histories, and so on—are not registered and given the benefit of extra and more thorough examinations, even though extra attention is indicated based on the statistical likelihood of disability associated with "high risk birth." (3) Services are not equitably divided between populous and more remote regions or between rich and poor districts of a given locality. And (4) some handicapped children are simply denied ser-

---

[9]Full commitment would be indicated if total service resources were likewise increased in the face of the increased demand generated by better and thorough identification.

vices and kept from society's full view by ignorant or guilt-ridden parents—most notably the "closet kids" reported in the newspapers from time to time. All of these factors diminish the prospects of complete identification; but several may be addressed and their effects lessened, presuming one honestly wants to provide identification and other services on as equitable a basis as possible to all of those who could benefit from them.

Later in this chapter we shall concentrate on the serious problems of the "missing cohort" aged 0 to 5, although we are well aware that other factors are operating to inhibit complete identification of those in need. This concern has been well summarized in a recent statement of the American Academy of Pediatrics:

> At present there is a serious obstacle to identification of health problems in the preschool child; only a small section of the child population receives continuous health care and supervision from infancy to school age. Early identification of handicapping among those children who receive health care from either the private or public sectors of the delivery of health care can be furthered by emphasizing the need for comprehensive screening procedures. But early identification of physical handicaps among those children who do not receive health supervision during infancy and childhood poses almost unsolvable problems. In our society children are not brought together regularly in groups until school age, and therefore it is currently almost impossible to conduct screening examinations on this population at an early age.[10]

The principle of early and correct identification, so prominent in the above statement, is a common one;[11] however, while not doubting its legitimacy, we shall discuss difficulties in implementing it in

[10]American Academy of Pediatrics, *Lengthening Shadows: A Report of the Council on Pediatric Practice on the Delivery of Health Care, 1970,* The Academy, Evanston, Illinois, 1971, pp. 56–57.

[11]The general case is spelled out in K. Eileen Allen et al., "Early Warning: Observation as a Tool for Recognizing Potential Handicaps in Young Children," *Educational Horizons,* Winter 1971-72, pp. 43–55, where Head Start, day care, and preschool nursery contacts with children are thought to be an underexploited and possibly important source of identification referrals. The case of early visual detection is made, for example, in R. W. Dockery, "The Value of Vision Screening in the Preschool Age Child," *Journal of the National Medical Association,* Vol. 52, 1960; and J. W. Oberman, "Vision Needs of American Children," *The Sight-Saving Review,* Vol. 36, Winter 1966, pp. 217–227. Similar arguments are common in hearing literature, as illustrated in A. Glorig, "Routine Neonate Hearing Screening: Summary and Evaluation," *Hearing and Speech News,* Vol. 39, No. 1, January-February 1971, pp. 4–7; and in C. P. Goetzinger et al., "Small Perceptive Hearing Loss: Its Effect on School Age Children," *Volta Review,* Vol. 66, 1964, pp. 124–132.

the next section of this chapter. In short, the problem of early preschool identification will not be resolved by any "easy" recommendation or "quick fix." Like the general system in which it is embedded, it is too complex for that.

Misidentification Identification presents, in one sense, the classic statistical problem of error types. In this setting, Type I errors occur when children who are not handicapped are screened and erroneously labeled handicapped; Type II errors occur when screening fails to detect children who are in fact handicapped.

Excessive Type I, or "false positive," errors would indicate that screening procedures are too conservative or perhaps unreliable. Too many "false positives," if referred for specialized diagnostic procedures, may overload scarce and expensive diagnostic resources and gradually erode diagnosticians' trust in the seriousness or worthiness of the screening program. Nor should the injurious effects of misidentification on child and parent be ignored. It is shocking to be told that you are the parent of a "defective" child; but it is also tragic to labor under this impression only to find that it is untrue. Some Type I errors are to be expected, however, when test subjects are very young and hence uncooperative, when the test instrument or device is known to have a significant margin of error, or when the testing personnel are inexperienced and make judgmental and procedural mistakes. Should any or all of these conditions hold in the actual test situation, several alternatives should be considered to reduce the impact of Type I error, since one "cries wolf" only so often until the cry is ignored.

- Personnel may be trained better, certified, supervised, and exposed to more screenings to gain experience.
- The test instrument may be evaluated and improved.
- One may work with a more "cooperative," i.e., an older or less impaired, population.
- Or, a second and third retesting may be performed on all positives initially screened to confirm the first identification and to minimize false positives before they are referred to a diagnostician.

Excessive Type II errors, in which handicapped children pass undetected, would indicate that the identification procedures are not discriminating enough. Too many "false negatives" could damage children by denying them needed services. Type II errors of identification should be expected when the handicap is slight, latent, or overshadowed by other more obvious problems, when the test instrument is faulty or too "coarse grained" to discriminate the condition, or when testing personnel are not properly trained and supervised. One should think about the following remedial actions if excessive Type II errors are encountered in a given identification program:

- Train the personnel better, certify them, and alert them to the often subtle, subjective cues that may signal the presence of a handicap.
- Improve the test instrument, especially to increase the level of resolution, to pick up more children with both severe and mild handicaps.
- Or, repeated tests could be given, both immediately and over time, with the same or similar complementary instruments to give the disability every opportunity to demonstrate its presence. Such a procedure is particularly suitable for progressive or degenerative disabilities, e.g., the Wardenburg syndrome as an etiology of deafness, and for "high risk" populations.

The special problems attendant to screening multiply handicapped and other hard-to-test children deserve special mention as a persistent source of misidentification, particularly in a total handicapped population that appears to include increasing percentages of congenitally and multiply handicapped children.[12] In the case of the mentally retarded child, for instance, there is no reason to believe that a "normal" screening test will reliably indicate either sensory competence or deficiency. It is also possible to confuse one handicap with another, as when a deaf child is incorrectly thought to be mentally retarded. Perhaps the mere presence of some impairment, such as mental retardation or a learning disability, should entitle the child to full diagnostic evaluation for other impairments. Statistically, there is reason to believe that children with one type of handicap have a greater than average probability of being impaired in a second way as well.[13]

[12]This observation is occurring more in the literature. For example, see J. T. Fenlason, "An Occupational Therapy Program for the Developmental Habilitation of Congenital Rubella Children," *American Journal of Occupational Therapy,* Vol. 22, November-December 1968, pp. 525–529.

[13]See M. D. Sheridan, "Vision Screening of Very Young or Handicapped Children," *British Medical Journal,* Vol. 2, 1960, pp. 453–462; Robert T. Blackhurst and Edmund Radke, "Vision Screening Procedures Used with Mentally Retarded Children—A Second Report," *The Sight-Saving Review,* Vol. 38, No. 2, Summer 1968, pp. 84-88; W. S. Schachat et al., "Ophthalmologic Findings in Children with Cerebral Palsy," *Pediatrics,* Vol. 19, April 1957, pp. 623–628; J. D. Schein and J. A. Salvia, "Color Blindness in Mentally Retarded Children," *Exceptional Children,* Vol. 35, April 1969, pp. 609–613; R. G. Suchman, "Visual Impairment Among Deaf Children," *American Journal of Ophthalmology,* Vol. 77, January 1967, pp. 18–21; R. T. Fulton and L. L. Lloyd, *Audiometry for the Retarded,* Williams & Wilkins, Baltimore, Maryland, 1969; and L. L. Lloyd et al., "An Operant Audiometric Procedure for Difficult-to-Test Patients," *Journal of Speech and Hearing Disorders,* Vol. 33, No. 3, August 1968, pp. 236–245.

Labeling and Stigmatization In the zealous endeavor to find the handicapped child, one often loses sight of the personal, familial, social, and legal consequences of the "simple" act of identification. To cite the most extreme case in recent history, it was a mere 35 years ago that Nazi Germany systematically exterminated thousands of humans "simply" labeled mentally defective. While far less lurid nowadays, the negative consequences of labeling still persist.[14]

Negative effects of labels on individual children should be minimized to the extent feasible, but some forms of labels are unavoidable. The mere act of providing special services implies the child is different, and at least implicitly "labels" the child in his or her own mind and in other children's minds. The labels may be formal or informal, but they will exist in some form. The Hobbs' study[15] on the classification of children found that some form of labeling or categorization of children to receive special services is both unavoidable and desirable. Categorization is desirable from the viewpoints of obtaining appropriate services for children in need, for planning and seeking support for programs, and for evaluation. Some sort of classification of groups, of children, if not individuals, is unavoidable, and so the aim should be to retain its usefulness while striving always to minimize the sometimes negative effects of labels. One could, for example, label each child only as having "exceptional needs," but use a more specific classification system *only* for data collection and reporting purposes.[16] For example, the individual child's file might contain data on various dimensions related to disability and special educational needs, but no label beyond "exceptional." Counting of children in various other specific categories for federal or other reporting could still be done from the detailed data, but such categorical reporting would only be for a group of children.

In a thorough recitation of the issues and legal precedents related to classification of handicapped children in and by schools, David L. Kirp has provided many of the legal underpinnings for a "Children's

[14]See John T. Chandler and John Plakos, *Spanish-Speaking Pupils Classified as Educable Mentally Retarded,* State Department of Education, Sacramento, California, 1969, which responded to the fact that in 1969 some school districts had as many as 85 percent "educable mentally retarded" with Spanish surnames. The problem was linguistic, not intellectual; the result was legislation to require intelligence testing in one's mother tongue and the consequent "delabeling" of *several thousand* EMR children throughout California.

[15]Nicholas Hobbs, *The Futures of Children: Categories, Labels, and Their Consequences,* Jossey-Bass Publishers, San Francisco, California, 1975.

[16]See California State Board of Education, "California Master Plan for Special Educaton," Sacramento, California, January 10, 1974.

Bill of Rights."[17] His discussion bears careful and thoughtful reading; we summarize here a few of the more salient issues he raised concerning the problem of labeling and stigmatization.

A basic principle guaranteed by the law is that a child's liberty may not be infringed upon unless adequate procedural protections are provided.[18] Specifically, courts have endorsed the concept that labeling a child mentally retarded or delinquent may not be used as a tactic to relinquish the obligation to educate the child, one area where this society has established a minimum demand and expectation for service.[19] One could likewise argue a related and more general case, that failure to classify a demonstrably needy and disabled child for the purpose of denying an expensive or scarce service would appear to be a denial of dubious legality.

The basic issues involved in the identification/classification act revolve about questions of the accuracy of the classification[20] and of the appropriateness of the proposed treatment.[21] The procedural "due process" guarantees afforded by the "Education for All Handicapped Children Act" passed in 1975[22] are substantial and should be beneficial in these two issue areas.

One possible outcome of an increased consciousness of the costs involved in labeling may be a more judicious use of the classification mechanism. Another outcome might be the extension of this considerable body of legal precedent from the substantive area of education to protect the rights of handicapped children more generally. Even if not more judicious, the labeling and classification processes are bound to become more public as wrongfully labeled people seek redress from the courts for real and imagined grievances.

The creation of functional classifications, another possible out-

[17]David L. Kirp, "Schools as Sorters: The Constitutional and Policy Implications of Student Classification," *University of Pennsylvania Law Review,* Vol. 121, No. 4, April 1973, pp. 705–797. (Republished under the same title as Reprint Number 1, Childhood and Government Project, The Earl Warren Legal Institute, Boalt Hall, University of California, Berkeley, California, 1973).

[18]*Wasson* v. *Trowbridge,* 382 F.2d 807 (2d Cir. 1967); *Goldwyn* v. *Allen,* 54 Misc. 2d 94 281 N.Y.S. 2d 899 (1967). See generally, Van Alstyne, "The Judicial Trend Toward Student Academic Freedom," *University of Florida Law Review,* Vol. 30, 1968. (Citations are from Kirp, op. cit.)

[19]Buss, "Procedural Due Process for School Discipline: Probing the Constitutional Outline," *University of Pennsylvania Law Review,* Vol. 119, 1971, pp. 611–612.

[20]*Kent* v. *United States,* 383 U.S. 541 (1966); and *Holmes* v. *New York City Housing Authority,* 398 F.2d 262 (2d Cir. 1968) (authority must articulate standards for admission to public housing).

[21]*Pennsylvania Association for Retarded Children* v. *Pennsylvania,* 334 F. Supp. 1257, 1260 (E.D. Pa. 1971).

[22]P.L. 94-142.

come of the legal machinery, has been advocated in the past.[23] It may develop as a way to scale a disabled person's total residual capabilities, and thereby replace mechanistic, simplistic, either/or labels such as "legally blind." Such functional classifications are implicit in our earlier argument calling for a *thorough* diagnosis and evaluation of the disability and the required services. For several reasons, therefore, efforts to create and execute such functional classification schemes appear to have considerable merit.

Current vision and hearing testing procedures, for example, attempt to determine the levels at which the subject fails an acuity test. For example, at what distance and size of figure on an eye chart, or at what level of dB of hearing loss, is he unable to perform? Such tests prove only that the subject cannot see or hear at the prescribed distance or with the noted level and tone of sound; they do not establish his total sensory capability. In contrast, one wonders what might happen if the test objective were to determine the person's aural and visual functional capability in reading, writing, mobility, and speaking or understanding speech. This is a very different conception of identification than presently exists, a conception whose objective is to evaluate the subject's residual capacity to function, and not to limit him by applying gross labels such as "blind," "deaf," or "deaf-blind."

The point here is the need to emphasize a person's best and total capability to function in a situation, as opposed to the present "worst case" emphasis that appears to underlie many labels. For people labeled "deaf-blind," this might mean the useful recognition that most have some residual capability in the aural and/or visual senses; very few are both profoundly deaf and totally blind. In fact, there is great diversity in the overall population labeled "deaf-blind"; diversity that must be recognized if proper service and a better service system are to be provided.

Inadequate Follow-Up

There is a major problem in getting children who fail screening tests to a place where they can receive competent, professional diagnostic services. That is to say, there are two breakdowns in the "Identification Process": between both the "Awareness" and "Diagnosis" and the "Diagnosis" and "Service" phases.

[23]S. M. Genensky, *A Functional Classification System of the Visually Impaired to Replace the Legal Definition of Blindness,* The Rand Corporation, RM-6246-RC, April 1970; and Jack Sokolow and Eugene J. Taylor, "Report of a National Field Trial of a Method for Functional Disability Evaluation," *Journal of Chronic Disability,* Vol. 20, 1967, pp. 897–909.

Breakdown in the first instance occurs when a child has been screened and is thought to be impaired, but nothing is done to get him to a competent source of diagnostic service. Breakdown in the second instance is thought to be less frequent, but is still notable; it occurs when the child has had a full diagnostic work-up but nothing is done to provide the services indicated by the nature and the extent of the disability and recommended by the diagnostician.

A screening program is nearly worthless without follow-up. The problem itself might be attacked simultaneously from several angles. General publicity about the nature and importance of detection of problems might help, for instance.[24] Parents who are so informed, either through the media, by school personnel, or by their physicians, might give the general problems more attention, being alert to recognize gross signals of disorders in the child and to search out competent care. The critical importance of the pediatrician and the general or family practitioner has not received the attention warranted. In their penetrating critique of neonatal hearing evaluation, Goldsen and Tait made several pertinent observations on this point.

- Pediatricians are in the most contact with the child in the 0–5 period, if the child is seen by a physician at all.
- Pediatricians are generally not sensitized to a full range of signs and symptoms indicative of sensory disorders.
- More should and could be done to improve on this situation by repeated exposure of the need for identification to the pediatrician in professional meetings, journals, inservice training, and other educational activities.
- Pediatricians do not normally have occasion to know and use audiologists (and other specialists in sensory problems), but this shortcoming could be reduced through individual initiative and through direct action by local medical societies.
- There is great and pressing need for more and better staffed well-baby clinics to increase the institutional chances that children in the "missing cohort" aged 0 to 5 will see a physician.

[24]The National Society for the Prevention of Blindness is to be commended for their program of dispensing free "Home Eye-Test Kits" for preschoolers. It is a simple test using a version of the illiterate "E" which can be used by the parent to spot fairly gross problems in about five minutes. Kits are obtainable from the Society by writing them at 79 Madison Avenue, New York, New York 10016. There is even a response card which the parent is asked to fill out and return to the Society so that they can evaluate the effectiveness of the program. On this return card, the parent may indicate that they did not use the test, that the child used and passed the test, or that the child was unable to pass a minimum standard and that an appointment for an eye examination had been made with a physician or optometrist (whose name and address are requested).

- The use of mobile hearing testing units, taken as part of a strong, general medical evaluation service, is an underutilized and underappreciated mechanism to realize contact with the 0-5 age group.[25]

Another and more difficult aspect of the breakdown phenomenon deserves more investigation: Why do parents either seek or not seek medical and other care for their children in the first place? What incentives operate in this matter? When we have completer answers to these "simple" questions, we will begin to know how to provide not only better screening follow-up but better services generally to our children.

Parental cooperation underlies an effective service program. Most parents respond well, but there is some proportion who, for whatever reason, will not take their children for more detailed examination or for a thorough medical workup, if that is called for. Delay can be a serious enemy for the impaired child. If there is difficulty in getting parents to obtain hearing aids for their children, for example, or if there is some problem with the parent's acceptance of special service regulations, then the parents need to be educated or the regulations modified. The school or public health nurse may be helpful in this regard. The recommended Regional Direction Center may have a pivotal responsibility in this task to ensure that the diagnostic examinations recommended by the screening program are made and made on time, and to check that services are having the effects they are supposed to have.

Follow-up is too important to be left to chance, and responsibility for it must be carefully and clearly defined early and throughout the handicapped child's life. It is time-consuming, frustrating, and demanding work, but doing it correctly has been demonstrated to have considerable positive benefits.[26]

[25]Robert Goldsen and Charles Tait, "Critique of Neonatal Hearing Evaluation," *Journal of Speech and Hearing Disorders,* Vol. 36, No. 1, 1971, pp. 3-18.

[26]The State of Michigan's vision screening program has been hailed in the literature as being exemplary. One of its key features is the well-developed follow-up procedure that forms an integral feature of the overall program. Parents are notified if their child fails the initial screening; a doctor's report form is included, which the parents are asked to have completed and returned to the Department of Public Health; if in six weeks no report is returned, a follow-up letter reminder is mailed out; and if that does not work, public health and school personnel are quite likely to pay a visit to the family to encourage them to make an appointment. It works. See Robert T. Blackhurst and Edmund Radke, "School Vision Screening in the State of Michigan," *The Sight-Saving Review,* Vol. 34, No. 1, 1964.

Insufficient Personnel Training and Certification

The need for well-trained and certified personnel has been noted occasionally in the literature as one explanation for uneven and unreliable screening programs.[27] The value of qualified screening technicians has been demonstrated over the years in the Michigan program.[28] The need for certification of those actually doing preschool aural and visual screening has been repeatedly noted in our interviews with speech, hearing, and vision specialists.

Comprehensive state screening programs are so few that there is reduced demand for these very particular technical skills. Black and his associates stress this point, noting that without sufficient jobs, there is little reason to train technical specialists, but without technical specialists, there is little reason to expect screenings to improve in either quality or quantity.

Failure to Exploit Technology

Adequate screening technology exists for school-age children; the problem is to screen very young preschool children. There are many embryonic technological developments in preschool identification, a point stressed in our review of "the state of the art" in the next section; however, the researcher soon forms the distinct impression that, lacking a central or at least recognizable focus for identification as a service,[29] much apparently promising embryonic technology is not being developed to see if it can become practical and be exploited.

For instance, promising but undeveloped technology for screening of neonates for hearing deficits has been reported in the open literature since at least the mid-1960s. There is little comparable literature or experience evaluating these promising techniques in depth, developing and determining their feasibility in an applications setting, or exploring their likely costs and benefits for limited, selected, or mass use. There are many promising technological tools around which, if evaluated, compared, and refined for large-scale applications, could undoubtedly help to strengthen the identification service.

In short, a remarkable variety of technology for preschool age

[27]J. W. Black, "Procedures for Children," *ASHA Reports No. 2*, 1967, pp. 27–38; and J. P. Moncur, "Judge Reliability in Infant Testing," *Journal of Speech and Hearing Research*, Vol. 11, 1968, pp. 348–357.

[28]Blackhurst and Radke, op. cit.

[29]The National Institute for Neurological Diseases and Stroke, and the National Eye Institute, have a long and commendable record of sensorineural research. There is a difference between much, if not most, of this kind of research and the more prosaic requirements of developing and evaluating identification techniques for mass screening programs.

screening exists in experimental form. The connection between research and applications, a connection associated with careful evaluation, studies of feasibility, and assessments of desirability, is not very well made in the current system.

IDENTIFICATION OF HEARING AND VISION DISORDERS

The costs and feasibility of identification programs of course must be considered. In broad terms, we recommend a "mixed scanning" approach to identification, by which we mean giving all children a minimum but sufficient opportunity to demonstrate impairments and, if once demonstrated, a maximum opportunity for thorough and accurate diagnosis.[30] It is infeasible, unnecessary, and too costly to gather finely detailed information on all youth of all ages. However, it appears necessary to improve on the present situation, in which an at-birth medical examination is often followed by almost a total blank until the child receives a school-entrance examination at age 5, and in which a large fraction of school-age youth are not screened for impairments. It would be desirable for both preschool and school-age children to have a greater opportunity to receive a more detailed examination, and, if found to be handicapped, to receive the best possible diagnostic confirmation of impairment. If "awareness" is fostered by low-cost screening procedures, the higher costs of carrying out detailed diagnostics are more readily justified.

In this section, we present detailed case studies of the feasibility and methodology of identification of various hearing and vision disorders in children of various ages.

Importance of Vision Screening Unlike adults, children are often unaware that their vision is impaired and therefore do not seek help. Furthermore, the lack of general awareness of the importance of vision tests, the inadequate numbers of trained personnel to conduct screening, and the costs of thorough testing, all work to the childrens' disadvantage, especially since the benefits of the screening are not directly reaped by the agencies typically funding the screening.

Vision screening is important, but currently it is not done comprehensively or very well. Preschool vision screening is especially underdeveloped despite several recent initiatives; for example, Head Start projects reported screening 680,000 children in 1968, and the National Society for the Prevention of Blindness reports that in the 1963-64 school year there were some 86 preschool screening projects working with 52,000 children, and in the 1964-65 school year there were some

---

[30]Amitai Etzioni, "Mixed Scanning: A 'Third' Approach to Decision Making," *Public Administration Review,* December 1967, pp. 385–392, explains the general concept.

290 projects screening 156,000 children. This is an encouraging trend, but the number of preschoolers screened is still a small fraction of the total.[31] For the sake of contrast, we estimated that in 1970 some 12.5 million children aged 5 to 17, or about one of every four children, had eye conditions requiring special care. Of course, not all of these children are severely enough impaired to be called handicapped, but they still benefit from an identification program, for example, by finding out that corrective lenses are required and subsequently by learning more in school.

It is hard to determine the prevalence of preschool vision problems, but we know that rates of referral from preschool vision tests have ranged from 1 to 30 percent in sample programs.[32] Rules of thumb indicate that refractive errors account for 70 to 75 percent of these referrals, muscle imbalance about 20 percent, and amblyopia ("lazy eye disorder") about 10 percent.[33] But these figures are no more than partial approximations of the actual needs of the total preschool population, needs which are not reliably known and met with services because the identification measurements are not being made. Trying to answer more specific questions about important subsets of the total preschool population is even more difficult. For instance, we know that multiply handicapped children as a class have more visual problems,[34] but precise prevalence rates are not known for specific combinations of impairments. Furthermore, it is often harder to screen and diagnose these especially handicapped children, but not much effort has been expended in designing and testing specialized instrumentation and procedures to serve them.[35]

[31]Jane S. Lin-Fu, *Vision Screening of Children,* Department of Health, Education, and Welfare, Health Services and Mental Health Administration, Maternal and Child Health Service, Washington, D.C., 1971. This is an excellent, concise work on the general topic.

[32]J. W. Oberman, "Vision Needs of America's Children," *The Sight-Saving Review,* Vol. 36, Winter 1966, pp. 217-227.

[33]E. M. Hatfield, "Progress in Preschool Vision Screening," *The Sight-Saving Review,* Vol. 37, 1967, pp. 191-207.

[34]M. C. Fletcher and M. M. Thompson, "Eye Abnormalities in the Mentally Defective," *American Journal of Mental Deficiency,* Vol. 66, September 1966, pp. 242-244; Michigan Department of Public Health, *Vision and Hearing Screening in Selected Classes for the Mentally Retarded, City of Detroit, Michigan,* U.S. Department of Health, Education, and Welfare, Social and Rehabilitation Service, Children's Bureau, Washington, D.C., 1966; and W. S. Schachat et al., "Ophthalmologic Findings in Children with Cerebral Palsy," *Pediatrics,* Vol. 19, April 1957, pp. 623-628.

[35]For general referral guidelines see R. B. Kugel, "Vision Screening of Preschool Children," *Pediatrics,* Vol. 50, December 1972, pp. 966-967, in which the following criteria for referral are recommended: (1) 3-year-olds with $20/50$ acuity or less, (2) 4-to-5-year-olds with $20/40$ acuity or less, (3) differences in two eyes of 20 or more, and (4) strabismus. Failing any of these, it is argued, is reason to retest before referral.

With identification through vision screening, the child has taken a necessary first step toward receipt of other services. The screening may, for example, result in referral of the child to a physician for a complete eye examination, and later to other personnel for sensory aids; it may make teachers aware of their students' eye conditions after diagnosis and service are rendered; or it may suggest possible service (e.g., for a child with corrected acuity of 20/70 or less) by a special education program. Screening is *not* diagnosis; it corresponds to the "awareness" phase of the identification process.

Basically, there are screenings by clinical history and screenings by vision tests.[36]

Vision Screening by Clinical Histories   Studies indicate a correlation between those who fail vision tests and those who either have a family history of eye problems or have demonstrated signs and symptoms of visual disorder. Clinical histories are valuable and important screening devices, although many identification programs do not compile them. It is no great task to extract the portion of a clinical history relevant to eye disorders; it comprises several simple components, such as the following:

- Is there a family history of visual problems?
- What was the mother's pregnancy history, including the possibility that she might have had rubella, toxoplasmosis, syphilis, or toxemia?
- What was the birth history?
- Were there neonatal problems, e.g., respiratory difficulty and the use of oxygen therapy?
- Are other handicapping conditions present?

Any significant positive findings should alert screening personnel to the increased odds that the child may have visual problems.

Signs and symptoms that often indicate visual problems include patient-supplied information about headaches, dizziness, sensitivity to light, and blurred vision, or observable signs such as crossed eyes, turned-out eyes, rapid eye movement (nystagmus), red, swollen, or puffy eyelids, watery eyes, and haziness in the pupils.

Behavior may also be indicative. Excessive blinking, squinting, rubbing, inattention to the blackboard, poor alignment in written material, holding books too near or far from the face, and poor performance in motor activities are all potential signs of trouble. Teacher and parent observations can be important, but they often appear to be overlooked or dismissed.

[36]Lin-Fu, op. cit., pp. 5–7.

Preschool Vision Screening The literature on vision screening of preschoolers is sometimes vague and inconsistent, and raises questions, while answering others.[37]

The general purpose of existing preschool vision screening programs relates mainly to the "Awareness" phase of the identification model developed earlier. The primary aim of these programs is to detect the existence of low-vision problems.[38] Problems of refraction, general development, and medical diagnosis are all relatively neglected with respect to this age group.[39]

A vision problem often cited as the object of preschool screening programs is amblyopia ex anopsia ("lazy eye blindness"). Treatment for it should not be delayed, as it may result in some permanent impairment of visual ability—impairment that is often avoidable if detected and treated at an early age.[40]

All that is attempted in most preschool tests is the detection of abnormal distance acuity, and if detected, there is some presumption that the child will be directed to competent professional examination and treatment—a presumption not guaranteed by routine or formal institutional devices.

For infants, most tests are reflex-oriented. If a stimulus provokes some expected response, it is assumed that the visual pathways are working. Reaction of the pupils to light, aversion of the eyes in a lateral direction in the opposite direction of that in which the infant's

---

[37]A sampling of some of the more satisfying of the general literature follows: O. Ffooks, "Vision Test for Children, Use of Symbols," *British Journal of Ophthalmology,* Vol. 49, June 1965, pp. 312-314; R. H. Bock, "Vision Screening for Infants," *Ophthalmologic Supplement,* Vol. 47, 1957; B. H. Schwarting, "Testing Infants' Vision—Apparatus for Estimating Visual Acuity of Infants and Young Children," *American Journal of Ophthalmology,* Vol. 38, 1954; H. F. Allen, "Testing Visual Acuity in Preschool Children," *Pediatrics,* Vol. 19, 1957; and J. N. Evans, "Visual Tests for Infants," *American Journal of Ophthalmology,* Vol. 29, 1946.

[38]Oberman, op. cit.

[39]The important work of A. Gesell, "Developmental Aspect of Child Vision," *Journal of Pediatrics,* Vol. 35, 1949, is a notable exception. See also R. W. Lowry, Jr., *Preschool Vision: Tests, Diagnosis, Guidance,* The American Optometric Association, St. Louis, Missouri, 1959, which is another valuable source.

[40]T. Gundersen, "Amblyopia ex Anopsia: A Preventable Form of Blindness," *Pediatric Clinics of North America,* Vol. 2, No. 2, 1955; C. W. Lepard, "Early Diagnosis of Visual Impairment in Children," *Postgraduate Medicine,* Vol. 24, 1958; R. W. Dockery, "The Value of Vision Screening in the Preschool Age Child," *Journal of the National Medical Association,* Vol. 52, 1960; D. Vaughn et al., *Eye Tests for Preschool and School Age Children with Special Emphasis on the Detection of Amblyopia ex Anopsia in Preschool Children,* California Medical Eye Council, Stockton, California, 1960; and O. Lippmann, "Vision of Young Children," *Archives of Ophthalmology,* Vol. 81, June 1969, pp. 763-775.

head is quickly turned (doll's eyes phenomemon), and response to a moving series of lines are all possible screening tests. Other reflex-oriented tests can also be used if the examining physician or nurse is alerted to the possible presence of visual problems and trained to perform them.[41]

For children from about age 1 to 2 years, subjective tests have been used.[42] Walking infants are asked to retrieve small, standardized objects from varying distances with each eye covered in turn. If the child can talk, several other tests can be used: picture tests,[43] direction tests,[44] and some very specific acuity tests.[45]

Medical examinations by pediatricians and general practitioners could be much more effective than they are, in practice, in the early detection of preschool visual problems. For instance, in a section of a standard pediatric textbook devoted to "Examination of the Pediatric Patient," Kempe and his colleagues recommend the following to the pediatrician:[46]

> Most newborns have the visual capacity to fix on a moving object as early as the first few minutes of life. Infants who do not follow a face at the first well child visit should be suspected of having a visual problem. Ophthalmoscopic examination should be done on one of the earliest possible visits in order to make the diagnosis of cataract, congenital glaucoma, or retinal abnormality.

[41]Frank W. Newell, *Ophthalmology: Principles and Concepts,* The C. V. Mosby Company, St. Louis, Missouri, 1969 ed., pp. 90–91. Dr. J. Terry Ernest pointed this out in an interview with G. D. Brewer, Chicago, Illinois, March 1972.

[42]Many of which are noted in E. S. Duke,*Textbook of Ophthalmology,* The C. V. Mosby Company, St. Louis, 1971; and Vaughn et al., op. cit.

[43]G. Osterberg, "A Sight-Test Chart for Children," *Acta Ophthalmology,* Vol. 14, January 1936, pp. 397–405; and C. Berens, "Visual Acuity and Color Recognition Tests for Children," *American Journal of Ophthalmology,* Vol. 46, 1958.

[44]A. E. Sloane and J. R. Callagher, "A Vision Test for Pediatricians' Use," *Journal of Pediatrics,* Vol. 28, 1946. The child is asked to point out the direction in which some object is facing, heading, etc. See also S. D. Liebman and S. S. Gellis (eds.), *The Pediatrician's Ophthalmology,* The C. V. Mosby Company, St. Louis, 1966.

[45]E.g., "STYCAR" tests (Screening Tests for Young Children and Retardates"); see M. D. Sheridan, "Vision Screening of Very Young or Handicapped Children," *British Medical Journal,* Vol. 2, 1960; and idem, "Vision Tests for Young Children, Normal and Handicapped," *Spastics Quarterly,* Vol. 11, March 1962, pp. 25–33.

[46]C. Henry Kempe et al., *Current Pediatric Diagnosis and Treatment,* Lange Medical Publications, Los Altos, California, 1972, pp. 124–125. The following are visual acuity tests in current usage for preschoolers: Snellen E. Test, Sjogren Hand Test (like the Snellen but uses hands and fingers), Landolt Broken Ring Test (variation of Snellen), California Clown Test—"Do-As-I-Do Vision Test" (another variation of the Snellen), matching letters tests, picture tests, symbol tests, miniature toy tests, etc. The point of this lengthy description is to show that it is not for want of instruments that preschool vision testing is not conducted.

And later in this same section:

> Five to 10 percent of preschool children have some kind of visual impairment. The illiterate E chart, Snellen chart, or Allen cards can be used for checking visual acuity, and each eye should be tested separately. The 5-year-old child should have a visual acuity of $20/30$ or better in both eyes, and there should be no significant difference between the two eyes. Amblyopia ex anopsia affects 2 to 5 percent of children and must be detected early before permanent loss of vision occurs.

In a subsequent section of Kempe devoted entirely to the pediatric eye, Ellis comments about the important and underutilized role of the mother in performing preschool visual acuity tests:

> Routine testing of visual acuity should be a part of every general physical examination. It is the single most important test of visual function. In children 4 years old or older, satisfactory visual acuity tests can usually be obtained with the use of Snellen test cards or illiterate E charts. . . . The mother, with her interest, can repeat the test at her leisure, and the final result is usually more accurate than testing done in the office by the pediatrician or his nurse.[47]

With respect to mass screening, several problems confront those interested in complete and reliable coverage of the preschool population.[48] Besides the general observation that there is no existing formal institutional mechanism to guarantee that the child will be screened before entering school, a problem noted previously, difficulties are reported in even those few instances where special efforts have been made to carry out these tests.

Screening tests themselves have not been standardized and misidentifications are not uncommon, or at least this seems to be the general point raised in several case settings where preschool vision testing has been tried on a large scale.[49] Given the problems with test

---

[47]Philip P. Ellis, "Eye," in ibid., pp. 197ff.

[48]Apell and Lowry, op. cit., and Hatfield, op. cit.

[49]D. M. Hufhines, "Preschool Vision Screening in Orange County, California: I. Community Organization," *The Sight-Saving Review*, Vol. 31, 1961, pp. 210–214; E. L. Russell, J. M. Kada, and D. M. Hufhines, "Orange County Vision Screening Project: II. Ophthalmologic Evaluation," ibid., pp. 215–219; Michigan Department of Public Health, op. cit.; idem, "Preschool Hearing, Vision Training Results Revealed," *Michigan Medicine*, Vol. 64, 1965; T. M. Colasuonno, *Preschool Vision Screening in Douglas County, Oregon*, National Society for the Prevention of Blindness, Publication P-255, New York, n.d., and idem, *Preschool Vision Screening in Louisville*, National Society for the Prevention of Blindness, Publication P-254, New York, n.d. The test instruments available in the area of mental retardation also are not infallible. See Lee J. Cronbach, "Five Decades of Controversy Over Mental Testing." *American Psychologist*, January 1975, pp. 1–14.

standardization, variation in the criteria used for referral, and the absence of reliable information on rates of clinical referral and follow-up, it is difficult to say much about any of the following points— all of which are necessary inputs and factors to be considered before making any recommendations about mass screening for preschoolers:

- The quality of screening techniques to be used
- The expected incidence and referral rates for various kinds of visual disorder
- The cost of a mass screening program for preschoolers
- The magnitude of the benefits that might accrue to the overall population as a result of such an undertaking

In light of critical unresolved questions, especially concerning whether potential benefits of mass screening of all children at a preschool age rather than age 5 outweigh the costs, we do not recommend *mass* screening for visual impairment in the *preschool* population. Rather, the value of the pediatrician and the family in the identification process is such that we have chosen to concentrate attention on them instead.

It has been noted that on the average parents are excellent diagnosticians, but that parental anxiety is often[50]

> compounded by professional denial of the diagnosis or by false reassurance. One-third of the parents interviewed by Meadow[51] and seen by Schlesinger . . . indicate that the first physician consulted denied the suspected deafness. Sixty percent of the parents in Meadow's study consulted four or more physicians prior to receiving a definite, accurate diagnosis.

One of the reasons that early diagnosis is often not accomplished is that physicians generally and pediatricians particularly are not well and thoroughly trained to detect early childhood hearing and vision disorders.

The pediatrician has a serious responsibility with respect to identifying all types of physical and mental handicaps in children, and he would be aided in discharging that responsibility if:

- Authorities responsible for medical school curricula would review those aspects devoted to pediatric examination to ensure that

[50]Hilde S. Schlesinger, "Diagnostic Crisis and its Participants," in Arthur G. Norris (ed.), *Deafness,* Vol. II, Professional Rehabilitation Workers with the Adult Deaf, Inc., Silver Spring, Maryland, 1972, pp. 29–34, at p. 30.

[51]K. P. Meadow, "Parental Responses to the Medical Ambiguities of Deafness," *Journal of Health and Social Behavior,* Vol. 9, 1968, pp. 299–309, as cited in ibid.

this material is covered and receives the serious attention it warrants.

- State boards certifying pediatricians would examine applicants to call attention to this responsibility and to ensure that certified pediatricians know how to conduct screening procedures for the various handicapping conditions appropriate for the age and general condition of the pediatric patient.
- Those responsible for pediatric residency programs would review their programs to ensure that screening procedures are learned and routinely carried out.

The parent's close contact with the preschooler should be exploited far more than it has been in the past. A parent may perform periodic initial screening of the preschooler at home as well as, or better than, would a massive, one-shot program.[52] The child is more relaxed, the mother has more time to carry out the basic tests and to repeat them until she gets stable results, and she has specific knowledge about the child that no one-time screener could be expected to match. Parents would be aided if:

- Programs such as that being conducted by the National Society for the Prevention of Blindness noted earlier were encouraged, evaluated as to effectiveness and cost, and then expanded if warranted.
- Parallel activities were supported to explore alternative testing instruments, practices, and corresponding results when parents test the preschool child in their home.

Finally, the nursery school—an expanding trend associated with heightened interest in early childhood education—is another underused resource. In this case the teacher and school nurse (if one is available) could be trained to recognize behavioral cues and perform screening. Again, this is not diagnosis; it is intended to pick up the grossest of sensory deviance as early as possible so that the child *suspected* of having problems may be identified and given professional diagnosis. The importance of follow-up and direction are critical and obvious in this case.

- Where procedures to license and certify preschool nursery personnel exist, we recommend that efforts be made to *instruct* and

[52]R. A. Savitz, T. Valadian, and R. B. Reed, "Vision Screening of Preschool Children at Home," *American Journal of Public Health*, Vol. 55, October 1965, pp. 1555–1562; R. R. Trotter, R. M. Philips, and K. Shaffer, "Measurement of Visual Acuity of Preschool Children by Their Parents," *The Sight-Saving Review*, Vol. 36, Summer 1966, pp. 80–87; and E. Press and E. Austin, "Screening of Preschool Children for Amblyopia: Administration of Tests by Parents," *Journal of the American Medical Association*, Vol. 204, May 27, 1968, pp. 767–770.

sensitize those personnel to be alert to the possible presence of handicapping problems.
• We recommend that clear standards and procedures of reporting suspected handicapping problems to parents and health and education authorities be created (where none currently exist) or reviewed and improved (where they do exist).

School-Age Vision Screening

Carefully controlled studies of the reliability of the available school vision screening tests and programs have not been done routinely or on a national comparative and evaluative scale.[53]

In those cases that have been monitored to some extent,[54] a number of consistent findings emerge:

• The programs are relatively expensive.
• Good screening programs, as measured solely by high rates of confirmation of true positives by diagnosticians, have trained and certified visual-technical specialists either closely supervising or actually conducting the test.
• Something on the order of 10 percent should be expected to "fail" the school vision screening programs, although the prevalence rates of disorders contributing to this rule of thumb are not well or reliably reported.
• Follow-up is a critical component in those programs thought to be relatively effective. That is, parents need to be informed of possible visual problems, they need encouragement and information about where to get competent diagnostic help, they may need financial assistance in obtaining the service, e.g., glasses and medical treatment, and they may need reminders to have the child examined further.

The State of Michigan has amassed a commendable record in its school vision program over the last 30 to 35 years.[55] As reported, this program is straightforward in its design and implementation and

[53]National Society for the Prevention of Blindness, *Vision Screening in Schools,* Publication 257, New York, 1961; and E. B. Guttmann, "School Vision Screening," *The Sight-Saving Review,* Vol. 26, Winter 1956, pp. 212–219.

[54]A. E. Sloane and R. A. Savitz, "Vision Screening," *International Ophthalmology Clinic,* Vol. 3, December 1963, pp. 803–809; Henrik L. Blum et al., *Vision Screening for Elementary Schools: The Orinda Study,* University of California Press, Berkeley, California, 1959; A. E. Sloane and P. Rosenthal, "School Vision Testing," *Archives of Ophthalmology,* Vol. 64, November 1960, pp. 143–150; and N. B. Belloc, "Vision Screening in the United States," *The Sight-Saving Review,* Vol. 32, No. 4, Winter 1962.

[55]Blackhurst and Radke, op. cit., and Michigan Department of Public Health, *Vision and Hearing Screening.*

could serve as a model for vision screening programs at the school level in other locations. Generally characterized as benefiting from good public education, high standards of personnel doing the testing, sound administration, and persistent follow-up procedures, the Michigan program has enjoyed confirmed true positives averaging around 90 percent over the years—a remarkable achievement. One result is that physicians respect the program and take its referrals seriously. Some 200 "vision technicians," employees of the Maternal and Child Health Division of the Michigan State Department of Public Health, have been recognized and suitably appreciated by public and policymaker alike as the essential ingredient in the program's success. The second key element is the administrative procedures of follow-up, created to ensure that the identification process does not break down before needed services are delivered. A notification is mailed to the parents when a child is found to have a vision problem. The notification includes a blank doctor's report that the parents are asked to have filled out and return to the Department of Public Health. If no report is received within six weeks, a follow-up letter is sent and the child's school nurse is notified. On their own initiative, Department personnel might then get in touch with the parents to inform them of local diagnostic services.

For school age visually impaired children we recommend that:

- Various apparently successful programs, including the Michigan model, be thoroughly evaluated for full details of their operation, costs, and benefits.

- A reproducible model or models for other states be developed, given the detailed findings of those thorough evaluations, which could serve for a full-scale implementation throughout the country.

- A comprehensive mass vision screening program be instituted throughout the United States, designed to reach every school-age child.

Importance of Hearing Identification

Serious and permanent hearing deficits occur in slightly more than ½ percent of the children, or about 490,000, aged 0 to 21; and for 10 percent of this group of handicapped children, their loss is profound and bilateral, resulting in a nonfunctional sense of hearing.[56] About 10 percent of all children have less severe but still significant hearing impairment (15 + dB).[57] The most frequent cause of children's hear-

[56]See Chap. 5 for details.
[57]D. Ling, "Early Identification and Epidemiology of Hearing Disorders," *Rehabilitation Digest*, Vol. 8. No. 1, 1971, pp. 5-9, at p. 6.

ing loss is recurrent chronic otitis media or serous otitis media (infection of the middle ear).[58] Even children with a single episode of otitis media may have some degree of hearing impairment for some period after the acute episode.

Although these hearing losses may not be too severe, they may occur at an unfortunate time and may be sufficient to inhibit the acquisition of language[59]—a setback that may affect the child throughout his school years.[60] If the losses are discovered and services provided before school begins, many of the learning, behavioral, and discipline problems that ensue from poor hearing and poor attention may be averted.

> Detection of such problems is as much a part of preventive pediatrics as is the immunization routine. Audiologic screening tests can be performed by nonprofessional technicians and should be a part of the preschool examination.[61]

Characteristics of Hearing Loss in the Youth Population

While the importance of early identification of hearing handicapped youth is undeniable, we know little about the characteristics of that population until they are about age 5 and over.

There are several types of hearing loss. *Sensorineural hearing loss* (or "nerve deafness") is due to a problem within the inner ear, in the nerves going from the inner ear to the brain, or in the brain itself. The loss may result from infection, trauma, toxic substances, degenerative disease, or congenital causes (see the "Medical Services" chapter). *Conductive hearing loss* occurs in patients with a normal inner ear

[58]V. Holm and L. Kunze, "Effect of Chronic Otitis Media on Language and Speech Development," *Pediatrics,* Vol. 43, May 1969.

[59]G. Bekesy, "Current Status of Theories of Hearing," *Science,* Vol. 123, 1956, pp. 779–783; J. B. Carroll, *The Study of Language,* Harvard University Press, Cambridge, Massachusetts, 1953; C. P. Goetzinger, "Effects of Small Perceptual Losses on Language and on Speech Discrimination," *Volta Review,* Vol. 64, 1965; and James E. Kavanagh, *The Genesis and Pathogenesis of Speech and Language,* National Institute of Child Health and Human Development, Department of Health, Education, and Welfare, Publication NIH 72-36, Washington, D.C., 1971.

[60]Lois L. Elliott and Ann B. Vegely, "Some Possible Effects of the Delay of Early Treatment of Deafness: A Second Look," *Journal of Speech and Hearing Research,* Vol. 11, December 1968, pp. 883–886; Lois L. Elliott and V. B. Armbruster, "Some Possible Effects of the Delay of Early Treatment of Deafness," in ibid., Vol. 10, 1967, pp. 209–224; M. M. Lewis, *Language, Thought and Personality in Infancy and Childhood,* Basic Books, New York, 1963; and A. R. Luria and F. Yudovich, *Speech and the Development of the Mental Processes in the Child,* Staples Press, London, 1966.

[61]Kempe et al., op. cit., p. 125; see also G. L. Wyatt, "Speech and Language Disorders in Pre-School Children: A Preventive Approach," *Pediatrics,* Vol. 36, 1965.

who are hard of hearing because something is wrong with the mechanism conducting the sound to the inner ear. Medical or surgical procedures, or amplification, may restore hearing partially or fully in such cases. *Congenital deafness* is probably present at birth or occurs soon thereafter. *Mixed hearing loss* involves both conductive and neural components. And *simulated hearing loss* results from causes that cannot be traced to organic disease, as in instances of involuntary, e.g., emotional or psychotic, disorders.[62]

Typically, hearing loss found in school audiometry programs is slight, conductive (not sensorineural), and transient (not permanent).[63] In urban schools, between 2 and 5 percent of children may require referral to physicians for medical attention and diagnosis.[64]

Most children with sensorineural loss are "hard of hearing" rather than deaf. This means that many of them can benefit greatly from hearing aids, despite the aural distortion that often occurs with this type of impairment. Sensorineural hearing loss usually occurs early in life and prevents or hinders the natural development of speech and language. Early diagnosis and treatment, together with effective teaching methods, could do much to reduce the total degree of functional handicap resulting from this type of hearing loss.

Measurement of Hearing

The current state of hearing measurement is relatively well developed and diverse, and is represented in a large and growing literature.[65]

Using an audiometer, the basic instrument, a competent audiometrist can test hearing by using air and bone conduction techniques. Hearing losses in children have been identified and measured at virtually all ages, with the possible exception of the first months of life.

[62]David D. DeWeese and W. H. Saunders, *Textbook of Otolaryngology,* The C. V. Mosby Company, St. Louis, 1968, pp. 275–276.

[63]E. L. Eagles, S. M. Wishik, and L. G. Doerfler, "Hearing Sensitivity and Ear Disease in Children," *Laryngoscope Monograph, 1967.*

[64]D. Ling, "Early Identification and Epidemiology of Hearing Disorders," *Rehabilitation Digest,* Vol. 8, No. 1, 1971, pp. 5–9; see also S. R. Silverman, "Clinical and Educational Procedures for the Deaf," in L. Travis (ed.), *Handbook of Speech Pathology,* Appleton-Century-Crofts, New York, 1957, p. 398.

[65]DeWeese and Saunders, op. cit., pp. 275–298; J. J. O'Neill and H. J. Oyer, *Applied Audiometry,* Dodd, Mead, New York, 1966, contains a technically detailed and thorough survey of the methods; A. Glorig (ed.), *Audiometry: Principles and Practices,* Williams & Wilkins, Baltimore, 1965, and I. M. Ventry and J. B. Chaiklin (eds.), "Multidiscipline Study of Functional Hearing Loss," *Journal of Audiological Research,* Vol. 5, 1965, pp. 179–262, have a comprehensive and detailed program that merits consideration.

The younger the child, naturally, the more sophisticated must be the instrumentation and the measurement specialist. This relates directly to our concept of the general identification process, in that gross screening ("awareness") tests may be done by a nurse or pediatrician in the office or nursery to pick up suspected hearing loss; solid diagnosis must be done where experience, specialized skill, and instrumentation are all more developed.

Ideally, screening tests should be done at birth and at all pediatric examinations so that possible hearing losses are picked up as early as possible. While this study is narrowly interested in children having hearing losses of about 40 dB and more, it is also important that children with lesser deficits of, say, 15 to 40 dB be identified so that parents and teachers can seek more specialized help if required. Rehabilitation can begin as early as the deficit is detected, which generally means as early as 6 months of age.[66]

Competent audiometrists are critical in the screening process. Ballenger enlarges on what constitutes "competency" here in the following terms:

> Adequate audiometry cannot be carried out by personnel who have not received suitable training and experience. In order to obtain accurate and useful clinical information, the audiometrist must have a satisfactory grasp of the basic principles underlying behavioral measurement. He must, in addition, be familiar with the audiologic patterns associated with the various types of hearing disorders. Finally, he must understand the limitations of electroacoustic instruments.[67]

Air conduction audiometry measures the sensitivity of the entire hearing system by placing an oscillator-driven earphone over the external ear. Because response derives from the entire hearing system, one is generally not able to isolate the point of hearing loss, if there is one.

Bone conduction audiometry measures the sensitivity of the sensorineural mechanism by placing a stimulus (tuning fork, bone conductor vibrator) directly to the patient's skull. So doing short-circuits the transmission mechanisms of the middle ear and helps to determine the type of hearing loss.

Hearing loss of 15 dB or more is one standard reference point for

[66]Marlin Weaver and Marion P. Downs, "Ear, Nose, and Throat," in Kempe et al., op. cit., pp. 221–245. For a general survey of the diagnostic literature, see L. M. DiCarlo et al., "Diagnostic Procedures for Auditory Disorders in Children," *Folia Phoniatrica,* Vol. 14, 1964. pp. 206–264.

[67]John Jacob Ballenger et al., *Diseases of the Nose, Throat, and Ear,* Lea & Febiger, Philadelphia, 1969 ed., pp. 581–599, at p. 581.

referral. Patients with that much loss should be considered candidates for special attention and services.[68]

Congenital deafness has been detected in infancy by exposing the child to acoustic stimuli and then recording his responses. Infants with significant hearing loss have been successfully fitted with hearing aids at one month of age.

The importance of taking the relevant clinical history as a routine part of the hearing screening process is as great here as it is for vision screening. Positive relationships exist between failures on hearing tests and family histories of ear disorder or those who have demonstrated signs and symptoms of hearing disorder. While this relationship is well known, the taking of clinical histories is not always a routine part of the child's hearing screening program. For example, audiologic high-risk registries (composed of those singled out in the clinical history process) have been important in detecting hearing losses in children as young as 6 months old. Without such registries, the earliest time that hearing loss is detected is commonly around 20 months.[69]

Testing very young children calls for patience and no little ingenuity. Children have little reason to want their ears tested, they often fear strangers and unnatural settings, it takes special effort to get them to listen attentively to sounds, and their responses are none too accurate. Finally, the child may not know what he has been missing, unlike the adult who may have enjoyed hearing in the past. The very young child's deficit probably has been with him since birth and seems perfectly "normal" to him, in a real sense of the term.[70]

To restress the main point of much of this discussion, it is generally agreed that early detection and treatment of hearing loss are crucially important.

> Every physician who is responsible for the care of infants should develop similar screening programs in the hospital nursery or at least check the infant's hearing at the first visit by the use of squeak toys and bells which have as close to pure tone sounds as possible. The newborn will only respond by a flicker of his eyelids or a very minute Moro response [body tremor in response to aural stimulus.][71]

[68]Howard P. House, F. W. Linthicum, Jr., and E. W. Johnson, "Current Management of Hearing Loss in Children," *American Journal of the Disabled Child,* Vol. 108, 1964, pp. 677–696; and A. Miller and L. Newburg. "Infant Orientation to Hearing Aids: A New Approach," *American Journal of the Disabled Child,* Vol. 113, 1967, pp. 466–468.

[69]Kempe et al., op. cit., pp. 124–125.

[70]Ballenger et al., op. cit.

[71]Kempe et al., p. 125; see also R. Carhart and J. Jerger, "Preferred Method for Clinical Determination of Pure-Tone Thresholds," *Journal of Speech and Hearing Disability,* Vol. 24, 1959, pp. 330–345; and H. Newby, *Audiology,* Appleton-Century-Crofts, New York, 1958.

Preschool Hearing Tests

Most 4-year-olds can be tested with conventional techniques. Children younger than 4, including the newborn, may also be tested with a variety of techniques, although diminished reliability and increased cost are to be expected. Davis and Silverman, for instance, divide hearing tests for the very young into three general classes: methods based on increased motivation, physiological audiometry, and electrophysical tests.[72]

The first class includes "games" and other devices designed to capture and maintain the child's interest in a conventional audiological examination. Children over 2½ years old normally play games and hence can be tested with these methods. The second class of tests depends on the behavioral reactions of the child, e.g., startle reactions, reflexes, awakening from sleep, and movements toward or away from a sound stimulus—the last of which, "orienting reactions," are thought to be the "best in the critical period from 6 to 12 months of age when identification and approximate assessment of impaired hearing are so important."[73] The third class is generally not suitable for mass screening at the current state of development, because of the size, cost, and demand for very specialized skills and instrumentation. As diagnostic aids, however, the third class is important; it includes electrodermal audiometry (galvanic skin responses to sound stimuli), electroencephalic audiometry (EEG patterns are assessed with respect to various sounds), and electric response audiometry (evoked response audiometry). These assessment techniques are known fairly well in the specialized audiologic community, but their administration is dependent upon earlier, grosser recognition that the child has some hearing impairment.[74] In terms of the identification model developed earlier, tests of the third class would clearly fall into the "Diagnosis" phase.

Given the fact that a large number of children are examined only at birth when identification is difficult, and then not again until their school entrance examinations, the need for some kind of preschool age identification program is clear, as is the need for physicians (especially pediatricians) to be alert for hearing problems during routine checkups.[75]

[72]Hallowell Davis and S. Richard Silverman (eds.), *Hearing and Deafness,* Holt, Rinehart and Winston, Inc., New York, 1970 ed., pp. 237–248.

[73]Ibid., p. 240.

[74]R. B. Eisenberg, "Auditory Behavior in the Human Neonate, I. Methodological Problems and the Logical Design of Research Procedures," *Journal of Audiological Research,* Vol. 5, 1965, pp. 159–177.

[75]*Conference on Newborn Hearing Screening,* Department of Health, Education, and Welfare, Public Health Service, Maternal and Child Health Service, Washington, D.C., 1971.

Hearing Tests at Various Ages of the Young

Screening At Birth There is a very large literature on screening at birth; its main points can be summarized as follows:

- It can be done, but it depends on the skill and training administered to screening personnel, e.g., nursery nurses who repeat simple reflex tests over the entire period that the newborn is in the hospital.[76]
- Responses are not too reliable. Both false positives and false negatives are commonplace. The need for repeated testing is clear.
- Based on the experimental evidence, mass screening techniques for the newborn are not reliable enough for consideration for large-scale implementation.[77]

This does not mean that efforts should be abandoned to develop better ways to conduct mass screening at birth; it merely affirms that current testing methods and procedures are not sufficiently reliable.[78] A promising innovation in this field is the "Crib-o-gram" system developed by Blair Simmons and his colleagues at the Stanford Medical School;[79] a full-scale evaluation, including follow-up of the identified children as they age, will be needed to confirm its value.

[76]Jean Robinson, "Screening Techniques in Babies," *Sound,* Vol. 4, No. 4, 1970, pp. 91–94; and Rayford C. Redell and Donald R. Calvert, "Factors in Screening Hearing of the Newborn," *Journal of Auditory Research,* Vol. 3, 1969, pp. 278–289.

[77]"[Because]results of mass screening programs are inconsistent and misleading . . . we urge increased research efforts, but cannot recommend routine screening of newborn infants for hearing impairment." Committee on Fetus and Newborn, "Joint Statement on Neonatal Screening for Hearing Impairment," *Pediatrics,* Vol. 47, No. 6, June 1971, p. 1085. See also Marion P. Downs, "The Identification of Congenital Deafness," *Transactions of the American Academy of Ophthalmology and Otolaryngology,* Vol. 74, 1970, pp. 1208–1214, tends to support this pessimistic assessment after reviewing the available evidence.

[78]The use of high-risk registries, for example, has been instrumental in narrowing the total population down to a more manageable subset of those likely to have hearing difficulties. For this group, every and all screening techniques would appear to be warranted. L. Bergstrom, W. G. Hemenway, and Marion P. Downs, "A High Risk Registry to Find Congenital Deafness," *Otologic Clinic of North America,* Vol. 4, 1971, pp. 369–399; and Marion P. Downs, "Audiologic Evaluation of the Congenitally Deaf Infant," *Otologic Clinic of North America,* Vol. 4, 1971, pp. 347–358.

[79]Basically, the movement of the child is carefully and automatically recorded in response to aural stimuli. "Abnormal" responses signal that the baby may have some hearing difficulties and indicate that the physician should administer more intensive diagnostic procedures. It has been reported in the press that some 6000 babies had been screened with the Crib-o-gram system between 1970 and 1973, and 300 "failures" were identified, of whom 8 were actually shown to have hearing loss in subsequent diagnostic workups. *Los Angeles Times,* September 23, 1973, Part 1, p. 3.

A recent summary by Bordley and Hardy advances the following comments about neonatal hearing screening—comments justified by a thorough review of the literature:

> Neonatal auditory screening appears to bear no relationship to subsequently identified hearing loss; in fact, 98 percent of the 248 children failing the audiometric test at age 8 years gave normal responses to sound stimuli of 65 dB to 75 dB during the newborn period. These findings are in accord with our past experience.[80]

Another summary evaluation of the considerable literature on neonatal screening adds the following cogent comments:

- Mild hearing loss is not routinely detectable, and unilateral loss is not detectable.
- The absolute number of missed children does not appear to be large, but the question is somewhat moot given the condition of the existing data.
- Screening procedures are not very good. There are too many false positives caused by a conservative orientation of the testers, who do not want to let a hearing impaired child slip through, and by operational problems connected to test administration.
- Follow-up on identified children is either not done or is done by nonspecialists, with the result that the problem of parents laboring under false positive identification looms somewhat large.
- Economic arguments about relative benefits derived from special training at age 1 versus age 3 or 4 are not well established. [There is] "no evidence to prove that detection at age four days for example, followed by immediate guidance and training, leads to a significant financial savings compared to when detection is accomplished and training is begun at four weeks, four months, or even two or three years."[81]

Screening at 0 to 2 Months Gross overall response to sound stimuli predominate in the 0- to 2-month range.[82] Electroencephalographic techniques, which record the brain's electrical activity after sensory

---

[80]John E. Bordley and Janet B. Hardy, "A Hearing Survey on Preschool Children," *American Academy of Ophthalmology and Otolaryngology*, Vol. 76, No. 2, 1972, pp. 349–354, at p. 353. This study implicitly calls attention to the pressing need for follow-up evaluation of children as they pass through the 0–5 period to determine the true rates of false positive reports for those children who in fact have received one of the many neonatal tests. Follow-up has been sparse so far.

[81]Robert Goldstein and Charles Tait, "Critique of Neonatal Hearing Evaluation," *Journal of Speech and Hearing Disorders*, Vol. 36, No. 1, 1971, pp. 3–18, at p. 10.

[82]E. F. Waldon, "Audio-reflexometry in Testing Hearing of Very Young Children," *Audiology*, Vol. 12, 1973, pp. 14–20.

stimuli, appear to have promise, but have not yet been demonstrated to be sufficiently valid, and much work is still in the early developmental stage.[83] Simple observational differences between "normal" and hearing disabled children have been noted; and Kaye has discerned significant patterns of sucking behavior.[84] Only slightly more involved were studies measuring the latency periods between the instance of aural stimulation and the crying response. Profoundly impaired babies of course did not respond; partially hearing babies would either not respond, would respond at significantly lengthier latency rates, or would not respond in synchronization with the stimulus.[85] Spectrographic analyses have been carried out that were reliably able to discriminate in the experimental setting between hearing and nonhearing babies.[86] In the older 7- to 12-month range, cries having higher pitches, greater pitch variability, and variations in intensity produced characteristic and different spectrographic signatures for normal and disabled children.

Screening at 3 to 24 Months Behavioral responses are observable by about the second month;[87] the infant is capable of being distracted by and of paying attention to sound. By the age of 4 months, eye movement in response to stimuli should be observable. The average 1-year-old is able to comprehend sounds and recognize parents; and by about 18 months can identify parts of his or her body and favorite toys.[88] By approximately 18 months, two- or three-word sentences should be regularly produced. If these abilities are not manifest at approximately these stages, parents should seek professional assis-

[83]Two fairly representative efforts are E. L. Lowell, "Electrophysiologic Tests of Hearing in Children," in E. H. Nober (ed.), *Trends in the Audiologic Assessment and Rehabilitation of Children,* Syracuse University Press, Syracuse, New York, 1967, pp. 41–50; and I. Rapin and L. J. Graziani, "Auditory-evoked Responses in Normal, Brain-damaged, and Deaf Infants," *Neurology,* 1967, pp. 881–894. See also V. Goodhill, "Deafness Research: Where Are We?" *The Volta Review,* Vol. 70, No. 8, 1968, pp. 620–629.

[84]H. Kaye, "The Effects of Feeding and Tonal Stimulation on Non-nutritive Sucking in a Human Newborn," *Journal of Experimental Child Psychology,* Vol. 3, 1966, pp. 131–134.

[85]J. K. Cullen et al., "The Development of Auditory Feedback Monitoring: I. Delayed Auditory Feedback Studies on Infant Cry," *Journal of Speech and Hearing,* Vol. 11, No. 1, March 1968.

[86]M. C. Jones, "An Investigation of Certain Acoustic Parameters of the Crying Vocalization of Young Deaf Children," Ph.D. thesis, Northwestern University, 1965 (University Microfilms, Ann Arbor, Michigan, 1965).

[87]J. Koch, "Conditioned Orienting Reactions in Two-Month-Old Infants," *British Journal of Psychology,* Vol. 58, 1967, pp. 105–110.

[88]J. Medioni and R. Tronche, "A New Method for Diagnosing Deafness in Young Children," *Bull. Information,* Vol. 13, 1967, pp. 9–16, describes a pure tone test using toys as a reward mechanism.

tance and diagnosis of suspected hearing loss. As we found in our parent interviews, however, parental suspicion is sometimes discounted by pediatricians as merely unnecessary anxiety. Judgment and sensitivity on the part of the physician is the key to identification in this early age period. Careful and consistent observation is called for by parents and doctors alike.[89]

Several small-scale screening programs for children in this age group were found in the literature; however, none seems to have comprehensive applicability.

- Much of the population in this age group is not routinely seen by a physician (no existing institutional mechanisms guarantee adequate coverage).
- Visiting nurses have been used, but they are few, are not all adequately trained in this field, are often overworked, and are not in contact with the total population.
- Public health clinics, well-baby clinics, etc., are not ordinarily set up to conduct this kind of screening nor do they serve a majority of the population.
- Reliance on high-risk registries would appear to have particular appeal for coverage of this age group.

Screening at 24 Months to 5 Years Screening is possible in this age range. By this time the child should be able to respond to sounds voluntarily. Simple tests can be performed by the physician, or even the parent if trained (see Table 7.1), and play-conditioning and finger-raising, both in response to commands, are commonly reported in the literature.[90] Failing these tests should be cause to seek out more competent diagnosis. The basic problems of doing screening for this age group have been summarized by Ballenger:[91]

- Fear of strangers and strange settings
- Fear of earphones
- Learning about the expected stimulus-response behavior inherent in most screening procedures (and thereby either volunteering response or failing to respond out of coyness or boredom)
- Maintenance of attention to the test

Despite these problems, the benefits of early preschool identification of hearing handicapped youth appear large in relation to the costs. Among the benefits are reduction of the potentially permanent inhibition of language and speech development by medical or surgi-

[89]Ballenger et al., op. cit.

[90]Philip Lichtenberg and Dolores Norton, *Cognitive and Mental Development in the First Five Years of Life—A Review of Recent Research,* National Institute of Mental Health, Chevy Chase, Maryland, 1970; and Davis and Silverman, op. cit.

[91]Ballenger et al., op. cit., Chap. 41.

cal treatment of the hearing loss, provision of sensory aids, and provision of preschool special educational services. Profoundly deaf and severely hard of hearing youth have the greatest need for these services before age 5, and they obviously cannot receive them until the handicap has been identified.

We have already mentioned several options for reaching preschool children, including a "high-risk registry" activated at the time of birth, working through well-baby clinics or nursery schools, and mak-

Table 7.1
SIMPLE CHART TO RATE HEARING

	Normal	Abnormal
Speech		
Does your child say a few words?	12–18 months	2 years and up
Can he say some words containing each of the following sounds?	Three-quarters of the sounds at two to three years	3 years and up
s (as in yes, bus, see, sock)		
sh (as in shoe, shut, fish)		
k (as in coat, cow, cup, cat)		
t (as in toe, teeth, top)		
Can strangers understand his speech?	Yes, from 18 to 24 months	No, two-and-a-half years and up
Language		
Is he putting two words together?	21–24 months	30 months and up
Does he talk in sentences?	Two to three years	Three years and up
Understanding		
Does he usually understand what you say to him?	Yes	No
Does he have to watch you in order to understand?	No	Yes
Responses to Speech (not noise)		
Does he hear you when you call him from a distance of several yards?	Yes	No
When in the same room do you have to raise your voice to get him to hear you?	No	Yes
Hearing Problems		
Do any relatives have hearing problems (other than through aging)?	No	Yes
Does he ever complain of earache?	No	Yes
Do you think he has any difficulty in hearing?	No	Yes

If the child is rated abnormal in speech only, the first area listed above, a hearing loss is not indicated. If the child is rated abnormal in two or more of the other areas, then hearing should be checked.

SOURCE: Ling, op. cit., p. 8.

ing simple screening tools available to parents for home use. But perhaps the most promising means of identifying preschool hearing or vision handicapped children is a type of "free checkup" system using pediatricians. Simple data/administrative procedures could be developed to aid in this type of identification. For instance, the simple form in Fig. 7.3 is used in Kansas. We would go further and recommend that each child be entitled to "free checkups" at various times between age 0 and 5, with an age 2 medical checkup to include quality screening for hearing, vision, and other impairments. These checkups could be performed by pediatricians or other service personnel, who could be reimbursed through National Health Insurance or some other program for every child they screen *and* report on to a health or other prescribed government agency. In brief, we recommend that:

- Various options for identification of 2 to 3 year old children for hearing handicaps be thoroughly evaluated with the goal of developing a reproducible model or models for full-scale implementation throughout the country.
- After viable models are developed, a comprehensive hearing identification program should be instituted throughout the United States designed to reach preschool-age children.

School Hearing Screening As with vision screening, carefully controlled studies of the reliability of the existing school hearing screening tests have not been routinely done on a national scale. It appears that "sweep frequency screening"[92] is a common method of choice, and is one of the simplest and most reliable methods. Other general findings include the following:

- Good screening depends significantly on the skill of the screener and the quality and calibration of the audiometer employed.
- Follow-up is the critical ingredient in a good, as opposed to unsatisfactory, hearing conservation program (as was the case with school vision screening).
- Teachers in the early elementary grades, if trained to observe and recognize behavioral clues, are an underutilized source of early identification.

By way of encouraging the thorough evaluation of all existing school hearing screening programs, the following general questions are offered for consideration. These should prove useful for those

[92]A. W. G. Ewing, "Sweep Frequency Method of Making Screening Tests of the Hearing of School Children," *British Medical Journal,* No. 4094, 1955.

Preschool Multiphasic Screening

Name of Child:				Physician's Name:	
Parent's Name:				Phone:	
Birthdate:					
Address:					USD No.

	Test	Retest	Referral	Remarks
Denver Developmental Screening Test				
Hearing				
Hemoglobin				
Immunizations—T. B. Skin Test				
Speech				
Physical Inspection				
Urinalysis				
Vision				

KSDH MCH

KANSAS STATE DEPARTMENT OF HEALTH

Copies: 1 School   3 Local Health Dept.
        2 Parents   4 Kans. State Dept. of Health

Fig. 7.3 Kansas form for preschool multiphasic screening.

192

actually involved and for those interested in the aggregate effectiveness of school hearing screening programs:

- Are true positive identifications routinely and systematically made as confirmed by competent diagnosis?
- Is the screening staff well trained and using technically reliable audiometers?
- Are new students screened?
- Are screenings done several times during the child's school career? (Some hearing disorders are degenerative, and a true negative at school entrance could become a false negative over time.)
- Are records complete and accurate?
- Have diagnostic procedures been reliable, and has follow-up worked satisfactorily?
- Have services, such as hearing aids, been provided to those in need?
- How is the local program generally regarded by specialists in the area?

Our recommendations for school-age hearing handicapped children parallel those for school-age vision handicapped children, and include a comprehensive mass hearing screening program designed to reach every school-age child.

For handicapping conditions in general, the status of identification services is much the same as for the hearing and vision case studies presented above. At present, there is no formal mechanism to screen and identify all handicapped children after they leave the newborn nursery and until they enter elementary school. In this case we are speaking of a medical examination designed to detect a range of potentially debilitating mental and physical conditions so that services may be offered at as early an age as is desirable to help alleviate the effects of the mental or physical disorders.[93] For children in or about to enter school, however, screening clearly is feasible for many types of disorders. The new federal "Education For All Handicapped Children Act"[94] requires that states "identify" all children residing in the state who are handicapped. However, the states will apparently be given great latitude in how they choose to identify those children.

We are particularly excited about the identification prospects of the recently mandated Child Health and Disability Prevention (CHDP) program in California. It is ambitious yet relatively simple in concept. (A description of the CHDP program is contained in the appendix to this chapter.) Its careful adaptation and adoption of

[93]The number of children who never see a physician in the period from 0 to 5 years of age may be as high as 25 to 30 percent of the total population of that age cohort. Interview with Dr. Frederick A. Frye, Department of Pediatrics, University of California Medical School, La Jolla, California, February 1972.

[94]P.L. 94-142.

some of its major tenets would go a long way, in our view, to improving the early identification of handicapped children. The program is not flawless; no program is, and we have reservations about the way California is implementing what otherwise appears to be an excellent program. (For example, the proposed Medicaid fee for a "developmental assessment" is a rather low $3.30.) Rather, it is a long-overdue, first step toward improved identification that responsible officials in other states should seriously consider emulating. The following recommendation includes some of the most desirable features of the California program.

We recommend that parents of children beginning their first year of school, or entering a school for the first time, be required as a condition of admission of the child to present to the school either (1) the results of an approved health and developmental screening by an approved professional, or (2) a statement that the parents have decided not to have their child receive the screening services. This screening is valuable but not infallible for two primary reasons: parents may choose not to have their children screened for various reasons; and screening methods for the detection of disorders at the age of 4 or 5 years are not as valid and reliable as we would like them to be. Nonetheless, most of the more severely disordered children can be detected with existing screening methods. Care must be taken, however, not to label children for whom the results of the screening and later diagnosis are not clear-cut. Before implementing this recommendation, the screening methods to be used would have to be carefully considered. If these recommendations were adopted, the Medicaid Early and Periodic Screening, Diagnosis, and Treatment program would pay for the screening for Medicaid-eligible children. The results of the screening would be forwarded to the state (to a Regional Direction Center, ideally), where they could be used to follow up to see that the various appropriate programs provide needed service at as early an age as is desirable, and to aid in planning future service programs. Implementation of privacy safeguards for people identified will be essential.

The federal government has had difficulty getting some states to implement the required Medicaid Early and Periodic Screening, Diagnosis, and Treatment program.[95] Consequently, to facilitate the provi-

---

[95]See U.S. General Accounting Office, *Improvements Needed to Speed Implementation of Medicaid's Early and Periodic Screening, Diagnosis, and Treatment Program,* MWD-75-13, Report B-164031(3), Washington, D.C., January 9, 1975; John K. Iglehart, "Health Report/HEW Plans to Fine States for not Implementing Program," *National Journal Reports,* January 11, 1975, pp. 59–61; and Anne-Marie Foltz, "Early and Periodic Screening, Diagnosis, and Treatment (EPSDT): The Development and Ambiguous Federal Policy," *Health Policy Project Working Paper Series,* Working Paper No. 2, Yale University School of Medicine, New Haven, Connecticut, June 1974.

sion of needed services, *we recommend that procedures be adopted (1) to help ensure that all Medicaid-eligible children and youth up to age 21 years receive early and periodic screening, unless such screening is formally refused, and (2) to help ensure that follow-up steps are taken to obtain diagnosis and treatment for those who need them.* The Regional Direction Centers (if created) would be useful in making referrals and coordinating needed services and follow-up.

The schools are an ideal setting for identification of handicaps in people of school age, since nearly all children are assembled, observed, and compared on a routine basis. Since screening of school children is feasible and not excessively costly, and the human and social cost can be great if young handicapped people do not receive timely special services, all children should be entitled to at least one screening to detect possible impairments.

We recommend that a screening program be established in every local school district to identify all handicapped children who need special education and other services. A school district cannot adequately serve children with handicaps and refer them for other services if it does not know who they are. We earlier suggested that a medical and developmental screening program reach children before they first enter school. Here we are recommending that the schools conduct a *screening* of all children when they reach a specified age (perhaps 7 or 8 or 9 years old) to identify any impairments that would not normally be detected by the preschool *medical and developmental screening* or that develop or become identifiable in the years after the preschool screening.

NEEDED IMPROVEMENT IN IDENTIFICATION PROGRAMS

A number of problems with and concepts for improving the identification service have been discussed in the course of this chapter and are summarized in the following recommendations:

Various existing physical and mental impairment identification programs, for both school-age and preschool-age children, should be thoroughly evaluated to learn details of their operation that contribute to effectiveness, and to assess their costs, benefits, and suitability for implementation throughout the country.

When that evaluation is complete, a comprehensive mass screening program for physical and mental handicaps should be instituted throughout the country designed to reach every young school-age child. The screening program we recommend would have two components:

- Parents of children beginning their first year of school, or entering a school for the first time, should be required as a condition of admission of the child to present to the school either (1) the

results of an approved health and developmental screening by
an approved professional, or (2) a statement that the parents
have decided not to have their child receive the screening services.

• A screening program should be established in every local school
district to identify all handicapped children who need special
education and related services. This would reach all children of
a specified age (perhaps 7 or 8 or 9 years old) to identify any
impairments that would not normally be detected by the preadmission health and developmental screening or that develop
or become identifiable after the pre-school screening.

High-risk registries appear desirable, especially for children at risk
in the 0- to 5-year age group not normally in contact with public
service institutions. *Registries should be improved where they exist,
and created where they do not. High-risk infants should be screened
at birth, at least once between birth and age 5, and again upon entering school.*

Persons in contact with preschool children, such as parents, day
care personnel, nursery school teachers, well-baby clinic personnel,
social workers, pediatricians, and nurses, *should be sensitized to the
possible existence and effects of various physical and mental impairments, and provided with knowledge of relatively simple tests for
signs and symptoms of such impairments. Existing institutional settings to catch the missing cohort aged 0 to 5 should be exploited as
fully as possible to improve the chances that a child will be identified.*

If detailed evaluation confirms its apparent desirability, *each child
could be given "free checkups" at various ages, with an age 2 medical
checkup to include quality screening for various impairments.* Reimbursement to pediatricians or other service personnel could be
through National Health Insurance or some other program, and
would follow their reporting the screening results to a health agency
or other prescribed government agency.

*Follow-up to see that the identified child receives diagnostic and
other needed services should be a component of every screening
program.*

*Procedures should be adopted (1) to help ensure that all Medicaid-
eligible children and youth up to age 21 years receive early and periodic screening, unless such screening is formally refused, and (2) to
help ensure that follow-up steps are taken to obtain diagnosis and
treatment for those who need them.*

*Efforts should be expended to collect all standards currently in op-
eration for screening programs throughout the country.* These stan-

dards should be summarized and analyzed with the end in view of developing a "model" code for screening, including all procedural details required to fully describe the elements in the identification process model.

State certification and licensing boards are encouraged to consider requiring general, family, and pediatric practice physicians to demonstrate proficiency in the various screening and diagnostic procedures. We further encourage such certification and licensing bodies to consider the need for improved and common standards for those paraprofessional and allied-skills professionals who conduct screening and diagnostic procedures, and for test instruments and procedures.

A program requiring physicians and teachers to report all handicapping conditions to parents, the State Department of Public Health, and the Department of Education should be carefully designed and implemented. We recognize the real possibility that privacy and service desirability norms may clash in this case, but believe that careful design of the procedures ensuring legal and moral safeguards is possible and desirable.

A coordinated and directed national research program should be supported, whose basic purpose is the production (research, testing, and development) of reliable mass screening instruments and procedures. Such work as exists at present is not well coordinated and generally is not directed to the operational aspects of implementation.

The Regional Direction Centers discussed in Chapter 8 would do much to focus local attention on and coordinate the general identification process, and direction is the next logical step in obtaining services after the child is identified.

Certain of the ideas developed in the prevention chapter are also relevant to identification, especially the discussion on genetic testing and screening and on a registry for children born abnormal or thought to be at high-risk of having some handicap.

CALIFORNIA'S CHILD HEALTH AND DISABILITY PREVENTION PROGRAM*

Parents of children beginning the first grade in the fall of 1975 will have to present to their school a CHDP Program Certification for School Entry, which is verification by the screening provider(s) that the child has received all or the equivalent of all of the required health screening services, or that the parents have decided not to have their child receive the health screening services.

CHILD HEALTH AND DISABILITY PREVENTION PROGRAM PURPOSES

The purposes of the CHDP Program are:

- To provide early and periodic assessments of the health status of children who are Medi-Cal beneficiaries under the age of 21, and of children who are entering 1st grade in the fall of 1975;
- To provide that on and after July 1, 1975, each child eligible for services, before enrollment in the 1st grade, shall have the opportunity to receive an efficiently provided health screening evaluation that is of the highest quality;
- To prevent physical and mental disabilities in children;
- To provide for the early identification and referral for treatment of children with potential handicapping conditions before they become chronic and irreversible damage occurs, and/or to lessen their impact on individuals so afflicted;
- To benefit the health and welfare of the citizens of this State by reducing the incidence of such conditions;
- To make maximum use of existing health care resources so that health screening programs are fully integrated with existing health services, that

*Material in this appendix was prepared by the Department of Health, Health and Welfare Agency, State of California, Sacramento, 1975. For more details see the Administrative Regulations for this program filed with the California Secretary of State, February 27, 1975 (Calif. Administrative Code, Title 17, Chapter 4, Subchapter 13).

health care professionals be appropriately represented and utilized in these programs, and that outreach programs be developed to stimulate the use of such preventive health services.

DEFINITIONS

For the purposes of the Child Health and Disability Prevention Program, the following definitions apply:

Child Health and Disability Prevention Program

"Child Health and Disability Prevention Program" means all activities including, but not limited to, planning, outreach and health education, periodic screening, referral for further diagnosis and treatment, follow-up, record-keeping, evaluation, and fiscal procedures related to a community-based program of early identification and referral for treatment of children with potentially handicapping conditions.

Outreach and Health Education Services

"Outreach and health education services" means the methods, including but not limited to simple notification, by which the eligible population is informed of the nature, scope and benefits of the program, and is motivated to participate in it. Outreach and health education services shall be designed to insure that the only reason eligible individuals do not participate in the program is because they intelligently and knowingly decline such participation for reasons unrelated to availability and accessibility of the health screening services.

Screening

"Screening" means the use of simple procedures to sort out from apparently well persons those who have suspected disease or abnormality and to identify those in need of more definitive study of potential physical, mental or other health problems.

Diagnosis

"Diagnosis" means the determination of the nature of a disease or disorder suspected as a result of screening.

Treatment

"Treatment" means the management and care of a child for the purpose of preventing or combating disease or disorder.

Early

"Early" means as soon as possible in the child's life in accordance with the regulations.

Periodic

"Periodic" means health screening repeated at appropriate intervals in accordance with the regulations.

Referral

"Referral" means the educational process by which the family understands the need for further diagnosis and treatment, and is assisted in obtaining the necessary diagnosis and treatment.

Follow-Through

"Follow-through" means the mechanism for confirming completion of the necessary diagnosis and treatment.

SCREENING SERVICES

The health screening services to be offered can be summarized as follows:

- Screening Evaluation of Health Status (SEHS)
     The SEHS will consist of collecting all available health information about the patient. The SEHS includes a history, physical examination, and dental and nutrition assessments.

- Developmental Assessment
     The developmental assessment shall be done by means of the (1) Denver Developmental Screening Test *or* (2) the approved alternate method in the community plan *or* (3) by less formal means for children who have been receiving continuous care by their physician for a minimum of six months.

- Immunizations, as needed, including:

DTP—Diphtheria and tetanus toxoids combined with pertussis vaccine.
TOPV—Trivalent oral polio virus vaccine.
MMR—Measles, mumps and Rubella, individually or in combination.
TD—Combined tetanus and diphtheria toxoids.

- Tuberculin Testing, by means of a standardized PPD or a tine test.

- Laboratory Tests, including blood tests for anemia, phenylketonuria (PKU), syphilis, sickle cell disease (when appropriate) and lead (under special conditions), and urine tests for sugar, protein and blood.

- Vision Screening
     Vision Screening shall consist of a history of eye problems, an inspection of the external eye, evaluation for strabismus, evaluation of the retinal (red) reflex, and in children who are mature enough to cooperate, screening for far visual acuity by means of a Snellen test. If conducted by a licensed optometrist or ophthalmologist, the Modified Clinical Technique (MCT) may be used.

- Hearing Screening

    Hearing Screening shall be appropriate to the age of the child. For children under 3 years of age, it shall be part of the SEHS, noting behavior of the child in response to sound as well as noting problems in speech and language development. For children over 3 years of age who are mature enough to cooperate, hearing screening shall be an individual pure tone audiometric screening test.

ELIGIBILITY DETERMINATION AND/OR VERIFICATION FOR STATE REIMBURSEMENT

In fiscal year 1974–75, the State will reimburse providers for screening services administered to Medi-Cal beneficiaries under 21 years of age and to those children entering first grade in September 1975 who are not eligible for Medi-Cal, but whose gross annual family income is at or below twice the AFDC minimum basic standard of adequate care (CHDP eligible).

Medi-Cal Eligibility

Medi-Cal eligibility is *verified* by obtaining a POE label or a copy of the child's Medi-Cal ID card which is valid for the month in which the service is rendered. The POE label or the copy of the valid ID card should be attached to the Confidential Screening/Billing Report.

CHDP Eligibility

CHDP eligibility is *determined* with the use of the CHDP Eligibility Determination Table (Attachment A). The provider informs the parent or guardian that the child may be eligible for the State reimbursement for screening services if the family income meets certain standards. The CHDP Eligibility Determination Table is given to the parent and the parent compares his family size with the gross annual (or monthly equivalent) family income specified in the Table for that family size. If the family income is at or below the level specified in the Table, the parent reports this to the provider and the child is eligible for State reimbursement for the screening services.

CHDP eligibility is *verified* when the parent or guardian completes the Eligibility Verification statement on the Confidential Screening/Billing Report.

USE OF THE CONFIDENTIAL SCREENING/BILLING REPORT

The Confidential Screening/Billing Report (PM 160) is designed to provide both billing and statistical information to state and local CHDP programs. Providers billing the state for screening services administered to Medi-Cal or CHDP eligible children are to use the PM 160. Fees for screening services are listed in Article 9 of the enclosed CHDP Program regulations.

A *sample* PM 160 with billing instructions on the reverse is included as Attachment B (tear-out). The actual Screening/Billing Report is a seven-part form and will be distributed by community CHDP programs located in local health departments.

The Screening/Billing Report is also to be used as an optional report of screening services provided to private pay patients in the CHDP Program. Instructions for submission of statistical information only are on the back of the Report.

REFERRALS FOR DIAGNOSIS AND TREATMENT

When a screening provider determines that a child needs diagnosis or treatment, the first referral is to be to the child's usual source of health care. If a referral is required and no regular source of health care can be identified, the screening provider must provide a list of at least three appropriate sources of care and assist in making an appointment. The screening provider is responsible for providing assistance, either directly or by agreements with appropriate agencies or individuals, to assure that referrals are completed. A screening provider may make self-referrals for diagnosis and treatment.

USE OF THE CONFIDENTIAL REFERRAL/FOLLOW-UP REPORT

Screening Provider

The screening provider is to complete the top half of a Confidential Referral/ Follow-up Report (PM 161) for each patient referred for diagnosis and treatment. If the patient is referred to more than one provider, a separate PM 161 must be completed for each provider. A Referral/Follow-up Report must be prepared even if follow-up will be done by the screening provider.

The screening provider is to give the last 3 copies of the Referral/Follow-up Report to the parent, guardian, or emancipated minor for transmittal to the provider to whom the patient is referred. A *sample* Referral/Follow-up Report with instructions is included as Attachment D. The actual Report is a five-part form and will be distributed by community CHDP Programs.

Provider of Diagnostic and Treatment Services

The provider of diagnostic and treatment services is to complete the bottom half of the Referral/Follow-up Report and mail the last copy to his local CHDP Program in a self-addressed envelope. To bill Medi-Cal for diagnostic services, he may submit a copy of the Referral/Follow-up Report with proof of Medi-Cal eligibility (POE label) in lieu of Medi-Cal prior authorization.

CHDP PROGRAM PARTICIPATION

Providers who wish to participate in the CHDP Program should read the enclosed information and review the regulations. Participation may be accomplished in several ways:

- Providers who wish to obtain state reimbursement for screening services must submit *one copy* of the Agreement to Participate as a Provider (Attachment B—tear-out) to their community CHDP Program. A list of community CHDP program addresses is enclosed as Attachment F.
- Agencies, organizations, and individuals establishing screening operations must also submit the additional information described on Attachments A and B to the Agreement to Participate as a Provider (Attachment C).

- Providers meeting program regulations will be approved as CHDP providers by their community CHDP program directors.
- Approved CHDP providers who have Medi-Cal provider numbers must use them to bill for screening services. Providers who do *not* have Medi-Cal provider numbers will be assigned CHDP provider numbers for billing at the time they are notified of approval.
- Providers who do *not* wish to obtain state reimbursement for screening services, but who do wish to certify children for school entry must notify their community CHDP program of their intent to provide the required screening services. They must also inform themselves about the requirements of CHDP program regulations.
- Providers who wish to participate as referral resources for diagnosis and treatment only are requested to submit the Agreement to Participate as a Provider to their community CHDP programs to assist them in estimating the adequacy of resources for diagnosis and treatment of disabilities suspected as a result of screening.

Please direct all questions about becoming a CHDP provider to the community CHDP program located in your local health department. See Attachment F for a list of community CHDP program addresses.

CONDITIONS FOR PARTICIPATION

Each screening provider shall forward to state and community CHDP programs all required reports on a timely basis.

Each screening provider who performs the Screening Evaluation of Health Status (SEHS) and wishes to submit a Screening/Billing Report to state and local CHDP programs shall issue Child Health Identification Cards to participants in the program. These cards are for identification only and do not serve as proof of eligibility for CHDP program reimbursement. Child Health Identification Cards will be distributed by community CHDP programs.

Each screening provider shall provide the child or his parent or guardian with a copy of the results of the health screening and evaluation, an explanation of the meaning of the results, and a separate certification of having received such screening services.

Each screening provider shall make arrangements for referral for diagnosis and/or treatment for all children identified as needing such services. Such arrangements shall be made as specified in Article 7 of the CHDP Program regulations.

Each screening provider shall determine the financial eligibility of persons seeking health services, and bill in accordance with the provisions of the CHDP Program regulations.

Prepaid health plans under contract with the State of California within the provisions of California Administrative Code, Title 22, Division 3, Article 8, shall, unless specifically exempted from doing so, meet the standards in this Article, and shall provide CHDP Program services to all Medi-Cal beneficiaries under 21 years of age that are enrolled in such prepaid health plans. Medi-Cal prepaid health plans may offer CHDP Program services to nonenrollees and shall notify the community CHDP Program director in writing of their intent to offer services to nonenrollees.

Each provider of screening services shall insure that:

- Screening services shall be made available to eligible children as defined in the CHDP Program regulations upon referral from any source, including self-referral, without regard to race, religion, sex, national origin, citizenship, marital status, or parenthood.
- Acceptance of screening services shall be voluntary, although outreach programs shall be designed and implemented by the State and communities in order to encourage maximum utilization of such services. Screening services shall not be provided to minors without obtaining written consent from their parent or guardian.
- Screening services shall be provided in a manner that respects the privacy and dignity of the individual. Children receiving State subvented screening services shall not be treated in such a way that they are identifiable from the rest of the population served.
- All information obtained by the screening agency staff as to personal facts and circumstances pertaining to eligible children and their families shall be treated as privileged communication, shall be held confidential, and shall not be divulged without written consent, except as may be necessary to provide emergency services to the child, or as required by the department to administer this program.
- Every effort shall be made to have one or both parents, or the guardian present during the screening procedure of minors, except in the case of emancipated minors.
- In order to make services accessible, screening clinics shall be scheduled at times convenient to working parents such as during evenings or on weekends.
- Bilingual staff shall be available whenever necessary to provide effective and efficient communication with children and parents who have difficulty with English.

CERTIFICATION FOR SCHOOL ENTRY

The Certification for School Entry (and Waiver) is to be completed by the screening provider(s) and/or the child's parent or guardian. It is either to be mailed directly to the child's school by the screening provider or given to the parent to be mailed or carried to the school.

Providers who submit the Agreement to Participate as a Provider and are approved by their community CHDP Program will receive Certification for School Entry Forms from their community CHDP Programs.

Providers who do not intend to bill the State for screening services but who wish to certify children for school entry must request Certification for School Entry forms from their community CHDP programs.

A copy of the Certification for School Entry (and Waiver) is enclosed as Attachment E.

Chapter 8

DIRECTION

OVERVIEW

In view of the considerable sums of money expended by government and the private sector, why are the care and services provided to handicapped youth so deficient in many important ways, and why do many children still receive no services, the wrong services, or inadequate services?

Certainly, it is not because the country lacks programs for handicapped youth—we have discussed over fifty major programs in our survey of the current federal effort, and there are hundreds of state, local, and private initiatives. Certainly, it is not because parents of the handicapped are resigned or lethargic—many of them make heroic efforts to secure services for their children. And certainly, it is not because of significant deficiencies in the quality of care available— the United States boasts some of the most advanced methods and technology ever devised.

Perhaps the easiest explanation would be to blame inadequacy of funds, and it is true that more money would certainly help. But resource insufficiency alone is not the answer to a basic problem that we find pervades nearly all aspects of the system: As it stands, the system currently delivering services to this nation's handicapped is so complex and disorganized as to defy efficient and effective operations.[1] Not all problems would be solved by pouring more money into the system without doing something about its disorganization and complexity. The more than $7 billion already spent annually could be used more effectively.

[1]Todd R. LaPorte (ed.), *Organized Social Complexity: Challenge to Politics and Policy,* Princeton University Press, Princeton, New Jersey, 1975. LaPorte deals extensively with the issues particularized in the instance of the handicapped service system.

Specialization, fragmentation, and bureaucratization without coordination and direction underlie poor system performance. The tangled array of service programs severely taxes parents' ingenuity, perseverance, and courage as they thread their way through the official labyrinth seeking services for their children. Fully two-thirds of the parents we interviewed said they had difficulty in obtaining appropriate services.[2] Their own words express their frustration and despair poignantly:

> The parents are over a barrel. . . . Whenever the mother of a "problem child" questions practices or "makes waves," the administrators threaten to exclude the child, and there is nothing that can be done about it.

> There is no parental counseling, no referral; we were willing to try just about anything.

> The woman offered help, and I almost cried because I was so grateful. . . .

> . . . a chain of talking and talking and talking . . . [and] stumbling around from place to place. . . .

> There are so many government agencies, the people don't know *where* to go.

> I don't even know what questions to ask.

Each major service program is designed to meet rather specialized needs; each has generated special constituencies and nurtured special interests; and each has its own separate budget, often not formulated according to any reasonable assessment of children's actual needs. Pity the unfortunate child who does not meet the letter or spirit of the law as "interpreted" in a federal or state bureau.

Some services are not a major responsibility of any program (see Table 8.1). We spend billions of dollars caring for handicapped children, but, as the preceding chapters demonstrate, we have traditionally spent very little on prevention or identification activities. This lack of responsibility for certain services is especially telling with respect to direction.

Direction is the periodic and systematic matching of a child's needs with the proper mix of available services to satisfy those needs. Individual needs change, for instance, as the child ages or improves in response to services; a system's capacity to serve is dynamic, too. To put it somewhat differently, then, direction is an information-based service designed to match individual needs and local service

---

[2]See Chap. 15 for a summary of these interviews.

Table 8.1
SERVICE COMPONENTS OF FEDERAL AND STATE AGENCY PROGRAMS FOR HANDICAPPED YOUTH

	Type of Federal and State Agency				
Type of Service	*Health*	*Welfare*	*Special Education*	*Vocational Services*	*Mental Health and Retardation*
Direction	—	m	—	—	—
Identification	m	—	m	—	—
Prevention	m	—	m	—	—
Psychological and counseling services	m	m	m	M	M
Medical/surgical treatment	M	m	—	m	m
Education	—	—	M	—	—
Special training	—	—	m	m	—
Vocational training	—	—	m	M	—
Job placement	—	—	—	M	—
Sensory aids/other equipment	m	m	m	m	—
Recreational/social activity	—	—	m	—	—
Personal care	m	—	m	—	M
Income maintenance	—	M	—	—	—
Personnel training	m	m	m	m	m
Construction of facilities	m	—	m	m	m
Research	m	—	m	m	m

NOTE: M equals major component; m equals minor component; a dash (—) indicates little involvement.

system capabilities as both change. It also provides coordination and continuity among the programs designed for meeting the child's needs.

Our society's service system is faced with an urgent need to become child-centered, not specialty-centered. Currently, agencies and professionals are responsible for providing only one or a select few specialized services. Even assuming that each agency and professional performs well, the fact still remains that each single service meets only a part of the child's overall needs. We must begin to regard our handicapped children less as a faceless statistical group, and more as individual fellow beings worthy of the utmost in respect and dignity—and attention. What is needed is a new institutional arrangement specialized to the job of looking at the child as a total human being.

The handicapped service system is not alone in suffering a lack of direction. We find it encouraging that a group of urban researchers, operating on a matter substantively separate from ours but conceptually similar to it, arrived at the same conclusion we did:

New institutional arrangements should be designed to use federal aids or grant conditions to help families learn about services that are available to them, to sort out what is available, to combine or help combine appropriately the many services (and their facility supports).[3]

This captures the essential spirit of what we mean by direction, but we develop and flesh out the concept considerably.

The remainder of this chapter discusses current service programs and their problems, desirable characteristics of a well-run direction service, some existing direction centers that are promising partial models, and some foreign models. The chapter concludes with a detailed discussion of recommendations for evaluating our proposed Regional Direction Centers for Handicapped Youth. When fully tested and developed for this population, the concept might be extended to include handicapped adults.

CURRENT PROGRAMS

As indicated in Table 8.1, the direction service is not a main order of business for any of the various types of federal or state agencies serving the handicapped. In one type of agency where such activities are carried out, public welfare, direction is not a central concern but occurs only tangentially as a social caseworker might be required or inclined to assess a client's needs, search out the appropriate services, and then monitor the results. However, this program is restricted to the poor, social workers generally have heavy caseloads and are not rewarded for "direction," and they do not have the information needed to direct the youth we are concerned with here. The Maternal and Child Health Service also sponsors programs that do limited noncomprehensive referral.[4] Vocational Rehabilitation programs can provide a comprehensive range of services, but these do not reach young children, and services must be aimed at achievement of a vocational objective. Schoolteachers and nurses sometimes help parents find other needed services. Pediatricians sometimes help direct the family. In some states, the "Commission for the Blind" agency provides limited direction service to a segment of the handicapped population.

In general, however, direction is a distinctly underdeveloped and undersupplied service that is no one's prime responsibility. Follow-up and redirection, implicit in the notions of "periodic and system-

---

[3]Selma J. Mushkin et al., *Services to People: State and National Urban Strategies,* Public Services Laboratory, Georgetown University, Washington, D.C., 1973, pp. 16–18.
[4]For details on each of these agency's programs, see later chapters of this book.

atic," are particularly underdeveloped. No one really provides this service except for isolated and dedicated professionals providing other services, who must make extraordinary and usually costly efforts to understand the overall system well enough to advise in areas outside of their particular service competence. Comprehensive information about the system is not generally available, and until it is, direction will remain stunted and erratic.

The upshot is that parents are confronted with an intricate maze for which there is no map, and are left almost entirely to their own devices to thread their way through it. Few of them know much if anything about the various programs when they start out, and there are too few guides that give the facts in plain unvarnished English on what is locally available and what to do to get it. But even the simple facts are not enough; parents need to be fairly sophisticated, and must set to work mastering the ins and outs of a complex, interlocking, and sometimes competing set of bureaucracies and professions. Even after they have succeeded in obtaining services for their children, the possibility remains that alternative services they are unaware of might do the job better. Although ignorance may be bliss, and a parent may report that he is "happy" with the services his child is currently receiving, it is regrettable that, without the aid of a quality direction service, he cannot tell if some other service might not be better for the child, short of experiencing it.

PROBLEMS WITH DIRECTION SERVICES

The symptoms of the system's direction deficiencies are everywhere evident. As with medicine, this disorder requires a thorough description of its signs and symptoms before any diagnosis can be advanced.

Parents are not made aware of all services available and all services their child is entitled to receive. There are no reliable sources of local information that routinely assist the parents of handicapped children. This lack of information and a systematic way of matching the child with the appropriate set of needed services is the major problem.

Records are generated by many different agencies as the child moves, characteristically in chain-like fashion, from one service provider to another. There is no comprehensive compilation of all information generated by the individual child, with the immediate result that rediagnosis and recertification are commonplace.

Data that are collected reflect specialized institutional biases. Measures tend therefore to be unidimensional and programmatic, and to miss much of what is happening to the individual.

Without the records a direction center could keep, problems arise in interpreting data. For instance, does an increase in the reported incidence of a disorder reflect an actual trend, or is the disorder merely being identified more vigorously? If such an increase is noted, is the information "translated" into messages to separate parts of the service delivery system so that adjustments should be anticipated at some future date to reflect the shift?

The tragedy of rubella-caused handicaps in children is an obvious case in point. Since at least 1964–1965, the rubella-caused bulge in the incidence rates of aural and visual handicaps has been known, but there is little evidence that separate parts of the service system were forewarned or that the system prepared for and responded adequately to these changes.

Data are usually outdated by the time they are finally reported, and once reported, they characteristically are cross-sectional not longitudinal. Planners have to resort to educated guesses to make marginal, time-dependent adjustments in service supply in the absence of time-series data on service demand.

Data often exist, but not in the public domain. Health information is particularly susceptible to this limitation, as in the case of the severely handicapped children of those wealthy enough to afford private services, or in those cases where a social stigma is associated with the disorder. No one has reliable information on how much aid is provided by churches, voluntary agencies, and specialized private agencies devoted to narrow classes of handicap.

The dissatisfied parent is often at a loss to know where to take his grievances, real or imagined, for settlement, or whether grievances are handled at all. Unfortunately, very few agencies are specialized to the redress of administrative or legislative oversight, and redress mechanisms within service agencies are generally very cumbersome, with the result that a parent has little or no effective recourse.

Families typically proceed serially from agency to agency. In the process they are liable to be "captured" by one agency whose services may appear to the parent to be adequate, or at least better than no service at all. The degree of misdirection owing to "capture" is simply unknowable, given the present state of information in the system. That it exists, however, is unquestionable; likewise indisputable is the knowledge that it results in a less than optimal or comprehensive delivery of required services.

One way of better understanding direction problems is to examine the process responsible for it from the perspectives of several of the main participants: parents, professionals, and agency decision makers.

Parents After all is said and done, the parent bears ultimate responsibility for the handicapped child. Our society has consistently and clearly operated to give a parent the widest possible latitude and license for child rearing.[5] However, a parent does not *have* to secure fully adequate health services, feed his child properly, provide a solid home environment, care about the emotional development of the child, or even feel and convey those basic instincts commonly labeled "love."[6] About the only area where society demands adequate minimum service is education, but as recent class-action law suits brought on behalf of the mentally retarded in several states show, even this minimal societal demand has not necessarily held for *handicapped* children.

Over-protective parents create problems of a quite different sort. Parents of handicapped children may internalize the guilt they associate with having a defective child; their resulting over-protection works to perpetuate the handicapped person in the role of the dependent child.[7] There are varying degrees and manifestations of the problem, but it is understandably common and ordinarily works to limit a child's participation in the decision-making and mistake-making process of growing up.[8]

Our society operates on the pervasive but erroneous assumption that the parents of handicapped children, like any other consumers, have unrestricted choices about the services they obtain for their children. In fact, most parents have neither the resources, nor the information on which to base choices.[9] Furthermore, existing institutions sometimes exacerbate the problem with unwitting incentives to use one service mechanism rather than another, e.g., insurance plans

[5]This is a main issue underlying weak and hard-to-enforce child abuse statutes. Parents with mental health disorders also present extraordinary problems that are frequently "insoluble," due in large part to this durable societal norm. See E. Pavenstein and V. W. Bernard (eds.), *Crises of Family Disorganization,* Behavioral Publications, New York, 1971, especially, V. W. Bernard, "Young Children of Mentally Ill Parents." See also Vincent Fontana's popularized account, *Somewhere a Child is Crying,* Macmillan, New York, 1973.

[6]This is not a frivolous point. It formed the basis for an interesting presentation by Mr. Fred Krause, Executive Director of the President's Committee for Mental Retardation, to the 24th Annual Convention, National Association for Retarded Children, Anaheim, California, November 1973.

[7]Olga Lurie, "The Emotional Health of Children in the Family Setting," *Community Mental Health Journal,* Vol. 6, No. 3, 1970, pp. 229–235.

[8]S. Chess, A. Thomas, and H. G. Birch, *Your Child is a Person,* Simon and Schuster, New York, 1965.

[9]William J. Horvath, "Organizational and Management Problems in the Delivery of Medical Care," *Management Science,* Vol. 14, 1968, pp. B275–B279. Horvath is one of the few investigators who have attempted a comprehensive view of the medical system. Such a perspective can be almost as revealing as it is distressing. See idem, "The Systems Approach to the National Health Problem," *Management Science,* Vol. 12, 1966, pp. B391–B395.

generally contain incentives that encourage differential use of facilities and services and discourage active exploration of creative and less costly alternatives.[10]

The reality of the situation is that the parent generally is an ignorant consumer.[11] He or she does not have all the information needed to assess the services received and to choose among alternative service providers. Both of these essential truths have consequences for the overall system.

Because parents do not have all the information needed to assess service well,[12] they may receive either too much or too little of that service. With medical services, for example, a person may be "overdoctored," receiving more services than the person actually needs or would buy if fully aware of their effectiveness; or the person may be "underdoctored," receiving fewer services than the person needs or would buy if less ignorant and more affluent. The latter case is an error more likely to afflict the poor;[13] the former is a rich person's error. Traditional market signals are not much help in resolving the matter.[14] There is no clear-cut relationship between the price of a service and its general quality or specific appropriateness for a given child. For example, a relatively inexpensive, but appropriate, correctly fitted, and well-maintained hearing aid certainly is better than a costly one that lacks these properties; but the ignorant consumer who does not know the difference may well put his trust in the costlier one because "they couldn't charge that much if it weren't really better."

When parents are unable to choose effectively among providers of a common service or to determine the appropriate mix of required services for the child, what do they do? Traditionally, they ask a physician. But physicians rarely have the amount and kind of informa-

[10]One of the main objectives of an ongoing National Health Insurance social experiment is to examine the effects of such embedded assumptions and incentives in as controlled an environment as is practicable. See Joseph P. Newhouse, *A Design for a Health Insurance Experiment*, The Rand Corporation, R-965-OEO, November 1972.

[11]Richard Zeckhauser clarified several of the key points in this portion of the discussion. Private conversation, February 1973.

[12]Arnold I. Kisch and Leo G. Reeder, "Client Evaluation of Physician Performance," *Journal of Health and Social Behavior*, Vol. 10, No. 1, 1969, pp. 51–58, is an eye-opening, empirical investigation of the main points.

[13]Frank Reisman et al. (eds.), *Mental Health of the Poor*, The Free Press, New York, 1968, esp. pp. 88–109.

[14]Tibor Scitovsky, "Some Consequences of the Habit of Judging Quality by Price," *Review of Economic Studies*, Vol. 12, 1944–45, p. 101; and Andre Gabor and C. W. J. Granger, "Price as an Indicator of Quality: Report on an Enquiry," *Economica*, Vol. 33, February 1967, pp. 43–70.

tion needed, either; it is understandable that physicians have few incentives to learn details about the whole local service system, or to take time away from their specialties to give advice about such diverse matters as special education, rehabilitation, or financial assistance—nor should they. Social workers often fill the information breach, but with a large and diversified clientele and with little or no specific preparation, this alternative is a far from optimal solution to the problem.

The problem has been discussed by economists from time to time.[15] One finding is that lack of information is a basic cause of the large and inequitable differentials in the amount and quality of services delivered by the private and public sectors and in different regions of the country.[16]

Professionals Professionals are commonly captives of their professions—their imperatives, perspectives, and tools. Psychiatrists, mostly liberal in their general views about humanity and human behavior, sometimes become very conservative when it comes to specific details about service delivery.[17] They wear psychiatrists' glasses. Ophthalmologists wear glasses of a different refraction and tint, teachers wear yet another, and so forth.

To be a specialist means that one has concentrated on a limited field of knowledge; however, there is a mismatch of impedances, to borrow a communication term and concept, between this specialized information and the general, comprehensive information required by the family of a handicapped child. The family needs a great deal of information, at not too detailed a level, compiled in an easy-to-understand format or package, and touching on all matters affecting the particular child and the child's chances in the future.

The artificial boundaries created by fractionalized professional groups have led to compartmentalization, not integration, of services available to handicapped children. Specialized services are required, but those providing them do not have the time to appreciate the client as a *whole* person. And a limited perspective, trained into the specialized professional and reinforced in daily practice, intensifies

---

[15]George Stigler, "The Economics of Information," *Journal of Political Economy,* Vol. 69, 1961, pp. 213–225.

[16]S. A. Ozaga, "Imperfect Markets through Lack of Knowledge," *Quarterly Journal of Economics,* Vol. 74, 1960, pp. 29–52.

[17]The issue has been treated clearly and compassionately in John E. Kysar, "Reactions of Professionals to Disturbed Children and Their Parents," *Archives of General Psychology,* Vol. 19, November 1968, pp. 562–570.

isolation from specialists in other fields.[18] In the words of another of our survey mothers,

> No one ever put all the pieces together. We only got the service that we asked for. No one ever tried to put all the clues together to move beyond the immediate problem. Doctors were not concerned. They kept coming up with the same diagnosis and did not listen to me or look through the histories.

"Putting the pieces together" is what direction is all about.

Little wonder that we find so many parents are distraught and bitter over the specialist's "lack of concern" and mystifying lack of information about other types of services the child needs. We demand entirely too much when we expect the specialist to be a generalist in providing complete information about the whole child—that is not the specialist's job, although people often imagine it to be, particularly the parents of a handicapped child.[19]

Agency Decision Makers   Specialization has its administrative and political features, and its implications are none too good for the handicapped child and the family. The number and diversity of the individual agencies have created a domestic situation of curious proportions, characterized by a strange construction put upon "responsibility." One is responsible only for actual events; if little or nothing happens, then it is hard to be "irresponsible," in the bureaucratic sense. Consequently, except in a crisis, the safest bureaucratic course is to change nothing. This is a possible rationalization, for example, of the observed noncommunication of research results to the more operational segments of the overall service system. Not only are the links among those specialized in research and those concerned with service delivery tenuous or nonexistent, but there are disincentives that reinforce customary behavior. An informational service should take this into account.

Bureaucratic pathologies, many of which are firmly rooted in the size and diversity of administrative systems, are well known and have been discussed in many standard works.[20] Disorderly symptoms are indicated in many aspects of the system serving handicapped children and youth; they include a penchant for treating administrative

---

[18]This point is made forcefully in R. E. Hoover, "The Ophthalmologist's Role in New Rehabilitation Patterns," *AMA Archives of Ophthalmology*, Vol. 78, No. 5, November 1967.

[19]Gerald E. Cubelli, "Some Dynamics of the Referral Process," *Rehabilitation Literature*, Vol. 31, July 1970, pp. 200-202.

[20]E.g., James G. March and Herbert A. Simon, *Organizations*, John Wiley & Sons, Inc., New York, 1958, pp. 36-47; and Peter Blau, *The Dynamics of Bureaucracy*, University of Chicago Press, 1955, passim.

systems in isolation, a failure to deal effectively with clients as total human beings, and restrictions that inhibit the client from having direct access to the administrative apparatus, a pathology thought to be especially severe for the poor.[21] Because of bureaucratic complexity, in short, there is less than comprehensive interest demonstrated for the client, and the system assigns no specific responsibility for the client's overall welfare and treatment. The responsibility is diffused throughout the system, and the more complex the system, the more the responsibility is diluted.

The informational implications of these pathologies are several. Specialized agencies at best collect data for their own narrow operational purposes, not for sharing with other agencies. As a result, there is no general source of factual information and material about the handicapped. Besides not transmitting even scanty operational data to other executive agencies, the system gives little help to legislative decision makers. Lacking even crude summary information, political decision makers have a hard time making rational, equitable, or humane judgments about new policies and programs on behalf of a defined clientele. Even if they were to get the facts, legislators have next to no resources to analyze and interpret them.[22] The size and specialization of the handicapped service system works to the advantage of well-organized groups who may present only that part of the case redounding to their limited clientele's advantage. The information market is distorted and grossly imperfect at present. Direction Centers could collect and pool much of the needed information.

One desirable recourse—and this represents a major reorientation—would be to devise procedures and institutions that could examine the effects of all pertinent services on the lives of the people who receive them.

DESIRABLE CHARACTERISTICS OF A DIRECTION SERVICE

Several general characteristics can be designed into a direction service to enhance its effectiveness. There is a need to structure direc-

[21]Gideon Sjoberg, Richard Brymer, and Buford Harris, "Bureaucracy and the Lower Class," *Sociology and Social Research,* Vol. 50, April 1966, pp. 325–337.

[22]The difficulty has been summarily treated in Donald C. Menzel, Robert S. Friedman, and Irwin Feller, *Development of a Science and Technology Capability in State Legislatures,* Institute for Research on Human Resources, University Park, Pennsylvania, June 1973, p. v.: "The professionalization (specialization) of public agencies has produced, in brief, a new problem: a substantial and steadily growing imbalance between executive and legislative capabilities to initiate, critique, and evaluate public proposals and ongoing programs. This problem is not due to inadequate expertise in state government; it is the result of the unequal and uneven distribution of existing expertise." (Italics omitted.) This is another way of stating the point we are making.

tion so that, consistent with the individual's and society's limited resources, handicapped persons have improved chances to become as independent as possible, and to round out their development with as many services as they can profit from. At the same time, the incentive systems that motivate agencies and professionals should be structured so as to marshal their full support behind handicapped persons and their families in their efforts to obtain the mix of services they need. Rather than an assortment of uncoordinated service agencies, many of them unknown to the handicapped person, and offering a tightly restricted range of services, handicapped people require some coordinated and flexible means of finding out what services are available and where to go to get the ones they need.

Two general perspectives are to be considered in designing an improved direction service: the individual's and the system's.

Individual Design Perspective   Because the current service system is demonstrably unresponsive in important ways, it is necessary to build in counterfragmentary, counterbureaucratic, and counterspecialist structures and incentives at a localized service delivery level to insure that equitable and effective care is received. The following list of requirements summarizes how this might be accomplished.

Develop a One-Stop, General Information Service. A well-publicized point of entry to the service system, and a one-stop source of information, could help answer the following types of questions for parents of handicapped children:

- Where does one obtain general help and guidance in rearing a handicapped child?
- What medical care is required and available; where is it located; how does one obtain it?
- What educational services are required and available; where are they located; how does one obtain them?
- Where are counseling services available to help the family to understand the special emotional demands created by having a handicapped child?
- What vocational opportunities and services are available; where are they located; how does one obtain them?
- How much will it cost, and where does one obtain financial assistance, if needed, to pay for the services required by the child?
- What should be done (or not done) to encourage a handicapped child to become as independent as possible?

Demand a Multidisciplinary Effort. Such an institution must strive to be as explicitly multidisciplinary as possible to avoid undue emphasis on certain types of services, to integrate the many specialized services the client needs, and to provide a client-oriented interface with the dispensing specialists.[23] Experts from various disciplines, with special skills in working with children with major different types of handicapping conditions, should be provided since the service needs and programs for serving those groups are significantly different.

Emphasize a Temporal Dynamic, Not Static, Orientation. There is a clear need to integrate the planning to meet an individual's service needs, and later to evaluate the effects of services so that changes in the child's needs are accounted for as they vary over time in response to changes in the life situation and in response to service provision.

Create Distinct Administrative Roles and Functions. A good direction service should be continually apprised of the status of all eligibility regulations and availability conditions for services from other agencies. It should maintain an active appointments process on behalf of handicapped clients, and in so doing it will generate a network of service contacts. The direction service should promote procedures for recall—for example, in the event that services become locally available or anticipated changes occur in the child's situation; and procedures for follow-up—for example, in the event the parents themselves do not or cannot obtain recommended services from other agencies.

Maintain Each Individual's Service Information. A direction service should compile and maintain records of all services each client receives, including updates, service terminations, and parents' assessments of their satisfaction with the service. These records would be made available to other service providers, with confidentiality safeguards invoked as appropriate. This information would be collected for the client's and the system's *mutual* benefit, in order to facilitate follow-up, coordination of other service programs in meeting the client's needs, and in the aggregate to provide information on needed improvements in the service system.

Foster Client Participation in the Direction Service. Active involvement by parents could at least partly relieve some of the negative feelings many of them have developed under the current system. Numerous researchers and commentators on the general subject of citizen participation offer evidence that the chance to participate can do much to alleviate people's sense of frustration and powerlessness,

[23]R. M. Flower, H. Gofman, and L. Lawson (eds.), *Reading Disorders,* F. A. Davis Company, Philadelphia, 1965, makes an exceptionally strong and lucid case for a multidisciplinary approach to handicapped care and service provision. The bases of their argument are implicitly founded on the general concepts of specialization developed earlier in this chapter.

and perhaps a little—admittedly, not much—to win over the alienated.[24] This design objective is not novel,[25] but the direction service appears to have a particularly attractive opportunity to realize it.[26]

Foster the Humane, Personal Dimension. Success for the service system can be defined in many ways, ranging from maximizing the individual's capabilities to planned dependence.[27] But however one defines success, it will be the greater if the system can win the child's trust and the trust of his family, and if an empathic service-provider gives enough of himself and of his time to understand *each* child and devise a personalized, comprehensive program fitted to the child's specific needs. The direction service is the best place to perform this function.[28]

Running the direction service efficiently of course will contribute to success but does not constitute success; efficiency should not be allowed to become an ingrown end in itself, to the detriment of personal attention to each child.

Together, these individual design characteristics for the direction service constitute a coalescent force and major supplement to the

[24]See, for example, R. K. Yin, W. A. Lucas, P. L. Szanton, and J. A. Spindler, *Citizen Organizations: Increasing Client Control Over Services,* The Rand Corporation, R-1196-HEW, June 1973; and R. K. Yin and W. A. Lucas, "Decentralization and Alienation," *Policy Sciences,* Vol. 4, September 1973, pp. 327–336. Both studies stress that increased participation of the sort envisioned here could do much to decrease the powerlessness and frustration many people feel when dealing with large and complex systems; they are not so sanguine about the likelihood of reducing alienation, a condition that appears to arise from a variety of factors not easily affected by increased participation alone.

Herbert Kaufman, "Administrative Decentralization and Political Power," *Public Administration Review,* Vol. 29, January-February 1969, pp. 3–15, has commented at length about the likely and mostly undesirable societal effects of centralization.

[25]Elliot L. Richardson has stressed the importance of the concept and the desirability of the objective in his "Significant Individual Participation," *Law School Record,* University of Chicago, Vol. 15, Autumn 1967; and Hans B. C. Spiegel has recorded the extent of citizen participation in a survey of federal programs in his "Citizen Participation in Federal Programs," *Journal of Voluntary Action Research,* Monograph No. 1, 1971.

[26]The case for a direction service is roughly outlined in W. Wolfensberger, *Toward Citizen Advocacy for the Handicapped,* USPHS Grant HD00370, Washington, D.C., January 15, 1971.

[27]L. L. Havens, "Dependence: Definitions and Strategies," *Rehabilitation Record,* Vol. 8, March-April 1967, pp. 22–28; Secretary of Health, Education, and Welfare, "Planning Guidance Memorandum—1972," February 15, 1972. The realistic point that some fraction of the handicapped population will never achieve "normal" levels of nondependence has been treated sympathetically by Leslie Gardner, "Planning for Planned Dependence?" *Special Education,* Vol. 58, March 1969, pp. 27–30.

[28]This is discussed in Charles B. Truax and Robert R. Carkhuff, *Toward Effective Counseling and Psychotherapy: Training and Practice,* Aldine, Chicago, 1967.

current fractionated system, in which "success" sometimes consists of shoehorning the client into a prefabricated single program instead of seeing how well the services can be made to fit the client's needs. Lawyer Thomas Gilhool, commenting on his successful class action on behalf of mentally retarded children in Pennsylvania, summarizes the distinction succinctly:

> This is a case where the class must fit the child instead of the child having to fit into any class room. . . . This is a new language, a new set of facts, and it will mean a new concept of oneself by those with handicaps of any variety.[29]

It is a concept well worth developing and one that is implementable through a direction service.

System Design Perspective   As the sheer number and complexity of agencies and professionals increase, the odds diminish that any one of them could provide for all of a handicapped client's needs. The concept of a "direction center" as a distinct social invention should enable many specialized talents to be brought to bear more effectively in the service of the child and his needs.[30] To this end, several desirable design characteristics, discussed below, will allow the direction center to relate and interact with the existing system[31].

Foster Comprehensiveness of Service Scope. All types of service needs affecting the handicapped child must be identified and accounted for by direction service personnel. The problem is to coordinate a variety of service professions. The direction service personnel could provide outreach, diagnostic, planning, referral, and follow-up services themselves or through consultants. Traditional providers of other services—e.g., medical, special education, vocational rehabilitation, and welfare—would still provide those services. Thus, the present service system would not be circumvented or duplicated, but rather would be complemented and made more effective by the direction centers.

Serve All Handicapped Youth in the Local Region. A direction center can achieve its maximum potential only if it is located close enough to the handicapped youth's home so that he can reach it

---

[29]*Los Angeles Times,* February 5, 1973, Part I, pp. 1, 11.
[30]Cubelli, op. cit.
[31]Working from different premises and considering a vastly different assortment of program areas, Peter Drucker has developed a compatible list of general objectives for public service institutions: "Managing the Public Service Institutions," *The Public Interest,* No. 33, Fall 1973, pp. 43–60; see esp. pp. 58–60.

without excessive travel, and if all handicapped youth in the region are served without discrimination.

Concentrate on Evaluation and Service Planning from the Individual's Perspective. Sound evaluation and planning of a single client's service package, and of the service system, depends on the collection of sound and complete information.

Before a child's total needs may be determined, past records must be compiled and gaps in the current package of services received must be sensed. Once an initial evaluation has been completed, a suitable list of goals (with a timetable for achieving those goals) may be developed. Once established, these goals become clues about the kinds and amounts of service needed in the short and longer terms. In the aggregate, such clues may signal needed current or future real-locations or adjustments in the overall service system. This process has been described by Knott for rehabilitation, although its application is clearly more general:

> Ideally, setting of goals is accomplished in patient evaluation and re-evaluation conferences where all the professions concerned may contribute suggested goals and methods of achieving them, and even more important, where agreement can be reached on a program of unified action.[32]

Evaluations of the system, its components, and overall performance are to be encouraged. What we have in mind was suggested by a current practice employed by several state Crippled Children's Service Directors. Over a period of time, some service providers perform more notably than others; they may have more positive medical results, work for lower fees, or generally be regarded more favorably by the parents and children. A valuable by-product of an on-going utility analysis and evaluation of all service received would be the identification of superior providers and of new and better services. Changes in the characteristics of the handicapped population could also be sensed, and therefore the need for compensating changes in the service system.

Stimulate an Active Outreach/Identification Program. As Chapter 7 demonstrates, the identification of handicapping conditions is not being vigorously pursued. A direction center could be an important agent in coordinating screening and case-finding activities, and en-

---

[32]Leslie W. Knott, "Evaluation Process in the Rehabilitative Program," *Med. Treatment,* Vol. 5, September 1968, pp. 693–699.

suring that follow-up procedures are instituted once a handicapped child is discovered.[33]

Concentrate on the Practicality and Feasibility of Services and Programs. Since not all parents of handicapped children can be fully informed and unbiased consumers, a distinct function for a direction center would be to monitor the match between a child's realistically determined needs and his or her ability to benefit from services received. While the problem of under- and over-service will always be with us, it doubtless could be reduced if sufficient attention were paid to this design characteristic. It could also be reduced as good evaluation information becomes available.

Serve as a Local Spokesman for Handicapped Persons Generally and for Individual Clients Particularly. The direction center, as conceived here, would be an important focus for citizen needs and expectations. It is a place in the system where grievances may be aired—a place that does not currently exist. Specifically, a direction center could become a local "court of appeals" to which bureaucratic and other grievances could be taken, particularly if there were reason to believe that the general rules or treatment were invalid or unjust in an individual case.

Reconfigure Existing Control and Incentive Systems. To attain maximum quality in the direction centers, new lines of authority and new professional identifications will probably have to be organized. In particular, a shift in traditional allegiances will be called for:

- Allegiance *not* to a currently existing professional field or specialty.
- Allegiance *not* to current programs, the people who operate them, or agencies that perpetuate them.
- Allegiance *not* to the status quo.
- Allegiance *not* to social and professional etiquette that frowns on the raising of unpopular issues.
- Allegiance to handicapped people, wherever they are, and to their needs, interests, and aspirations.[34]

Operate as a Separate Public Agency Primarily Concerned with Direction. Direction and coordination should be provided as the primary service of the program, so that attention is not diverted to the

[33]W. Hoff has elaborated this point with skill and compassion. See his "Why Health Programs are not Reaching the Unresponsive in our Communities," *Public Health Reports,* Vol. 81, July 1966.

[34]Proposed by Benjamin C. Johnston, "Advocacy for the Handicapped," paper presented at the Fourth Southeast Regional Conference of the American Association of Workers for the Blind, July 27, 1972.

meeting of other pressing service demands. The Direction Center should be separate from other major direct service programs in the bureaucracy, so that it is not captured by those programs, and so that too much emphasis is not placed on direction to certain services. Further, the direction service program should be part of the public rather than the private service sector, since it is unlikely that the public sector programs could be coordinated by the private sector.

To operate in this new mode, it is fairly obvious that a direction center will have to be independent of existing service agencies. One idea might be to create a line of authority and control running from the various local direction centers directly to an advisory council at a higher level of government,[35] which, in turn, does not report to any of the existing service agencies, but rather to the governor. Funds for the direction center would thus flow from a line in the budget separate from other services for the handicapped.

Satisfy Existing Federal Requirements for Service Integration. A legal requirement to coordinate federal grant-in-aid programs exists in the form of the A-95 review process, a provision of Title IV of the Inter-Governmental Cooperation Act of 1968. There is no reason to assume that provisions of A-95 cannot be carried out on behalf of citizens in a target population, such as the handicapped, as well as generally throughout a geographic area. *Regional* direction centers could receive a legal boost via amendments and clarification of the basic existing A-95 provisions. The objective of these adjustments would be to coordinate programs, but to do so directly on behalf of the individual intended service recipients. An already existing regional bias in current federal administrative practice may contribute to the implementation of direction centers; furthermore, a regional bias appears to square with the realities of the size of, and practical means of serving, the handicapped population generally.

EXISTING PARTIAL MODELS OF DIRECTION CENTERS

Many current programs are partial approximations to the design characteristics just described. The following discussion has several purposes: to show that each design characteristic is feasible; to indicate where one might wish to conduct more detailed studies and analyses to assess relative strengths and weaknesses before trying to implement features of the illustrated cases; and to confirm the appropriateness of the design characteristics themselves (for example, direction

---

[35]A similar recommendation appears in New York State Committee for Children, *A Child Advocacy System in New York State,* Albany, New York, November 30, 1971. We discuss the New York proposal in a following subsection.

services that incorporate relatively more of the characteristics are "better" than those that incorporate fewer).

Partial models exist in many locations, because the problems of direction are general. Here, we review programs in only a sample of those locations (first in the United States, then in foreign countries). No one model, to the best of our knowledge, is complete enough to be labeled "ideal" and, hence, apt to be easily transferred and replicated. But several of them embody promising features.

The first three partial models we discuss are ambitious activities, representing three quite different strategies of implementation for our recommended direction service. In late 1971, the New York State Committee for Children proposed to Governor Rockefeller that an ambitious "Child Advocacy System" be implemented as rapidly as possible to alleviate many direction-related crises;[36] the Maryland State Department of Education, using ESEA Title VI funds, has designed and begun to implement a "Maryland State Data System for the Handicapped";[37] and the program of Regional Diagnostic, Counseling, and Service Centers for the mentally retarded of California, in operation since 1965,[38] has been widely acclaimed as a breakthrough in service provision.

We have selected these three activities for first presentation because individually they embody and extend the concept of direction in tangible ways, and because collectively they represent a close approximation of the direction service we recommend on a national basis. We believe that most of our direction design characteristics could be realized by a selective, thoughtful, and careful amalgamation of the better features of these examples.

New York State's "Child Advocacy" System The New York State Committee for Children has devised a highly interesting plan. Reporting to the governor in November 1971, the Committee recommended the creation of a State Child Advisory Commission and local advocacy councils that "would have the power and the duty to review present services to children, to suggest changes and to represent the interests of children."[39]

This concept included a state-level commission, "independent of existing departments of state government and able, therefore, to keep

[36]Ibid.

[37]Maryland State Department of Education, *Data System for the Handicapped: Toward the Implementation of the Maryland State Data System for the Handicapped,* ESEA, Title VI Proposal, March 21, 1972.

[38]*California Statutes of 1965,* AB 691, Chap. 1242, pp. 3106–3108.

[39]New York State Committee for Children, p. 1.

as its central responsibility a concern for the welfare of all children."[40]
Locally, the intent of the proposed system would be carried out by
"advocacy councils with a responsibility for all children in their localities, with the power to gather information, respond to felt needs,
and recommend changes as indicated."[41]

Costs were intended to be minimized by manning the local councils with voluntary personnel. The recommended budget for the first
year of operation of the State Commission was $950,000, some
$350,000 of which was earmarked for staff support and travel, and the
balance "to be used to support the development of a number of pilot
programs at the local advocacy council level."[42]

The composition of the State Commission was recommended to be
100 members, from a variety of prescribed professions, socioeconomic strata, and age categories. Parents would constitute at least a
51 percent majority but no more than 70 percent. Commissioners
would serve by gubernatorial appointment for terms ranging from
one to three years. The State Commission itself would report directly
to the governor on matters of policy and operational significance
affecting the lives of children in New York.

The local advocacy councils are intended to be major points of
citizen access for direction service, and would report directly to the
State Commission on their operations and findings. It was hoped that
compiling legal compendia and rosters of locally available services
would satisfy information deficiencies, and that review, evaluation,
and fact-finding would improve performance. Various specific duties
and powers are also spelled out, which approximate some of our
direction service design characteristics.[43]

The Child Advocacy System concept is interesting and important
for several reasons:

- It recognizes the need to complement the existing system, and to
  do so with clear lines of authority and control running directly
  to the governor, rather than running through the existing service
  agencies.

[40]Ibid.

[41]Ibid., pp. 1-2.

[42]Ibid., p. 8. Also (p. 2), "the Commission shall seek federal funds as they become
available."

[43]In a recent, sensation-provoking report, "Juvenile Injustice," seven present and
former judges and a number of senior administrators of the New York Family Court
charged that the system was failing to such an extent that "changes must be made
before yet another generation of children is destroyed." Peter Kihss, "Children's Justice
Called a Failure by Judicial Panel," *The New York Times,* October 29, 1973, pp. 1, 25.
This represents yet another manifestation of the general problem, but this time as it
appears in the treatment of children by the judicial system.

- It stresses the perspective of the individual and his family, not that of the existing system or its specialized constituents.
- It values the importance of information as a resource to be used in a two-way communication process: direction to the parents and feedbacks about performance to those most generally responsible for that performance.

Maryland State Data System for the Handicapped Maryland officials have begun implementation of a state data system for the handicapped that collects and centralizes information from the state's current scattered programs. They have generated an important piece of emerging direction service, but the "piece" suffers from want of being integrated into a general concept and overall direction system, such as the one proposed in New York.

The technical problems associated with any large, information-based activity, such as direction, are certainly many and difficult; however, they are manageable if due consideration is given to system design and early implementation.[44]

A technically adequate "Data System for the Handicapped" (DSH) is being implemented in Maryland and reportedly has over 70,000 children registered.[45] The Maryland proposal for this data system, requesting early implementation funding, called for $123,144 and contains an impressive list of reasons and anticipated benefits for the system,[46] most of which have been generalized in our direction design characteristics. Among the striking facts already discovered during implementation is the finding that the average lag time between the identification of a handicap and the commencement of services is excessively long: 500 days for the hearing impaired and 131 days for any handicapped child requiring residential school services. It was also found that of the handicapped children known and registered in the DSH, approximately 7000 were identified but not yet served.[47]

An issue with the DSH, as with all public data systems, relates to privacy safeguards.[48] It is a problem that threatens both present and future efforts to manage information on and for the handicapped;

---

[44]Besides the Deaf-Blind Centers Information System reported on later in this chapter, the following related development is notable: C. Vallbona et al., "An On-line Computer System for a Rehabilitation Hospital," *Methods of Information Medicine*, Vol. 7, January 1968; for a less technical description of this system, see Nancy De Sanders, "Computer's Basic Plans Help Doctors Initiate Rehabilitation Regimen," *Modern Hospital*, Vol. 113, November 1969, pp. 97–100.

[45]*Education Daily*, Vol. 6, No. 200, October 18, 1973.

[46]Maryland State Department of Education, op. cit., pp. 16, 23.

[47]*Education Daily*, same issue, p. 3.

[48]Ibid.

however, ways to resolve the problem are presented in the excellent 1973 Report of the Secretary's Advisory Committee on Automated Personal Data Systems,[49] compiled for the Secretary of HEW. It would be unfortunate if the inroads made in Maryland toward resolving the technical information problems of direction were subverted for non-technical issues and reasons that are in principle resolvable. Another problem noted by those responsible for the Maryland system is the reluctance of some parents to have their child labeled as "handicapped." Data forms and the official name of the system are being changed to alleviate this problem.

California's Regional Centers[50]   In 1963, the California State Assembly created a subcommittee to investigate the problems confronting the mentally retarded generally and to make legislative recommendations. It did so in response to many fundamental questions about the care provided to the mentally retarded in California,[51] and before deciding whether to increase the state's investment in residential mental institutions. In 1965, the subcommittee reported its findings—and they were startling:

• The mental hospital represented the only major means for the mentally retarded to receive state aid.
• Long waiting lists impeded even this one option.
• These people do not need all of a hospital's services, but, in the "all or nothing" situation then prevailing, they often got them anyway.
• Little or no help of any kind was locally available from the public service sector.[52]

[49]*Records, Computers, and the Rights of Citizens,* DHEW/OS Report No. 73-94, 1700-00-116, Washington, D.C., 1973. A summary of this live and important issue is contained in R. E. Cohen, "Justice Report/Nixon Administration Weighs Restrictions on Use of Criminal History Data Banks," *The National Journal,* October 27, 1973, pp. 1599–1607.

[50]Documentation describing the regional centers is complete and clearly presented. See, e.g., Edgar W. Pye, *California's Regional Centers: Gateway to Services for the Retarded,* Bureau of Mental Retardation Services, State Department of Public Health, Berkeley, Calif., 1970; State Human Relations Agency, *Lanterman Mental Retardation Services Act,* Sacramento, Calif., 1971; and "Lanterman Mental Retardation Services Act," *Liaison,* Vol. 2, No. 2, March 1973 (Sacramento, California). Performance data are not as complete or available.

[51]One source specifically notes the importance of the creation of the President's Panel on Mental Retardation in 1962 as a stimulus for California to look more carefully at problems confronting its mentally retarded. Pye, op. cit., p. 1.

[52]Report of the Assembly Committee on Ways and Means, Subcommittee on Mental Health Services, State of California, Sacramento, California, 1965.

The subcommittee recommended the creation of regional diagnosis, counseling, and service centers for the mentally retarded—a recommendation contained in Assembly Bill 691, 1965, truly a landmark piece of legislation.[53]

The "regional centers" thereby created were to provide the following services:

- Diagnosis
- Counseling on a continuing basis
- Provision of state funds to vendors of services, when, lacking such services, the only recourse would be institutionalization
- Maintenence of a registry and individual case records
- Systematic follow-up and reactivation of cases if needed
- Assistance in state hospital placement when necessary
- Education of the public about needs and capabilities of the handicapped
- Staffing according to standards set by the State Department of Public Health

The regional centers idea started in 1966 with two pilot projects, one in Los Angeles and one in San Francisco, operating on a budget of some $600,000. By FY 1974 it had grown to an overall $22.2 million proposition, with 14 centers operating throughout the state and a small additional number being discussed.[54] Of course, this budget is not all for direction, as many other types of services are purchased.

Regional centers have been embedded in an institutional framework that in 1971 included 13 Mental Retardation Program Area Planning Boards, responsible for planning and coordinating all mental retardation services in their respective planning areas[55] and representing parents (25 percent), professionals (50 percent), and representatives of the general public (25 percent) in each of its 14-to-19-member bodies.[56] At the state level there is a Mental Retardation Program Advisory Board, responsible for developing a statewide plan based on county and area proposals and for advising the state executive and legislative bodies about the status and needs of the mentally retarded

[53]*California Statutes of 1965,* AB 691, Chap. 1242, pp. 3106–3108 (cited provisions at p. 3107).

[54]In recognition of his central and faithful role in the invention and implementation of the regional centers, new and expanded legislation bore the name of Frank Lanterman, Assemblyman, 47th District, Pasadena: "Lanterman Mental Retardation Services Act of 1969," *California Statutes of 1969,* AB 225, Chapter 1594.

[55]Lucian B. Vandegrift, Secretary of Human Relations, State of California, *Mental Retardation Program: Suggested Procedure for Area Planning,* Human Relations Agency, Sacramento, Calif., July 15, 1970.

[56]*Lanterman Mental Retardation Services Act,* p. 9. These people must also reside within the planning area.

throughout the state.[57] Budgetary and primary responsibility for implementing the plan rests with the Human Relations Agency, its Office of Mental Retardation, and other of their subordinate activities.

The regional centers themselves are staffed somewhat differently in each situation, reflecting local needs and the availability of personnel; however, the staff and the caseload of the Golden Gate Regional Center in San Francisco are at least illustrative. In addition to a director and associate director, it includes a senior staff physician, a public health nurse, a chief of administrative services, a chief counselor, a supervisory counselor, and ten staff counselors". . . whose professional training is in social work. And the counselors are stationed in the communities for which we relate our services."[58] The active caseload reported on January 1, 1970, was 450, of whom 230 were receiving services provided and paid for, in whole or part, by the regional center.[59]

The regional centers strive to follow a "Case Management Flow Process," the details of which were described for us by Dr. Charles Gardipee, Chief of the California Bureau of Mental Retardation Services, in the following terms:

- *Screening,* with the option to refer the client out of the regional center to some other more appropriate service, if required.
- *Intake interview,* with an option to refer out. At this point a complete information file is collected from all public sources and, to the greatest extent possible, private ones as well.
- *Initial case staffing,* where information developed in the intake interview is evaluated by a committee or board of the regional center, including social workers, doctors, and medical administrators.
- *Case staffing* and creation of a plan for the handicapped client, tailored to his needs to the extent services are locally available.
- *Execution* of the plan.
- *Review and evaluation* of the plan and the client's progress based on the criteria established during the case staffing and planning phase.[60]

[57]The Board's composition is defined by terms of California's AB 225 of 1969 and includes voting members: two from the public at large, a parent of a mentally retarded child who is a patient in a state hospital, a parent of a mentally retarded child who is not in a state hospital, a county supervisor, and one member from each of the following professions: medicine, psychology, social work, nursing, education, and law. Appointments to the Board are shared on a formula basis by the Governor, the Chairman of the Senate Rules Committee, and the Speaker of the Assembly. Service is without material compensation.

[58]Pye, op. cit., p. 7.

[59]Ibid., p. 9. The 450 figure is static and does not represent an annual figure.

[60]Interview, March 6, 1972.

The average annual professional costs for each regional center are estimated to be approximately $250,000 for purposes of this analysis, although in practice this estimated average probably varies considerably (see Table 8.2). The State Budget for FY 1972 allotted the following funds to these regional-center-related activities: case funding and identification, $1.6 million; case evaluation, $3.9 million; and case management, $1.8 million; for a total of $7.3 million. A simple average for each functional activity per center funded in FY 1972 would then be $123,000, $300,000, and $138,000, respectively, or a total of about $560,000 per center per year. Since this program is in its initial rapid expansion phase with attendant initial staffing and facility costs and the caseload during that phase consists of persons requiring, primarily, initial intake and direction, meaningful long-term average annual costs per case are not available.

Population characteristics for each of the regional centers are shown in Fig. 8.1. Summary statistics for the program's first five years are shown in Table 8.3 and Fig 8.2. Note that for the California regional centers there is a great deal of variation in total catchment size (from 185,000 in Mendocino-Humboldt-Del Norte to 7.034 million in Los Angeles) and in travel times to a regional center. The extreme variation represented by Los Angeles has resulted in the planned addition of two or perhaps three additional regional centers for the greater Los Angeles basin. Travel times are not directly reflected in the state budget.

For completing a thorough evaluation of the California regional centers, these data are plainly unsatisfactory, but they are instructive

Table 8.2
ESTIMATED PROFESSIONAL PERSONNEL COSTS PER ANNUM
FOR CALIFORNIA REGIONAL CENTERS

Position	Cost Per Center
Director (M.D.)	$ 30,000
Associate Director	20,000
Staff Physician	25,000
Public Health Nurse	15,000
Chief, Administrative Services	15,000
Chief Counselor	20,000
Supervisory Counselor	18,000
Staff Counselors: 10, at $12,000	120,000
Total	$263,000

SOURCE: Interview with Dr. Charles Gardipee, March 6, 1972.

NOTE: The total shown does not include overhead charges and supporting staff. The more inclusive State Budget estimates provide for a total of $560,000 per year per center.

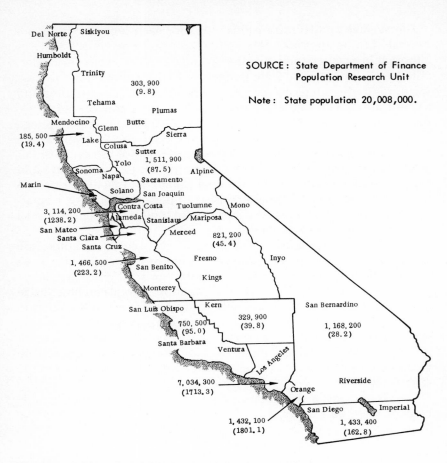

Del Norte / Siskiyou

Humboldt

Trinity

303, 900
(9. 8)

Tehama

Plumas

Mendocino Butte
Glenn

185, 500
(19.4) Lake

Sierra

Colusa

Sutter

Yolo 1, 511, 900
(87.5) Alpine

Sonoma Napa Sacramento

Marin

Solano San Joaquin

3, 114, 200
(1238.2) Alameda Stanislaus Mariposa

Contra Costa Tuolumne Mono

San Mateo

Santa Clara

Santa Cruz

Merced

821, 200
(45.4)

1, 466, 500
(223.2) San Benito

Fresno Inyo

Kings

Monterey

San Luis Obispo Kern San Bernardino

750, 500
(95.0)

329, 900
(39.8)

1, 168, 200
(28.2)

Santa Barbara Ventura

Los Angeles

7, 034, 300
(1713.3)

Riverside

Orange

San Diego Imperial

1, 432, 100
(1801.1)

1, 433, 400
(162.8)

SOURCE: State Department of Finance
Population Research Unit

Note: State population 20,008,000.

Fig. 8.1 California Regional Center program, 1971: area populations and population densities (persons per square mile).

for the purpose of extending the concept of the regional center to a national scale.

The regional centers program has many positive aspects. The families we interviewed who were fortunate enough to make it through the waiting lists and received regional center service uniformly praised the service and the center's personnel; the physicians we contacted were generally favorably disposed to it on the grounds that the centers had access to information that they did not and that was of great use to the families; and state public health administrators of the program were also supportive. The centers are beset, however, by several recognized and persistent problems that bear careful examination, although we note them here only in summary fashion:

- Regional centers have some power over state mental institutions, and this can lead to direct conflict. Under the regional center concept, the state hospital is only one of many service-vendors that may be planned for the individual child.
- Interaction with the so-called "Short-Doyle" program (to provide a local alternative to the mental hospitals) has had the effect of rapidly loading the regional centers with clients. The shift from state institutional to local care has been rapid.
- Animosity connected with the hospital closure issue has spilled over to the regional centers program, pitting rural legislators (who stand to lose important and nonfungible local industries), psychiatric technicians (who stand to lose their jobs), and other miscellaneous groups, against the regional center concept and practice.

Table 8.3
CALIFORNIA REGIONAL CENTER PROGRAM FROM INCEPTION
THROUGH DECEMBER 31, 1971

Number of Regional Centers, December 1971		
Fully operational	9	
Initiating services	1	
Awaiting final approval of contracts	3	
Statistics (last quarter of calendar year 1971, estimated)		
Total referrals and requests for assistance (1/66–12/71)	25,000	
Total intake processes initiated (1/66–12/71)	9,800	
Caseload, December 31, 1971	6,000	
(NOTE: this does not include some 500 individuals and/or families who, each month, receive some type of Regional Center assistance prior to initiation of the intake process.)		
Inactive cases, December 31, 1971	880	
Closed cases (deceased, diagnosed not mentally retarded)	330	
Purchase of services, December 1971		
Individuals and/or families receiving purchased services	2,000	
Clients in residential placements (subtotal of above)	750	
Total budgets for Regional Center Program[a]		
Fiscal Year 1971–1972	$10,252,272	
Fiscal Year 1972–1973	$14,367,000	
Costs per case-month of care (1970–1971)	$	%
Purchase of services	78	51
Direct Center services		
(costs attributable to diagnosis and counseling)	59	39
Regional Center administrative costs	13	9
Bureau administrative costs	2	1
Total	$152	100%

SOURCE: California State Department of Finance.
[a] $22.2 million in Fiscal Year 1974.

- Local problems have been noted, particularly in the early stages of locating and implementing the regional centers: Zoning is frequently used to prevent the location of centers in incorporated areas, funding for facilities is sometimes hard to obtain or obtained only at premium rates, and community acceptance of mentally handicapped people in their midst is not always positive.
- Waiting times tend to be long. Not only has deinstitutionalization contributed to this, but the extent of unmet demands was not well estimated, in the following sense: If one has a real but "marginal" problem, travel to a distant facility for care becomes a seriously inhibiting consideration; however, when the facility is relatively closer at hand, the travel constraint lessens and service is demanded.
- Local service facilities have not been created or expanded as fast as the demand for service.
- Follow-up and evaluation (noted in the "Case Management Flow Process") are very hard to carry out in practice. There are no well-known criteria, and a variety of needed, specialized services is not always locally available; i.e., if a service received is not appropriate or satisfactory, there is often no readily accessible alternative.
- Given all of these systemic features, it is to be expected that the regional centers have not been able to realize their full potential to case-find, coordinate, and evaluate at the individual level.
- Because the regional center is structured within the existing service bureaucracy in California, it is susceptible to pressures to favor one or another existing type of service program, rather than being independent and fully child-centered.
- The regional centers rely very heavily upon social workers to execute the program at the client level. Social workers have many commendable skills; however, one should be alert to ensure that social worker norms and modes of operation do not become the norms and modes of operation for the regional centers. One manifestation of this would be a "style" characterized by long-term case management (a task of the Department of Social Welfare) and not one of short-term case-finding, coordination, and evaluation (relatively "unique" functions not presently done by any line agency as a main order of business).

Direction is an important service that has many unique features not routinely performed by existing agencies. To the extent that direction is not recognized as a different concept and service, and to the extent that direction is attempted within the existing, unreconstituted bureaucratic framework, one would expect limitations of its full realization and potential. The need for new, clear lines of author-

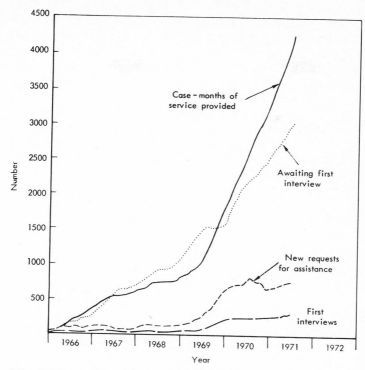

Fig. 8.2 California Regional Center program (5-month moving averages). SOURCE: California State Department of Finance.

ity and control is evident in this case (a need explicitly recognized in the foregoing New York State proposal).

Deaf-Blind Centers As a result of two separate pieces of legislation passed in the aftermath of the rubella epidemic of 1963–65,[61] Deaf-Blind Centers were mandated and translated into policies and programs by the U.S. Office of Education.[62] The Deaf-Blind Regional Center program has many desirable features—prototypical "lessons learned" for our proposed regional direction center concept.

Basically, the Deaf-Blind Centers were designed to provide the following services: comprehensive diagnostic and evaluative services; programs for adjustment, orientation, and education, integrating all necessary professional and allied services; effective consultative ser-

[61]P.L. 90-247, January 2, 1968; and P.L. 91-230, April 13, 1970.
[62]U.S. Office of Education, *Policies and Procedures, Centers, and Services for Deaf-Blind Children, ESEA, Title VI, Part C,* April 1969.

vices for parents, teachers, and others, to enable them to play a direct role in the lives of children, and to assist in their adjustment, orientation, and education.[63]

Because they are intended to provide a full range of services to a severely handicapped subset of the total handicapped population, the Deaf-Blind Centers do not meet many of the design objectives for a purely direction-oriented service. This is not to say that Deaf-Blind Centers are not worthwhile or that they do not provide much needed services; it is to say that because a choice has been made to serve a very special and quite small population, it has been possible to include within the single institution the delivery of a full range of services. Were the choice made to serve a larger group of handicapped children, as we propose in the direction center concept, then *full provision* of services within the same institution would probably not be feasible, either because the number of clients would be too large or because too many centers would be required.

In a study of the Deaf-Blind Centers from an information system design perspective, EXOTECH Systems, in June 1971, provided some valuable ideas for consideration in the proposed direction center concept. According to EXOTECH, information about this most severely handicapped subset of the total population was "by any standard poor in quantity and low in quality,"[64] and the report detailed what might be done to improve matters on both scores. The partially implemented, prototypical DBCIS (Deaf-Blind Center Information System) that EXOTECH selected was in some senses a good and reasonable choice. The deaf-blind population is small and not too difficult to identify (about 5000 deaf-blind children are known to exist in the total population). The great complexity of the problems facing a deaf-blind child[65] actually had some positive effects for the information system. If an accounting, registry, and direction system could be

[63]Section 622, P.L. 91-230, "Education of the Handicapped Act."

[64]EXOTECH Systems, Inc., *An Information System for Regional Centers for Services to Deaf-Blind Children,* BEH/OE/DHEW, Contract No. OEC-0-70-4923, Washington, D.C., June 30, 1971, p. xiv.

[65]The following is a mere sample of the extensive literature: E. F. Cicenia et al., "The Blind Child with Multiple Handicaps: A Challenge," *International Journal for the Education of the Blind,* May 1965, pp. 105–112; A. Kaye, "The Multiple Handicapped Child: A Challenge to Programming," *Special Education Review,* Vol. 20, 1963, pp. 1–8: H. R. Myklebust, *The Deaf-Blind Child,* Perkins School for the Blind, Watertown, Mass., 1956; and two reports on progress achieved in California's various programs for the deaf-blind: Berthold Lowenfeld, *Report on Multihandicapped Blind and Deaf-Blind Children in California,* California State Department of Education, Division of Special Schools and Services, Sacramento, May 1968; and Laurice S. Jenkins, *Follow-up Study on the First Annual Deaf-Blind Institute,* California School for the Blind, Berkeley, 1972.

built to serve the deaf-blind, then it should be feasible to extend the design to other handicapping conditions if problems associated with increasing the scale of the system can be solved. There is much truth in the EXOTECH study's concluding remark that, "Taken as a whole, the Deaf-Blind Center Information System will serve as a model for application to the entire field of the handicapped."

One reservation about simply transferring and expanding the Deaf-Blind Centers, however, is that as institutions, they are at once both too specialized *and* too generalized to satisfy the design objectives set out for a direction service. Deaf-Blind Centers are narrowly focused on the special needs of a limited subgroup, and they provide a general range of services, of which direction is only one of the less important (relatively speaking). In all likelihood the Deaf-Blind Center concept would therefore be infeasible if scaled up from serving a national population of about 5000 to serving one close to 10 million (the gross estimate of total handicapped children).

Because direction is a neglected but vital service, we are prompted to concentrate on procedures for improvement. The DBCIS is one such procedure, and its adaptation and incorporation into the proposed Regional Direction Center appears to be a relatively effective way to satisfy several of our design objectives.

Young Adult Institute and Workshop of New York   Since 1957, the Young Adult Institute and Workshop of New York has provided the mentally retarded and other young adult handicapped with preemployment training, which the Institute calls "Adjustment Counseling."[66] While the program is mainly aimed at vocational placement and job preparation, its information content is of more general interest. Social, communicative, and employment skills are taught to ease the transition into the "normal" community.[67] However, the most interesting aspect of the program for our purposes is the extensive network of service providers and potential employers maintained by Institute staff. The demonstrated success rates of the program attest to the importance of such specialized information for a limited range of purposes—in this case, placement. It would be valuable to expand the concept and practice into more general application.

[66]Thomas-Robert Ames, "Program Profiles: A Program for Transition to Independence," *Mental Retardation,* Vol. 8, April 1970, pp. 49–51.

[67]B. Macleech et al., *An Exploration of the Advisability of Developing a Research and Demonstration Project Concerned with Elevating the Readiness for Vocational Rehabilitation of Multiply-Handicapped Young Adults,* Young Adult Institute and Workshop, Inc., New York, 1966.

New York University Deafness Research and Training Center   Using
the existing facilities of New York University, the Deafness Research
and Training Center employs a multidisciplinary team to expand the
menu of vocational services usually available to the deaf. This effort
has been labeled the "Community Service Delivery Model," whose
stated purpose is to develop, within the deaf community, "sophisti-
cation . . . as to the acquisition of social services . . . [and] competence in community agencies for serving deaf people."[68] To accomplish these objectives, the CSDM strives to make the community's
existing services work to the best advantage of the deaf. Service responsibility is primarily left to others, while the CSDM is oriented
toward referral and guidance of its clientele and toward educating
the community at large about the needs and capabilities of the deaf.

Many elements of this effort appear to satisfy the design characteristics we have laid out for a direction service. However, it is appropriate to caution would-be emulators on several possibly troublesome
features of the CSDM: it is located within a university and hence lies
outside the political mainstream; it is a modest operation, from all
indications; and it appears to have a decided research bias. All of
these aspects should be considered seriously before one attempts to
reproduce the model on a wholesale basis elsewhere.

Comprehensive Vocational Rehabilitation Programs   As a result of
1958 amendments to the Vocational Rehabilitation Act, several feasibility studies were conducted to determine whether the severely educationally limited deaf (those reading at a third-grade level or less)
could be integrated into the community if supported by general purpose rehabilitation centers oriented to providing a comprehensive
range of adjustment and guidance services instead of being limited to
vocationally related services.

Some of the results of these feasibility studies were encouraging.
The design objectives of comprehensive, multidisciplinary, and personalized service provision operated to good effect. Likewise, it
proved meritorious to have a single point of access through which a
variety of services could be matched with the specialized needs of
these seriously limited people.[69]

[68]Frank Bowe et al., "Delivery of Community Services to Deaf Persons," *Journal of
Rehabilitation of the Deaf,* July 1973, pp. 15–29.
[69]C. A. Lawrence and G. M. Vescovi, *Deaf Adults in New England: An Exploratory
Service Program,* SRS/DHEW, Final Report RD-1516-S, Washington, D.C., 1967; and
S. N. Hurwitz, *Habilitation of Deaf Young Adults,* SRS/DHEW, Final Report RD-1804-S,
Washington, D.C., 1971.

Family Counseling for the Adult Deaf   Short-term counseling to help the deaf adult with his special problems (including diagnostics, translator services, family counseling, placement assistance, and so forth) has been shown to be promising in the three or four limited applications where it has been tried.[70] The main message from all these applications is that the marginal utility of information about the availability of needed services is high, but the cost of providing that information is not. The principle is fundamental to the general concept of direction.

San Francisco Speech and Hearing Center   A well-known article by Donald R. Calvert and Suzanna Baltzer[71] embodies some creative though somewhat limited fragments of the direction design. The study concentrated on deaf preschoolers and demonstrated that a management program stressing "normalization" had some noticeable payoffs for the children's development and achievement. Professionals from the Speech and Hearing Center periodically visited the children's homes to evaluate their needs and then to match those needs with the capabilities of the Center and of other agencies that cooperated with the Center in providing additional services. The effort was multidisciplinary, professional, and essentially one-stop for those parents fortunate enough to benefit from the program. Furthermore, the benefits of preschool education for the deaf were "built into" the program from the start.

The small size of the preschool deaf population in the immediate area necessitated enlarging the catchment area to include northern and central California, Nevada, and southern Oregon. The resulting distances, travel time, and displacement from the family in those cases where children had to come to the Center for medical treatment must count as less than desirable features of an otherwise interesting program.[72]

[70]R. Falberg, "Community Services for Deaf People in Kansas City: A Description and Report," *Journal of Rehabilitation of the Deaf,* Vol. 3, October 1969, pp. 42–62; W. A. Ethridge, "Community Referral Sources," ibid., July 1969, pp. 103–111; and J. Kane and C. Shafer, *Personal and Family Counseling Services for the Adult Deaf,* DHEW, Final Report RD-2560-S, Washington, D.C., 1968.

[71]"Home Management in a Comprehensive Preschool Program for Hearing Impaired Children," *Exceptional Children,* Vol. 34, December 1967, pp. 253–258.

[72]Other problems noted included the Center's dependence on "soft" money; the fact that there were insufficient numbers of professionals trained to deal with preschoolers; and that there were few standards to rely on in teaching the very young deaf.

Brookline Early Education Project (BEEP)   Heralded as "the nation's first major school-based program to provide comprehensive educational and health services to children during infancy and the early years of life," BEEP is an ambitious program designed to capitalize on the mother as teacher and constant observer of her child.[73] The implicit assumption underlying much of the thinking is that the parent is an underused resource and with training and guidance could do much to educate and protect the health of the child. For our purposes, the most interesting aspect of BEEP is that it will have a referral service to help the parents find specialized medical care, and a provision to ensure that the handicapped within BEEP's otherwise normal population will be followed up once they are identified. The project is funded privately by the Carnegie Corporation and the Johnson Foundation.

The project is far more elaborate and ambitious than the direction service we are proposing. It is commendable for its intention to track *all* children throughout the preschool years to promote their intellectual growth and ensure that any handicaps are discovered promptly.

American Foundation for the Blind: Pilot Projects   Two pilot projects undertaken on the initiative of the American Foundation for the Blind were conducted on behalf of preschool visually impaired children in Minnesota and New Hampshire. Their basic purpose closely resembled the direction center concept, in that they were exploring ways to coordinate local services on behalf of the handicapped child. The pilot projects may be followed by demonstration models in other areas of the country.

Judging solely by the size of the preschool visually impaired population, it would seem that size or scale difficulties would prevent such a scheme from providing sufficiently numerous or diverse services if a small catchment area is used, and that, on the other hand, an overly large catchment area would also impede the effort just as it has somewhat reduced the effectiveness of direction services for preschool hearing impaired in the San Francisco Center and in the Deaf-Blind Centers nationally. Direction, to repeat the theme, is a universally needed service whose fullest potential will be realized only when it is offered to all handicapped children, no matter what their condition.

Pennsylvania: Commonwealth Child Development Committee   The Governor of Pennsylvania attacked the problem from another direction. By virtue of Executive Order No. 35, in 1972, a Commonwealth

[73]*Education Daily,* March 9, 1973, pp. 5-6.

Child Development Committee was established to oversee and coordinate the "merger of all federal funding for medical problems of children into one agency, with sufficient capacity to conduct cost analyses and impact evaluation of programs."[74] As we shall point out in the recommendations portion of this chapter, it is critically important that there be some recognized authority outside of the existing chain of bureaucratic command to which the proposed Regional Direction Centers may report. In principle, the Commonwealth Child Development Committee, with an expanded and clarified charter, could serve this purpose quite well.

Satellite Facilities To anticipate a possible objection to the creation of Regional Direction Centers—that they may entail excessive investment in plant—it seems useful to note here that, unlike a hospital or formal educational facility, a direction center requires only minimal, relatively unspecialized, and unadorned space.

The concept of satellite facilities, although not new, may be relevant in this case. Satellites have been shown to increase service demand by lessening the geographic constraint through the imaginative use of a variety of small, cheap, flexible, and sometimes mobile facilities.[75] Interesting examples include building space within public housing units, and even surplus firehouses.[76]

Many of these examples confirm that small size and low overhead cost are often an advantage in the delivery of information-laden services such as referral, planning, scheduling, and follow-through. A smaller setting, with fewer clients and a smaller staff, can make scheduling easier, shorten waiting times, and enable people to get more thorough individual attention.[77]

Observations on Promising Partial Models In practice, direction is at best a primitively developed and poorly understood concept and ser-

---

[74]March 30, 1972.

[75]Most of the literature on this subject is thoroughly surveyed in J. R. Lave and S. Leinhardt, "The Delivery of Ambulatory Care to the Poor: A Literature Review," in William Cooper (ed.), "Urban Issues II," Special Supplement to *Management Science,* Vol. 19, No. 4, December 1972. An early statement of the satellite concept that gained some attention is Jerry A. Solon et al., "Patterns of Medical Care: A Hospital's Outpatients," *American Journal of Public Health,* Vol. 50, December 1960, pp. 1905–1913; this piece is cited to remind the reader that these ideas are not new, only pregnant.

[76]"Physician's Assistant: Medicine Acts to Meet Manpower Need," *Dental Survey: Journal of Dental Practice,* April 1969; M. I. Levinson, "Missouri Clinic Occupies Converted Firehouse," *Hospitals,* Vol. 41, December 1967, pp. 48–57.

[77]Richard M. Bailey, "Economies of Scale in Medical Practice," in Herbert Klarman (ed.), *Empirical Studies in Health Economics,* The Johns Hopkins Press, Baltimore, 1970.

vice. While the foregoing examples embody many attractive and interesting features, they remain only scattered fragments of the larger and more inclusive system defined by our direction design characteristics. The following summarizes a few of our observations:

- Direction is in a primitive state, although the need for it is acknowledged in the prototypes and experiments reviewed.
- Data systems—stressing both operational information and information about the local context that could be used by service recipients—are virtually nonexistent or, in the case of Deaf-Blind Centers and the State of Maryland, in a design and early implementation stage.
- Direction systems appear to yield high payoffs in those limited instances where even the most elementary information has been collected and used.
- The incremental cost of direction information is slight, compared with its marginal utility to the service recipient.
- A variety of direction service strategies exists in some crude form, but those responsible have not developed the strategies well or systematically; they are more "accidents" that grew out of some other purpose than they are deliberate creations in their own right.
- The critical elements in a direction strategy appear to be the following: mixture of services, definitions of the served population, catchment population size, catchment spatial features, staffing mix, follow-up, expedited flow of individual clients through the center, and independence from existing service agencies.

FOREIGN MODELS

Foreign models have many constructive lessons to offer about direction and other services.[78] Rather than describing each program in exhaustive detail, the following discussion mentions only a select few interesting features that exemplify the direction concept and service, and indicates where an interested party might begin looking for further information on the issue.

An excellent, general summary of European activities has been completed and published by the Council of Europe. The section en-

[78]In 1972, S. M. Genensky visited eight Western European countries in the course of a project on sensory aids sponsored by the Social and Rehabilitation Service of the Department of Health, Education, and Welfare; he was particularly involved with closed circuit television for the partially sighted. G. D. Brewer remained primarily in Germany for a month as a guest of DATUM e.v. (Bonn-Bad Godesberg), where he was able to pursue inquiries about the German system and approach, and to obtain information about systems in other European countries.

titled, "Education of Parents and the Community," embodies many direction concepts.[79]

Sweden The Swedish tradition of excellence in the general area of health carries over especially to the care of handicapped children.[80] Besides attaining nearly total identification and registry of the population by virtue of the coverage guaranteed under the National Social Insurance Board, there are multiple institutional arrangements to ensure that the handicapped child and his family are informed about and receive needed services.[81] In this regard, the Central Registry has been pivotal in coordinating many of the more specialized services and in planning for the total needs of Sweden's handicapped population. It is reported that the Registry engages in monthly updates "in order to detect at as early a stage as possible increases in the incidence of certain types of malformation."[82] Around 90 percent of all children are given the equivalent of a multiphasic screening by the time they reach one year of age; such screenings are delivered in Child Welfare Centers located throughout the country. Follow-up and direction to all needed and available services are done mainly by nurses attached to the Child Centers. These Centers also conduct routine eye tests as early as age four, which results in a 3 percent rate of referral for services nationally; ear tests are also done, resulting in a 5 to 10 percent referral rate.[83]

Care Boards, to plan, evaluate, and coordinate services to the mentally retarded of all ages, have consistently worked to "normalize" the life experiences of children by virtue of the Boards' physical location near ordinary schools and their encouragement of both families and educators to integrate the handicapped child into as many normal

[79]Council of Europe, *Social Co-operation in Europe: Social Rehabilitation of Physically and Mentally Handicapped Persons,* Strasbourg, 1972, hereinafter cited as "COE."

[80]Obligatory Health Insurance has been in force since 1955, and extensive preventive pediatric care dates from the 1930s. Besides a general child allowance provided all parents, a special handicapped child allowance of approximately $75 per month is provided on the supposition that being a parent of a handicapped child creates a chronic and additional financial burden, even over and above that accounted for directly by insurance payments for treatment and other defined services. This minimum allowance is adjustable upward, subject to a family-means test. Furthermore, the government either provides or covers the cost of transportation to receive services.

[81]Bo Hellstrom, "Society and the Handicapped Child in Sweden," *Journal of the American Medical Women's Association,* Vol. 24, March 1969, pp. 224–232; Eva Lindstedt, "Blind People in Sweden: A Socio-medical Study," *Acta Ophthalmologica,* Vol. 45, 1968, pp. 1146–1158; and Leopold Lippman, "Sweden Remembers—and Provides for—the Handicapped," *Mental Retardation,* August 1969.

[82]Hellstrom, op. cit., p. 235.

[83]Lindstedt, op. cit.; Hellstrom, op. cit.

routines as possible.[84] This concept has been extended to preschoolers in Integrated Play Schools, whose function it is to mix impaired children, such as the deaf or blind, with normal ones, encouraging the former to develop to a full potential and educating the latter to the simple fact that handicapped children are, after all, people too.[85]

Denmark From all indications, services to Danish handicapped people are also excellent relative to those in many other countries.[86] While driven generally by terms of the National Assistance Act, which "makes it the State's duty to care for all persons afflicted by any form of handicap and in need of special assistance,"[87] the Danish system is in transition. Prior to the execution of terms of the Public Health Security Act in April 1973, the system was a mixed, public-private one wherein the public component was concerned primarily with planning, evaluation, and coordination, and the private sector was largely responsible for service provision.[88] Since April 1973, coordination and comprehensive service integration have been rationalized and placed under public control. Policies are set and interpreted at the national level; they are administered in 14 county-level jurisdictions (each having about 250,000 citizens), and in over 275 municipalities. Revenue is shared with the central government to pay for service provision. Direction occurs primarily at the municipal level, although a well-defined chain of authority and responsibility passes directly to the central government, aided by a general ombudsman system.[89]

Early identification is stressed; so is early education, "preferably immediately after the diagnosis has been made so that educational-psychological treatment can be started at the earliest possible stage."[90]

A remarkable feature of the Danish approach is the use of Home Advisory Services (HAS), which offer to send a specially trained nurse for about three weeks into the homes of the handicapped to counsel,

---

[84]COE, op. cit., p. 19. Schools for the Blind, located in Stockholm and Orebro, have as residents only the most severely impaired; otherwise, they emphasize a parent-child instructional program that ranges in duration from two to nine months.

[85]Hellstrom, op. cit., pp. 232–233.

[86]E. Johnson, "Modern Implementation of Denmark's Tradition of Health Care Delivery," *Health Services Reports,* Vol. 88, No. 7, August-September 1973, pp. 624–630.

[87]COE, op. cit., p. 40.

[88]Ibid., p. 38.

[89]Johnson, op. cit., p. 630.

[90]Kurt Kristensen, "Educational Care of Children with Extremely Low Vision," Paper read at the Conference of International Council of Educators of Blind Youth, Madrid, July 25-August 2, 1972. Kristensen characterizes the Home Advisory Service in his paper.

educate, and assess the progress of the child and the efficacy of services currently received. This service pursues nearly all of the purposes cited in our direction design objectives, plus an additional one—to help ensure that the client *continuously* receives maximum benefit from the services he receives. Another interesting service of the HAS is the creation of individualized training programs for preschoolers that emphasize the parent's role; the program works as much with the parent (to relieve guilt, for example, and to train the parent to help the child) as it does directly with the child.

Belgium Many notable direction concepts have also been institutionalized in Belgium, although the experiences there are less comprehensive than in Sweden or Denmark. The National Rehabilitation Fund, created in 1963, is a basic element of enabling legislation for handicapped programs; because of it, a number of specialized schools, training programs, public education efforts, and financing initiatives have been undertaken or supported. For instance, the Fund has made direct approaches to the National Federation of Industries and was instrumental in changing physician certification procedures to include required instruction in the full service needs of the handicapped.[91]

Much direction, in the form of planning and service coordination, is evidently done through specialized schools for the deaf or blind. Schools also favor integrated research, testing, and screening practices;[92] they are in many aspects configured and operated along the lines of the Deaf-Blind Centers in the United States, a factor limiting the simple transfer of the institutional concept for many of the same reasons cited earlier for the U.S. case.

Two appointed bodies, having considerable parental participation, exist at the national level: The Central Council for the Handicapped concerns itself with the general implications (present and future) of policies affecting the handicapped, and the Central Family Council (dating only from 1967) tends to be oriented toward specific problems facing families of handicapped children. Both contribute in special and important ways to improved direction.

France Much like that in Belgium, the French system allows voluntary (often officially sanctioned) bodies to take the lead in providing services to the handicapped. Public agencies provide some supervi-

[91]COE, op. cit., pp. 24, 46–47.
[92]O. Perrier, "A propos de l'enseignement de la réadaptation de l'enfant handicapé d'ouie," *Acta Otorhinolaryngol Belgique,* Vol. 23, 1969, pp. 585–594.

sory and financial assistance and carry out rather specialized direction on behalf of categorical subsets of the handicapped population. For example, special inspectorates such as the Commission Départementale d'Orientation des Infirmes ensure that the quality, or at least the legality, of services provided to the young and to handicapped youth is maintained.

The complex "Social Aid Acts" basically underwrite a portion of the total costs of the handicapped and do so through complicated transfer arrangements with individual départements (roughly, "states"), municipalities, and quasi-public institutions. The Ministry of Labor, Employment, and Population is a major conduit of these funds at the national level.

An important, powerful voluntary organization is the National Federation of Associations of Parents of Handicapped Children (UNAPEI), which functions to educate the public in general, but concentrates on providing parents with information and direction. This is done through "family representatives" and a vigorous publications program.[93]

Schools specialized to specific disorders exist,[94] and from all reports, carry out many direction-oriented activities on behalf of those enrolled.[95]

Germany Through a special "microcensus" taken in April 1966, it was estimated that somewhere between 450,000 and 500,000 school-aged, handicapped youth were located in the Federal Republic of Germany. A direction deficiency has hampered service delivery in Germany, where

> . . . many organizations, institutions, and public authorities work on rehabilitation of the disabled. [The term "rehabilitation" has an all-encompassing meaning.] For the disabled, the distribution of competence [a very subtle word in German more connoting responsibility than it does wisdom or knowledge] is often confusing; coordination is hence required on both the individual plane . . . and on the institutional and organizational plane, to guarantee continuous cooperation among all entities concerned about the setting up of necessary rehabilitation centers.[96]

[93]COE, op. cit., pp. 19, 20, 24, 38, 41, 48.

[94]One such is the Institut National des Jeunes Aveugles [National Institute of the Young Blind].

[95]Jean Crouzet, "Le rôle de l'ophtalmologiste vis-à-vis des enfants déficients visuels," *Bulletin des sociétés d'ophtalmologie*, Vol. 70, February 1970, pp. 212–221.

[96]"German Note on General Programs and Action Taken to Abet Coordination of Rehabilitation Work," Bonn: Ministry of Youth, Family, and Health; and Strasbourg: Council of Europe, PA/REHAB/71, June 7, 1971, pp. 1–2. We have assembled and reviewed a modestly representative German-language literature on these topics.

Discussion and analyses preceding a national decree of October 28, 1969,[97] enabling the creation of rehabilitation institutions, focused on many of the same direction-related issues confronting the United States in 1974.

The "solution" to these issues is a many-faceted, and only recently widely implemented, collection of laws, directives, decrees, and appeals. It is worth noting the general character of the solution to get an inkling of what a strategy favoring a massive frontal assault on the direction problem could portend if adopted elsewhere. A desire to improve coordination, access, efficiency, and equity—in short, a concern for better direction—is the *only* common discernible thread knitting these activities together.

To extend and create rehabilitation centers, the Ministry of Labor and Social Affairs allocated some 10 million DM in 1969 and 15 million DM in 1970. These funds are supplemented by large but undeterminable amounts from several federal ministries, most notably the Ministry for Youth, Family, and Health—the designated "cooperative and co-action" institution. The funds are being expended in five broad categories:[98]

- Centers of medical rehabilitation (e.g., Wildbad, Heidelberg)
- Rehabilitation centers for specific disorders, e.g., heart (Bad Krozingen), brain (Bad Godesberg), eyes (Marburg)
- Vocational training centers
- Sheltered workshops
- Special facilities for children, e.g., day care, kindergartens, special schools
- Homes for disabled persons

In addition to expansion and construction of facilities, complementary training programs to staff the new buildings were instituted. Reconciliation and redrafting of conflicting federal legislation have begun (e.g., the "Federal Social Assistance Act," the "Youth Welfare Act," the "Severely Disabled Persons Act," the national insurance codes, the "Employment Promotion Act," and many lesser pieces of legislation all existed in some form but were not always mutually consistent, much less coordinated). "Harmonization" of conflicting federal and state laws and practices has been encouraged (German states have considerable power under the federal system, and this has proven to be particularly troublesome for easy achievement of the

[97]Basically a modification by decree of Section 62 of the Employment Promotion Act. The Act was a legal precedent calling for cooperation and coordination of employment and rehabilitation for all citizens that the decree seized upon and *generalized* to cover all services and *specialized* to focus on the handicapped.

[98]Interviews, Ministry of Youth, Family, and Health, Bonn, June 1972.

coordinative objectives). A consolidation of highly fragmented data into one information system has been recommended, along with the collection of needed new data. And multiple appeals for cooperation have been made to service providers at all levels of government, to industry and the trade unions, to the churches, to private agencies, to educational institutions, to the families of the handicapped, and to the population at large.

While it is too soon to make any overall assessments, these various activities have, if nothing else, raised the level of public awareness about the problems of the handicapped,[99] and have already produced a host of specific improvements.[100]

Given the many similarities between the German situation with respect to a direction service in 1968 or 1969 and the current situation in the United States, a careful monitoring and assessment of Germany's implementation difficulties and realized (as opposed to expected) outcomes appears called for.

The Netherlands Serving Dutch handicapped persons is the express responsibility of municipal authorities, although the central government has taken on many informational service activities. Programs for the mentally handicapped have been stressed, doubtless because of their relatively greater numbers in a small total handicapped population, although direction and identification services are generally available to all.

Various institutional forms coordinate, plan, and deliver services. Foremost among these are 32 "Day Centers," each composed of a multidisciplinary team whose main task is to provide child- and family-oriented information, planning, guidance, and help; a strong, voluntary, national Parent's Association for the Mentally Handicapped, which has influenced legislation and serves as a "court of appeals" for parental grievances; and a Central Advisory Council on Care of the Mentally Handicapped. The Central Advisory Council has evidently concentrated its efforts on "normalization" activities—in-

---

[99]As only one tangible example, a nationwide lottery whose proceeds benefit handicapped children is conducted with much anticipation, interest, and participation on a periodic basis. Results are announced on the "A Ray of Sunshine" television show.

[100]A number of "Guides to Services for the . . ." and compilations of locally available services, resources, and institutions have begun to appear. Judging by the sheer number and variety of entries they commonly contain, they must be a considerable aid to families searching for help. One excellent handbook is the 175-page *Bundessozialhilfegesetz* (BSHG), issued by the Ministry of Youth, Family, and Health, Verlag Reckinger, Siegburg, June 1971. The handbook is categorized according to an extensive list of services, disorders, and pertinent laws, all discussed in simple terms. It is a "model" of sorts, easily replicated.

directly, with respect to changing public attitudes through a vigorous media program, and directly, by supporting the integration of the handicapped into ordinary schools to the maximum extent possible and by developing and disseminating correspondence courses for the families of severely handicapped children unable to participate fully in regular programs.[101]

Switzerland   Several features distinguish the Swiss delivery system, especially as it treats the informational services. The national Assurance Invalidité (AI) is financed 50 percent from private contributions of individuals, employers, and others, and 50 percent from the state. It maintains over 3000 local offices, each an accessible source of *referral* for a comprehensive range of services for some 2000 citizens. A Federation of Associations of Parents of the Mentally Handicapped[102] works to educate the public and to reflect and advise on policy proposals (through an Advisory Council), and serves as a local spokesman in individual instances (mainly through an organization known as Pro Infirmis). The most visible of these efforts is an annual month-long public relations campaign.[103]

United Kingdom   Under national health or security legislation, such as the "Social Security and Supplementary Benefits Act," assistance is generally provided to the handicapped.[104] However, a distinctive feature of the British system is a concern for independent assessment of the quality and equitability of services. That concern is best embodied in "Her Majesty's Inspectors"—objective, impartial, and usually personally respected people reporting directly to the appropriate Minister—in a number of program areas,[105] and in professional certification demands contained in the National Health Service regulations.[106] Additionally, two more specific direction activities have been observed: efforts by the Department of Employment and Productivity to coordinate job openings with individual capabilities by working directly with physicians,[107] and a general purpose, hospital-based in-

---

[101]COE, op. cit., pp. 24, 48.

[102]Much as in The Netherlands, the relative sizes of Switzerland's different handicapped populations tip the scales in favor of the mentally retarded. However, concern in fact is generalized.

[103]COE, op. cit., pp. 23, 43, 45, 47, 49.

[104]Ibid., p. 38.

[105]James Lumsden, "A Very Special Inspectorate," *Special Education,* Vol. 60, April 1971, pp. 18–22; and Department of Education and Science, *HMI: Today and Tomorrow,* Her Majesty's Stationery Office, London, 1970.

[106]COE, op. cit., p. 27.

[107]Ibid., p. 47.

formation system designed to provide a full range of practical information to the handicapped and their families.[108]

A general preference for "normalization" is evident in extraordinary efforts to integrate handicapped children into ordinary schools to the greatest extent possible,[109] efforts that appear to work reasonably well, for the deaf at least.[110]

Observations on Foreign Models   It is hard to make detailed, general conclusions about the variegated array of European activities and systems, but certain features stand out, most of them related to the direction service:

- Direction services are better organized and developed in many European countries than in the United States.
- Regardless of governmental form or degree of service coverage supported publicly, nations with superior direction facilities and institutions tend to provide better and more extensive services.
- Each of various desirable features or characteristics of a direction service has been implemented, to a greater or lesser extent, in foreign applications, thereby supporting the feasibility of each feature in practice.
- Registration of the handicapped, often a routine by-product of a health insurance program (irrespective of the specific details of implementation of that program) can contribute significantly to early and periodic identification and to the periodic and systematic matching of the child's needs with a proper mix of services.
- More extensive and comprehensive services are provided in those settings where distinct lines of communication link parents with local, intermediate, and central governmental officials; i.e., "feedbacks" in the system are important.
- The provision of a full range of services through regional centers is

[108]The design is explicitly oriented toward the client and not the administrator or service provider. Jean Cullinan, "Information Service for the Disabled," *Nursing Times,* Vol. 64, January 1958, p. 76. Created in 1964, the Information Service is the product of the joint efforts of the Disabled Living Activities Group of the Central Council for the Disabled, and the King Edward's Hospital Fund for London.

[109]"No handicapped pupil should be sent to a special school who can be satisfactorily educated in an ordinary school." Ministry of Education Circular No. 276, June 1954.

[110]Ministry of Education, *Survey of Deaf Children Who Have Been Transferred from Special Schools or Units to Ordinary Schools,* Her Majesty's Stationery Office, London, 1963. The Survey found that except for the *most severely* impaired, about ⅓ were "successful," ⅓ "moderately successful," and ⅓ had been "failures" and returned to special units. See also Kathryn Meadows and Lloyd Meadows, "The Education of Deaf Children in England," *American Annals of the Deaf,* Vol. 113, September 1969, pp. 777–785.

feasible if the total (and hence total handicapped) population served by the center is absolutely small, or if the population served is made small by differentiating according to specific handicapping conditions. None of the countries we investigated combined both *full* service provision and *total* coverage of the entire handicapped population in a single national institutional setting.

- A potential option is to concentrate on a *single* service on behalf of the *total* population—an eventuality ruled out for any but the most generally demanded service, such as direction—and to provide this service through locally accessible institutions whose individual activities are coordinated by some superior authority.
- Because of severe contextual differences between the U.S. and foreign settings, none of the foreign models is entirely suitable for transfer en bloc to the United States, but many of them have desirable features that could be adopted in a United States direction service.

RECOMMENDATIONS FOR EVALUATING REGIONAL DIRECTION CENTERS

We have identified and described a serious lack of direction services in the current system serving American handicapped children and youth. In the process, we specified several design characteristics for an improved direction service, and reviewed existing partial models that embody one or more of these characteristics and therefore could supply valuable inputs to a new and superior direction service for the United States.

We particularly commend certain aspects of the *conceptual approach* embodied in the New York State "Child Advocacy System," the *technical innovation* represented in Maryland's "Data System for the Handicapped," and a modified *institutional version* of California's Regional Direction Centers. Our proposed Regional Direction Centers for Handicapped Youth (RDCs) would be the result of judicious selection of the better features of these and other examples.

Specifically, we have three major recommendations, the first of which is:

Full-scale evaluations should be undertaken of the most promising existing partial models for providing direction service, to learn their strengths, weaknesses, and implications for an expanded, nationwide network of regional direction centers for handicapped children.

Our preliminary estimates of the eventual cost, composition, modus operandi, and institutional structure of these centers follow.

Cost   Our initial planning estimate is that each local center could be operated for about $100 per handicapped child per year. This would mean that if the child and his family received comprehensive direction service every four years on the average, then $400 would be available to provide that direction. This amount appears adequate for at least minimum quality direction, and may be a high estimate if volunteer help is used extensively, as in the New York Child Advocacy model.

One offsetting cost reduction would come from elimination of the need for other agencies to provide their present inefficient and partial direction based on little comprehensive information about the service system. In view of the potential for standardized, accurate, and rapidly accessible management information (currently nonexistent or available in only the most rudimentary forms), this $100 expenditure would provide significant benefits. Additional humane, quality-of-life benefits to the children and parents from receipt of appropriate services are not calculable, but must be very significant. Benefits deriving from savings in services not needed by the youth later in life because of timely identification, evaluation of needs, and case management are also not calculable, but would be significant in the individual case and probably positive in the aggregate. The savings in rediagnosis and recertification realized by a simple transfer of client records from the center to various other servers will be considerable, but not reliably calculable. The savings to be realized by a timely and accurate sensing of shifts in the number and character of the handicapped population—resulting from rubella or other epidemic problems, for example—could be significant but are not reliably calculable. The savings that would result from more efficient matching of the needs of a handicapped population with the locally available services are not measurable, using available data, but would be positive.

In brief, the cost per child for a direction service is not in itself excessively high, and the potential benefits and late savings from that service could be large, but cannot be accurately estimated.

Composition of Staff   The staff composition of individual centers will undoubtedly vary from site to site in reponse to local requirements and the availability of personnel. However, we think that a staff composed like the list in Table 8.4 would be a reasonable model and point of departure for individual sites. A representative table of organization is presented in Fig. 8.3; it shows the structural equivalence given to information collection and management; administration and case management; and service counseling and parent direction. The last-named is worth additional comment.

In addition to the direction provided by the center's permanent staff (by all staff members, not merely those we call Direction Counselors in Table 8.4), an unexploited and valuable source of counseling and direction is the parent of the handicapped child. Much of the day-by-day direction could be left to Parent Counselors who are members of the RDC's clientele and who would be available to help other, more recent initiates into the center's program and into the local service milieu. These Parent Counselors could be trained by and consult with the RDC's own permanent staff. Besides providing some much needed manpower, in an honest sense "ideally" suited to the parent information task, this innovation might do much to relieve the "What can the families do?" problem consistently noted in our family interviews and by professionals in the system; it is also a constructive step toward the participation objective.

Table 8.4
STAFF COMPOSITION MODEL FOR RDC

Director—a physician

Associate Director/Data Management—a data specialist
Associate Director/Administrative Services—a skilled administrator
Associate Director/Direction Services

Special educator
Vocational rehabilitation specialist
Social worker
Public health specialist
Psychologist
Direction counselors
Data management technician
Parent counselors (volunteers)
Consultant specialists on particular handicapping conditions
Consultant lawyer

Direction Counselors would be trained specifically for the RDC's purpose. They would not be social workers, psychologists, or counselors as conventionally defined. They would constitute an important professional specialty that does not currently exist; their socialization, training, and orientation would be designed from the beginning to

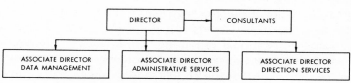

Fig. 8.3   RDC Table of Organization.

conform to the objective of serving the handicapped child and his family.

Parent Counselors and the professional staff of the RDC, with their knowledge of local information and conditions, could jointly develop correspondence courses and information booklets for use of the families served by the RDC. The courses developed and disseminated currently by the John Tracy Clinic in Los Angeles, which has pioneered in work with hearing handicapped youth, are a model of what is needed. Thousands of parents have benefited from these courses, but the courses' general potential has scarcely been tapped. Local information and conditions could be built into similar course material by the Parent Counselors and the RDC professional staff. Such courses can minimize costly face-to-face counseling time and enhance the benefits.

We recommend the early and more widespread use of correspondence courses, whether or not the more ambitious concept of the RDC is adopted.

Because some of the service specialists could not be effectively utilized full time, they could be hired on a consultant basis. A certain number of days' worth of consulting time would be allotted for use at the discretion of the RDC Director.

Modus Operandi The major direct contacts that the child and his family will have with the RDC will be the initial intake and several other natural "milestones" related to the child's age and stage in the life process. For example, the "Case Management Flow Process," developed in California's regional centers, is a sound beginning and could serve as the intake or basic introduction to the RDC. That process includes the following steps: initial screening; intake; case staffing and plan formulation; plan execution; and periodic review and evaluation. We would amend this process somewhat to increase the "throughput," or rapidity, of the RDC's service to clients. By defining *major* and *minor* periodic reviews and updates, annual costs per child could be held down. Major review periods would occur at initial discovery of the handicap; when the child reaches five years of age and is about to enter school; at nine years of age, when a detailed evaluation of school progress and prospects would be carried out; at fifteen years of age, when vocational services would become salient; and at twenty years of age, the "exit" age, to make a thorough assessment of the individual's needs and point out available services for adults, such as vocational retraining. Minor review periods would occur when the parent raised a specific question between the major reviews. In the event that the child's family moved from one region to another, this could signal the "Case Management Flow Process" to begin anew to match the child's needs with what is locally available.

Institutional Structure The RDCs would be configured somewhat like the model outlined in Fig. 8.3. These centers would be placed in a chain of command linking them directly to a State Advisory Council, which itself does not report to any existing agency providing other services such as health and education. To the greatest extent possible, this separate chain of command and compensation is needed to restructure incentives and to avoid "capture" by the existing service system. Finally, at the national level, we believe that a *strong* Office for Handicapped Individuals within the Office of the Secretary of HEW would do much to focus attention on the needs of and serve as a spokesman for handicapped children and would serve admirably as a focus for coordinating existing services and all State Advisory Council and RDC activities. The Office for Handicapped Individuals could have access to the information generated by the RDCs, and could be a vast improvement over the present multitude of uncoordinated groups that compete for resources at the federal level.

The following is our second major recommendation:

Based on an evaluation as noted above, a thorough implementation analysis should be conducted and five to ten pilot RDC projects should be created in locations throughout the country. Such pilot operations should themselves be carefully observed to ensure that subsequent, full-scale implementation is carried out rapidly and with an absolute minimum of difficulty.

The need for direction is too important to permit implementation of the services to be sidetracked for reasons that could be avoided by sufficient foresight and planning. The pilot efforts would check out initial estimates of cost, modus operandi, staff composition, location, etc., and would serve as definitive factual examples upon which to base full-scale implementation.

Conducting pilot projects over a one-to-three-year period also "buys time" to accomplish several necessary jobs preliminary to full-scale implementation. It allows time for better design of the data system; it allows time for the legislative process to work through the many ramifications of the concept; it allows some time for the training of the specialized Direction Counselors; and it allows time for the idea's full impact to be absorbed by those who will benefit from and provide the services. The pilot project approach is one way to reduce risks without unduly inhibiting the adoption of the concept.

Our final recommendation:

*If the pilot projects demonstrate the viability of the Regional Direc-
tion Center concept, then improvements in the Regional Direction
Center design suggested by the pilot projects should be incorporated,
and the concept should be expanded as rapidly as possible into a
nationwide network of Regional Direction Centers for Handicapped
Youth.*

While we have noted the benefits such a proposal would afford to
the families and children, it is important to stress that the present
service system is also likely to benefit handsomely, because timely
and efficient provision of services can eliminate duplication of effort
and clients' need for other services later in life. We note again in
closing this chapter that one of the aims of Regional Direction Centers is to complement and make the present system more efficient,
and they would operate within the context of the present service
system without major disruption of its present structure. However, if
the information-based direction service is effectively provided, then
localized conflicts may arise as the unevenness in the quality of existing service programs becomes apparent. When fully tested and developed, the Regional Direction Center concept might be extended to
include handicapped adults.

Chapter 9

MEDICAL SERVICES

OVERVIEW

Medical programs that bestow large benefits on the lives of all handicapped children are summarized here as best we can, given the dearth of programmatic information and data on the status and needs of the handicapped population. While there are three main federally supported medical programs serving handicapped youth—Medicaid, Maternal and Child Health Service, and Crippled Children's Service—many more are to be found in rehabilitation programs, in Department of Defense programs for military dependents, in the Veterans Administration, in NIMH, in Project Head Start, and so forth.

Children are entitled to good health care, and handicapped children are no different from normal ones in this regard, except that they need more services and resources. The total contribution to "good health" that accrues to all children, including the handicapped, comes from a wide assortment of publicly and privately provided health services.

Federally supported programs providing health services are estimated to have assisted at least 1 million handicapped youth in FY 1971. A total of over 1½ million children were reported to have been served by the different health programs, but some unknown amount of double-counting is included because of youth receiving service from more than one program. Total federal and state expenditures in this area were at least $314 million in FY 1971, of which the federal share was $205 million and the state share was $109 million. State and local expenditures not known or reported to the federal government would raise the total even further. The breakdown of these figures, shown in Tables 9.1 and 9.2, indicates that the largest single program in this area is Medicaid, which serves youth from financially needy families. The second largest is the Crippled Children's Service which is designed to serve children having nearly all types of handicapping conditions. Table 9.3 shows the funds expended by type of handicap (based on data of questionable reliability).

The medical services can be considered as a delivery system, represented by a mix of models, functions, rationales, and processes that cannot be adequately described collectively. Medicaid, for instance,

Table 9.1
ESTIMATED FEDERAL AND STATE HEALTH PROGRAM EXPENDITURES FOR HANDICAPPED YOUTH, 1971

	Expenditures		
Program	Federal	State	Total
Crippled Children's Service	$ 58,598,000	$ 29,299,000[a]	$ 87,897,000
Other maternal and child health programs	25,000,000	[b]	25,000,000
Medicaid	105,548,000	80,255,000	185,803,000
Community health care—rubella immunization	16,000,000[c]	[b]	16,000,000
Other state and federal public health programs[d]	[b]	[b]	[b]
Total	$205,146,000	$109,554,000	$314,700,000

SOURCE: See later portions of this chapter for data sources and estimation methods.

[a] Amount required to match federal CCS funds only. The actual total state and local contribution may be as much as twice the amount shown.

[b] Not estimated.

[c] FY 1970.

[d] For a description of these programs, not primarily intended to serve handicapped youth, see the subsection entitled "Other Public Health Programs" in this chapter.

Table 9.2
ESTIMATED NUMBER OF HANDICAPPED YOUTH RECEIVING HEALTH SERVICES, 1971

Program	Number of Handicapped Youth
Crippled Children's Service	485,000
Other maternal and child health programs	81,000[a]
Medicaid	1,097,000
Community health care—rubella immunization	(b)
Other state and federal public health programs	(b)

SOURCE: See later portions of this chapter for data sources and estimation methods.

[a] Note that this is an estimate of *handicapped* youth served, not *total* served, and hence may appear at first glance to be undersized.

[b] Not estimated.

Table 9.3
**ESTIMATED FEDERAL AND STATE EXPENDITURES FOR HEALTH SERVICES
TO YOUTH BY TYPE OF HANDICAP, 1971**

Type of Handicap	Estimated Expenditures
Visual impairment	$ 28,663,000
Hearing impairment	28,415,000
Speech impairment	61,315,000
Crippling and other health impairments	101,001,000
Mental retardation	54,354,000
Emotional or other nervous disorders	27,946,000
Learning disability	13,006,000
Total	$314,700,000

SOURCE: See later portions of this chapter for data sources and estimation methods.

is a reasonably good example of the Controllership model, functioning primarily through federal control of all but the delegated provision of services (which the states and localities do) and rationalized as a program that provides needed redistribution of resources and basic support for services that would otherwise not be provided. The Maternal and Child Health Service, including the Crippled Children's Service, are by comparison best described as species of the Special Revenue Sharing Model; but even here there are some subtle but important differences.

CCS programs concentrate heavily on medical treatment, typically are operated by doctors, and stress quality medical care for a range of handicaps that encompasses the "simplest" clubfoot to extraordinarily exotic disorders. MCHS programs, however, encompass a bewildering variety of some 200 distinct services and activities, which are not consistently provided in all states and localities, and stress identification through screening and registration mechanisms and prevention via immunization and other disease specific programs.

A distinction between CCS and MCHS is summarized in terms of our concept of the Plus in the Special Revenue Sharing, Plus model. In this case, the Plus is not exercised by federal officials in either MCHS or CCS, although they have the rudiments of an information system with which it could be in CCS. Quality control is built into the CCS program through professional, historical, and structural guides that may or may not be reproducible for other related health service programs. The MCHS and CCS programs are grant providing mechanisms, rationalized primarily according to redistribution of resources arguments and secondarily by basic service support.

Crippled Children's Service

As of 1972, Crippled Children's Service programs were reaching some 491,000 children aged 0–21, and 29.5 percent of those served were aged 4 or less. CCS provides medical services to youth in financially needy families, although the determination of financial need is left to state officials. Males have traditionally outnumbered females over the years, and in 1970 the breakdown by sex of the total caseload was 54.5 percent male and 45.5 percent female. Racial characteristics are recorded only to the extent of listing whether the recipient is "white," "all other," or "not reported," and this breakdown was respectively, 66.8 percent, 24.0 percent, and 9.2 percent.

The bulk of the services provided were for physician visits and medical treatment; however, some 82,000 were served as hospital inpatients. About 90,000 were listed as multiple handicap recipients. Three general classes on impairment account for 69.8 percent of the total CCS caseload: impairment of the bones and organs of movement (25.2 percent), diseases of the nervous system and sense organs (24.2 percent), and congenital malformations (20.4 percent). The word "crippled" in the program title is presently a misnomer, since the program serves youth with virtually all types of medical problems.

Large variations exist on a state-by-state comparative basis, as compared with national averages of impairment covered, the extent of multiple handicapping reported, and the amounts of resources expended per recipient. For example, as contrasted with the national percentage breakdowns for the top three disease classes, Wisconsin reported 39.6 percent of its caseload was concerned with diseases of the nervous system and sense organs, but Kansas had only 8.3 percent; for diseases of the bones and organs of movement, Vermont reported 52.1 percent of its caseload in this category, while Oklahoma had only 6.6 percent; and for congenital malformations, Connecticut reported 39.8 percent of its caseload devoted to this disease class, and Oklahoma had only 5.2 percent. With respect to the reporting of multiple handicaps, Minnesota led all other states, with 53.5 percent of its total caseload reported as multiply handicapped (compared with a national average of 18.5 percent) but, on the other end of the scale, Rhode Island reported only 2.6 percent similarly handicapped. When considering per client federal expenditures on a state-by-state basis, the discrepancies are quite pronounced. These figures range from a low in Washington, D.C., of $26.90 to a high of $249.17 in Ohio, as contrasted with a national average federal per client value of $117.76.

Program highlights and distinguishing features of the CCS program include the following: high standards are maintained by the liberal use and control of the program by medical specialists; local needs are reflected in marginal variations in coverage that exist from state to state (this does not explain the wider variations that have been noted, however); the medical community has generally accepted CCS as "one of its own" programs as distinguished from the Title XIX and welfare-related health programs; and operational data are routinely and comprehensively collected according to a common format from all states to enable programmatic analyses.

CCS is reaching only a fraction of those who might benefit from it. Categorical coverage, as determined locally according to available resources and local preferences for certain classes of impairments over others, contributes to inequitable coverage from state to state and within the same state at different phases of the fiscal year. Planning and resource guidance information, and indeed coordination of related health centered services for handicapped children, do not exist to any noticeable extent. Nonetheless, the CCS model is a durable, time-tested one that has some general applicability—from all indications we received in interviews, from the survey questionnaire, and from our review of the few analyses made of it.

Maternal and Child Health Service

Other programs sponsored by Maternal and Child Health Service are widely diverse and rather difficult to appraise. Doubtless, underlying many program initiatives is the need to be both comprehensive and humanitarian; however, the actual results obtained are difficult to assess or trade off with other competitive services because of vague objectives, inadequate resources, poor coordination, and lack of accountability data.

In FY 1972, the MCHS budget, exclusive of CCS funds, was $177 million to improve and expand medical services related to maternal and child health, but the portion accruing to handicapped children is not clearly indicated.

One must take great care to separate each of the MCHS programs in making any summary assessments of the total activity. For instance, some 56 facilities to support the Maternal and Infant Care (M&I) program were funded in FY 1973 at a cost of some $46.332 million; Intensive Care of Infants was supported at a rate of $900,000 in some eight separate facilities; and programs for Children and Youth (C&Y) were conducted in 59 facilities at a cost of $52.842 million in the same period. Each program is intended to accomplish different objectives, and each must be carefully appraised by matching its objectives against its accomplishments. The M&I and C&Y programs were aimed specifically, for example, at urban slum areas and brought medical treatment services to thousands of mothers and children who otherwise would not have benefited. In the most general sense, these programs have had some preventive impact on the total handicapped population, reducing to some extent the number of children who otherwise might have later been "handicapped." However there are problems in accounting for these programs in the context of an analysis of *services to the handicapped*.

These programs include a variety of activities and services related to the health of handicapped and nonhandicapped preschool and school-aged children (e.g., vision and hearing screening and rubella immunization campaigns). During FY 1972, over 300,000 mothers received maternity nursing services, but we cannot say how many of these women actually bore handicapped offspring, or more difficult yet, how many handicapped children were prevented as a result of these nursing visits. Mental retardation clinics served 57,000 children, but over 2 million youth in the United States are retarded. PKU screening was given to 9 of 10 live births in FY 1972, some number of PKU children were detected, and remedial treatments were begun. Although data are not available, these programs undoubtedly had many beneficial impacts, although how far-reaching is unknown. It may be because a carefully documented case for their effectiveness is not easily made, among a host of other explicit reasons, that they have been the target of much federal interest as possible candidates for special revenue sharing.

Medicaid

Medicaid reached some 8.3 million youth aged 0–21, with medical services in FY 1971 at a total dollar cost of $5939 million. Eligibility for these funds and services is determined according to the family's financial need in addition to the child's medical needs. Available data do not show how many of what kinds and degrees of handicaps are truly represented in these totals. To arrive at wholly reliable data on the handicapped youth served by Medicaid would require a case-by-case investigation and reconstruction and, even at that, there would still be problems because of the ways certain types of handicaps have been noted for the record; e.g., in some states, social workers, not mental retardation specialists, determine whether or not a youth is mentally retarded. Without better data, we utilized data on the proportion of the U.S. population under age 22 that is handicapped to make order of magnitude estimates of the handicapped served by Medicaid. We estimate that some 1 million children were both Medicaid recipients and handicapped in FY 1971; in dollar terms, this amounts to $105 million for the federal share, and $186 million total, including the state shares. One noteworthy feature of this program is the provision for mandatory, early, and periodic screening, diagnosis, and treatment of all Medicaid-eligible children.

Other Public Health Services

There are other public health-related services supported with federal resources that relate to children generally and therefore have some hard-to-estimate effects on handicapped children as well. We summarize several formula and grant programs designed to provide comprehensive and improved local health care; e.g., "Hill-Burton" construction programs, health services development projects, dental care and screening, and several community service activities. Because the objectives of some of these programs are, to varying degrees, vague and rationalized in humanitarian terms, it is difficult to assess to what degree certain of these individual programs have accomplished their objectives. Examples of Veterans Administration, Defense, and other efforts that relate to health services for handicapped children are noted, not because the number of children or size of resources expended are large, but because the existence of these programs illustrates how fragmented health services to handicapped children are.

Basic Observations

Our basic observations about federal and state health programs for handicapped children follow:

- The provision of services is fragmented in this system, composed as it is of a melange of organized public, quasi-public, voluntary, and private agencies. There is little effective organized cooperation at the federal level; there is at best haphazard orchestration of services at the local and state level; and there is no systematic means by which relative service priorities and performance are being assessed.
- Evaluation and monitoring of program performance are not systematically or routinely done, and any coherent data base for these purposes is notable (with only minor exceptions) mostly by its absence.
- *Inequity* of service exists as measured and estimated along a variety of dimensions. However, *inadequacy* of service provision does *not* appear to be as great a problem as in other service areas. The rich have excellent medical services if they are willing to search them out and pay for them; and the poor, due mainly to the Medicaid and Crippled Children's programs, do have an institutional mechanism to which they can appeal for medical

assistance for their handicapped children. The mere existence of services says nothing, however, about differences in the quality of those services.
- Most medical programs are *not* aimed primarily at handicapped children but are distinctly oriented to provide general health services.

ROLES AND GOALS

There is a striking contrast between MCHS and CCS program operations when considered from the perspective of our four federal institutional models. Superficially, both appear in practice to be examples of Model III, Special Revenue Sharing; however, the big difference is the Plus factor. To oversimplify somewhat, MCHS, particularly the formula grant portion of it, is operating without much of the evaluation and control Plus, but CCS programs have partially structured the Plus factor into their operations in a number of interesting ways. For CCS the decisive factor includes strong elements of professional medical control; i.e., the insertion of professional norms and incentives by virtue of the proportion of doctors who actually operate CCS programs, the requirement for board certification of specialists who provide CCS services, and the locally exercised option of not honoring services provided in substandard or overpriced facilities. The primitive data elements needed to carry out rigorous and routine aggregate and more specific state and local program assessments exist in a common format and could be used to far greater advantage than they have been in the past. If such *were* done, a better approximation of our Plus concept and model would result.

Our models concept has indicated what appears to be a critical structural difference between effective and not-so-effective collections of programs. In fact, we note that as of March 1973, Pennsylvania has recognized this distinction and capitalized on the Plus features of CCS by collapsing all MCHS activities into CCS, thereby capturing some scalar economies in administrative overheads as well as a better measure of control.

Functions performed under MCHS and CCS auspices include investments in facilities and services (especially for various MCHS programs), some slight direct service provision (special clinics for mentally retarded children provided under the 1967 "Child Health Act"), and an only partly realized potential for data collection and accountability (CCS almost exclusively). The prime function is making grants so that the states might provide the services themselves, and this is rationalized in terms of the familiar balance wheel or redistribution argument.

Besides the redistributive rationale, which is far and away the most persuasive explanation for both programs, MCHS has some elements of internalizing externalities underlying its existence, particularly as pertains to screening for vision, hearing, and PKU, and to providing immunizations—general services in which the "whole population benefits" argument is salient.

In terms of the process categories of policy invention, execution, and so forth, we must separate our discussion of the two basic programs.

For MCHS, it is clear that the estimation, implementation, evaluation, and termination phases have been ill-developed or underdeveloped. Under implementation, what for instance happened to the 10 million or so children who received visual screenings under MCHS auspices in 1972, especially those who were found to have defective vision? Were follow-up and treatment services provided to those in need? Did anyone keep track of the potential users of medical services to see that they received what they required? If other disorders were suspected at the time of visual screening, were the appropriate consultative services and treatments arranged? Deficient implementation in this regard could easily result from the fragmented nature of the services actually provided. Termination has been largely overlooked; and without any routine determination and evaluation of the applicability and efficiency of MCHS programs, termination cannot be given well-reasoned consideration.

CCS programs are generally well implemented and well estimated (i.e., state directors have a fairly good "sense" of the size of the served populations and what it is costing them to provide services). The primary areas requiring attention are evaluation and termination, and a beginning has been made to carry out evaluations based on comprehensive and common data collected in all the states. Termination or reduction in service, such as it is, is carried out at at the state level in response to fluctuating demand for services by children having various disorders and financial requirements. There is no standardized pattern of termination or reduction of service provision from state to state, a fact that has led to incredible variations and inconsistencies regarding kinds of disease and levels of family financial capacity that will be covered, factors which change during the fiscal year as funds are either in ample or scarce supply. Termination or reduction in services then is a fluctuating, capricious activity exercised entirely at the state level.

Medical services represent a mix of models, functions, rationales, and processes, and cannot be adequately described as a single, collective entity. Considering Medicaid, for instance, we see an example of a group of services that approximates our Controllership model, where the prime function is the delegation of service delivery to the states and localities but where most resources, policy/program control, and innovative and stimulative functions derive from the federal level. These functions have been rationalized basically according to redistribution of resources and welfare arguments. In policy or process terms, there is little evidence that detailed scientific estimation was ever done to determine just how many handicapped individuals at what cost would be eligible for services. Implementation has not been particularly successful because of coordination problems, inflexible eligibility categories, and other conflicts at the local level of service delivery. It is nearly impossible to evaluate the specific impact of Medicaid on handicapped children because relevant information is collected according to welfare interests and not according to the medical needs of the served population. There are even some questions about evaluating Medicaid as a more general purpose program, an issue attested to by frequent U.S. General Accounting Office probings of specific activities and by the demands that resulted in constructing a new Medicaid Management Information System for the program.

MEDICAL SERVICE PROGRAMS

Maternal and Child Health Service

Background Amendments to the "Social Security Act of 1935" authorized grants to the states for maternal and child health and for health services to crippled children. Demonstration projects were also enabled in the basic 1935 legislation.[1] The fundamental concerns of the Maternal and Child Health Service are roughly characterized as preventive health services, child health supervision, and the fostering of good parent-child relations. Thus, most MCHS funds are not expended on handicapped youth, but rather on ways that may promote health and prevent physical or mental handicaps.

In 1965, amendments to the "Social Security Act" provided project grants to train professionals in Crippled Children's Services and for

---

[1]Title V, Section 501 of the Social Security Act funds the states to provide services for reducing infant mortality and otherwise promoting the health of mothers and children. It also provides the following for crippled children or those who are suffering from conditions leading to crippling: services for locating such children, and for medical, surgical, corrective, and other services, as well as care and aftercare and facilities for diagnosis and hospitalization. A basic source document is U.S. Department of Health, Education, and Welfare, *Maternal and Child Health Services of State and Local Health Departments,* MCHS Statistical Series No. 2, 1971 (hereafter referred to as MCHS Statistical Series No. 2).

so-called "Children and Youth Projects"—comprehensive health services for children in high-density, low-income areas.[2]

The "Child Health Act of 1967", once again amending the basic "Social Security Act", moved the MCHS further into preventive services (prenatal care, PKU, malnutrition, rubella, etc.), family planning, more comprehensive health services for preschoolers, and identification programs. The total current program's services include maternity, medical clinics, (public health) maternity nurses visitations, classes for expectant parents, well-baby clinics, pediatric clinics, school health programs, dental care for children and pregnant women, and immunizations against preventable diseases. The act also provides for special clinics for mentally retarded children. These clinics, established by a number of states, provide for diagnostic, evaluation, counseling, treatment, and follow-up services. In addition, a proportion of the annual budget is set aside for special projects in support of mentally retarded children.

Budget The FY 1972 MCHS total budget of $238.714 million is broken down in Table 9.4. About 2.5 percent went for research, and 6.3 percent was earmarked for personnel training. Ninety percent of the funds were divided about equally between state grants and project grants. The descriptions and comments in these subsections apply to

[2]William M. Schmidt, "Public Health: Then and Now," *American Journal of Public Health,* Vol. 63, No. 5, May 1973, pp. 419–427, for a historical overview of child health programs in the United States.

Table 9.4
MATERNAL AND CHILD HEALTH SERVICE, FY 1972 BUDGET

Type of Service	*Expenditures*
Grants to states	
Maternal and Child Health Service	$ 59,250,000
Crippled Children's Service	62,272,000
Project grants	
Maternity and infant care	43,428,000
Children and youth	47,400,000
Dental health of children	1,180,000
Training of service personnel	15,071,000
Research	6,035,000
Direct operational costs of MCHS	4,078,000
Total	$238,714,000

SOURCE: U.S. Department of Health, Education and Welfare, *Justifications of Appropriation Estimates for Committee on Appropriations—FY 1973,* Vol. I, pp. 223–235.

all of the MCHS programs *except* the Crippled Children's Service state grant program, which is discussed separately.

Service Description   Maternal and Child Health Service activities have a vast diversity of program objectives. To promulgate a policy as broad as "reducing infant mortality and otherwise promoting the health of mothers and children"[3] is literally to champion "motherhood." Problems arise in trying to identify programs that are effective in realizing these vague policy objectives. Programs actually undertaken by individual states are numerous and diverse, and generally so dilute the limited available resources that they lose the leverage to mount a concerted effort on a manageable subset of mother and child health problems.

For instance, about 334,000 mothers received services under the Maternity Medical Clinic program in 1971, but this accounts for less than 9 percent of all live births in the United States; expectant parent classes were offered by most of the states, but only 87,760 individuals attended them nationwide in 1970; general pediatric clinics provided services to around 200,000 children in 1970, but this represents only some 0.2 percent of the total population who might have benefited from these services.[4]

Let us consider some of the larger classes of MCHS services in more detail.

Support, in whole or part, is given to more than 150 mental retardation clinics to provide diagnosis, evaluation, and the development of a treatment and management plan for the individual child. In addition, 15 special clinics have been established for multiply handicapped children. While these clinics apparently are meeting some individual needs within that population, it is questionable whether these efforts are sufficient to the task. For example, it is estimated that there are roughly 2.5 million children under age 20 who are mentally retarded; however, the mental retardation clinics, a limited program, at best serviced only 57,000 children in 1971, and these services were mostly limited to diagnosis and counseling.[5]

Screening for the prevention of mental retardation because of phenylketonuria (PKU) has been a most successful MCHS undertaking. The tests are simple and inexpensive and in 1971 were adminis-

[3]MCHS Statistical Series No. 2, pp. 1–3, quote at p. 1.
[4]Ibid.
[5]Information on the mental retardation clinics is from U.S. Department of Health, Education, and Welfare, *Justifications of Appropriation Estimates for Committee on Appropriations—FY 1973*, Vol. I, p. 224 (hereafter referred to as *Justifications of Appropriation Estimates*).

tered to more than nine out of ten newborn children in the United States. It is estimated that this preventive program has discovered one PKU baby in every 16,000 live births, and discovery is the important first step in preventing PKU-caused retardation.

The children and youth project grants reached an estimated 400,000 children through 59 projects in 1971.[6]

Millions of children received basic immunizations under MCHS supported programs in FY 1971: smallpox, 1.087 million; pertussis, 1.633 million; tetanus, 2.137 million; polio, 2.204 million; measles, 1.257 million; and rubella, 3.783 million.[7]

Other services provided under MCHS sponsorship are noted in Table 9.5. Of specific interest are the screening programs for visual and hearing defects. Such services are provided with MCHS assistance. In FY 1971, screening programs conducted under the C&Y program found some 14,404 children with visual defects and 5800 children with hearing deficiencies.[8] Information on rates of referral and follow-up services for youth identified by this program is not generally available. Follow-up activities typically are weaker than those activities designed to identify handicapping conditions.

Table 9.5
EXAMPLES OF SERVICES PROVIDED WITH MCHS SUPPORT, 1971 AND 1973

Service	1971 Provisional	1973 Estimate
Mothers receiving prenatal and postpartum care in maternity clinics	334,000	400,000
Women receiving family planning services	752,000	752,000
Public health nursing visits to		
Mothers	566,000	566,000
Children	3,290,000	3,290,000
Children attending well child clinics	1,500,000	1,500,000
Children receiving screening tests for:		
Vision	8,977,000	10,000,000
Hearing	5,677,000	6,250,000

SOURCE: U.S. Department of Health, Education, and Welfare, *Justifications of Appropriation Estimates for Committee on Appropriations—FY 1973.* Vol. I. p. 225; for more detailed breakdowns, see also idem, *Maternal and Child Health Services of State and Local Health Departments,* MCHS Statistical Series No. 2, 1971.

[6]Secretary's Committee on Mental Retardation, *Mental Retardation Activities,* U.S. Department of Health, Education, and Welfare, January 1971.

[7]The MCHS Statistical Series No. 2; and U.S. Department of Health, Education, and Welfare, *Children Who Received Physician's Services Under the Crippled Children's Program,* MCHS Statistical Series No. 3, 1970.

[8]*Justifications of Appropriation Estimates,* p. 230.

Crippled Children's Service

Background   The "Social Security Act of 1935" also provided for federal aid to state Crippled Children's Services. Grants-in-aid are given to extend and improve services to crippled children and to those suffering from conditions that lead to crippling. The emphasis is on service to rural and economically depressed areas. Such services are provided as locating crippled children, providing medical, surgical, corrective, and other assistance for diagnosis, hospitalization, and post-hospitalization care. Special demonstration projects are also provided, as is a special contingency fund for mentally retarded programs.

The state share is determined according to a formula that takes into account the number of children under 21, the financial needs of the state (as determined by its per capita income), and the relative number of rural children in the state. States are required to match, on a dollar-for-dollar basis, one-half of the federal funds; but the other half, including funds for "special projects," is exempted from the matching requirement.[9]

Beginning in 1963, CCS began to open up to a wider range of disabilities by relaxing definitions and including additional services in the coverage. The program is now serving many types of handicapped children, not just the crippled. CCS funds have never been lavish, but the program has many excellent features, not the least of which is a fairly thorough reporting system.

According to state officials interviewed in a variety of different types of agencies, the Crippled Children's Services represent a particularly bright spot in services to handicapped children generally. We asked ourselves and those involved in administering the program what it was about CCS that made it appear to be relatively successful. The answers suggested were as follows:[10]

- Medical and other health specialists are used routinely for consultation.

[9]For additional details, see U.S. Department of Health, Education, and Welfare, *Health Services for Mothers and Children Under Title V, Social Security Act,* MCHS/PHS/DHEW; and Public Health Service, *Services for Crippled Children,* PHS Publication No. 2137.

[10]These generalizations were gleaned from direct interviews in five states and from a careful search through the Rand survey questionnaire responses. Specific references supporting many of these points are H. W. Porterfield, "A Physician Looks at the Crippled Children's Program," *Ohio's Health,* Vol. 23, No. 3, March 1971, pp. 21–24; and H. W. Wallace, R. Cohen, and R. Siffert, "Advisory Committees and Consultants in Programs for Crippled Children," *Public Health Report,* Vol. 83, August 1968, pp. 652–658.

- Medical and health specialists are used for patient care, and the physician-patient relationship is enhanced.
- High standards tend to be maintained through periodic evaluation by peer groups of individual physicians and of the institutions delivering the services and by advisory committees who consider the highest level policies for the program at the state level.
- The program is tailored by each state, is in touch with local needs, and responds flexibly to those needs.
- The program has evolved and is sensitive to changes in the character of the recipient population.
- The "nonpolitical" nature of the program means that it is neither subject to election year vicissitudes nor to general distaste shown by many physicians for welfare-based and oriented care, e.g., Title XIX medical care.
- There is a minimum of administrative overhead, and a maximum of acceptance by the medical community as one of its "own" programs.
- Monitoring and evaluation in terms of requirements for a minimum of comprehensive operational data collection are evident (but not well utilized generally in terms of rigorous analyses and evaluation follow-through).

The concept of "medical care" has been interpreted in the broadest possible sense, as the CCS program has evolved since 1935, to the point where the programs may include nearly all categories of long-term or chronic illness as well as most services that reasonably might be expected to improve the individual's health condition.

According to one recent assessment,[11] the use of medical advisory committees is one keystone feature of the CCS program, and most CCS directors used this method to guide the planning and administration of their program. Additionally, planning for the total needs of the individual handicapped child is a hallmark function of the CCS program.[12]

Number and Character of the CCS Population Table 9.6 shows the number and rate of children receiving physician services (the most prevalent service provided under CCS) for 1950, 1960, and 1970. As compared with the estimated total number of handicapped children in the United States—over 9 million in 1971—the half-million served

[11]Wallace, Cohen, and Siffert, op. cit.

[12]In our interviews with CCS officials in Illinois and California, we learned, for example, that private physicians in all states often use the CCS planning function on behalf of patients and their families who receive no other assistance from the government; that is, the planning and diagnosis functions or services are important and used even by those who in all other respects are able to provide for their children's needs.

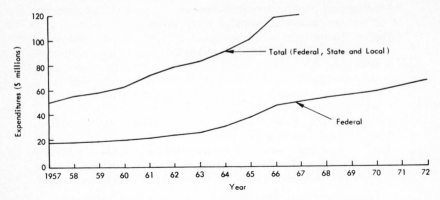

Fig. 9.1   Growth in expenditures for Crippled Children's Services.

SOURCE: James W. Moss, *Background Paper on Special Programs for Handicapped Children and Youth for the 1970 White House Conference on Children and Youth,* U.S. Department of Health, Education, and Welfare, Office of Education, BEH, December 1970; and U.S. Department of Health, Education, and Welfare, *Justifications of Appropriation Estimates for Committee on Appropriations.*

yearly is not a particularly large proportion; however, the program more than doubled in the two decades. The total federal share of this program has increased in the 1960–1972 period from about $19.5 million to $62.272 million. The amount of the state contribution to match federal funds is $31.136 million. Figure 9.1 shows the relative contributions to CCS from states and localities and federal sources over the period.

Data on the number served are reported in Table 9.7 by age, sex, and race. Note that this program is reaching significant numbers of children under age 5, unlike most other programs for handicapped

Table 9.6
NUMBER AND RATE OF CHILDREN RECEIVING PHYSICIAN SERVICES:
1950, 1960, 1970

Year	Number of Children Served	Rate per 1000 Population[a]
1950	214,405	4.0
1960	354,883	4.9
1970	491,855	6.1

SOURCE: U.S. Department of Health, Education and Welfare, *Children Who Received Physician's Services Under the Crippled Children's Program, FY 1970,* MCHS Statistical Series No. 3, December 1971, p. 7.

[a] Number served per 1000 population under 21 years of age.

Table 9.7
AGE, SEX, AND RACE OF CHILDREN RECEIVING PHYSICIAN SERVICES, 1970

Characteristic	Number 1970[a]	Percent 1970[a]
Age	491,855	100.00
<1	18,937	3.8
1–4	126,461	25.7
5–9	148,125	30.1
10–14	112,595	22.9
15–17	51,220	10.4
18–20	32,153	6.5
Unknown	2,364	0.6
Sex	491,855	100.0
Male	267,509	54.4
Female	224,003	45.5
Unreported	343	0.1
Race	491,855	100.0
White	328,537	66.8
All others	117,990	24.0
Unreported	45,328	9.2

SOURCE: U.S. Department of Health, Education, and Welfare, *Children Who Received Physician's Services Under the Crippled Children's Program, FY 1970,* MCHS Statistical Series No. 3, December 1971, p. 9.
[a] California estimated.

youth. At a maximum of 75 percent, the relatively low proportion of whites (as compared with their numbers in the general population) indicates that a CCS program objective to reach the economically disadvantaged may in fact be partly realized.

Handicapping Conditions As shown in Table 9.8, three general classes of disease account for about 70 percent of all reported conditions in the current CCS caseload. The total number of reported conditions (613,023) exceeds the total number of children served (491,855) by an amount roughly approximating the number of multiply handicapped children in the CCS population. It is a rough approximation because we do not know how many children have more than one handicapping condition, more than two, and so on.

Large variations exist on a state-by-state basis, as compared with national averages of impairment covered, the extent of multiple handicapping reported, and resources expended per recipient. For example, as contrasted with the national percentage breakdowns for the top three disease classes, Wisconsin reported that 39.6 percent of its caseload was concerned with diseases of the nervous system and sense organs, but the figure for Kansas was only 8.3 percent.

Table 9.8

NUMBER OF CONDITIONS IN CHILDREN SERVED BY DIAGNOSTIC CLASS, 1970

International Classification of Disease	Number	Percent of Total
Infective and parasitic diseases	12,016	1.9
Neoplasms	8,265	1.3
Allergic, endocrine system, metabolic and nutritional diseases	6,649	1.0
Diseases of blood and blood-forming organs	2,399	0.3
Mental, psychoneurotic and personality disorders	28,013	4.5
Diseases of nervous system and sense organs	148,413	24.2
Diseases of the circulatory system	13,099	2.1
Diseases of the respiratory system	6,083	0.9
Diseases of the digestive system	20,025	3.2
Diseases of the genito-urinary system	4,474	0.7
Deliveries and complications of pregnancy, childbirth, and puerperium	405	0.0
Diseases of the skin and cellular tissue	2.952	0.4
Diseases of the bones and organs of movement	154,854	25.2
Congenital malformations	125,510	20.4
Certain diseases of early infancy	5,238	0.8
Symptoms, senility, and ill-defined conditions	11,373	1.8
Accidents, poisonings, and violence	21,015	3.4
Provisional or deferred diagnosis	12,207	1.9
Examination made, no abnormality reported	30,033	4.8
Total[a]	613,023	100.0

SOURCE: U.S. Department of Health, Education, and Welfare, *Children Who Received Physician's Services under the Crippled Children's Program, FY 1970,* MCHS Statistical Series No. 3, December 1971, p. 18.

[a] Excludes information for the state of Maine.

Table 9.9 presents the CCS caseload for hearing and vision handicaps. Of the 491,855 reported to the receiving services under CCS, some 13.4 percent, or 82,144, were reported as having some sort of aural or visual impairment. We consider this a conservative estimate based on our observation about the wide variation in reporting of multiple handicapped children on a state-by-state basis.

Budget Grant allocations for the various states for FY 1971 and 1973 again reveal major state-by-state variation. In fact, on a raw per capita basis of total state population aged 0–21, we see that federal expenditures range from a high in Alaska of $1.28 to a low in California of $0.31, as compared with a national average expenditure per young person of $0.69. When considering the per client federal expenditures for the CCS caseload on a state-by-state basis, the discrepancies are even more pronounced. The average per client expenditures range from $26.90 in Washington, D.C., to $249.17 in Ohio, as com-

Table 9.9
CCS CASELOAD OF AURAL AND VISUAL DISORDERS, 1970

Type of Disorder	Percent of Total CCS Caseload	Number of Conditions Treated	Estimated Size of Vision and Hearing Handicapped Population Aged 0–21, 1970
Aural			
Otitis media without mention of mastoiditis	2.7	17,139	
Mastoiditis	0.1	1,005	
Conductive hearing impairment	1.7	11,003	
Sensory-neural hearing impairment	2.0	12,833	
Other central nervous impairment resulting in hearing loss	0.1	791	
All other hearing impairments	1.1	6,835	
All other disorders of the ear and mastoid	0.5	3,331	
Congenital malformation of the ear	0.2	1,698	
Total aural disorders	8.4	51,493	490,000
Visual			
Refractive errors	1.3	8,519	
Strabismus	2.5	15,903	
Blindness	0.1	601	
All other eye disorders	0.8	5,147	
Congenital cataract	0.2	1,425	
Congenital ptosis (eye)	0.1	677	
Total visual disorders	5.0	30,651	193,000
Total aural and visual disorders	13.4	82,144	683,000

SOURCE: U.S. Department of Health, Education, and Welfare, *Children Who Received Physician's Services Under the Crippled Children's Program, FY 1970,* MCHS Statistical Series No. 3, December 1971, Tables 14 and 15, abstracted. Population estimates (last column) taken from Chap. 5.

pared with a national average of $117.76. CCS serves a small percentage of the handicapped youth aged 0–21 in each state; the percentage varies widely across states.[13] Why these variations exist is not clear, but they are related to differences in the relative wealth of the states and the number of live births in each per annum (the basic factors considered in the formula calculations) as well as to differences in the kinds and numbers of various disorders served, to the amount of service given to each individual, and to local market considerations for health services. On a state-by-state basis, it is extremely hard to believe that per capita or per client CCS expenditures are equitable.

[13]For detailed state-by-state data, see Chap. 8 of the Rand Corporation Report R-1220, op. cit.

Medicaid

Under Title XIX of the Social Security Act, as amended, medical payments are being made to some indeterminate number of handicapped children from financially needy families. FY 1971 federal expenditures were $3,373,865,665.[14] The total payments for vendor medical bills under the Title XIX program, including the state contribution, were $5,939,236,000 in FY 1971.[15] We note that this program is in a stage of rapid growth. Understanding of Medicaid is complicated to a considerable extent by the diversity of programs that the states offer.[16] The federal contribution in Medicaid varies from 50 to 83 percent based on a state's per capita income. While coverage must be given to all persons receiving income maintenance under the Social Security Act and children under 21 in families must be covered, the states may also cover "medically needy" persons who require financial assistance with medical bills but do not need income maintenance in general.[17]

Number Receiving Medicaid   An estimated 8.3 million different children under age 21 received assistance under Title XIX in the category of Medical Assistance in FY 1971.[14] We are unable to determine just what proportion of these totals is handicapped because information on the child's medical condition, i.e., the kind, extent, and degree of handicap, is not compiled from the individual's case files into basic state reports. Also, the transitory receipt of medical services makes it extremely difficult to account for who is in the program receiving what kinds of services at any particular time.

According to HEW's midmonth quarterly summary for May 1971,[18] both handicapped and nonhandicapped youth represented at least

[14]U.S. Congress, House, Hearings before a Subcommittee of the Committee on Appropriations, *Departments of Labor and Health, Education, and Welfare Appropriations for 1973—Part 5,* 92d Cong., 2d Sess., p. 316.

[15]U.S. Department of Health, Education, and Welfare, *Trend Report,* Social and Rehabilitation Service, DHEW Publication No. SRS 73-03101, October 6, 1972.

[16]U.S. Department of Health, Education, and Welfare, *Characteristics of State Medical Assistance Programs Under Title XIX of the Social Security Act,* 1970 ed. For example, only 17 states covered all financially needy individuals under age 21 in 1970.

[17]U.S. Congress, House, Hearings, loc. cit., p. 317. The 1972 amendments to the Social Security Act provided for Medicare protection to persons who have received Social Security disability benefits for at least two years. This provision will not only benefit disabled adults, but also disabled youth. The Social Security Administration will also assume responsibility for determining eligibility for Medicaid in conjunction with Supplemental Security Income disability determinations.

[18]U.S. Department of Health, Education, and Welfare, *Medical Assistance (Medicaid) Financed under Title XIX of the Social Security Act,* Social and Rehabilitation Service, DHEW Publication No. SRS 72-03150, October 27, 1971.

35.2 percent of the total Title XIX caseload and accounted for at least 23.7 percent of expenditures in May 1971, or about $138 million of the total $582.7 million. Lacking better data, we estimate that the number of handicapped children served by Medicaid is the same as the proportion of the U.S. population under age 22 who are handicapped.

We also assume, for lack of better data, that the expenditure per handicapped child is the same as that for all children in the Medicaid program. Thus we estimate that in FY 1971 Medicaid served 1.097 million handicapped children at a cost to the federal government of $105.548 million. Including costs to the states, the total is an estimated $185.803 million. Because handicapped youth in general need more medical services than normal youth, we view these estimates as the minimum amount of resources the program is using to serve the handicapped.

Federal-Level Program Assessments Interviews were conducted with officials in the responsible federal agencies (Medical Service Administration and Assistance Payments Administration of the Social and Rehabilitation Services), state agencies, and local agencies. What the most senior personnel in the Assistance Payments Administration had to say about Medicaid seems worth summary comment.[19] One interesting observation had to do with the "last resort" nature of the Title XIX caseload. It was surmised that many handicapped children who find their way into the program have simply been "missed" by other agencies or by physicians who are not aware of alternative programs such as the Crippled Children's Service program. In some cases, however, the Medicaid program is the "only resort." The needs for individual level diagnosis and direction were stressed.

It was indicated that the states have so much diversity in the kinds of services provided, definitions of eligibility, and accounting systems used that it is practically impossible to sort out and keep track of the caseload. Most agreed that the delivery of this type of service should be done at the local and individual level; however, the accounting and evaluation aspects of this program were weak but are improved greatly by a newly designed Medicaid Management Information System that states can adopt.

Rarely do records of health services rendered accompany the child when he goes for services under Title XIX. Furthermore, it was asserted that these records are seldom obtained; rather a completely

---

[19]Interview, Assistant Payments Administration, U.S. Department of Health, Education, and Welfare, March 14, 1972.

new medical record work-up on each child is instituted. While we cannot estimate the costs involved with redundant rediagnosis and recertification, the existence of such apparently common practices is not in the best interests of either the child or the efficient execution of the services.

Federal officials were especially pleased that the 1967 Amendments provided that early and periodic screening, diagnosis, and treatment of Medicaid-eligible children be made a required aspect of Title XIX programs. However, compliance and full implementation of these provisions have been hard to attain from the states. Data accounting for total numbers of individuals screened, referral rates, disease incidence, and follow-up measures undertaken are beginning to be collected, but the results are incomplete. To the basic question, "How many children were screened under this program?" asked by the Medical Services Administration of SRS in January 1973, 26 states either did not reply or did not have implemented programs. Data on disease incidence were even more fragmentary and incomplete.[20]

Other Public Health Programs

A number of other health-related programs that must have at least some effect on handicapped children have been identified.

Comprehensive Health Care and Communicable Diseases   Three separate programs are known to emphasize comprehensive health care and the improvement of prevention services, both relevant to handicapped children. These are Communicable Disease Prevention and Control, Health Services Development—Project Grants, and Comprehensive Public Health Services—Formula Grants and Migrant Health Grants.

Headquartered in Atlanta in the Epidemiology Program of the Communicable Disease Center, the "Communicable Disease Prevention and Control"[21] program is responsible for national surveillance activities that in 1971 included reports on hepatitis, salmonellosis, influenza, and diphtheria. Besides direct observation, the FY 1972 expenditure of some $1.709 million provided for consultation, technical assistance, and training for each of the state health agencies.

Communicable Disease Control is also funded under Section 317 of the basic "Public Health Service Act," and some proportion of the

[20]Correspondence, Early and Periodic Screening Diagnosis and Treatment Program, Medical Services Administration, July 31, 1973. Signed by M. F. Abdalla, Program Analyst, Office of Program Planning and Evaluation. Data provided from same source.

[21]"Public Health Services Act," amended, sections 301, 311, 315, and 361–69.

$7.213 million of FY 1971 expenditures for a variety of immunization activities affected children.[22]

The concept of developing comprehensive health services at the local level has been embodied in the "Health Services Development—Project Grants"[23] program. New projects are developed and initially supported, some training is done, and priority has recently been given to constructing comprehensive health centers. Project grants are made to the states directly by the Division of Health Care Services of the Community Health Care Service in the Health Services and Mental Health Administration. In FY 1971 about $108 million was awarded in support of 43 comprehensive health service projects, including $30 million for 16 neighborhood health centers. Other projects funded in FY 1970 included $16 million for rubella immunization; $19.3 million for 27 comprehensive health service programs; $12.8 million for rat control; and $25.5 million for chronic disease programs.[24] Certainly some of these resources benefited handicapped children, but estimating just what proportion that might be is difficult. The rubella prevention program is the only one primarily and directly aimed at the problem of preventing handicapping conditions. For women contracting rubella in their first trimester of pregnancy, the chances of giving birth to a handicapped child are high: about a 15 percent chance of visual impairment; a 20 percent chance of hearing impairment; a 5 percent chance of both deafness and blindness; and a 5 percent chance of mental retardation or orthopedic impairment.[25]

The "Comprehensive Public Health Services—Formula Grants"[26] program monitored by the Office of Program Planning and Analysis of the Community Health Service granted on the order of $90 million in FY 1971 to the states for a wide variety of innovative and developmental services. The program gave some preference to services for "high risk" populations, including the poor. It is impossible to determine what fraction of the basic line goes to handicapped children, although some of it obviously does.

The Division of Health Care Services of Community Health Services, HSMHA, is also responsible for the "Migrant Health Grants"

[22]Additionally, some $16 million was expended for venereal disease control under provisions of this program. *Catalog of Federal Domestic Assistance,* Update, Office of Manpower and Budget, November 1972. p. 186.1.

[23]PHS, Title III, Sec. 314(e), amended; P.L. 89-749; P.L. 90-174; and P.L. 91-515.

[24]*Catalog of Federal Domestic Assistance,* p. 156.

[25]D. E. Hicks, "Comparison Profiles of Rubella and Non-rubella Deaf Children," *American Annals of the Deaf,* Vol. 115, pp. 86–92, March 1970. See also, D. Calvert, *Report on Rubella and Handicapped Children,* U.S. Department of Health, Education, and Welfare, May 1969, pp. 1–6.

[26]PHS Act, Title III, Section 314(d), amended.

program[27] for improving the "health status of migratory seasonal workers and their families to that of the general population."[28] Some proportion of the FY 1971 expenditures of about $14.0 million benefited the children of migratory workers through organized family health clinics. How many of those children are handicapped or how many handicapping conditions were prevented as a result of those services is not known.

Construction   The so-called "Hill-Burton Program"[29] is one of the largest single federal sources of construction funds. Its stated objective has been to provide hospitals, public health centers, laboratories, outpatient facilities, emergency rooms, neighborhood health centers, long-term care centers, rehabilitation facilities, and related health facilities. It has been, in effect, the omnibus hospital construction legislation. In this role, in FY 1971, some 450 separate projects providing around 10,000 new or modernized beds at a cost of $172 million were undertaken. Handicapped children benefited certainly, but there is little reasonable basis for estimating what fraction of Hill-Burton money is directly attributable to this class of individuals.

Dental Health[30]   A 1969 amendment to the "Social Security Act" was designed to promote the dental health of preschool and school-aged children, particularly in low-income areas; $860,000 in grants were made to the state health departments in FY 1972. The program has been in operation only a very short period and has stressed prevention and identification of dental conditions. Some training of paraprofessional personnel has been undertaken, and funds for direct service (i.e. treatment) have also been made available.

Veterans Administration   The VA runs a program for handicapped children of veterans. Chapter 35 of the basic enabling legislation provides "Restorative Training" for the wives, widows, and dependents of those who have suffered service-connected disabilities.[31] It is especially Part 5 of Chapter 35 that allows the VA to aid damaged, handicapped, and congenitally malformed children.

The VA has commendable provisions to inform these children that

[27]P.L. 90-574, P.L. 91-209, and 42 U.S.C. 242h.

[28]*Catalog of Federal Domestic Assistance,* p. 173.

[29]PHS Act, Title VI; P.L. 88-443 and P.L. 91-296.

[30]Social Security Act, amended, Title V, Section 510; P.L. 90-248. *Health and Services for Mothers and Children Under Title V, Social Security Act,* 1969.

[31]Title 38 U.S.C., Chapters 31, 34, 35, and 36 are the relevant pieces of legislation that have enabled the VA to serve handicapped children. See particularly Chap. 35.

they might receive services. When the eligible child reaches age 13, a letter is sent to the parent or guardian informing him or her of the benefits available under the code. The VA Regional Offices serve as the points of contact and provide diagnostic and rehabilitation services in the main. "Damaged" children begin receiving benefits at age 14, and it was "estimated" by officials in the VA's Rehabilitation and Educational Services Division that some 200,000 children had received or were presently receiving such services.[32] The program is designed to diagnose and then rehabilitate the child; occupational objectives are foremost in the program.

In 1972, the VA's Prosthetics and Sensory Aids Division was providing eligible children with audiological diagnoses in some 35 clinics spread over the country, and hearing aids were being fitted and evaluated if needed. Services for blind, eligible children were primarily given through three VA Hospitals (Palo Alto, New Haven, and Hines-Chicago); prosthetics are available from some 20 specialized centers throughout the country.[33]

We were unable to obtain detailed population data on these children beyond the approximation of the total number who were receiving services of all varieties. Nor could we obtain any specific cost breakdowns.

Department of Defense   Under provisions of P.L. 89-614, September 1966, the "Dependent's Medical Care Act," health care benefits for dependents of servicemen are provided if the dependents are severely mentally retarded or have a serious physical handicap. According to a deductible schedule based on the service member's rank and pay, the law provides for up to $350 per month for diagnosis, inpatient, outpatient, and home teatment, training, rehabilitation, and special education, institutional care in public and private nonprofit institutions, and transportation to and from these facilities. The program is small compared with the mainline agencies and programs that we concentrate on, but it is indicative of the fragmentation that exists among divisions of the federal government. An ongoing and proper accounting of children served under this and other highly specialized programs is clearly a federal task, but no one has yet taken up the task of collecting the data centrally or in any way that would lend itself to analysis and programmatic evaluation.

[32]Interview, Division of Rehabilitation and Educational Services, Veterans Administration, August 8, 1972.

[33]Interview, Division of Prosthetic and Sensory Aids, Veterans Administration, August 9, 1972. Work includes the evaluation of laser cane systems and reading devices for the blind as well as hardware for orthopedic handicaps.

Department of Interior/Department of Health, Education, and Welfare The Bureau of Indian Affairs of the Department of Interior transferred its responsibility for providing health services to the Indian Health Service in Health Services and Mental Health Administration of DHEW.[34] The program provides some 51 Public Health Service Indian Hospitals, 79 health centers and school health centers, over 300 other health stations, and contracts for services arrangements with private and community hospitals. Eligibility is extended to the nearly one-half million "American Indian and Alaska Natives," as determined by proximity to a reservation or by community recognition and self-identification as "Indian." Some proportion of the FY 1972 total expenditure of $154 million[35] benefits handicapped Indian children.

RESEARCH: THE NATIONAL INSTITUTES OF HEALTH

The nature of the research performed by the National Institutes of Health (NIH), makes it extremely difficult to measure the effects of specific programs on the health and welfare of handicapped children. We indicate child-specific research aimed at reducing the incidence of handicaps in general, which, of course, must also reduce handicaps among the young. The reader is warned, however, that our inclusion and exclusion of various items as child-specific research are judgmental. These items may or may not correspond to lists drawn up by people in the member institutes, by officials in the Department of Health, Education, and Welfare, or by other observers.

This section describes the NIH programs most directly relevant to handicapped youth. It is also difficult to estimate the dollars that accrue directly to handicapped children and flow through these member institutes. With the single exception of the National Institute of Child Health and Human Development (NICHD), the research is usually not child-specific, but disease-specific, and hence difficult to associate with population subgroups. Nevertheless, we have conservatively estimated that some $60 to $65 million of NIH research could be *directly* associated with handicapped children. The bulk of this amount comes from NICHD and the National Institute of General Medical Services (NIGMS). The following subsections, which are devoted to program descriptions, discuss this total estimate. The NIH expenditures on research for and about handicapped children are considerable, compared with the special education and vocational rehabilitation research expenditures of $17 million and $7 million, respectively.

[34]42 U.S.C. 2001–2004a.
[35]*Catalog of Federal Domestic Assistance,* p. 157.

The NIH present a clear example of our Catalytic model. While concentrating primarily on the innovative and stimulative features of research, NIH also provide some direct investments in facilities (e.g., genetic research and trauma centers). These functions are rationalized by (1) information brokerage arguments, (2) the importance of acquiring research economies of scale (both of talent and supporting capital investments), (3) the linking of research with professional channels of communication in order to evaluate and disseminate new knowledge, and (4) arguments that emphasize making known the general beneficial nature of the NIH work to citizens in every state.

The NICHD and NIGMS contribute the largest share of research directly aimed at reducing the diseases and disorders of handicapped children. In NICHD, the program most closely concerned with handicapped children is in mental retardation, while NIGMS has concentrated a large portion of its effort on genetic diseases and trauma research. Other basic research efforts include:

- Sensory-neural studies under the auspices of the National Institute for Neurological Diseases and Stroke (NINDS).
- Studies of congenital and developmental abnormalities and more specific diseases of the eye by the National Eye Institute (NEI).
- Cleft lip and palate work by the National Institute of Dental Research (NIDR).
- Heart and lung studies, including the development of improved surgical and prosthetic equipment, by the National Heart and Lung Institute (NHLI).
- Studies of allergic, immunological, and infectious diseases, including venereal disease and other bacteriological and viral infections, by the National Institute of Allergy and Infectious Disease (NIAID).
- Research on chronic renal failure and inherited diseases of metabolism, by the National Institute of Arthritis, Metabolic, and Digestive Diseases (NIAMDD).

NIH programs do produce results; but given the unpredictable nature of research, it is very hard to calculate many direct and immediate payoffs from the work. In summary, our main observations are that:

- A very small fraction of the NIH health research is handicapped-child specific.
- Of research on handicapped youth for all services, the NIH medical contribution is by far the largest.

National Institute of Child Health and Human Development (NICHD)

The NICHD, like the other NIH institutes, makes grants available to research organizations, hospitals, health departments, institutions of higher education, and other nonprofit organizations primarily for basic research and research training. The institute also supports research through the contract mechanism. The five major programs of the institute are (1) perinatal biology and infant mortality, (2) growth and development, (3) mental retardation, (4) population and reproduction, and (5) adult development and aging. The first three deal directly with child health.

In FY 1972, nearly $50 million was awarded in grants and contracts in the Child Health programs of NICHD, as shown in Table 9.10, and an additional $6 million was spent on intramural research, conferences, scientific information dissemination, and other direct operations. The number of grant applications received annually has been increasing rapidly, with the result that NICHD has been able to support a diminishing proportion of those who apply each year.[36]

Of the three NICHD programs directly concerned with child health, the greatest emphasis on handicapped youth is found in the Mental Retardation program. Its primary mission is to develop and support research aimed at preventing mental retardation, and when this is not possible, to ameliorate its effects. In FY 1972, the NICHD investment in mental retardation grants and contracts totaled $19 million. A major aspect of the program has been the development and implementation of 12 Mental Retardation Research Centers, authorized by Congress in 1963. All are now operational. Core support for their administration, facilities, and program planning was $5.86 million in FY 1972. In addition to the core grants, research and training grants in these centers support more than 600 investigators from a broad range of basic, clinical, and applied sciences. They provide a resource for multidisciplinary and collaborative research between biomedical and behavioral scientists to better understand the complex causes, pathogenesis, and modes of prevention, treatment, and amelioration of mental retardation.

Although the main emphasis in the Growth and Development and the Perinatal Biology and Infant Mortality programs is on the normal development of infants and children, much of the research supported by both programs provides basic knowledge that is ultimately

[36]Letter from L. Freedman, Chief, Program Statistics and Analysis Branch, NICHD, to G. Brewer, The Rand Corporation, June 7, 1973.

Table 9.10
NATIONAL INSTITUTE OF CHILD HEALTH AND HUMAN DEVELOPMENT: GRANTS AND CONTRACTS IN CHILD HEALTH, FY 1972

Mechanism of Support	Total	Perinatal Biology and Infant Mortality	Growth and Development	Mental Retardation
A. Funds (in thousands)				
Research grants	$36,988	$10,321	$12,039	$14,628
Training grants	6,269	2,316	2,524	1,428
Fellowships	573	279	248	45
RCP awards[a]	1,931	632	895	404
Total grants	45,760	13,547	15,706	16,506
Contracts	4,020	510	1,191	2,318
Total grants and contracts	49,780	14,058	16,898	18,824
B. Number of Projects				
Research grants	551	224	228	99
Training grants	84	31	36	17
Fellowships	58	27	27	4
RCP awards[a]	80	26	37	17
Total grants	773	308	328	137
Contracts	34	10	8	16
Total grants and contracts	807	318	336	153

SOURCE: NICHD, Program Statistics and Analysis Branch, June 7, 1973.
[a] Research Career Program.

essential for the treatment or prevention of handicapping conditions. Both programs also support some research directly concerned with health problems that could result in permanent handicaps.

The Growth and Development program supports research in the mechanisms of biological growth, developmental immunology, developmental pharmacology, nutrition, physical growth, developmental behavioral biology, learning and cognitive development, human communication and personality, and social growth.

As an example of research in child growth and development, several longitudinal projects are under way to assess the severity and permanence of the effects of malnutrition on physical and mental development. Another example is research on learning disorders and dyslexia. To elucidate the processes involved, research is being conducted to increase knowledge of the developmental maturation of brain function. NICHD expenditures for grants and contracts for research training in child growth and development amounted to $17 million in FY 1972.

The Perinatal Biology and Infant Mortality program promotes a coordinated program of research and training that will enhance understanding of pregnancy and maternal health, embryonic development, fetal growth, and infant well-being through the first year of life. Efforts are directed toward reducing the country's infant mortality rate, ameliorating infant morbidity, and shortening the time lag between the production of new knowledge and its incorporation into health-care delivery. Some of this research directly bears on handicap prevention. Examples include research on the consequences of maternal complications during pregnancy, such as toxemia and diabetes, and on factors adversely affecting fetal development, such as malnutrition. Also relevant is research on neonate adaptation to postnatal life, including the problems engendered by such disorders as respiratory distress, hyperbilirubinemia, hypoglycemia, and erythroblastosis fetalis. In FY 1972, support for all programs in perinatal biology and infant mortality amounted to $14 million.

National Institute for Neurological Diseases and Stroke (NINDS)[37]

A major program area of research grant support is in the communicative disorders (hearing, language, and speech), amounting to approximately $10 million in FY 1973. A directed research program is also under way on communication disorders. Interesting features of the program include (1) the development of a means to test for hearing loss in early infancy, (2) studies of diseases connected with childhood hearing loss, (3) research to improve hearing aids generally, (4) research tracing the implications of high fever for hearing loss, and (5) investigations into the possibilities of developing other sensory channels when the "ordinary" ones become inoperative.

The perinatal research project in 14 collaborating institutions is studying neurological and sensory disorders in approximately 60,000 children. This project was funded at $7.5 million in FY 1973, and is directly concerned with caring for handicapped children who have cerebral palsy; congenital defects; brain damage; minimal brain dysfunction; mental retardation; and hearing, language, and speech defects.

Epilepsy has been a long-time interest of NINDS, and continuing work is in progress to determine better surgical and chemical means for treating and correcting it. A directed program of contract-support

[37]Interview, Dr. O. Malcolm Ray, Extra-Mural Programs, NINDS, March 15, 1972.

research is also under way in developing and field testing new anti-convulsant drugs. The epilepsy program was funded at approximately $4 million in FY 1973.

In its broad charter to study diseases of the nervous and sensory systems, NINDS is concentrating on the development of certain prostheses for the blind. Roughly categorized, this research is concerned with (1) the neurological pathways that produce sensations of sight, (2) determining how these pathways might be replicated or stimulated when they are not functioning naturally, and (3) surgical and chemical means for correcting deficiencies of these systems.

National Eye Institute (NEI)

Under Title IV, Part F of the "Public Health Service Act," the NEI had an estimated total research budget of $24.95 million in FY 1973. By category of disease, $6.2 million was devoted to the retina and choroid, $3.7 million to sensory motor disorders, $3.0 million to corneal diseases, $2.7 million to glaucoma, and approximately $530,000 to congenital and developmental abnormalities. The remaining bulk of the budget was spread rather widely among a number of other disease classes.[38]

The primary program emphasis of NEI is on basic research in anatomy and biochemistry of the eye. Being phased out are Model Reporting Area programs, which are voluntary state associations for the registry of the blind, on the grounds that they "are just not valid and they certainly are not very reliable."[39] It is hard to assess the child-specific portion of NEI's effort. At the least, $530,000 is being spent on congenital defects; determining the proportion of the more basic and general work that affects children depends on the assumptions one makes about the proportion of children in the total population who will not be afflicted as a result of research-based improvements in eye health.

National Institute of Dental Research (NIDR)

Cleft lip and cleft palate occur relatively frequently in the general population. NIDR estimates that between 6000 and 7000 children are born annually with cleft lip or palate, for whom corrective surgery and rehabilitative services total some $100 million per annum. NIDR support for research into cleft lip and palate and related malforma-

---

[38]U.S. Department of Health, Education, and Welfare, *Justifications of Appropriation Estimates for Committee on Appropriations—FY 1973,* Vol. IV, p. 146 (hereafter cited as *Justifications of Appropriation Estimates*).

[39]Interview, Staff of the Program Planning Division, NEI, March 16, 1972.

tions and disorders amounted to approximately $2 million in FY 1970.[40]

National Heart and Lung Institute (NHLI)

The Medical Applications Program of NHLI is concentrating some $10 million on devices to detect, prevent, and treat medically handicapping conditions of the heart and lung. For example, research and development is being financed for a heart-assist pump, improved oxygenation equipment to aid in open heart surgery, and artificial prosthetic devices to replace diseased and damaged portions of the heart. While the research is not child-specific, the equipment under development will be used in the care and treatment of many children with heart and lung disorders.

National Institute of Allergy and Infectious Diseases (NIAID)

NIAID supports work toward discovering methods for controlling allergic, immunological, and infectious disease problems. Major programs and centers for allergic diseases are in operation, but the number of children who are served and who benefit from these efforts is not readily estimable. General research into bacterial and staphylococcal infections is also under way with NIAID support, estimated at $1.795 million for FY 1973. Drug resistance mechanisms, venereal diseases, and viral infectious diseases are specifically considered in the NIAID budget, and the work doubtless helps reduce handicaps in children to some unknown extent. It is interesting to note that with venereal disease again reaching epidemic proportions among the nation's youth (as well as adults), the total budget for venereal disease research was only $500,000 in FY 1973.[41]

National Institute of Arthritis, Metabolic, and Digestive Diseases (NIAMDD)

The NIAMDD makes grants for a variety of research enterprises, several of which have some direct bearing on handicapped children and youth. For instance, NIAMDD supports work in orthopedics (mostly related to arthritic conditions), diabetes, and "other inherited diseases of metabolism," in which cystic fibrosis is the one most directly related to children, although a variety of diseases and syndromes are presently being studied with an eye to the development of preventive

[40]Memo from Mr. Bruce Carson to the Assistant Secretary for Health and Scientific Affairs, March 3, 1972.
[41]U.S. Department of Health, Education, and Welfare, *Justifications of Appropriation Estimates,* pp. 13–22.

techniques. Endocrinology, including digestive diseases and studies of nutrition, are also carried out under NIAMDD auspices.

Under the Kidney and Urologic Diseases segment of the NIAMDD budget, $10.162 million was earmarked for studies in FY 1973. Chronic renal diseases are classed with several other degenerative urological diseases, and all are being attacked; the total estimated research budget was $10.162 million in FY 1973. One child suffering from chronic renal failure requires, by a conservative estimate, about $25,000 per year to sustain life. This means that only 150 to 200 children can be supported for the same amount of money that the NIAMDD budget devoted to research on this problem. Or, put another way, it is surprising how little money is being spent on investigating the causes and cures of the disorder as compared with the large amounts that are being spent on its treatment.

National Institute of General Medical Sciences (NIGMS)

The programs of NIGMS are extremely varied, but its research on prevention and treatment of trauma, genetically caused handicaps, and improvements in anesthesiology applies directly to the population of handicapped children.

Beginning in 1971, the establishment of 12 genetic research and training centers, at an average cost of $600,000, was authorized in medical centers throughout the country. (Einstein College of Medicine in New York is one such center.) These centers are working in four broad program areas, including (1) the identification of carriers of genetic disease, (2) mapping of human chromosomes, (3) genetic control of the human cell, and (4) establishing a bank of human cell culture lines to enhance the practice of genetic medicine. NIGMS estimates that "one out of every 250 newborn babies has major chromosome defects that lead inevitably to mental retardation, sterility, or serious physical abnormalities."[42] Work for genetics and genetics centers was funded at a rate of $33.5 million in FY 1973.

The trauma program focuses on ways to minimize or prevent the crippling effects often found in victims of automobile accidents or those who are severely burned. It is estimated that trauma (primarily as a result of accidents) claims the lives of more children between the ages of 1 and 14 than the next six leading causes of death combined. Some fraction of the estimated total of $8.3 million in the FY 1973 Clinical Sciences budget went for trauma research and centers.

Another specific program within NIGMS's budget for General Clinical Sciences is directed toward improving procedures for help-

[42]Ibid., p. 61.

ing premature infants suffering from acute respiratory distress. The exact amount of this cannot be determined from the budget, but is something less than the total $2.17 million that was allocated for Anesthesiology and Diagnostic Radiology Centers taken together.[43] In total, the portion of the NIGMS's annual budget primarily relevant to handicapped youth is at least $33.5 million.

MEDICAL TREATMENT OF HEARING AND VISION DISORDERS

This section is a case study of the methods, costs, and efficacy of providing medical services for handicapped youth. Taking up vision and hearing disorders in turn, this section presents data on prevalence, descriptions of disorders, common methods of treatment, likelihood of successful treatment, and approximate costs.

Prevalence statistics are not currently available in sufficient detail or comprehensiveness to allow more than the most general assessment of needs in the population based on the etiology or cause of sensory impairment. For etiologies of eye disorders, the NIH-compiled "Model Reporting Area" data are probably the best available in terms of comprehensiveness. However, there are some serious weaknesses with these MRA data: they represent returns from only 16 states; the system is voluntary, with all the problems that entails for timely and reliable information collection; and the data are so gross that meaningful detailed disaggregation according to etiology, degree of handicap, and several other potentially important categories is not possible. Prevalence data on the etiology of hearing disorders are, if anything, even less useful; the national health surveys are prime sources of information, but they are not fully reliable, nor are the data presented in the most useful fashion.

Time-series information of sufficient reliability, coverage, and detail to be useful for policy purposes does not exist. If one conceives of the policymaking process, in one sense at least, as being responsive to changes in the needs and characteristics of a context, e.g., a target population,[44] a politically bounded setting, a problem or legislative area, then this absence of any longitudinal information from which timely signals about changes could be determined is distressing.

The descriptive information presented below about vision and hearing disorders was collected and summarized from numerous

---

[43]Ibid., pp. 61, 68.

[44]It has been pointed out that fundamental changes occur in the handicapped population, the result in part of improved medical treatment techniques. Ben E. Hoffmeyer, "The Multiple Handicapped Child: A Product of Improved Medical Care," *Medical Times,* August 1951, pp. 807–815.

sources, including medical texts, journal articles, interviews, and conference proceedings. This information is included to give the reader an idea of what the various handicapping disorders are, what causes them, what representative literature exists, and what some of the common methods of treatment involve. Lacking adequate data on prevalence by affection or etiology, we have been only slightly successful in suggesting which among the disorders are relatively more frequent, dangerous, and so forth. General comments about the likelihoods of success for any given treatment of choice are presented, but these assessments will not necessarily pertain in any particular case. Success of treatment varies with the patient's age, state of general health, degree of present impairment, etiology, timeliness and appropriateness of treatment, the skill of those administering the treatment, and a multitude of other factors. In fact, the success rates noted for various treatments are probably biased upward because they have been gleaned from interviews with practitioners in highly specialized, up-to-date, and highly respected practices and institutions. There is no certainty that a general practitioner with little specialized training and fewer specialized resources at his command will attain similar rates of success. Our basic question was of the following form: "If a patient with condition 'x' is treated with the best possible medical care available, what are the odds that the treatment will be successful?"

Widespread realization of these "optimal" success rates appears less related to marginal improvements in technique than to institutional changes that would result in making the appropriately specialized skills available to all of those who need them. Research and hoped-for breakthroughs, as for instance being able to successfully treat most sensorineural deafness,[45] will certainly result in spectacular and highly beneficial outcomes—when they occur; however, improvement in reducing the aggregate incidence of disability is currently possible simply by making the known procedures and technical skills more accessible to those in need. Our comments and recommendations regarding the identification and direction services (Chapters 7 and 8) are aimed at this issue.

A major problem with medical treatment for disorders capable of causing sensory handicaps in children is what we have termed the informational services. Treatment procedures exist to correct, stabilize, or alleviate a large number of the primary conditions causing

---

[45]See John R. Lindsay, "Profound Childhood Deafness: Inner Ear Pathology," *The Annals of Otology, Rhinology, and Laryngology,* Supplement No. 5, Vol. 82, March-April 1973.

handicapping. But if the child is not identified early enough, properly diagnosed, and then directed to competent medical treatment, the likelihood that a skilled ophthalmologist or otologist will be able to retrieve the situation is *greatly* diminished. Furthermore, the costs for such medical treatment are sometimes absolutely high but usually relatively low as compared with lifetime service costs associated with reduced sensory capacity. Magnificent technologies and highly skilled physicians exist, but the institutional mechanisms needed to ensure that the children in need get to these services either do not exist, or languish at a stage of inadequate development. *Without adequate identification and direction, the system is simply not achieving its potential.*

Presuming that the child has been identified, properly diagnosed, and well directed, important considerations must still be taken into account before medical treatment begins. No generally applicable comments can be made about these except to say that each must be seriously considered by the physician, the patient, and the patient's family and that the process is fundamentally unique to each case.

- What are the risks of complication from the proposed treatment? From diagnostic procedures?
- What are the dollar costs of tests and treatments? How much testing is "enough," given resource limitations? Time limitations? Should the patient's ability to pay enter into the medical decision, and if it does, what are the likely consequences for the patient's well-being? For the likelihood of cure? For long-term societal costs?
- What are the patient's general characteristics with respect to age, sex, and general health? How do any of these enter into the assessment of what should be done by way of recommending treatment?
- What are the possibilities for spontaneous change in the patient's condition? What might happen if nothing is done? If some action less than "total" medical intervention is taken? If total intervention is undertaken? Does one adopt a conservative or a more daring approach in the individual case? With what consequences? Who benefits from and who pays for those consequences?
- What are the patient's general feelings about the desirability of likely outcomes? What are the medical feelings? Societal feelings?
- How do considerations of malpractice suits enter into physician's calculations about various courses of treatment? What is the current "going rate" for various procedures and treatments?

- What is the orientation of the institution where the treatment will be administered? Is it a research facility where higher-risk procedures might be adopted? Is it a more conventional setting where "state of the art" talent and supporting resources are not so readily available?

This is a far from complete list, but it does give one a sense that the decision to pursue a course of medical treatment is far from automatic, even presuming that the disorder is well and properly diagnosed. These decisions are made in "real time" by the physician and patient.

Vision Disorders: Prevalence Data

Data on the prevalence of specific eye disorders causing vision impairment are not complete. Some of the most reliable detailed estimates are those reported for the "Model Reporting Area" (MRA) legal blindness prevalence rates. These data are compiled through the voluntary association of 16 states and represent about one-fifth of the total U.S. population.[46] However, these data are of limited value since legally blind youth are only a fraction of the visually handicapped population of concern to this study. Supplementary, but dated, information on age-specific details of the visual impaired population is contained in the National Society for the Prevention of Blindness "Fact Book."[47]

In spite of the questionable quality of the data, several gross features of that portion of the legally blind population reported in MRA statistics are worth noting. (See Tables 9.11, 9.12, and 9.13.) First, somewhere between 15 and 20 percent of the total have either "unknown," "undetermined," or "not specified" causes of blindness. Second, prenatal cataracts, retinal disease, and retrolental fibroplasia

[46]Harold A. Kahn and Helen B. Moorhead, *Statistics on Blindness in the Model Reporting Area, 1969–1970,* National Eye Institute, DHEW Publication No. (NIH) 73-427, Washington, D.C., 1973. States reporting in the MRA included: Connecticut, Georgia, Kansas, Louisiana, Massachusetts, New Hampshire, New Jersey, New Mexico, New York, North Carolina, Oregon, Rhode Island, South Dakota, Utah, Vermont, and Virginia.

[47]National Society for the Prevention of Blindness, *Estimated Statistics on Blindness and Vision Problems,* NSPB, New York, 1966; worldwide data of even less reliability are reported in Leonard T. Kurland et al., *Epidemiology of Neurologic and Sense Organ Disorders,* Harvard University Press, Cambridge, Massachusetts, 1973. Elizabeth Macfarlane Hatfield, "Blindness in Infants and Young Children," *Sight-Saving Review,* Vol. 42, No. 2, Summer 1972, pp. 69–89, has produced a detailed study of prevalence data collected on children aged 0 to 6 for the National Society for the Prevention of Blindness in a one-time survey. Hatfield's specific estimates differ somewhat from the MRA data but not sufficiently to change any of the following discussion.

account for the largest proportions of the reported total. (Each disorder is described in the next subsection.) And third, prenatal influence is far and away the most prevalent etiology class for those age 19 and under, with 57 percent of the total new additions to the registers of legally blind persons. (We caution that legally blind persons are a minority of the visually handicapped population, and other groups of visually handicapped persons will have different prevalences of etiologies.)

This prenatal influence class includes coloboma, absence of part or all of the eye; congenital cataracts; glaucoma; albinism; hereditary retinal degenerations; and other disorders described in the next section. Because little is known about the exact prenatal factors, how-

Table 9.11
ESTIMATED PREVALENCE OF LEGAL BLINDNESS BY SITE AND TYPE OF EYE AFFECTION, U.S., 1960 AND 1962

Site and Type of Affection	Number of Persons by Age, 1960			Number of Persons by Age, 1962		
	All Ages	Under Age 5	Ages 5–19	All Ages	Under Age 5	Ages 5–19
Eyeball						
Glaucoma	54,120	140	1,630	56,190	140	1,670
Myopia	20,980	210	1,700	21,770	220	1,740
Other	20,810	520	5,380	21,560	540	5,530
Total eyeball	95,910	870	8,710	99,520	900	8,940
Cornea	18,330	50	600	19,050	50	630
Lens						
Cataract	84,880	400	4,040	88,130	420	4,150
Other	1,630	30	210	1,690	30	220
Total lens	86,510	430	4,250	89,820	450	4,370
Uveal tract	19,120	110	1,670	19,840	110	1,720
Retina						
RLF[a]	12,610	600	11,930	12,710	370	12,060
Other	100,610	250	2,590	104,480	260	2,660
Total retina	113,220	850	14,520	117,190	630	14,720
Optic nerve	40,690	260	3,330	42,240	270	3,430
Vitreous	730	[b]	40	770	[b]	50
Undetermined and not specified	10,490	210	2,300	10,870	220	2,370
Total, all sites	385,000	2,780	35,420	399,300	2,630	36,230

SOURCE: National Society for the Prevention of Blindness, *Estimated Statistics on Blindness and Vison Problems*, NSPB, New York, 1966, p. 52, Table 14.

[a] Retrolental fibroplasia.

[b] No data or less than 5.

Table 9.12
AGE-SPECIFIC RATES OF PERSONS ON MRA REGISTERS, BY CAUSE, 14 STATES, DECEMBER 31, 1970
(Rate per 100,000)

Cause	All Ages	Under Age 5	Ages 5–19
Glaucoma	16.2	0.1	0.2
Myopia	4.3	0.1	2.4
Cornea or sclera	6.9	0.2	0.8
Cataract, total	19.2	1.9	6.4
Prenatal	5.7	1.9	6.0
Other	13.5	0.0	0.4
Uveitis	7.5	0.2	1.3
Retinal disease, total	36.6	1.0	6.0
Prenatal	10.5	0.8	4.2
Diabetic	6.9	0.0	0.0
Other	19.2	0.2	1.7
Retrolental fibroplasia	3.7	0.9	8.1
Optic nerve	13.5	1.4	5.3
Multiple afflictions	6.4	0.0	0.2
Other	15.9	3.7	12.7
Unknown	16.3	1.1	4.8
Total	146.5	10.5	48.3

SOURCE: Kahn and Moorhead, op. cit., p. 135.
NOTE: Table excludes New York and Massachusetts because of reporting difficulties for age specific data.

Table 9.13
PERCENTAGE DISTRIBUTION OF FIRST ADDITIONS TO REGISTERS BY ETIOLOGY CLASS, ACCORDING TO AGE: MRA, 1970

Etiology Class	All Ages	Under Age 5	Ages 5–19
Infectious disease	2.3	12.0	7.1
Injury or poisoning	3.6	8.9	5.1
Neoplasm	1.1	4.7	3.9
Diabetes	12.7	0.0	0.5
Senile degeneration	24.6	0.0	0.0
Vascular disease	2.6	0.0	0.0
Other general disease	1.4	3.6	1.5
Prenatal influence	14.4	56.8	57.4
Multiple etiologies	7.7	0.0	0.8
Unknown to science	12.3	0.0	3.4
Not reported or determined	17.4	14.1	20.4
Total	100.0	100.0	100.0

SOURCE: Kahn and Moorhead, op. cit., p. 75, Table 17d.

Table 9.14
NUMBER OF PERSONS ON MRA REGISTERS BY VISUAL ACUITY
AND AGE, AS OF DECEMBER 31, 1970

Acuity	All Ages	Under Age 5	Ages 5–19
Absolute blindness	10,518	126	1,397
Light perception	11,296	108	1,235
Light projection	1,114	8	103
Less than 5/200	15,891	29	786
5/200 to less than 10/200	9,674	10	576
10/200 to less than 20/200	15,757	19	1,190
20/200	22,449	17	2,399
Restricted field	7,218	0	234
Unknown	5,430	201	1,233
Total	99,347	518	9,153

SOURCE: Kahn and Moorhead, op. cit., p. 113, Table 27b.

ever, making even informed "guesses" about research priorities is basically impossible.

The need for identification procedures is supported by recognizing how poor are the existing data on causes, and by noting the low *reported* prevalence below age 5 compared with ages 5 to 19. We cannot overstress the need to do something about the nonexistent data upon which hundreds of millions of dollars of programs and policies are being "planned" and "evaluated," nor the need to deliver specialized medical treatment services to presently unidentified children under age 5.

Table 9.14 is a breakdown of the legally blind population by degrees of reported visual acuity.

Vision Disorders: Description and Medical Treatment

Some of the more common visual disorders affecting children are briefly sketched out in this section, including a brief discourse on common treatment methods. Also included is a general idea of the likelihoods of outcomes of treatment and attempts at prevention of the disorder. None of what follows is meant to be construed as definitive; on the contrary, our basic purpose is a merely descriptive orientation. The interested reader is strongly encouraged to consult one of the listed general sources for more detailed coverage.[48]

[48]A general, layman's account is contained in Bernard Seeman, *Your Sight: Folklore, Fact, and Common Sense,* Little, Brown, Boston, 1968. Among the large number of more technical treatments, we found the following to be of general use: Frank W. Newell, *Ophthalmology: Principles and Concepts,* The C. V. Mosby Company, St. Louis, 1969 ed.; and Philip P. Ellis, "Eye," in C. Henry Kempe et al., *Current Pediatric Diagnosis and Treatment,* Lange Medical Publications, Los Altos, California, 1972 ed., pp. 197–213.

Prevalence data on etiology are not sufficiently detailed to give one a very good idea about the relative rates of occurrence and expectations of a handicapping condition resulting from any given disorder, and the ordering of specific disorders in what follows thus does not represent relative prevalence.

Strabismus Some 5 percent of all children have a deviation in the eyes either inward, outward, or vertically. Strabismus may be observed at or shortly after birth or may develop up to about 3 years of age. The disorder can often be diagnosed by simple inspection or one of several simple tests, e.g., corneal light reflection or the cover test. Such tests are important because a child may have strabismus that is not readily observable. Early treatment of strabismus is important because, uncorrected, it may lead to inadequate development of central vision. (See below, amblyopia ex anopsia.) The importance of preschool identification screening of children must be stressed because treatment tends to be more effective, and the prevention of lost vision through amblyopia greater, the earlier the disorder is identified, diagnosed, and treated.

Exercises, corrective lenses, and/or "patching" the good eye to force development of macular vision in the underdeveloped eye are all treatments encountered.[49] In addition, surgical intervention to correct the deviation may be necessary, and has a greater likelihood of effecting a functional cure if it occurs early in life rather than being delayed until the child reaches 4 or 5 years of age.

Strabismic or Suppression Amblyopia This term, meaning weak or dull vision, describes a disorder in which the affected eye is not providing adequate sensory information, even though there usually is no medically observable damage to the eye. Loss of vision from disuse, strabismic or suppression amblyopia (amblyopia ex anopsia), is a specific form of the disorder that is prevalent in children. Other forms exist, e.g., those caused by toxic substances, diabetes, complications of diphtheria, and hysterical disorders. Early identification and correction of the ex anopsia form are critical in a sight conservation program; hysterical causes are sometimes dealt with successfully by specialized psychological or psychiatric means; and a variety of medications exist to treat the toxic forms. Patching of the good eye for periods of as great as three months is used to encourage proper

[49]Gunter K. Von Noorden, "Strabismus: Annual Review," *Archives of Ophthalmology,* Vol. 84, 1970, pp. 103–122; and Gunter K. Von Noorden and A. E. Maumenee, *Atlas of Strabismus,* The C. V. Mosby Company, St. Louis, 1967.

fixation. If patching is not sufficient, pleoptics is a method of choice of some physicians for additional treatment.[50] If the cause is strabismus, the treatment is as for that disorder.[51]

Retrolental Fibroplasia (RLF)   Essentially, RLF is due to excessively high oxygen concentrations or levels in the blood of premature or respiratorially distressed infants. First occurrences of the condition were noted in the 1940s, and in the mid-1950s it was listed "as the chief cause of blindness in infants."[52] While the mechanisms responsible for the disorder (development of a fibrous mass leading to a possible detachment of the premature infant's retina) are not completely known, it is known that excessive oxygen is the precipitating agent. In the premature or otherwise respiratorially distressed infant, high concentrations of oxygen may be required for several days after birth. Excessively high concentrations in the infant's blood cause the RLF. The role of the ophthalmologist is important in conducting oxygen therapy in infants. Frequent tests of the arterial blood oxygen content should be made to determine whether the levels of oxygen received are excessive and may cause damage to the retinal vessels. Periodic ophthalmoscopic examinations may also be conducted, although assessment of damage to the retinal vessels may be difficult.[53]

It is distressing that, some 20 years after its causative mechanisms were identified, this essentially preventable disease is still showing up at all in published Model Reporting Area data for those under the age of 5 years (at a rate of 0.9 per 100,000). The rate for ages 5 to 19 is 8.1 per 100,000.[54] In interviews it was suggested that in the obstetrician's understandable desire to save the life of a distressed newborn, or in the case of oxygen therapy's being administered more generally throughout the newborn population, some RLF is being caused that

[50]Pleoptics is a relatively new orthoptic technique in which the eye is stimulated with a bright light, causing a circular afterimage (as when one fixes on a bright light and then "sees" a colored circle when the eyes are closed). The eye is then made to fix on smaller and smaller targets until fixation is improved. It is expensive because equipment is expensive and a course of treatment may be prolonged and of high frequency.

[51]Von Noorden, op. cit.

[52]F. H. Adler, *Gifford's Textbook of Ophthalmology,* 6th ed., Saunders, Philadelphia, 1957, p. 358. See also, A. Patz, "A New Role of the Ophthalmologist in Prevention of Retrolental Fibroplasia," *Archives of Ophthalmology,* Vol. 78, 1967, p. 565.

[53]Frank W. Newell, *Ophthalmology: Principles and Practices,* The C. V. Mosby Company, St. Louis, 1969 ed., p. 258. This work has a very thorough section on RLF, its treatment, and methods to be used in the premature nursery. See also J. D. Baum and J. P. Tizard, "Retrolental Fibroplasia: Management of Oxygen Therapy," *British Medical Bulletin,* Vol. 26, 1970, pp. 171–174.

[54]Kahn and Moorhead, op. cit., p. 135.

could be averted if an ophthalmologist were consulted or if the doctor in attendance were fully aware of the possible damage that otherwise life-saving therapy was doing to his patient's vision.

Nystagmus Nystagmus refers to the rhythmical movement of one or both eyes. It is involuntary and ranges in severity from slight, hard-to-observe, and nonhandicapping to rapid, readily detectable, and debilitating. Basically, nystagmus results because the eye is unable to fix or focus. Nystagmus occurs in a variety of forms; it is usually congenital in youth. Congenital ocular nystagmus due to sensory defects can be caused by any disorder inhibiting fixation in an infant, e.g., scarred cornea, damage to the macula, cataract, and as a result of albinism.

Congenital ocular nystagmus due to defects in the neurological mechanism for fixation is also found in youth. A third entity, called Spasmus Nutans, exists; beginning at a few months of age, a child may develop nystagmus of the eyes which persists up to an age of perhaps 1 or 2 years. There is no known cure for nystagmus, and treatment is seldom effective.[55] In addition to the above types, nystagmus can be due to a serious central nervous system disorder such as a brain tumor, and this cause should be differentiated.

Myopia Myopia is a common disorder, familiarly referred to as "nearsightedness." Myopia is a relative imbalance between the refractive power of the eye's cornea and lens and the length of the eyeball, such that light rays do not focus on the macula but form an image somewhere in front of it, with the result that objects at a distance are blurred, and the blurring increases with distance.

Myopia can be hereditarily caused, it can occur because of damage to the cornea, such as by abcess or injury, or it can result from defects of the eyeball, such as an abnormally curved cornea, an abnormally round lens, or an abnormally long globe. Generally, when one eye is myopic, the other becomes so in time.

In something over 90 percent of the cases, myopia is moderate and is self-limiting by the age of about 20 or 21. It is the other 10 percent that concerns us as a cause of handicapping in children. Complicated or progressive myopia, the more severe form of the disorder, has been known in extreme instances to contribute to the tearing and detachment of the retina and to degeneration of the macula—events leading to blindness if not treated correctly and early.

There is no known cure or preventive method for myopia. The need for early and correct identification and diagnosis to improve

[55]Newell, op. cit., pp. 423–425.

vision and identify progressive myopia is clear. In more severe instances, even glasses may be inadequate.[56]

Astigmatism   Astigmatism can be caused when the cornea, the front or "window" part of the eye, is not perfectly rounded, or can also be caused by irregularity of the lens. These irregularities cause an improper focusing of light rays at a series of points rather than at a single point as in a normal or a myopic eye. In mild forms, the afflicted person may be unaware of astigmatism; in more severe forms, it may be handicapping. Astigmatism can be corrected by spectacles in most cases. *Irregular astigmatism* occurs when the cornea is irregular and misshapen, usually because of trauma, ulcers, injuries, disease, etc., to the cornea itself and due to keratoconas. Irregular astigmatism usually cannot be corrected by spectacles, but contact lenses can in some cases overcome the visual disability. In some advanced and severe cases contact lenses may not be sufficient and corneal transplants may be necessary.[57]

Cataract   Cataract is a cloudiness of the lens preventing the passage of light to some extent and hence inhibiting vision. Cataract has many causative agents. Among them are general diseases such as diabetes, galactosemia, hypoparathyroidism, hyperparathyroidism, and rubella. In addition, injuries from direct trauma or from radiation can cause cataracts, as can long-term steroid therapy.

Depending on the size and type of cataract, vision is impaired to a variable degree. Impairment may be slight or so great as to only allow perception of light.

No known medication will "cure" cataracts, even though a great deal of research energy has been expended to find something that might dissolve, absorb, retard, or prevent their formation and development. Surgery is the method of choice to relieve the disorder and has been known and effectively used since ancient times in the older person. The treatment of congenital cataracts depends to a large degree on reasonable expectation for improvement for vision. In many cases, cataracts present since birth result in an irreversible loss of vision (amblyopia ex anopsia) which cannot be overcome by surgery. Removal of a cataract extremely early in life may result in improved vision; in many cases removal of congenital cataracts later in life is not effective in improving vision because of irreversible amblyopia ex anopsia.

[56]A. E. Sloane, *Manual of Refraction,* Little, Brown, Boston, 1970 ed.
[57]Ibid.

Cataract is preventable to some extent. Because rubella has been clearly implicated as a causative agent, pregnant women should avoid exposure to the disease, or better yet should be vaccinated against it before becoming pregnant. Trauma and radiation-caused cataract can be prevented by simple avoidance tactics.[58]

Toxoplasmosis Caused by a microscopic parasite, toxoplasmosis exists in both congenital and acquired forms. In the congenital form, a variety of presenting symptoms has been demonstrated, e.g., skin rash, jaundice, central nervous system disorder, hydrocephalus, mental retardation. The acquired form may occur at any age, and, as with the congenital form, choroid and retinal involvement is known. Accurate diagnosis is hard to attain because the symptoms resemble those of a number of quite different disorders. Treatment involves careful administration of one of a number of sulfa drugs and corticosteroids to reduce and eliminate lesions to the eye. Drug therapy is complex, and great care must be exercised. While research into the disorder has been vigorous, preventive measures are not generally agreed upon. It is suspected that pregnant women should avoid all contact with cat feces, as that method of transmission of the congenital form of toxoplasmosis has been identified.[59]

Coloboma During the first trimester of pregnancy, the development of the eyes is most critical. Occasionally, a portion of the eye does not form, and what results is a coloboma, a missing part of the eye's structure. Depending upon the severity of the coloboma, the choroid, part of the retina, and/or the optic disc can all be involved. Most commonly, the coloboma results in an absence of part of the iris. If the coloboma affects large or central parts of the choroid and retina or optic nerve, vision may be greatly impaired and by and large treatment cannot be effective.

Aniridia Aniridia is a developmental defect in which all or part of the iris is absent. As with other developmental problems, there is some reason to suspect hereditary factors and there is usually some

---

[58]Gunter Von Noorden, S. J. Ryan, and A. E. Maumenee, "Management of Congenital Cataracts," *Transactions of the American Academy of Ophthalmology,* Vol. 74, 1970, pp. 352–359; and Ellis, op. cit., p. 205.

[59]H. A. Feldman, "Toxoplasmosis," *Pediatrics,* Vol. 22, 1958, pp. 559–574; A. E. Maumenee (ed.), *Symposium: Toxoplasmosis, with Special Reference to Uveitis,* Williams & Wilkins, Baltimore, 1962; M. J. Hogan, S. J. Kimura, and G. R. O'Conner, "Ocular Toxoplasmosis," *Archives of Ophthalmology,* Vol. 72, 1964, pp. 592–600; and Newall, op. cit., pp. 376–377.

additional complicating factor contributing to visual impairment. Cataract, glaucoma, and other disorders often accompany aniridia, and the disorder is unfortunately usually binocular.

Albinism   In cases of albinism where there is no pigment in the eye (albinism may affect only the eye or may be more generally distributed over the body), visual problems almost always will follow. Besides acute sensitivity to light, those affected with albinism usually have some degree of nystagmus and often are myopic as well. Albinism is a genetically related disorder; about one in three cases result from consanguineous reproduction, e.g., children produced by brothers and sisters or close cousins, and others are the result of spontaneous mutation. Procreation by two albinos always results in albinistic offspring. No one knows how to cure or correct albinism, and for the visual component of it, all that can be done is to correct the visual deficit with spectacles and to protect the eye from damage by blocking the sun's rays with appropriately tinted lenses.

Macular Degeneration   A number of hereditary conditions impair vision as a result of abnormal changes in the macula, the center of the retina and the location of one's best vision. There are a number of hereditary diseases that result in degeneration of the macula. Usually, macular degeneration is seen in the older person; when it occurs in the younger person, it is usually a hereditary form, and by and large there is no effective treatment for them. Reduction of color vision capability is one of the earlier signs, and this is in time followed by loss of central vision and a general diminution of the imaging capacity.

Retinitis Pigmentosa   Resulting in, among other things, defective night vision, retinitis pigmentosa is mainly diagnosed in children over the age of 14, and the disorder progresses through adulthood until a greatly reduced or a total loss of vision occurs. It is binocular and is thought to result from the primary degeneration of the pigment layer of the retina. It is incurable and not preventable, and there is a distinct hereditary tendency.

Retinoblastoma   Retinoblastoma is a relatively rare malignant growth in children. It is sometimes traceable to a family history of the disorder. The disease can become apparent from birth through several years of age. Involvement of both eyes may not be simultaneous, and only about 25 percent of the cases are bilateral. One sign of the disorder is the so-called "cat's eye" or white or yellow reflex in the pupil of the eye due to detachment of the retina or the presence of a large tumor. Early detection of a retinoblastoma is critical, as the disease is capable of progressing along the optic nerve and into the brain, out of the eye into the orbit, or via the blood to other bodily organs, with a high likelihood of fatality. Treatment, in any case a truly life-saving operation, involves the removal of the affected eye with special care taken to ensure that the tumor has not spread as far as the optic nerve. In the unilateral case, attention is then given to the second eye to detect the earliest signs of the disease. In the bilateral case, the better eye is salvaged, if possible, and x-ray and chemotherapy are undertaken. Parents having survived retinoblastomas should be advised concerning procreation, as the odds are significantly greater that they will produce similarly affected children: if one parent has survived a retinoblastoma, it is about a 50-50 chance that a child will be afflicted. If one child has a unilateral retinoblastoma and there is also a family history of that disorder, chances are about 40 percent that the next child will also be afflicted; with no prior family history the chances the next child will also be afflicted drop to about 4 percent. In the unilateral case, spontaneous or somatic mutation is the more common cause and accounts for 80 to 90 percent of all cases; the family form accounts for only about 5 per-

Hypermetropia Farsightedness or hypermetropia is a disorder of the eye in which light rays striking the eye would be in focus at a point behind the retina. This disorder can be adequately treated with spectacles. If uncorrected the condition could lead to strabismus.

Dislocated Lenses Either because of developmental problems, metabolic disease such as cystinosis, or because of trauma, usually a sharp blow to the head, the lens may become completely or partially displaced. If only partially, the lens is referred to as subluxated. In the congenital or developmental case, the disorder is often associated with defective formation of the ligaments supporting the lens, has been traced to genetic origins, and is often found in conjunction with other deformities in the body, such as excessively long bones. Complications of dislocation include glaucoma, cataract, and uveitis.

Glaucoma Basically, glaucoma is a disorder of the eye in which pressure within the eye is excessively high. This condition may lead

[60]Sir Stewart Duke-Elder, *System of Ophthalmology: Diseases of the Retina,* Vol. 10, The C. V. Mosby Company, St. Louis, 1967. See also, W. A. Bedford, C. Bedotto, and P. A. MacFaul, "Retinoblastoma: A Study of 139 Cases," *British Journal of Ophthalmology,* Vol. 55, 1971, pp. 19–27.

to damage to the optic nerve, which can be permanent and lead to total blindness. In glaucoma, the normal drainage of fluid produced within the eye is obstructed to some degree, either because of a developmental congenital disorder (some authorities believe it to be a membrane growing over the normal drainage system), because of uveitis, resulting in clogging or damage to the drainage system, or because of adherence of the iris to cover the drainage system, which can be secondary to developmental abnormalities in which the lens adheres to the cornea or iris or secondary to a dislocation of the lens. *Primary glaucoma* is a glaucoma which is not associated with an identifiable pre-existing disorder. *Secondary glaucoma* refers to a glaucoma which is due to some other pre-existent disorder such as uveitis, a dislocated lens, or trauma. Blunt trauma to the eye can result in glaucoma which is insidious and may take several months or perhaps years to develop.

Glaucoma demands early, accurate, and complex treatment by an ophthalmologist. The congenital glaucoma is usually treated surgically. That and other forms may also be treated topically with eye drops, systemically with a variety of medications, and surgically by a number of procedures, all of which are meant to reduce pressure within the eye.[61]

Optic Atrophy   Many threats to the optic nerve, the main pathway of visual images to the brain, exist: glaucoma, tumors of the eye and brain, trauma associated with skull fractures, circulatory disorders, infections of the eye or brain, complications of diabetes, anemia, or toxic poisoning, and unknown congenital causes. There is no known means to restore the optic nerve once it has atrophied. Because it is a debilitating complication of several other ocular disorders, research, prevention, and treatment of those primary causes all contribute to the lessening of blindness from this cause.

Corneal Ulcers and Scars   The number of possible causative agents is large and includes, for example, viral infection, trauma, chemical agents, gross vitamin A deficiency, bacterial agents, and so forth. Symptoms include pain and unusual sensitivity to light, overproduction of tears, and the reduction of vision. Treatment for residual visual impairment may be carried out after the eye has been made healthy and includes corneal transplantation and contact lenses.

[61]B. Becker and R. N. Shaffer, *Diagnosis and Therapy of Glaucoma,* The C. V. Mosby Company, St. Louis, 1965 ed.

Keratitis An inflammation of the cornea, keratitis, is divisible into three basic types: *interstitial keratitis,* usually syphilitic in origin, involving the intermediate layers of the cornea; *deep keratitis,* caused by trauma or infectious agents such as mumps; and *superficial punctate keratitis,* thought to be mainly infectious in origin, and usually treatable. The basic threat posed by the disorder is the scarring it leaves in its wake, with resultant loss of visual acuity.

Burns Eyelid burns are treated like burns elsewhere in the body, with special care to prevent infection of the eye and deep lid scarring. Preventive antibiotic and corticosteroid therapy may be indicated to reduce chances of infection and to reduce inflammation; such therapy is usually topical, as is therapy designed to minimize corneal scarring. Chemical burns of the cornea require prompt and copious irrigation and subsequent evaluation of the extent of damage and needed medical treatment. Ultraviolet burns of the cornea, e.g., from sunlamp exposure or skiing in bright light without tinted lens protection, may require antibiotic therapy and patching of the eye to reduce chances of infection and discomfort.[62]

Fracture of the Orbit Usually a traumatic shock to the head or a fist to the eye is responsible for fracture of the orbit. This is a serious disorder that can have a number of complications, e.g., double vision. Significant displacement of the bone surrounding the eyeball requires prompt and skillful surgical intervention. Depending on the severity of the fracture, sight may be impaired.[63]

Contusions of the Globe (Including Hyphema) Blood in the anterior chamber of eye—hyphema—and an assortment of other sight-threatening results, are known to occur as a result of trauma in and around the eye. Care depends upon the nature and severity of the contusion and the extent of complications resulting from it, e.g., hyphema, retinal detachment, vitreous hemorrhage, glaucoma, rupture of the eyeball, and complications that can occur well after the initiating trauma.[64]

Foreign Bodies Depending upon the nature of the body and the extent of eye injury it causes, a foreign object in the eye can be sight-

[62]R. R. Tenzel, "Trauma and Burns," *International Ophthalmological Clinic,* Vol. 10, 1970, pp. 55–69.
[63]B. Becker and T. K. Lyle (eds.), *Fractures of the Orbit,* Williams & Wilkins, Baltimore, 1970; and H. B. Stallard, *Eye Surgery,* Williams & Wilkins, Baltimore, 1965 ed.
[64]Duke-Elder, "Mechanical Injuries," op. cit., Vol. XIV, Part I, 1972; and A. Callahan, *Surgery of the Eye: Injuries,* Charles C. Thomas, Springfield, Illinois, 1950.

threatening. Many foreign bodies in the cornea can be removed simply with a moist, sterile cotton applicator; others may require minor surgical treatment with prophylactic antibiotic therapy; intraocular foreign bodies necessitate more involved procedures with a poor prognosis for visual function.[65]

Retinopathy   Hemorrhages or changes in the blood vessels nourishing the eye are common signs of retinitis; blank, diminished, or distorted vision, as well as sensitivity to light, are symptoms. Retinitis has many suspected causes, including diabetes, high blood pressure, rheumatism, burns from the sun's rays, leukemia, and kidney disease. Infectious causes include untreated corneal or scleral disorders. Parasites, chemicals, and allergic materials have also been implicated in retinopathy. The problem is not so much with the disorder itself, but with the damage left in its wake, especially if undetected and untreated.

Uveitis   Diseases of the iris (iritis), ciliary body (cyclitis), and the choroid (choroiditis) can cause handicapping conditions. Although specific causes such as viral infections, injury, or systemic illnesses can cause uveitis, the bulk of the cases of uveitis are due to unknown etiology. While the disorders in general are treatable, their possible complications warrant special consideration, e.g., glaucoma and cataract.[66]

Medical Treatment Costs of Vision Disorders

Table 9.15 presents a sample of treatment costs for medical services available to those suffering from vision disorders. These data are a sample of charges in 1973 for high-quality care in a specialized practice, and may vary considerably for different parts of the country and for different practices. These estimates are for professional medical specialist fees only; payments for other aspects of medical care, such as days of hospitalization, are excluded.

Two features stand out from this summary sample of treatment costs. First, good-quality medical care can be had, but it can also be costly in the absolute sense. However, the appropriate tradeoff is between the cost of such care and all costs involved in a lifetime of being handicapped or more severely handicapped than one would be if good medical care were received. In this sense, good-quality medical treatment is probably a "bargain." Second, the finest special-

[65]D. Paton and M. F. Goldberg, *Injuries to the Eye, Lids, and the Orbit,* Saunders, Philadelphia, 1968.
[66]T. F. Schlaegel, *Essentials of Uveitis,* Little, Brown, Boston, 1969.

Table 9.15
SAMPLE TREATMENT COSTS FOR VISION DISORDERS IN CHILDREN, SPECIALIZED PRACTICE, CALENDAR YEAR 1973

Item	Charge ($)	Item	Charge ($)
Service group/routine/MDs		Gonioscopy	20
Office visit	12	Gonioscopy, infant	60[a]
Initial comprehensive diag-		Gross external examination	
nostic ophthalmic exami-		with ophthalmoscopy and	
nation	30	refraction	30
Initial hospital consultation	35	Gross external examination,	
Routine hospital visit	20	as above, with cyclopegic	
Diagnostic group/X-ray		of mydriatic	40
Eye, for foreign body	40	Orthoptic and/or pleoptic	
Eye, for localization of		evaluation	25
foreign body	60	Orthoptic and/or pleoptic	
Facial bones, limited	30	training (30 min)	15
Facial bones, complete and/		Visual fields: plotting, cen-	
or orbits	50	tral and/or peripheral	20
Facial bones, complete with		Tonometry	15
nasal bones	60	Tonography	30
Nasal bones	28	Provocative test(s) for glau-	
Nasolacrimal duct	50	coma, including water	
Optic foramina	30	drinking, and/or mydriat-	
Skull, limited	25	ic, and/or dark room test	20
Skull, complete	35	Ophthalmoscopy (fundos-	
Tumor localization, ocular	70	copy) with mydriasis,	
Diagnostic group/laboratory		direct and/or indirect	
Blood count, complete	5	methods	20
Culture sensitivity	10	Ophthalmoscopy, as above,	
Hydroxycorticosteroid	25	with general anesthetic	40
Culture	10	Ophthalmoscopy, as above,	
Diagnostic/optometry/		with contact lens	30
ophthalmic		Ophthalmoscopy, as above,	
Eye examination, including		with intravenous (fluores-	
visual acuity, ophthalmos-		cein)	50
copy, tonometry, gross		Ophthalmoscopy, as above,	
visual fields, muscle bal-		with ophthalmodyna-	
ance, and slit lamp		mometry	40
microscopy	35	Fitting and evaluation of	
Eye examination, as above,		contact lens	b
with refraction	45	Miscellaneous and office	
Eye examination, as above,		procedures	
with plotting of central		Injection	5
and/or visual fields	50	Medication	c

[a] Includes 7 days follow-up.
[b] Fee varies ($250 minimum).
[c] Fee varies.
[d] Plus 4 postoperative office visits per year for 3 years = $144.

[e] Minimum fee.
[f] Plus 6 postoperative office visits = $72.
[g] Plus 9 postoperative office visits = $108.

Table 9.15—Continued

Item	Charge ($)	Item	Charge ($)
Surgical nurse	50c	Sclerotomy, posterior, with or without drainage of fluid	250
Special reports	c		
Surgical procedures		Sclerotomy for glaucoma, with scissors, punch, trephine, or cautery	350f
Enucleation of eye, without implant	400d		
Enucleation of eye, with implant	450d	Scleral resection, any type, with graft	700d
Evisceration of eye	400d	Iridotomy	140
Suture of eye for wound or injury	(c)	Iridotomy, with transfixation of iris	150
Removal of embedded foreign body	15e	Iridotomy, photocoagulation or laser	200
Removal of embedded foreign body under slit lamp	20e	Excision of lesion of iris	400f
		Iridocyclectomy	600f
Keratectomy, lamellar, partial	300e	Iridectomy, any type	300f
		Iridencleisis	350f
Keratectomy, lamellar, complete	350e	Iridodialysis	300f
Pterygium, simple	200e	Cyclodiathermy, initial	250
Pterygium, complicated	(c)	Cyclodiathermy, subsequent	120
Curettage and cauterization of corneal ulcer	40e	Cyclocryotherapy, initial	180
Corneal transplant, lamellar	700d	Cyclocryotherapy, subsequent	90
Corneal transplant, penetrating	800d	Cyclodialysis, initial	350f
		Cyclodialysis, subsequent	180f
Aspiration of aqueous, diagnostic	30	Discission, initial	150f
		Discission, subsequent	70f
Aspiration of vitreous prolapse	200d	Discission, secondary membrane, simple	150f
Goniotomy	250	Discission, secondary membrane, complicated	250f
Paracentesis	30		
Removal of intraocular foreign body, anterior chamber	400d	Aspiration of lens material for cataract, one or more stages	500
Severing corneal-vitreal adhesions	(c)	Extraction of lens, unilateral, one or more stages (e.g., cataract, subluxated lens)	700d
Air injection into anterior chamber	30		
Sclerotomy, posterior, with removal of intraocular foreign body by magnetic extraction	400f	Discission of anterior hyaloid (e.g., pupillary block)	150f
		Reattach retina, retinopexy, with or without drainage of subretinal fluid, initial	600d,e
Sclerotomy, posterior, with removal of intraocular foreign body by nonmagnetic extraction	450f	Reattach retina, retinopexy, with or without drainage of fluid, subsequent	(c)

Table 9.15—Continued

Item	Charge ($)	Item	Charge ($)
Reattachment with scleral buckling, resection, implant, initial	900e	Excision of meibomian gland (chalazion), single	40
Reattachment, as above, subsequent	c	Excision of meibomian gland (chalazion), multiple, same lid	40
Repair of retinal breaks or schisis, one or more stages during same period of hospitalization, photocoagulation and/or cryotherapy	300e	Excision of meibomian gland (chalazion), multiple, different lids	50
Photocoagulation, initial	300	Conjunctive, removal of foreign body, surface	20e
Photocoagulation, subsequent	150	Conjunctive, removal of embedded foreign body	20e
Diathermy or cryotherapy	c	Conjunctiva, evacuation of cysts	20e
Muscle surgery, initial	450	Biopsy of conjunctive	25
Muscle surgery, subsequent	c	Excision of lesion of conjunctiva, benign	30e
Muscle transplant	500	Excision of lesion of conjunctiva, malignant	c
Orbitotomy with exploration	350	Suture of conjunctiva	30e
Orbitotomy with drainage of intra-orbital abscess	350	Conjunctivoplasty, free graft using conjunctiva	350
Orbitotomy with removal or intra-orbital tumor or foreign body	c	Conjunctivoplasty, free graft using buccal mucous membrane	400
Excision of lesion of orbit, requiring bone flap	650	Conjunctival flap for corneal ulcer	150
Orbital decompression	600	Drainage of lacrimal gland, abscess or cyst	120
Extenteration of orbit, without skin graft	600g	Drainage of lacrimal sac: dacryocystotomy or dacryocystostomy	60
Extenteration of orbit, without skin graft, including orbital bone	c	Excision of lacrimal gland	350f
Retrobulbar injection	20e	Excision of lacrimal sac	350f
Retrobulbar injection, alcohol injection	60	Dacryocystorhinostomy	400g
Retrobulbar injection, air or opaque contrast medium for radiography	30	Conjunctivocystorhinostomy	450d
Blepharotomy with drainage of abscess of meibomian glands or stye	20e	Closure of punctum by cautery	25
		Dilation of punctum	20e
		Probing of nasolacrimal duct	20e
		Probing and/or irrigation of canaliculus	20

ized medical care in the world is relatively useless, irrespective of its costs, if there are inadequate identification and diagnosis services in operation locally.

Hearing Disorders: Prevalence Data

Data on the causes of hearing impairment in the young are neither comprehensive nor reliable. Data are better for visual disorders. For example, Model Reporting Area data exist on prevalence with respect to site and type of affection for youth aged 0 to 5 and 5 to 19 years, and on age-specific prevalence numbers and rates with respect to cause. Comparable data do not exist for hearing disorders, although a few special studies shed some light on these matters. Some of the best, but limited, available etiological information is contained in the national health surveys. Those data are in many cases over 10 years old, however, and are limited by many sampling and technical problems; but the information in Table 9.16 does show that illness and congenital causes generally are the most prevalent for youth under the age of 6. The utility of these data is compromised by the fact that over one-third of the youth surveyed had "unknown" or "other" etiologies, or simply did not respond to the survey questionnaire.

Data on the medical aspects of hearing impairment available through federal surveys have many specific limitations. For example, the national health interview survey data[67] are self-reported by survey respondents without reference to detailed medical diagnosis; are summarized in too gross a detail ("Diseases of ear" are reported as a summary category including seven international classification code numbers); are categorized by too gross a set of age categories (e.g., "under 45 years"); exclude institutionalized hearing impaired persons; and are often over 10 years old. The national Health Examination Survey[68] involved professional reporting, but only very limited information on etiologies was collected, institutionalized persons

---

[67]See, for example, "Current Estimates from the Health Interview Survey, United States—1968," *Vital and Health Statistics,* Series 10, No. 60, Public Health Service, Washington, D.C., June 1970; and Augustine Gentile, Jerome D. Schein, and Kenneth Haase, "Characteristics of Persons with Impaired Hearing, United States, July 1962–June 1963," *Vital and Health Statistics,* Series 10, No. 35, Public Health Service, Washington, D.C., April 1967; and "Prevalence of Selected Impairments, United States, July 1963–June 1965," *Vital and Health Statistics,* Series 10, No. 48, Public Health Service, Washington, D.C., November 1968.

[68]See, for example, "Hearing Sensitivity and Related Findings Among Children, United States," *Vital and Health Statistics,* Series 11, No. 114, Public Health Service, Washington, D.C., March 1972; "Hearing Status and Ear Examination Findings Among Adults, United States, 1960–1962," *Vital and Health Statistics,* Series 11, No. 32, Public Health Service, Washington, D.C., November 1968; and "Hearing Levels of Children by Demographic and Socioeconomic Characteristics," *Vital and Health Statistics,* Series 11, No. 111, Public Health Service, Washington, D.C., February 1972.

Table 9.16
PERCENTAGE DISTRIBUTION OF PERSONS WITH BINAURAL HEARING IMPAIRMENT, BY CAUSE ACCORDING TO AGE AT ONSET: U.S., 1962-1963

Cause	All Ages	Under Age 6	Ages 6 to 16
Illness	20.9	33.2	41.7
Accident	13.5	6.5[a]	11.5
Hereditary or congenital	4.0	24.9	4.0[a]
Presbycusis (old age, degenerative)	4.9	NA	NA
Unknown	39.9	19.3	30.0
Other and nonresponse	16.8	16.0	12.8
Total	100.0	100.0	100.0

SOURCE: Augustine Gentile, Jerome D. Schein, and Kenneth Haase, "Characteristics of Persons with Impaired Hearing, United States: July 1962-June 1963," *Vital and Health Statistics,* Series 10, No. 35, Public Health Service, Washington, D.C., April 1967, pp. 35-36, Table 16, abstracted.
NOTE: NA = not available.
[a] Data do not meet standards of reliability and precision.

were not included, and published reports provide only very gross categorical breakdowns.

Because of these limitations, we rely primarily on other sources—special studies and medical textbooks for the most part—for information on prevalence of hearing disorders by age, etiology, and affection.

Hearing loss appears to be directly related to other conditions, such as mental retardation,[69] cerebral palsy,[70] cleft palates,[71] allergies,[72] goiter,[73] tonsillitis,[74] and vitamin deficiency.[75] Our general recommendation for the creation of high-risk registers as an integral part of a strengthened identification program (Chapter 7) would at least

[69]C. Webb et al., "Incidence of Hearing Loss in Institutionalized Mental Retardates," *American Journal of Mental Deficiency,* Vol. 70, 1966, pp. 563-568.
[70]W. Hatchuel, "The Importance of Performing Adequate Hearing Tests in Children with Cerebral Palsy," *South African Medical Journal,* Vol. 36, 1962, pp. 237-238.
[71]D. J. Fahey, "Otologic Care of Cleft Palate Cases," *Laryngoscope,* Vol. 75, 1965, pp. 570-587. In an interesting, comprehensive, multidisciplinary cleft palate program at Los Angeles Children's Hospital, as many as 75 percent of those enrolled contract disorders capable of causing hearing loss if not properly, correctly, and persistently treated. Interview, Dr. Frederick Linthicum, Otologic Medical Group, Los Angeles, December 14, 1973. This is a startling and not generally known finding.
[72]Hallowell Davis and S. Richard Silverman, *Hearing and Deafness,* Holt, Rinehart and Winston, Inc., New York, 1970 ed., pp. 106, 114.
[73]W. R. Trotter, "The Association of Deafness with Thyroid Dysfunction," *British Medical Bulletin,* Vol. 16, 1960, pp. 92-98.
[74]John Jacob Ballenger, *Diseases of the Nose, Throat, and Ear,* 11th ed., Lea & Febiger, Philadelphia, 1969, pp. 206-216; and L. G. Waggoner, "Secretory Otitis Media," *Harper Hospital Bulletin,* Vol. 22, 1964, pp. 50-58.
[75]A. Yassin and M. Taha, "Sensory Neural Deafness in Pellagra," *Journal of Laryngology,* Vol. 77, 1963, pp. 992-1000.

be a start toward finding and preventing hearing loss in children known to possess other related conditions.

The need for detailed, timely, and improved prevalence data by etiology is clear. (This observation holds for vision handicapped children as well.) Detailed prevalence data would go a long way toward informing and rationalizing research priorities and medical service planning. Adequate information also might be usefully employed in informing pediatricians. For instance, if there is an upswing in the number of children in a region or locality suffering from a specific disorder, it is important for pediatricians to know about it and be on the alert; persistence of the disorder signals that perhaps something more fundamental is happening to the population and warrants more detailed investigation. Finally, better information on prevalence could be converted into educational materials for the average parent, e.g., information on the signs of serous otitis media, what the parent should do, and what might happen if early and correct care is not undertaken.

Hearing Disorders: Description and Medical Treatment

This section briefly sketches some of the more common hearing disorders affecting children and mentions common treatment methods. It also comments on the likelihood of successful treatment or prevention. None of what follows pretends to be definitive; the interested reader is strongly encouraged to consult the general sources listed in the footnotes for more detailed information.

Many, if not most, external ear, eardrum, and middle ear disorders are treatable with a high likelihood of success in correcting or avoiding a handicapping condition. The critical factors are early identification, correct diagnosis, and skillful treatment. Most sensorineural ("nerve deafness") disorders are not so successfully treatable, and the likelihood of a lifelong handicapping condition is much greater. The key factors in sensorineural disorders are early identification, stabilization or cure of the underlying disorder, if appropriate and possible, and then vigorous rehabilitation to minimize the handicapping effects of the disorder.

Prevalence data on etiology are not sufficently detailed to give one a very good idea about relative rates of occurrence and expectations of a handicapping condition resulting from any given disorder; the ordering of specific disorders in what follows therefore does not represent relative prevalence.

Serous Otitis Media   Serous otitis media is perhaps the most commonly encountered ear disorder in younger children. It has been implicated in a large fraction of the cases of hearing impairment, although we do not know what the fraction might be, given the poor quality of data available on hearing disorders in children. The term "serous otitis media" describes the collection of fluid in the middle ear, and it may be acute or chronic. The disorder is caused by any condition that results in blockage of the eustachian tube and may be congenital, due to infection or allergy, or may be caused by enlarged adenoids. In any event the middle ear becomes partially closed, and gases in it are partially absorbed. This situation leads to a collection of fluid and infection in about 25 percent of the cases.

Treatment depends on the specific causative agent. For congenital causes, such as an immature eustachian tube, treatment may be continuous until the child matures or "grows out of" the disorder's cause; in the case of cleft palate, the prognosis is not so simple and probably will call for a great deal of specialized attention in the child's life. For most cases, one treats the underlying disorder; aspiration of the middle ear fluid may be required; myringotomy (incision of the eardrum) is frequently resorted to and with it the placement of a hollow plastic tube to prevent the incision from healing and to ensure that the middle ear is open. In the case of allergic causes, one works to identify the allergic material, treats the condition through avoidance or desensitization, and simultaneously works to keep the middle ear from becoming or staying infected. Medication alone often suffices to open and clear the ear, as in the case of antihistaminics, decongestants, and mechanical techniques to inflate the passageway to the middle ear. Failure to treat properly may result in hearing loss.

Prognosis for treatment administered by competent physicians is nearly 100 percent success for all cases except cleft palate. In the case of myringotomy, however, there may be repeat surgeries to replace the ventilation tube. In a relatively few cases, it may become necessary to perform a mastoidectomy, a more radical procedure, to ensure control or elimination of the serous otitis media.[76]

Acute Otitis Media and Mastoiditis   A more serious variant of serous otitis media, this disorder is the inflammation and infection of the middle ear and the mastoid air cell system by one of several agents,

---

[76]B. Senturai, "Classification of Middle Ear Effusions," *Annals of Otolaryngology, Rhinology, and Laryngology,* Vol. 79, 1970, pp. 358–370; G. Thomas, "Management of Chronic Middle Ear Effusion," *California Medicine,* Vol. 110, 1969, pp. 300–304; H. Silverstein et al., "Eustachian Tube Dysfunction as a Cause for Chronic Secretory Otitis with Children," *Laryngoscope,* Vol. 76, 1966, pp. 259–273; and Ballenger, op. cit., Chapters 44 and 45.

e.g., pneumococci, streptococci, staphylococci, viruses, and *Hemophilus influenzae*. It is important to mention these disease agents, for proper treatment requires that the infection be cultured and the appropriate antibiotic be administered in sufficient strength and for a sufficiently long time to control the disease. Treatment is of primary importance because of the numerous, and mostly unpleasant, complications that may occur in the unchecked case of acute otitis media, e.g., meningitis, abscesses, mastoiditis, and hearing loss. With adequate care, which is mainly the selection and application of the appropriate antimicrobial agent and the administration of oral and topical decongestants, prognosis and the odds of cure are virtually 100 percent. The key is in continuous and competent treatment.[77]

Chronic Otitis Media and Mastoiditis   This form of otitis media results from infection of the middle ear and the mastoid via the eustachian tube or the external auditory canal; it may also result from the formation of a cholesteatoma, a "bone-like" cystic growth in the ear (considered below). Water is often found to be the main cause of the chain of events leading to infection, entering either through the external auditory canal or through infected droplets driven into the ear when sneezing or blowing the nose. As with other forms of otitis media, the basic problem is to control the disorder to avoid damaging complications. Chronic otitis media may form granulations and polyps, which in turn may break down the bony structure around the middle ear, which in turn could lead to abscess in the brain, meningitis, or infection of the labyrinth in the ear.

Treatment of chronic otitis media is both preventive and therapeutic; one should not blow the nose hard, sneezing should be done with an open mouth, and swimming and bathing should be done only with a cotton plug covered with vaseline or with a lambswool plug in the affected ear. Debris in the ear should be periodically removed. Topical applications of corticosteroids and specific antibiotics (determined after the infection is cultured and identified) are normally recognized as treatments of choice. As soon as the infection is controlled, and this may take as long as six or more months of careful management, it may be necessary to reconstruct the ear surgically, a procedure usually not undertaken until the patient is around

[77]M. M. Rubenstein, "The Treatment of Acute Otitis Media in Children," *American Journal of Disabled Children,* Vol. 109, 1965, pp. 308–313; E. H. Townsend, "Otitis Media in Pediatric Practice," *New York Journal of Medicine 1964,* pp. 1591–1597; and W. Hemenway et al., "Treating Acute Otitis Media," *Postgraduate Medicine,* Vol. 47, 1970, pp. 110–115, 135–138.

6 to 9 years of age, when the likelihood of upper respiratory infection declines.

With proper and persistent treatment, cure and prevention of hearing impairment should be nearly 100 percent. It should be stressed, however, that treatment of serous otitis media in general is not a "one-shot" process, and some cases may require repeated visits and surgeries. These are the facts of the disorder, and they should be reflected in medical treatment and assistance programs and provisions.[78]

Otitis Externa Otitis externa is basically a skin disorder. Infection is introduced into the ear, where the eardrum (tympanic membrane) may become infected and softened with bacterial growth. This growth, if unattended, may spread to the lymph nodes and other surrounding tissue or may perforate the eardrum. Treatment consists of removal of the softened tissue, and the administration of antimicrobial drops and systemic antibiotics (based on a culture and identification of the infectious agent). "Cure" is possible in about 95 percent of the cases, if treatment is properly administered and continuous care is given. The disorder has a persistence and rate of recurrence that may involve repeated care through adulthood.[79]

Perforation of Eardrum (Tympanic Membrane) Eardrum perforation can be caused by a number of factors and agents, such as trauma or acute otitis media. In rare cases, scarlet fever and rheumatic fever have been linked to perforations. Treatment consists of keeping water out of the ear to control and prevent infection, removal of softened tissue, and repeated application of topical anti-infectives. When the infection, if present, has been controlled, surgery may be called for to repair the drum, to prevent reinfection, and to improve hearing. In approximately 50 percent of the cases, cure will be "spontaneous" merely with the appropriate administration of antibiotics; however, in many of the remaining cases, surgery will be required to repair the damage. Surgery is successful in nearly all cases; hearing impairment will be mild but not disabling in some 25 percent of the

[78]J. Frederickson, "Otitis Media and Its Complications," *Archives of Otolaryngology,* Vol. 90, 1969, pp. 387–393; R. E. Jordan, "Secretory Otitis Media in Etiology of Cholesteatoma," *Archives of Otolaryngology,* Vol. 78, 1963, pp. 261–264; Ballenger , op. cit., pp. 646–655; and James L. Sheehy, "Surgery of Chronic Otitis Media," *Otolaryngology,* Vol. 2, Harper & Row, Medical Department, Hagerstown, Maryland, 1972, Chapter 10.

[79]"Otitis Externa," *British Medical Journal,* Vol. 1, 1969, pp. 70–71; E. H. Jones, *External Otitis: Diagnosis and Treatment,* Charles C Thomas, Springfield, Illinois, 1965; and Ballenger, op. cit., pp. 606–613.

cases, and there will be no measurable impairment in the other 75 percent. The success rate of treatment depends on careful and correct management of the infection, if that is the cause, and then upon skillful surgery by a qualified otologist.[80]

Bullous Myringitis Blisters will sometimes form on the eardrum itself in conjunction with an upper respiratory infection. The disorder produces extraordinary pain in most cases until the blister(s) rupture. The disorder is treated more or less symptomatically, e.g., through using local heat and hydroscopic and anaesthetic drops. The likelihood of successful treatment is nearly 100 percent. Surgical rupture of the blisters is *not* recommended because of the chance that infection may be spread to the sterile middle ear.[81] This disorder threatens the patient's hearing only if left untreated (and even then the probability of complication is slight) or if treated improperly (with subsequent infection of the middle ear).

Labyrinthitis The inner ear may become inflamed through infection of the middle ear, surgical accidents, or meningeal infections (from nerve bundles connecting the ear with the brain). Nausea, vertigo, and general loss of balance are all common symptoms of labyrinthitis. Treatment consists of bed rest, medication to control motion sickness, and antibiotics to control the infection. Corticosteroids are sometimes used to reduce the inflammation. Unless untreated or improperly treated, cure should be virtually assured without hearing impairment.[82]

Mumps Mumps can cause deafness, as can other infectious diseases of childhood. (Scarlet fever, typhoid fever, diphtheria, etc., have been brought under control and cause very little hearing disorder in modern settings.) Basically, the viral agent attacks the Organ of Corti and other segments of the inner ear, destroying the tissue. As a result, very little can be done medically to restore hearing, although if nerve involvement has not been too great, sensory aids and rehabilitation can be of great assistance in reducing the handicapping of the condi-

---

[80]P. H. Beales, "Acute Otitis Media," *Practitioner,* Vol. 199, 1967, pp. 752–760; E. L. Derlacki, "Repair of Central Perforations of the Drum," *Archives of Otolaryngology,* Vol. 58, 1953, pp. 405–417; and Kempe et al., p. 228.

[81]B. Palmer, "Hemorrhagic Bullous Myringitis," *Ear, Nose, and Throat Monthly,* Vol. 47, 1968, pp. 562–565.

[82]See Ballenger, op. cit., Chapter 48, where the disorder is treated mainly as a complication of other ear disorders.

tion. Prevention is the best course, however; and one should get the appropriate vaccinations.[83]

Measles and Other Viral Agents   Measles and other viral agents have been implicated in hearing loss; in fact, in the 1920s and 1930s, meningitis was the commonest clearly identified cause of acquired deafness in children. Vaccines and antibiotics have changed this drastically, with the one exception that certain of the antibiotics that are effective in treating the primary disorder are themselves capable of damaging the inner ear and hence causing deafness. If treatment of the viral agent is not done in a timely fashion, bilateral hearing impairment usually results.[84]

Eighth Nerve Tumors   Fortunately rather rare, although exact prevalence data are not available, tumors in the area of the inner ear are capable of producing sensorineural hearing loss and, if left untreated, weakening and damage of facial muscles and nerves, and death. If the tumor is detected early enough and is sufficiently small, it may be surgically removed. Morbidity and mortality from large tumors are both quite high. Diagnosis is a complex operation involving x-rays, audiometry, and other clinical findings.[85]

Cholesteatoma   When debris from the surface of the ear finds its way into the middle ear or mastoid following a perforation of the drum, a skin-lined cystic growth filled with hardened debris—cholesteatoma—may result. There are three general types, and treatment depends upon early and accurate diagnosis. In the congenital type, cystic growths are present in the temporal bone or in the mastoid at or near birth. In the primary acquired type, entrance through a perforation of the eardrum of hardened debris then develops into a growing cystic mass; in the secondary acquired type, entrance is much the same as in the primary, although the continuity of the growth is not notable as with primary. Infection is a decided possibility either in conjunction with the cholesteatoma or as a result of degeneration of the bone invaded by the disease. Diagnosis is complex and involves radiography of a highly specific variety.

Treatment of the disease involves surgical removal and reconstruction. Control of the disease and the likelihood of successful treat-

---

[83]Kempe et al., op. cit., p. 232; and Davis and Silverman, op. cit., pp. 120–122.
[84]Davis and Silverman, op. cit., p. 120.
[85]Ballenger, op. cit., pp. 764–767, and W. H. House, "Transtemporal Removal of Acoustic Neurinomas," *Archives of Otolaryngology,* Vol. 80, 1964, pp. 599–756.

ment are highly dependent upon early detection and surgical technique. It is unusual for one suffering from the disease to escape without some hearing loss, although in specialized facilities control of it may be as great as 95 percent. Removal of the mastoid and repair of the eardrum, the common treatment of choice, will in most cases result in normal or slightly reduced hearing in some 10 to 25 percent of the cases, moderate, but usable hearing in about 50 percent of the cases, and moderate but acceptable hearing with the proper sensory aid in the remainder. Here again, the success of surgery and hearing conservation is critically dependent upon early identification, correct diagnosis, and skillful treatment.[86]

Foreign Bodies Lodged in the Ear   An incredible variety of foreign objects can find their way into the ear. Irrigation will remove something like 50 percent of them, and simple surgical removal the rest. Success of treatment is nearly 100 percent, with the warning that inept efforts to remove the offending object are themselves a possible source of serious damage to the ear. For instance, beans (often used as fillers in children's toys) should not be irrigated with water because they swell when moist. And children being worked on without anaesthesia occasionally jump and hence cause injury. Sufficient cases of damage are known to make note of these "simple" problems. Well-meaning but unskilled efforts to remove the foreign body should be resisted.[87]

Cerumen   Some people are predisposed to produce excessive cerumen secretions (wax) in the ear. If not removed, wax can restrict and even close the ear canal and apply pressure to the eardrum. In single episodes, treatment, consisting of removal of the debris and irrigation of the canal, is virtually 100 percent certain of restoring the ear to health. Some people have a chronic problem with cerumen, however; for them, treatment is more one of "control" than a "once-and-for-all" proposition and may be required at unpredictable intervals through their lives.

Trauma to Organ of Corti   Skull fractures in and around the auditory canal and the middle and inner ear may cause permanent and total hearing loss. Concussion without fracture can also cause some hearing loss, which sometimes is not permanent. It is impossible to assess

[86]Ballenger, op. cit., pp. 648–652; and interview with Dr. Frederick Linthicum, Otologic Medical Group, Los Angeles, December 14, 1973. Treatment may be spread out over a one-year period and progress in several surgical steps.

[87]B. M. Merkel, "Foreign Bodies in the Ear Canal," *Journal of the Iowa Medical Society*, Vol. 47, 1957, pp. 744–746.

the likelihood of hearing loss in general, as it is basically a function of the extent and location of the fracture or the severity of the concussion.[88] Observation is certainly required, including competent diagnosis, and surgery may be indicated to repair the fracture.

Drug Effects on the Auditory Nerve   Several drugs are known to cause deafness by attacking and causing permanent injury to the Organ of Corti. Quinine, sometimes used to induce abortion, or even to induce labor by unknowing obstetricians, can cause irreparable damage. Certain antibiotics, primarily in the mycin group, are also known to cause deafness and hearing loss. Susceptibility to hearing loss varies from patient to patient, and loss may not be spontaneous but may occur at some time after the drugs have been administered. One otologist respondent in this study went so far as to recommend that antibiotics, particularly the mycins, be administered only in "life-threatening situations with continuous monitoring of kidney function to insure that toxic levels of the drugs had not been achieved." Very little can be done once the nerve has been damaged in this fashion, short of rehabilitative therapy.[89]

Hearing Loss Due to Noise   Temporary hearing loss is known to nearly everyone, from such causes as working around noisy industrial equipment, being near a discharging firearm, or riding a "go-cart" or motorcycle for some period of time. Usually, hearing returns to normal within a few hours or days; however, explosive sounds or continuous exposure to excessive noise can cause permanent hearing loss, as in the cases of rock musicians, children who persist in playing records at peak volume, and children who have cap pistols fired close to their ears. Treatment involves removal of the offending sound source or wearing of ear plugs, and rehabilitation. Because it involves the deterioration of the hair cells and nerve, surgical treatment is not possible. Persons already having some hearing impairment should be cautioned about exposure to loud and excessive noise over a period of time.[90]

Hereditary or Congenital Hearing Disorders   The term "congenital" literally means "at birth," although in common statistical usage the term has lost much sharpness of meaning: many instances are known where a child's impairment is called congenital, but in fact was the

[88]H. Schuknecht, "Head Injury," *Archives of Otolaryngology,* Vol. 63, 1956, pp. 513–528.

[89]James L. Sheehy, "Ototoxic Antibiotics," *California Medicine,* Vol. 94, 1961, pp. 363–365.

[90]Davis and Silverman, op. cit., pp. 114–119.

result of some infectious agent attacking the ear in infancy (e.g., meningitis) or of the injudicious use of antibiotics with damage occurring some time later. A few of the better known congenital disorders are listed and described below.

Maternal rubella: As is described in detail in the "Prevention" chapter, maternal rubella, particularly when contracted in the first three months of pregnancy, is capable of causing an insidious assortment of handicaps, not the least of which is congenital hearing impairment of often marked severity. Ex post facto, there is no treatment except rehabilitation.

Congenital malformations of the Organ of Corti: Two basic classes of this disorder exist: hereditary and "misadventures of fetal life." In the first class, it is thought to be transmitted by a recessive gene in the more common case, and by a dominant gene which also is linked to kidney malformations. Both cases result in bilateral and severe impairment. Misadventures include maternal rubella, administration of ototoxic drugs (as noted above), and damage from other, unspecified viral agents. A number of specific syndromes have been identified describing specific ways in which the Organ of Corti and the inner ear may be malformed and dysfunctional, e.g., Waardenburg, Mondini-Alexander, and Schiebe. As with other inner ear disorders, treatment prospects are not good. The major concern is to identify the child as soon as possible to ensure that rehabilitation progresses as well as possible.[91]

Erythroblastosis fetalis: As a result of Rh sensitivity, the infant may suffer from hearing loss. The critical combinations are an Rh-positive father and an Rh-negative mother. Particularly in second and subsequent births the condition, commonly known as "newborn jaundice," can attack the central nervous system through a protein reaction, and the auditory system is susceptible to the disorder. Treatment is massive transfusion of the infant, e.g., "exchange transfusion" if indicated by serum bilirubin level, and placement of the infant on a high-risk registry for subsequent close examination, early identification, and appropriate rehabilitation. Lowered oxygen levels in the blood aggravate the problem. Prevention is partly possible through inoculation of the Rh-negative mother with an anti-Rh antibody.[92]

[91]H. Davis, "The Young Deaf Child: Identification and Management," *Acta Oto-Laryngologica,* (Supplement), Vol. 206, 1964, pp. 1–258; Ballenger, op. cit., pp. 769–773; and Kempe et al., op. cit., pp. 231–232.

[92]Davis and Silverman, op. cit., pp. 122–123; J. G. Hall, "On the Neuropathologic Changes in the Central Nervous System Following Neonatal Asphyxia with Specific Reference to the Auditory System in Man," *Acta Oto-Laryngologica,* (Supplement), Vol. 188, 1964, pp. 331–338; and C. Friedman, *Rh Isoimmunization and Erythroblastosis Fetalis,* Appleton-Century-Crofts, New York, 1969.

Stenosis and atresia of external auditory canal: A narrowed canal may be caused through infection or may be congenital. In the former case, treatment consists of removal of the infection and the debris it leaves, and repair of any damage done to the canal or the middle ear. Damage may also result from surgical misadventure. Repairing the damage requires a highly skilled technique but is successful in approximately 90 percent of the cases. Depending upon the seriousness of the narrowing and damage, there may be no hearing loss at all, but occasionally moderate impairment results (especially in the congenital case). Bone-conduction hearing aids and prompt rehabilitation should alleviate the handicap.[93]

Congenital malformation of the eardrum: There may be congenital malformations of the external ear, the auditory canal, and the eardrum, in which all or part of any or all of these items is missing or deformed. Surgical restoration is usually called for if the disorder is bilateral; if unilateral, surgery may be postponed because of possible damage to the facial nerve. Success rates depend largely on the degree and site of the malformation; likewise, hearing loss depends on the severity of the disorder and the success of restorative efforts.[94]

Otosclerosis: Because of abnormal bony growth, usually at or near the stapes or stirrup, hearing gradually becomes impaired. Otosclerosis is hereditary and occurs more commonly in females. It is rare for the disorder to manifest itself before about the age of 15 years. For those whose nerve has not been involved, surgical treatment is possible and successful in between 80 and 90 percent of the cases. Depending upon the extent, if any, of nerve involvement, hearing can be totally restored. Repeated operations in the case of initial nonrestoration have been successful.[95]

Medical Treatment Costs of Hearing Disorders

A sample of treatment costs for medical services available to those suffering from hearing disorders is presented in Table 9.17. These data are a sample of charges in 1973 for high-quality care in a specialized otologic practice, and may vary considerably for different parts of the country and for different practices. These estimates are for professional otologist's fees only; payment for other aspects of medical care such as days of hospitalization are excluded.

[93]Ballenger, op. cit., pp. 600–613; David D. De Weese and William H. Saunders, *Textbook of Otolaryngology,* The C. V. Mosby Company, St. Louis, 1968 ed., pp. 345–346, where the Treacher-Collins syndrome is discussed; and Kempe et al., op. cit., p. 225.

[94]James A. Crabtree, "Tympanoplastic Techniques in Congenital Atresia," *Archives of Otolaryngology,* Vol. 88, 1968, pp. 89–96.

[95]Otologic Medical Group, *A Discussion of Otosclerosis,* Los Angeles, 1972 (pamphlet); Kempe et al., op. cit., p. 229; and Ballenger, op. cit., Chapter 49.

Table 9.17
SAMPLE TREATMENT COSTS FOR HEARING DISORDERS IN CHILDREN,
SPECIALIZED PRACTICE, CALENDAR YEAR 1973

Item	Charge ($)	Item	Charge ($)
Service group/routine/MDs		Hearing aid test/check	20
Office visit	12[a]	Special audiologic evalu-	
Initial comprehensive diag-		ation	50
nostic otologic examina-		SISI only	5
tion	35	Stenger test	10
Initial hospital consultation	35	Recruitment test	5
Routine hospital visit	12	Impedance test	10
Diagnostic group/X-ray		Delayed feedback	15
Plain mastoid	35	Electrical promontory testing	250
Plain sinus series	35	CROS evaluation	10
Polytome mastoid X-ray	80	Diagnostic/vestibular testing	
Polytome otologic survey	60	Electronystagmography	35
Poly-petrous pyramid X-ray	80	Eng positional	15
Skull, complete	35	Eng interpretation and report	15
Pelvic scan	5	Special vestibular testing	[b]
Implant series	60	Diagnostic/allergy testing	
Diagnostic group/laboratory		and treatment	
Culture sensitivity	10	Terpene and Petro tests	55
Blood count, complete	5	Terpene or Petro retest	6
Protein, total serum,		Complete allergy test	230
chemical	8	Allergy injection	5
Child's panel	36	Allergy medication	10[c]
Hydroxycorticosteroid (17		Histamine titration	10
OHCS)	36	TOE/dust/inhalants	50
Lipoprotein phenotypes	25	Pollen and inhalant testing	115
Diagnostic/audiology		Foods testing	115
Initial hearing test	15	Recheck pollen and inhala-	
Return hearing test	10	tion	50
Unilateral speech	5	Recheck individual food	6[d]
Bilateral speech	10	Miscellaneous and office pro-	
Bekesy unilateral SISI	15	cedures	
Bekesy bilateral SISI	25	Myringotomy, unilateral	40[e]
Tone decay	5	Myringotomy with tube, uni-	
Hearing aid evaluation	35	lateral	50[f]

[a] Factor used in calculation of repeat visits.
[b] No maximum fee.
[c] Minimum; no maximum fee.
[d] For each food tested.
[e] Plus $25 for subsequent visits.
[f] Plus $35 for subsequent visits.
[g] Plus $60 for subsequent visits.
[h] Special charge.
[i] Basic fee covers all procedures, including 6 months of postoperative care; any additional fees required are noted.

[j] Plus 6 postoperative office visits = $72.
[k] Fee varies.
[l] Plus 2 postoperative office visits per year for life to clean cavity.
[m] Plus 2 postoperative office visits per year for life.
[n] Plus 3 postoperative office visits.
[o] Fee varies around average.
[p] Plus 8 postoperative office visits.

Table 9.17—Continued

Item	Charge ($)	Item	Charge ($)
Myringotomy with tube, bilateral	80[g]	Revision of tympanoplasty without mastoidectomy	1000[n]
I.V. histamine	15	Tympanoplasty with mastoidectomy	1200[n]
Injection	5	Tympanoplasty with revised mastoidectomy	k
Medication	b	Revised tympanoplasty with mastoidectomy	k
Surgical nurse	50	Labyrinthectomy TR/canal	600
Special reports	b	Labyrinthectomy TR/lab	900
Surgical procedures[i]		Vestibular nerve sec TL	1000[o]
Myringotomy, unilateral	150[j]	Vestibular nerve sec MF	1500[o]
Myringotomy, bilateral with tube	200[j]	Facial nerve repair	1500
Myringotomy, unilateral with tube	150[j]	Facial nerve graft	1500
Adenoidectomy	100	Facial nerve decompression	1000
Tonsillectomy	200	Shunt—optic/periodic	700[o]
Myringoplasty	800	Biopsy of eac.	250
Revision of myringoplasty	k	Petrosectomy	1500[n]
Mastoidectomy, simple	800	Cholesteatoma removal, primary	1500[n]
Mastoidectomy, radical	1000[i]	Exostosis, removal	700
Mastoid obliteration	1000[m]	Tumor removal, glomus jugular	2500[p]
Mastoidectomy, mod. radical	1000[m]	Tumor removal, glomus tympanicum	1500[p]
Revision of mastoidectomy	k	Tympanotomy	k
Stapes mobilization	1000	Tympanosympathectomy	k
Stapes exploration	1000	Meatoplasty	k
Stapedectomy	1000	Oval window fistula repair	k
Revision of stapedectomy	k	Acoustic neuroma, removal	2500[p]
Stapes fenestration	1000		
Revision of stapes fenestration	k		
Tympanoplasty without mastoidectomy	1000[n]		

As with vision disorders, Table 9.17 makes it apparent that high-quality medical care can be had, and can also be costly in the absolute sense. Again, however, the appropriate tradeoff is between the cost of such care and all costs involved in a lifetime of being handicapped or more severely handicapped than one would be with good medical care. In this sense, medical treatment is probably a "bargain." We should also call attention to the discrepancy between this fee schedule and the top fees payable under federally supported medical treatment programs. Many of the fees in Table 9.17 exceed maximum governmental program limits. Finally, we repeat the observation that the finest specialized medical care in the world is relatively useless, irrespective of its costs, if local identification and diagnosis services are inadequate.

NEEDED IMPROVEMENT IN MEDICAL SERVICE PROGRAMS

A significant number of potentially handicapping disorders can be prevented, reduced, or eliminated altogether with skilled medical treatment. The major problem is not the quality of medical treatment but the fact that so many handicapped children are not receiving it. Lacking early identification, accurate diagnosis, and timely direction, the best medical treatment in the world may well be practically and tragically irrelevant.

For example, many of the disorders causing vision and hearing handicaps, even the more exotic of them requiring highly specialized attention, can be treated at remarkably low cost relative to the expected lifetime costs incurred by a handicapped person. On cost grounds alone, a convincing argument often can be made that the best medical treatment available represents a profitable social investment, since it reduces future claims on society and the public treasury. To deny or limit these services is to risk being penny-wise and pound-foolish. Add to the cost-argument even the most elementary humanitarian concerns, and the case for providing medical services to those who need them becomes virtually incontrovertible.

The limited and inelastic population of gifted and highly skilled physicians could be better utilized than it presently is if the population in need were actively identified (see Chap. 7) and if the "invisible intelligence network" currently linking the population with doctors were made visible through an improved direction service concentrated at the regional level. (See our recommendations in Chap. 8.) Effective direction could overcome the consumer's ignorance of where to get appropriate medical care; and adequate National Health Insurance for all citizens, together with other supplementary services such as transportation, could surmount the economic deterrent.

The provision of good medical care to the nation's handicapped youth is not a "blue sky" objective. The tradeoff, in rational terms, is between lifetime quality-of-life and economic costs for a permanent disability and possibly one-time and relatively limited costs for proper medical treatment, with all that might entail for the aggregate reduction in the number and extent of handicapped persons in the population.

The Maternal and Child Health Service provides support for the operation of a multitude of varied and disconnected programs. The limited available resources have been spread so thin that they lose the potential leverage to mount a concerted effort to solve a manageable subset of maternal and child health problems. For instance, about 334,000 mothers received services under the Maternity Medical Clinic program in 1971, but they accounted for less than 9 percent of all live births in the United States; most states offered expectant parent classes, but only 87,760 parents attended them nationwide in 1970; general pediatric clinics provided services to around 200,000 children in 1970 but this represents only about 0.2 percent of the total population who might have benefited from these services.

We recommend that the Office of the Secretary of HEW conduct a full-scale evaluation of all MCHS-supported programs with an end in view of concentrating future resources on the most critical needs and most effective programs. The remaining programs would be candidates for termination. Research studies on specific disorders should be transferred to the cognizant National Institute of Health.

The Crippled Children's Service program is financially closed-ended, and states do what they think best with the limited funds available to them. One option is to concentrate on one or a few extremely high-quality programs for a limited number of handicapped children. This strategy often bears fruit in the innovative, high-quality care for which CCS has been justly applauded. But given a fixed or slow-growing total budget and fast-rising costs, this concentration means that other children are not served at all. On the other hand, a state official may spread his resources over as many children as possible so as to offer services on something like an equitable basis. Dilution of service coverage and quality is the hazard with this option. At some point, it is no longer financially desirable for a physician to accept the CCS payment schedules, which are often lower than prevailing private rates. In several interviews, physicians reported a dangerously thin margin between their merely breaking even on a CCS patient and actually losing money. (We have heard of certain specialized physicians and groups who have declined CCS clients on these grounds alone.) In short, the CCS program can deliver high-quality services, but is financially unable to meet the total needs of the eligible population.

It is a stated federal goal to make high-quality, comprehensive medical services available throughout the country. As basic first steps toward that goal, someone has to figure out where the best individual programs are operating, determine what makes them "best," what they cost, and how they work, and then figure out what resources it will take to make the "best" generally available.

Commitment and money have been forthcoming to some extent in provisions encompassing the financially open-ended Medicaid program, which partially duplicates the responsibility of the CCS program to provide medical treatment to financially needy families with handicapped youth.

Pending resolution of difficulties experienced with the present Medicaid program, and pending the adoption of National Health Insurance or some other program to make high-quality comprehensive medical care available to all youth, we recommend that the CCS program be retained and expanded.

While the basic services provided under Medicaid are undoubtedly an improvement over the previous situation, the program's welfare basis and the prevalence of welfare administration have caused other difficulties besides those related to medical data collection, evaluation, and reporting. Some states have shown reluctance to match Title XIX dollars, an understandable eventuality where "welfare" has taken on important negative connotations, particularly at election time. Standards for the health care provided under Medicaid have not been generally established, an omission traceable to the relatively lower participation of health professionals in the state planning and programming processes, as compared with the CCS program. Program emphasis has been on treatment, but since 1967 there have been provisions for mandatory early and periodic screening, diagnosis, and treatment of Medicaid-eligible children. Compliance and full implementation of these provisions have been hard to attain from the states. Data accounting for total numbers of individuals screened, referral rates, disease incidence and follow-up measures undertaken are beginning to be collected, but the results are incomplete. The basic problem in this case is that the states have little incentive to seek out any more children than are already on the rolls and receiving Medicaid assistance. And, as with CCS, the payment schedule reportedly is often significantly lower than private rates; that deterrent, coupled with red tape and slow payments, has reportedly led more than a few physicians to avoid Medicaid patients. Relative to other federally supported health programs, two other features of Medicaid merit careful attention: it is meant to be comprehensive in covering the financially needy population, and it is financially open-ended. Both are necessary preconditions if one is interested in providing a full range of health services to all eligible and needy members of the population.

In the short run, pending the adoption of National Health Insurance or some other program designed to make quality comprehensive medical care available to all youth, we have two recommendations.

Consideration should be given to integration of CCS and Medicaid program operations in the states. The desirable comprehensive and financially open-ended nature of the Medicaid program could benefit from some of the apparently better program administration features of CCS, which also provides for medical treatment for handicapped youth in financially needy families. A thorough evaluation of methods and effects of integration should precede implementation.

Significantly improved management procedures should be implemented to yield much better Medicaid program management information; to cut delays; to improve the equity of eligibility standards; to ensure that mandatory provisions are implemented (e.g., screening); and to permit revision of medical payment schedules to reflect the realities of the medical marketplace (for example, the schedules would be tied to an escalator provision sensitive to a medical cost-of-living index compiled by the Bureau of Labor Statistics). Coverage for all Supplementary Security Income recipients should be assured (see the Income Maintenance chapter below).

Pressure continues to exist for a national health insurance program. Besides Administration proposals, various plans have been initiated in the Congress.[96] The government can, in effect, make sure an insurance policy is available to parents so that the care of a handicapped child does not become an economic catastrophe to them.

Realistic estimation of the costs and effects of the various proposals has begun. The selection process leading to a final decision of whether any proposal will be enacted into law will take considerable time, given the incredible variety of interests involved and the large fiscal implications of the proposed concepts. Finally, implementation will certainly not take place overnight. In short, whatever form National Health Insurance takes if and when it becomes law, it will not be an operating program for some time. Consequently, the short-term recommendations noted above for improvements of MCHS, CCS, and Medicaid should not be disregarded.

We endorse the concept of National Health Insurance as a long-term solution, provided that it includes coverage of comprehensive

---

[96]A concise summary of these plans as of the fall of 1973 is contained in John K. Iglehart, "Health Report: HEW's National Medical Insurance Plan Includes Major Cost-Sharing Requirement," *National Journal Reports,* October 20, 1973, pp. 1570–1571.

*medical services to all handicapped youth in need and provides for
the special needs of handicapped persons.*

In the longer run, NHI could do much to reduce the current reliance of the handicapped on scattered noncomprehensive medical programs that do not serve significant proportions of those in need. The legitimate specialized needs of the handicapped can best be served if NHI includes certain features. For example, any program made into law should explicitly provide for continuity of treatment during the transition from the current to the new system, and should take into account prevention, screening, extended medical treatment, medically related sensory aids and other equipment, pre-existing conditions, extraordinary transportation costs related to medical care, and catastrophic contingencies.

The effects of various NHI proposals on the handicapped population deserve special attention from HEW. In particular, the Office for Handicapped Individuals or some other appropriate entity within HEW might review and react to *all* NHI proposals by providing assessments of their likely effects on the lives of the handicapped.

Consider that one Administration proposal for NHI limited preventive care to family planning, maternity, and well-child care.[97] But a single vaccination program for rubella, even though poorly coordinated and needing some sustaining attention, has saved millions of dollars in continuing medical and other service costs. The preventive aspects of the NHI proposals do not appear to have been well enough researched nor their implications well enough considered, especially from the point of view of present and *future* handicapped citizens. (See the chapter on prevention.)

NHI could also provide comprehensive identification of handicaps or disorders leading to handicaps by providing medical screening at age 2, which we recommend in the chapter on identification. No one currently has direct responsibility for this needed service, and no one is likely to assume it unless directed to do so.

Another provision of one proposed NHI plan, which calls for an independent and objective assessment of its likely effect, relates to the coverage of eye examinations, eyeglasses, hearing aids, and dental services for children through the age of 12. The selection of the 12-year-old cut-off age appears at first glance to have been made arbitrarily. The realistic and legitimate needs of the young handicapped population aged 13 to 21 are not represented in this provision as formulated. As discussed in Chap. 11, sensory aids are sometimes expensive but generally appear cost-beneficial; but no current pro-

---

[97]As reported in Iglehart, op. cit., p. 1570.

gram assures that all children needing aids can receive them. NHI is one clear way to rectify the omission.

The "Government Assurance Program" aspect of one of the Administration's proposals contains several commendable features. One of them is that it provides guarantees, as it were, to those unable to obtain private coverage through the main provisions of the proposal. However, care must be taken that handicapped children with "preexisting conditions" are not denied coverage for medical needs related to their handicaps because those conditions preexisted the insurance coverage. In a basic sense, handicapped people differ from the actuarial populations used to calculate expected medical payouts in an insurance program, and special consideration must be given to this fact.

Limits on the amount of medical insurance coverage for handicapped youth need to be set with cognizance of possible very high bills for extended medical treatment or short-term remedial treatment. Failure to cover expensive medical treatment may cost the system even more in the long run by increasing the costs of other services. Similarly, it could be more expensive for society in the long run if a family failed to obtain medical services because it could not afford the relatively small cost of transportation to a distant special medical facility.

Chapter 10

EDUCATION

OVERVIEW

This chapter contains information about federal programs and roles in the education of handicapped children; data on special education programs in the states; and recommendations for improving special education programs.

To compete successfully with his nonhandicapped counterparts in society, a handicapped person needs at least equal educational opportunities. Public support of special education is doubly important, since education in this country, unlike health, has traditionally been a public responsibility, and the parent of a handicapped child will find limited alternatives in the private sector for his child's education. If private special education *is* available, there is no insurance plan to help defray the cost.

Because the learning process requires the coordination of physical and mental skills, many handicapping conditions become evident in the public school through formal school identification programs (e.g., vision and hearing screening) and informal methods (e.g., teacher observation). Once a handicapped child has been identified, medical or other services available in the public education system may be necessary, in addition to special educational assistance.

Government spending for the "excess cost" of special education above the cost of regular education was estimated by a recent study to be over $4.7 billion in FY 1976, or about $1200 per physically or mentally handicapped child served.[1] Of this total, that study estimated the federal, state, and local shares to be 14, 55, and 31 percent respectively. The same study estimated that about 9 percent of the

[1]W. H. Wilken et al., *State Aid for Special Education: Who Benefits?* National Foundation for the Improvement of Education and the National Conference of State Legislatures, Washington, D.C., October 1, 1976, pp. I-2, I-3.

328

school age population participated in some form of special education in FY 1976. Great variation exists in these statistics across states, however,[2] and the 9 percent figure includes some unknown amount of double counting and counting of many children who are inadequately served.

In FY 1977, the October 1976 and February 1977 P.L. 94-142–required counts of the number of different children receiving special education showed an average of approximately 3.7 million children being given some service.[3]

The above figures are marked increases above the levels of the early 1970s. In 1971 special education programs in the United States assisted an estimated 3,046,000 physically or mentally handicapped youth under 22, or 6.6 percent of the public school enrollment. Total annual special education expenditures were an estimated $2.7 billion, of which the federal share was 12 percent in FY 1972.

In 1975 there were about 20 major federal programs aiding the education of handicapped children. Public Law 94-142, the new "Education for All Handicapped Children Act," was passed in November 1975. This new Act was basically superimposed on existing federal special education programs without changing them, even though P.L. 94-142 potentially represents a major revised federal role in both funding and control of special education programming.

The 1977 federal programs of primary concern to this study are:

EHA-B (P.L. 94-142)
ESEA-Title I (P.L. 89-313)
ESEA-Title IV
Early Education
Headstart
Deaf-Blind Services
Learning Disabilities
Severely Handicapped
Vocational Education
Regional Post-Secondary Education
Higher Education
Gallaudet College
NTI for Deaf
Personnel Preparation
Recruitment and Information

[2]Ibid. For additional statistical and descriptive material, see F. J. Weintraub et al. (eds.), *Public Policy and the Education of Exceptional Children,* The Council for Exceptional Children, Reston, Virginia, 1976; and *Yearbook of Special Education: 1975–1976,* Marquis Academic Media, Chicago, 1975.

[3]*Insight,* The Council for Exceptional Children, Reston, Virginia, June 3, 1977, p. 5.

Regional Resource Centers
Media Services and Captioned Films
American Printing House for the Blind
Library of Congress
Handicapped Research

By the term "handicapped children" in this chapter we mean people aged 0 to 21 years who have sufficient mental or physical impairment to require significant special educational services. The federal definition of handicapped children in P.L. 94-142, the "Education for All Handicapped Children Act," is

> . . . mentally retarded, hard of hearing, deaf, speech impaired, visually handicapped, seriously emotionally disturbed, orthopedically impaired, or other health impaired children, or children with specific learning disabilities who by reason thereof require special education and related services.

> The term "children with specific learning disabilities" means those children who have a disorder in one or more of the basic psychological processes involved in understanding or in using language, spoken or written, which disorder may manifest itself in imperfect ability to listen, think, speak, read, write, spell, or do mathematical calculations. Such disorders include such conditions as perceptual handicaps, brain injury, minimal brain dysfunction, dyslexia, and developmental aphasia. Such term does not include children who have learning problems which are primarily the result of visual, hearing, or motor handicaps, of mental retardation, of emotional disturbance, or of environmental, cultural, or economic disadvantage.[4]

By the term "special education" we mean special services in a variety of settings, ranging from a residential institution, to a special school, to a special class, to a regular class with a resource room or a part-time special teacher or a consultant advising the regular teacher. It includes diagnostic services, counseling, speech therapy, training in activities of daily living, and other services, as well as education in conventional classroom subjects. The federal definitions of special education and related services follow:

> The term "special education" means specially designed instruction, at no cost to parents or guardians, to meet the unique needs of a handicapped child, including classroom instruction, instruction in physical education, home instruction, and instruction in hospitals and institutions.

[4]20 U.S.C. 1402 as amended.

The term "related services" means transportation, and such developmental, corrective, and other supportive services (including speech pathology and audiology, psychological services, physical and occupational therapy, recreation, and medical and counseling services, except that such medical services shall be for diagnostic and evaluation purposes only) as may be required to assist a handicapped child to benefit from special education, and includes the early identification and assessment of handicapping conditions in children.[5]

Available data on incidence rates for handicaps in school age children have already been reviewed (Chap. 5). The estimates of the total prevalence of exceptionalities among school-age children are typically in the 9 to 12 percent range.[6]

Improvement in the education of handicapped children is clearly needed. This need exists despite the rapid expansion and evolution that has taken place in special education in recent years. Several major trends are observable:

- Federal and state court rulings and legislation are being implemented, making appropriate special education mandatory for all handicapped children.
- Increased numbers of handicapped children are being served (up from 6 percent in the early 1970s to approximately 9 percent of school-age children now).
- Special education expenditures are rising rapidly (approximately doubling since the early 1970s).
- Increased use is being made of "individualized education programs" designed to meet the specific needs of the child.
- A shift is underway toward provision of services in the "least restrictive environment" that is satisfactory for the child (popularly called "mainstreaming").
- A major shift away from local agencies and toward state and federal agencies is evident in both *funding* and *control.*

Despite the large expenditures for special education, the recent legal mandates that handicapped children have a right to an appropriate public education, and recent dramatic improvements in ser-

---

[5]P.L. 94-142.

[6]See, for example, R. A. Rossmiller, J. Hale, and L. Frohreich, *Educational Programs for Exceptional Children: Resource Configurations and Costs,* Department of Educational Administration, University of Wisconsin, Madison, August 1970; Patricia A. Craig, "Counting Handicapped Children: A Federal Imperative," *Journal of Education Finance,* Vol. 1, No. 3, Winter 1976; and P. Craig and N. McEachron, "The Development and Analysis of Base Line Data for the Estimation of Incidence of the Handicapped School Age Population," Research Note EPRC 2158-19, Stanford Research Institute, Menlo Park, California, January 3, 1975.

vices, several problems still exist: many youth are not receiving needed special educational services, or are receiving the wrong or inadequate services; inequities prevail in the availability of special educational services; gaps exist in the services offered within geographic areas; policy-relevant information on the costs and effects of different services is insufficiently available; coordination of the service system is inadequate; and, most important, the resources devoted to these youths' needs are insufficient. For example, the "Education for All Handicapped Children Act" included the following statement of findings:

1. There are more than eight million handicapped children in the United States today;
2. The special educational needs of such children are not being fully met;
3. More than half of the handicapped children in the United States do not receive appropriate educational services which would enable them to have full equality of opportunity;
4. One million of the handicapped children in the United States are excluded entirely from the public school system and will not go through the educational process with their peers;
5. There are many handicapped children throughout the United States participating in regular school programs whose handicaps prevent them from having a successful educational experience because their handicaps are undetected;
6. Because of the lack of adequate services within the public school system, families are often forced to find services outside the public school system, often at great distance from their residence and at their own expense.[7]

A breakdown of federal expenditures is shown in Tables 10.1 and 10.2 for FY 1972 and FY 1977 for the three major types of programs: those for instruction of handicapped students (81 percent of expenditures in FY 1977); those designed to produce resources such as teachers and instructional materials (17 percent); and those sponsoring research (2 percent). Note that federal expenditures grew from about $315 million to the current $542 million plus, or 72 percent in five years.

Total federal, state, and local expenditures by type of handicap are shown for FY 1972 in Table 10.3. The mentally retarded received the largest fraction of total expenditures—an estimated 45 percent—while speech impaired, emotionally disturbed, and learning disabled each received 10 or 11 percent.

[7]P.L. 94-142, Section 3(b).

Table 10.1
SUMMARY OF FY 1972 FEDERAL PROGRAMS FOR
EDUCATION OF HANDICAPPED CHILDREN

Program	Budget ($ million)	Estimated Number of Youth Served (year)
Education	245.966	—
EHA-B	37.500	204,836 (1970)
ESEA-Title I		
Local Education Agencies	28.000	180,000 (1972)
P.L. 89–313	56.381	107,698 (1970)
ESEA-Title III	20.100	134,047 (1971)
Headstart	33.384	37,900 (1973)
Vocational Education Act	38.384	221,342 (1972)
Higher Education Act	0.436	—
Federal Schools for Deaf		
Gallaudet College	7.888	1,583 (1971)
NTI for Deaf	2.907	395 (1971)
Kendall School	1.212	208 (1971)
Model Secondary School	2.524	100 (1972)
Special Target Groups		
Deaf-Blind Centers	7.500	2,300 (1971)
Early Education	7.500	2,000 (1971)
Learning Disabilities (EHA-G)	2.250	—
Instructional Support	57.906	—
Teaching Personnel		
EHA-D	35.145	—
Education Professions Development Act	6.100	—
Regional Resource Centers (EHA-C)	3.550	—
Media		
EHA-F	10.500	—
American Printing House for the Blind	1.580	—
Library of Congress	1.031	—
Research	10.994	—
Research (EHA-E)	10.994	—
Total	314.866	—

ROLES AND GOALS

The following are the stated objectives and priorities of the federal government with respect to education of handicapped children:

(a) The U.S. Office of Education is committed to assuring equal educational opportunities for all handicapped children. The efforts of the Office of Education in meeting this commitment are coordinated through the Bureau of Education for the Handicapped.

Table 10.2
**SUMMARY OF FY 1977 FEDERAL PROGRAMS FOR EDUCATION OF
HANDICAPPED CHILDREN**

Program	Budget ($ million)	Estimated Number of Children Receiving Special Education	Primary Target Population of Handicapped Children
Education			
EHA-B (P.L. 94–142)	110	406,000	All
ESEA-Title I (PL. 89–313)	111	207,000	State operated and supported schools
ESEA-Title IV	21	?	School age
Early Education	22	14,000	Preschool age
Headstart	47.5	35,000	Preschool age disadvantaged
Deaf-Blind Services	16	5,000	Deaf-Blind
Learning Disabilities	5	8,700	Learning disabled
Severely Handicapped	3	1,800	Severely handicapped
Vocational Education	48.2	310,000	All with vocational needs
Regional Post-Secondary Education	2	1,500	Post-secondary age
Higher Education	?	?	Post-secondary age physically disabled
Gallaudet College	41	2,000	Post-secondary age deaf
NTI for Deaf	13	680	Post-secondary age deaf
Instructional Support			
Personnel Preparation	40	(a)	All
Recruitment and Information	1	(b)	All with information and referral needs
Regional Resource Centers	10	(c)	All with identification and service prescription needs
Media Services and Captioned Films	16	—	All
Amer. Print. House Blind	3	—	Blind
Library of Congress	22	—	Blind and physically handicapped
Research			
Handicapped Research	11	—	All
Total	>542	(d)	

SOURCES: See text.
ᵃA total of 33,000 personnel were trained.
ᵇApproximately 50,000 people were provided information.
ᶜApproximately 90,000 children were given referral services, and 2,900 personnel were trained.
ᵈThe number of *different* children served cannot be determined from the available data since the same children are sometimes served through more than one program.

Table 10.3
SUMMARY OF TOTAL SPECIAL EDUCATION EXPENDITURES AND NUMBER SERVED, BY TYPE OF HANDICAP, FY 1972[a]

Type of Handicap	State & Local ($ million)[a]	Federal ($ million)	Total ($ million)	Expenditures per Child Served ($)	Total Number Served	Percent of Total Served
Mentally retarded, trainable	260.0	45.5	305.5	2064	148,000	4.9
Mentally retarded, educable	840.0	75.9	915.9	1217	752,000	24.7
Hard of hearing	55.0	13.6	68.6	1247	55,000	1.8
Deaf	91.0	42.5	133.5	4767	28,000	0.9
Speech impaired	251.0	21.8	272.8	197	1,383,000	45.4
Visually impaired	66.0	19.2	85.2	3043	28,000	0.9
Emotionally disturbed	258.0	35.0	293.0	1472	199,000	6.5
Crippled	210.0	10.0	220.0	1718	128,000	6.5
Learning disabled	250.0	32.1	282.1	1227	128,000	4.2
Other health impaired	84.0	19.2	103.2	1086	230,000	7.5
Total	2364.0	314.9	2678.9	879	95,000	3.1
					3,046,000	100.0

[a] See the later text of this chapter for data sources and methods of estimates.

335

(b) Education of handicapped children has been adopted by the U.S. Office of Education as one of its major priorities. The six objectives designed to implement this priority are:

(1) To assure that every handicapped child is receiving an appropriately designed education;

(2) To assist the States in providing appropriate educational services to the handicapped;

(3) To assure that every handicapped child who leaves school has had career educational training that is relevant to the job market, meaningful to his career aspirations, and realistic to his fullest potential;

(4) To assure that all handicapped children served in the schools have a trained teacher or other resource person competent in the skills required to aid the child in reaching his full potential; and

(5) To secure the enrollment of preschool-aged handicapped children in Federal, State, and local educational and day care programs.

(6) To encourage additional educational programming for severely handicapped children to enable them to become as independent as possible, thereby reducing their requirements for institutional care, and providing opportunities for self-development.[8]

Furthermore, P.L. 94-142 states that the intention or objective of Congress is "to assure that all handicapped children have available to them, within the time periods specified . . ., a free appropriate public education."

While education is primarily a nonfederal responsibility, the principal rationale for federal involvement is the current lack of equal educational opportunity for handicapped children.

At the state level, special education is also of very high priority. A 1975 survey of state officials found that of 42 areas of need for children and their families, the need of the handicapped child was rated first priority.[9]

We note that "equal education opportunity" for handicapped children does not mean either equal resources or equal objectives for both handicapped and nonhandicapped children. In general, the educational resources and goals established for each handicapped child will be different and based on the child's needs and potential.

---

[8]*Code of Federal Regulations,* Title 45, Public Welfare, Part 121, Definitions; General Provisions, Section 121.3.

[9]E. R. La Crosse, *State Trends and Priorities in Services for Children and Their Families,* Education Commission of the States, Report No. 90, Denver, Colorado, May 1976.

Council for Exceptional Children personnel have defined equal opportunity in terms of "equal access to differing resources for differing objectives."[10]

A list of federal programs aimed at educating handicapped youth is shown in Table 10.4; they are grouped into three basic classifications, according to whether funds are used primarily for instruction of handicapped students, production of resources in support of instruction, or research and development in education of the handicapped. The programs are also classified by the function that the federal government is fulfilling in the particular program. The X marks indicate the major federal function in each current program. Here again, assignment of roles and functions to programs cannot be made neatly. It should be emphasized that assignment of the primary or major role is based on our opinions.

The multifaceted federal role in special education is in a state of transition.[11] Since the federal government supplies only 14 percent of the total special education funds, the present federal role is not a dominant one, but appears to be a changing and hybrid mixture of roles. As Table 10.4 shows, the various programs serve a number of very different functions. However, the primary federal role prior to passage of the "Education for All Handicapped Children Act" in 1975 was one of catalyzing or stimulating expansion and improvement of special education. As P.L. 94-142 is implemented and the federal efforts and role grow, the primary federal role will become one of basic service support. Without question, special education has been stimulated to expand and improve greatly in recent years. One cannot ascertain the extent that this is a result of federal programs, however, since other forces have also contributed to the stimulation. Those other forces include increasingly effective lobbying efforts by professional and parent groups as well as court decisions affirming the right of handicapped children to an appropriate education.[12] Clearly, however, the federal special education programs have aided and contributed to the expansion and improvement of special education at the state and local level.

---

[10]F. J. Weintraub and A. Abeson, "Appropriate Education for All Handicapped Children: A Growing Issue," *Syracuse Law Review*, Vol. 23, 1973, p. 1056.

[11]For a recent discussion of alternative federal roles in education in general, see the Congressional Budget Office issue paper, *Elementary, Secondary, and Vocational Education—An Examination of Alternative Federal Roles*, Washington, D.C., January 1977.

[12]Office of Planning, Budgeting, and Evaluation, *Annual Evaluation Report on Programs Administered by the U.S. Office of Education, FY 1975,* Office of Education, Department of Health, Education, and Welfare, Washington, D.C., September 1976, p. 17.

The hybrid federal role is being carried out through an assortment of functional mechanisms, including court orders; research and development; seed money; demonstrations and experiments; direct investments in facilities, services, and personnel; service policy mandates and regulations; and practically any other conceivable function

Table 10.4
PRIMARY FUNCTION OF FEDERAL PROGRAMS FOR EDUCATION OF HANDICAPPED CHILDREN

Program	Provision of Services		Provision of Funds With Accompanying Regulations		
	Economy of Scale	*Internalize Externalities*	*Basic Service Support*	*Redistribution of Resources*	*Stimulation*
Education					
EHA-B (P.L. 94–142)			X[b]		
ESEA-Title I (P.L. 89–313)			X		
ESEA-Title IV					X
Early Education					X
Headstart				X	
Deaf-Blind Services	X				
Learning Disabilities					X
Severely Handicapped					X
Vocational Education					X
Regional Post-Secondary Education					X
Higher Education			X		
Gallaudet College	X				
NTI for Deaf	X				
Instructional Support					
Personnel Preparation		X			
Recruitment and Information					X
Regional Resource Centers					X
Media Services and Captioned Films	X				
Amer. Print. House for Blind	X				
Library of Congress	X				
Research					
Handicapped Research		X			

a See Chap. 4, "Functional Mechanisms," for a full discussion of these column headings.
b Prior to its revision of P.L. 94–142 in 1975, the primary function of the EHA–Part B program was stimulation.

that one might define. Federally supported special education for the handicapped is such a widely variegated class of activities that it is difficult to generalize about it. The products of each of the 1977 federal programs are shown in Table 10.5.

Likewise, the rationales used to justify federal involvement are multiple and variegated. Some definable programs are currently rationalized (whether implicitly or explicitly, it matters little) in terms of redistribution of resources arguments (e.g., Headstart). Another cluster is most accurately labeled as stimulative (e.g., ESEA-Title IV, Learning Disabilities, and Handicapped Early Education). Some programs are primarily managed at the federal level because of economies of scale considerations (e.g., Gallaudet College, media services, and the American Printing House for the Blind). Still another cluster could be rationalized in terms of internalization of externalities (e.g., training teaching personnel under the "Education of the Handicapped Act," and most research support). And finally, some programs such as P.L. 94-142 provide direct service support on the primary rationale that current state and local resources are inadequate to achieve equal educational opportunity for handicapped children.[13]

Later in this chapter we present and discuss the validity (or lack thereof) of the rationales usually advanced in support of a *federal* role in existing special education programs for handicapped children.

In terms of dollar support devoted to each of the different functions, the picture is changing. In 1971, approximately 44 percent—the largest share—of total federal expenditures was classifiable under the stimulation category; some 9 percent was classifiable under resource distribution arguments; 20 percent was under internalization of externalities; 18 percent was under basic service support; and 11 percent was under economies of scale. The predominant functions being carried out in 1971 under the stimulation rationale were demonstrations and experiments and the provision of seed money as parts of the "Education for the Handicapped Act" (Title VI-B), the ESEA-Title III, and the "Vocational Education Act."[14] By 1977, the total federal special education budget had grown by 72 percent, and the emphasis was shifting from stimulation to basic service support. The percentages devoted for the different functions were 21 percent stimulation, 9 percent resource redistribution, 20 percent economy of scale, 9 percent internalization of externalities, and 41 percent basic service support. By 1982, if P.L. 94-142 appropriations match authorizations and the budget for all other special education programs stays the

---

[13]P.L. 94-142, Section 3(b).
[14]See text later in this chapter for sources of data.

Table 10.5
PRODUCTS OF FEDERAL PROGRAMS FOR EDUCATION OF HANDICAPPED CHILDREN

Program	Program Products						
	Instruction of Handicapped Students	Related Services to Students	Trained Teachers	Other Trained Personnel	Facilities	Materials	R&D
Education							
EHA-B (P.L. 94-142)	X	X	X	X	X	X	
ESEA-Title I (P.L. 89-313)	X	X			X	X	
ESEA-Title IV	X	X				X	X
Early Education	X	X				X	X
Headstart	X	X				X	
Deaf-Blind Services	X	X	X	X		X	X
Learning Disabilities	X	X	X	X		X	X
Severely Handicapped	X	X	X	X		X	X
Vocational Education	X	X	X	X		X	
Regional Post-Secondary Education	X	X				X	
Higher Education	X	X				X	
Gallaudet College	X	X	X	X		X	X
NTI for Deaf	X	X	X	X		X	X
Instructional Support							
Personnel Preparation			X	X			
Recruitment and Information		X	X	X		X	
Regional Resource Centers		X	X	X		X	X
Media Services and Captioned Films		X	X	X		X	X
Amer. Print. House Blind		X				X	
Library of Congress		X				X	
Research							
Handicapped Research							X

same, basic service support will comprise 91 percent of the federal expenditures for the education of handicapped children.

CURRENT FEDERAL PROGRAMS

This section describes the current federal education programs in three groups, according to whether funds are used primarily for direct support of education of handicapped children, for indirect support of instruction through the production of educational resources such as teachers and materials, or for research.

Federal Programs for Instruction of Handicapped Children

Handicapped Preschool and School Program—Aid to States Created by P.L. 94-142, this program has the potential to change dramatically the federal role in both preschool-age and school-age special education toward one of "basic service support." If P.L. 94-142 appropriations match authorizations, and if special education is assumed to cost approximately twice as much as regular education, the federal government share of special education excess costs would rise from the current 14 percent[15] to at least 40 percent by 1982. Total 1982 appropriations under P.L. 94-142 alone would be over $3 billion, more than is currently spent on Title I of the "Elementary and Secondary Education Act," and more than triple what the federal government currently spends for all other special education programs.

The federal role in control of special education service delivery policy also has the potential to increase markedly since the financial support is accompanied by various "strings": e.g., the mandate that by 1980 *all* handicapped children be identified and provided a free appropriate public education; a requirement that the currently unserved and the inadequately served severely handicapped youth be served first; various requirements regarding individualized education programs with annual reevaluations, due process procedures, and service in the least restrictive environment that is appropriate for the child; plus other requirements summarized later in this section. These controls come even if the full authorized funds are not appropriated, but the strength of the controls will depend on how federal regulations are written, interpreted, and enforced. Perhaps the most significant aspect of the new law is the universal service standard—the requirement that to be eligible for federal funds each state must provide an appropriate special education to each of its handicapped children. This universal service standard itself represents a rather radi-

---

[15]W. H. Wilken et al., *State Aid for Special Education: Who Benefits?*, pp. I-2, I-3.

cal departure from federal policy in other categorical education programs. It also imposes a "matching" requirement on states and localities; they must "match" the federal funds in an amount sufficient to achieve the full service standard and other service policy mandates of P.L. 94-142. Inadequate state and local resources as well as a civil rights argument were used to justify federal funding of P.L. 94-142.

The Congress finds that—

State and local educational agencies have a responsibility to provide education for all handicapped children, but present financial resources are inadequate to meet the special educational needs of handicapped children; and it is in the national interest that the federal government assist state and local efforts to provide programs to meet the educational needs of handicapped children in order to assure equal protection of the law.[16]

Before summarizing the details of P.L. 94-142, it is useful to note the program it replaces as Part B of the "Education of the Handicapped Act." This replacement exemplifies the major federal shift from primarily playing a catalytic or stimulative role toward playing a basic service support role.

Prior to 1975, grants were made to states to support education of handicapped children through initiation, expansion, or improvement of programs at the preschool, elementary school, and secondary school levels. The stated purpose of the "Education of the Handicapped Act" (EHA-Part B) was to stimulate state and local investment in special education. This stimulation was attempted primarily through the demonstration mechanism since there was no matching requirement to obtain federal funds under this program. Grants were allocated to the states, based on the number of children in each state between the ages of 3 and 21. In FY 1970, the program supported education for 204,836 youth.[17] The FY 1972 budget under EHA-Part B was $37.5 million.[18]

In FY 1977, the EHA-Part B budget (advance funded from FY 1976) was $110 million, and approximately 406,000 children were being at least partially served with those funds.[19]

[16]P.L. 94-142, Sec. 3(b).

[17]U.S. Bureau of Education for the Handicapped, *Aid to the States, Information System, National Report*, Education of the Handicapped Act Part B, September 1971.

[18]U.S. Congress, House, Subcommittee of the Committee on Appropriations, *Hearings, Part 2, Office of Education and Special Institutions*, 92d Cong., 2d Sess., 1972, p. 403.

[19]U.S. Department of Health, Education, and Welfare, *Justifications of Appropriation Estimates for Committee on Appropriations, Fiscal Year 1977*, Education Division.

For readers unfamiliar with the details of the revised EHA-Part B program created by P.L. 94-142, the following summary is presented:[20]

> . . . P.L. 94-142 sets out to make certain that without exception, every one of the Nation's handicapped children (defined as "mentally retarded, hard of hearing, deaf, speech impaired, visually handicapped, seriously emotionally disturbed, orthopedically impaired or other health impaired children, or children with specific learning disabilities") receives "special education and related services."

The scope of assistance inherent in this goal might seem to suggest that the most noteworthy aspect of the bill is the size of the outlays it implies, and in fact the numbers do get big. What most observers see as being of greater significance, however, is the fact that the policies expressed in the law are binding irrespective of what happens as regards the size of appropriations. Those policies clearly are worth noting, and they include the following:

- A free public education will be made available to all handicapped children between the ages of 3 and 18 by no later than September of 1978 and all those between 3 and 21 by September of 1980. Coverage of children in the 3-to-5 and 18-to-21 ranges will not be required in States whose school attendance laws do not include those age brackets. Nevertheless, it is now national policy to begin the education of handicapped children by at least age three, and to encourage this practice P.L. 94-142 authorizes incentive grants of $300 over the regular allocation for each handicapped child between the ages of three and five who is afforded special education and related services.

- For each handicapped child there will be an "individualized educational program"—a written statement jointly developed by a qualified school official, by the child's teacher and parents or guardian, and if possible by the child himself. This written statement will include an analysis of the child's present achievement level, a listing of both short-range and annual goals, an identification of specific services that will be provided toward meeting those goals and an indication of the extent to which the child will be able to participate in regular school programs, a notation of when these services will be provided and how long they will last, and a schedule for checking on the progress being achieved under the plan and for making any revisions in it that may seem called for.

- Handicapped and nonhandicapped children will be educated together to the maximum extent appropriate, and the former will

[20]The following material is excerpted from L. V. Goodman, "A Bill of Rights for the Handicapped," in *Programs for the Handicapped,* Office for Handicapped Individuals, U.S. Department of Health, Education, and Welfare, Washington, D.C., n. d.

be placed in special classes or separate schools "only when the nature or severity of the handicap is such that education in regular classes," even if they are provided supplementary aids and services, "cannot be achieved satisfactorily."

- Tests and other evaluation material used in placing handicapped children will be prepared and administered in such a way as not to be racially or culturally discriminatory, and they will be presented in the child's native tongue.

- There will be an intensive and continuing effort to locate and identify youngsters who have handicaps, to evaluate their educational needs, and to determine whether those needs are being met.

- In the overall effort to make sure education is available to all handicapped children, priority will be given first to those who are not receiving an education at all and second to the most severely handicapped within each disability who are receiving an inadequate education.

- In school placement procedures and in fact in any decisions concerning a handicapped child's schooling, there will be prior consultation with the child's parents or guardian, and in general, no policies, programs, or procedures affecting the education of handicapped children covered by the law will be adopted without a public notice.

- The rights and guarantees called for in the law will apply to handicapped children in private as well as public schools, and youngsters in private schools will be provided special education at no cost to their parents if the children were placed in these schools or referred to them by State or local education agency officials.

- The States and localities will undertake comprehensive personnel development programs, including inservice training for regular as well as special education teachers and support personnel, and procedures will be launched for acquiring and disseminating information about promising educational practices and materials coming out of research and development efforts.

- In implementing the law, special effort will be made to employ handicapped persons.

- The principles set forth a few years ago in Federal legislation aimed at the elimination of architectural barriers to the physically handicapped will be applied to school construction and modification, with the Commissioner authorized to make grants for these purposes.

- The State education agency will have jurisdiction over all education programs for handicapped children offered within a given State, including those administered by a noneducation agency (a State hospital, for example, or the welfare department).

- An advisory panel will be appointed by each governor to advise the State's education agency of unmet needs, comment publicly on such matters as proposed rules and regulations, and help the State develop and report relevant data. Membership on these panels will include handicapped individuals and parents and guardians of handicapped children.

Many of these policies have at one time or another been advocated by individual educators or by professional associations. Several have in fact been established within particular States, either by legislative action or as a consequence of court suits brought on behalf of handicapped children. And for more than five years, OE's Bureau of Education for the Handicapped (and particularly its Deputy Commissioner, Edwin W. Martin) have been urging a national goal of providing education for all handicapped children and of doing so by 1980—a principle and a target date now spelled out in the law. In short, the concepts involved are not new. The difference is that through P.L. 94-142 they have become requirements, and accommodation to them is a condition of being eligible to receive support under the Act's funding provisions.

Like so many other aspects of the Act, those provisions are both lofty and innovative, entailing some noteworthy changes in the ways by which Federal education dollars have traditionally been distributed. Allocation of the current $100 million annual appropriation for the State grant program, for example, is based on a funding formula by which the number of children in a State between the ages of 3 and 21 is multiplied by $8.75. Starting with FY 1978, however, State allocations are to be determined by a radically different formula which at the same time rewards extra effort to educate handicapped children and calls upon the federal government to take on an increasing share of the cost.

The first element of the new formula's equation again involves the 3-to-21 age range but includes only those youngsters in that range who are handicapped and who are receiving special education. Thus the more handicapped children the State sets out to educate, the more money it will be entitled to. [To address the potential problem of overcounting for the purpose of obtaining more federal funds, a maximum of 12 percent of the state's school-age population may be counted as handicapped.] The second element is a specified percentage of the national average public school expenditure per child. For FY 1978 the proportion of the overall allocation for which a given State will be eligible is to be determined by multiplying the number of handicapped children being served by five percent of the national average expenditure. At the current expenditure rate that would translate into an estimated overall authorization of $378 million.

For FY 1979 the multiplication factor doubles, with the number of children being served multiplied by *ten* percent of the national per pupil expenditure. Thereafter it continues to rise by an additional ten percent annually for another three years, to a permanent level of 40 percent—that is, the number of handicapped children being served in the State times 40 percent of the National average per pupil expenditure.

Based on the current per pupil expenditure, that could mean a FY 1981 authorization of more than $3.16 billion, and even that figure might be low, depending on whatever changes inflation or other factors might work on national average expenditures during the next four years. It is important to note, however, that the actual amounts of money to become available will depend in large measure on the President's budget and the subsequent actions of the Congressional Appropriations committees. Authorization amounts frequently far exceed actual appropriations. . . .

If the Commissioner finds there to be a "substantial" failure to meet the various provisions of P.L. 94-142—either by a State or by an intermediate or local agency within the State—the law says he "shall" withhold further payments under the Act and that he "may" withhold funds earmarked for education of the handicapped under the Elementary-Secondary and Vocational Education Acts.

Action also might be taken by the parents of individual children, for the Congress went to considerable pains to spell out various procedural safeguards. It is now required, for example, that parents or guardians have an opportunity to examine all relevant records bearing on the identification of children as being handicapped, on evaluating the nature and severity of their disability, and on the kind of educational setting in which they are placed. The latter issue is expected to be of particular concern to parents who feel their handicapped children have been unfairly denied access to regular classes. Schools are called upon to give written notice prior to changing a child's placement (and a written explanation if it refuses a parent's request for such a change), and statements of this kind are to be in the parents' native tongue.

In the event of objections to a school's decision, there must be a process by which parents can register their complaints. That process must also include an opportunity for an impartial hearing which offers parents rights similar to those involved in a court case—the right to be advised by counsel (and by special education experts if they wish), to present evidence, to cross-examine witnesses, to compel the presence of any witnesses who do not appear voluntarily, to be provided a verbatim report of the proceedings, and to receive the decision and findings in written form.[21]

The P.L. 94-142 grants are given to the states. However, beginning in FY 1979, 75 percent must be passed on to localities in proportion to the number of handicapped children served, except that:

- Federal dollars may only be used by localities for the excess cost of special education above the average annual per pupil expenditure for all children.
- Federal dollars may not supplant state and local dollars until all handicapped children in the state are receiving a free appropriate public education.
- Funds are not passed through to the local district if that district is not entitled to at least $7500. This encourages special education consortia in order to more effectively use federal dollars and more effectively serve the children.
- The state may refuse to pass through dollars if the local district does not conform to state plan requirements or to service delivery policy requirements set forth in P.L. 94-142; if the local district doesn't apply; if the special education program within the district is of insufficient size and scope; or if the local district is already providing full service to all handicapped children with state and local funds.[22]

Elementary and Secondary Education Act—Title I Title I primarily provides grants to local education agencies for the education of children from low-income families. These funds are used to expand and improve educational programs which contribute to meeting the exceptional needs of educationally deprived children. Since handicapped children are a part of this target population, they can also benefit from the increase in school resources. However, these grants are not specifically targeted for mentally and physically handicapped children, and we do not have data on the number of handicapped children served in 1976 with these resources.[23]

[21]Ibid.

[22]P.L. 94-142, Sec. 5.

[23]In FY 1972, unlike today, in many states special education was not mandated by law. Title I money could be used to provide special educational services to handicapped children where such services were not mandated by state law. The number of handicapped youth receiving educational support under this "nonmandated" portion of Title I in FY 1972 was an estimated 180,000. (See U.S. Congress, House, Subcommittee of the Committee on Appropriations, *Hearings, Part 2, Office of Education and Special Institutions,* 92d Cong., 2d Sess., 1972, p. 271.)

Perhaps the largest impact of ESEA-Title I on the handicapped population comes through an amendment to that Act, P.L. 89-313, which provides funds to state agencies for special education in schools supported or run directly by the state. Participating youth must be less than 21 years old and have not completed grade 12. An estimated 108,000 handicapped youth whose special education was the direct responsibility of a state agency benefited under P.L. 89-313 provisions in FY 1970.[24] By FY 1977, $111 million in expenditures provided service to approximately 207,000 children and youth.[25]

To encourage service in the least restrictive environment, a handicapped child who leaves a school operated or supported by the state agency to participate in a local special educational program is eligible for P.L. 89-313 funds. However, he must continue to receive an appropriately designed education program if the state transfers the P.L. 89-313 funds attributable to that child to the local agency.

The federal government plays two different roles in Title I. For the most part, it acts to redistribute resources in providing compensatory education to educationally deprived children. The argument is that some school districts do not have adequate financial resources to carry out compensatory education. The size of the federal grant is based on the number of children between ages 5 and 17 who come from low income families, who receive Aid to Families with Dependent Children, and who are in publicly supported institutions for neglected, delinquent, or foster children. Expenditures of $1725 million are expected to aid about 4,275,000 children in FY 1977 (the majority of whom are not mentally or physically handicapped).[26] In Title I, the federal government shifts resources to make the distribution of educational resources more nearly equitable.

It is difficult to interpret the P.L. 89-313 aspect of Title I as primarily one of redistributing resources, however. The P.L. 89-313 formula requires that the allocation of federal funds to a state be equal to the maximum authorization, which is based on the number of eligible handicapped children in average daily attendance (ADA) in all eligible state-operated and state-supported schools multiplied by 40 percent of the state's per pupil expenditure (or not less than 80 percent nor more than 120 percent of the national average).[27] This formula

[24]U.S. Bureau of Education for the Handicapped, *Aid to the States Information System, National Report,* September 1971.

[25]U.S. Office of Management and Budget, *Catalog of Federal Domestic Assistance,* Sec. 13.428, November 1976.

[26]Ibid.

[27]National Advisory Committee on the Handicapped, *The Unfinished Revolution: Education for the Handicapped, 1976 Annual Report,* U.S. Department of Health, Education, and Welfare, 1976.

obviously has some redistributive effect. Since poor states tend to spend less on education per capita than rich states, they will receive more than 40 percent of their average expenditures because of the minimum floor set by the national average. Although poorer states will get more as a percentage of current expenditures than richer states get per ADA, they will get less money in absolute terms than the richer states get per ADA.

The rationales generally offered for a strong federal role in redistributing resources are based on both the large amount of resources necessary to operate an adequate program and the wide range of financial capability among the states. In programs serving large numbers of persons, such as welfare and compensatory education, both of these arguments have some credibility. However, in the case of special education in state operated and supported institutions, there is more room for argument. The point is that state funds for state operated or supported schools could be greatly increased without dramatically affecting the size of the total state budget. Under such circumstances, the need for redistribution of resources from state to state is far from clear.

The P.L. 89-313 program functions primarily to provide basic service support. In effect, the federal government is saying that it will pay each state approximately $536 for each eligible handicapped child counted in average daily attendance at state operated and state supported schools or transferred from those schools to local schools. The federal government has not assumed a basic support role for education in general. Until passage of the "Education for All Handicapped Children Act" in 1975, this P.L. 89-313 program was the only major basic special education support program operated by the federal government.

Until every youngster in a state institution is receiving some special education, the ability of states to receive more P.L. 89-313 funds by increasing coverage also should have a stimulative effect.

Educational Innovation and Support P.L. 93-380[28] permits states to consolidate funds from the innovation portion of Title III of the Elementary and Secondary Education Act with Title V (which is for strengthening state departments of education) and with Title VIII (which is for dropout prevention and school health and nutrition programs). The money is consolidated by ESEA-Title IV and must be used for purposes similar to those authorized by the three consolidated programs. This is permitted if federal consolidated appropri-

---

[28]Part C, Sec. 431.

ations for the three component programs exceed a minimum figure; FY 1977 appropriations of $185 million permit the consolidation.[29]

The ESEA-Title III program, "Supplemental Education Centers and Services, Guidance Counseling and Testing," is intended to assist schools in the establishment and development of exemplary elementary and secondary school educational programs. To ensure that part of these funds go to special education, states are required to spend at least 15 percent of their Title III allotment on education and related services for handicapped children. The language of ESEA-Title III makes clear that the federal function is one of stimulation:

> The Commissioner shall assist in the provision of vitally needed educational services not available in sufficient quantity or quality, and to stimulate and assist in the development and establishment of exemplary elementary and secondary educational programs to serve as models for regular school programs.[30]

Innovation and stimulation are brought about by the demonstration effect, since Title III money is not distributed on a matching basis. The formula used is based primarily on each state's total population between the ages of 5 and 17 years. A reported total of at least 134,047 handicapped youth received a portion of their services under this program in FY 1971.[31]

Under the "Educational Innovation and Support" program which consolidated Titles III, V, and VIII, the rule about spending at least 15 percent of the funds for specific learning disabled and other handicapped children applies to the consolidated total, not just the Title III portion.[32] Approximately $21 million of the FY 1977 funds went for handicapped children.[33] The federal role in the consolidated program is primarily one of stimulation through demonstration. It can also be considered partially a basic service support program and partially an R&D program (to the extent that innovative exemplary projects are developed prior to and during their functioning as demonstrations).

[29]U.S. Office of Management and Budget, *Catalog of Federal Domestic Assistance,* Sec. 13.571, November 1976.

[30]P.L. 89-10 as amended by P.L. 93-380, Sec. 310.

[31]Compiled from 1972 Title III state reports to the U.S. Office of Education. Five states (Kentucky, Maryland, Montana, New Hampshire, and Pennsylvania) and the District of Columbia are excluded from this total because the state report either was not available or was inadequately prepared. The program total excludes Texas, which reported serving 375,000 at an average Title III per pupil expenditure of $2.37.

[32]F. J. Weintraub et al. (eds.), *Public Policy and the Education of Exceptional Children,* The Council for Exceptional Children, Reston, Virginia, 1976.

[33]U.S. Dept. of Health, Education, and Welfare, *Justifications for Appropriations Estimates for Committee on Appropriations, Fiscal Year 1978, Education Division,* vol. I.

Special education projects in the consolidated Title IV program stress direct services. The projects address areas such as placement of handicapped children in the least restrictive environment commensurate with their needs, the use of resource rooms, diagnostic-prescriptive teaching, individualized instruction, the use of paraprofessionals, the organization of curriculums around learning problems, education of the severely handicapped, early childhood education, vocational education, and evaluation.[34]

In FY 1975, about 16 percent of the projects funded (approximately 300 out of 1900) were partially or exclusively concerned with education of handicapped children.[35]

Early Education for Handicapped Children The purpose of this demonstration and outreach program is to aid state and local education agencies in developing model preschool and early education programs for handicapped children aged 0 to 8 years. A total of 224 experimental preschool projects were funded in FY 1977 to develop models applicable to many different handicapping conditions and environmental settings. Projects are supposed to be structured such that other communities can replicate them in whole or in part.

Projects that have received three years of demonstration funds from this program and that have other sources of funds to continue direct services to children, can apply to this Early Education program for "outreach" funds to assist and stimulate increased early education of handicapped children not directly served by the project. Twenty-four projects received "outreach" funds in 1976.[36]

While this program provides direct services to approximately 14,000 young children[37] (up from 2000 in FY 1971), the primary purpose of the program appears to be development, demonstration, and dissemination of the results of exemplary experimental preschool and early childhood projects. The federal government pays 90 percent of project costs, and FY 1977 appropriations were $22 million.[38]

The program is intended to be stimulative, in terms of both its

---

[34]National Advisory Committee on the Handicapped, *The Unfinished Revolution: Education for the Handicapped, 1976 Annual Report,* U.S. Department of Health, Education, and Welfare, 1976.

[35]Ibid.

[36]Ibid.

[37]U.S. Department of Health, Education, and Welfare, *Justifications of Appropriation Estimates for Committee on Appropriations, FY 1977, Education Division.*

[38]U.S. Office of Management and Budget, *Catalog of Federal Domestic Assistance,* Section 13.444, November 1976.

demonstration and its matching effects. To the extent that R&D is conducted by the funded projects, the program can be justified by the internalization of externalities argument that is used to support federal involvement in all types of R&D programs.

The program claims an outreach impact on 47,250 children in 525 projects that are complete replications of an Early Education program demonstration project and in 1050 projects that are partial replications.[39]

Headstart   The Headstart program provides diagnostic, educational, health, nutritional, and other services to preschool-age children from economically disadvantaged families. (90 percent of the enrollees' families must have income below the poverty line.) The program also provides for staff training. Authorizing legislation for Headstart states that at least 10 percent of the preschool-age enrollment opportunities in each state shall be reserved for handicapped children, and that services shall be provided to meet their special needs. Accordingly, 35,000 enrollees should have been handicapped in FY 1977 (10 percent of the total 350,000), and expenditures for those handicapped children should have been at least $47.5 million (10 percent of the $475 million total).[40]

Reserving a number of positions, rather than earmarking money, was a new approach meant to benefit handicapped children. This approach potentially assures better accountability because it is easier to count handicapped children than it is to calculate the amount of resources going to a particular group of children.

Reservation of places also creates certain incentives for Headstart administrators. If handicapped children are more expensive to serve than nonhandicapped children, then more than 10 percent of the funds will be going to handicapped children. Given limited resources, the administrator has several choices: he or she can serve children who have a range of types and severities of handicapping conditions and operate a reduced size project from what enrollment would be in the absence of handicapped children; the handicapped children admitted can be those with the milder exceptionalities and hence less expensive service needs; or, contrary to the intent of the authorizing legislation, handicapped children can be given about the same level of service as nonhandicapped children. The latter case would appear on its face to be far from optimal, although it is prob-

[39]U.S. Department of Health, Education, and Welfare, *Justifications of Appropriation Estimates for Committee on Appropriations, FY 1977, Education Division.*

[40]U.S. Office of Management and Budget, *Catalog of Federal Domestic Assistance,* Section 13.600, November 1976.

ably better to have some service for handicapped children, as opposed to none.

Since Headstart, like ESEA-Title I, is targeted on economically disadvantaged children, a primary rationale for federal involvement is to redistribute resources from richer to poorer segments of the population. Earmarking 10 percent of the enrollment positions for handicapped children was initially an attempt to stimulate increases in preschool services for these children. Now that 10 percent of those served are handicapped, earmarking ensures that they continue to receive their share of the redistributed resources.

The ESEA-Title I program, however, does not earmark a fraction of enrollment positions or dollars for handicapped children. Thus, the federal government is taking a different approach with economically disadvantaged children of different ages.

Centers and Services for Deaf-Blind Children   This program is aimed at a special target group of handicapped children who are both deaf and blind. A recent increase in the prevalence of deaf-blind children (though still a very low incidence population) was brought about in part by the rubella epidemic of 1964–1965 and left many children without access to appropriate educational services. Services were available to some deaf and some blind children, but sensorially multihandicapped children add another dimension of complexity to the education process. The federal program of 10 regional centers for deaf-blind children was an attempt to overcome this gap in service to this severely handicapped group. An estimated total of 2300 were served in FY 1971.[41] The FY 1977 appropriations of $16 million will result in service to 4216 children full time, 300 children on a part-time basis, and 417 children at home.[42] About two-thirds of the population is served, and by 1981 the federal plan calls for reaching 100 percent of the population.[43] In addition to direct service to children and counseling of their families, in 1976 approximately 3000 teachers and aides were provided inservice training on services to deaf-blind children.[44] The extremely low prevalence of this handicap, and hence the geographic dispersion of the target population, made it difficult for

---

[41]U.S. Congress, House, Subcommittee of the Committee on Appropriations, *Hearings, Part 2, Office of Education and Special Institutions,* 92d Cong., 2d Sess. 1972, p. 420.

[42]U.S. Office of Management and Budget, *Catalog of Federal Domestic Assistance,* Section 13.445, November 1976.

[43]U.S. Office of Education, *Forward Plan FY 1977–1981,* July 22, 1975, p. 8.

[44]U.S. Department of Health, Education, and Welfare, *Justifications of Appropriation Estimates for Committee on Appropriations, FY 1977, Education Division.*

many states to individually provide quality services at a reasonable cost to this group. Regional centers allow the federal government to capture the economies of scale existing for educating these children.

Learning Disabilities Program   Part G of the "Education for the Handicapped Act" provides for model centers to meet the needs of children with specific learning disabilities.

With a FY 1977 budget of $5 million, approximately 8700 children are being served in 35 projects.[45] In addition, a separate project provides technical and other assistance to the model centers. Approximately 7800 teachers were trained last year under this program.[46]

In addition to R&D and personnel training, the centers provide testing and evaluation to identify learning disabled children, help plan programs to meet the needs of those children, and disseminate information about effective new methods and techniques.[47]

The purpose of the program is to stimulate state and local provision of comprehensive identification and diagnostic, prescriptive, and educational services for children with specific learning disabilities.

On June 17, 1977, the "Education of the Handicapped Amendments of 1977," P.L. 95-49, was passed to reauthorize the "Education for the Handicapped Act," with the exception of this Part G, the Learning Disabilities program. In the future, the functions of Part G will be fulfilled by programs funded under other parts of the "Education for the Handicapped Act," particularly under Part E, the Research and Demonstration Projects program.

Severely Handicapped   This program awards contracts for up to three years to demonstrate programmatic practices to meet the educational and training needs of severely handicapped children and youth. With FY 1977 appropriations of just over $3 million, a total of 1804 children are participating in 32 projects.[48] Program estimates are that of 1.4 million severely handicapped youth aged 0–19 years, only about 352,000 were receiving special educational services from all sources of funding in FY 1973.[49]

[45]U.S. Office of Management and Budget, *Catalog of Federal Domestic Assistance,* Section 13.520, November 1976.

[46]National Advisory Committee on the Handicapped, *The Unfinished Revolution: Education for the Handicapped, 1976 Annual Report,* U.S. Department of Health, Education, and Welfare, 1976.

[47]Ibid.

[48]U.S. Department of Health, Education, and Welfare, *Justifications of Appropriation Estimates for Committee on Appropriations, Fiscal Year 1977, Education Division.*

[49]Ibid.

The primary intent of this demonstration program is to stimulate improved services for severely handicapped youth. All projects are to contain both a replicable model demonstration program providing direct services, and a strategy to widely disseminate exemplary project results to both professional and other personnel. A total of 310 staff members are estimated to be receiving inservice training in FY 1977.[50]

The program is not intended to support R&D or personnel preparation other than through inservice training.

Vocational Education The "Vocational Education Act" provides that 10 percent of the basic grant funds allocated to each state must be spent on handicapped youth. These funds are used to maintain, extend, and improve vocational education in various types of schools, including high schools, state-operated schools for handicapped youth, community colleges, and area vocational schools. The program requires a 50 percent matching with state and/or local funds. Federal funds are distributed by a formula based on the state's population aged 15–65 years and per capita income in the state.

The term "vocational education" means:

> . . . vocational or technical training or retraining designed to prepare individuals for gainful employment as semiskilled or skilled workers or technicians or subprofessionals or to prepare individuals for enrollment in advanced technical education programs, but excluding any program to prepare individuals for employment in occupations generally considered professional or which require a baccalaureate or higher degree; and such term includes vocational guidance and counseling; job placement; the training of persons engaged as, or preparing to become teachers in a vocational education program or preparing such teachers to meet special education needs of handicapped students.[51]

A total of 221,342 handicapped youth were served in FY 1972.[52] In FY 1977, of the estimated 17,596,000 students enrolled in vocational education, approximately 310,000, or 1.8 percent, were handicapped.[53] At least 10 percent of the $482 million federal FY 1977 ap-

[50]U.S. Office of Management and Budget, *Catalog of Federal Domestic Assistance,* Section 13.568, November 1976.

[51]P.L. 90-576, Section 108.

[52]Letter from H. F. Duis, Program Support Branch, DHEW/OE/BAVTE, to J. S. Kakalik, The Rand Corporation, May 9, 1973.

[53]U.S. Department of Health, Education, and Welfare, *Justifications of Appropriation Estimates for Committee on Appropriations, Fiscal Year 1977, Education Division.*

propriations, or $48.2 million, were supposed to go for service to handicapped persons.[54] With the 50:50 state and local match, $96.4 million should be going for service to handicapped people, which equals about $310 per handicapped person served. If 10 percent of the dollars are in fact reaching 1.8 percent of the students served, then this program is spending 5½ times more per handicapped person served than it is spending per nonhandicapped person. Even so, 1.8 percent is far less than the 9 to 12 percent of the student population who are handicapped.

The "Vocational Education Act" requires that cooperative arrangements be made for coordinating activities among the state vocational education agency, the state special education agency, the state vocational rehabilitation agency, and other state agencies with responsibility for educating handicapped people. At the federal level, the vocational education funds are subject to fiscal and legal management through the O.E. Bureau of Occupational and Adult Education, but the Bureau of Education for the Handicapped is to cooperate in administering these funds to help ensure coordinated programming.

The rationale for this vocational education program is primarily that of stimulating expanded and improved vocational education services. The teacher training component of the program can be justified by the externality of benefits argument that applies for all education and related service personnel training programs.

Regional Post-Secondary Vocational, Technical, and Adult Education for Deaf and Other Handicapped People This $2 million program provided funds in FY 1977 for 9 projects for post-secondary vocational, technical, and adult education of deaf and other handicapped people. Approximately 1500 handicapped people were served in FY 1977.[55] Priority is given to multistate regions and large population centers. The program provides support services for handicapped persons enrolled in institutions of higher education, including junior and community colleges and vocational and technical schools. The goal is "to stimulate the development and operation of 'specially designed or modified programs of vocational, technical, post-sec-

---

[54]U.S. Office of Management and Budget, *Catalog of Federal Domestic Assistance,* Section 13.493, November 1976.

[55]U.S. Department of Health, Education, and Welfare, *Justifications of Appropriations Estimates for Committee on Appropriations, Fiscal Year 1977, Education Division.*

ondary, or adult education for deaf and other handicapped persons'."[56]

Note that an economy of scale argument can be used to rationalize federal support of multistate regional special education programs for low incidence populations such as older deaf youth desiring a college education, or deaf-blind children and youth. Such a rationale does not apply, however, to higher incidence groups of handicapped people who are sufficiently prevalent to permit individual states to mount an appropriate, economical, special education program for the group. For higher prevalence groups, federal involvement demonstrates effective service models to stimulate states to act. At the low FY 1977 level of funding, the program cannot be justified as basic service support necessitated by inability of lower levels of government to provide the necessary funds.

Higher Education: Special Services to Disadvantaged Students

Grants are made to accredited education institutions to encourage and assist disadvantaged students to complete their post-secondary education. FY 1977 appropriations for this program were $23 million.[57] The target population includes low-income students, those with physical disabilities, and those of limited English-speaking ability. An estimated 100,000 students received aid, of which an unknown number were handicapped.[58]

We have no reasonable means of estimating what fraction of the total of $23 million went for physically handicapped students in FY 1977. (FY 1972 expenditures for handicapped youth were $436,000.)

The federal government, by redistributing resources from the general taxpaying population to the disadvantaged population, is apparently attempting to correct underinvestment in education for these students in earlier years of their elementary and secondary education. For students with physical disabilities, who receive special services more due to current need rather than to past underinvestment in their education, the primary function of the program appears to be direct service support.

[56]National Advisory Committee on the Handicapped, *The Unfinished Revolution: Education for the Handicapped, 1976 Annual Report,* Washington, D.C.

[57]U.S. Office of Management and Budget, *Catalog of Federal Domestic Assistance,* Section 13.482, November 1976.

[58]U.S. Dept. of Health, Education, and Welfare, *Justifications of Appropriations Estimates for Committee on Appropriations, Fiscal Year 1978, Education Division,* vol. II.

Gallaudet College   The federal government sponsors Gallaudet College in Washington, D.C., which provides an undergraduate and graduate program for deaf individuals, a graduate school program in the field of deafness, and adult education for deaf people.[59]

The federal government also operates the Kendall School for deaf children, which is a preschool program, and the Model Secondary School for the Deaf.[60] Both are located in Washington, D.C., and not only provide basic educational services to their students, but also are used for research and demonstration on methods of teaching deaf children.

In creating and supporting Gallaudet College and the National Technical Institute for the Deaf (discussed in the next subsection), the federal government has in a sense nationalized higher education for deaf students in order to achieve economies of scale for this very low incidence target population.

Support for the Kendall School and the Model Secondary School can be justified by the externality argument that applies to all R&D. Research into better practices in teaching deaf children obviously has payoffs to all states, and any single state would be likely to underinvest in such R&D because that state would not reap all the benefits resulting from such research. Association of these two schools with Gallaudet College should enhance the effectiveness of all three programs because of the economies of scale and the concentration of a large number of experts on deafness and service to deaf individuals.

In 1971 Gallaudet served 1583; the number at Kendall was 208; and the Model Secondary School was being planned. The number served in 1978 will be approximately 2000 at Gallaudet, 210 at Kendall, and 350 at the Model Secondary School.[61] Total FY 1977 appropriations were about $41 million.[62]

The National Technical Institute for the Deaf   Created by P.L. 89-36 in 1965, the National Technical Institute for the Deaf is located at the Rochester Institute of Technology and specializes in post-secondary school vocational training of deaf people to prepare them for employment. NTID also trains professionals to serve the deaf and conducts research. The primary rationale for federal support of this program is the economy of scale argument used for Gallaudet College.

In 1971 the Institute served 395 students, a number that had ex-

---

[59]P.L. 83-240.

[60]P.L. 89-694.

[61]*Appendix, the Budget of the United States Government, FY 1978*, p. 365.

[62]P.L. 94-439, *Departments of Labor and Health, Education, and Welfare Appropriations Act, 1977.*

ceeded 680 by FY 1977.[63] FY 1977 appropriations were approximately $13 million.[64]

Federal Programs to Provide Instructional Support

The federal government also supports programs that provide resources for the education process, as opposed to direct support of that process.

Personnel Preparation   To increase the number of teachers and other personnel specialized in the education of handicapped children, funds are available in Part D of the "Education of the Handicapped Act." Programs for training personnel presently engaged in or preparing to engage in teaching or providing related services for handicapped children and financial assistance to students pursuing a career in special education are operated with this mandate.

Federal sponsorship to increase the supply of trained personnel is an example of the recognition of the externalities involved. Highly trained personnel are mobile. If one state trains teachers and other specialized personnel who eventually migrate elsewhere, that state receives smaller benefits for its investment. Federal support helps to compensate for this and also reduces total training costs. Hence, most special education professionals are being trained in programs supported by the federal government; for example, 17,731 students finished training under programs supported by the U.S. Bureau of Education for the Handicapped in FY 1970.[65]

Another federal program, authorized by the "Educational Professions Development Act,"[66] sponsors student fellowships and grants to colleges for personnel training programs in the area of child development and special education for handicapped children. This program is aimed at producing many different types of trained education personnel, not just those in special education. The overall program has been scaled down in recent years, however. As a recent Office of Education *Forward Plan* indicates, "the continuing teacher surplus has eliminated the justification for large scale support of preservice training, at least at this time."[67] That same plan notes the continuing

[63]National Advisory Committee on the Handicapped, *The Unfinished Revolution: Education for the Handicapped,* 1976 Annual Report, U.S. Department of Health, Education, and Welfare, Washington, D.C.

[64]P.L. 94-439, *Departments of Labor and Health, Education, and Welfare Appropriations Act, 1977.*

[65]U.S. Office of Management and Budget, *Catalog of Federal Domestic Assistance,* Section 13.451, update to 1972 issue.

[66]P.L. 90-30.

[67]U.S. Office of Education, *Forward Plan FY 1977-1981,* July 23, 1975.

need for training specialized talent in shortage areas, including both preservice and inservice training related to the education of handicapped children. The *Forward Plan* suggests, for efficiency reasons, that those activities be part of the handicapped programs rather than aggregating them under a single broad authority such as the "Education Professions Development Act."[68]

The FY 1977 funding level for personnel preparation under Part D of the "Education of the Handicapped Act" is $40 million; approximately 33,000 individuals are being trained.[69] Priority training areas are: early childhood education, education of severely handicapped children, training of paraprofessionals, physical education and recreation training, vocational education, interdisciplinary personnel training, general special education, training of regular educators, postdoctoral training, and development of new instructional models for training.[70] Funds can be used for the training of teachers, supervisors, administrators, researchers, teacher educators, speech correctionists, and other special services personnel such as specialists in physical education and recreation, music therapy, and paraprofessionals.[71] Funds are used for preservice/full-time training of special educators (approximately $21.8 million and 6800 personnel in FY 1977), for inservice continuation preparation for special educators (approximately $7.6 million and 12,600 personnel), for special education training for regular classroom teachers (approximately $3.7 million for inservice training of 10,500 regular teachers, plus $3.2 million to help colleges of education revise their programs for preservice training to regular teachers).[72]

Recruitment and Information   The program, established under Part D of the "Education of the Handicapped Act," has two purposes: (1) to encourage people to enter occupations in the field of special education; and (2) to disseminate information and provide referral services for parents and other interested persons to help them locate appropriate educational services for individual handicapped children. With FY 1977 funds of only $1 million, the program is concentrating predominantly on its second "information and referral" pur-

---

[68]Ibid., p. 10.

[69]U.S. Office of Management and Budget, *Catalog of Federal Domestic Assistance,* Section 13.451, November 1976.

[70]U.S. Department of Health, Education, and Welfare, *Justifications of Appropriation Estimates for Committee on Appropriations, Fiscal Year 1977, Education Division.*

[71]Ibid.

[72]Ibid.

pose.[73] Less than 5 percent of the funds went for special education personnel recruitment.

Although both purposes of this program can involve the use of mass media techniques, the justification for having a single program pursue two such diverse purposes is unclear. In reality, however, the recruitment portion of this program is so small as to be practically nonexistent.

Nationally, the largest component of the information and referral effort is known as "Closer Look," operated through the Special Education Information Center. The Center uses national radio and television to advertise the availability of its information and referral services. Each inquiry to the Center receives an individual response. In 1976 the Center received about 50,000 inquiries, about half from parents of handicapped children.[74]

The Center staff also develops and distributes informational materials (a newsletter reaches about 200,000 parents) and provides technical assistance about information and referral services to a wide variety of state, local, and private agencies.[75]

While there are obvious economies of scale to developing general information and referral materials (including radio and TV ads) at the national level, specific referrals for actual services must be made in light of the specific needs of a child and the specific service programs available locally. Specific information and referral services, as opposed to general information and referral applicable to broad groups of handicapped children, can best be provided locally or regionally. To stimulate the establishment of local information and referral units, in FY 1977 this national program planned to provide assistance grants for the establishment of local information units, as well as technical assistance to agencies interested in establishing such units.[76]

Regional Resource Centers Sponsored under Part C of the "Education of the Handicapped Act," 13 centers advise and offer technical services to personnel for improving the education of handicapped children. The emphasis is on the development and application of exemplary handicapped child identification, appraisal, and individ-

[73]Ibid.

[74]National Advisory Committee on the Handicapped, *The Unfinished Revolution: Education for the Handicapped, 1976 Annual Report;* and U.S. Department of Health, Education, and Welfare, *Justifications of Appropriation Estimates for Committee on Appropriations, Fiscal Year 1977, Education Division.*

[75]Ibid.

[76]U.S. Department of Health, Education, and Welfare, *Justifications of Appropriation Estimates for Committee on Appropriations, Fiscal Year 1977, Education Division.*

ualized education programming practices.[77] In addition, in FY 1977, 10 of the centers were to operate Direction Centers (a one-stop source of information and referral to match the child's needs with available services). (See the Epilogue.)

Centers' activities include support of demonstration models, training of personnel, dissemination of information, testing and evaluation of children, development of educational programs for referred children, and collaborative efforts with the media centers described elsewhere in this section.

The essential difference between the Regional Resource Centers and the media centers is that the former focus on appraising and prescribing special educational needs of children, while the latter focuses on media and materials.

In FY 1976, approximately 90,000 handicapped children were provided with referral services, and about 2900 personnel were trained in special education programming skills. The FY 1977 budget was approximately the same as for FY 1976, $10 million.[78]

One rationale for having a separate federal program focus on appraisal and prescriptive services is that these "identification and evaluation" services have been relatively neglected and underdeveloped in the past. Thus, the program is primarily to stimulate improvement and expansion of these two services through demonstration, personnel training, and dissemination of information. There should also be economies of scale achieved by providing such stimulation through regional centers rather than through every state.

Media Services and Captioned Films for the Deaf   Part F of the "Education of the Handicapped Act" makes available a free loan service of captioned films and instructional media to the deaf. It also provides services to all types of handicapped people by acquiring and distributing educational media, materials, and equipment, by assisting with training of teachers and others in media use, and by funding media-related research. FY 1977 appropriations were $16 million.[79]

The National Center on Educational Media and Materials for the Handicapped and depositories around the country can be of assistance to local education agencies in supplementing their media inventory. The program's Area Learning Resource Center Network provides educational media and materials to states, as well as

[77]U.S. Department of Health, Education, and Welfare, *Justifications of Appropriation Estimates for Committee on Appropriations, Fiscal Year 1977, Education Division.*
[78]Ibid.
[79]P.L. 94-439, *Departments of Labor and Health, Education, and Welfare Appropriations Act, 1977.*

demonstrations and technical assistance. CBS television broadcasts a newscast five nights a week which is captioned by this program. FY 1977 appropriations included $500,000 for recordings for the blind and physically handicapped.[80]

The primary rationale for federal involvement in this area is the economy of scale that can be achieved. The primary justification for involvement in media research and personnel training is based on the same internalization of externalities argument that is used to support all federal research and personnel training programs.

American Printing House for the Blind An 1879 federal act created this private nonprofit institute which manufactures and distributes educational materials and apparatus nationwide to blind and multiple-handicapped children and adults. The APHB works in cooperation with the previously described Media Services and Captioned Films program. Federal expenditures under this program were $1.6 million in 1972, and $3 million were appropriated for FY 1977.[81] The APHB also receives revenues from a number of other sources. This national level production of educational materials for blind people primarily is justified by the economies of scale achieved in such manufacture.

Library of Congress: Books for the Blind and Physically Handicapped A media program run by the Library of Congress provides free loan books and magazines in Braille and on records for blind and physically handicapped people. This material is distributed to libraries throughout the country for circulation to individual readers. The program reached some 120,000 readers in 1969,[82] and reached an estimated 478,000 annually in FY 1977,[83] with appropriations of approximately $22 million.[84] Federal involvement in this program is called for because of the economies of scale that are available in the production of media.

[80]U.S. Department of Health, Education, and Welfare, *Justifications of Appropriation Estimates for Committee on Appropriations, Fiscal Year 1977, Education Division.*

[81]P.L. 94-439, *Departments of Labor and Health, Education, and Welfare Appropriations Act, 1977.*

[82]Nelson Associates, Inc., *A Survey of Reader Characteristics, Reading Interests, and Equipment Preferences,* Washington, D.C., 1969, p. 111.

[83]U.S. Office of Management and Budget, *Catalog of Federal Domestic Assistance,* Section 42.001, November 1976.

[84]P.L. 94-440.

Federal Research Programs

A significant percentage of the money devoted to education of handicapped children could be classified as research. For example, in the development of model projects under ESEA-Title IV, the Early Childhood program, and several other of the "stimulation" programs, much of the innovative work could be classified as research and development. For the purposes of this section, however, research programs are limited to those whose primary purpose is research.

Handicapped Education Research and Development   Part E of the "Education of the Handicapped Act" provides grant funds for research and development purposes.

R&D project grants are made to improve the educational opportunities of handicapped children, as well as to improve physical education and recreation programs for these children. Dissemination of the results of R&D are considered to be an important part of the program. Project grants cover a wide range of areas, including early childhood education, full school services, career education, education for the severely handicapped, and personnel development.

The federal research role is based on the notion of internalizing externalities. That is, research has nationwide benefits, yet costs about the same whether funded by local, state, or federal governments. Since some of the benefits of a research project will accrue external to any single state or locality, single states and localities might underinvest in research compared to the federal government. Those benefits which are external to single states, however, are internal when viewed from the federal level. Hence, on a cost-benefit basis, the federal government can justify a higher research budget than lower levels of government can. The federal government in this case acts as a consortium of states in funding needed research and then sharing the research results.

FY 1977 appropriations were $11 million,[85] and approximately 115 projects were awarded funds.[86]

FEDERAL FUNDS FOR EDUCATION OF HANDICAPPED CHILDREN

Having summarized federal programs that are directly and indirectly related to educating handicapped children, we now examine the size of the federal financial commitment. First, the federal program for the

[85]U.S. Office of Management and Budget, *Catalog of Federal Domestic Assistance,* Section 13.443, November 1976.
[86]U.S. Department of Health, Education, and Welfare, *Justifications of Appropriation Estimates for Committee on Appropriations, Fiscal Year 1977, Education Division.*

education of handicapped children is put into perspective by estimating its total cost and then showing this cost as a percentage of federal expenditures on education, state expenditures on special education, and total outlays for education. Second, federal expenditures are broken down by the level of instruction—preschool, elementary, secondary, and higher education. Third, expenditures are shown by the function that the federal government is playing in the education process. Finally, federal expenditures are shown by type of handicapping condition. For comparative purposes, we present overview but not detailed data for both 1972 and 1977.

Expenditures for Education of Handicapped Children

An estimate of federal expenditures for educating the handicapped in FY 1972 is presented in Table 10.6. The total is approximately $315 million, with 78.1 percent allocated to direct support of the education of handicapped children, 18.4 percent to support of instruction through teacher training and media services, and 3.5 percent to research. Only 5 percent of the total federal funds spent on education went for education of the handicapped in FY 1972. Federal expenditures also make up only a small part of the total expenditures on special education. The FY 1972 state and local contribution to special education has been estimated at approximately $2.3 billion in FY 1972.[87] This means that the federal government was bearing 12 percent of the cost of special education. The federal government paid about 7 percent of the total FY 1972 national expenditures for elementary and secondary education.[88]

An estimate of federal expenditures for educating handicapped children in FY 1977 is shown in Table 10.7. The total is over $542 million, up 72 percent over 1972. Of the 1977 total, 81 percent went for instruction of handicapped students; 17 percent went to produce resources such as teachers and materials; and 2 percent went for research. As indicated at the start of this chapter, the federal government is bearing about 14 percent of the excess cost of special education above the cost of regular education.

[87]These estimates were derived from the reports filed by the state under EHA-B. The reliability of the data is in great doubt. Many of the estimates were made by taking an estimate of the number of children of each disability receiving some sort of service and multiplying by the unit cost of delivering some special education to that particular handicapped group. These estimates were based neither on a census of handicapped students nor on a careful cost analysis of the resources actually flowing to the handicapped group. The estimate presented is also biased downward because it does not include state expenditures for teacher training as was done in the estimate of federal expenditures.

[88]*Hearings,* p. 372.

Table 10.6
FY 1972 FEDERAL FUNDS FOR EDUCATION OF HANDICAPPED CHILDREN
($ million)

Program	Budget (Fiscal Year 1972)	Provision of Services		Provision of Funds With Accompanying Regulations		
		Economy of Scale	Internalize Externalities	Basic Services Support	Redistribution of Resources	Stimulation
Education	245.966					
EHA-B[a]	37.500	—	—	—	—	37.500
ESEA-Title I						
Local Education Agencies[b]	28.000	—	—	—	28.000	—
P.L. 89-313[b]	56.381	—	—	56.381	—	—
ESEA-Title III[c]	20.100	—	—	—	—	20.100
Headstart[d]	33.384	—	—	—	—	33.384
Vocational Education Act[e]	38.384	—	—	—	—	38.384
Higher Education Act[f]	0.436	—	—	—	0.436	—
Federal Schools for Deaf[g]						
Gallaudet College[h]	7.888	7.888	—	—	—	—
NTI for Deaf[i]	2.907	2.907	—	—	—	—
Kendall School[h]	1.212	—	1.212	—	—	—
Model Secondary School[i]	2.524	—	2.524	—	—	—
Special Target Groups						
Deaf-Blind Centers[a]	7.500	7.500	—	—	—	—
Early Education[a]	7.500	—	—	—	—	7.500
Learning Disabilities (EHA-G)[a]	2.250	—	—	—	—	2.250

	Total					
Instructional Support	57.906	—	—	—	—	—
Teaching Personnel[k]						
EHA-D	35.145	—	35.145	—	—	—
Education Professions Development Act	6.100	—	6.100	—	—	—
Regional Resource Centers (EHA-C)[a]	3.550	3.550	—	—	—	—
Media						
EHA-F[a]	10.500	10.500	—	—	—	—
American Printing House for the Blind[l]	1.580	1.580	—	—	—	—
Library of Congress[m]	1.031	1.031	—	—	—	—
Research	10.994	—	—	10.994	—	—
Research (EHA-E)[n]	10.994	—	—	10.994	—	—
Total	314.866	34.956	55.975	56.381	28.436	139.110
Percent	100.0	11.1	17.8	17.9	9.0	44.2

a U.S. Congress, House, Subcommittee of the Committee on Appropriations, *Hearings, Part 2, Office of Education and Special Institutions,* 92d Cong. 2d sess, 1972 (hereafter cited as *Hearings*), p. 403.

b *Hearings,* p. 271

c "The Big Package for Education for the Handicapped," *American Education,* May 1972, p. 39.

d Office of Child Development Headstart Program—State Worksheets, as reported in *Education Daily,* September 12, 1972.

e *Hearings,* p. 584. Ten percent of Vocational Education funds are earmarked for the handicapped.

f An estimate of the percentage of program funds under this Act that were received by the handicapped was not available for 1972. Therefore, the 1973 estimate (taken from *Hearings,* p. 245) was multiplied by the ratio of 1972 to 1973 program funds to obtain the estimates presented here. Estimates of the total program were obtained from U.S. Department of Health, Education, and Welfare *Justifications of Appropriation Estimates for Committee on Appropriations, FY 1973,* Vol. III, *Office of Education,* Department of Health, Education, and Welfare, Washington, D.C., p. 220.

g All estimates exclude construction costs.

h *Hearings,* p. 1162.

i *Hearings,* p. 1107.

j *Hearings,* p. 1122.

k *Hearings,* p. 403. Includes teacher education, physical education and recreation training, and recruitment and information components of EHA.

l *Hearings,* p. 1065.

m Estimate for the Library of Congress-Books for the blind and Physically Handicapped program was obtained by multiplying the fraction of total readers under age 22 by the FY 1972 estimate in "Budget Justification: Library of Congress Division for the Blind and Handicapped," 1972.

n *Hearings* p. 433.

Table 10.7
FY 1977 FEDERAL FUNDS FOR EDUCATION OF HANDICAPPED CHILDREN
($ Million)

| Program | Budget (Fiscal Year 1977) | Primary Function | | | | |
| | | Provision of Services | | Provision of Funds With Accompanying Regulations | | |
		Economy of Scale	Internalize Externalities	Basic Service Support	Redistribution of Resources	Stimulation
Education						
EHA-B (P.L. 94–142)	110	—	—	110	—	—
ESEA-Title I (P.L. 89–313)	111	—	—	111	—	—
ESEA-Title IV	21	—	—	—	—	21
Early Education	22	—	—	—	—	22
Headstart	47.5	—	—	—	47.5	—
Deaf-Blind Services	16	16	—	—	—	—
Learning Disabilities	5	—	—	—	—	5
Severely Handicapped	3	—	—	—	—	3
Vocational Education	48.2	—	—	—	—	48.2
Regional Post-Secondary Education	2	—	—	?	—	2
Higher Education	a	—	—	—	—	—
Gallaudet College	41	41	—	—	—	—
NTI for Deaf	13	13	—	—	—	—

a Some unknown fraction of $23 million was for physically handicapped youth.

Instructional Support						
Personnel Preparation	40	—	40	—	—	—
Recruitment and Information	1	—	—	—	—	1
Regional Resource Centers	10	—	—	—	—	10
Media Services and Captioned Films	16	16	—	—	—	—
Amer. Print. House Blind	3	3	—	—	—	—
Library of Congress	22	22	—	—	—	—
Research						
Handicapped Research	11	—	11	—	—	—
Total	>542	112	51	221	47.5	112.2
Percent	100.0	20	9	41	9	21

Expenditures by Level of Instruction

The emphasis of the federal program for education of the handicapped is at the preschool and elementary level. Approximately 63 percent of FY 1972 federal funds went to this level of instruction, with 30 percent to secondary education, and only about 7 percent to post-secondary or higher education. The federal government spends a much larger percentage of its total education funds on higher education than it does for special education of the handicapped. Given the relatively large percentage of the handicapped who do not go on to college, this difference in emphasis appears reasonable.

Expenditures by Federal Function

The relatively small size of the federal expenditures for education of handicapped children almost precludes several of the functions as viable alternatives. Given the high cost of special education, it would be impossible for the federal government to fulfill a major or basic service support function at FY 1972 budget levels. Given the dispersion of both wealth and income in this country, it would take a larger commitment on the part of the federal government than that in FY 1972 to serve as an effective balance wheel through redistribution of resources.

Table 10.6 includes an estimate of the funds devoted to each function. In the table each program is identified with a primary individual function. Secondary functions of each program may also be important if the federal government is performing a dual role. The largest percentage of FY 1972 funds went to the role of stimulation (44 percent), which is in agreement with the pronouncement by the Bureau of Education for the Handicapped that federal policy at that time was to stimulate state and local participation in special education.[89] Provision of services to achieve economies of scale and to internalize externalities received 11 and 18 percent of the funds, respectively. Funds for redistribution of resources accounted for only 9 percent of the special education budget in FY 1972 and were part of similar larger programs where budget levels may make this role practical. The federal government provided basic service support to only a very specialized group—those in state-operated or state-supported facilities for the handicapped—and this accounted for 18 percent of the special education budget. As shown in Table 10.7, by 1977 the federal emphasis was shifting from stimulation toward basic service support as P.L. 94-142 was implemented. The percentage of the federal special

[89]E. Martin, *Hearings,* p. 360.

Table 10.8
FEDERAL EXPENDITURES ON EDUCATION OF THE HANDICAPPED

Type of Handicap	Expenditures
Blind (American Printing House for the Blind)	$ 1,580,000
Deaf (Federal Schools for the Deaf)	14,531,000
Deaf-Blind (Model Centers for the Deaf-Blind)	7,500,000
Learning disabled	2,250,000
Noncategorical for type of disability	289,005,000

education funds used for stimulation was down to 21 percent, whereas 41 percent went for basic service support.

Expenditures by Type of Disability

The bulk of federal expenditures for education of the handicapped is not allocated on a categorical basis to any specific handicapped group. Table 10.8 presents an estimate of the amount of money specifically allocated to a disability in FY 1972; 92 percent was noncategorical aid.

When the money is not earmarked by the federal government, the state governments are allowed to spend according to their own preferences among disabilities—subject to federal review, of course. Table 10.9 presents an estimate of how the funds were allocated among the various handicapping conditions for the two largest FY 1972 federal programs, EHA-B and P.L. 89-313.

Table 10.9
DISTRIBUTION OF FY 1972 FEDERAL EXPENDITURES FOR EHA-B AND P.L. 89-313 BY HANDICAPPING CONDITIONS[a]
(by percent)

Type of Handicap	EHA-B	P.L. 89-313	Total
Mentally retarded, trainable	10.0	39.5	26.3
Mentally retarded, educable	29.3	13.8	20.8
Hard of hearing	5.6	1.0	3.1
Deaf	6.4	16.6	12.0
Speech impaired	9.1	1.1	4.7
Visually impaired	4.4	6.4	5.5
Emotionally disturbed	11.4	15.1	13.5
Crippled	3.5	3.3	3.3
Learning disabled	12.6	0.9	6.1
Other health impaired	7.7	2.3	4.7
Total Percent	100.0	100.0	100.0

[a] Estimates are from the U.S. Bureau of Education for the Handicapped, *Aid to the States Branch Information System, National Report,* EHA-B, FY 1970, p. 8; and P.L. 89-313, p. 9.

The table shows that nearly half of the federal funds for these two programs went to the mentally retarded, split fairly evenly between the trainable and educable. Only 13.5 percent of the funds went to the emotionally disturbed.

SPECIAL EDUCATION PROGRAMS IN THE STATES

Resources for education of the handicapped are largely state and local. Operation of institutions for mentally retarded, blind, and deaf youth are an integral part of education programs in many of the states. In terms of money and children served, however, the larger state program is one of direct transfer of funds to local school districts or private schools for operation of special education programs.

This subsection describes the programs sponsored by the states in terms of the number of people affected and the amount of funds devoted to each program. From the standpoint of federal policy, however, it is perhaps more important to attempt to determine why state programs are the way they are. That is, we will examine the determinants of spending on special education. If some states spend more, because of income, for example, there may be a *priori* evidence for the need of federal redistribution of resources.

To compile this description of programs, we used three different data collection methods. First, we visited five states to obtain background information on a cross section of state programs. Second, we sent a questionnaire to all the states, requesting information on their programs for education of the handicapped. Third, we used reports filed with the federal government by the state education agencies about their programs.

Although the questionnaires provided a large volume of information, they were not an entirely satisfactory method of gathering information. Some states supplied excellent responses, but many did not. An accurate national picture could not be compiled from the returned questionnaires. Therefore, those data were used mainly as checks against information supplied to the federal government, and for examples of different kinds of programs that exist in the states.

State and Local Expenditures

One difficulty in analyzing program expenditures for educating the handicapped is the lack of reliable data. Much of special education is intermingled with the regular school program, making it difficult to identify the additional cost of special education. Moreover, in the residential schools, where the handicapped are isolated from the regular program, only a fraction of the total cost goes for instruction.

This fraction cannot be easily identified in the financial records of the schools.

Estimates of expenditures on special education, then, are not very reliable and will vary from source to source, depending on the assumptions made about allocating cost between the regular and the special programs. Table 10.10 presents estimates of state and local spending on education of handicapped children that were prepared by personnel in the various state departments of education.[90] While the estimates are not precise, they are valuable in two ways. First, they give an order of magnitude picture of the total amount of funds being devoted to education of the handicapped. This is useful in assessing the size of the program against the size of the problem. Second, these figures show the distribution of funds among handicapping conditions, thus enabling the planner to see where funds are going and to locate any apparent gaps in service in a particular state or nationwide.

The table shows that, of the total $2.364 billion expended in FY 1972, a large percentage of state and local funds went for the education of mentally retarded children. Approximately $1.1 billion was spent by these levels of government on both trainable and educable mentally retarded children. In other terms, 46 percent of the state and local effort, as measured by dollars expended, was going to the mentally retarded. The emotionally disturbed received 11 percent of state and local funds. The speech impaired, learning disabled, and crippled groups each received between 8 and 11 percent of the funds in FY 1972.

Number of Children Receiving Educational Services

The total number of students served is also a measure of the size of the program, while the percentage of those in need who receive special education services is a measure of the gaps in service that may exist in particular states or in particular handicapping conditions.

Estimates of the total numbers served in FY 1972, by handicap, are presented in Table 10.11. The total number of handicapped children receiving service was estimated at 3.046 million, or 6.6 percent of the

[90]These estimates were taken from the state plans submitted in 1972 by each state to the Bureau of Education for the Handicapped. From discussions with personnel in various states responsible for making these estimates, it became clear that their methodology could not lead to accurate estimates. For example, one state estimated the cost by multiplying the number of handicapped served by $1000, with little regard to the disability. In other cases it appears that when the State Education Agency was not responsible for residential schools, the costs of these schools were excluded from the estimates. The analysis presented in this section should be interpreted with this data reliability problem well in mind.

Table 10.10
ESTIMATED STATE AND LOCAL EXPENDITURES ON EDUCATION OF THE HANDICAPPED, 1972–73[a]
($ thousand)

State	Mentally Retarded Trainable	Mentally Retarded Educable	Hard of Hearing	Deaf	Speech Impaired	Visually Impaired	Emotionally Disturbed	Crippled	Learning Disabled	Other Health Impaired	Total
Alabama	960	7,539	300	581	840	161	454	322	504	427	12,088
Alaska	275	2,244	381	105	190	84	402	85	1,058	127	4,954
Arizona	1,085	7,906	120	0	609	165	1,026	209	483	803	12,408
Arkansas	1,091	1,609	0	1,304	46	923	70	115	142	31	5,332
California	27,560	62,800	14,700	10,500	15,225	7,000	0	81,900	78,750	0	298,435
Colorado[b]	1,585	5,518	0	0	2,046	341	1,876	1,183	4,996	2,508	20,067
Connecticut	5,551	8,416	2,820	0	3,282	1,157	6,770	3,255	8,777	0	40,278
Delaware	1,744	2,524	13	475	540	0	1,228	540	1,552	1,593	9,805
Florida	5,008	27,728	2,160	2,480	5,040	1,120	9,040	4,432	6,256	0	71,520
Georgia	2,220	11,412	834	1,745	11,142	3,915	4,762	0	2,840	3,227	42,475
Hawaii	1,358	2,821	95	607	65	96	493	383	1,221	224	7,367
Idaho	430	1,542	10	5	518	7	0	11	622	0	3,791
Illinois	8,805	47,295	1,365	11,850	18,195	2,430	23,385	12,675	15,585	5,325	174,585
Indiana	5,669	10,399	143	1,432	3,798	1,362	983	717	267	118	28,617
Iowa	1,750	7,320	1,080	360	4,270	380	2,875	655	1,320	778	24,565
Kansas	1,186	6,849	399	0	1,917	185	1,165	1,082	738	554	15,876

NOTE: Column totals do not add to the United States total. When costs are shared among disabilities, they are listed in the "more than one" category on the federal reporting form. Costs in this category were arbitrarily distributed among the disability totals in proportion to the total state and local expenditures for that disability.

[a] These statistics were compiled from *Description of Projected Activities for Fiscal Year 1973 for the Education of the Handicapped*, an annual report submitted to the Bureau of Education for the Handicapped by the fifty states under EHA-B. Completed forms from two states were not available.

[b] Colorado did not break down its total expenditures by disability. It was assumed that 1972–73 expenditures followed the same pattern as in 1968–69. All 1968–69 data were obtained from *Summary Statistics-Expenditures, FY 1969*, State-Federal Information Clearinghouse for Exceptional Children, Reston, Virginia.

Kentucky	1,312	8,074	619	258	4,451	147	889	1,829	1,252	0	18,935
Louisiana	650	5,000	100	40	1,500	70	600	140	850	400	10,850
Maine	560	740	26	805	297	202	173	251	334	108	3,713
Maryland	3,165	4,236	633	462	1,117	448	1,307	438	6,893	4,987	24,616
Massachusetts	3,421	19,189	469	4,267	3,489	1,942	12,402	3,489	6,763	0	55,435
Michigan	27,397	46,044	5,296	6,920	17,253	4,298	9,893	8,715	0	0	153,896
Minnesota	6,408	15,162	0	2,957	4,255	1,075	19,800	1,507	19,800	130	61,547
Mississippi	553	5,010	121	806	506	319	28	303	373	2	8,023
Missouri	0	19,877	652	0	33,751	129	808	712	912	1,162	58,253
Montana	500	1,170	145	300	1,525	250	100	160	0	450	4,700
Nebraska	2,468	6,106	269	1,078	11,939	613	897	526	155	0	26,624
Nevada	375	1,697	125	62	500	50	1,062	250	0	0	4,247
New Hampshire	1,288	2,724	118	979	550	211	1,181	75	2,034	312	9,476
New Jersey	5,544	12,600	840	1,932	8,400	2,184	9,072	756	5,292	6,132	84,000
New Mexico	1,040	4,131	67	132	1,490	192	276	112	562	135	8,562
New York	42,123	139,557	4,399	15,666	14,832	12,889	97,744	44,170	0	15,309	403,650
North Carolina	2,519	17,054	2,769	0	3,007	2,415	1,391	673	762	583	31,316
North Dakota	224	1,155	19	0	733	40	154	643	133	49	3,152
Ohio^c	29,600	97,200	0	7,000	16,200	2,400	0	5,000	24,400	7,800	174,200

cOhio reported only state expenditures. It was estimated that state expenditures were 50 percent of the total, as that percentage is typical of the region.

Table 10.10—continued

State	Mentally Retarded		Hard of Hearing	Deaf	Speech Impaired	Visually Impaired	Emotionally Disturbed	Crippled	Learning Disabled	Other Health Impaired	Total
	Trainable	Educable									
Oklahoma	705	5,163	172	37	1,098	255	187	112	2,347	187	10,797
Oregon	1,697	4,800	440	412	1,808	1,919	706	390	1,200	616	12,239
Pennsylvania	13,193	50,862	1,336	1,518	13,524	2,899	5,566	6,287	0	5,692	100,879
Rhode Island	1,300	1,800	1,400	0	720	300	1,320	150	3,800	100	10,890
South Carolina	779	8,761	227	100	1,206	198	998	293	681	0	13,698
South Dakota	250	1,500	100	500	200	400	200	900	250	75	4,375
Tennessee	2,707	11,625	350	150	1,900	275	975	2,970	2,700	3,600	28,452
Texas	6,834	32,085	1,375	1,525	5,969	2,114	5,072	2,933	16,918	10,449	85,277
Utah	1,680	3,546	125	235	1,682	97	1,668	166	4,769	0	14,348
Vermont	425	1,044	206	253	192	105	217	349	299	98	3,190
Virginia	3,968	28,939	1,752	0	2,370	0	2,551	846	1,000	1,170	47,755
Washington	3,187	6,728	442	609	2,605	254	2,684	551	991	1,033	30,057
West Virginia	583	3,166	112	19	605	26	24	102	26	168	4,834
Wisconsin	7,670	2,815	1,610	3,718	6,441	3,275	4,567	2,015	2,205	652	64,509
Wyoming	240	1,029	31	186	373	73	192	38	544	20	3,256
D.C.	3,190	1,591	826	557	1,104	328	1,994	817	270	1,037	11,919
Total	260,000	840,000	55,000	91,000	251,000	66,000	258,000	210,000	250,000	84,000	2,364,000
Percent	11	35	2	4	11	3	11	8	11	4	100

Table 10.11
HANDICAPPED CHILDREN RECEIVING EDUCATIONAL SERVICE, BY DISABILITY, FY 1972

State	Mentally Retarded		Hard of Hearing	Deaf	Speech Impaired	Visually Impaired	Emotionally Disturbed	Crippled	Learning Disabled	Other Health Impaired	Total
	Trainable	Educable									
Alabama	2,208	13,884	347	777	8,550	426	616	452	620	540	28,420
Alaska	140	900	160	50	70	35	166	40	400	50	2,011
Arizona	952	6,153	60	0	6,090	61	799	163	376	473	15,127
Arkansas	1,800	7,377	0	342	5,010	224	329	146	845	357	16,430
California	11,000	47,000	3,000	3,000	130,000	2,500	0	58,000	60,000	0	313,900
Colorado	0	8,584	1,716	451	23,184	233	6,241	533	0	1,250	42,192
Connecticut	2,962	5,260	1,573	0	13,033	464	9,044	2,424	9,501	0	44,261
Delaware	650	2,800	8	155	4,000	95	910	200	920	580	10,318
Florida	3,450	26,000	11,410	1,400	33,590	1,050	7,500	7,000	9,000	0	100,400
Georgia	3,683	31,666	1,085	630	28,232	1,100	3,479	0	2,557	4,108	76,540
Hawaii	733	2,409	152	176	3,960	51	193	155	1,339	100	9,268
Idaho	492	1,700	53	109	4,786	80	0	32	2,908	0	10,160
Illinois	7,040	37,840	9,100	2,480	97,000	1,617	26,510	7,600	12,463	5,320	206,970
Indiana	5,420	18,968	200	927	48,616	374	745	402	190	106	75,948
Iowa	1,450	7,883	430	70	20,414	280	9,464	854	1,400	970	43,215
Kansas	945	7,735	256	0	16,000	180	1,300	770	1,170	1,300	29,656
Kentucky	1,464	13,560	1,040	288	19,000	143	850	2,044	984	0	39,373
Louisiana	1,000	13,500	300	100	32,000	150	1,000	200	1,700	1,000	50,950
Maine	665	2,900	98	336	3,700	283	320	405	800	102	9,609
Maryland	3,165	21,180	633	462	22,435	448	1,307	438	6,893	4,987	61,948
Massachusetts	1,969	12,106	1,087	1,377	32,934	730	3,345	5,500	16,480	0	75,528
Michigan	11,522	42,393	2,399	828	91,488	1,818	6,181	7,539	0	0	164,168
Minnesota	4,284	12,500	0	1,200	28,560	400	27,500	500	0	0	75,344
Mississippi	886	8,623	118	310	9,556	192	74	580	528	400	20,927
Missouri	0	19,877	652	0	33,751	129	808	712	912	1,162	58,003

Table 10.11—continued

State	Mentally Retarded Trainable	Mentally Retarded Educable	Hard of Hearing	Deaf	Speech Impaired	Visually Impaired	Emotionally Disturbed	Crippled	Learning Disabled	Other Health Impaired	Total
Montana	510	1,700	53	60	3,000	103	600	750	1,733	45	8,554
Nebraska	2,240	6,043	281	305	17,047	246	913	378	1,302	136	28,891
Nevada	300	1,600	70	30	2,800	50	950	200	0	0	6,000
New Hampshire	619	1,999	263	213	5,050	108	463	50	1,304	244	10,313
New Jersey	6,043	20,661	691	1,654	61,023	1,875	26,274	1,178	5,748	24,625	149,772
New Mexico	1,040	4,590	75	265	2,980	385	276	125	625	150	10,511
New York	12,961	49,842	3,666	2,984	118,658	3,069	27,927	11,938	0	5,670	236,715
North Carolina	3,293	38,000	1,645	0	34,000	1,300	2,000	515	2,500	600	83,853
North Dakota	180	1,240	12	0	4,500	60	1,217	115	1,117	160	8,601
Ohio	14,760	53,239	0	2,436	93,035	1,089	0	1,650	18,645	6,576	191,430
Oklahoma	1,243	11,013	186	462	13,597	157	180	158	5,325	1,511	33,832
Oregon	887	4,670	325	398	14,500	250	650	444	7,000	700	29,824
Pennsylvania	6,200	43,233	1,500	600	80,500	2,050	2,200	2,187	0	1,980	140,450
Rhode Island	300	2,500	4,200	0	7,200	281	600	150	3,800	300	19,331
South Carolina	1,200	20,500	830	170	19,000	600	8,000	1,250	2,000	0	53,550
South Dakota	600	2,000	150	150	5,000	150	400	300	3,000	150	11,900
Tennessee	2,850	15,500	350	150	20,000	275	650	3,300	2,700	4,800	50,575
Texas	10,996	44,221	1,830	910	85,683	1,879	6,881	4,052	24,291	15,467	196,210
Utah	1,293	3,258	259	284	9,928	155	1,293	103	9,282	0	25,855
Vermont	313	1,181	236	87	1,440	86	430	72	1,049	300	5,194
Virginia	2,310	16,845	1,020	0	17,775	0	1,485	1,092	2,500	4,497	47,524
Washington	2,895	10,284	349	412	2,278	245	4,054	509	2,599	1,061	24,686
West Virginia	900	6,625	200	30	8,000	37	45	100	45	198	16,180
Wisconsin	3,985	15,474	676	377	32,352	436	1,580	432	851	2,433	58,596
Wyoming	150	710	65	49	2,150	165	120	280	620	300	4,609
D.C.	1,476	2,177	283	191	5,630	113	756	230	128	292	11,276
Total	148,000	752,000	55,000	28,000	1,383,000	28,000	199,000	128,000	230,000	95,000	3,046,000
Percent	4.5	24.9	1.8	1.0	45.4	0.9	6.5	4.2	7.5	3.2	100.0

SOURCE: Estimated 1972–73 students to be served from *Description of Projected Activities for FY 1973 for the Education of Handicapped Children.*

Table 10.12
INCIDENCE RATES FOR HANDICAPS
(In percent)

Speech impaired	3.5
Emotionally disturbed	2.0
Mentally retarded	2.3
Learning disabled	1.0
Hard of hearing	0.5
Deaf	0.075
Crippled or other health impaired	0.5
Visually impaired	0.1
Multihandicapped	0.06

SOURCE: *Short Term Analysis Issue in Education for the Handicapped,* prepared by the Office of Program Planning and Evaluation, Bureau of Education for the Handicapped, and Exotech Systems, Inc., November 1971.

total enrollment in publicly supported elementary and secondary schools.[91]

Figures on total enrollment for special education service are more revealing when they are shown as the number receiving service as a percentage of those who require service. Wholly reliable estimates of the size of the handicapped youth population are not available. For our purposes, however, it seems sufficient to use the estimates published by the Bureau of Education for the Handicapped. The incidence rates shown in Table 10.12 for school-age youth were used in determining the number of handicapped children to be served. The incidence rate for all handicaps combined is 10.1 percent.[92]

These particular estimates are low compared with some of the percentages used by the states to estimate the number needing service. Compelling evidence of the state-by-state variation in the definitions of various types of handicaps or of variations in the actual incidence rates is shown in Table 10.13, which lists the percentage served by state and by disability for FY 1972. The table shows too many cases of

[91]K. A. Simon and W. V. Grant, *Digest of Educational Statistics,* U.S. Department of Health, Education, and Welfare, DHEW Publication No. (OE) 72-45, 1971, p. 24.

[92]Higher incidence rates than those used in this book are being reported by some states in their estimates of the size of the handicapped population. (See *Description of State Special Education Programs, FY 73,* submitted to the Bureau of Education for the Handicapped, U.S. Department of Health, Education, and Welfare.) Nebraska estimates that 5 percent are emotionally disturbed and 7 percent are learning disabled. North Dakota estimates 3 percent emotionally disturbed and 5 percent learning disabled. One study reported finding the use of incidence rates up to 20 percent for the learning disabled (M. Fleischmann, *Report of the New York State Commission on the Quality, Cost and Financing of Elementary and Secondary Education,* Vol. II, Albany, N.Y., 1972, p. 9.44). There are also lower estimates of incidence, as low as 0.05 percent for emotionally disturbed and 0.5 percent for the learning disabled (Rossmiller, Hale, and Frohreich, p. 121.)

Table 10.13
ESTIMATED PERCENT OF HANDICAPPED SERVED BY SPECIAL EDUCATION PROGRAMS, 1972-73

State	Mentally Retarded	Hard of Hearing	Deaf	Speech Impaired	Visually Impaired	Emotionally Disturbed	Crippled and Other	Learning Disabled	Total All Handicaps
Alabama	75.03	7.44	111.10	26.20	45.68	3.30	21.28	6.65	30.55
Alaska	41.95	29.69	61.85	1.86	32.47	7.70	16.70	37.11	18.70
Arizona	63.65	2.47	0.00	35.85	12.57	8.23	26.21	7.75	31.25
Arkansas	80.29	0.00	91.76	28.80	45.07	3.31	20.24	17.00	33.14
California	50.47	12.02	80.11	74.39	50.07	0.00	232.31	120.16	63.02
Colorado	63.51	58.40	102.33	112.72	39.65	53.10	60.68	0.00	71.98
Connecticut	46.58	41.00	0.00	48.52	60.46	58.93	63.17	123.81	57.82
Delaware	100.92	1.08	139.05	76.89	63.92	30.61	104.96	61.90	69.60
Florida	79.64	141.93	116.10	59.69	65.30	23.32	87.07	55.98	62.60
Georgia	125.71	17.75	68.71	65.98	89.97	14.23	67.20	20.91	62.76
Hawaii	67.02	14.92	115.14	55.51	25.02	4.73	25.02	65.70	45.59
Idaho	47.80	5.32	72.89	68.58	40.12	0.00	3.21	145.85	51.08
Illinois	68.26	63.67	115.67	96.95	56.56	46.37	90.39	43.60	72.58
Indiana	76.58	2.89	89.27	100.32	27.01	2.69	7.34	1.37	54.99
Iowa	54.71	11.59	12.58	78.64	37.75	63.80	49.18	18.87	58.41
Kansas	66.06	8.96	0.00	80.02	31.51	11.38	72.47	20.48	52.04
Kentucky	77.49	24.68	45.55	64.40	16.96	5.04	48.50	11.67	46.83
Louisiana	60.65	5.77	12.83	87.96	14.43	4.81	23.09	16.36	49.14
Maine	59.79	7.56	172.82	40.78	109.17	6.17	39.12	30.86	37.16
Maryland	102.05	12.21	59.39	61.80	43.19	6.30	104.61	66.46	59.87
Massachusetts	43.53	15.47	130.61	66.94	51.93	11.90	78.25	117.24	53.86
Michigan	95.80	19.61	45.12	106.83	74.30	12.63	61.62	0.00	67.26
Minnesota	69.52	0.00	152.42	77.74	38.11	130.99	17.15	0.00	71.96
Mississippi	65.19	3.72	65.18	43.05	30.28	0.58	20.18	8.33	33.08

Missouri	73.13	11.03	0.00	81.60	10.92	3.42	31.71	7.72	49.20
Montana	49.01	5.41	40.80	43.72	52.53	15.30	81.09	88.39	43.74
Nebraska	92.99	14.51	105.01	125.77	63.52	11.79	26.54	33.62	74.79
Nevada	65.40	11.08	31.67	63.34	39.59	37.61	31.67	0.00	47.62
New Hampshire	60.27	27.85	150.38	76.40	57.19	12.26	31.13	69.05	54.74
New Jersey	64.66	7.70	122.82	97.10	104.42	73.16	287.40	32.01	83.62
New Mexico	79.08	4.85	114.14	27.50	124.37	4.46	17.77	20.19	34.04
New York	62.71	16.84	91.37	77.86	70.48	32.07	80.87	0.00	54.50
North Carolina	135.82	24.89	0.00	73.49	98.34	7.56	16.87	18.91	63.59
North Dakota	35.28	1.37	0.00	73.46	34.28	34.77	31.43	63.82	49.27
Ohio	104.94	0.00	115.29	94.35	38.65	0.00	58.40	66.18	68.12
Oklahoma	63.48	4.43	73.38	46.28	18.70	1.07	39.76	63.43	40.40
Oregon	45.28	12.18	99.45	77.64	46.85	6.09	42.88	131.18	56.03
Pennsylvania	73.56	10.27	27.38	78.72	70.16	3.76	28.52	0.00	48.19
Rhode Island	54.35	375.01	0.00	91.84	125.45	13.39	40.18	169.65	86.52
South Carolina	131.15	23.07	31.51	75.46	83.40	55.60	34.75	27.80	74.62
South Dakota	60.56	16.07	107.15	76.53	80.36	10.71	48.22	160.72	63.91
Tennessee	79.70	6.99	19.98	57.09	27.47	3.25	161.84	26.97	50.65
Texas	120.08	18.31	60.69	122.45	93.98	17.21	195.26	121.50	98.38
Utah	63.41	16.60	121.35	90.90	49.67	20.72	6.60	297.45	83.06
Vermont	55.47	40.30	99.05	35.13	73.44	18.36	63.53	89.58	44.46
Virginia	69.57	17.04	0.00	42.42	0.00	6.20	93.37	20.88	39.80
Washington	65.16	7.94	62.47	7.40	27.86	23.05	35.71	29.56	28.14
West Virginia	74.02	9.05	9.05	51.71	8.37	0.51	13.48	1.02	36.70
Wisconsin	70.42	11.25	41.84	76.94	36.29	6.58	47.69	7.08	48.89
Wyoming	40.80	14.18	71.28	67.02	180.03	6.55	126.57	67.65	50.41
D.C.	96.57	34.41	154.84	97.80	68.71	22.98	63.48	7.78	68.73
Avg. percent served	80.45	21.38	71.61	76.66	54.76	19.27	86.65	44.65	59.23

over 100 percent of the population being served, indicating that the definitions and incidence levels are not consistent across the states. An example would be separating hard-of-hearing and deaf children by different definitions.[93]

The percentage served also depends on the assumptions made about the proper base population. It could be argued that the base population should be the age cohort from 0–21. Certain types of handicapped children below the age of 5 need special educational services and hence should be included in order to estimate those still needing service. Another line of reasoning is that the schools can only serve those who attend. Applying the handicapped incidence rates to the school population is one way of estimating how many handicapped children are in the regular school system and are not receiving special educational services, but are receiving normal instruction.[94]

Using public school attendance population as a base also eliminates the bias introduced by the implicit assumption, which is made when general population data in an age range are used as a base, that those not served in the public schools are not served at all. Table 10.14 shows the percentage served for various base populations.

When the population base is the general population age cohort that is served by the public schools, 5–17 years, the percentage served is considerably higher than when all youth (0–21) are taken as the base.[95] From the preceding discussion we conclude that the public schools are serving a majority, but not nearly all, of those handicapped children of traditional school age. But there is great variation

[93]It could also be argued that the states are overestimating the number actually served. In one state, for example, the estimate was derived by multiplying the number of special education classes offered by the maximum permissible class size. This would lead to an upward bias in the estimates. There is no evidence, however, that this was just an isolated example. Some states combined their hard-of-hearing and deaf into one category. This gives the impression that they are serving a high percentage of one of the disabilities and zero percentage of the other. This same phenomenon occurs with the learning disabled, retarded, and the emotionally disturbed. The reader is advised that some of these coverages of over 100 percent are due to differences in classification.

[94]The implicit assumption in this estimation method is that the incidence rates are the same for the school population as they are for the general population, and the same for all ages.

[95]An often quoted figure is that 60 percent of the handicapped are unserved by special education. This calculation uses the 0–20 age cohort as the base population. Incidence rates for ages 0–4 are assumed to be one-half of those for the 5–20 age cohort. See "Short Term Analysis Issue in the Education for the Handicapped," prepared by Bureau of Education for the Handicapped and Exotech Systems, Inc., November 1971.

Table 10.14
PERCENT OF HANDICAPPED SERVED IN FY 1972
ASSUMING DIFFERENT POPULATION BASES

Population Base	*Percent Served*
General population	
Age cohort	
0–21 years	36
0–17 years	44
5–17 years	59
School population enrollment	65

across states and across the types of handicaps, leaving much room for improvement in the amount and equity of special education services delivered. Many handicapped youth are not being served, however, because they are either too old or too young by traditional school age standards, or have dropped out or never been admitted to the public school.[96] If one assumes that the general population 0–21 age cohort is the proper population to use, then some 64 percent of the handicapped are not being served. This is approximately 5.3 million children. If one assumes the public schools should be serving just those enrolled (aged 5–17), neglecting the private school population, then perhaps 1.7 million children are not being served. No matter what one assumes, many youth are not served, and if the policy were to increase the number served, then a two-pronged attack would be needed: First, special education for those in school would have to be expanded. Second, younger and older youth (generally not considered the province of the public school) would have to be included in the programs.

This analysis also demonstrates that numbers can be selected to substantiate almost any position. In any event, policy should be based not only on the number served, but also on the type and quality of service being received. Variations in the amount of program input resources are discussed later in this section. Though this would be a logical place to discuss variation in program output, such a discussion is not within the scope of this book. Even if it were, it would not be too enlightening because of the dearth of information on the effectiveness of special education programs.

Though it is difficult to get an estimate of the percentage served because of the various assumptions underlying each estimate, we can say something about the percentage served for each handicapped

---

[96]We were unable to locate reliable data on the number served in private schools.

group, holding the assumptions constant. Table 10.13 reveals that a relatively large percentage of the mentally retarded were being served in FY 1972 compared with the emotionally disturbed and the learning disabled. The hard of hearing and the emotionally disturbed were the most underserved categories. Table 10.13 also shows the variation in the percentage served among states. The minimum percentage served in the mentally retarded category was 35 percent in North Dakota, but only 13 states fell below 60 percent served. The chances that a mentally retarded child was served were fairly good no matter what state he lived in. The same cannot be said for the emotionally disturbed. Because of the variation in the percentage receiving service for the emotionally disturbed, the probability that an emotionally disturbed child was served varied greatly from state to state, and the variation among school districts may have been even greater than among states. A look at intrastate programs, however, is outside the scope of this research.

The last column in Table 10.13 shows that there was a large variation in the percentage served among states.

State and Local Expenditures Per Handicapped Student

The percentage served in any handicapped category is not an adequate indicator of the quality of the program that is being offered. Rossmiller found that the costs for special education vary quite widely. In the sample districts used in that survey, the cost per pupil for a program for the educable mentally retarded varied from $826 to $2358.[97] The same wide variation was found among the states. Table 10.15 presents the average FY 1972 state and local special education expenditure per handicapped child served, by type of disability. The United States average was $776 per handicapped student. The reported average annual special education expenditure for a speech-impaired student was $170; for a deaf child it was $3067. The reported variation across the states for all handicapped children was extreme: from $213 in the lowest state to $1705 in the highest (excluding Alaska). The reported variation across states within a single handicap was even more striking. For example, the range for deafness was from less than $100 per pupil to nearly $10,000 per pupil annually; however, these figures understate the amount of funds going to the handicapped. The handicapped youth also receive services from the regular education program, and in some states these services may not have been reported in estimating the funds for educating the handicapped. The estimates presented here are the funds reported by the

[97]See R. A. Rossmiller, James Hale, and Lloyd Frohreich, *Educational Programs for Exceptional Children: Resource Configurations and Costs,* University of Wisconsin, Madison, August 1970.

states for special education only. We do not believe these reported data represent the total cost of educating children who receive some special education services. As an example of data inconsistencies, the reported FY 1972 expenditures for special education averaged $776, which was less than the average expenditures of $858 for the education of nonhandicapped youth.[98] Other sources have used much higher estimates of the total average per pupil expense for educating handicapped children; e.g., the U.S. Senate Labor and Public Welfare Committee used $1470.[99] Inspection of the budgetary data from the states, broken down by type of handicap, indicates that the expenditures were typically "line item" budget expenses identifiable as special education. Thus, for a speech-impaired student the reported $170 was probably the excess cost of speech therapy above the cost of his education in a regular classroom. For a deaf child, on the other hand, the $3067 reported expense was probably total rather than excess cost, since the deaf child would most typically be served in a special education classroom rather than in a regular classroom. If the speech-impaired are removed from the calculation of average per pupil expenditures, the average figure jumps from $776 to $1271. Because of the lack of reliable special education cost data, total and excess costs are difficult to estimate. For instance, the total cost figure of $1470 used by the Senate committee cited earlier, uses the assumption that the excess cost of educating the handicapped child is one-half of the total cost. What the cost of special education should be is inextricably tied to the type and structure of the program (special classrooms, itinerant special teachers, etc.), proportions of handicapped youth being served, and the effectiveness of the program.

Part of the reported variation in expenditures across states is due to problems in defining the types of handicapping conditions. Some states grouped their deaf and hard of hearing into one category, for example, while others did not. Such groupings will distort the amount spent on each disability. Some portion may also be attributed to different assumptions made about what costs to include in the cost-estimating procedures used by the states. One state, for example, estimated that service costs were $1000 per student for most major types of disability. Still, most variation is probably due to the different resource levels provided in each state. Again, however, one can say that some states pay more for special education, but there is virtually no information on whether these states are achieving more.

[98]*U.S. Statistical Abstract,* U.S. Government Printing Office, Washington, D.C., 1971.
[99]As reported in "Handicapped School Children, Caught in School Aid Debate," *National Journal,* Vol. 5, No. 6, February 10, 1973.

Table 10.15
ESTIMATED AVERAGE EXPENDITURE PER HANDICAPPED STUDENT SERVED, 1972-73
(Dollars)

State	Mentally Retarded		Hard of Hearing	Deaf	Speech Impaired	Visually Impaired	Emotionally Disturbed	Crippled	Learning Disabled	Other Health Impaired	Total
	Trainable	Educable									
Alabama	435	543	865	748	98	378	737	712	813	791	425
Alaska	1,964	2,493	2,381	2,100	2,714	2,400	2,422	2,125	2,645	2,540	2,463
Arizona	1,140	1,285	2,000	0	100	2,705	1,284	1,282	1,285	1,698	820
Arkansas	606	218	0	3,813	9	4,121	213	788	168	87	325
California	2,506	1,336	4,900	3,500	117	2,800	0	1,412	1,313	0	951
Colorado	0	643	0	0	88	1,464	301	2,220	0	2,006	476
Connecticut	1,874	1,600	1,793	0	252	2,494	749	1,343	924	0	910
Delaware	2,683	901	1,625	3,065	135	0	1,349	2,700	1,687	2,747	950
Florida	1,452	1,066	189	1,771	150	1,067	1,205	633	695	0	712
Georgia	603	360	769	2,770	395	3,559	1,369	0	1,111	786	555
Hawaii	1,853	1,171	625	3,449	16	1,882	2,554	2,471	912	2,240	795
Idaho	874	907	189	46	108	88	0	344	214	0	373
Illinois	1,251	1,250	150	4,778	188	1,503	882	1,668	1,251	1,001	844
Indiana	1,046	548	715	1,545	78	3,642	1,319	1,784	1,405	1,113	377
Iowa	1,207	929	2,512	5,143	209	1,357	304	767	943	802	568
Kansas	1,255	885	1,559	0	120	1,028	896	1,405	631	426	535
Kentucky	896	595	595	896	234	1,028	1,046	895	1,272	0	481
Louisiana	650	370	333	400	47	467	600	700	500	400	213
Maine	842	255	265	2,396	80	714	541	620	418	1,059	356
Maryland	1,000	200	1,000	1,000	50	1,000	1,000	1,000	1,000	1,000	397
Massachusetts	1,737	1,585	431	3,099	106	2,660	3,708	634	410	0	734
Michigan	2,378	1,086	2,208	8,357	189	2,364	1,601	1,156	0	0	937
Minnesota	1,496	1,213	0	2,464	149	2,688	720	3,014	0	325	817
	624	581	1,025	2,600	53	1,661	378	522	706	33	383

Missouri	0	1,000	1,000	0	1,000	1,000	1,000	1,000	1,000	1,000	1,004
Montana	980	688	2,736	5,000	508	2,427	167	213	0	10,000	549
Nebraska	1,102	1,010	957	3,534	700	2,492	982	1,392	119	0	922
Nevada	1,250	1,061	1,786	2,067	179	1,000	1,118	1,250	0	0	708
New Hampshire	2,081	1,363	449	4,596	109	1,954	2,551	1,500	1,560	1,279	919
New Jersey	917	610	1,216	1,168	138	1,165	345	642	921	249	561
New Mexico	1,000	900	893	498	500	499	1,000	896	899	900	815
New York	3,250	2,800	1,200	5,250	125	4,200	3,500	3,700	0	2,700	1,705
North Carolina	765	449	1,683	0	88	1,858	696	1,307	305	972	373
North Dakota	1,244	931	1,583	0	163	667	127	5,591	119	306	366
Ohio	2,005	1,826	0	2,874	174	2,204	0	3,030	1,309	1,186	910
Oklahoma	567	469	925	80	81	1,624	1,039	709	441	124	319
Oregon	1,913	1,028	1,354	1,035	125	7,676	1,086	878	171	880	410
Pennsylvania	2,128	1,176	891	2,530	168	1,414	2,530	2,875	0	2,875	718
Rhode Island	4,333	720	333	0	100	1,068	2,200	1,000	1,000	333	563
South Carolina	649	427	273	588	63	330	125	234	341	0	256
South Dakota	417	750	667	3,333	40	2,667	500	3,000	83	500	368
Tennessee	950	750	1,000	1,000	95	1,000	1,500	900	1,000	750	563
Texas	621	726	751	1,676	70	1,125	737	724	696	676	435
Utah	1,299	1,088	483	827	169	626	1,290	1,612	514	0	555
Vermont	1,358	884	873	2,908	133	1,221	505	4,847	285	327	614
Virginia	1,718	1,718	1,718	0	133	0	1,718	775	400	260	1,005
Washington	1,101	654	1,266	1,478	1,144	1,037	662	1,083	381	974	1,218
West Virginia	648	478	560	633	76	703	533	1,020	578	848	299
Wisconsin	1,925	182	2,382	9,862	199	7,511	2,891	4,664	2,591	268	1,101
Wyoming	1,600	1,449	477	3,796	173	442	1,600	136	877	67	706
D.C.	2,161	731	2,919	2,916	196	2,903	2,638	3,552	2,109	3,551	1,057
U.S. average	1,757	1,045	936	3,067	170	2,186	1,214	1,530	1,015	822	776

Table 10.16
STATE AND LOCAL EXPENDITURES FOR SPECIAL EDUCATION PER ADA, FY 1972

Type of Handicap	Average Expenditure Per ADA
Mentally retarded, trainable	$ 4.61
Mentally retarded, educable	14.61
Hard of hearing	1.19
Deaf	1.69
Speech impaired	5.98
Visually impaired	1.20
Emotionally disturbed	4.51
Crippled	2.30
Learning disabled	4.87
Other health impaired	1.58
Total	$43.83

Another measure of state and local effort is the amount spent on education of the handicapped in comparison with the total number of children (handicapped and nonhandicapped) in the public school system. While a state may be spending a large amount per child served, it may not be serving a large percentage of the handicapped. By looking at the amount spent, normalized for total public school population size, we get a better idea of fiscal effort being put forth in each disability category.

Table 10.16 shows the average amount reported spent by each state in FY 1972 on each handicap for each youth (handicapped and non-handicapped) in the public school system. Only $44 per total average daily attendance in FY 1972 was spent on handicapped children, while the average expense for elementary and secondary education was $858.

Determinants of State and Local Spending

If one objective of federal policy is to stimulate state and local spending on special education, it is important to understand the determinants of that spending. Just why state and local districts spend at various levels is a complicated issue. Some simple models of state and local behavior can help clarify the issue.

Per pupil spending on special education should reasonably be a function of per capita income. The higher the income, the more one would expect to be spent on the education of the handicapped. This is true of regular education,[100] and it is reasonable to believe that it would be the same for special education.

[100]S. M. Barro, *The Impacts of Grants in Aid to State and Local Education Expenditures,* The Rand Corporation, Santa Monica, California P-4385, 1970, p. 21.

Spending on special education should also be a function of whether such education is mandated. Even without legislation, many local districts would provide such services. Legislation, however, would have an effect on some districts that would not otherwise provide it. Therefore, it is hypothesized that state and local education expenditures would be affected positively by legislation mandating the provision of special education services.

The amount spent on special education may also be a function of population density, although whether high population density should increase or decrease emphasis on special education is not clear. Low population density areas might have fewer handicapped youth per school district because travel times would limit the geographic size and, hence, the population size a school district serves. Since it is reasonable to expect that economies of scale will make special education relatively less expensive when large numbers of pupils are involved, the expenditure rate may be inversely related to population density. The low-density district may simply not offer special education, since the small size program and high cost could outweigh benefits. However, if the high density district were to offer the program, their spending per capita on special education would obviously exceed that of the low density district. This would imply that special education expenditures were positively related to density. Therefore, population density exerts two conflicting forces on special education expenditures.

Another possible determinant is the method of financing special education within each state. Whether the state reimburses all excess costs, matches local spending, or provides flat grants will make a difference in the behavior of the local district. Unfortunately, it was not possible to get adequate data on this variable to include in this description. It should be gathered, however, for extensions of this research.

The model that has been discussed is assumed to be linear:

$$S = a + bI + cM = dD,$$

where S = special education expenditures per ADA,
I = per capita income,
M = 1 if mandated, O if not mandated in 1971,[101]
D = population per square mile.

[101]States that only provided permission for the local districts to have special education or required a minimum of children (greater than one) for special education were considered not to have mandated special education. Information on existing legislation was taken from The Council for Exceptional Children, *Digest of State and Federal Laws: Education of Handicapped Children,* Reston, Virginia, 1971.

Using 1971 data,[102] the following coefficients of the model were estimated:[103]

$$S = 36.3 + .020I - .003D + 6.56M$$
$$ (5.2) \quad (.3) \quad (1.6) \qquad R^2 = .53.$$

Income has by far the most significant coefficient and is related to large changes in the special education expenditure variable. The model estimates that for every dollar increase in per capita income, two cents goes to special education per ADA. This could mean that Connecticut would spend some $46 more than Mississippi because of the income effect. Since the mean value of S is $36, it shows the dramatic relation to special education that incomes may have.

The density variable is not statistically significant. It could be that the two conflicting forces potentially caused by density just cancel one another out. Using state data, however, probably results in too high a level of aggregation to see behavior in individual school districts. The impact of density should be studied more closely with data from school districts.

Mandating legislation was hypothesized to have a positive impact on spending and, in fact, had a positive statistical relation. The coefficient, however, is only significant at approximately the 15-percent level of confidence.

The preference of states for dividing funds between special and regular education was also subject to investigation. A model similar to the one above was hypothesized, where the ratio of special education expenditures to total current expenditures on the total school program was regressed against the variables measuring density, mandated legislation, and per capita income. The estimated model is shown below:

$$S/E = -1.01 + 1.10 M + - .0005 D + .0017 I$$
$$ (1.68) \quad\quad (-.32) \quad (2.75) \quad R^2 = .30,$$

where S/E = Special Education Expenditures/Current Expenditures for Public Elementary and Secondary Schools.

Once again, the density variable is not significant in explaining differences in emphasis on special education among the states. Whether the state has mandated legislation, however, is related (10-percent confidence level) to spending preferences.

[102]Data on average daily attendance were taken from the *Digest of Educational Statistics*, p. 26. Income data were taken from the *U.S. Statistical Abstract*, p. 121. The income data were for 1969, but because income is a slow-moving function, the year lag should not distort the analysis. Data on population density were also obtained from *U.S. Statistical Abstract*, p. 13.

[103]The *t*-ratios are shown in parentheses below each equation.

Again, income is highly correlated with the amount of funds going to special education. The coefficient of the income variable is significant at the 1-percent level of confidence. This means that not only do high income states pay more for special education, but they also give it more emphasis relative to regular education.

We noted previously that percentage of handicapped served was related to the density of the state. Here, however, we have seen that both special education to expenditures per ADA and special education expenditures as a percentage of total expenditures are not related to density. This implies that, while the less densely populated states are serving fewer students, they are spending more on each of those served. To verify this, we used the same type of model and showed that expenditures per pupil served are negatively related to density.

The utility of such models is restricted by inconsistencies in the cost data cited earlier. But these exploratory models do indicate some of the major factors relating to special education expenditures. Further analyses with other potentially explanatory variables are needed before we can draw firm policy conclusions.

Total Governmental Expenditures for the Education of Handicapped Children

Previous subsections have examined federal and state and local spending separately. The programs supported by these funds are for the most part not distinct, and federal funds are intermingled with state and local funds in their operation. To obtain an idea of the scope and composition of the funds going to handicapped children, it is necessary to look at the total contribution each level of government makes.

As Table 10.17 indicates on a state-by-state basis (for those states reporting data), the federal government contributes about 14 percent of the special education funds. However, the variation across states is extreme—from 3 percent federal funds in Tennessee to 44 percent in Oklahoma (all in FY 1975).

State and local expenditures by disability were presented in Table 10.10. Most of the federal funds are not allocated by disability. Table 10.18 presents the state and local expenditures and an estimate of the federal allocation of funds among handicapping conditions for FY 1972. This estimate was made by assuming that federal funds that could not be classified directly[104] were distributed in the same proportion as EHA-B funds in FY 1972. The distribution of EHA-B funds

---

[104]Federal programs classified directly were Federal Schools for the Deaf, American Printing House for the Blind, EHA-B, P.L. 89-313, Deaf-Blind Centers, and EHA-G.

Table 10.17
SPECIAL EDUCATION REVENUE ALLOCATED TO HANDICAPPED CHILDREN
AGE 6 TO 21, BY SOURCE, FY 1975[a]

States	Amount	Percent of Special Education Revenue From: State Sources	Local Sources	Federal Sources
Alabama	N.R.[b]	—	—	—
Alaska	N.R.	—	—	—
Arizona	$ 32,176,133	50.7	44.7	4.6
Arkansas	13,245,536	50.9	21.1	28.1
California	N.R.	—	—	—
Colorado	65,007,738	58.6	25.2	16.2
Connecticut	77,627,594	65.9	27.7	6.4
Delaware	20,617,000	69.0	23.0	8.0
Florida	147,759,000	51.5	29.0	19.5
Georgia	64,537,000	81.6	8.3	10.1
Hawaii	N.R.	—	—	—
Idaho	13,734,000	67.8	20.8	11.4
Illinois	384,712,477	29.9	42.1	28.0
Indiana	54,991,000	53.4	40.6	6.0
Iowa	36,461,000	29.5	61.5	9.0
Kansas	33,846,000	74.0	19.9	6.1
Kentucky	28,665,172	72.1	14.7	13.2
Louisiana	46,242,694	89.2	0.0	10.8
Maine	11,962,255	36.4	36.4	27.2
Maryland	85,961,000	47.7	39.5	12.8
Massachusetts	210,430,000	44.3	28.6	27.1
Michigan	202,453,626	56.8	37.0	6.2
Minnesota	N.R	—	—	—
Mississippi	18,524,702	44.3	20.7	35.0
Missouri	51,645,459	54.5	37.1	8.4
Montana	14,442,730	93.2	0.0	6.8
Nebraska	21,860,000	51.2	40.7	8.1
Nevada	N.R.	—	—	—
New Hampshire	17,724,580	27.9	56.4	15.7
New Jersey	N.R.	—	—	—
New Mexico	14,790,000	83.4	4.9	11.7
New York	372,745,248	52.7	41.5	5.8
North Carolina	81,731,000	63.0	10.8	26.2
North Dakota	8,064,000	65.6	26.4	8.0
Ohio	N.R.	—	—	—
Oklahoma	29,838,628	25.6	30.4	44.0
Oregon	30,525,000	31.7	46.0	22.3

SOURCE: W. H. Wilken and David O. Porter, *State Aid for Special Education: Who Benefits?* National Foundation for the Improvement of Education and the National Conference of State Legislatures, Washington, D.C., October 1, 1976, Table I-12.

[a] NCSL calculations derived from ESEA-Title V1-B State Plan Amendments, U.S. Bureau of Education for the Handicapped, FY 1976.

[b] No report available.

Table 10.17—continued

States	Amount	Percent of Special Education Revenue From:		
		State Sources	Local Sources	Federal Sources
Pennsylvania	213,743,000	78.6	15.5	5.9
Rhode Island	N.R.	—	—	—
South Carolina	41,006,636	78.7	0.9	20.4
South Dakota	5,885,000	14.4	70.8	14.8
Tennessee	113,668,461	58.7	38.2	3.1
Texas	N.R.	—	—	—
Utah	23,865,823	—	—	—
Vermont	6,537,000	48.5	27.8	23.7
Virginia	N.R.	—	—	—
Washington	N.R.	—	—	—
West Virginia	N.R.	—	—	—
Wisconsin	98,969,000	36.3	58.7	5.0
Wyoming	6,342,252	35.0	61.2	3.8
Total[c] (dollars)	$2,702,337,744			
Total[c] (percent)		54.8[d]	30.8[d]	14.4[d]

[c] Reporting states only.

[d] Unweighted mean. Weighted mean for state share is 52.9 percent.

closely resembled the distribution of state and local funds among handicapped groups. Since the state and local expenditures played a dominant role in shaping the program, it is not unreasonable that the remaining federal funds (teacher training, research, Title III, etc.) will be used ultimately in proportion to the size of the state and local program.

Total expenditures on education of handicapped youth were approximately $2.7 billion in FY 1972. Recall that this is an estimate of the amount budgeted for special education of handicapped students. Some handicapped students also receive services as part of the regular school program budget.

Table 10.18 indicates the average cost per handicapped child served in FY 1972, by disability. Education for the aurally or visually impaired is by far the most expensive.

One federal government goal is to provide an appropriate education to 100 percent of the handicapped population. Table 10.19 shows an estimate of the increase above the 1972 level in the annual special education expenditures necessary to achieve this objective. In this estimate the federal roles in training and research would be expanded in proportion to the change in the population served. A fur-

Table 10.18
TOTAL SPECIAL EDUCATION EXPENDITURES BY TYPE OF HANDICAP IN FY 1972

Type of Handicap	State and Local ($ million)	Federal ($ million)	Total ($ million)	Per Child Served ($)
Mentally retarded, trainable	260.0	45.5	305.5	2064
Mentally retarded educable	840.0	75.9	915.9	1217
Hard of hearing	55.0	13.6	68.6	1247
Deaf	91.0	42.5	133.5	4767
Speech impaired	251.0	21.8	272.8	197
Visually impaired	66.0	19.2	85.2	3043
Emotionally disturbed	258.0	35.0	293.0	1472
Crippled	210.0	10.0	220.0	1718
Learning disabled	250.0	32.1	282.1	1227
Other health impaired	84.0	19.2	103.2	1086
Total	2364.0	314.9	2678.9	879

ther assumption was that the average cost of serving children is equal to the marginal cost of expanding service. The number presently unserved in the age 5 to 17 general population was derived previously.

As shown in Table 10.19, an estimated $2.5 billion per year would have to be added to the special education expenditures to provide elementary and secondary education to 100 percent of the handi-

Table 10.19
INCREASE ABOVE FY 1972 SPECIAL EDUCATION EXPENDITURES NEEDED TO SERVE ALL HANDICAPPED YOUTH AGED 5–17 YEARS

Type of Handicap	Incremental Number	Incremental Expenditures ($ million)[a]
Mentally retarded	289,000	393
Hard of hearing	204,000	254
Deaf	11,000	52
Speech impaired	423,000	83
Visually impaired	24,000	73
Emotionally disturbed	835,000	1229
Crippled	(b)	(b)
Learning disabled	287,000	352
Other health impaired	36,000	52
Total	2,109,000	2488

[a] Assuming 1972 service quality, service cost, and value of the dollar.
[b] Crippled are included with "other health impaired."

capped youth aged 5 to 17 at FY 1972 service quality, service cost, and dollar value levels. Over 48 percent of this increase would go toward educating the emotionally disturbed, who presently consume only 10 percent of the expenditures. An attempt to serve all handicapped children would require a large change in the percentage of funds going to each disability group. A possible implication of this need for a large change from current practice is that the 100 percent service level cannot be reached by just adding money to the total program. Such additions are likely to be allocated among handicaps in much the same way as the current budget because of institutional forces that tend to make budget proportions rigid. To increase funds for a particular disability would require changes in the mix of programs and types of skilled personnel in the education service system.

Four important qualifications must be put on the implications of this information. First, estimates of incidence levels of disabilities and marginal costs are based on data of questionable quality. Second, the appropriate measure of the population size against which to apply the incidence levels is a matter of judgment. Third, some of those handicapped but not served by special education are presently in school, and the increase in special education expenditures, if they were to be served, would be partially offset by a reduction in the regular educational services that would no longer be delivered. Fourth, continuing high inflation will mean much more than $2.5 billion will be required to reach the full service goal. The more important qualification is that this information does not imply any normative judgment about what the proper allocation of resources among the disabilities should be, or the proper amount of resources needed per child to obtain a quality education. Since many handicapped children now being served may not be being served appropriately, the added cost may be much greater than our estimate.

The cost estimates presented in Table 10.19 attempt to answer the question, "What increase in special education expenditures would be necessary to enroll 100 percent of the handicapped children in programs of today's present quality?" Equity considerations would argue that 100 percent coverage is a proper objective, but it should not be a solitary one. Another consideration is the effectiveness of programs in altering behavior or teaching cognitive skills. If programs for the emotionally disturbed, for example, are not effective in restoring mental health, it would not be good policy to expand them just to increase the equity coverage. Estimates of the marginal benefits of increased expenditures, however, are well outside the scope of this report.

COSTS AND EFFECTIVENESS OF SPECIAL EDUCATION

Lack of Information for Planning Reliable analyses of the cost and effectiveness of special educational services require information that is not presently available. Given the high cost and importance of these services, this lack of essential planning information is critical, and we recommend a major federal effort to rectify the situation. The program is attested to by the U.S. Office of Education's own evaluation reports.[105] In the 1973 report's evaluations of all education programs serving the handicapped, all but two contained a statement like the following, "No formal evaluations have yet been conducted of this program and its effectiveness cannot be ascertained from reports now available." And the remaining two programs were "evaluated" in that report in terms of the number of teachers trained and the volume of media services offered. In the 1975 report, the situation had not improved much relative to measures of either cost or the effect of the programs on the children.

In brief, no one has sufficient information to evaluate adequately the effects of any of these special education programs. At the project level, evaluation information is often required as a condition of funding, but our observations suggest that such project level evaluations are more often perfunctory than substantive.

In the absence of reliable evaluation information, we venture some order-of-magnitude estimates in the following subsections.

Program Cost We have estimated that the average annual special education expenditure per child served in the United States was $879 for all handicaps combined in FY 1972, but ranged from $197 for the speech impaired, to $1247 for the hard of hearing, to $3043 for the visually impaired, to $4767 for the deaf. Since the speech impaired generally are served on a part-time basis by itinerant specialists, the $197 figure is thought to be the excess cost of serving one such child above the average regular education expenditures of $776 per child. However, since most deaf children are not educated in a classroom with "normal" children, the $4767 figure is thought to be close to the total annual cost of educating one such child; hence we arrived at an excess cost of $4767 minus $776, or about $4000 per year, using FY 1972 methods of education and the average student-teacher ratio of

---

[105]U.S. Office of Education, *Annual Evaluation Report on Education Programs, FY 1972,* March 1973; and *Annual Evaluation Report on Programs Administered by the U.S. Office of Education, FY 1975,* September 1976.

about 6 to 1.[106] Using the same reasoning, the average excess cost for visually handicapped youth is between $2267 and $3043; an estimate of approximately $2600 is probably the correct order of magnitude. Of course, this is for FY 1972 methods of educating these children and could reasonably be as high as $4000 for the totally blind and as low as $800 for the partially sighted. We caution that if services were to be expanded to reach *all* handicapped youth, the mix of types and degrees of handicaps would change, and hence the overall average costs would change.

One 1970 study of costs[107] indicated major variations in reported special education costs among school districts, which partially reflect differences in the special education programs offered and partially reflect variations in resource prices and accounting methods. Costs are expected to change significantly as the nation moves from predominantly special classes toward serving more handicapped children in regular classes.

Economic Benefits Data are not available on future earnings and future services required as a function of the type and amount of special education given to a child. Hence, we cannot say definitely if these expenditures are justified on an economic benefits basis. We can, however, say what these economic benefits would have to be in order to justify special education on a purely economic benefits basis. (This is a very narrow way of measuring program effect. We do not subscribe to it, and we will discuss other criteria of effect shortly.)

Let us assume that a child receives special education services at an excess cost of $800 a year for 12 years. He then enters the labor force and works until he is 55. What increase in monthly income will equal the cost of special education if both costs and income are discounted at 8 percent? The answer is that the handicapped child must earn some $108 a month more after receiving special education services to justify the program in these simplistic terms. It is not difficult to conceive of the 12 years of special education raising the earnings of the handicapped by this small amount—about 63 cents an hour. Thus, it appears that extra expenditures on the order of $800 per year can be justified on purely economic benefits terms (however, data are not

---

[106]Average student-teacher ratios used here and later in this section were calculated from data in U.S. Bureau of Education for the Handicapped, *Handicapped Children in the U.S. and Special Education Personnel Required,* August 1970.

[107]R. A. Rossmiller, J. Hale, and L. Frohreich, *Educational Programs for Exceptional Children: Resource Configurations and Costs,* University of Wisconsin, Madison, August 1970.

available to prove this conclusively). On the other hand, the increase in earnings necessary to offset a $4000 per year excess expenditure for special education is about $540 a month. Expenditures of $4000 per year for a severely handicapped child may or may not be justified on purely economic benefits terms; however, economic benefits are only one of many factors that should be considered.

An economic benefit/cost analysis conducted by Conley, using national data, showed that "educational services provided to the mildly retarded can be justified on the basis of earnings alone. . . . It is, in fact, self-defeating not to provide these services, since this would sacrifice a large long-run gain for a small short-run gain."[108] He was unable to support the same conclusion for moderately and more severely retarded youth, but he did not consider the major economic benefits of averting institutionalization of these people, nor did he consider the important quality-of-life benefits.

Academic Achievement   Difficulties also are encountered when the effectiveness of special education programs is considered from the viewpoint of academic achievement. We attempted to collect data only for the two illustrative handicaps of hearing and vision. While studies of the intelligence of hearing and vision handicapped children indicate that as a group they generally are normal, they are still handicapped in their ability to learn by their impairment in receiving or communicating information. Consequently, both students and education agencies may have to exert a great deal of extra effort if these youth are to reach normal academic achievement levels. While the data on achievement testing of these youth are incomplete and not representative of all sensorially handicapped students, they suggest that there is significant room for improvement. For example, test results for 12,000 hearing-impaired students in special educational programs throughout the United States indicated that they were achieving at a grade equivalent level approximately half that of normal school children.[109]

Similar types of data on visually handicapped children were not located.

[108]R. Conley, *The Economics of Mental Retardation,* The Johns Hopkins Press, Baltimore, 1973.

[109]*Academic Achievement Test Performance of Hearing-Impaired Students: United States,* Office of Demographic Studies Report, Series D, Number 1, Gallaudet College, Washington, D.C., 1969. This is one in a series of publications that provide much useful information on current education programs for the hearing impaired.

Quality-of-Life Effects   Earlier we suggested several scales for measuring the effects of a program on the quality of life of handicapped youth. Since statistically reliable data are not available to use any of those scales, we are forced to rely on opinion: the parents of hearing and vision handicapped children we surveyed gave extremely high ratings to the value of special education; and the consensus in the literature and among education professionals we interviewed at the federal level, and in five states, indicates that program effects outweigh costs and that all handicapped youth should receive special educational assistance.

Since special education for the most severely handicapped may not be justifiable on purely economic benefits grounds, it also must be considered on these quality-of-life, humanitarian grounds. Again, we point out that statistically reliable comprehensive evaluations of the impact of special education programs have not yet been conducted, nor is the abundant literature on the impact of single projects adequate to support the major program decisions that must be made.

Of course, it is possible that the educators who say more funds should be devoted to these programs are incorrect, and that the legislators who have significantly increased funds for them are incorrect, and that the parents whose children are part of these programs are mistaken in their judgment on their usefulness. But our considered judgment is that these programs yield good and effective results.

Equity of Service Distribution   One possible objective of the service system is to distribute services equitably or "fairly"—for example, to give similar treatment to every handicapped child with the same type and degree of disability. But by nearly any definition of equity that might be chosen, the distribution of special education services is grossly inequitable. In terms of the likelihood of a 5-to-17-year-old youth receiving any special educational assistance, the variation across states is extreme: For example, from apparently serving less than 10 percent of the visually handicapped in two states to serving most of them in five other states; from apparently serving less than 10 percent of the hearing handicapped in five states to serving most of them in at least four other states. (These figures are obtained by applying national prevalence data to the individual states for FY 1972.)

In terms of the amount of assistance received per child in a special education program, as measured by average reported special education expenditures in FY 1972, the variation across states is extreme: from less than $500 for each hearing or vision handicapped student served in several states to more than $3000 in several other states.

Intrastate variations in service levels are probably as large as, if not larger than, interstate ones. Given the large variation in expenditures among school districts for regular education programs, it can only be expected that these same variations hold with respect to special education. Nonetheless, a child's receipt of special educational assistance, and the amount he receives, are unmistakably and strongly dependent on where his parents live. This means that many handicapped children will either be denied educational service because of where they live, or they will be forced to move to districts where quality services are available (1 in every 10 of the families we surveyed *had* moved to obtain special education for their children). Such a system is undesirable from several standpoints. First, it creates disincentives for local districts to sponsor outstanding special education programs. If they do, they are likely to attract handicapped children from outside the district and necessarily raise the budget of the school or divert resources from the regular education program. Second, it requires that families having handicapped children bear the burden of moving costs, possible loss of jobs, etc., to obtain adequate public service. Third, it means that the children of some who cannot or will not move will receive inadequate special education services. Our analysis has suggested that handicapped youth receive more assistance (as measured by expenditures per child served) in higher-income states. Some of these differences in expenditures are due to price differences between states. The differences are so large, however, that most of them must be attributed to differences in service levels.

Preschool-age and postschool-age youth also are less likely to receive special educational assistance.

NEEDED IMPROVEMENT IN SPECIAL EDUCATION PROGRAMS

Crucial improvements needed in the delivery of special educational assistance to handicapped youth are discussed here; our recommendations appear in italics.

Increase the fraction of school-age handicapped youth receiving appropriate special educational assistance, and concomitantly increase trained personnel and the comprehensiveness of special educational assistance available in each geographic area.

Principal arguments in favor of these increases are: Parents we interviewed overwhelmingly point to special education as their child's most important need; these increases would reduce the inequity of present service delivery; the courts and federal legislation have mandated such service as a "right"; such assistance appears to be cost-beneficial in an economic sense, as well as humanitarian, for the less severely handicapped; and such assistance appears to be justifiable on humanitarian grounds for the more severely handicapped. The principal argument against this increase is the cost.

While other issues are also extremely important, in our view the most imperative issue area in 1977 was finance and the insufficiency of funds to implement court-ordered and legislatively-mandated special education services, and hence provide equal educational opportunity for all handicapped children.

As the National Advisory Committee on the Handicapped indicated in its 1976 report: "The basic overriding need is of course to close the gap that sees half of the nation's handicapped children not receiving an education appropriate to their needs."[110] Existing laws are not ideal in every respect, but the provision of special education is inhibited more today by lack of funding than by lack of legislation.

From the federal viewpoint, a major issue is: What should the federal role be in financing special education? The 1975 "Education for All Handicapped Children Act" represents a major potential shift in the federal funding role in education. If P.L. 94-142 appropriations match authorizations, the federal government share of special education excess costs would rise from the current 14 percent to at least 40 percent (assuming special education costs approximately twice as much as regular education). Total 1982 appropriations under P.L. 94-142 would be over $3 billion, more than is currently spent on Title I of the "Elementary and Secondary Education Act".

Since providing the P.L. 94-142 mandated appropriate special educational services to all handicapped children and youth prior to 1980 requires substantial increases in both funds and trained personnel, it is questionable whether the resources can be marshalled in time to meet the deadline. An August 1976 survey of State Legislature education committee chairmen found only 26.5 percent saying "yes," they could meet the goal, while 12.2 percent said "no" and the remainder were not sure.[111]

Four 1976 conferences of state policy makers concerned with P.L. 94-142 concluded that

> . . . full implementation will be difficult to achieve within the specified time period. . . . A primary issue is the early deadline of 1980 to achieve a free and appropriate education for all handicapped chil-

[110]National Advisory Committee on the Handicapped, *The Unfinished Revolution: Education for the Handicapped—1976 Annual Report,* U.S. Department of Health, Education, and Welfare, Washington, D.C., 1976.

[111]National Conference of State Legislatures, *Press Release on State Education Committee Chairmen Survey on School Finance,* Washington, D.C., 1976.

402   Needs of Handicapped Children

dren. . . . It seems improbable that deficits incurred over a history of schooling can be removed over a short time period.[112]

The federal government has at least two major options with respect to funding under P.L. 94-142. The first would be a relatively large increase of federal appropriations to meet the intent of P.L. 94-142. In this case the federal government will be funding a significant portion, but still not the majority, of the excess cost of special education. Initially the federal funds would go primarily for expanding services to the unserved and the inadequately served handicapped children. In the event that federal appropriations do not approach the level of those authorized under P.L. 94-142, then it is possible and even probable that the states and localities will not be able to provide free appropriate public education to all handicapped children by the dates mandated in the law.

The second major option the federal government has relative to funding is to provide only very modest increases over FY 1977 levels, i.e., to set P.L. 94-142 appropriations well below the levels authorized in the law. This second option, however, would almost surely cause states and localities to demand changes in P.L. 94-142 to remove some of the controls and mandates on service delivery. The states generally agree with the intent and objectives of P.L. 94-142,[113] but do not necessarily like all of the detailed methods prescribed for reaching those objectives and do not want to have to fully implement all features of the law in the absence of substantial federal funds to do so. The rather strong P.L. 94-142 regulations are not likely to be accepted or seen as legitimate by states and localities in the absence of substantial federal funding to help implement the mandated improvements in special education. The FY 1977 level of federal financial effort is in fact rather minimal relative to the mandates of P.L. 94-142 and relative to state and local financial effort.

To meet the intent of the current law and court rulings mandating an appropriate education for all handicapped children, *the federal government should appropriate the substantial sums of money authorized by P.L. 94-142.*

While education is primarily not a federal responsibility, the lack of equal educational opportunity for handicapped children is the primary rationale for federal involvement. Several arguments can be

[112]Ian McNett (ed.), *The Education for All Handicapped Children Act, Public Law 94-142, A Summary and Analysis of Four Regional Conferences,* The Consortium on the Education for All Handicapped Children Act, Institute for Educational Leadership, George Washington University, Washington, D.C., 1976.

[113]John J. Calahan and William H. Wilken, *The Federal Role in School Financing: A View from the States,* The Rand Corporation, Washington, D.C., February 1977.

marshalled to justify the federal government's assuming a larger share of the financial burden of special education. First, the poorer districts and states are at an economic disadvantage in serving their handicapped youth. Second, costs to the federal government of rehabilitation and welfare for the handicapped population can be reduced by investment in special education. Third, the state and local institutional framework for resource allocation decisions may embody incentives against providing services to minorities such as the handicapped, and federal financial intervention in this case may be justified in order to protect the handicapped minority's rights and to alleviate the current lack of equal educational opportunity for handicapped children. And a fourth argument that might be advanced is that some level of government should fill the large unmet need; state and local governments are not doing the job and have inadequate resources; therefore, the federal government should provide categorical financial aid. Court rulings have the effect of forcing increases in the number of handicapped youth served by state and local agencies, and are becoming an important prod to equitable treatment. The lack of service to a large fraction of handicapped youth is partially caused, one might assume, by current program inertia and high start-up costs, in which case the federal government should also adopt a major stimulative role.

An equity argument in support of federal financial aid is that poorer states do not have the resources for an adequate special education program, and the federal government, while giving aid to all states, might favor poorer states and in effect transfer funds from wealthy to poor states in order to enhance equal educational opportunity.[114] Of course, every state *does have* sufficient resources to support an adequate special education program, but it must choose to do so. For example, only about 1 out of 10 school-age youth are handicapped; if state officials wanted to spend twice as much per handicapped child as per nonhandicapped child, and they increased the fraction of handicapped youth served by special education from 50 to 100 percent, the total education budget would need to increase by only about 5 to 7 percent, depending on one's assumptions about the percentage presently excluded from school altogether. Since primary and secondary education accounts for only about 32 percent of

---

[114]A case for nonlocal funding of all the excess costs of special education is made in F. J. Weintraub et al., *State Law and Education of Handicapped: Issues and Recommendations,* The Council for Exceptional Children, Reston, Virginia, 1971, and in L. C. Pierce et al., *State School Finance Alternatives,* Center for Educational Policy and Management, University of Oregon, Eugene, May 1975.

state and local expenditures,[115] only about a 2 percent increase in total state and local expenditures would be needed to finance the needed expansion in special education services in this example. It is not fair, however, to view special education needs in isolation from the other pressing problems faced by states and localities. Poorer states are at a disadvantage in providing many social services. To provide a uniformly high standard of service could mean high state and local tax rates, which, in the long run, might not be in the best interests of the poor states or the nation as a whole. Therefore, the equity argument provides support for allowing the federal government to help special education financially, thereby allowing all states, rich and poor, to provide an equivalent level of service for equal tax effort. Another equity argument for federal funding is that the incidence of handicapping conditions varies geographically, and this uneven distribution of handicapped children implies an unequal financial burden. Further, the migration of families with handicapped children to states thought to have exemplary special education places an additional "unfair" financial burden on those states.

An externality of benefits argument in support of federal financial aid for special education is that its benefits are bestowed upon the nation as a whole, in the form of an informed and well-trained citizenry, and that federal welfare and other service costs for handicapped persons are reduced when special education is provided.[116] According to this argument, without federal support the handicapped person, and state and local authorities, might underinvest in special education to the detriment of society, because some benefits of special education do not accrue to the single individual, state, or locality. A highly mobile populace and federal funding of other noneducation services are two causes of benefits accruing beyond state boundaries. To have a nationally optimum level of investment in special education, then, the tenor of this argument is that federal supplement is required to equate total marginal social benefits with total marginal social costs.[117] Nevertheless, it is difficult to construct a case where the external (interstate) effects of special education are

[115]Education accounted for 40.5 percent of state and local general expenditures in 1969 (*1971 Statistical Abstract,* p. 404). Higher education accounted for 20 percent of all educational expenditures (ibid., p. 403). Therefore only about 32 percent of all funds went for primary and secondary education.

[116]See R. Conley, *The Economics of Mental Retardation,* The Johns Hopkins Press, Baltimore, 1973.

[117]See Samuel B. Chase, Jr. (ed.), *Problems in Public Expenditure Analysis,* The Brookings Institution, Washington, D.C., 1968, pp. 44–45, for a discussion of the analysis of external effects for public expenditure decision making.

large in relation to the intrastate effects. The most serious deprivations inflicted by small investment in special education will be borne by the handicapped and their families, not by other citizens.

Another argument for federal financial aid for special education is that there is a large unmet service need resulting in a lack of equal educational opportunity for handicapped children; some level of government should meet the need; state and local governments are not meeting the need; and therefore the federal government should. A counterargument is that regulation without financial aid might be sufficient, a contingency discussed later in this section. In considering this argument for financial aid, it is important to try to understand why state and local levels of government are not meeting the need. One possible explanation is that local decision makers do not view special education as a high priority program relative to other demands for the limited available funds. That is, the compelling demands on the limited state and local resources are such that state and local governments cannot now provide an appropriate education for all handicapped children, even though they are mobilizing greater resources for their special education programs. Another possible explanation is that the inherent ability of one level of government to raise increased funds under the current tax structure is greater than that of other levels of government. Some state government fiscal surpluses in recent years, for example, have facilitated increased state funding of education for equalization purposes. At the present time, however, it is not clear which level of government will have the most surplus (or least deficit) in future years. Another possible explanation for insufficiency of funds in special education rests on the institutional structure of resource allocation: who makes decisions, and the incentives facing the decision maker. A simplistic model of this decision-making process at the local level includes the public, the school board, and the superintendent. In preparing the budget, the superintendent faces pressure from both the parents and the employees of the district. Confronted by increasing costs of providing regular education, the superintendent may perhaps feel compelled to maintain support of the majority of both groups, to the disadvantage of handicapped children and their parents, a small minority by comparison. The school board is responsive mainly to voters. Assuming that a board member wants to be reelected, coalition-building among the majority of parents and nonparents who live and vote in the school district naturally follows. Parents are primarily concerned with *regular* education, and nonparents are often resistant to increases in the tax rate; together, these two groups are a force against increasing school expenditures. Parents without handicapped children are generally concerned with visible signs of progress in their child's education, along with other indicators of the overall quality of the school. In appealing to these interests, a school board may emphasize programs that boost student achievement scores on statewide tests or that stress intermural athletics. Again, as with any minority group, it is hard for the handicapped to exert a heavy influence on the board's decisions. The model presented above is overdrawn for the purpose of emphasis. Decision making at the local school district level is not as simple as the model suggests. Our model, however, is not in basic disagreement with the findings of more careful examinations of the school budgeting process.[118]

While much the same argument can be made for state-level decision making, the federal government, for a variety of complex reasons, has lately been in the forefront in protecting the rights of minorities. Should federal dollars be spent in support of the handicapped children to protect their rights? The federal government appears to be the most likely candidate to redress grievances.

If financial aid is provided by the federal government, earmarking funds for special education is probably required since any noncategorical revenue-sharing would not alter the local decision–making incentive structures that have in the past helped create a large fraction of unserved handicapped youth.

If federal financial aid is given to states and localities, regulations could be implemented to earmark the funds for special education and to encourage the states to offer a comprehensive range of quality services to meet the needs of youth of each age, with each type and degree of handicap. However, such regulations are more likely to be politically feasible and effective if the federal government were to assume a major financial role.

Further, a big problem is that the P.L. 94-142 controls and the mandate to serve all children came before big federal money flows. Unfortunately, P.L. 94-142 mandates a free appropriate public education for all handicapped children aged 3–18 years no later than September 1978, while only providing one-fourth of the maximum funding level in the Act in that year. The Act does not provide the full 40 percent funding level until the 1981–1982 school year. Thus, the states and localities face the prospect of having to fund services themselves for a greatly increased number of children between 1978 and 1982 when the maximum level of federal financing becomes available. Even if

[118]Thomas James, James A. Kelly, and Walter I. Garms, "The School Budget Process in Large Cities," in Michael W. Kirst (ed.), *The Politics of Education at the Local, State, and Federal Levels,* McCutchan Publishing Corporation, Berkeley, California, 1970, pp. 74–89.

appropriations equal authorizations, a serious problem will exist in the first year or two of the implementation of P.L. 94-142. A recent report made an estimate of the amount of federal money available to local agencies per handicapped child and concluded, "It is reasonable to question whether the amounts provided will be large enough to cover the expenses generated by the comprehensive identification, planning, and procedural safeguard provisions incorporated in the legislation."[119] If the added costs of implementing the legislation exceed the finances provided, then there is an incentive to delay participation or to start off on the wrong foot, with implementation and compliance that is more apparent than real—this is true even if all parties involved agree with the goal of an appropriate public education for every handicapped child. P.L. 94-142 should be changed to phase in the required improvements in special education as funds become available. This could be done by advancing the time at which large scale funds become available, delaying the time of required improvements, or both.

The courts offer another creative source for potentially powerful regulation, as evidenced in recent federal court decisions requiring state and local authorities to provide education service to certain classes of handicapped children. Though the courts can be and have been effective in getting some excluded children into the educational service system, this population is only a fraction of those entitled to but not receiving an appropriate special education. Many handicapped children in the regular school system do not receive needed special services, or they may be ruled ineligible for service because of administrative restrictions related to age. Redressing all the inequities facing handicapped youth through court action on a case-by-case, handicap-by-handicap basis may be a feasible approach, but it is also a difficult and inefficient cure. It is difficult for the courts to specify exactly the quantity and quality of special education services that must be delivered, given critical individual differences in needs among the handicapped. However, courts could reaffirm the rights of equal protection of all children by requiring that special education services be given, without specifying the level of service. It could be argued that since court rulings are based on both state and federal constitutions, then both state and federal governments should also provide the funds to implement the rulings.

While the greatest spur to the increased provision of special educa-

[119]Joel Berke et al., "Change in Education: Three Policy Papers on the Implementation of the 'Education for All Handicapped Children Act'," P.L. 94-142, Education Testing Service, Washington, D.C., February 1976.

tion probably has been court decisions providing that handicapped children have a right to a public education, the fact remains that funds are still insufficient to serve all those in need, and many remain unserved. The first two major legal cases are relatively recent—1971: *Pennsylvania Association for Retarded Children v. Commonwealth of Pennsylvania,*[120] which provided that every school-age, mentally retarded Pennsylvania child has a right to a public education; and *Mills v. Board of Education of District of Columbia,*[121] which extended the principle to all handicapped children. Since 1971 dozens of similar cases have been completed or are pending in a majority of the states,[122] but government has not yet responded with the dollars necessary to provide services to fulfill the right of handicapped children to an education and to fully implement the states' "mandatory" special education legislation.

In the area of personnel preparation, the federal effort in recent years has been focused primarily on preservice training of special educators, and the Bureau of Education for the Handicapped estimates that about 260,000 additional special education teachers will be required to provide an appropriate education for all handicapped children.[123] About 30,000 new special education teachers graduated in academic year 1973–1974.[124] While additional new full-time *special* educators are needed, the current major shift toward serving handicapped children in the least restrictive environment makes it imperative that new *regular* teachers also receive preservice training on serving handicapped children in the regular classroom. Many current special educators also will need inservice training in serving children effectively in the least restrictive environment rather than primarily in the more traditional special classes. In light of the overall decline in school enrollments, regular staff cutbacks are more likely in the near future than are regular staff increases. Hence, currently employed regular teachers will be the primary group of professionals serving handicapped children in the regular classroom for years to come, and they will need inservice training to give them the needed skills. A recent report of the National Advisory Council on Education Professions Development found:

[120]334 F. Supp. 1257 (E.D. Pa. 1971).

[121]348 F. Supp. 866 (D.D.C. 1972).

[122]U.S. House of Representatives, Committee on Education and Labor, *Education for All Handicapped Children Act of 1975,* Report No. 94-332, June 26, 1975, p.3.

[123]W. F. Pierce, U.S. Office of Education, Statement Before the Subcommittee on Handicapped, Committee on Human Resources, United States Senate, March 22, 1977.

[124]Comptroller General of the United States, "Training Educators for the Handicapped: A Need to Redirect Federal Programs," U.S. General Accounting Office, Report B-164031(1), Washington, D.C., September 28, 1976.

The major conclusion is that a majority of the two million teachers now in the schools have had little if any training in the education of handicapped children. It also appears that the majority of students now in preparation in the field of education are receiving little training in the education of handicapped children.[125]

Data presented earlier for the Bureau of Education for the Handicapped FY 1977 personnel preparation program indicate that only 17.3 percent of the $40 million appropriation is going for training of regular teachers. However, in recent years the Bureau has been expanding its expenditures and efforts for training regular teachers.

To implement P.L. 94-142 fully and provide an appropriate education for all handicapped children, additional special education teachers will need to be trained, regular education teachers who will begin to serve more handicapped children in the regular classroom will need to be trained or retrained, and support staff to help identify and diagnose handicapping conditions will need to be trained. A major difficulty will be in developing cost-effective programs to train or retrain regular classroom teachers to serve handicapped children in the "mainstream" when that type of service is appropriate. Edwin Martin, Director of the Bureau of Education for the Handicapped, recently pointed out in an address to the National Advisory Committee on the Handicapped that the special education field is so broad that limited inservice training cannot hope to provide the background regular classroom teachers need to deal with the many different special educational needs of handicapped children.[126] The report by the National Advisory Council on Education Professions Development pointed out that:

Whatever direction mainstreaming takes at the local level, it is clear that the role and responsibilities of the regular classroom teacher are greatly changed as a result of the inclusion of handicapped children in the classroom.

Teachers will need to exercise a wide range of skills. . . . Many of these skills will not have been required of a teacher in his or her previous classroom experience. . . .

Judging from our review of certification regulations and education curricula, preparation is very inadequate. Without a significant effort toward a reconciliation of needs and capabilities through retraining and the provision of supportive services to regular teachers, many fear that mainstreaming will result not only in deteriorated education for handicapped children, but will bring about less effective education for all students. . . .

[125]National Advisory Council on Education Professions Development, "Mainstreaming: Helping Teachers Meet the Challenge," Washington, D.C., Summer 1976.
[126]*Education Daily,* October 21, 1976, p. 4.

The Education for All Handicapped Children Act requires each State to provide training for virtually all teachers with any responsibility for the handicapped. However, the retraining of every public school teacher is quite improbable and could be very expensive. For example, even a simple provision of tuition reimbursement for a 10-credit special education package (insufficient as this might be) for a 10 percent of the workforce of teachers would cost close to $100 million each year.

In reality, the funds required for such an effort are not now available.[127]

A recent report to Congress on training educators of handicapped children found:

The Department of Health, Education, and Welfare (HEW) needs to improve its programs which assist in preparing teachers for the handicapped.

- The majority of handicapped students spend most of their school day in regular classrooms, yet regular classroom teachers generally have not received training in the skills needed to effectively teach them.
- Handicapped students vitally need vocational instruction, yet they are intentionally excluded from the schools' vocational training programs by teachers untrained in methods for teaching the handicapped.

Although more handicapped students are being integrated into regular classrooms and educators believe training regular classroom teachers is essential to the effective education of the handicapped, HEW has done relatively little to encourage this special training. HEW's programs for preparing teachers for the handicapped have mainly involved (1) stimulating growth in the capacity of colleges to prepare specialists for educating the handicapped and (2) financially supporting college students entering the field of special education.

Since the federal programs of this type began, the capacity of colleges to prepare specialists for educating the handicapped has greatly increased, and, according to school district special education administrators, is now adequate to fulfill the anticipated demand.
. . .

To increase the impact of HEW's teacher-preparation programs in areas of major need, the Secretary of HEW should direct the Office of Education to:

[127]National Advisory Council on Education Professions Development, "Mainstreaming: Helping Teachers Meet the Challenge," Washington, D.C., Summer 1976.

- Provide a major emphasis on programs for training the Nation's regular classroom teachers to effectively deal with the handicapped, in cooperation with state and local education agencies and institutions of higher education.
- Discourage the use of Bureau of Education for the Handicapped funds for paying stipends for full-time students, except where such stipends are deemed essential and other sources of student assistance are not available.
- Emphasize the need for applying individualized instruction techniques to the handicapped in supporting projects—such as those for preparing and using paraprofessionals—designed to extend the regular classroom teacher's ability to reach individual students.
- Develop and implement a plan to provide vocational educators with the skills and abilities needed to effectively deal with the handicapped in the regular classroom.[128]

The emphasis on use of federal personnel preparation funds for the education of handicapped children should be expanded to include a major focus on inservice training of regular educators, vocational educators, and special educators, although appropriate preservice training of these three groups should not be slighted in the process. All regular and special and vocational education personnel preparation, both preservice and inservice, should include techniques for educating handicapped children. The primary rationales for federal involvement in personnel training are twofold: additional trained and retrained personnel are necessary to allow effective implementation of P.L. 94-142 and provision of an appropriate education for all handicapped children; and since skilled personnel are mobile, benefits of training them accrue outside the boundaries of any single state, and partial federal funding is necessary to achieve a socially optimum level of investment in personnel training.

[128]Comptroller General of the United States, "Training Educators for the Handicapped: A Need to Redirect Federal Programs," U.S. General Accounting Office, Report B-164031(1), Washington, D.C., September 28, 1976.

Chapter 11

EQUIPMENT

OVERVIEW

Various types of physical equipment such as orthotic and prosthetic devices and sensory aids can be extremely effective in increasing the functional abilities of handicapped children and youth. Despite what may seem to be high initial costs of such equipment, most is decidedly cost-effective. We present here an illustrative detailed look at sensory aids and other equipment for hearing and vision handicapped children.

This chapter discusses various types of sensory aids and related equipment currently in use, such as corrective lenses and other optical vision enhancement devices, closed circuit television systems, talking books, large-print and braille reading material, canes, guide dogs, hearing aids, captioned films, and speech training aids.

The chapter also discusses promising devices that either are not yet fully developed or are not yet widely used, intended to aid in reading, writing, mobility, speech training, and speech perception. They include such devices as hearing aids that not only amplify but also modify the frequencies at which aural information is presented, electrocortical prostheses, and devices for converting visual information to tactile or aural information, or for converting aural information to tactile or visual information.

This chapter also briefly describes the population needing sensory aids, presents information on the costs and the effects of current and potential aids, reviews the multitude of government programs concerned with these aids, and presents recommendations for program improvement.

We believe that nearly all hearing and vision handicapped youth need and can benefit from some type of sensory aid. A majority of them, however, do not have the aids they need. For example, the device most often used is the hearing aid, yet only about one-third to one-half of the hearing handicapped youth have hearing aids, and the use of such aids depends strongly on family income. Current annual expenditures on sensory aids for handicapped youth are impossible to determine accurately because they are generally part of a larger budget in one of the many programs concerned with such devices. We can make an estimate, however, by adding known expenditures for aids; doing so yields a total of at least $40 million a year in public and private expenditures, while the correct figure is probably on the order of $50 million. To provide aids to all sensorially handicapped youth that need them would cost at least another $50 million annually.

The National Academy of Sciences Committee on Prosthetics Research and Development estimated that in 1970, $64 million was expended on prosthetics and orthotics (braces, artificial limbs, etc.) for 3.5 million people of all ages who could use them. While we have no reliable data on government expenditures for all devices used by youth, we estimate they are on the order of $20 to $30 million per year.

Nearly all types of public agencies serving handicapped youth expend some funds on sensory aids and other equipment, but no agency has major responsibility for perfecting and disseminating these aids. The federal government engages in a variety of activities connected with aids; it directly provides certain aids, it funds aids through various programs, and it stimulates aid development by research in still other programs. The aids themselves, however, are usually dispensed by private dealers or organizations, and private funds are often used to purchase them.

Several problems afflict current programs concerned with aids. Programs are numerous, fractionated, and unorganized. Too few youth needing aids have them. If one believes that access to an aid should be a function of the child's need, not family income, then there are inequities in distribution. Considerable progress has been made in creating new aids, but many of these are not properly tested and guided through the many steps needed to convert a promising prototype device into a rationally designed production model. And mechanisms for assuring that production models are widely distributed among the handicapped consumers need much improvement.

AIDS FOR VISUALLY HANDICAPPED PEOPLE

Among the many sensory aids and other equipment for the visually handicapped are corrective lenses, other optical and electro-optical vision enhancement devices such as binoculars and closed circuit television systems, talking books, tape recorders, large-print and braille reading material, braille writers, canes, guide dogs and other mobility aids, and devices that convert visual information to aural or tactile information (for example, the Optacon reading device and special timepieces).

Over the years, many survey papers on sensory aids and other equipment for the functionally blind and partially sighted have been published. For example, Sloan[1] has surveyed head-worn, hand-held, and stand-mounted optical magnifiers for the partially sighted, and Nye and Bliss[2] have surveyed various reading, writing, and mobility aids for the functionally blind and some reading and writing aids for the partially sighted. Proceedings of several conferences on aids for the visually handicapped contain detailed descriptions of various types of aids.[3] In view of the thoroughness of these and other reports, we did not generate still another detailed listing and description of such devices. Rather we have chosen to review the various types of sensory aids and other equipment that improve or show promise of improving the educational and vocational prospects, as well as the overall quality of life, of the visually handicapped population.

Recall that we consider a person visually handicapped if the visual acuity in his better eye with corrective lenses is no better than $20/70$, or if the visual field is so restricted that he cannot maneuver safely in an unfamiliar environment without the assistance of a guide dog, cane, or sighted person. An acuity that is no better than $20/70$ with correction lies in the approximate range in which a person is unable to read ordinary newsprint. Of the approximately 193,000 visually handicapped youth aged 0 to 21 in the United States, only about 7 percent have either no sight or so little sight that they must be regarded as functionally blind rather than functionally partially sighted. Further, only about 30 percent of the legally blind need to be functionally blind. By functionally blind we mean the person is visually handicapped; unable, with or without the aid of an optical or image enhancement device, to use his eyes to read printed or handwritten

[1]L. L. Sloan, *Recommended Aids for the Partially Sighted,* National Society for the Prevention of Blindness, Inc., New York, 1966.

[2]P. W. Nye and J. C. Bliss, "Sensory Aids for the Blind: A Challenging Problem with Lessons for the Future," *Proceedings of the Institute of Electrical and Electronic Engineers,* Vol. 58, No. 12, December 1970, pp. 1878–1898.

[3]See, for example, *Proceedings of the International Congress on Technology and Blindness,* Vols. I–IV, American Foundation for the Blind, New York, 1963; *Proceedings of the International Conference on Sensory Devices for the Blind,* St. Dunstan's, 191 Marylebone Road, London, 1966; *Proceedings, 1972 Carnahan Conference on Electronic Prosthetics,* Report UKY TR60-72-EE4, University of Kentucky, Lexington, December 1972.

material as the literate sighted do or to recognize familiar objects as the illiterate sighted do; and unable to maneuver safely in an unfamiliar environment without the assistance of a guide dog, a cane, or a sighted person. As Genensky has pointed out, the problems of the partially sighted are distinctly different from those of the functionally blind, and, further, these two subsets of the visually handicapped population, in general, need distinctly different sets of services and sensory aids.[4] However, nearly all of the visually handicapped need some type of aid when reading and writing, and all of the functionally blind and many of the partially sighted need some type of mobility aid.

Corrective Lenses

The most important type of sensory aid needed by the great majority of the partially sighted is corrective lenses. We were unable to locate reliable data on how many handicapped youth possess them, but it is very clear that these lenses significantly upgrade the quality of life of the partially sighted and should improve their ability to benefit from other services such as education. At a typical cost of perhaps $150,[5] with replacement every three years, starting at age 2, and using an 8 percent discount rate, we calculate that lifetime average earnings would have to be increased by at least 12 cents per hour to offset the cost. If a more expensive type of optical aid were needed, costing perhaps $300 and lasting 10 years, then the average earnings would have to increase at least 10 cents per hour to offset costs.[6]

Reading and Writing Aids

For about 150 years, braille or other embossed writing has been used for reading and writing by some of the legally blind population. At no time, however, has a majority of that population used braille—even today the figure is perhaps less than 10 percent.[7] This is due to many

[4]S. M. Genensky, *A Functional Classification System of the Visually Impaired to Replace the Legal Definition of Blindness,* The Rand Corporation, RM-6246-RC, April 1970. See also L. H. Goldish, "The Severely Visually Impaired Population as a Market for Sensory Aids and Services: Part One," *The New Outlook,* June 1972, pp. 183–190.

[5]Corrective lenses typically cost $100 to $200, including professional fees. Low-vision aids range in cost from a few dollars for a simple magnifier, to $1000 to $1300 for a CCTV system, to $3500 for an electro-optical to tactile reading device. Special low-vision spectacles typically cost $150 to $500 in 1973.

[6]If a 4 percent discount rate were used, the foregoing figures would be approximately 6½ and 4½ cents per hour, respectively.

[7]*Rehabilitation Engineering—A Plan for Continued Progress,* Committee on Prosthetic Research and Development, National Academy of Sciences, Washington, D.C., April 1971.

factors, including the complexity of the braille code, the relatively low reading speeds usually attained, the large and awkward size of braille volumes, the limited braille literature, and a perceived stigma associated with its use by many of the newly functionally blind. Reading speeds of up to 200 words per minute have been recorded for rapid braille readers, but the average range is 60 to 120 words per minute. However, since most legally blind people can or could visually read ordinary or enlarged printed material with the aid of appropriate optical or image enhancement devices, a primary dependence on braille is not necessary.

People who can be functionally partially sighted should *not* be summarily channeled into the use of braille. The fact that they often are is due to the crude and regrettable dichotomization of the population into the sighted and the legally blind. Some partially sighted people are channeled not only into braille for reading and writing but also into mobility training with the long cane or guide dog, and hence are conditioned to act, think, and feel as if they were functionally blind. This can put severe and unnecessary restrictions on their educational and vocational opportunities.

Among the functionally blind, there has been a tendency in recent years to use taped material to supplement and sometimes replace braille, perhaps because taping can be faster than embossing braille and is a relatively compact way to store information. Tapes have at least one serious drawback: the problem of gaining rapid access to specific items at various locations along their length.

Talking books in the form of tapes or records are also used by about 18 percent of the legally blind, and about 75,000 people read large-print books.[8]

Attempts have been made to speed up the rate and ease with which printed material can be converted into braille. Nye and Bliss[9] describe some of the work that has gone on to achieve these goals.

Historically, most of the research and development expenditures on devices to assist the visually handicapped have been spent on projects concerned almost exclusively with the needs of the functionally blind. A 1971 National Academy of Sciences Report[10] indicates that at least $1.383 million was spent in 1970 by the Social and Rehabilitation Service, Veterans Administration, Office of Education, and the National Eye Institute on research and development concerned with such devices. Analyses of the constituent data suggest

---

[8]Ibid.
[9]Nye and Bliss, op. cit.
[10]*Rehabilitation Engineering—A Plan for Continued Progress.*

that over 90 percent of that sum was spent on projects aimed at helping less than 8 percent of the visually handicapped population, namely, the functionally blind. Even if we exclude the partially sighted who are not legally blind, our calculations indicate that more than 90 percent of the research and development dollars went to help less than 31 percent of the legally blind (i.e., the functionally blind), and hence less than 10 percent of those dollars went to help the more than 69 percent of the legally blind who are partially sighted. The research and development projects reported included those assisting the partially sighted to read printed material with their residual vision, and those assisting the functionally blind to cope with printed material using one of their nonvisual senses, to read braille, and to get around with a cane or other sensing devices. The projects also included those aimed at developing methods for preparing special material for use by the functionally blind. Medical projects aimed at treating or understanding ocular pathologies are not included—such projects do not involve the design, fabrication, testing, or evaluation of a device or process aimed at helping the visually impaired to cope with their education, vocation, or the general environment. It should also be noted that the National Academy of Sciences project compilation is said to be incomplete. Even so, it is hard to believe that the heavy bias of research and development dollars and projects toward the functionally blind is due primarily to incomplete reporting.

Responding to the issue, the Social and Rehabilitation Service (SRS) and the Veterans Administration have made efforts to change the balance of emphasis and funding just described. For example, the SRS lent support to the research that led to the Rand Corporation's development of closed circuit TV (CCTV) systems that help the partially sighted to use their eyes to read printed and handwritten material, to write with a pen or pencil, and to carry on other operations that require precise eye-hand coordination.[11] The key to the systems' value is that magnification can be combined with increased contrast and with contrast reversal.

CCTV systems are being used in schools, in libraries, on the job, and in the home. The Veterans Administration and the California Department of Vocational Rehabilitation, among others, now make CCTV systems available to partially sighted clients for use in school and on the job. Reading rates of 80 to 120 words per minute are

[11]S. M. Genensky, H. E. Petersen, H. L. Moshin, R. W. Clewett, and R. I. Yoshimura, *Advances in Closed Circuit TV Systems for the Partially Sighted,* The Rand Corporation, R-1040-HEW/RC, April 1972. Neither Rand nor any of its staff engaged in research on CCTV systems for the partially sighted have any interest in any company that manufactures, distributes, or sells such systems.

typical, and some users reach 200 words per minute. These are approximately the same rates as are achieved with braille, but with CCTVs *all* printed or written material can be read, not just specially prepared (braille) material, and any item that will fit under the camera can be examined visually.

The development of CCTV aids illustrates that human engineering of devices is very important. The most successful CCTV systems are quite simple and easy to operate and have rational designs. Roughly speaking, a CCTV system for the partially sighted consists of a TV camera, a zoom lens, a TV monitor with some added electronics, a bright light, and a movable platform on which the item to be viewed is placed. Merely putting such parts together is not enough to produce a good CCTV system, however, and several inadequate systems have come and gone. One must carefully choose the component parts, make design modifications in either the camera or monitor or both, and configure the instrument so that the viewer can use it with ease while seated in a natural and comfortable position.

A CCTV system has certain advantages over other reading aids for the partially sighted. For example, (1) it does not require the generation of special reading material, such as large-print books, because it can present magnified images of various sizes on its TV monitor, and (2) the images can be brighter and of higher contrast than is possible with any pure optical device. It can also present an image with the contrast reversed—for example, black type on a white background can be presented as white type on a black background; and it can view low-contrast material, such as most newspaper type, and display it as high-contrast white letters on a black background or black letters on a white background. These features, too, are beyond the capability of a purely optical aid. The result is that with the aid of contrast reversal and other image enhancement techniques, many partially sighted people, who could not read or write using other types of devices, are able to read print with their eyes and write with a pen or pencil.[12]

Mehr, Frost, and Apple[13] made a careful comparison of optical aids and CCTV systems with the help and cooperation of 40 partially sighted veterans. They found that these veterans' reading rates were higher and reading durations were much longer with a CCTV system than with an optical aid. The veterans were also able to write much

[12]Genensky et al., op. cit.

[13]E. B. Mehr, A. B. Frost, and L. E. Apple, "Experience with Closed Circuit Television in the Blind Rehabilitation Program of the Veterans Administration," *American Journal of Optometry and Archives of the American Academy of Optometry*, Vol. 50, No. 6, June 1973, pp. 458–469.

more clearly and neatly with a CCTV system. All the subjects could do this with the help of a CCTV system, but only 63 percent of them could do it with the help of an optical aid.

Among the many devices that have been explored or developed for use by the functionally blind, one of the most promising is the Optacon, which was designed by Bliss and his colleagues at Stanford University and the Stanford Research Institute, and which is now manufactured by Telesensory Systems, Inc., of Palo Alto, California. This electro-optical to tactile reading aid permits the functionally blind to read ordinary printed material, letter by letter, by moving a probe over the material with one hand and with the other hand sensing a tactile image of each letter being viewed by the probe. The probe contains an array of sensing diodes, and the trough in which the sensing index finger is placed contains a tactile sensing element corresponding to each of these diodes. When the probe views a symbol, for example, a "B," the only tactile elements that stimulate the sensing finger are those that correspond to diodes that are viewing the printed "B." According to Telesensory Systems, over 200 Optacons are currently in use, and as of December 1972, the company estimated that new orders were coming in at the rate of about 35 per month. Optacon sold for about $3500 per unit. Telesensory Systems advertise that people read with the device at rates as high as 80 words per minute, and one official of the Veterans Administration indicated that rates of perhaps 40 to 50 words per minute were typical in his limited experience.[14]

At first glance, being able to read ordinary printed material at the rate of 50 words per minute does not sound very impressive. It sounds much more so, however, when we consider that after the development of Optacon and other electro-optical to tactile or electro-optical to auditory devices, it was possible for the functionally blind person to read printed material himself rather than having a sighted person read to him. To anyone who is functionally blind (or even partially sighted), being able to read even at a very low speed means less dependence upon others and more privacy and personal satisfaction. For example, a rate of 50 words per minute allows the functionally blind to read their own mail and short magazine articles. Even so, it must be recognized that such a slow rate is not conducive to reading full-length books. Consequently, Optacon and other similar devices, as currently configured, should not be looked upon as a replacement for sighted readers or for all materials in braille or on

---

[14]Interview with R. Bennett, Veterans Administration Hospital, Palo Alto, California, November 1972.

tapes or records. They should, however, be looked upon as useful supplements to the more traditional techniques for enabling the functionally blind to read.

Mach Laboratories of Dayton, Ohio, with financial support from the Veterans Administration since at least 1957, has carried on research aimed at helping the functionally blind to read ordinary printed material. We have been told by Mach Laboratories that they now have an electro-optical to auditory reading aid for the functionally blind that they intend to offer for sale. This device, the Stereotoner, uses an electro-optical probe consisting of a vertical line of sensors that is moved across the printed line by the user. The Stereotoner transmits musical tones to the user's ears. The higher and louder sounds appear to come from the user's right, and the lower and softer sounds from his left. The high notes are induced by the tops of letters like "h," "k," and "t," and the lower notes by the bottoms of letters like "g," "p," and "q." Mach Laboratories is making 85 Stereotoners. The Veterans Administration is purchasing 50 for about $1875 each, 15 will be turned over to the National Academy of Sciences for evaluation, and 20 are for sale to any organization or person who might want them.

Work is going on at various rates at Mach Laboratories, MIT, and Haskins Laboratories on devices that scan printed material electro-optically and produce either an audible letter-by-letter spelling of words (called spelled speech) or an actual word-by-word audible rendition.

For example, Haskins Laboratories has been experimenting with a device that scans the printed work letter by letter, determines whether it has the combination and permutation of letters in its memory unit and, if it does, produces an audible rendition of the word. If it does not, it produces an audible spelling of the word.

Mach Laboratories is working on a device called the Cognodictor, which is said to be capable of recognizing both capital and lowercase letters, but not punctuation marks, numbers, and other special symbols. It produces an audible rendition of those letters, and it has some buffering capability, which permits the spelled speech to sound less mechanical—for example, "T-H-E M-A-N I-S T-A-L-L" is rendered more like "THE MAN IS TALL." The device is said to have a 2- to 3-percent error rate; and it requires that the user keep the electro-optical probe on the line, that he adjust it for differences in letter size, and that he be able to recognize the tactile image revealed to four fingertips on the hand he uses to move the probe across the printed line, when and if the Cognodictor cannot recognize a printed symbol. Mach Laboratories states that the Cognodictor, which currently is said to need modification, permits reading rates of 80 or 90 words per minute.

As Nye and Bliss[15] point out, the devices under design at Haskins Laboratories and at MIT, which are meant to produce speech that is adequately recognizable and appealing to the ear, will probably be expensive and far beyond the reach of the individual functionally blind user, if they ever reach the production stage. They might be purchased however, by large libraries and other facilities that serve many functionally blind people.

A subject of recent research interest and funding by the National Institutes of Health is electrocortical visual prosthesis, the stimulation of visual sensations by means of electrodes implanted in the brain. While it is possible to create arrays of visual sensations in this way, this type of prosthesis is still at an embryonic state, and it is unlikely to be of practical use to the blind in the near future.

Mobility Aids

A 1963–1964 National Health Survey[16] found that 36 percent of persons who could not read newsprint used an aid such as a cane, guide dog, or other person for mobility; and a 1971 report by the National Academy of Sciences estimated that more than 50 percent of the legally blind have canes.[17] According to Nye, however, only about 15 to 20 percent of the legally blind have had cane-travel training—that is, instruction in the efficient and effective use of a cane.[18] Some of the visually impaired use a cane as no more than a signal to motorists and pedestrians.

The American Foundation for the Blind lists about ten organizations that raise or train guide dogs and teach functionally blind people how to use them, but only about one percent of the legally blind do so. Many people who serve the functionally blind, and some of the blind themselves, look upon these helpful creatures with disfavor, often because they believe that dependence on a dog prevents a functionally blind person from achieving genuinely independent mobility. They feel that a blind person has a better kinesthetic grasp

---

[15]Nye and Bliss, op. cit.

[16]*Characteristics of Visually Impaired Persons, United States, July 1963–June 1964,* National Center for Health Statistics Report, Series 10, Number 46, HEW, Washington, D.C., August 1968.

[17]*Rehabilitation Engineering—A Plan for Continued Progress.*

[18]P. W. Nye (ed.), *Evaluation of Mobility Aids for the Blind,* Proceedings of a Conference, June 22–23, 1970, at Airlie House, Warrenton, Virginia, sponsored by the Subcommittee on Sensory Aids of the Committee on the Interplay of Engineering with Biology and Medicine, National Academy of Engineering, Washington, D.C.

of the environment while using a cane, and that it forces him to handle travel problems more realistically. They may admire and love dogs, but they nevertheless look upon them as potential obstacles to a functionally blind person's obtaining a job, and they may argue heatedly that guide dogs must be walked, fed, and otherwise cared for, and hence prolong or interfere with their masters' day.

The most acceptable mobility aid to date for the functionally blind appears to be the long cane specially designed by R. E. Hoover. This simple device permits a functionally blind person to detect obstacles on or near the ground several feet in front of him, and thus gives him time to take evasive action. It does not warn him of overhanging obstacles such as scaffolding or casement windows, however, and it can fail to warn him of depressions quickly enough and of objects that might endanger his upper body. Several techniques have been tried to reduce those dangers, but none has yet gained wide acceptance. The most promising may be the laser cane developed by Haverford College and Bionics Instruments, Inc. It is composed of the Hoover cane and three lasers, each of which scans a region of interest to the traveler: head level, mid-section, and ground level. The laser cane also has a ranging capability that indicates to the traveler roughly how far he is from a potential hazard. All three lasers trigger a single tactile warning device that presses against one of the traveler's index fingers. Two of the lasers also give him auditory warning: the head-level laser activates circuitry that produces a high-pitched sound, and the ground-level laser generates a low-pitched sound. About 18 laser canes are now in use or on order by the Veterans Administration.

The ultrasonic spectacles developed by L. Kay, in conjunction with the Hoover cane, also appear to be of interest. They emit an ultrasonic signal which, when reflected back from an obstacle, produces an audible binaural signal and gives the traveler some indication of the direction of and distance to the obstacle.

A less sophisticated device that also may become a useful supplement to the Hoover cane is the Travel Pathsounder, developed by Russell and the MIT Sensory Aids Evaluation and Development Center. Worn on the chest, this device detects obstructions up to 6 feet in front of the traveler. When it does so, it emits a ticking sound that grows more rapid as the traveler gets closer to the obstacle. When he is within 30 inches of the obstacle, the ticking sound gives way to an urgent beeping.

While most partially sighted people do not or should not need to use a cane or other guidance device, they nonetheless may need some guidance instruction. By learning to use the visual cues that remain within their capability, they can do things that the normally sighted would regard as virtually impossible at first glance.

Simple and effective techniques can often be used. For example, glare frequently prevents partially sighted people from seeing whether a traffic light is red or green straight in front of them when they want to cross a street. But oftentimes they can look off at a right angle and see when the traffic light turns yellow and red for crosswise traffic. Coupling that knowledge with the sounds and sight of traffic movement, they can deduce when they have the green light with them. A skeptic may admit this is ingenious but doubt that the partially sighted could also detect oncoming cars. The answer is that most of these people can hear vehicles coming and can see what Genensky calls "the essence," or "Gestalt," of the car soon enough to take precautions. After all, a pedestrian does not need to know the make and year of an oncoming car to tell whether it is a hazard.

Genensky has also described the value of binoculars as a reading, writing, and mobility aid.[19] They permit many partially sighted people to do such things as read the number and route name on the front of a bus, read street signs, view traffic signals and "walk-don't walk" signs, read street numbers and names of stores, and view merchandise in a store or in its show windows.

Another electro-optical to tactile aid that may prove useful to the functionally blind for mobility and other purposes has been researched by P. Bach-y-Rita.[20] This device, called a tactile television system, converts information gathered by a TV camera into a coarse tactile image on a person's back or stomach by means of an array of vibrating electromechanical stimulators. This allows recognition of some objects. Starkiewiecz and Kuprianowicz[21] have stimulated the skin of the forehead in an attempt to achieve similar results.

AIDS FOR HEARING HANDICAPPED PEOPLE

Sensory aids for the hearing handicapped include hearing aids, captioned films and TV, speech training and speech perception aids that convert aural information to visual or tactile, and devices to aid activities of daily living, such as "doorbells" that flash lights and a teletype-like device for use with a telephone.

[19]S. M. Genensky, *Binoculars: A Long-Ignored Aid for the Partially Sighted,* The Rand Corporation, R-1402-HEW, November 1973.

[20]P. Bach-y-Rita, "A Tactile Vision Substitution System Based on Sensory Plasticity," in T. D. Sterling et al., (eds)., *Visual Prosthesis: The Interdisciplinary Dialogue,* Academic Press, New York, 1971, pp. 281–290.

[21]W. Starkiewiecz et al., "60-Channel Electrophthalmy with $CdSO_x$ Photoresistors and Forehead Tactile Elements," in ibid., pp. 295–300.

Recall that in this book we consider persons aurally handicapped if they have frequent difficulty understanding normal speech, or worse. In terms of average decibels of hearing loss in the better ear in the 500 to 2000 Hz range, that is considered to be about 40 dB or more (ISO). A more detailed survey-document in this field has been published by the National Institute of Neurological Disease and Stroke;[22] it notes problems with both definitions and prevalence data, but suggests that the most widely accepted definition of a deaf person is one "in whom the sense of hearing is nonfunctional for the ordinary purposes of life." In average decibels of loss in the better ear, that level is approximately in the range of 85 to 90 dB and up. Our review of prevalence data suggests that approximately 50,000 U.S. youth aged 0 to 21 years can be considered deaf, and another 440,000 youth are aurally handicapped but not deaf. One new source of prevalence data is a national speech and hearing survey of a random sample of 38,884 public school subjects in the United States.[23] Preliminary analysis of data from that survey,[24] which excluded students in special schools or special classes, indicates that our estimate of 490,000 hearing handicapped youth aged 0 to 21 with loss greater than 40 dB may be a little low. Consequently, our estimates of need for sensory aids may be low.

Nearly all of the 440,000 partially hearing youth—those who are aurally handicapped but not deaf—need hearing aids.[25] A small fraction of the hard of hearing may not be able to benefit from hearing aids, for example, those with dysacusic disturbances primarily characterized by garbled hearing. The approximately 50,000 deaf youth have distinctly different needs for aids since their sense of hearing is essentially nonfunctional. There are two different classes of deafness: congenitally deaf youth have an impairment that occurred before language and speech were acquired; adventitiously deaf youth have a sense of hearing that became nonfunctional through illness or accident, generally after language acquisition. Speech perception aids are desirable for both types of deaf youth. Speech training aids are most

---

[22]*Human Communication and Its Disorders: An Overview*, NINDS Monograph No. 10, Bethesda, Md., 1969.

[23]F. M. Hull et al., "The National Speech and Hearing Survey: Preliminary Results," *ASHA, A Journal of the American Speech and Hearing Association*, September 1971.

[24]F. M. Hull and J. A. Willeford, *National Speech and Hearing Survey Progress Report, Part II*, Colorado State University, Fort Collins, May 9, 1972.

[25]H. Davis and S. R. Silverman (eds.), *Hearing and Deafness*, 3d ed., Holt, Rinehart and Winston, Inc., New York, 1970, for example, cite a hearing level of 40 dB or worse in the better ear as the range in which a hearing aid generally is needed.

desirable for the congenitally deaf, but can also be useful in helping adventitiously deaf youth to maintain a reasonably high quality of speech. However, while high-quality hearing aids are available, much remains to be accomplished in the development of speech training and speech perception devices.

The degree of *unaided and uncorrected* hearing loss, like the degree of unaided vision loss, is not a good measure of the degree of permanent sensorial handicap, because it does not take into account how well the hearing impaired person can *function* with an aid or after medical or surgical correction. For example, a hearing impaired person can have a very severe unaided and uncorrected hearing loss due to a malfunction or degeneration of the eardrum or one or more of the small bones in the middle ear, but surgical intervention may improve hearing so much that the person has no need for a hearing aid and has little or no difficulty with normal speech. A youth's need for a sensory aid therefore should not be established until he or she has received an otologic examination by a qualified physician.

Hearing Aids

A hearing aid is basically a microphone to pick up sound, an electronic device to amplify and perhaps modify the sound in other ways, and an earphone. The many models available differ from one another in various ways, such as aesthetically, in the amount of sound amplification, in the relative amplification of different frequencies of sound, and in their ways of controlling very loud sounds. Some aids modify the frequencies of sound to give the person more information in the frequency range within which he can hear best. An earmold provides a tube to convey sound from the earphone to the eardrum. Historically, hearing aids made a tremendous leap forward in utility with the advent of small transistorized versions in the early 1950s.

If the inner ear and the auditory nerve or the auditory cortex in the brain are insensitive, a hearing aid may be useless; but if the problem is a lack of conduction of sound to the inner ear, a hearing aid normally yields beneficial results. Again, an otologic examination by a qualified physician may suggest a medical or surgical method of alleviating the hearing loss, and should be conducted before a hearing aid is dispensed to a child. After a hearing aid is selected, the youth or the family need information on its use, care, and maintenance, as with other types of aids, and the family may need advice on how to *motivate* the child to use the aid.

Hearing aids for young children can be a problem because the instruments need to be physically robust, it is difficult to obtain good impressions of small ears for earmolds, and rapid ear growth makes it difficult to maintain good earmold fit—but early fitting is especially important to facilitate language development.[26]

For further summary information on hearing aids, the reader can refer to several publications.[27]

In addition to personal hearing aids, group hearing aids exist. I. J. Hirsh[28] describes the development of group aids and how they have been used in teaching persons with very serious hearing losses. One of the most successful has been the induction loop transmitter. It consists of one or more loops of wire that encompass a classroom and are connected to one or more microphones, which are used by the teacher and the students to communicate with one another. Each student wears a special hearing aid, which is equipped with an induction coil that picks up signals from the room-encompassing loop. This arrangement permits the students to move around the room freely and still listen in to the discussion.

Frequently, persons with severe hearing impairment are able, albeit unevenly, to hear sounds at frequencies below 1000 Hz and down to about 125 Hz with their residual hearing. At least two types of experimental instruments have been developed that try to take advantage of this residual capability. One is called a low-frequency extended-range amplification system. It delivers amplified signals down to about 80 or 100 Hz. The hope is that extending the range of a hearing aid down to those frequencies, rather than settling for the conventional cut-off at 300 to 400 Hz, may give the listener auditory clues with respect to a male voice, and thus enhance the listener's chances of understanding what that voice is saying.

Another type of instrument modifies the energy distribution of the sound across frequencies and delivers more of that energy at frequencies at which the person's hearing is best. For example, the energy in the entire range of speech-sound frequencies may be shifted

[26]F. Kleffner, "Hearing Losses, Hearing Aids, and Children with Language Disorders," *Journal of Speech and Hearing Disorders,* May 1973.

[27]D. Ling, "Conventional Hearing Aids: An Overview," *The Volta Review,* September 1971; E. L. H. Corliss, *Hearing Aids,* National Bureau of Standards Monograph 117, Washington, D.C., October 1970; K. W. Berger, *The Hearing Aid: Its Operation And Development,* The National Hearing Aid Society, 24261 Grand River Avenue, Detroit, Michigan, 1970; *Hearing Aid Performance Measurement Data and Hearing Aid Selection Procedures, Contract Year 1970,* Veterans Administration, Report 1B 10-124, Washington, D.C., 1970.

[28]"Use of Amplification in Educating Deaf Children," *American Annals of the Deaf,* Vol. 113, November 1968, pp. 1046–1055.

into a compressed lower-frequency range, or only the higher sound frequencies may be filtered out and the information transposed and presented at lower frequencies. Erber has reviewed a number of experiments carried out to test the value of these techniques in the communication training of the hearing handicapped. He found no conclusive evidence that either technique was or was not of significant value.[29]

Aids to hearing by means of electrocortical aural prostheses are roughly at the same stage of development as electrocortical visual prostheses, namely, the feasibility study stage. Research on implants in the brain is interesting and may someday result in useful sensory aids, but is unlikely to do so in the near future.

In 1962, of the binaurally hearing impaired population in the United States who could hear and understand a few spoken words without an aid, about 29 percent of those of all ages, and 31 percent of those under age 45, used hearing aids.[30] The usage rate among families with annual incomes over $7000 was about twice that for families with incomes under $2000 per year. Of persons who could not hear and understand spoken words without an aid, 43 percent of those of all ages, and 40 percent of those under age 45, used a hearing aid. The basis for selecting the aid was a doctor's or clinic's prescription in about one-third of the cases; hearing aid dealers' advice accounted for another third; and the remainder based their selections on advertising, the recommendation of a layman, or on a reason unknown to us. Of persons who had ever used an aid, 68 percent of those who cannot hear and understand spoken words without an aid, and 61 percent of those who can hear and understand a few spoken words without an aid, reported they were very satisfied or fairly satisfied with the aid. While we could locate no reliable data on the use of hearing aids by children, the relatively low usage rate for persons of all ages suggests that only a fraction of the children that could benefit from a hearing aid presently have one. That fraction is probably less than one-half and may be as low as one-third.

It is clear that by improving hearing ability, these aids can significantly improve the quality of life of these handicapped youth and also improve their ability to benefit from education and to succeed vocationally. Hearing aids generally range in price from approximately $100 up to $700, with a high-quality aid typically costing $300

[29]N. P. Erber, "Evaluation of Special Hearing Aids for Deaf Children," *Journal of Speech and Hearing Disorders,* Vol. 36, No. 4, November 1971, pp. 527–537.

[30]*Characteristics of Persons with Impaired Hearing, U.S. July 1962–June 1963,* National Center for Health Statistics Report, Series 10, No. 35, U.S. Department of Health, Education, and Welfare, Washington, D.C., April 1967.

to $350. Using a typical cost of $350 and assuming annual operating expenses of $60, with replacement every two years for children aged 2 to 10 and every five years thereafter, and using an 8 percent discount rate, we calculate that lifetime average earnings from ages 18 to 55 would have to be increased by at least 39 cents per hour to offset the cost. At an assumed discount rate of 4 percent, the breakeven point in earnings is 19 cents per hour.

We are obliged to rely on analyses of the "breakeven point" type since no data exist on the change in economic benefits due to use of a sensory aid. Note that, for simplicity, we have described the breakeven point in terms of earnings alone, but other benefits may also accrue, notably a reduction in the cost of providing various services to the handicapped person. Thus, the actual earnings increase needed to offset the cost of the aid would be, say, 19 cents less some amount to account for the decrease in cost of providing other services later in the child's life. The largest cost reduction can be in education, if the aid so improves hearing that the child no longer requires expensive special education services. Ling reports that "owing to the use of hearing aids, a large proportion of children who formerly received their education in special schools have been able to compete and conform with their normally hearing peers in regular classes. Many severely hearing impaired children who would formerly have been trained as deaf are now correctly treated as hard of hearing."[31]

While the typical cost of $300 to $350 for a hearing aid seems low in view of the benefits, this is by no means a negligible sum for the poor and often may be prohibitive. Recall the strong correlation between level of income and hearing aid use.

Directions for research to improve hearing aids further are outlined in a National Academy of Sciences report,[32] which also makes recommendations on early screening and diagnosis, methods of stimulating language development, and the distribution of existing aids and services.

In 1968, about 400,000 hearing aids were sold in the United States. A comparison of the rate of sales per 1000 population in various areas of the world reveals that the United States and Canada have relatively high usage.

[31]Ling, op. cit.

[32]*Directions for Research to Improve Hearing Aids and Services for the Hearing Impaired,* Committee on Hearing, Bioacoustics and Biomechanics, Working Group 65, National Academy of Sciences—National Research Council, Washington, D.C., 1972.

1968 SALES PER 1000 POPULATION

United States and Canada	2.05
Western Europe	1.06
Eastern Europe and Russia	0.40
Middle and Near East	0.04
Far East and Oceania	0.14
Africa	0.02
Latin America	0.09

SOURCE: Berger, op. cit.

A later report by O. Bentzen and J. Courtois[33] presented data suggesting that the number of patients with hearing aids per 100,000 inhabitants was strongly dependent on government programs, as is shown below, where we cite the two countries with highest usage rates and the two countries with the lowest usage rates, by three categories of programs.

Country and Type of Program	*Patients with Hearing Aids per 100,000 Inhabitants*
Hearing aids fully paid for by the state	
Denmark	483
Sweden	363
England and Wales	250
New Zealand	182
Hearing aids partly paid for by the state	
U.S.A.	237
Norway	205
Uganda	1
Ceylon	0.6
Hearing aids fully paid for by patients	
El Salvador	170
Surinam	12
Madagascar	1
Tanzania	0.1

Speech Training and Speech Perception Aids

Several surveys of aids to help the deaf learn to speak and other aids to help them understand human speech have appeared in the litera-

[33]"1970 World Statistical Analysis of Hearing Aid Fittings," *National Hearing Aid Journal*, October 1971.

ture.[34] Some of the instruments they describe convert auditory information into tactile signals, such as the Vocoder built at the Speech Transmission Laboratory in Stockholm. If speech sounds are converted to tactile stimuli, for example, the deaf person receives tactile clues to what another person is saying which supplement information obtained by lip reading, and also receives tactile feedback to help maintain the quality of his or her own speech. Other instruments convert auditory information into visual signals, such as the visible speech translator (VST), built at the Bell Telephone Laboratories, and the LUCIA, built at the Speech Transmission Laboratory. If speech sounds are converted to visible displays, for example, the deaf person can be shown and trained to know what certain sounds "look like" and hence to recognize them when spoken by another person; or the displays can show the person whether his or her speech "looks" as it should to be understandable. These visible displays can be relatively simple, such as light bulbs that are turned on by a certain tone of sound and whose brightness depends on the volume of the sound, or they can be a relatively complex electronic device that analyzes the frequency components of the sound, displays the results as a pattern on a TV-type screen for an indefinite period of time so they can be studied, and stores the video display for future reference. Advocates of audio-to-tactile speech perception and training aids for the deaf argue that the perception of time patterns and rhythms through the skin appears to resemble that encountered in hearing. Supporters of audio-to-visual speech training aids argue that visual models of desired speech patterns can be shown to a student, the student can then practice and have the results stored, and then both the patterns of the student and the desired patterns can be analyzed and compared in detail by teacher and student. Pickett appears to have reservations concerning the value of audio-to-tactile aids, because the skin has a limited capacity for frequency analysis compared with the ear or the eye.

H. Upton of Bell Helicopter Company has developed another auditory-to-visual aid aimed at helping a profoundly deaf or even a severely hard of hearing person to supplement information obtained about other person's speech by lip reading and the use of a hearing

---

[34]J. M. Pickett, "Status of Speech Analyzing Communication Aids for the Deaf," *IEEE Transactions on Audio and Electrical Acoustics,* Vol. AU-20, No. 1, March 1972, pp. 3–8; idem, "Some Applications of Speech Analysis to Communication Aids for the Deaf," *IEEE Transactions on Audio and Electrical Acoustics,* Vol. AU-17, No. 4, December 1969, pp. 283–289; H. Levitt, "Speech Processing Aids for the Deaf: An Overview," *IEEE Transactions on Audio and Electrical Acoustics,* Vol. AU-21, No. 3, June 1973; H. Levitt and P. Nye, *Sensory Training Aids for the Hearing Impaired,* Subcommittee on Sensory Aids, Committee on the Interplay of Engineering with Biology and Medicine, National Academy of Engineering, Washington, D.C., 1971.

aid. The aid consists of a set of tiny light bulbs mounted on eyeglass frames; different bulbs flash on and off in response to different sounds in speech.[35]

Levitt suggests that speech perception aids are as yet only of marginal assistance, but he concludes that speech training aids have already met with a "moderate degree of success."[36]

In summary, speech training and speech perception aids hold considerable promise but are not yet in widespread use because they have not been fully developed and methods of using them have not been fully evaluated and disseminated.

A different class of speech perception aids includes captioned films and captioned television. The technology has been developed to provide captions for network television programs but make the captions visible only to viewers who have specially modified TV sets.[37] The modification reportedly costs less than $100.

In the previous discussion of sensory aids for the visually handicapped, we cited a National Academy of Sciences Report that estimated research and development expenditures of at least $1.383 million, or $1.08 per patient, for the blind and partially sighted in FY 1970. The corresponding figures for the hearing handicapped were only $702,000, or $0.41 per patient. In view of the state of the art of sensory aids we have described, and the sizes and needs of the two populations, it appears that more emphasis than exists presently on sensory aids for the hearing handicapped would be justified, as well as increases, in general, of expenditures for research on aids for both the hearing and the vision handicapped populations.

AIDS FOR DEAF-BLIND PEOPLE

There has been a recent growth of interest in what modern technology can do to help the deaf-blind people. At the outset, technologists embarking on work in this area must be aware that only a minority of deaf-blind people have no usable residual hearing *and* no usable residual vision. Most have some residual capability with one or both senses.[38] We in no way wish to imply that technologists should devote their efforts exclusively to that majority; but we believe it would be mistaken zeal to stake everything on finding devices or techniques

---

[35]Pickett, "Status of Speech Analyzing Communication Aids."

[36]Levitt, op. cit.

[37]R. Perkins (ed.), *Proceedings of the First National Conference on Television for the Hearing Impaired,* Southern Regional Media Center for the Deaf, University of Tennessee, Knoxville, December 1971.

[38]L. Guldager, "The Deaf-Blind: Their Education and Needs," *Exceptional Children,* Vol. 36, November 1969, pp. 203–206.

for the most severely handicapped segment of the deaf-blind population.

Many of the aids developed for persons with either impaired hearing or impaired vision are adaptable to serve many of the deaf-blind,
and we need not repeat our discussion of those aids here. In addition, the visual-to-tactile and aural-to-tactile conversion devices we
discussed earlier, if *developed and adapted,* could prove valuable to
profoundly deaf-blind youth.

EQUIPMENT PROGRAMS

Nearly all types of public agencies serving handicapped youth expend some funds on sensory aids, but no agency has major responsibility for perfecting and disseminating these aids. Some school systems purchase classroom sensory aids, and sometimes even personal
aids. HEW's Media Services and Captioned Films Program develops
and supplies sensory aid materials. The Vocational Rehabilitation
agencies purchase hearing aids, corrective lenses, and other reading,
writing, and mobility aids for the visually handicapped. Under the
Medicaid and the Crippled Children's Service programs, states can
purchase sensory aids. Welfare funds also sometimes are used for this
purpose. The Library of Congress supplies talking books and braille
materials through a system of regional libraries in every state.

Other chapters describe such federal programs that do some developing, disseminating, and purchasing of sensory aids. Federal agencies involved include the Bureau of Education for the Handicapped,
the Library of Congress, the Veterans Administration, the Rehabilitation Services Administraton, the Assistance Payment Administration,
the Medical Services Administration, the Maternal and Child Health
Service, the National Institutes of Health, the American Printing
House for the Blind, the National Academy of Engineering, the National Academy of Science, the National Science Foundation, and the
National Bureau of Standards.

The current federal role in the provision of sensory aids is hetero-
geneous; in some programs the federal government provides the aids
directly, in other programs it provides funds for aids that are secondary to the other primary services being funded, and research is
funded in many different programs.

The current system for providing sensory aids is unorganized and
fractionated, with duplication in some cases, but without any mechanism for ensuring that children who need sensory aids receive them.
The funding of sensory aids is partially governmental, through a multitude of programs, and partially private. The actual dispensing of the

two commonest types of aids, corrective lenses and hearing aids, is typically private but with governmental regulation in many states.

For example, in 1971 about 25 states licensed and regulated hearing aid dealers,[39] and other states have passed regulatory legislation since then. Some form of minimum training for dealers is generally required for licensing, and a few states specifically prohibit selling a hearing aid to a child who has not had an examination by an otolaryngologist or a written recommendation to have such an examination. A recent project sponsored by Ralph Nader describes the present hearing aid service system in detail, strongly criticizes it, and makes several recommendations for improvement, including stronger regulation of the industry.[40]

The mechanisms used to provide sensory aids in some other countries are distinctly different from those in the United States. K. W. Berger[41] has reviewed foreign mechanisms for providing hearing aids; the following are some of his findings: In Australia a scheme was introduced in 1968 whereby qualified recipients might rent an aid from the government for about $10 a year. Belgium has a governmental program wherein the hearing impaired person gets a prescription for a hearing aid and then obtains a grant, which is renewed every five years, to purchase a hearing aid, with the amount of the grant based on the type of hearing loss. Since 1951, Denmark has furnished free hearing aids, with free replacements every five years. All hearing aids sold under Norway's health plan must be approved by a central state testing authority, and personalized hearing aids are furnished free to children under 20 years of age and parents with children under 20. Other Norwegians needing aids are given grants toward their purchase. In Sweden, children under 16 are supplied with personalized hearing aids free of charge, while for others a grant is available every 8 years toward the purchase of a hearing aid. In Switzerland, starting in 1959, the federal health insurance program has furnished free personalized hearing aids to hearing impaired persons under 65.

NEEDED IMPROVEMENT IN EQUIPMENT PROGRAMS

Recommendations for improving the quality, quantity, and distribution of equipment and sensory aids have been divided into two groups: those that involve the equipment and sensory aids directly, and those that are related to complementary services that can make

[39]For a digest of those states' regulations, see "Current Information: State Licensing of Hearing Aid Dealers," *National Hearing Aid Journal,* Vol. 24, No. 9, 1971.

[40]E. L. Griesel and W. L. Wilson, *Paying Through the Ear: A Report on Hearing Health Care Problems,* Public Citizens Retired Professional Action Group, Public Citizen, Inc., P.O. Box 19404, Washington, D.C., 1973.

[41]Berger, op. cit.

an equipment and sensory aids program more effective or eliminate the need for the equipment or sensory aid altogether. Sensory aids were rated as one of the top three most important services by the families we interviewed who had sensorially handicapped children. Hearing aids and corrective lenses were the aids most often mentioned as being valuable; however, these aids may have been singled out by the families because they are the types most likely to be needed and are also the best-known aids.

All handicapped youth who can benefit from equipment and sensory aids should be assured of having them. The judicious choice of an aid can make the youth functionally less handicapped, lessen his or her need for other special services such as education in a special classroom, and improve the effectiveness of other services such as education and job training. Most sensory aids appear to be cost-effective and to improve the youth's quality of life significantly, especially the two types of aids most often needed: corrective lenses and hearing aids. Depending on the type of aid needed, the youth or the parents may also need to be trained to use and maintain the device.

Coordinated and intensified effort is needed in support of research and development programs aimed at designing and testing new aids for the handicapped and at converting promising prototype devices into fully human-engineered production instruments. Some of the new devices currently in the research and development stages show promise of giving the visually handicapped ready access to normal printed material, and of significantly improving their mobility; and they show promise of giving the hearing handicapped significantly improved speech perception capability.

Certain services are ancillary but necessary to the effective provision of equipment and sensory aids.

Many children may not receive needed sensory aids because their handicap is not identified. In our earlier chapter on "identification," we recommended screening all children for hearing and vision impairment. An early identification program would be particularly helpful to preschool hearing handicapped youth, who should be fitted with hearing aids as early as possible so that language development is facilitated.

The provision of a direction service could give parents and teachers needed information on the value of various types of equipment and aids available, on which aids are appropriate for the child, and on where to obtain them. This direction service would coordinate the presently fragmented delivery system.

Since an impairment can often be stabilized, alleviated, or eliminated medically or surgically, *we recommend that a medical specialist examine the child before sensory aids are dispensed.*

Chapter 12

MENTAL HEALTH AND MENTAL RETARDATION PROGRAMS

OVERVIEW

The proliferation of federal programs supporting services to children who are mentally retarded or have mental health disorders has been discussed in earlier chapters, along with other programs aimed at the general population or at all types of handicapped persons rather than specifically at the mentally handicapped. This chapter presents an overview of programs aimed primarily at mentally handicapped people; discusses the federal role in those programs; and presents available descriptive data, including estimates of program expenditures and number of persons served. Since the scope of our research did not include analysis of ways of improving the mental health and mental retardation programs discussed in this chapter, we will not be presenting any recommendations.

Programs primarily providing services to mentally handicapped people are estimated to have assisted over 700,000 youth aged 0–21 in 1970. Total program expenditures for youth were at least $898.2 million in 1970, of which the federal share was $74.7 million, or 8.4 percent. The breakdown of these figures, shown in Tables 12.1 and 12.2, indicates that the expenditures were predominantly for residential inpatient care of people who were mentally retarded (54 percent) and had mental health disorders (30 percent). However, the greatest number of youth were served in outpatient facilities for the emotionally disturbed. The two largest federal programs were the Developmental Disabilities program, primarily serving retarded persons, and the NIMH Community Mental Health Center (CMHC) program. A breakdown of the estimated expenditures by type of handicap is shown in Table 12.3; the retarded or otherwise developmentally disabled received the largest share, with 61 percent.

Table 12.1
ESTIMATED MENTAL HEALTH AND RETARDATION PROGRAM EXPENDITURES
FOR HANDICAPPED YOUTH, 1970

Program	Expenditures	
	Federal	Total
Residential care: mental retardation	—	$479,529,000
Inpatient care: mental health disorders	—	267,000,000
Outpatient care: mental health disorders		
(except Community Mental Health Centers)	—	64,000,000
NIMH (including CMHC)	49,000,000	54,000,000
Developmental disabilities (FY 1972)	25,000,000	33,000,000
President's and Secretary's Committees on		
Mental Retardation (FY 1971)	660,000	660,000
Total	$74,660,000	$898,189,000

SOURCE: For data sources and estimation methods, see "Mental Health and Mental Retardation Programs," in this chapter.

Table 12.2
ESTIMATED NUMBER OF HANDICAPPED YOUTH RECEIVING
MENTAL HEALTH AND RETARDATION SERVICES, 1970

Program	Number of Handicapped Youth
Residential mental retardation care	103,073
Inpatient mental health care (FY 1969)	149,000
Outpatient mental health care (FY 1969)	570,000
Developmental disabilities (FY 1971)	88,000

SOURCE: For data sources and estimation methods, see "Mental Health and Mental Retardation Programs," in this chapter.

Table 12.3
ESTIMATED EXPENDITURES FOR MENTAL HEALTH AND RETARDATION
PROGRAMS FOR YOUTH BY TYPE OF HANDICAP, 1970

Handicap	Estimated Expenditures
Mental retardation, developmental disability	$549,189,000
Mental health disorder	349,000,000
Total	898,189,000

SOURCE: For data sources and estimation methods, see "Mental Health and Mental Retardation Programs," in this chapter.

There is no clearly defined federal role, nor are there even well-understood federal goals, underlying the provision of services to populations of youth with mental health disorders or mental retardation.

With respect to the mentally retarded, even the basic diagnosis of "mental retardation" is a fundamental operational problem. For example, in the Mental Retardation Clinics operated under the auspices of the Maternal and Child Health Service, nearly half of those referred and medically diagnosed were not mentally retarded at all. In the Developmental Disabilities program, we found that the definition issue, not having been resolved in the basic legislation, was referred by the Secretary to a study group for deliberation. On this score, we do not fault those responsible for the various programs, but merely note that the issue is a terribly difficult one, having grave implications for program planning, funding, and evaluation.

It is hard to plan when information is in short supply, but this is the case for practically every program we observed which touched the lives of mentally handicapped children and youth.

The question of cost is also thorny, but here at least there are some data, much of which indicate that the general skyrocketing of medical expenses has also affected mentally handicapped children, irrespective of whether they are inpatients or outpatients, although the effect on the former is far greater than on the latter. The cost factor is one of the major elements (others being humanitarian concern for better care and more normal alternatives to a mental institution) that account for the trend away from institutionalization and toward outpatient care for mentally retarded children.

Mentally retarded people in hospitals account for the greatest expenditures, even though only about 1 in 25 mentally retarded youth receives residential inpatient services. Since 1950, the institutionalized and mentally retarded portion of the total population for all ages has grown only slightly. The proportion of youthful residents has grown, however, especially those under age five, whose inpatient rate per 100,000 of their cohort's population nearly quadrupled between 1950 and 1970. The average costs per patient-day for maintaining persons in institutions basically tripled between 1960 and 1970, reaching a figure of $12.70. These costs vary considerably across the states; five states spent less than $7 per patient-day in 1970, while six states spent over $15.

Of youth served who have mental health disorders, 21 percent are inpatients, while 66 percent are served in psychiatric outpatient clinics, 11 percent in Community Mental Health Centers, and 2 percent in day treatment centers. The trend to lessen the ratio of mental health inpatients to outpatients, noted for all ages combined, is not mirrored in the child and youth subset of the population, where the ratio has remained relatively stable or even increased slightly. Costs have not remained constant, particularly for institutionalized people, who in 1970 numbered some 150,000 in the 0–21 age range and whose mental health inpatient maintenance costs totaled at least $267 million.

In our investigation of federal programs for the mentally handicapped, we were struck by the dispersion of effort throughout the government; nonetheless, several federal programs concentrate on these populations, and we examined them in some detail.

The National Institute of Mental Health has six distinct programs that bear directly on these populations. (1) The Community Mental Health Centers program is the largest; (2) child-specific mental health research is the next largest; followed (in descending order of total expenditures, not necessarily by the fraction that is child-specific) by (3) mental health training grants; (4) St. Elizabeths Hospital; (5) mental health fellowships; and (6) hospital improvement grants.

A second focus is the Developmental Disabilities Act. In FY 1972 it was funded at $49.54 million, some portion of which benefited children and youth.

The following summarizes our observations about mental health and mental retardation programs for handicapped youth:

- The federal share of the total expended on programs primarily intended for the mentally handicapped population is not large.
- Population and cost data are not well known, even by those having direct operational responsibility for programs. High-quality evaluation is practically nonexistent, but given the poor status of primary data on the populations, that is to be expected. In short, no one really knows who is doing what to whom and with what effect.
- Coordination among the array of programs for the mentally handicapped is more a bureaucratic goal than actuality.
- Research is neither large-scale nor is it generally child-specific. Compared with estimated expenditures of more than $800 million a year for maintenance of the population, and because of the lack of knowledge, the total of all research seems quite low.
- Is service provision inadequate? Many say so. The problem of funding is pervasive, as it has been for nearly all of the services and programs we report on. One result of increased budgetary pressures at the state and local levels has been the closing of state institutions for the mentally handicapped. Instead of being an alternative to institutionalization, community based pro-

grams have become increasingly an underdeveloped replacement.

• Is service provision inequitable? Probably, but data to assess the nature and extent of inequity are not readily available.

ROLES AND GOALS

In no other area is there more confusion about the appropriate federal role as there appears to be with respect to people with mental retardation or mental health disorders. All of our characteristic role models exist in some federal mental health or mental retardation program, but each exists only partially, and none is developed sufficiently well that it dominates. The amorphousness of the system is partly explained by the sheer number of functionally disparate agencies that have programs affecting mentally retarded and emotionally disturbed children.

The Direct Operations model is, for instance, partially evident at St. Elizabeths Hospital. For the mentally ill and some few retarded in their CMHC in Washington, D.C., this is a prime source of direct service, and it is located administratively within the National Institute of Mental Health. Partial examples of the Controllership model are also to be found. There is the Community Mental Health Center program, whose funds are basically provided from federal (NIMH) sources, whose guidelines and policies are set down in federal offices, whose research component is even separately mandated with federal funds, but whose services are delivered by the states and localities. A form of the Special Revenue Sharing model exists to a certain extent in the Developmental Disabilities program, whose annual budget of $50 million or so in 1971 primarily benefited state planning and coordinating bureaucracies. Another form of Special Revenue Sharing, but with some degree of the evaluation Plus, also exists in the Maternal and Child Health Service's Mental Retardation Clinics. The Catalytic model is embodied to some degree in the research and training efforts of NIMH, in some of the research efforts of the Rehabilitation Services Administration, and in some of the activities sponsored by the Bureau of Education for the Handicapped in the Office of Education. However, there appears to be little real coordination among these assorted research efforts.

In fact, if a single model of the existing system were to be contrived, it would have to be called the "Disorganization" model.

Lacking clearly stated objectives or well-delineated authority, functions are likewise numerous and underdeveloped. Some research and development is going on, but, even using liberal estimates of its extent, the total effort is clearly less than the unanswered questions, the size, or even the maintenance costs of the afflicted population would suggest to be adequate. Seed money projects are being run in many programs, but none alone, or even in the aggregate, appears to be solving the problems. Demonstrations abound, attended with much rhetoric and political fanfare; but, given the poor state of basic information, no one really knows how well these efforts have fared or whether they are worth more widespread adoption.

There have been large investments in services, hospitals, manpower, and research, but there is no way to measure their payoffs or to determine whether another mix of investments might not have done the job as well or better.

The policy process responsible for the legislation, programs, and the overall system serving the mentally handicapped is also underdeveloped. Because research and development efforts are small in relation to needs, not coordinated to any large degree, and detached from the many agencies meting out services to the population, the initial or invention phase of the process is embryonic. Estimation is largely nonexistent because data are insufficient for more than crudely estimating the needs of the population. Selection remains an isolated, basically political, process, generally unsupported by factual information about the needs and demands of the population. Implementation has a few isolated bright spots; but, in the overall perspective, no one really knows what is working well and why. Evaluation is a piecemeal proposition not closely related to the prior phases of the policy process, e.g., invention, estimation, and selection. And in decisions to terminate services, as in the case of state mental hospital closures, budgetary reasons appear to have been as influential as concern over the effects on the specific afflicted populations.

MENTAL HEALTH AND MENTAL RETARDATION PROGRAMS

Previous chapters have described agencies providing services to children with any type of physical or mental handicap. Special education, public welfare, and vocational rehabilitation agencies serve all handicapped persons; Maternal and Child Health and Crippled Children's Service programs also have disease categories and coverage for both physically and mentally handicapped youth. This section discusses agencies primarily serving persons commonly said to be mentally retarded or to have a mental health disorder.

Mental Retardation

Mental retardation is a common problem in all societies. Defining the terms that describe the disorder is at best a problematic undertaking and at worst an impossible one.[1] Reacting to a variety of descriptors of mental retardation (e.g., age at onset, IQ, mental age, educability), the American Association on Mental Deficiency attempts to combine the concepts of functional proficiency and measured intelligence, which seems a reasonable enough place to begin:

> Mental retardation refers to subaverage general intellectual functioning which originates in the developmental period and is associated with impairment in adaptive behavior.[2]

Notwithstanding definitional (and other) problems, the 1970 White House Conference on Children, using estimates made by an earlier Presidential Committee,[3] stated that in 1970 there were about 2.5 million mentally retarded children in the United States under the age of 20. Of these, some 75 percent were mildly retarded (educable), 15 percent were moderately retarded (trainable), 8 percent were severely retarded (many trainable), and 2 percent were profoundly retarded (unable to care for themselves).[4] This estimate squares reasonably well with work done by Ronald W. Conley in his pioneering effort on measuring the economics of mental retardation programs. Conley considers a wide variety of data in making estimates of mental retardation, disaggregated by age,[5] which are 679,000 children aged 0–4, and 1,916,000 aged 5–19, for a total of 2,595,000 aged 0-19. It is important to note that these estimates are for the *total* young retarded population, not those identified and receiving services, a considerably smaller figure, as we shall see momentarily.

[1]The definition problem is thorny to say the least. We cannot resolve it here, but refer the interested reader to the following representative works: R. Heber, "Mental Retardation: Concept and Classification," in E. R. Trapp and Paul Himelstein (eds.), *Reading on the Exceptional Child,* Appleton-Century-Crofts, New York, 1962, pp. 69–81; American Association on Mental Deficiency, *A Manual on Terminology and Classification in Mental Retardation,* Monograph Supplement to the *American Journal of Mental Deficiency,* 1961; and E. A. Doll, "The Essentials of an Inclusive Concept of Mental Deficiency," *American Journal of Mental Deficiency,* Vol. 46, 1941, pp. 214–219.

[2]AAMD, *A Manual on Terminology.*

[3]The President's Committee on Employment of the Handicapped, *Report,* Washington, D.C., n.d. (reference to Chart 87). Another important source book is Joint Commission on Mental Health of Children, *Crisis in Child Mental Health: Challenge for the 1970s,* Harper & Row, New York, 1969.

[4]White House Conference on Children 1970, *Profiles of Children,* Government Printing Office, Washington, D.C., 1971, p. 51.

[5]A preliminary report is contained in R. W. Conley, "An Assessment of the Economic and Non-Economic Costs and Benefits of Mental Retardation Programs," in J. S. Cohen et al., *Benefit-Cost Analysis for Mental Retardation Programs: Theoretical Considerations and a Model for Application,* Institute for the Study of Mental Retardation and Related Disabilities, Ann Arbor, Michigan, 1971.

The 1970 White House Conference also estimated that among the 100,000 to 200,000 babies born each year who are mentally retarded, one-fourth of their disorders are linked to genetic abnormalities, infections of the mother during early pregnancy, birth accidents, postnatal infections, or trauma. "In the remaining cases, inadequacies in prenatal and perinatal health care, nutrition, child rearing and social and environmental opportunities are suspected as causes of retardation."[6] That is not a great deal of information with which to formulate policy, but it is representative of the current state of knowledge about the root causes of mental retardation, a subject clearly needing much more systematic attention.[7]

Budget Allocations for Mentally Retarded Persons of All Ages   In 1970, the Secretary's Committee on Mental Retardation calculated total obligations for mental retardation activities for all age groups throughout the Department of Health, Education, and Welfare.[8] Summary data presented in Table 12.4 break down the $557.7 million spent by HEW in FY 1970, and attest concisely to the grossly fragmented authority and responsibility in services for the mentally retarded. A similar picture could be shown for each of the other types of handicaps. The Social and Rehabilitation Service (SRS) led the five major segments of HEW in expenditures for FY 1970, with a total estimated for all SRS accounts of $287.9 million. Of this total, grants to states for medical assistance ($100.0 million), income maintenance ($79.2 million), and basic state vocational rehabilitation ($54.5 million) were the largest components of assistance to the mentally retarded. Income maintenance represented all of the Social Security Administration's $145.1 million share. The Office of Education added $71.4 million, the bulk of which came from funds under Title I of "Elementary and Secondary Education Act." Health Services and Mental Health Administration ranked fourth overall with a total expenditure of $31.2 million. And the National Institutes of Health added some $21.5 million, nearly half of which was for research on child health.

Those expenditures are for persons of all ages. Earlier chapters have already discussed most of the items in Table 12.4 for children, in the course of describing general types of service agencies. Several pro-

---

[6]White House Conference, *Profiles of Children.*

[7]One's expectation that research into the causes and cures for mental retardation would be likewise diffuse is borne out by examination of the pertinent programs of institutes in the National Institutes of Health.

[8]Secretary's Committee on Mental Retardation, *Mental Retardation Activities of the Department of Health, Education, and Welfare,* U.S. Department of Health, Education, and Welfare, January 1971.

Table 12.4
U.S. DEPARTMENT OF HEALTH, EDUCATION, AND WELFARE:
OBLIGATIONS FOR MENTAL RETARDATION ACTIVITIES, FY 1970 AND 1972
(In $ thousand)

Activity	1970	1972 Budget Estimate
Health Services and Mental Health Administration		
Services		
Comprehensive Health Planning and Services	525	0
Maternal and Child Health and Welfare	12,990	12,990
Total	13,515	12,990
Training		
Mental Health Research and Services	441	400
Comprehensive Health Planning and Services	50	0
Maternal and Child Health and Welfare	14,765	19,336
Total	15,256	19,736
Research		
Mental Health Research and Services	600	0
St. Elizabeths Hospital	0	0
National Health Statistics	0	0
Maternal and Child Health and Welfare	1,842	1,600
Total	2,442	1,600
Construction		
Hill-Burton	0	0
Other		
Mental Health Research and Services (abstracts)	0	0
Total, HSMHA	31,213	34,326
National Institutes of Health		
Training		
Neurology and Stroke Activities	6,171	4,676
Child Health	1,471	1,431
Total	7,642	6,107
Research		
Neurology and Stroke Activities	4,795	4,974
Child Health	9,089	11,879
Total	13,884	16,853
Total, NIH	21,526	22,960

SOURCE: Secretary's Committee on Mental Retardation, *Mental Retardation Activities of the Department of Health, Education, and Welfare,* Department of Health, Education, and Welfare, Washington, D.C., January 1971, pp. 71–75.

[a] Data not available.

[b] Includes Child Welfare Training Programs.

[c] Includes Child Welfare Research and Demonstration and Special Programs for the Aging, Title IV, Research and Demonstration.

Table 12.4—continued

Activity	1970	1972 Budget Estimate
Office of Education		
Services		
Title I, ESEA, Educationally deprived children	33,000	35,600
Title III, ESEA, Supplementary centers	3,650	4,900
Education for the Handicapped Act, Part B	9,200	10,160
Education for the Handicapped Act, Part C, Section 623	590	950
Vocational Education Act, Part B	11,500	11,500
Total	57,940	63,110
Training		
Education for the Handicapped Act, Part D	10,391	10,500
Education Professions Development Act	1,400	1,400
Total	11,791	11,900
Research		
Cooperative Research Act	76	—
Education for the Handicapped Act, Part E	1,602	1,600
Total	1,678	1,600
Other		
Library Services and Construction Act	15	30
Total, Office of Education	71,424	76,640
Social Security Administration		
Income Maintenance		
Estimated Benefit Payments from Trust Funds	143,000	176,800
Trust Fund Obligations Incurred to Adjudicate Claims of Beneficiaries	2,100	2,500
Total, SSA	145,100	179,300
Social and Rehabilitation Service		
Services		
Rehabilitation Services and Facilities		
Basic State Grants	54,500	74,100
Innovation	223	0
Expansion Grants	108	144
Facility Improvement Grants	3,600	3,400
Formula Grants for the Developmentally Disabled	0	5,608
Services for the Developmentally Disabled	20,172	18,975
Total	78,603	102,227
Grants to States for Public Assistance		
Child Welfare Services	—	a
Medical Assistance	100,000	100,000
Special Programs for the Aging		
Foster Grandparents Program	5,800	5,000
Title III Community Grant Programs	100	50
Total	5,900	5,050
Total (services)	184,503	207,277

Table 12.4—continued

Activity	1970	1972 Budget Estimate
Social and Rehabilitation Service		
Training		
Rehabilitation Services and Facilities		
Vocational Rehabilitation	1,282	290
Services for the Developmentally Disabled	3,359	4,600
Health Services Activities	113	0
Total	4,754	4,890
Research and Training		
Research and Training Centers[b]	902	950
Total (training)	5,656	5,840
Research		
Research and Training		
Research and Demonstrations[c]	1,216	695
Social and Rehabilitation Activities Overseas (special foreign currency program)	300	400
Total (research)	1,516	1,095
Construction		
Rehabilitation Services and Facilities		
Formula Grants for the Developmentally Disabled	0	5,607
Construction of University Affiliated Facilities	0	0
Construction of Community Service Facilities	16,870	0
Rehabilitation Facilities and Construction Grants	123	0
Total	16,993	5,607
Total (construction)	16,993	5,607
Income Maintenance		
Grants to States	79,200	116,700
Total, all SRS activities	287,868	336,519
Office of the Secretary		
Secretary's Committee on Mental Retardation	(111)	110
President's Committee on Mental Retardation	580	650
Total, Office of the Secretary	580	760
Total, all activities	557,711	650,505

grams have not been mentioned before, however, because they are provided through agencies primarily serving the mentally impaired. We shall cover these in this chapter.

Institutions Serving the Mentally Retarded The 1970 Annual Census of Patients in Public Institutions for Mentally Retarded indicates that while the rate of first admissions per 100,000 population is relatively stable or slightly decreasing for all age cohorts (Table 12.5), both the percentage representation and the rate per 100,000 for all those under

Table 12.5
NUMBER, PERCENT DISTRIBUTION, AND RATE PER 100,000 POPULATION OF FIRST ADMISSIONS TO PUBLIC INSTITUTIONS FOR THE MENTALLY RETARDED: UNITED STATES, 1950–1970

Year	Total	<5	5–9	10–14	15–19	20–24	25–34	35 and Over
				Number				
1950	10,960	1,743	2,337	2,557	2,022	729	780	792
1955	12,092	2,266	3,086	2,825	1,913	611	668	723
1960	13,534	2,264	3,734	3,532	2,312	507	455	730
1965	15,008	2,031	4,486	4,155	2,659	639	440	598
1970[a]	12,063	1,668	3,405	3,114	2,378[b]	422[c]	468	588
				Percent				
1950	100.0	15.9	21.3	23.3	18.5	6.7	7.1	7.2
1955	100.0	18.7	25.5	23.4	15.8	5.1	5.5	6.0
1960	100.0	16.7	27.6	26.1	17.1	3.7	3.4	5.4
1965	100.0	13.5	29.9	27.7	17.7	4.3	2.9	4.0
1970[a]	100.0	13.8	28.2	25.8	19.7	3.7	3.9	4.9
				Rate Per 100,000				
1950	7.3	10.7	17.6	22.9	19.4	6.6	3.3	1.2
1955	7.5	12.4	18.0	21.2	18.0	6.5	2.8	1.0
1960	7.6	11.1	19.9	20.8	17.8	5.0	2.0	1.0
1965	7.8	9.9	21.9	21.9	15.9	5.1	2.0	0.7
1970[a]	6.0	9.5	16.7	15.1	8.4[d]	8.4[d]	1.9	0.7

SOURCE: U.S. Department of Health, Education, and Welfare, *Public Institutions for the Mentally Retarded—Trends in Caseload, Manpower, Expenditures,* Social and Rehabilitation Service, July 1968 (updated to 1970).

[a] Data for 1970 in this table and Table 12.6 are based on 1970 Annual Census of Patients in Public Institutions for Mentally Retarded. 1970 data shown in other tables in this chapter are based on another survey. Therefore, there are minor discrepancies in the numbers.

[b] For 1970 age 15–20   [c] For 1970 age 21–24.   [d] For 1970 age 15–24.

age 19 is increasing; furthermore, it is more pronounced for those aged 5 or less (Table 12.6). As of the 1970 census, one in every twenty-five, or 99,058, of the total estimated number of mentally retarded persons aged 21 or less in the United States was resident in a public institution.[9] At a daily expenditure rate of $12.70 per resident patient,[10] the estimated annual expenditure rate is $459,233,000 for mentally retarded youth.

[9] Estimate based on linear interpolation of data shown in Table 12.6.

[10] U.S. Department of Health, Education, and Welfare, *Residents in Public Institutions for the Mentally Retarded, Current Facility Reports, July 1, 1969–June 30, 1970,* Social and Rehabilitation Service, 1971. Some small but undetermined percentage of these funds is from federal sources. In addition, some small but again undetermined percentage may also be reported in education budgets.

Table 12.6
NUMBER, PERCENT DISTRIBUTION, AND RATE PER 100,000 POPULATION OF RESIDENTS IN PUBLIC INSTITUTIONS FOR THE MENTALLY RETARDED: UNITED STATES, 1950-1970

Year	Total	<5	5-9	10-14	15-19	20-24	25-34	35 and Over
				Number				
1950	128,145	1,949	7,146	13,922	18,912	16,785	27,962	41,469
1955	143,548	3,617	11,643	17,429	19,769	15,739	27,897	47,454
1960	163,730	3,474	14,512	23,744	25,727	18,101	27,459	50,713
1965	187,305	3,933	17,457	28,797	32,419	22,370	28,741	53,588
1970[a]	187,177	7,198	21,474	29,247	36,373[b]	19,062[c]	27,727	46,096
				Percent				
1950	100.0	1.5	5.6	10.9	14.7	13.1	21.8	32.4
1955	100.0	2.5	8.1	12.1	13.8	11.0	19.4	33.1
1960	100.0	2.1	8.9	14.5	15.7	11.0	16.8	31.0
1965	100.0	2.1	9.3	15.4	17.3	11.9	15.4	28.6
1970[a]	100.0	3.9	11.5	15.6	19.4	10.2	14.8	24.6
				Rate Per 100,000				
1950	85.3	11.9	53.7	124.9	181.6	151.6	118.8	64.1
1955	88.4	19.8	67.9	130.6	185.7	167.3	118.4	67.2
1960	91.9	17.1	77.2	139.8	197.9	177.1	123.6	66.2
1965	97.6	19.2	85.1	151.9	194.1	178.8	132.8	66.0
1970[a]	92.8	41.9	108.0	140.6	161.1[d]	161.1[d]	112.7	54.4

SOURCE: U.S. Department of Health, Education, and Welfare, *Public Institutions for the Mentally Retarded—Trends in Caseload, Manpower, Expenditures,* Social and Rehabilitation Service, July 1968 (updated to 1970).

[a] Data for 1970 in this table and Table 12.5 are based on 1970 Annual Census of Patients in Public Institutions for Mentally Retarded. 1970 data shown in other tables in this chapter are based on another survey. Therefore, there are minor discrepancies in the numbers.

[b] For 1970 age 15-20.   [c] For 1970 age 21-24.   [d] For 1970 age 15-24.

State mental hospitals sometimes serve the mentally retarded as well as the mentally ill, and there too the trend seems reasonably well established that in the past 20 years the percentage distribution of adults is slowly but steadily decreasing while that of children is increasing (see Table 12.7). An estimated total of 4015 mentally retarded persons aged 21 or less were served in state mental hospitals in 1970.[11] Using the average total annual measurable cost of $5055[12] per person served in 1970 leads to an estimated annual expenditure rate of at least $20,296,000 for mentally retarded youth in state mental hospitals.

Data for private institutions are sketchy. The only informational reporting requirement that routinely generates data merely notes the

[11] Estimate based on linear interpolation of data shown in Table 12.7.
[12] Conley, p. 79.

Table 12.7

NUMBER AND PERCENT DISTRIBUTION OF RESIDENT PATIENTS DIAGNOSED AS MENTALLY DEFICIENT IN STATE MENTAL HOSPITALS BY AGE: UNITED STATES, 1950–1970

Year	Total	<15	15–24	25–34	35–44	45–54	55–64	65+
				Number				
1950	48,226	582	4,636	9,337	10,520	10,362	7,639	5,150
1955	47,620	481	3,526	8,584	10,599	10,601	7,997	5,833
1960	43,486	424	3,271	6,782	9,627	9,892	7,907	5,583
1965	35,727	748	4,101	5,526	8,210	8,942	7,360	4,840
1970	30,327	1,147	4,097	4,168	5,038	6,249	5,405	4,223
				Percent				
1950	100.0	1.2	9.6	19.4	21.8	21.5	15.8	10.7
1955	100.0	1.0	7.4	18.0	22.3	22.3	16.8	12.2
1960	100.0	1.0	7.5	15.6	22.1	22.7	18.2	12.8
1965	100.0	1.9	10.3	13.9	20.7	22.5	18.5	12.2
1970	100.0	3.8	13.5	13.8	16.6	20.6	17.8	13.9

SOURCE: Unpublished data from National Institute of Mental Health, HSMHA, reproduced in Secretary's Committee on Mental Retardation, *Mental Retardation Activities of the Department of Health, Education, and Welfare,* U.S. Department of Health, Education, and Welfare, Washington, D.C., January 1971, p. 38.

number of facilities in each state and crudely identifies the types of programs available. In 1969 there were 708 private facilities offering services for the mentally retarded throughout the United States; California (250), Ohio (43), and Pennsylvania (43) accounted for nearly half of the total. Four states reported no private institutions at all: Alaska, Arkansas, Idaho, and Wyoming.[13]

State Cost Factors for the Institutionalized Mentally Retarded On a national average, daily maintenance expenditures for the mentally retarded in public institutions nearly tripled from 1960 to 1969.[14] While growth rates have climbed steadily upward in all states, not all state growth rates have conformed to the average. First consider the five states with the highest average daily rates in 1970: California ($16.38), Georgia ($15.92), Colorado ($15.73), Pennsylvania ($15.38), and Kansas ($15.26). (Alaska is a special case and also the most expensive at $35.62; we disregard it for the purposes of calculating trends

[13]Unpublished data from the National Center for Health Statistics' 1969 survey of the Master Facility Inventory.

[14]Kenneth McCaffree, "The Cost of Mental Health Care Under Changing Treatment Methods," in H. Schulberg et al. (eds), *Program Evaluation in the Health Fields,* Behavioral Publications, New York, 1969, pp. 452–457, provides a brief, well-rounded discussion of costing problems.

and rates of change.) The 1960 group average for these five states was $5.01 per day per patient; this figure was $15.73 in 1970, an increase of 214 percent. On the other hand, consider the five states having the lowest daily rates in 1970: Mississippi ($4.61), South Dakota ($6.28), Alabama ($6.37), Idaho ($6.53), and North Dakota ($6.62). The 1960 group average for these states was $2.61 per day per patient; this figure was $6.08 in 1970, an increase of 133 percent.[15] Costing services to mentally retarded children is difficult; it is next to impossible to figure out what society will eventually have to pay because of *not* providing services.

MCHS Mental Retardation Clinics[16]   The Maternal and Child Health and Crippled Children's Service programs support in whole or part some 154 mental retardation clinics in which some 60,800 children received diagnostic and counseling services during FY 1971. Male patients out-numbered females at a consistent rate of 3 to 2 in all age categories; the 5-to-9-year-old cohort was the most frequently served (45.1 percent of the total); and the median age of those receiving services was 7.2 years.[17]

New patients are referred to the clinics most frequently by private physicians (31.7 percent of the total); schools are second (18.4 percent); hospitals are third (16.5 percent); and public health services are fourth (9.0 percent).

Of the 27,988 new referred patients in 1971, only 49.1 percent were classified as mentally retarded—a clear demonstration of how difficult it is to determine what mental retardation means in operational terms and then arrange for appropriate services. The problem is even worse for those who were classified by etiology.[18] For 32.2 percent of

[15]U.S. Department of Health, Education, and Welfare, *Public Institutions for the Mentally Retarded—Trends in Caseload, Manpower, Expenditures,* Social and Rehabilitation Service, July 1968 (updated to 1970).

[16]Most of the statistical data in this section are taken from Maternal and Child Health Service, U.S. Department of Health, Education, and Welfare, *Mental Retardation Clinic Services, 1971,* Washington, D.C., 1972.

[17]Expenditures and youth receiving these services have already been counted under the appropriate MCHS and CCS headings in the "Medical Services" chapter.

[18]The classification of mentally retarded or mentally ill is not to be taken casually. See T. Szasz, *Law, Liberty, and Psychiatry,* Macmillan, New York, 1963; O. G. Simmons, *The Mental Patient Comes Home,* John Wiley & Sons, Inc., New York, 1963; and a host of others who have been deeply concerned with the labeling problem and its various, mostly unpleasant, side effects. An excellent empirical case detailing the problems of public opinion and mental health is presented in H. J. Halpert, *Public Opinions and Attitudes Toward Mental Health,* Public Health Service Publication No. 1045, Washington, D.C., 1963.

the new patients, the diagnosis was "Uncertain cause—functional reaction alone manifest"; for an additional 16.9 percent, the diagnosis was "Unknown cause—structural reactions manifest." In all, then, retardation had unknown causes in 49.1 percent of the 79.6 percent of the patients who were classified. It appears that research is needed into possible ways of improving basic data collection on the reasons for patients' mental retardation and, in time, into the basic causes of retardation itself.

When the generic categories of causation are further broken down into the specific classifications (for details see our chapter on "Prevention"), we find that the largest group ("Uncertain cause—functional reaction alone manifest") breaks down principally into the vague and unilluminating categories of "Other," 13.13 percent, and "Cultural-familial," 8.78 percent. For the second most prevalent generic classification, "Prenatal influence," congenital causes were the most reported at a total of 9.76 percent, and Mongolism was second at 8.15 percent. The "Other" category of "Unknown cause—structural" is as nonilluminating as "Other" for "Uncertain cause—functional." In the case of "Trauma," anoxemia at birth was the most frequently reported cause at 5.76 percent.

Diagnostic difficulty is further revealed by the fact that, of the new patients referred in FY 1971, 38.9 percent were reported as having "no retardation in measured intelligence." Add reported "borderline" patients (20.5 percent), and the two subgroups together account for 59.4 percent, well over half of the total new referred patients whose level of intelligence was determined.

MENTAL HEALTH DISORDERS

Population Characteristics Since 1955, there has been a dramatic shift toward outpatient care for the emotionally disturbed and mentally ill of all ages. (See Table 12.8.) Inpatient care as a proportion of total care decreased from 77.4 percent in 1955 to 39.1 percent in 1971. Of the total care in 1955, some 48.9 percent was accounted for by state and county mental hospitals; by 1971 this had decreased to 18.1 percent. The contribution of the Community Mental Health Centers, which carried some 19.1 percent of the 1971 caseload, has also become significant.

While the trend was made possible by the development of psychotropic medications, cost considerations have certainly contributed to that trend. The total daily expense for each patient in nonfederal

Table 12.8
MENTAL ILLNESS, ALL AGES: PATIENT CARE BY TYPE OF FACILITY, 1955–1971
(In thousands and percentages)

Type of Facility	1955	1968	1969	1971
Outpatient				
Psychiatric outpatient	379	1507	1603	1668
	(22.6)	(44.7)	(43.9)	(40.1)
Community Mental Health Centers	NA	272[a]	373[a]	797[a]
	—	(8.0)	(10.3)	(19.1)
Day treatment services	NA	NA	NA	75
	—	—	—	(1.8)
Total outpatient	379	1779	1976	2540
Inpatient				
State & county mental hospitals	819	792	767	754
	(48.9)	(23.4)	(21.0)	(18.1)
Private	123	118	124	145
	(7.3)	(3.5)	(3.4)	(3.5)
General hospitals (with psychiatric service)	266	559	535	556
	(15.9)	(16.5)	(14.7)	(13.3)
Residential treatment centers	NA	NA	NA	NA
Veterans Administration	88	134	187	169
	(5.3)	(3.9)	(5.1)	(4.09)
Community mental health centers	(a)	(a)	(a)	(a)
Total inpatient	1296	1602	1613	1624
Total all facilities	1675	3381	3589	4164
	(100.0)	(100.0)	(100.0)	(100.0)

SOURCE: 1955, 1968, and 1969 data from U.S. Department of Commerce, *Statistical Abstract of the United States 1972*, p. 76. (Derived from U.S. Department of Health, Education, and Welfare, *Statistical Note 23*, Public Health Service, April 1970, and *Statistical Note 58*, Public Health Service, January 1972.)

1971 estimates from Mrs. Shirley Willner, co-author of *Statistical Note 23*, Biometry Division, NIMH, March 21, 1973 telephone conversation.

NOTE: Estimated. Includes resident patients at beginning of year or those on active rolls of outpatient clinics, plus those admitted during year.

[a] The total CMHC caseload, both in- and outpatient, is listed under the outpatient category.

psychiatric hospitals in 1950 was $2.43; in 1960 it had climbed to $4.91; and by 1970 the figure was up to $16.63.[19]

The concept of cost associated with mental illness presents some theoretical and practical difficulties beyond the province of this book. However, in a thorough consideration of these problems, Rashi

[19]U.S. Department of Commerce, *Statistical Abstract of the United States 1972*, Washington, D.C., 1972, p. 74, Table: "Hospital Expense per Patient Day: 1950–1970." Comparable rates for all hospitals in each of the three periods were as follows: 1950 = $7.98; 1960 = $16.46; and 1970 = $53.95.

Fein, in 1958, judged that the total direct and indirect costs of mental illness in the United States were in the neighborhood of $3.0 billion per year.[20] (He did not disaggregate his estimate for children and youth.)

Overview data on services for children with mental health disorders are shown in Table 12.9. The number of child inpatients increased slightly between 1966 and 1969 from 15.1 percent to 20.7 percent. Still, the majority of children served—66.3 percent of the total—are served through psychiatric outpatient facilities, while the comparable figure for the general population is 40.1 percent. The relative use of inpatient care has not declined for the 0–21 age group, particularly for state and county mental hospitals (the class of facilities where the most marked decline occurs for the total population).

Estimated total expenditures in 1970 for inpatient care of handicapped children were $267 million, assuming that the per day figure of $16.63 in nonfederal psychiatric hospitals is valid for young patients, and assuming that the average days in mental hospitals is the same for a child as it is for the average person.[21]

The growth rate in number of children receiving service from outpatient psychiatric clinics is less than the growth rate for adults. Males consistently outnumber females among those who receive services by nearly two to one.[22] Disregarding sex-linked causes of mental illness, this consistent overrepresentation should be investigated more thoroughly to determine whether sex discrimination in the identification and provision of service exists.[23]

[20]Rashi Fein, *Economics of Mental Illness,* Basic Books, New York, 1958; these numbers are not "hard," as attested to in this caveat: "The large differences between the estimates contained in this study and some of the popular estimates of the costs of mental illness certainly bear witness to the fact that one should approach published data on costs with a high degree of caution." p. 125.

[21]Unpublished data of the American Hospital Association of Chicago, reported in *Statistical Abstract of the United States 1972,* indicate a 1970 rate per 1000 population of 862 total days in mental hospitals. Thus, the 203,211,926 United States residents spent an estimated 175.2 million patient-days in mental hospitals in 1970.

[22]U.S. Department of Health, Education, and Welfare, *Outpatient Psychiatric Clinics—Annual Statistical Report Data on Patients, 1959–1965,* Public Health Service, National Institute of Mental Health.

[23]Two evaluations of institutions and current practices for the mentally ill must be noted and recommended: the first, D. L. Rosenhan, "On Being Sane in Insane Places," *Science,* Vol. 179, Jan. 19, 1973, pp. 250–258, for the graphic information it presents with respect to the classification and general powerlessness of the institutionalized mentally ill; and the second, P. H. Hoch and Joseph Zubin (eds.), *The Evaluation of Psychiatric Treatment,* Grune and Stratton, New York, 1964, for the excellent job it does of collecting into one place a variety of competent professional views on the difficult subject of psychiatric evaluation.

We attempted to ascertain current total expenditures for outpatient services for mentally disturbed youth by contacting various NIMH personnel. We were unable to locate anyone there who was able to provide or knew of good data on nonfederal expenditures. The most current data available were for 1971 for CMHC. We estimated total

Table 12.9

MENTAL ILLNESS, AGED 0-21: PATIENT CARE EPISODES BY TYPE OF FACILITY, 1966, 1968, 1969

(In thousands and percentages)

Type of Facility	1966[a]	1968[a]	1969[b]
Outpatient			
Psychiatric outpatient	399	526	477
	(84.9)	(77.0)	(66.3)
Community Mental Health Centers	NA	52[c]	80[d]
	—	(7.0)	(11.1)
Day treatment services	NA	NA	13
	—	—	(1.8)
Total outpatient	399	578	570
Inpatient			
State & county mental hospitals	27	26	54
	(5.9)	(4.0)	(7.5)
Private	8	7	11
	(1.7)	(1.0)	(1.7)
General hospitals (with psychiatric service)	28	32	53
	(6.0)	(5.0)	(7.5)
Residential treatment centers	8	26	21
	(1.7)	(4.0)	(3.4)
Veterans Administration	NA	NA	2
	—	—	(0.3)
Community Mental Health Centers	NA	(c)	8
	—	—	(1.1)
Total inpatient	71	91	149
Total all facilities	470	669	719
	(100.0)	(100.0)	(100.0)

SOURCE: 1966 data from Beatrice Rosen, Morton Kramer, Richard Redick, and Shirley Willner, *Utilization of Psychiatric Facilities by Children,* U.S. Department of Health, Education, and Welfare, NIMH, Mental Health Statistics, Series B, No. 1, 1968.

1968 data from White House Conference on Children, *Profiles of Children,* 1971, p. 105, Table 50; and the National Health Education, Committee, Inc., *What are the Facts About Mental Illness in the United States?* New York, 1971.

1969 data came from Shirley Willner in telephone conversation of March 21, 1973.

[a] Data are computed for 0-18 only.

[b] Data are for 0-21.

[c] Combines both in- and outpatient care.

[d] Outpatient only.

outpatient expenditures for mental health treatment of youth aged 0–21 to be approximately $84 million, multiplying the total 1969 youth care episodes by the average estimated cost per episode for CMHCs in 1971.

The need for better and more detailed information is supported and elaborated on by Eveoleen Rexford in these pointed comments:

> As a nation we have not been able to look honestly at the scope of the problem of emotional disturbance in children and youth nor at the size and quality of the resources available to cope with these children. We have not developed the systematic surveys, the categories of conditions, the conceptual models, nor the adequate reporting and analyzing systems to know where we are.
>
> However concerned we may be about the lacunae in our information regarding emotionally disturbed children identified by psychiatric facilities, the total situation may be far more serious. Many of the children residing in correctional institutions, welfare homes, state schools, and foster homes undoubtedly suffer from emotional and behavioral disturbances. They may be labeled dependent, neglected, delinquent, or retarded and there is no way under present circumstances to include them in a comprehensive mental health survey. Each grouping of institutions has its own nomenclature and its own programming. There are those who believe that the reform schools and correctional institutions of the country are the sites of the same neglect of mentally disturbed young individuals as the state hospitals' back wards were of adults.[24]

SOME FEDERAL PROGRAMS FOR MENTALLY HANDICAPPED CHILDREN

Attaining reasonable services for children with a mental health disorder or mental retardation depends delicately on knowing the size and composition of the afflicted populations and then providing appropriate services, including research, diagnosis, counseling, treatment, and other assistance. This admirable objective is hampered by sketchy demographic and expenditure information and by the multiplicity of existing programs.[25] We concentrate here on the larger and more important of those programs.

The National Institute of Mental Health NIMH is responsible for seven programs that bear directly on handicapped children and

---

[24]Eveoleen Rexford, as quoted in Joint Commission on Mental Health of Children, *Crisis in Child Mental Health*, pp. 257–258.

[25]Secretary's Committee on Mental Retardation, *Mental Retardation Financial Assistance Programs*, U.S. Department of Health, Education, and Welfare, July 1971, lists no less than 54 separate programs run by a variety of agencies having some relevance to mentally retarded individuals.

youth: (1) Community Mental Health Centers, (2) Mental Health Research, (3) Hospital Improvement Grants, (4) Fellowships, (5) Training Grants, (6) St. Elizabeths Hospital, and (7) Scientific Communication and Public Education.

Community Mental Health Centers: The last 20 years have seen a trend to shift the locus of service delivery from residential institutions to the clients' communities.[26] Congress gave a major impetus to that trend when it made NIMH a prime executor of provisions of the "Mental Retardation Facilities and Community Mental Health Centers Construction Act,"[27] whose multiple objectives are all aimed at creating a network of local centers for the distribution of mental health services. The Act provides for resources (1) to establish the initial operation of Community Mental Health Centers through a flexible grant mechanism to meet a portion of the costs of professional and technical personnel, (2) to provide a share of construction funds (one-third to two-thirds of costs, and more if the site is located in a designated poverty area), and (3) to generally improve the organization and allocation of mental health services at the local level. Each of the centers created under this Act provides limited inpatient care, outpatient care, 24-hour emergency service, partial hospitalization, consultation, and some education. The guidelines under which NIMH is assisting states also stipulate that "centers are encouraged to develop rehabilitation services, training activities, and research and evaluation programs."[28] To accomplish these considerable objectives, a total of $478.9 million was expended for the program between its inception in 1965 and 1971 to develop some 452 centers, of which 300 or so were operational in whole or in part at the end of 1971.[29]

[26]The trend is documented earlier in this section. Reasons often cited for this shift in service emphasis include the need to provide an alternative to hospitalization, the need to provide services to low income groups, and the need to integrate forms of care at the local level; see H. G. Whittington, *Psychiatry in the American Community,* International Universities Press, New York, 1966, for the historical viewpoint and a setting of the context.

General literature, reporting on selected aspects of the trend, includes A. R. Foley et al., *The Community Mental Health Center, An Analysis of Existing Models,* Joint Information Service, American Psychiatric Association, Washington, D.C., 1964; R. M. Glasscote et al., *Partial Hospitalization for the Mentally Ill: A Study of Programs,* Joint Information Service, American Psychiatric Association, Washington, D.C., 1969; and George James, "The Present Status and Future Development of Community Mental Health Research—A Critique from the Viewpoint of Community Health Agencies," *Annals of the New York Academy of Sciences,* Vol. 107, May 23, 1963.

[27]42 U.S.C. 2681–2687.

[28]U.S. Department of Health, Education, and Welfare, *Justifications of Appropriation Estimates for Committee on Appropriations, FY 1973,* Washington, D.C., 1972, Vol. I, p. 40 (hereafter cited as *Justifications of Appropriation Estimates*).

[29]Ibid.

In 1971, the program served about 797,000 people of all ages; in 1969 it was estimated that 87,800 children and youth were served, of whom 7700 were inpatients and 80,100 were outpatients.[30]

Under a separate provision of the basic Act,[31] some $10.0 million was expended in FY 1972 for a Child Mental Health Program to stimulate innovative approaches to expanding the range of services offered children through the CMHC vehicle. For that money, 32 projects were funded in FY 1973 for a variety of purposes, all of them child-oriented.[32]

HEW's Office of Child Development and NIMH have announced plans to integrate Headstart children into the facilities and services provided under the CMHCs. Emotionally disturbed, mentally retarded, and physically handicapped Headstart children (especially those in the first two categories) will be eligible.

Mental Health Research: The character and style of research programs sponsored by NIMH are as follows:

- Much of the work has been investigator-initiated.
- Research interests have been richly diverse, and research attention has been diffuse and subject to periodic realignments as areas of specific interest waxed and waned.
- Child-centered research (as contrasted to generic, human-centered, or even disease-specific research) has not been treated as a separate domain until recently, and then only as "add-ons" to ongoing efforts.

Because child mental health is not a precisely defined specialty, it is difficult to identify the child-specific portions of NIMH's total research program. Nonetheless, the budgets and previous investigations of this problem offer some guidelines.

Mental Health Research Grants[33] amounted to $82.47 million in FY 1972 and were estimated at $86.47 million in FY 1973.[34] About 1485 separate projects were funded (including 192 so-called "Small Grants" not exceeding $5000) to seek new knowledge about mental diseases, finance clinical research, and apply the results to mental health problems. NIMH's Divisions of Special Mental Health Problems and Extra-Mural Research Programs have primary responsibility for the child-specific portion of the overall research program. Four specific lines in the budget appear to pertain to children directly. The

[30]CMHC population data were provided by Ms. Shirley Willner, Biometry Division, NIMH, telephone conversation, March 21, 1973.

[31]"Community Mental Health Centers Act," Part F., Section 271.

[32]*Justifications of Appropriation Estimates,* p. 52.

[33]"Public Health Service Act," 301 (d); P.L. 78-410.

[34]*Justifications of Appropriation Estimates,* pp. 20–25.

Early Child Care segment amounted to $2 million in FY 1973, Crime and Delinquency added $4.1 million, Child Mental Health Research (not to be confused with the Child Mental Health portion of Community Mental Health Centers) had $1.5 million of the inclusive Mental Health Services line of $9.089 million earmarked, and some portion of the $2.18 million that was expended for Metropolitan Problems must have been related to children.[35]

Reporting in early 1971, the Ad Hoc Committee on Child Mental Health observed that only $10.23 million of the total $77.75 million research budget for FY 1970 could be directly attributable to "Primary Child Mental Health Support."

A contrast is evident between such figures and NIMH's statement that "Activities directed at improving the mental health of children carry the highest priority for NIMH."[36] Those research activities are directed toward the following goals:

- Coordination of children's services, particularly at the level of the community mental health facility.
- Expansion of preventive programs, also by means of the community mental health centers.
- Development of ways to reduce hospitalization of children.
- Support of mental-health-oriented day care, nursery, and kindergarten programs.
- Improvement in referral services for minorities, emphasizing the community health center's role.
- Creation of special services for the adolescent dropout and drug user.

This is a large and admirably intentioned list of goals, but one must wonder how far $10 million, or even $20 million, will go toward achieving it.

Hospital Improvement Grants: Designed to improve the care and treatment of the mentally ill in state hospitals, Mental Health Hospital Improvement Grants[37] are small, special-purpose, project-oriented grants. Projects average about $83,000 (with a maximum annual grant of $100,000 allowed over a period of ten years), and total support for the program was $6.9 million in FY 1972 and FY 1973. All states but one have these grants, responsibility for which, as of 1972, was transferred to the HEW Regional Offices.[38] Some benefit accrues to handi-

---

[35]*Catalog of Federal Domestic Assistance,* p. 170.

[36]*Justifications of Appropriation Estimates,* pp. 23–24.

[37]"Public Health Service Act," Section 303(a) (2). Section 303(a) (1) Mental Health—Hospital Staff Development Grants, is related.

[38]Of the 302 eligible state mental hospitals, some 179 had received grants.

capped children (the mentally ill and emotionally disturbed, who are inpatients for the most part), but the amount is not measurable.

Mental Health Fellowships: A manpower training component of NIMH's multifaceted role is contained in the Mental Health Fellowship program, which in FY 1972 and FY 1973 was funded at a level of $8.7 million.[39] Two basic classes of awards are made, research development for established professionals and fellowships for pre- and post-doctoral students. Of the 657 awards made in FY 1973, 35 percent, or 230, were directly related to child mental health problems, and 29 were in other specialized areas having some relationship to children and youth.[40] A rough estimate of child-related fellowships, using simple proportions, would therefore be $3.6 million.

Mental Health Training Grants: To cover a portion of the costs incurred by educational institutions in training mental health professionals in an assortment of fields and to provide stipends to those receiving the training, the Training Grants program was established and funded in FY 1973 at a level of $96.35 million.[41] Behavioral Sciences, with $24.28 million, was the major beneficiary, followed in descending order by Psychiatry ($20.473 million), Social Work ($12.678 million), Experimental and Special ($7.743 million), and Psychiatric Nursing ($7.259 million). There is no information that would enable a breakdown by child-specific expenditures; however, some preference has been given to those preparing for careers in child mental health.[42]

St. Elizabeths Hospital: Organizationally placed within NIMH in 1969, St. Elizabeths Hospital provided treatment and rehabilitation services for some 3300 inpatients and 2650 outpatients of all ages in 1972. Through its Division of Clinical and Community Service, the hospital also operates a Community Mental Health Center for the southeast sector of Washington, D.C., and conducts mental health research and training programs. The total obligation in FY 1973 was estimated at $55.86 million, of which the federal share totaled $28.27 million.[43]

St. Elizabeths does not serve many children and youth. It has a 30-bed children's ward, but the bulk of the 0–24 age group is served in

[39]*Catalog of Federal Domestic Assistance,* pp. 169–170.

[40]*Justifications of Appropriation Estimates,* pp. 36–37. The Division of Manpower and Training Programs (Behavioral Sciences Training Branch) is the responsible section of NIMH.

[41]*Catalog of Federal Domestic Assistance: Update to 1972,* pp. 169–170.

[42]*Justifications of Appropriation Estimates,* p. 32. The Division of Manpower and Training Programs and a variety of its constituent branches have responsibility.

[43]*Justifications of Appropriation Estimates,* pp. 78–95, at pp. 81, 85. The balance of operating expenses is mainly obtained from "non-federal sources," i.e., receipts and reimbursements for care.

the Community Mental Health Center. In FY 1972, a total of 696 individuals aged 0–24 were served, but St. Elizabeths has made no breakdowns by inpatients and outpatients. Nor is it known what fraction of the total is accounted for in the CMHC contribution.[44]

Scientific Communications and Public Education: Funded at $7.298 million in FY 1972 and FY 1973, this program operated both the National Clearinghouse for Mental Health Information (NCMHI) and the National Clearinghouse for Drug Abuse Information (NCDAI). The program distributes thousands of pamphlets, brochures, articles, and other items to the public on mental health activities.

Developmental Disabilities The basic Act defines a developmental disability in the following terms:

> . . . a disability attributable to mental retardation, cerebral palsy, epilepsy, or another neurological condition of an individual found by the Secretary to be closely related to mental retardation or to require treatment similar to that required for mentally retarded individuals, which disability orginates before such individual attains age eighteen, which has continued or can be expected to continue indefinitely, and which constitutes a substantial handicap to such individuals.[45]

Because the original Act, P.L. 91-517, did not identify neurological handicapping conditions other than mental retardation, cerebral palsy, and epilepsy, a number of requests to expand the number of eligible categories were made in 1971 and 1972, and the Secretary referred the matter to a study group for advice.[46] A second, related difficulty arose over the meaning of "substantial handicap," and this issue has been resolved in the following manner: "Services provided in a particular community *under this Act* will depend on the needs and existing resources of that community."[47]

The act is intended to provide services, facilities, and manpower training through three mechanisms: (1) formula grants to states—for administration, planning, services, and construction, (2) service projects—hospital improvement, rehabilitation service projects, and initial staffing, and (3) university-affiliated facilities—concentrated

[44]Data obtained in telephone conversation with Mrs. Lyles, Biometry Division, St. Elizabeths Hospital, March 22, 1973.

[45]*Guidelines for Services and Programs for Developmentally Disabled Persons,* U.S. Department of Health, Education, and Welfare, Social and Rehabilitation Services Administration, Division of Developmental Disabilities, May 1972, p. 1. The appropriate legal source for the citation is 42 U.S.C. 2691, Title IV, Section 401 (1).

[46]*Federal Register,* Vol. 37, No. 176, Sept. 9, 1972, p. 18424.

[47]*Guidelines for Services and Programs for Developmentally Disabled Persons,* p. 2.

mainly on the training of service and research personnel.[48] To accomplish these programs, some $49.54 million was expended in FY 1972.[49]

State grants[50] are designed to help coordination and planning activities at the state level to improve the flexibility and responsibleness of services delivered to the developmentally disabled. As a result, State Planning and Advisory Councils are required, as is a National Advisory Council on Services and Facilities for the Developmentally Disabled. It was estimated that 43,000 were served in FY 1972.[51] Most state grants were in the $400,000 range.[52]

Service projects, which are also matched,[53] included $10.075 million for initial staffing, $7.0 million for service projects, and $6.5 million for hospital improvements in FY 1972,[54] a year in which some 132,000 persons were served and around 10,000 received training under these projects.[55]

University affiliated facilities included 34 centers, whose "core" support was partly financed, and stressed demonstrations and interdisciplinary training for professionals to serve the developmentally disabled. The average grant was around $125,000 per year per center, and it has been estimated that 15,000 received some training in FY 1972.[56]

Developmental Disabilities is best regarded as a supplemental program aimed specifically at a difficult subset of the handicapped population that often has been slighted, or for which more detailed planning and orchestrating of available services and resources were needed at the state and local levels. An estimated 175,000 people were served in FY 1972, some considerable proportion of which consisted of children and youth aged 0–21. The total of federal and

[48]*Justifications of Appropriation Estimates,* Vol. VI, "Social and Rehabilitation Service," p. 163.

[49]Ibid.

[50]The federal share of the match for services was 75 percent in FY 1973, and up to 90 percent for areas designated as poverty areas by the Secretary. For construction projects, the range was up to two-thirds for regular grants and up to 90 percent for poverty areas.

[51]*Justifications of Appropriation Estimates,* Vol. VI, p. 122.

[52]The top three state recipients were closely followed by Ohio ($937,000), Illinois ($851,000), and Michigan ($768,000). *Justifications of Appropriation Estimates,* Vol. VI, pp. 172–173.

[53]The federal share ranges between 66 and 90 percent, but averages somewhere around 75 percent for the 670 separate projects funded in FY 1972.

[54]*Catalog of Federal Domestic Assistance,* p. 341.

[55]*Justifications of Appropriation Estimates,* Vol. VI, p. 126.

[56]Ibid., pp. 127–128. Construction authorized under this segment of the Act was being phased out in FY 1972 and accounted for only $31,000 of the $4.281 million actually expended here; no construction funds were budgeted in FY 1973.

matching resources expended was on the order of $66.0 million in FY 1972.[57]

U.S. Senator Jennings Randolph summarized changes in the developmental disabilities legislation that were made in 1975.

The basic provisions of this law are:

First, an extension of the demonstration, the training, and operational grants for university affiliated facilities and a new program of satellite centers to serve as clinical outreach facilities of the university affiliated facilities;

Second, an authorization for a special projects section, including the existing projects of national significance and projects previously funded under the "Vocational Rehabilitation Act" and the "Public Health Service Act";

Third, an authorization of a new $150,000 minimum for each State;

Fourth, a strengthening of State planning councils by clarifying and enlarging their functions and insuring sufficient stature of the council within the State;

Fifth, an increased membership of the National Advisory Council to include the heads of each of the agencies of the Department of Health, Education, and Welfare that have the responsibility of administering programs for the handicapped;

Sixth, a removal of the requirement from the previous act which required that each construction project had to be approved by the Secretary of Health, Education, and Welfare;

Seventh, a requirement of the Secretary to insure that recipients under the act shall take affirmative action to employ and advance the employment of handicapped individuals;

Eighth, the establishment of an evaluation system by the Secretary and a phased plan for each State's implementation of an evaluation system;

[57]We were unable to find hard information on how many aged 0–21 are in fact served under this program. Richard Walker, statistician in Program Evaluation, Division of Developmental Disabilities, Rehabilitation Services Administration, indicated to us that these data are "not available." (Telephone conversation, March 23, 1973.) Lacking some reliable information from those responsible for the program, we have made an arbitrary estimate that half of the 175,000 total were aged 0–21, and that half of the $66.0 million gross expenditure for both federal and matching sources benefited children too. We prefer not to make arbitrary estimates, but the current state of the data makes it necessary. For an evaluation of this program, see C. W. Larson and J. Weichers, *Survey of Operation of the Developmental Disabilities Services and Facilities Construction Act of 1970 (P.L. 91-517) in States,* Department of Health, Education, and Welfare, Rehabilitation Services Administration, October 31, 1972 (study document).

Ninth, a change in the definition of the term "developmental disability" to include autism and dyslexia if the latter results from mental retardation, cerebral palsy, epilepsy or autism;

Tenth, a requirement that the Secretary determine other handicapping conditions which should be included in the definition of a developmental disability; and

Eleventh, a new title on the rights of handicapped persons to protect such rights; mandate an individual written habilitation plan for each developmentally disabled person being served in a program funded under this act; and mandate an advocacy system in each State to protect and advocate the rights of persons with developmental disabilities.[58]

President's Committee on Mental Retardation   This important group was constituted to provide both policy and program assistance and expertise at the highest levels of the executive branch.[59] Its task is to increase public awareness, coordinate governmental units serving the mentally retarded, and evaluate operations from a strategic perspective. Perhaps the most subtle contribution of the committee is its obligation to view the whole spectrum of services provided to an identified target population—a rare and heroic undertaking, given the complex and ponderous overall system.

For the $550,000 expended on the President's Committee in FY 1972,[60] a variety of policy studies and papers were produced of the kind characterized by earlier, much-read efforts such as MR 69: *Toward Progress: The Story of a Decade,* and MR 70: *The Decisive Decade.*[61]

In 1971, The Secretary's Committee on Mental Retardation attempted to estimate and integrate all HEW expenditures for the mentally retarded.[62] While the effort was only partly successful, the perspective taken—i.e., a comprehensive one for a target population—was quite insight provoking. The coordination, fragmentation, and information deficiencies that we frequently note in the study were obvious in the Committee's 1971 report as well. The Secretary's Committee expended $110,000 in FY 1972.[63]

[58]P.L. 94-103, October 4, 1975, as reported in *Insight, the Council for Exceptional Children Government Report,* Reston, Virginia, Vol. 12, Holiday Issue, 1976.
[59]The President's Committee is authorized under Executive Order 11280, May 11, 1966.
[60]*Catalog of Federal Domestic Assistance,* p. 698, for a fuller description of activities.
[61]Both documents are available from the Government Printing Office.
[62]Secretary's Committee on Mental Retardation, *Mental Retardation Activities of the Department of Health, Education, and Welfare,* Department of Health, Education, and Welfare, Washington, D.C., January 1971.
[63]Table 12.4 above.

Chapter 13

VOCATIONAL SERVICES

OVERVIEW

All Handicapped Youth

sp̂eech Vocational rehabilitation and employment programs in the United States are designed to assist physically and mentally handicapped persons to achieve gainful employment, which may include family work, sheltered employment, or gainful homebound work. In 1970, the programs assisted over 100,000 physically or mentally handicapped youth under age 22. The Vocational Rehabilitation program provided a comprehensive set of services through state agencies for 101,000 handicapped youth whose cases were closed in 1970. Seventy-seven percent of those youth accepted for vocational rehabilitation services were rehabilitated. The total expenditure for VR and other employment services for youth in FY 1972 was an estimated $202.254 million, of which federal and state shares were 83 and 17 percent, respectively.

Table 13.1 shows a breakdown of the expenditures for the three major programs: Vocational Rehabilitation, the Committees on Employment for the Handicapped, and Employment Services. Over 75 percent of the expenditures are for the basic state-federal Vocational Rehabilitation program that provides a wide variety of services to individuals through state agencies. Data shown in Table 13.2 indicate that the most prevalent types of handicapped youth given vocational services are those with mental retardation (29,654, or 29 percent), mental health disorders (24,032, or 24 percent), orthopedic impairments or absence of extremities (16,465, or 16 percent), and other health impairments such as cardiac, respiratory, and digestive disorders (15,987, or 16 percent).

Federal involvement in civilian vocational rehabilitation began in 1920 with a 50:50 matching grant program to states to provide vocational training, counseling, prosthetics, and placement services to physically handicapped persons. Since then, the federal role has expanded markedly so that now the federal government funds 80 percent of the basic VR program; supports service to all types of physically or mentally disabled persons with a substantial handicap to employment but with "high" vocational potential; allows provision of virtually any service that a client might need; supports research, the construction of physical plants, and the training of professional personnel; and gives special attention to the needs of low-incidence population groups. Step by step, the evolution of federal assistance in VR can be interpreted as one of perceiving the unmet needs of disabled persons and providing otherwise unavailable funds to help meet those needs.

Although the federal government provides the greatest share of funding for VR programs, the state role is also a major one because states operate the VR agencies, subject to federal guidelines. And state personnel directly provide certain services such as counseling and placement, but contract with vendors for other services such as medical and occupational training.

Since available detailed statistics on the VR program were not disaggregated by client age, it was necessary for us to analyze data from individual client reports (DHEW Form RSA-300—Case Service Re-

Table 13.1
SUMMARY OF ESTIMATED TOTAL EXPENDITURES ON VOCATIONAL SERVICES TO YOUTH AGED 0-21, FY 1972

Federal Expenditures	
Federal administration of VR services	$ 1,705,000
VR research and demonstration	6,700,000
Training VR personnel	6,925,000
Construction and improvement of VR facilities (1971)	9,820,000
Grants to states for basic VR program[a]	124,943,000
Special VR service projects	13,900,000
Presidential Committee on Employment for Handicapped	152,000
Employment services	3,750,000
Total	$167,895,000
State Expenditures	
Construction and improvement of VR facilities (1971)	$ 2,264,000
Basic VR program (1971)	31,759,000
Special VR service projects	336,000
Total	$ 34,359,000
Total Federal and State Expenditures	$202,254,000

SOURCE: See section "Vocational Rehabilitation Programs," in this chapter for data sources and estimation methods.
[a] Exclusive of funds for construction and improvement of VR facilities.

Table 13.2
SUMMARY OF VOCATIONAL REHABILITATION OF YOUTH, BY DISABILITY GROUP

Handicap Group	Number Accepted for Service, FY 1970 Closures	Number Successfully Rehabilitated, FY 1970	Number Rehabilitated as Percent of Number Accepted, FY 1970 Closures	Percent of Basic Program Expenditures on Handicap Group, FY 1970	Approximate Total State and Federal Expenditures on Handicap Group, FY 1972[a]
Blind	332	249	77	1.2	$ 2,427,000
Partially sighted, legally blind	1,235	964	78	3.3	6,674,000
Other visual impairments	5,197	4,443	85	5.7	11,528,000
Deaf, unable to talk	1,145	900	79	1.5	3,034,000
Deaf, able to talk	1,267	1,081	85	1.7	3,438,000
Hard-of-hearing	1,931	1,672	87	2.2	4,450,000
Orthopedic impairments or absence of extremities	16,465	13,520	82	23.7	47,934,000
Mental health disorders	24,032	15,974	67	16.5	33,372,000
Mental retardation	29,654	22,862	77	23.7	47,934,000
Other health impairments	15,987	13,249	83	16.7	33,776,000
Speech impairments	1,608	1,378	86	1.9	3,843,000
Other impairments	2,172	1,524	70	2.0	4,045,000
Total	101,015	77,816	77	100.0[b]	$202,254,000[b]

SOURCE: See section "Vocational Rehabilitation Programs," in this chapter for data sources.

[a] Assumes total FY 1972 expenditures are distributed across handicaps in the same proportions as the FY 1970 Basic VR program expenditures were.

[b] Columns do not total exactly due to rounding.

ports). The following summary data were compiled at The Rand Corporation for age 0–21 clients and referrals whose cases were closed in FY 1970. The states had 184,068 youth referrals, of which 55 percent were accepted for service, and 77 percent of these were rehabilitated. Nearly all young clients were between 14 and 21, nearly two-thirds were male, four-fifths were white, and the median grade completed was 11. The majority of applicants were supported by their family or friends, and only 9 percent received public assistance.

The largest single source of referrals to the program was the school system; only 15 percent were not referred by someone connected with a public or private service agency. Only 5 percent of those not accepted were reportedly referred elsewhere by VR personnel. The number of successful rehabilitations per 100,000 general population aged 14–21 averaged 260 but ranged from less than 100 in some states to over 500 in others. Referrals accepted varied across states, from 46 to 70 percent, as did the success rate for those accepted, from 46 percent in one state to 90 percent in another. The relative emphasis on different types of handicaps also varied considerably across the states.

Of youth referred for VR services, only 11 percent were rejected as unqualified to receive service. The most frequent reasons for not accepting youth were that they refused service; or were unable to be located or contacted or had moved; or failed to cooperate. Of reasons that youth accepted into the program were not rehabilitated, the most prevalent were that they could not be located or contacted, or had moved.

For successful clients, only 11 percent were working during the week preceding referral. Average weekly earnings at closure were $76. The estimated annualized earnings of all rehabilitated youth rose from $20.637 million at referral to $279.851 million at closure.

The average times from referral to acceptance and closure were 6 and 21 months, respectively. Three-quarters of the rehabilitated youth received job training, one-third received physical or mental restorative services, slightly less than one-third received income assistance, and one-third received other services.

Total expenditures averaged $1300 per person served, or $1687 per person rehabilitated. The average total expenditures per youth rehabilitated varied across the states from $800 to $4500. Expenditures by type of handicap varied from $1356 per youth with a mental health disorder who was vocationally rehabilitated to $6514 per blind youth rehabilitated.

In addition to the basic VR program, there are four major vocationally oriented programs: Committees on Employment of the Handicapped that promote employment opportunities for the physically and mentally handicapped population; a Civil Service program aimed at increased federal employment of the handicapped; a vending stand program in government buildings for visually impaired persons; and the Employment Service Agencies that offer counseling and job placement referrals.

In our survey of all state vocational rehabilitation agencies, problems in the present system cited most often were insufficient funds; inadequate coordination among different agencies providing services to handicapped persons; tardiness and unpredictability of federal funding levels; and the very few attempts made to reach out and locate persons needing vocational services.

In summary, we have five principal observations on vocational services for handicapped youth:

1. The program for older youth offers a very comprehensive package of services and appears generally successful in meeting the objective of gainful employment.
2. It is not surprising, but nonetheless worth emphasizing, that many authorities feel that present service funding levels are inadequate, and that more handicapped could be successfully served if budgets were increased. Funds directly supporting professional personnel training and facilities construction also are low in relation to the need.
3. VR program data are the best available for any federally supported program serving handicapped youth. The utility of the data in understanding and comparing various state programs would be increased, however, if the statistics presented were more disaggregated. More programmatic analysis of these data might also help to explain reasons for variations in success rates and other significant differences across state agencies and to identify excellent program elements that could profitably be disseminated.
4. Inequities in the level of service to the client, in the fraction of the population served, and in the different types of handicaps treated exist across states.
5. The issue of "creaming" of referrals, in which some counselors reportedly select the least handicapped (as opposed to the severely handicapped) to increase the number of successful clients, is an important one that needs further attention and investigation.

Hearing and Vision Handicapped Youth

General Description of Services The Vocational Education program described in Chap. 10 expends an estimated $6.1 million per year for hearing and vision handicapped youth, but data are not available on program effects for these youth. Vocational or career education is not well developed even for "normal" youth, and the options available to sensorially handicapped youth through this program appear very limited.

The largest vocational service program is Vocational Rehabilitation, which provided a wide variety of different services through state agencies to over 11,000 hearing and vision impaired youth whose cases were closed in FY 1970. In a sense, the need for VR to provide services normally thought to be the earlier responsibility of other programs represents a shortcoming of those other programs. For example, nearly half the clients need and are provided medical or medically related services by VR.

The $31.6 million per year expended on VR for hearing and vision impaired youth results in an 84 percent success rate for the 52 percent of such referrals accepted, with success consisting basically of a favorable prognosis after 30 days of gainful employment. Visually impaired youth receive nearly twice the total expenditures that hearing impaired youth receive, and nearly half the expenditures for the visually impaired go for youth who either have one good eye or some other visual impairment with acuity better than $20/70$—youth who are not handicapped according to the criteria used in this book.

Across the states there is extreme variation in the number of successfully rehabilitated youth per 100,000 population aged 14 to 21. For example, the number of totally blind youth rehabilitated per 100,000 ranged from less than 0.1 to a high of 2.2. The figures for deaf youth unable to talk ranged from less than 1 to as high as 9, and for other hearing impaired youth from less than 1 to 17.

At the time of referral, only 14 percent of the rehabilitants were "gainfully employed" and over half were nonworking students; at time of closure, 86 percent were in the competitive labor market, 8 percent were homemakers, and 3 percent were employed in sheltered workshops. The average weekly earnings at closure were $84, and about one-third earned less than $64—the 1970 national minimum wage of $1.60 per hour for a 40-hour workweek—despite being in the VR program for an average of 19 months from acceptance to closure, and despite basic program expenditures of $2103 per youth rehabilitated. Expenditures per youth rehabilitated varied extremely across the states for youth with the same type of degree of handicap. They averaged, for example, $6167 for a totally blind youth, $2068 for a deaf youth unable to talk, and $1678 for a youth with some other hearing impairment. Note that 3 times as many resources are expended per totally blind youth as are expended per deaf youth who is unable to talk.

Later in this chapter we present our benefit-cost analysis of the VR program. Our main conclusion is that the program appears to offer society a handsome return on its investment regardless of the youth's *type or degree* of hearing or vision handicap. We analyzed the sensitivity of benefits and costs to variations in the data and assumptions, and even with what we consider a demanding test, using much more conservative assumptions than most previous evaluators have used, the program still appears to offer economic benefits to society and to taxpayers that exceed the costs for all eight categories of hearing and vision handicapped youth we analyzed. Add the enhanced quality of life of the youth served, and the VR program is all the more laudable.

The federal government also supports other vocational programs, such as the State Employment Service agencies which provided job information or placement services to about 11,000 hearing and vision handicapped youth in 1970 and expended about $35 per client.

Exclusive of vocational education, which was discussed in Chap. 10, we estimate that all other government expenditures on vocational services for hearing and vision handicapped youth totaled $31.6 million in FY 1972.

Need for Vocational Services The relatively higher unemployment and underemployment rates among the hearing and vision handicapped, as compared with the nonhandicapped, are thought to be due to such factors as employers' underestimation of the handicapped persons, employers' "fear of the unknown," the relatively lower educational levels of some handicapped groups, and the relatively longer on-the-job training period that may be required—but not to lower average mental ability and not to lower average physical ability (other than the ability to see or hear).[1] Although these young persons' abilities to perform in certain occupations are impaired, there is an abundance of other occupations in which they can be as productive as persons without sensory handicaps. Hence there is no physical or mental reason why they, as a group, cannot be as fully employed, as productive in the work force, and as well paid as their counterparts who have no sensory handicaps.

To set a perspective on the magnitude of this need, recall that there are about 50,000 profoundly deaf youth aged 0 to 21 in the United States, and another 440,000 hard of hearing youth who at least have frequent difficulty understanding normal speech (an average uncorrected hearing loss in the better ear in the speech frequency

---

[1] See, for example, H. Davis and S. R. Silverman (eds.), *Hearing and Deafness,* 3d ed., Holt, Rinehart and Winston, Inc., New York, 1970, Chapter 20.

range of approximately 40 dB or more, ISO). There are also about 13,000 totally blind and 180,000 partially sighted youth who are unable to read normal newsprint (an acuity with correction in the better eye of approximately 20/70, or correspondingly significant restriction of visual field). To get an order of magnitude estimate of the number of youth that would have to complete a vocational service program each year if all youth were to be served once, consider the number of hearing and vision handicapped youth that enter the potential client population each year. For example, dividing the number of youth aged 0 to 21 by 21 produces an estimate that each year about 2400 profoundly deaf, 21,000 hard of hearing, 600 totally blind, and 8600 partially sighted youth reach an age where they become part of the potential client population. That is, to keep up with the need on a continuing basis, the vocationally handicapped fraction of these approximately 33,000 hearing and vision handicapped youth must complete service each year. Of course, the distribution of ages of sensorially handicapped youth is not uniform from age 0 to 21, but in the absence of more reliable age-specific data, making that assumption allows us to make an order of magnitude approximation of the number of such youth entering the potential client population each year.

In FY 1970, VR case closures for deaf youth numbered over 100 percent of the 2400 estimate just mentioned of deaf youth annually entering the client population; case closures for "other hearing impaired" youth numbered about 10 percent of the 21,000 figure mentioned above; case closures for totally blind youth numbered about 50 percent of the 600 figure mentioned above; case closures for partially sighted youth, as we define them, numbered about 1800 (or 21 percent of the 8600 figure mentioned above); and case closures numbered over 4600 for visually impaired youth who are not visually handicapped by our definitions, such as those youth with "one good eye" or "other visual impairment."[2]

Thus, with respect to the number in need, the VR program appears to be doing quite well in serving the most severely hearing and vision handicapped youth. It also appears to be placing relatively low emphasis on service to less severely hearing *handicapped* and to less severely visually *handicapped* youth, while placing relatively high emphasis on mildly visually *impaired* youth who are outside our definition of visually *handicapped*. Several explanations are possible for this program behavior: the mildly *visually impaired* youth may be

[2]While data are not available to document what constitutes "other visual impairment," our interviews with state VR personnel in California suggest that they are strabismus ("crossed eyes"), amblyopia ("lazy eye"), and relatively mild refractive errors (less than 20/70 with correction in the better eye).

more vocationally handicapped than the less severely *hearing handi-capped* youth; the two groups may both be vocationally handi-capped, but hearing handicapped youth are not as fully identified and known to the VR agency; VR counselors may be giving severely or multiply handicapped clients labels that incorrectly indicate a mild handicap, so as to lessen stigmatization; or the often-heard charge of "creaming," or accepting easy clients for service to bolster success rates, may be true for the visually impaired youth population.

The Rehabilitation Services Administration has maintained that all of these sensorially handicapped youth are vocationally handicapped and need VR services.[3] If one defines need in very strict terms, such as current unemployment—ignoring potential need due to expected unemployment after school graduation and due to underemploy-ment[4]—then some fraction of these youth would not need voca-tional services because they could find jobs without VR or employ-ment service assistance. Service levels to meet the need clearly depend upon one's assumptions. At one extreme, all hearing and vision handicapped youth could be given full VR service in an at-tempt to prevent expected underemployment and unemployment. At the other extreme, only handicapped youth with at least, say, three months of unemployment would be given placement service, with none receiving VR services. A more moderate position would be that all profoundly deaf and totally blind youth can expect vocational difficulties and will need VR services before or just after they finish school; while less severely handicapped youth—the partially sighted and hard of hearing—would need to be screened to detect the frac-

---

[3]For example, the HEW report *Hearing and Speech: Obligations Fiscal Year 1970 to Fiscal Year 1974,* the Rehabilitation Services Administration summary of programs for the deaf, the hard of hearing, and the speech impaired, indicates that "Americans who are vocationally handicapped by varying degrees and kinds of communication disor-ders exceed 20,000,000 in number" (p. 7), while the same report indicates that the prevalence of handicapping communicative disorders affects "over 20,000,000 Ameri-cans" (p. 2).

[4]U.S. Department of Health, Education, and Welfare, *Justifications of Appropriation Estimates for Committee on Appropriations—FY 1973,* Vol. 1, p. 114, presents an esti-mate of youth who are "the under-employed and the unemployed (40% and 26% of handicapped school leavers, respectively)." Kenneth Trouern-Trend, *Blindness in the United States: Review of the Available Statistics with Estimates of the Prevalence of Blindness and Its Economic Impact,* The Travelers Research Center, Inc., Hartford, Con-necticut, November, 1968, discusses the loss of earnings due to vision handicaps. For a discussion of the underemployment problems of deaf persons, for example, see Davis and Silverman, op. cit.; and A. B. Crammatte, *Deaf Persons in Professional Employ-ment,* Charles C Thomas, Springfield, Illinois, 1968. J. E. Weinrich provides a summary of the literature on unemployment and earnings of deaf persons in "Direct Economic Costs of Deafness in the U.S.," *American Annals of the Deaf,* August 1972.

tion who are also significantly vocationally handicapped. That fraction would need full VR services, while the remainder would need placement assistance; and only if that placement assistance were insufficient would they receive full VR services. This latter moderate position incorporates two major concepts: there is a continuum of degree of need for vocational services, and the programs should be flexible enough to assess each youth's need and be able to respond with different levels and types of services as the youth's need changes over time.

While the number of youth needing VR service is a matter of judgment, it is apparent from our later benefit-cost analysis that this program has humanitarian and economic benefits that exceed the cost of the program for the average youth in each category of type and degree of sensory handicap. It is also apparent that benefits would increase if the program were expanded. There is little question that, at the least, placement assistance *may* be needed by each sensorially handicapped youth, since these youth all have a major handicap that limits their vocational options in ways that are not fully understood by potential employers.

The parents of the handicapped youth we surveyed[5] rated job training and placement services as less important than education, medical care, and sensory aids, but most of them had handicapped children who were not yet of working age. Three-quarters of the youth who had worked at all had had problems, and the majority of these felt their handicap was the major reason.

ROLES AND GOALS[6]

Initial federal involvement in vocational rehabilitation occurred in 1917 with services provided to disabled World War I veterans. Civilian disabled were first included in 1920 under the "Smith-Fess Act," which provided federal grant-in-aid programs to states for vocational

[5]See Chap. 15 for details.

[6]Historical information in this section is compiled from the following sources: U.S. Congress, Senate, Committee on Labor and Public Welfare, *Rehabilitation Act of 1972,* 9⌐ ' Cong., 2d sess., S. Report 92-1135, September 20, 1972; U.S. Department of Health, ⌐tion, and Welfare, *An Introduction to the Vocational Rehabilitation Process,* Vo-⌐l Rehabilitation Administration, Report 68-32, July 1967; U.S. Department of ⌐ducation, and Welfare, *Statistical History: Federal-State Program of Vocational* ⌐*tion, 1920–1969,* Rehabilitation Services Administration Report, June 1970; ⌐ment of Health, Education, and Welfare, *Caseload Statistics: State Voca-* ⌐*litation Agencies: 1971,* Social and Rehabilitation Service, DHEW Publica-⌐72-25401, December 1971; and U.S. Department of Health, Education, ⌐*te Vocational Rehabilitation Agency: Program Data, FY 1971,* Social ⌐Service, DHEW Publication No. (SRS) 72-25016, March 1972.

training, counseling, prosthetics, and placement services for physically handicapped persons. States received funds according to population on a 50:50 matching basis. Preferential employment opportunities were given to blind persons in 1936 when the "Randolph-Sheppard Act" permitted licensing of vending stands to them in federal buildings or federally sponsored buildings.

The federal role increased significantly in 1943: (1) to include persons who were mentally ill or mentally retarded; (2) to accept separate state agencies for the visually handicapped into the program; and (3) to provide "any services necessary to render a disabled individual fit to engage in a remunerative occupation."[7] Under (3), the most significant new provisions included were medical, surgical, and other physical restoration services.

In 1954,[8] the federal role was again expanded. Besides helping states pay for VR services to disabled persons, the federal government would help train service personnel, alter or expand rehabilitation facilities and workshops, and extend rehabilitation knowledge through research and demonstration grants. The financing provisions were also modified so that both the state's population and its per capita income were considered in the allocation formula. The federal share varied from 50 to 70 percent and averaged about 60 percent of the total of federal plus state expenditures. Federal funding of up to 75 percent was made available to encourage state program improvement and extension to disability groups and geographic locales not being adequately served.

The "Vocational Rehabilitation Act Amendments of 1965" increased the federal share of funding to 75 percent; allowed a person to receive services for a short time (up to 18 months in some cases) while his employment potential was evaluated; prohibited states from using economic-need tests in deciding whether to give diagnostic, counseling, and placement services; provided funds for constructing *new* facilities and workshops; and extended from 2 to 4 years the length of time a person could receive professional training assistance.

In 1967, provision was made for a National Center for Deaf-Blind Youth and Adults; and services were extended to migratory agricultural workers. Services were expanded to include follow-up after placement, and families of disabled persons could be served under the 1968 Amendments.[9] In addition, the federal share of funding increased to 80 percent in 1968. A major amendment passed, but has never been funded, that allows for vocational evaluation and work

[7]P.L. 78-113, *1943 Amendments to Social Security Act of 1935.*
[8]P.L. 83-565, *1954 Amendments to Social Security Act of 1935.*
[9]P.L. 90-341, *1968 Amendments to Vocational Rehabilitation Act.*

adjustment services to persons who are disadvantaged (but not necessarily physically or mentally disabled) "by reason of their youth or advanced age, low educational attainments, ethnic or cultural factors, prison or delinquency records, or other conditions that constitute a barrier to employment."[10]

The "Rehabilitation Act of 1973"[11] replaced the "Vocational Rehabilitation Act" (29 U.S.C. 31 et seq.). The new act will revise the VR program, but will not radically change its basic aspects. The basic program will still provide grants to states, with guidelines, for provision of a wide variety of services to physically and mentally handicapped persons so that they may prepare for and engage in gainful employment. Emphasis is to be placed on serving first those persons with the most severe handicaps.[12]

A major provision of the proposed "Rehabilitation Act of 1972,"[13] which would have substantially enlarged program goals by removing the restriction that the rehabilitation be strictly vocationally oriented, was not adopted. Under the "Rehabilitation Act of 1973," however, a study is to be conducted to develop methods of serving persons for whom a vocational goal is not feasible.

The Act also provides for one-year advanced funding; research, including several specified projects; grants for special projects and demonstrations that hold promise of expanding or otherwise improving rehabilitation services to the handicapped, including people with spinal injuries, older blind people, the deaf, migratory agricultural workers, and seasonal farm workers. The Act also provides for a National Center for Deaf-Blind Youths and Adults; grants for construction of rehabilitation facilities; mortgage insurance for rehabilitation facilities; and funds for personnel training. The Act calls for the preparation of a long-range projection for the provision of comprehensive services to the handicapped (this provision is not limited to VR programs).

The Office of the Secretary of HEW is given responsibility for planning, evaluation, and coordination of all programs providing services

[10]Section 15 of *Vocational Rehabilitation Act,* as amended.

[11]P.L. 93-112.

[12]As specified in the Act, the term "severe handicap" means a disability that requires multiple services over an extended period of time and results from amputation, blindness, cancer, cerebral palsy, cystic fibrosis, deafness, heart disease, hemiplegia, mental retardation, mental illness, multiple sclerosis, muscular dystrophy, neurological disorders (including stroke and epilepsy), paraplegia, quadriplegia and other spinal cord conditions, renal failure, respiratory or pulmonary dysfunction, and any other disability specified by the Secretary in regulations he shall prescribe.

[13]U.S. Senate Report 92-1135.

to the handicapped, and for providing a central clearinghouse for information and resource availability (resulting in the creation of a national Office for Handicapped Individuals). The Act also establishes a federal Interagency Committee on Handicapped Employees and an Architectural and Transportation Barriers Compliance Board, and forbids discrimination against the handicapped in work done under federal grants and contracts.

The present role of the federal government is dominant. It funds 80 percent of the basic VR programs; supports employment service to all types of physically or mentally disabled persons with a substantial handicap but with "high" vocational potential; allows provision of virtually any service that a client might need; supports research, the construction of physical plants, and the training of professional personnel; and gives special attention to the needs of low-incidence population groups such as the deaf-blind. Over time, federal assistance in VR has been a step-by-step progression in perceiving the unmet needs of disabled persons and providing otherwise unavailable funds to help meet those needs.

States also play a major role, however, because they operate and directly provide VR services. They contribute up to 20 percent of all funds expended and operate within broad guidelines set up by the Federal Rehabilitation Services Administration.[14] The state rehabilitation agencies tailor their programs within the guidelines to suit local situations. While state personnel directly provide certain services to individuals, such as diagnostic evaluation, counseling, rehabilitation planning, and placement, private vendors under state contract often perform other services, such as medical/surgical treatment, physical restorative and vocational training.

The State-Federal Vocational Rehabilitation Program is "designed to return physically and/or mentally handicapped persons to gainful employment and meaningful lives. . . . The (FY 1973) goal is to serve 1,195,000 disabled individuals, of which 253,000 will be public assistance recipients. This 253,000 represents approximately 85 percent of the disabled public assistance recipients who could benefit from rehabilitation services under the present state of the art. . . . An estimated 326,000 individuals will be rehabilitated into gainful employment, of which 66,000 will be public assistance recipients."[15]

The program is strictly vocational, and physically or mentally

[14]For rules and regulations, see the *Federal Register: Vocational Rehabilitation Programs and Activities,* Vol. 34, No. 200, October 1969.

[15]U.S. Department of Health, Education, and Welfare, *Justifications of Appropriation Estimates for Committee on Appropriations—FY 1973,* Vol. VI (hereafter cited as *Justifications of Appropriation Estimates*).

handicapped persons may be provided "any goods and services necessary to render [them] fit to engage in a gainful occupation. . . . The handicapped person served, however, must have a "substantial handicap to employment, which is of such a nature that vocational rehabilitation services may reasonably be expected to render him fit to engage in a gainful occupation, including a gainful occupation that is more consistent with his abilities and capabilities."[16] That is, he must need the services and have reasonable potential to benefit from them. He may also be served to evaluate his rehabilitation potential. The term gainful occupation is interpreted broadly to include "employment in the competitive labor market; practice of a profession; farm or family work . . . ; sheltered employment; and home industries or other gainful homebound work."[17]

Other objectives of federal rehabilitation programs in the states include increasing the knowledge of rehabilitation techniques and their application, and increasing the supply of manpower and facilities for serving the disabled.

As far as we could determine during our interviews, the objectives used in practice are consistent with the officially stated objectives. Several people indicated, however, that rehabilitation counselors and state administrators tend to try to maximize the number of successful rehabilitations. This tendency, known as "creaming," supposedly emphasizes the acceptance and service of less severely vocationally handicapped persons and persons needing the least costly services. It also supposedly emphasizes selection of occupations in which training and placement is relatively easy. Examples of increasing the number of reported successes at low cost would be to provide a pair of eyeglasses or a hernia operation to an employed applicant and then send him back to his current job. On the whole, however, VR objectives are clearly stated and seem to be well understood and adhered to in the states.

The federal role in rehabilitation is best characterized in terms of our Controllership model because individual states are responsible for providing rehabilitation services under strong federal guidelines and primarily with federal funds.

The federal functions of providing research and development resources, "seed money," demonstrations, and data standardization and collection are all reasonably well developed. Twenty Special Centers and 16 Regional Research Institutes are currently fulfilling the

16*Federal Register,* October 1969.
17*Federal Register,* October 1969.

R&D and demonstration functions in ways noted later in this chapter. And we were most favorably impressed by the quality and quantity of VR data that the federal government collected from all the states; of all the programs we considered, the VR data are the best available in allowing comprehensive program evaluations. These data allow some additional measure of control over all rehabilitation programs. The control mechanism has been indirectly stressed through the Form RSA-300 data collection procedures; comprehensive program evaluations using these data are a rather underdeveloped but potentially important phenomenon.

The rationales most routinely used to explain the federal rehabilitation role are the provision of otherwise unavailable resources, the needed stimulation of new devices and rehabilitation techniques, and the need for a balance wheel redressing fiscal inequities among the states in their ability to provide services.

VOCATIONAL REHABILITATION PROGRAM

Characteristics of the State-Federal Program[18]

Youth Caseload, FY 1970 Closures Of a total of 184,068 persons aged 0–21 who were referred or applied for VR services in FY 1970, 101,015 (55 percent) were accepted, and of these 77,816 (77 percent) were successfully rehabilitated.[19]

Table 13.3 shows caseloads and success rates by state. Note the considerable variation across states in the number of successful rehabilitations per 100,000 population aged 14–21, the relevant age range of youth in the VR program. For example, the national average is 260 per 100,000, but Oregon and California successfully serve less than

[18]Data presented on persons under age 22 have been computed at The Rand Corporation from FY 1970 "Case Service Reports," DHEW Form RSA-300, submitted by states on each individual applicant at the time of case closure, and computed from a 1972 Rand Corporation Survey of state VR Agencies. Population data are from the 1970 U.S. Census of Population. Data on VR clients of all ages are drawn from the following U.S. Department of Health, Education, and Welfare publications: *Caseload Statistics—State VR Agencies—1971; Justifications of Appropriation Estimates; State Vocational Rehabilitation Agency Program Data—FY 1971; Statistical History—Federal-State Program of Vocational Rehabilitation, 1920–1969;* and several issues of *Statistical Notes,* Rehabilitation Services Administration publication series.

[19]That is, both the client and employer gave a favorable employment prognosis after a month on the job. Data describe FY 1970 case closures only. Thus, data such as expenditures for active cases not closed during that year are excluded; however, data on expenditures for the FY 1970 closures include expenditures incurred in previous years if the case was open prior to FY 1970.

Table 13.3
VOCATIONAL REHABILITATION YOUTH CASELOAD BY STATE, FY 1970 CLOSURES

State	Youth Aged 0–21			Number Rehabilitated per 100,000 Population Aged 14–21	Rehabilitated as Percent of all Ages Rehabilitated	Accepted as Percent of Referred	Rehabilitated as Percent of Accepted
	Referred	Accepted	Rehabilitated				
U.S. Total	184,068	101,015	77,816	260	29.5	55	77
Alabama	3,048	2,024	1,487	278	24	66	73
Alaska	371	200	105	216	29	54	53
Arizona	1,334	624	461	170	30	47	74
Arkansas	1,230	817	547	193	10	66	67
California	10,775	5,007	2,745	94	19	46	55
Colorado	2,231	1,391	1,007	286	35	62	72
Connecticut	1,976	1,377	1,079	260	41	70	78
Delaware	434	252	165	205	23	58	65
D.C.	2,359	1,210	917	825	28	51	76
Florida	9,800	4,506	3,239	355	27	46	72
Georgia	6,531	3,770	2,902	408	26	58	77
Hawaii	707	425	238	194	37	60	56
Idaho	660	342	285	252	40	52	83
Illinois	8,479	4,622	4,116	262	34	55	89
Indiana	3,397	1,764	1,591	204	60	52	90
Iowa	4,184	2,442	1,937	462	47	58	79
Kansas	1,202	777	510	148	35	65	66
Kentucky	4,045	2,408	1,992	404	23	60	83
Louisiana	4,286	2,765	2,162	364	42	65	78
Maine	712	333	247	169	36	47	74
Maryland	5,142	3,067	2,404	426	31	60	78

Massachusetts	3,825	2,070	1,630	200	39	54	79
Michigan	6,577	4,568	3,296	243	40	69	72
Minnesota	3,638	1,716	1,498	260	33	47	87
Mississippi	2,362	1,078	847	334	26	46	79
Missouri	7,025	3,248	2,473	369	38	46	76
Montana	701	375	315	292	35	53	84
Nebraska	1,349	842	652	292	46	62	77
Nevada	507	249	114	176	21	49	46
New Hampshire	386	209	143	134	33	54	68
New Jersey[a]						
New Mexico	1,041	520	303	185	38	50	58
New York	8,843	5,349	3,830	156	36	60	72
North Carolina	7,328	3,359	3,006	363	27	46	89
North Dakota	651	422	371	367	21	65	88
Ohio	7,508	4,002	3,115	197	38	53	78
Oklahoma	4,479	2,534	1,994	524	31	57	79
Oregon	1,060	622	291	93	15	59	47
Pennsylvania	15,346	7,758	5,835	351	31	51	75
Rhode Island	1,381	828	704	494	37	60	85
South Carolina	4,611	2,574	2,269	513	26	56	88
South Dakota	716	396	338	315	52	55	85
Tennessee	3,545	2,037	1,752	296	12	57	86
Texas	7,548	4,689	3,616	209	26	62	77
Utah	1,535	966	790	436	40	63	82
Vermont	332	187	134	193	28	56	72
Virginia	6,884	3,846	3,126	435	33	56	81
Washington	2,905	1,437	1,008	193	39	49	70
West Virginia	2,699	1,368	1,118	423	18	51	82
Wisconsin	5,681	3,338	2,897	434	32	59	88
Wyoming	418	232	158	311	32	56	68

[a] Data not available.

100 youth per 100,000, whereas Oklahoma and South Carolina successfully serve over 500 per 100,000. Also note that the acceptance rate varies by state from 46 percent in several states to 70 percent in Connecticut, and the success rate per youth accepted varies across states from 46 percent in Nevada to 90 percent in Indiana. Various hypotheses can be formulated to explain these differences, and testing of such hypotheses in subsequent research should yield important policy implications.

The emphasis on youth in the state programs ranges from 10 percent of rehabilitations of all ages in the 0–21 age group in Arkansas to 60 percent in Indiana. Of course, these numbers must be considered with the knowledge that some states might be serving more difficult cases on the average than others; but despite statistical difficulties, the data indicate significant differences in the programs across states. And the differences cannot all be attributed to statistical fluctuation. They suggest differences in program effectiveness as well as geographic inequity across states in the fraction of handicapped youth served.

Our analysis indicates that national summary data should be presented in enough detail by type and severity of handicapped client so that a clearer picture of each state program's successes is available. The overall total number of successfully rehabilitated clients can be very misleading and could be improved by disaggregation. In-depth studies, beyond the scope of this project, are needed to analyze the most effective state programs and to disseminate this information to states with less effective programs. Changes in program rules and regulations are one method of attempting to correct the geographic and age inequities in the proportion of youth served.

Table 13.4 shows clients by type of handicap. Although program objectives are clearly defined, handicapping conditions are not, permitting states to exercise a great deal of judgment and making comparison across states difficult. Note that mental and physical impairments each account for about half of the youth served. Mental health disorders and mental retardation each account for about one-quarter of those accepted, while orthopedic and other health impairments each account for about one-sixth of those accepted.

Since at least two-thirds of those accepted in each handicap group are successfully rehabilitated, it appears that the states have developed fairly good methods of screening out applicants with the lowest rehabilitation potential. The applicant rejection rate is 45 percent for reasons discussed later.

Comparing the incidence of various impairments in VR clients and in the U.S. population, as estimated by the U.S. Bureau of Education for the Handicapped (BEH),[20] is interesting but difficult to interpret because neither VR nor BEH definitions of handicapping conditions are clear, and because a physical impairment (e.g., slight speech impairment) may not constitute a significant vocational impairment. BEH estimated that 53 percent of the aged 5–19 handicapped population have a mental handicap (23 percent retarded, 20 percent emotionally disturbed, and 10 percent learning disabled), whereas about 50 percent of clients aged 14–21 under VR agency auspices have a mental impairment. The tabulation below compares BEH percentages of the total youth handicapped population and VR percentages of clients served, by various impairments. These comparisons suggest that the VR agencies are placing a relatively heavy emphasis on serving visual, orthopedic, and other health impaired youth.

Handicap	BEH	VR
Visual impairments	1.0	7.2
Hard of hearing	5.0	2.1
Deaf	0.8	2.6
Speech impairments	35.1	1.8
Crippled or other health impairments	5.0	34.4

Illustrative comparisons of all youths rehabilitated in FY 1970 with rehabilitations of all ages are shown in Table 13.5. Mental health disorder, exclusive of alcoholism and drug addiction, was about the same for youths as it was for clients of all ages.

Table 13.6 shows the number of youth successfully rehabilitated per 100,000 population aged 14–21 in each state by type of handicap. Some agencies, like Montana's, place heavy emphasis on orthopedically or other health impaired youth, whereas others, such as the District of Columbia's, primarily serve the mentally handicapped.

As we stated earlier, while there are undoubtedly differences in incidence rates of various handicapped conditions by state, the differences cannot be nearly as great as the differences states report in the proportion of VR youth clients that they treat with various handicaps. For example, Indiana rehabilitates 8 youths with mental health impairment per 100,000 population in the 14–21 age range, while the District of Columbia rehabilitates 313. Arizona and California each

---

[20]Incidence levels were derived by BEH from a number of sources. See U.S. Bureau of Education for the Handicapped, *Rationale for Estimates of Handicapped Children and National Manpower Needs,* October 1971.

Table 13.4
VOCATIONAL REHABILITATION YOUTH CASELOAD BY HANDICAP GROUP, FY 1970

Handicap Group[a]	Referred		Accepted		Rehabilitated		Accepted as Percent of Referred	Rehabilitated as Percent of Accepted
	Number	Percent	Number	Percent	Number	Percent		
Blind	561	0.3	322	0.3	249	0.3	57	77
Partially sighted, legally blind	1,823	1.0	1,235	1.2	964	1.2	68	78
Other visual impairments	11,377	6.1	5,197	5.1	4,443	5.7	46	85
Deaf, unable to talk	1,553	0.8	1,145	1.1	900	1.2	74	79
Deaf, able to talk	1,938	1.1	1,267	1.3	1,081	1.4	64	85
Hard of hearing	4,207	2.3	1,931	1.9	1,672	2.1	46	87
Orthopedic impairments or absence of extremities	30,358	16.5	16,465	16.3	13,520	17.4	54	82
Mental health disorders	45,641	24.7	24,032	23.7	15,974	20.5	53	67
Mental retardation	47,141	25.6	29,654	29.4	22,862	29.4	63	77
Other health impairments	31,492	17.1	15,987	15.8	13,249	17.0	51	83
Speech impairments	2,913	1.6	1,608	1.6	1,378	1.8	55	86
Other impairments	5,064	2.8	2,172	2.2	1,524	2.0	43	70
Total	184,068	100.0	101,015	100.0	77,816	100.0	55	77

a Definitions of handicaps given in the U.S. Department of Health, Education, and Welfare, "Statistical Reporting Procedures," *Rehabilitation Services Administration Manual*, Ch. 13, are grouped here as follows:

Blind is totally blind, no light perception (code 10).

Partially sighted is legally but not totally blind (code 11).

Other visual impairments are visual defects but not within the definition of legal blindness (codes 12, 13, 14).

Deafness, unable to talk (code 20); deafness, able to talk (code 21), and other hearing impairments (code 22) are not further defined in the RSA reporting instructions to the states.

Orthopedic impairments or absence of extremities are orthopedic deformities or functional impairments, and absence or amputation of extremities (codes 30 to 39 and 40 to 44).

Mental illness is psychotic disorders (code 50), psychoneurotic disorders (code 51) and other mental disorders (code 52).

Mental retardation is subjectively and lengthily defined as basically an IQ below 85 on an individualized test plus the presence of maladaptive behavior associated with subnormal intellectual functioning.

Other health impairments include impairments related to neoplasms, allergic, endocrine system, metabolic and nutritional diseases, diseases of blood and blood-forming organs, and nervous system, cardiac, circulatory, respiratory, digestive or genito-urinary disorders (codes 60 to 67).

Speech impairments include cleft palate and harelip, speech imperfections, stammering and stuttering, laryngectomies, aphasia, and other speech impairments (code 68).

Other impairments as used here mean anything not classified in above codes plus alcoholism (code 520) and drug addiction (code 521).

Table 13.5

Handicap	Percent of VR Rehabilitations by Age	
	Age 0–21	*All Ages*
Visual impairments	7.2	8.8
Hearing impairments	4.7	5.6
Orthopedic impairments	17.4	21.5
Other health impairments	17.0	21.8
Mental retardation	29.4	11.8

rehabilitate 14 orthopedically impaired youth per 100,000, while Oklahoma succeeds with 154. Taking all handicaps as a group, Oregon and California rehabilitate 93 youth per 100,000, while the District of Columbia rehabilitates 825.

According to the 1970 U.S. Census of Population, approximately 4 million youth reach age 14 each year. Applying the BEH estimates of handicap incidence rates in the population aged 5–19 means that approximately 400,000 additional handicapped youth enter the eligible age range for VR services annually. It is the vocationally impaired fraction of 400,000 that the VR program should serve if it is to fill the need on a continuing basis. Our analysis of client data reported to the federal government indicates that the state VR agencies in 1970 had 46 percent of 400,000 referred to them, accepted about 25 percent (101,015) of that number, and successfully rehabilitated 77,816. Since we have no reliable estimate of the total youthful handicapped who are vocationally impaired, we cannot reliably estimate the unmet need. As we discuss later, however, the greatest proportion of those not accepted for service are not rejected for lack of a physical, mental, or vocational handicap, but for other reasons. Thus, it is reasonable to assume that significantly more than 25 percent of handicapped youth can benefit from vocational services.

Source of Referrals Nearly all FY 1970 case closures reported the source of the client referral. Table 13.7 shows that the largest single source of referrals is the school system, which accounts for about 40 percent of the total. The health system refers only a small proportion—less than 15 percent. Also note that only about 15 percent of the youth were self-referred or came because of referral by some individual who was not connected with the public or private system serving the handicapped.

Table 13.6
SUCCESSFULLY REHABILITATED YOUTH PER 100,000 POPULATION: VARIOUS HANDICAP GROUPS BY STATE, FY 1970

State[a]	Blind	Partially sighted, legally blind	Other Visual impairments	Deaf, Unable to Talk	Deaf, Able to Talk	Hard of Hearing	Orthopedic Impairments	Mental Health	Mental Retardation	Other Health Impairments	Speech	Other Impairments	Total All Handicaps
U.S. totals Number in this handicap group	249	964	4,443	900	1,081	1,672	13,520	15,974	22,862	13,249	1,378	1,524	77,816
Percent in this handicap group	0.3	1.2	5.7	1.2	1.4	2.1	17.4	20.5	29.4	17.0	1.8	2.0	100.0
Rate per 100,000 population age 14-21	1	3	15	3	4	5	45	53	75	44	5	5	260
Alabama	0.7	4	16	2	2	5	52	39	87	57	6	4	216
Alaska	0.0	6	18	2	8	6	28	47	66	23	2	8	278
Arizona	0.7	2	2	3	3	1	14	54	75	12	1	3	170
Arkansas	0.7	4	6	3	2	7	42	32	38	50	3	6	193
California	0.9	2	3	3	3	1	14	26	27	11	1	3	93
Colorado	1.1	4	13	3	5	3	62	66	89	28	3	8	286
Connecticut	1.4	8	3	1	3	2	21	129	68	14	3	8	260
Delaware	0.0	5	12	1	3	5	31	63	32	40	6	4	205
D.C.	0.9	6	33	5	5	6	41	313	247	119	7	41	825
Florida	0.3	3	16	3	3	6	40	95	118	58	6	7	355

[a] State figures are rate per 100,000 population aged 14-21.

485

Table 13.6—continued

State[a]	Blind	Partially sighted, legally blind	Other Visual impairments	Deaf, Unable to Talk	Deaf, Able to Talk	Hard of Hearing	Ortho-pedic Impairments	Mental Health	Mental Retardation	Other Health Impairments	Speech	Other Impairments	Total All Handicaps
Georgia	0.8	4	21	2	3	4	51	74	152	82	5	6	408
Hawaii	0.8	3	3	4	2	4	20	37	60	52	2	5	194
Idaho	0.0	2	17	4	7	12	86	11	36	73	2	4	252
Illinois	0.8	3	15	4	6	7	43	68	63	46	4	2	262
Indiana	0.3	2	21	4	4	6	69	8	32	46	8	1	204
Iowa	0.4	3	25	7	7	12	92	114	106	79	10	6	462
Kansas	1.7	2	4	1	4	3	46	23	34	17	3	4	148
Kentucky	1.4	2	22	3	4	9	67	87	95	71	6	28	404
Louisiana	0.4	5	38	1	2	17	120	34	73	63	8	7	364
Maine	0.0	4	10	6	4	0	35	37	42	24	1	3	169
Maryland	2.0	4	23	4	6	9	38	106	137	75	8	11	426
Massachusetts	0.0	4	11	2	5	4	41	34	56	38	2	2	200
Michigan	1.4	3	16	3	8	7	54	23	77	39	7	4	243
Minnesota	1.0	2	3	1	2	6	49	59	89	42	4	2	260
Mississippi	0.8	3	14	2	3	5	48	17	88	44	3	1	334
Missouri	0.4	3	22	5	4	10	61	50	158	41	3	7	369
Montana	0.9	2	27	2	10	11	99	19	43	58	8	8	292
Nebraska	0.4	4	16	0	6	5	50	74	72	39	5	6	292

Nevada	0.0	0	6	3	3	5	18	56	51	29	2	3	176
New Hampshire	0.0	8	6	0	1	2	25	25	44	17	3	1	134
New Jersey[b]													
New Mexico	1.2	5	4	4	6	2	45	22	68	23	2	3	185
New York	2.2	2	6	5	4	4	30	23	44	31	2	4	156
North Carolina	0.6	5	24	5	3	4	40	53	150	66	7	4	363
North Dakota	1.0	3	18	3	3	7	105	79	69	54	13	13	367
Ohio	0.6	4	13	4	6	4	37	33	51	33	5	5	197
Oklahoma	0.8	3	30	3	4	9	154	110	77	108	11	11	524
Oregon	0.6	3	4	1	2	1	12	29	26	10	1	2	93
Pennsylvania	0.2	3	32	2	2	13	53	72	79	83	9	2	351
Rhode Island	1.4	4	30	5	5	11	55	197	79	76	14	18	494
South Carolina	0.0	2	18	1	5	5	58	100	215	93	7	9	513
South Dakota	0.9	3	27	5	6	8	97	29	44	76	15	3	315
Tennessee	0.2	5	15	4	2	7	59	50	92	50	7	1	296
Texas	0.5	3	17	3	2	4	27	35	89	25	3	2	209
Utah	1.1	5	11	9	3	9	61	192	103	38	3	6	436
Vermont	0.0	0	2	4	6	1	23	26	99	20	3	7	193
Virginia	0.4	3	10	2	3	6	43	118	158	80	7	4	435
Washington	0.4	2	4	3	3	4	34	63	54	22	2	3	193
West Virginia	1.1	6	31	7	1	14	70	36	80	14	13	17	423
Wisconsin	0.9	3	15	4	3	7	69	137	127	4	5	18	434
Wyoming	0.0	0	22	0	12	10	77	98	28	47	6	10	311

[b] Not available.

Table 13.7
SOURCE OF YOUTH REFERRAL TO STATE VR AGENCIES, FY 1970 CLOSURES
(By Percent)

Referral Source	Not Accepted	Not Rehabilitated	Rehabilitated
Educational institutions	38.7	35.1	46.9
Elementary or high school	34.2	28.0	38.6
School for handicapped	1.8	4.7	4.8
Other educational institutions	2.7	2.4	3.5
Hospitals and sanatoriums	5.3	11.4	6.8
Health organizations and agencies	4.1	5.1	5.0
Welfare agencies	7.8	6.4	5.0
Other public organizations and agencies	25.5	25.5	16.0
Correctional or court agency	7.0	15.7	6.7
Employment service	6.1	4.5	4.5
Other public	12.4	5.3	4.8
Other private organizations and agencies	1.0	0.8	0.9
Individuals	17.6	15.7	19.4
Self-referred person	5.3	4.1	5.7
Physician	2.5	2.9	4.2
Other individual	9.8	8.7	9.5
Total (percent)	100.0	100.0	100.0

Problems noted are the poor coordination between VR and the schools and a deficiency in VR outreach efforts. Two prime recommendations for handicapped children by a National Citizens Advisory Committee on Vocational Rehabilitation were aimed at alleviating these problems.[21] Some progress in coordination has been noted in recent years, at least at the agency administration level.[22]

Referral Destination Of youth referred or applying to VR agencies, only 5 percent of those not accepted are reported as being referred elsewhere by VR personnel. If this low figure indicates that VR personnel are not offering referral guidance to youth they do not accept

[21]*Report of the National Citizens Advisory Committee on Vocational Rehabilitation,* submitted to the Secretary of Health, Education, and Welfare, June 26, 1968, p. 2. Recommendations for handicapped children included "Establishment of cooperative school-rehabilitation programs in all schools, public and private, in both urban and rural locations, including a central repository of health and rehabilitation records," and "Evaluations of disabled children for rehabilitation purposes by vocational rehabilitation personnel at regular intervals to help prepare the child for a meaningful adult vocational career."

[22]See, for example, M. S. Hester, Director-in-Charge, *Workshop on Evaluation and Recommendations Relating to the National Conference for Coordinating Vocational Rehabilitation and Educational Services for Deaf People,* Delgado College, New Orleans, Louisiana, February 12–13, 1971, HEW Publication No. (SRS) 72-25030.

for service, then a great opportunity exists for improving the quality of "direction" services at very low cost. Data in Table 13.8 indicate that youth are most often referred to educational institutions (22 percent) or to other public agencies (for example, of the 39 percent going to other public organizations and agencies, 13 percent are sent to the employment service).

Outcomes of Referrals to VR Agencies Although 45 percent of referred youth aged 0–21 are not accepted into the VR program, only 5 percent are rejected as having no disabling condition, only 4 percent have no vocational handicap, and only 2 percent have too severe a handicap or an unfavorable medical prognosis. As Table 13.9 shows, the most frequent reasons for nonacceptance are that the youth re-

Table 13.8
AGENCIES YOUTH REFERRED TO BY VR AGENCIES, FY 1970 CLOSURES

Referral to:	*Percent*
Educational institutions	22
Hospitals and sanatoriums	4
Health organizations and agencies	13
Welfare agencies	16
Other public organizations and agencies	39
Other private organizations and agencies	2
Individuals	4
Total	100

Table 13.9
OUTCOMES OF REFERRING YOUTH TO VR AGENCIES

Outcome	*Percent Referred*
Accepted	52
Extended 6- or 12-month evaluation	3
Not accepted	45
Unable to locate or contact, or moved	8
Handicap too severe or unfavorable medical prognosis	2
Youth refused services	13
Death	<1
Client institutionalized	<1
Transfer to another agency	<1
Failure to cooperate	6
No disabling condition	5
No vocational handicap	4
Other, or reason not given	6
Total	100

fused the services (13 percent); the agency was unable to locate or contact the referred youth, or he had moved (8 percent); or the youth failed to cooperate (6 percent). The significant point is that most unaccepted youth are not reported to be unqualified to receive service but are not served for other reasons.

Reasons Youth Not Rehabilitated   Of all closures not rehabilitated in FY 1970, fully one-third of the youth could not be located or contacted or had moved. The next two most prevalent reasons were refusal of services or failure to cooperate. Only 9 percent reportedly failed because of too severe a handicap or an unfavorable medical prognosis. Table 13.10 documents reasons for closures not rehabilitated from an extended evaluation status (10 percent), before services began (33 percent), and after services were initiated (57 percent).

Other Client Attributes   The following are summary demographic and other case-data on VR clients for FY 1970.

- Nearly all VR agency clients are 14 or older. The mode of the age distribution is 16–19, near the end of the formal schooling age range.

Table 13.10
REASONS YOUTH NOT REHABILITATED IN VR PROGRAM

| Reason | *Percent of Closures:* | | | *Percent of Total Closures Not Rehabilitated* |
	From Evaluation Status	*Before Rehabilitation Services Began*	*After Rehabilitation Services Began*	
Unable to locate or contact, moved	2	10	21	33
Handicap too severe, or unfavorable medical prognosis	2	2	5	9
Youth refused services	2	10	8	20
Death	0	1	2	3
Client institutionalized	1	2	4	7
Transfer to another agency	0	0	1	1
Failure to cooperate	1	5	9	15
No disabling condition	0	0	0	0
No vocational handicap	0	0	0	0
Other, or reason not given	2	5	7	13
Total	10	33[a]	57	100[a]

[a] Rows and columns do not total precisely due to rounding.

- Of youth referred to or applying for VR, 38 percent were female, 62 percent male. The percentage breakdown is the same for those successfully rehabilitated.
- In education, excluding clients from mental retardation classes, the median grade completed was 11 both for referrals and for those served but not rehabilitated, and 12 for those successfully rehabilitated. Employers' use of the high school diploma as a job prerequisite may partially explain the higher success rate with those who completed grade 12.
- A total of 20 percent of the youth accepted for VR services had secondary disabling conditions, most often orthopedic, mental health, mental retardation, or other health impairments.
- Of youth successfully rehabilitated, 81 percent were Caucasian and 18 percent were black; 78 and 21 percent of all referrals or applicants were Caucasian and black, respectively. For comparison, the 1970 Census of Population indicated that 87 percent of the U.S. population was Caucasian.
- As would be expected with young clients, over two-thirds reported family and friends as their prime source of support. Of those accepted for service, 7 percent were primarily self-supporting from current earnings, interest, dividends, or rental income. That figure was higher—12 percent—for hearing and vision handicapped youth.
- Only 9 percent of youth referred for VR services were receiving public assistance at referral. At closure, only 3 percent of successful rehabilitants needed public assistance. About 2 percent were allowed SSDI benefits. Although the VR somewhat reduces current welfare costs, future reductions should be the most significant, as the youths become adults and may no longer receive family support.
- The average time between referral and acceptance for service was 6 months, and from acceptance to closure 15 months, for a total of 21 months. Hearing and vision impaired youth spent an average of 19 months between acceptance and closure, for a total of 25 months.
- The median annual income for families of youth referred to state VR agencies was approximately $3600. Nearly one-third had less than $1800, and only 17 percent had over $7200. For families of hearing and vision handicapped youth, the median was $4500; only 17 percent had under $1800, and 21 percent had over $7200.

Earnings   A full 100 percent of successfully rehabilitated youth were "gainfully employed" at closure. Only 11 percent had worked during the week preceding referral, with average weekly earnings of $51. Average reported earnings at closure were $76.

Of hearing and vision impaired youth, 14 percent were gainfully employed at time of referral, with average reported weekly earnings of only $8; that figure rose to $84 at closure. The highest average earnings at closure, $93, were for youth with one good eye. Only about two-thirds of the youth earned more than $64, the minimum wage for a 40-hour work-week, and less than 20 percent earned over $100. At time of referral, over half were nonworking students; at time of closure, 86 percent were in the competitive labor market, 8 percent were homemakers, and 3 percent were employed in sheltered workshops.

For comparison, the median May 1970 weekly earnings of salaried workers aged 16 to 24 were $88 and $112 for females and males, respectively.[23]

In aggregate terms, the estimated total annualized earnings based on weekly earnings of all rehabilitated youth rose from $20.637 million at the time of referral to $279.851 million at the time of closure.

Services Provided to Youth   All VR clients receive some services directly from the state agency's rehabilitation counselors, such as vocational planning, counseling, and job placement. In addition, most receive one or more specialized services for individuals:[24]

- Diagnostic and evaluation—including transportation, hospital and professional fees for medical, psychological, social, and vocational diagnostic and evaluation services to determine eligibility or scope of other services needed.
- Restorative—medical or medically related services to correct or substantially modify a physical or mental condition.
- Training—including training materials, tools, and equipment; training in a college, university, high school or elementary school, business school, vocational school; or on-the-job and training in personal and vocational adjustment.
- Income maintenance—basic living expenses, if necessary.
- Service to other family members—services that contribute substantially to rehabilitation of the handicapped youth.
- Other services—including reader or interpreter services, occupational tools and equipment, initial stocks, licenses, or transportation.

Youth who are not rehabilitated receive fewer services on the average, primarily because one-third of their cases are closed before any services are given. Nearly all clients receive diagnostic and evaluation services, but less than 33 percent require physical or mental restor-

[23]M. P. Flaim and N. Peters, "Usual Weekly Earnings of American Workers," *Monthly Labor Review,* Vol. 95, No. 3, March 1972, p. 30.

[24]See U.S. Department of Health, Education, and Welfare, *Vocational Rehabilitation Manual,* "Statistical Reporting Procedures," Chap. 13, July 1969.

ative services. Seventy-six percent of those rehabilitated receive training, while only 56 percent of those not rehabilitated are trained. Less than 30 percent need income maintenance while receiving other VR services, and only 2 to 3 percent of the youths' families receive special services. The mix of services delivered to rehabilitated VR clients of all ages differs from the mix delivered to youth, since nearly half of all clients receive restoration, while only 47 percent of all clients receive training.

Expenditures for Youth VR in FY 1970 Estimated expenditures for persons aged 0–21 under the state-federal VR program in FY 1970 were $131.305 million. This figure translates into $1300 per youth served, $1687 per youth successfully rehabilitated, and $6.49 for each person aged 14–21 in the United States in 1970. Table 13.11 shows the expenditure rates across states; for example, Maryland and Utah spend less than $800 per youth rehabilitated, while Alaska spends more than $4500, and the expenditures per total population aged 14–21 vary from $1.74 in Oregon to $10.51 in Wyoming. Table 13.12 gives the expenditures by disability group.

Table 13.11

ESTIMATED EXPENDITURES FOR YOUTH VR BY STATE, FY 1970 CLOSURES

State	Total Cost of Services (000)	Service Cost as Percent of Total Expenditures[a]	Estimated Total Expenditures[b] (000)	Average Expenditures		Expenditures per Total Population Aged 14–21
				Accepted	Rehabilitated	
U.S. total	$73,531	56	$131,305	$1,300	$1,687	$ 6.49
Alabama	2,290	55	4,164	2,057	2,800	7.78
Alaska	180	38	474	2,370	4,514	9.74
Arizona	623	52	1,198	1,920	2,599	4.42
Arkansas	846	72	1,175	1,438	2,148	4.15
California	2,795	52	5,375	1,073	1,958	1.84
Colorado	1,182	64	1,847	1,328	1,834	5.25
Connecticut	1,006	50	2,012	1,461	1,865	4.85
Delaware	172	30	573	2,274	3,473	7.12
D.C.	387	35	1,106	914	1,206	8.22
Florida	2,254	48	4,696	1,042	1,450	5.15
Georgia	1,928	67	2,878	763	992	4.04
Hawaii	250	45	556	1,308	2,336	4.54
Idaho	171	47	364	1,064	1,277	3.22
Illinois	4,324	63	6,863	1,485	1,667	4.36
Indiana	1,302	69	1,887	1,070	1,186	2.41

[a] U.S. Department of Health, Education, and Welfare, *State Vocational Rehabilitation Agency: Program Data FY 1971,* Social and Rehabilitation Service, DHEW Publication No. (SRS) 72–25016, March 1972.

[b] Assuming services cost as percentage of expenditures is same for both youth and adults.

Table 13.11—continued

State	Total Cost of Services (000)	Service Cost as Percent of Total Expenditures[a]	Estimated Total Expenditures[b] (000)	Average Expenditures		Expenditures per Total Population Aged 14–21
				Accepted	Rehabilitated	
Iowa	1,371	50	2,742	1,123	1,416	6.54
Kansas	384	54	711	915	1,394	2.05
Kentucky	1,107	49	2,259	938	1,134	4.51
Louisiana	2,118	67	3,161	1,143	1,462	5.39
Maine	340	60	567	1,703	2,296	3.88
Maryland	647	35	1,849	603	769	3.27
Massachusetts	2,399	68	3,528	1,704	2,164	4.32
Michigan	2,138	45	4,751	1,040	1,441	3.50
Minnesota	907	51	1,778	1,036	1,187	3.09
Mississippi	976	43	2,270	2,106	3,188	6.28
Missouri	2,320	58	4,172	1,284	1,687	6.22
Montana	259	67	387	1,032	1,229	3.58
Nebraska	582	57	1,021	1,213	1,566	4.57
Nevada	96	29	331	1,329	2,904	5.10
New Hampshire	140	54	259	1,239	1,811	2.43
New Jersey[c]						
New Mexico	287	45	638	1,227	2,106	3.79
New York	7,621	70	10,887	2,035	2,843	4.42
North Carolina	2,152	51	4,220	1,256	1,404	5.08
North Dakota	435	58	750	1,777	2,022	7.43
Ohio	2,785	44	6,330	1,582	2,032	4.02
Oklahoma	1,420	63	2,254	890	1,130	5.92
Oregon	295	54	546	878	1,876	1.74
Pennsylvania	9,060	67	13,672	1,762	2,343	8.22
Rhode Island	653	59	1,107	1,337	1,572	7.76
South Carolina	1,037	42	2,469	959	1,088	5.58
South Dakota	423	56	755	1,907	2,234	7.02
Tennessee	1,182	56	2,111	1,036	1,205	3.55
Texas	2,530	53	4,774	1,018	1,320	2.76
Utah	343	57	602	623	762	3.31
Vermont	227	47	483	2,583	3,604	6.97
Virginia	2,156	61	3,534	919	1,131	4.91
Washington	678	50	1,356	944	1,345	2.59
West Virginia	1,257	72	1,746	1,276	1,562	6.60
Wisconsin	3,033	69	4,396	1,317	1,517	6.58
Wyoming	289	54	535	2,306	3,386	10.51

[c] Not available.

While the estimated average expenditure rate per youth rehabilitated was $1687, the rates per blind and partially sighted youth rehabilitated were $6514 and $4437, respectively. In contrast, average expenditures per rehabilitated mentally retarded youth and deaf youth who are unable to talk were only $1361 and $2151, respectively. Even allowing for the differences in services needed by various handicap groups, there clearly are large unexplained differences in the expenditure rates for the various handicap groups.

Estimated expenditures for hearing and vision handicapped youth were $20.408 million. Of that amount, $11,428,000 was for the "cost of services" and the remainder was for the cost of state counselors and for operation of the state agency.[25] Average total expenditures per youth accepted were $1765, while expenditures per youth successfully rehabilitated were $2103. Expenditures per rehabilitant decreased with degree of severity, from $6167 for a blind youth to $1362 for a youth with "other visual impairment," and from $2068 for a deaf youth unable to talk to $1678 for a youth with "other hearing impairment." Note that 3 times as much is expended per blind youth as is expended per deaf youth who is unable to talk.

VR Expenditures in FY 1972[26]

Basic State-Federal Program In FY 1972 the federal expenditures for the basic VR state grants were $560 million with an additional $58,148,891 for service projects to all age groups. The states devoted an estimated additional $141,762,553 and $1.400 million for the basic VR program and service projects, respectively. Of the federal funds, approximately $134 million of the basic state grant and $13.9 million of the service project monies were for services to persons aged 0–21.[27] The portion of state funds used for the basic VR program and for service projects that reach youth aged 0–21 were estimated to be $34.023 million and $336,000, respectively.

For clients of all ages, the service projects in 1972 included $42,098,891 for grants to expand services to the handicapped beyond that possible under the basic state-federal VR program. Expansion grants focused on handicapped persons who were disadvantaged or severely disabled. An additional $1 million was expended on projects to develop employment opportunities for handicapped persons in particular industries. Another $2 million was spent on training individuals for new career opportunities in service to the handicapped. A total of $550,000 was for initial staffing of new or renovated rehabili-

[25]Assuming, for lack of better data, that all expenditures are distributed by type of handicap in the same proportions as "cost-of-services" expenditures are distributed by type of handicap.

[26]FY 1972 data from U.S. Department of Health, Education, and Welfare, *Justifications of Appropriation Estimates.*

[27]Assuming the 24 percent of total FY 1970 basic state grant expenditures devoted to serving handicapped persons aged 0–21 also is valid for FY 1972 and for service projects.

Table 13.12

ESTIMATED EXPENDITURES FOR YOUTH VR BY DISABILITY GROUP, FY 1970 CLOSURES

Handicap Group	Total Cost of Services (000)	Estimated Total Expenditures[a] (000)	Average Expenditures per Youth		Percent of Expenditures Incurred by Handicap Group	Average Cost of Services per Youth		
			Accepted	Rehab		Not Accepted	Accepted	Rehab
Blind	$ 908	$ 1,622	$5,037	$6,514	1.2	$31	$2,796	$3,227
Partially sighted, legally blind	2,395	4,277	3,463	4,437	3.3	27	1,927	2,179
Other visual impairments	4,193	7,488	1,441	1,685	5.7	13	791	877
Deaf, unable to talk	1,084	1,936	1,691	2,151	1.5	17	941	1,081
Deaf, able to talk	1,224	2,186	1,725	2,022	1.7	15	958	1,048
Hard of Hearing	1,624	2,900	1,502	1,734	2.2	14	824	910
Orthopedic impairments or absence of extremities	17,373	31,024	1,884	2,295	23.7	13	1,044	1,142
Mental health disorder	12,133	21,666	902	1,356	16.5	19	484	557
Mental retardation	17,422	31,111	1,049	1,361	23.7	21	575	632
Other health impairments	12,262	21,897	1,375	1,653	16.7	16	751	827
Speech impairments	1,440	2,571	1,598	1,866	1.9	12	886	982
Other impairments	1,471	2,627	1,209	1,724	2.0	17	660	701
Total	$73,531	$131,305	$1,300	$1,687	100.0	$18	$ 713	$ 804

[a] Assumes that the United States average of 56 percent of total expenditures on "services to individuals" holds for each group of handicapped youth. Only 1 percent of the youth accepted into the VR programs are eligible to have the Social Security Trust Fund pay costs. These costs are included in the totals presented above.

tation facilities. $12.5 million was for rehabilitation facility improvement, including $7.85 million for training workers, $4.45 million to increase and improve professional services to the handicapped, business management, and other aspects of rehabilitation facilities. The remaining $200,000 was for short-term technical assistance to rehabilitation facilities by consultants.

Training VR Personnel In providing skilled manpower to meet VR program needs, the FY 1972 federal appropriations were $27.7 million—$26.2 million for 440 long-term training projects and $1.5 million for 100 short-term training projects. It has been estimated that 3700 new state rehabilitation program staff positions and 1000 additional private program staff positions are required in FY 1973 to serve the project client load. Thus, the present training program meets only a fraction of the need for new vocational rehabilitation staff. In addition, it is estimated that 30,000 jobs are presently available for health-related rehabilitation personnel such as occupational and physical therapists and speech pathologists.[28] Since 25 percent of the clients in state VR agencies are 21 and under,[29] and assuming approximately that percentage of VR staff members' time is devoted to younger clients on the average, then we estimate $6.925 million of the total funds devoted to training personnel will benefit handicapped youth.

Construction and Improvement of Rehabilitation Facilities Development of new facilities and improvement of old ones are funded principally under Secs. 2 and 12 of the "Vocational Rehabilitation Act." In FY 1972 the total Sec. 12 expenditures were $3.051 million for one facility construction project; and no funds were requested by HEW for this section for FY 1973.[30]

Section 2 is the basic federal grant-in-aid program to the states. Actual total federal and state matching Sec. 2 expenditures for facilities in FY 1971 were $45,288,730; of this total, $37,012,785 was to assist in establishing rehabilitation facilities and workshops, $968,997 was capital expense for state agency operated rehabilitation facilities, and $7,306,948 was for construction.[31] Compared with the high cost of

[28]Information above is condensed from *Justifications of Appropriation Estimates.*

[29]U.S. Department of Health, Education, and Welfare, Form RSA-300, *Case Service Report—Federal State Program of Vocational Rehabilitation,* FY 1970.

[30]*Justifications of Appropriation Estimates.* For a more detailed discussion of legislation relating to facilities, see U.S. Department of Health, Education, and Welfare, *Rehabilitation Facility Needs in the 1970s,* Rehabilitation Services Administration, Monograph No. 1.

[31]U.S. Department of Health, Education, and Welfare, *State Vocational Rehabilitation Agency; Program Data, Fiscal Year 1971.*

facilities, these direct federal and state expenditures are relatively minor. It is apparent that most current funding of construction and improvement of facilities does not come directly from the federal and state governments. Rather, those facilities are largely created by other funding sources. Over the long run, however, they are indirectly and partially financed by payments to facilities for serving clients of the state-federal VR program. Again assuming that approximately 25 percent of the clients accepted into the state VR agencies are 21 and under, and assuming approximately that percentage of the facilities is devoted to younger clients, we then estimate approximately $12.085 million is spent annually to construct and improve rehabilitation facilities utilized for youth.

SRS Administered Research and Demonstration   In FY 1972, the U.S. Social and Rehabilitation Service (SRS) administered Research and Demonstration funds relevant to handicapped youth that were included as part of the $19.255 million devoted to rehabilitation and employability, $525,000 expended on Social Security programs, and $13.941 million devoted to special centers, or roughly $32 million in all.[32] While all of the expenditures are relevant to handicapped youth in that they may yield results that will improve services to younger disabled persons, they are also obviously relevant to disabled adults and to aged and low-income persons. Of the $32 million in Research and Demonstration funds, we estimate that $6.7 million, or 21 percent, goes to handicapped youth, since approximately 21 percent[33] of the U.S. population who have some chronic physical or mental condition that may result in limited activity are under 22.

Federal Administration of the Social and Rehabilitation Service Program   The operational costs of administering the Social and Rehabilitation Service within the U.S. Department of Health, Education, and Welfare were $44.175 million in FY 1972. The SRS staff totaled 2382 that year,[34] of which 368 were in the Rehabilitation Services Administration.

We estimate that the percentage of total program expenditures on VR assistance to handicapped persons up through age 21 is 25 per-

[32]*Justifications of Appropriation Estimates.*

[33]U.S. Department of Health, Education, and Welfare, *Limitation of Activity and Mobility Due to Chronic Conditions, United States, July 1965–June 1966,* National Center for Health Statistics, PHS Publication No. 1000, Series 10, No. 45. We note that as in any case in which one allocates overhead costs, the estimate is somewhat artificial because we do not really know what the overhead expenditures would have been if there were no handicapped youth to consider.

[34]*Justifications of Appropriation Estimates.*

cent of total VR expenditures.[35] Assuming the administrative expenditures are proportional to staff size, and that staff time is divided in roughly the same way as expenditures within each program, we estimate that $1.705 million of the SRS administration cost can reasonably be allocated to VR activities for handicapped youth.

OTHER VOCATIONAL PROGRAMS

Besides the basic state-federal VR program, there are four major vocationally related programs: Committees on Employment of the Handicapped; federal employment of the handicapped; the vending stand program for the visually handicapped; and the Employment Services Program. The focus of these four programs is on employment rather than on vocational rehabilitation.

Committees on Employment of the Handicapped

The Presidential Committee on Employment of the Handicapped, the corresponding Governors' Committees on Employment of the Handicapped in the 50 states, and hundreds of local committees promote employment opportunities for the mentally and physically impaired. Primarily, these committees endeavor to educate potential employers and the public regarding the vocational abilities of the handicapped, rather than provide individual placement services. Many of the committees are also active in backing legislation to remove barriers to employment of the handicapped, including physical obstacles in architecture and transportation.

The FY 1972 budget estimate for the Presidential Committee was $726,000 for persons of all ages. Since approximately 21 percent of the U.S. population who have some chronic physical or mental condition that may limit their activities are under age 22,[36] we estimate that 21 percent of the $726,000 budget, or $152,000, goes to handicapped youth. Governors' Committee budgets and staffs are small. The Massachusetts Committee, for example, runs on $450 annually, with two staff members loaned from the state employment service. Illinois is exceptional, with a relatively high annual budget of $146,000.[37] At these still low levels of expenditure, the committees cannot develop an extensive, high-quality set of public and employer education material; nor can they fund extensive campaigns in the media.

[35]Based on analysis of U.S. Department of Health, Education, and Welfare Form RSA-300.

[36]U.S. Department of Health, Education, and Welfare, *Limitation of Activity and Mobility Due to Chronic Conditions, United States, July 1965–June 1966,* National Center for Health Statistics, PHS Publication No. 1000, Series 10, No. 45.

[37]Financial data from staff members of the Illinois and Massachusetts Governors' Committees on Employment for the Handicapped.

Federal Employment of the Handicapped

The Civil Service Commission provides assistance to handicapped persons seeking federal employment. Budget obligations in FY 1970 and FY 1972 were $70,000 and $72,000, respectively.[38]

The Randolph-Sheppard Vending Stand Program

In FY 1971 a total of 3454 blind and visually handicapped persons operated vending stands in governmental buildings and earned an average of $6540 each from the businesses.[39] It is assumed that only a small fraction of the operators are under 21.

Employment Services

In FY 1970 the federal government budgeted $348 million for grants to states for employment services, including interviewing, counseling, and job placement referrals for individuals. This amount averaged $35 for each of the 9.957 million applicants for services in that year. The objective of these services is not vocational rehabilitation, but the matching of potential employees with employers. Special attention reportedly is given to the physically and mentally handicapped and other disadvantaged groups.

The total nonagricultural placements of handicapped persons of all ages in the United States in FY 1969 by the Employment Service program were 324,000; and that number grew about 22,900 from 1966 to 1969.[40]

Difficulties with the Employment Service program were noted in the *1973 Manpower Report of the President:* ". . . with the ES caught in an avalanche of new responsibilities, its effectiveness—as measured by the number of job placements made—has declined sharply in recent years. . . . Between 1966 and 1970 . . . ES non-farm placements dropped 30 percent . . . contacts with employers dropped 20 percent . . . accompanied by a decline of one-third in the number of job openings obtained. . . . The number of placements of disadvantaged workers also fell."[41]

During our five-state interviews with VR and employment service personnel,[42] several observations on the employment service program

[38]*Catalog of Federal Domestic Assistance,* Executive Office of the President, Office of Management and Budget, 1972.

[39]U.S. Department of Health, Education, and Welfare, *Justifications of Appropriation Estimates for Committee on Appropriations—FY 1973,* Vol. VI.

[40]Data from Manpower Administration, U.S. Department of Labor, Washington, D.C.

[41]U.S. Department of Labor, Washington, D.C., March 1973, pp. 31, 47.

[42]1972 interviews with VR personnel in Arkansas, California, Illinois, Massachusetts, and Wyoming, and with ES personnel in Massachusetts and Illinois.

were made which, if accurate, bear further investigation: (1) information on each job and client were said to be generally insufficient to permit effective matching of the handicapped client's abilities with job requirements; (2) employment service personnel were said to have such high client loads in most states that they often were unable to provide good placement service to handicapped persons; and (3) specialists in serving handicapped persons were said to be insufficient in number, with the result that personnel without special training often served handicapped persons.

BENEFIT-COST ANALYSIS OF VOCATIONAL SERVICES FOR HEARING AND VISION HANDICAPPED YOUTH

Previous studies have concluded that the VR program for handicapped persons has yielded benefits that considerably outweigh the cost of the program. For example, a 1967 study by the U.S. Vocational Rehabilitation Administration found that each dollar of cost in FY 1966 generated an estimated $35 in increased clients' earnings and value of work activity over their working lives.[43]

A more thorough study, using more conservative assumptions, has been made by Ronald W. Conley.[44] His analysis of the VR program focuses on economic costs and benefits, makes sophisticated use of available data, and clearly states the assumptions used in making estimates. With 1967 data, Conley estimates that for each dollar of the social cost of rehabilitation services, an increase in lifetime earnings of a little less than $5 accrues (at a 4-percent discount rate on future increased earnings). He also estimates that "the increased taxes paid by the rehabilitants and the reduction in tax supported payments for their maintenance amount to perhaps as much as 25 percent of the total increase in earnings." Critical assumptions underlying these and all other estimates relate to how one estimates what earnings would have been without rehabilitation, and what the employment record of the rehabilitant will be over his lifetime.

In the following analysis, we will use Conley's methodology, with some significant adaptations. First, previous analyses have generally dealt with the program as a whole, not with disaggregations by type and degree of handicap and by age of the recipient. We will investi-

[43]U.S. Department of Health, Education, and Welfare, Vocational Rehabilitation Administration, *An Exploratory Cost-Benefits Analysis of Vocational Rehabilitation,* Washington, D.C., August 1967.

[44]*The Economics of Vocational Rehabilitation,* The Johns Hopkins Press, Baltimore, 1965; and see idem, "A Benefit-Cost Analysis of the Vocational Rehabilitation Program," *The Journal of Human Resources,* Vol. 4, No. 2, April 1969, for one of the best of these benefit-cost studies and a review of others. See also Rand Report R-1220-HEW, Chapter 5, for citations of other analyses.

gate the program's costs and benefits for eight categories of hearing and vision handicapped youth, and will also look at differences based on sex and race. Second, although the data for the VR program are generally better than data for any other program we investigated, benefit-cost analyses must still resort to assumptions where data are incomplete. We will vary certain of those assumptions and note the sensitivity of estimated benefits to the variations.

The analyses in the remainder of this section will concentrate on economic benefits, which are only one of the various types of benefits on which this program can be evaluated. Earlier in this chapter we presented available data on other classes of criteria, such as degree of change in nondependence and equity of service distribution. Data are not available for one of the most significant classes of effects, changes in the overall quality of life of youth served. As will be seen, the VR program appears justified by its economic benefits alone. Other unquantified but very significant major types of benefits add still more support for this program.

Benefit-Cost Methodology

For a more detailed description of the methodology we are using with certain adaptations, the reader is referred to Conley's works.[45] The methodology is briefly discussed here to lay out its underlying assumptions. We first describe components of cost, and then discuss the calculation of economic benefits.

Basic Program Costs   The basic program costs include those of administration, vocational counselors, case services,[46] and the establishment and support of rehabilitation facilities and workshops. When considering the effectiveness of the total program, it is possible to use the budget as an indicator of the program cost. However, if we want to make distinctions among the various groups participating in the program, we must try to disaggregate the cost. The only expenditure that is kept in a client's file is that for case services, such as medical diagnostics, treatment, or vocational training. The other costs are generally treated as "overhead" and are not attributed directly to individual clients by the agency. To do an analysis by handicap, race, age, or sex, we must devise some means of allocating overhead costs to each type of client. Two possible methods of allocation suggest themselves. First, those "overhead" costs could be attributed on a per capita basis. This would be an accurate approximation if these ser-

[45]Conley, *The Economics of Vocational Rehabilitation,* and idem, "A Benefit-Cost Analysis."
[46]Called "Cost of Services" in the preceding section.

vices (e.g., counseling and guidance) were independent of the length and cost of the service program that is designed to help the client. Another approach, and the one adopted for this analysis, is to allocate all costs in proportion to the amount of costs of case services for the individual clients.[47] This implies that the types of clients who receive the most in case services, such as medical treatment and training, also consume a higher proportionate share of counseling and other expenditures. Because high service costs are likely to be associated with the most difficult cases, such an allocation scheme is not unreasonable. Some clients, however, have no "cost of case services," and are successfully rehabilitated with, for example, only counseling and placement services from VR agency personnel. The assumption of allocating all costs in relationship with case service costs would imply that these types of clients were served at no cost. However, since those who have zero cost of case service are only a small fraction of the total, and are distributed across all handicap types, the resultant error is likely to be small.

Maintenance Cost   The cost of income maintenance payments is not counted as a cost to society in the benefit-cost analysis. This stems from the fact that the cost to the group that pays the income transfer payment is equal to the benefits that accrue to the recipients of the income transfer payment; cost and benefits of the transfer cancel each other out when society as a whole is considered. This is not to say that they are canceled out if we are considering any group *within* society, such as taxpayers. In the case of taxpayers, income maintenance costs would be considered because most recipients of the income transfer payments are not representative taxpayers. Conley estimates that approximately 7 percent of the program cost goes for income maintenance. It was not possible to get a better estimate of the actual amount of program funds going for maintenance for hearing and vision handicapped youth. We therefore adopted Conley's figure.

Adjustment for Carryovers   The VR program has been growing steadily over the past decade. If the total annual expenditures were divided by the number of successful rehabilitations in a given year to obtain an average unit cost, the estimate would be biased upward because most clients are served more than one year. To adjust for this bias, Conley reduced the estimate of program cost by 2 percent. Our

---

[47]In 1970 the ratio of basic program costs to the cost of case services was approximately 1.78.

cost data are in a somewhat different form from Conley's. We have the cost of case services for all FY 1970 closures. Therefore, we do not have cost data on persons who entered the program but were not closed in 1970. However, the overhead rate used here would be biased upward slightly. Because of the growth in the program, a downward adjustment of 2 percent of the basic program cost is made.

Other-Party Costs Some clients receive services that are not financed by the VR agency and hence do not show up in the budget of the agency or in the expenditure record of the client. Conley has estimated that such expenditures amounted to 4 percent of the annual program costs, and we use this estimate.

Repeater Costs Some of the clients in the program have previously received service from the VR agencies. Others, especially youth, will receive additional service in the future. Conley argues that both these past and future costs should be included as part of the incremental social costs for the current year's rehabilitants. Since Conley's data indicated that 22 percent of the year's rehabilitants were or would become rehabilitation "repeaters," and assuming that future service costs are the same as the present average cost of rehabilitation, the program cost should be increased by approximately 22 percent to account for these "repeat" costs.

It is important to count program costs in benefit-cost analysis if in fact the benefits from these expenditures are also measured. It is not clear, from the methodology presented later for estimating benefits, that the benefits from past and future VR expenditures on a single client are incorporated into Conley's model. For example, past expenditures should be reflected in the income that the client has been receiving. Since the client's income upon entering the program is subtracted from his future income to obtain an estimate of net benefits, benefits flowing from past expenditures do not appear to be included in Conley's analysis. Conley's methodology on repeaters will be used in the base case.

Research, Training, and Construction Costs This year's clients are also recipients of the benefits of previous research, staff training, and past expenditures on construction of facilities. These costs must be amortized to estimate the program's true cost. Conley found that public expenditures for these categories were about 20 percent of the annual basic program cost, and that private support in these categories was about 5 percent of basic program cost. This meant that an estimate of the cost of research, training, and construction programs that could be allocated to this year's program would be equal to 25 percent of this year's basic program cost.

Opportunity Cost   One of the social costs of the VR program is the opportunity cost associated with the production that is lost when the client forgoes the labor force and enters the program. Conley estimates this production loss as equal to 35 percent of the first year's earnings of the successful rehabilitants after they leave the program. He estimates

> forgone earnings [based] on the earnings reported by rehabilitants during the three months prior to acceptance (1962–64). These earnings averaged around 40 percent of those at closure, and given that it requires 85 percent of a year to complete rehabilitation, then forgone earnings would be equal to about 35 percent of estimated annual earnings at closure.[48]

Two features of his analysis appear questionable. First, he considers the forgone earnings only of those successfully rehabilitated. But unrehabilitated clients also had to forgo earnings—a small but real cost of the program that should be included. Second, since real data on earnings at acceptance were available, it would seem only reasonable to use those data instead of approximations. It is especially important to do so in our case because the ratio of the two earnings is not likely to hold constant among age groups. For totally blind or profoundly deaf youth, for example, this ratio is closer to 8 percent. Since the Conley methodology is being used in the base case, however, his methodology is adopted here and will be modified in the sensitivity analysis later in this section.

Benefits   We emphasize that the VR program produces several types of benefits for both the client and society. There are obvious psychic and other benefits to the client, notably self-sufficiency, but in this section we are concerned with the economic benefits that can be attributed to the services provided by the program.

Three major parameters must be specified to find the total increase in earnings from the VR program: the number of years the client will work, the differential in earnings for each year between what he earns after VR services and what he would have earned without them, and the discount rate. The specification or estimation of each parameter is discussed below.

Number of Years Worked   To estimate the number of years worked, Conley assumes that unless the rehabilitant suffers vocational failure

[48]Conley, "A Benefit-Cost Analysis," p. 241.

or dies, he works until he retires at the age of 65. Conley's mortality rates are taken from experience with Railroad Retirement Disability annuitants. This group has high mortality rates compared with the population in general. Conley makes this conservative assumption noting that this is the "worst possible" case for the VR program. If the VR program is cost-beneficial under this assumption, it is even more beneficial under less stringent assumptions.[49] These mortality rates are very unrealistic for hearing and vision handicapped youth. Only 50 percent of those who are rehabilitated between the ages of 16 and 19 are assumed to live to be 40 years old. That figure soars to 96 percent if one uses 1959 mortality data for the general population.

A critical assumption concerns the amount of unemployment later in life. The number of years worked after rehabilitation and before reaching age 65 must be adjusted to reflect periods of possible unemployment. As described in the next section, Conley argues that the decrease in earnings due to unemployment is offset by the increase in productivity (as measured by earnings) of those who retain their employment.

Earnings Differential   Conley estimates the increase in productivity among successfully rehabilitated clients due to VR services as follows:

> We will accept our conclusions from the follow-up studies that 80 percent of all rehabilitants are still gainfully employed five years after closure and that their average earnings are about 25 percent higher than the average earnings of rehabilitants in the year of closure, and we will further assume that these successful rehabilitants will continue to be employed at these higher wages until death or retirement. Given these assumptions, it follows that the increase in earnings due to rehabilitation during any time period after rehabilitation will vary with the number of rehabilitants still employed (since the loss of earnings among live rehabilitants of working age who fail to maintain their employment is offset by the increased earnings of successful rehabilitants). Total increased output due to rehabilitants will, therefore, be equal to the average number of years worked by rehabilitants still employed five years after closure multiplied by the increase in earnings between acceptance and closure.[50]

A 1972 follow-up survey of 4146 VR service recipients in six states one, two, and three years after closure, conducted by National Ana-

---

[49]This kind of analysis is termed *a fortiori*. It is explained in G. H. Fisher, *Cost Considerations in Systems Analysis,* Elsevier Publishing Company, New York, 1971.
[50]Conley, "A Benefit-Cost Analysis," pp. 234–235.

lysts, Inc.,[51] suggests that the assumption about the percentage working five years after closure is too high. Our later sensitivity analysis accordingly considers what the economic benefits would be if the figure were less. The National Analysts report indicates that in the 12 months following closure, 47 percent of the rehabilitants worked without interruption, 29 percent did not work at all, and 57 percent were working for pay when interviewed. Comparable figures for nonrehabilitants were 19 percent, 60 percent, and 24 percent, respectively. Over a 36-month period following closure, the percentage employed for pay at the time of the interview decreased only slightly, to 55 percent. The average amount of time worked for pay averaged just over 7 months per year, but varied from about 6 months per year up to 9 months per year, depending on sex and race. However, rehabilitants under age 30 fared better; approximately 67 and 77 percent of females and males, respectively, were working for pay at the time of the interview.

The National Analysts study also presents new data on the percentage increase in earnings, one, two, and three years after closure. In constant-value dollars, mean monthly earnings of 0- to 24-year-old rehabilitants increased about 25 to 35 percent for males and 20 to 30 percent for females. For rehabilitants of all ages at the end of one, two, and three years, earnings increased 30, 32, and 32 percent, respectively. However, even if Conley's assumption of a 25-percent increase in earnings over a five-year period after rehabilitation is accurate, it may not be appropriate to label this as a benefit of the VR program. Employer-conducted or on-the-job training, not the VR program, may have increased the skills of the rehabilitants after the time of closure.

A large possible error, however, is introduced if it is assumed that the increase in output is equal to the difference in earnings at acceptance and at closure for the youth. Although this may be a justifiable assumption for those who have already been in the labor force, it loses credibility for those who enter the VR program before entering the labor force and sometimes before leaving school, and therefore have no earnings at acceptance.[52] It is difficult to believe that at least some of the less severely handicapped (e.g., those with $20/70$ vision, or one good eye) could not qualify for jobs without VR training. Our

[51]National Analysts, Inc., *A Follow-Up Study of Closed Vocational Rehabilitation Cases, Final Report to the Social and Rehabilitation Service, U.S. Department of Health, Education, and Welfare,* Contract No. SRS-69-54, April 1972.

[52]Only 12 percent of hearing and vision handicapped youth under age 22 were reported as working at acceptance. Over 50 percent were students when they were accepted into the program.

doubts are strengthened by the National Analysts study, which found that 78 percent of the rehabilitants under age 30 thought they could have obtained their present positions without VR services.[53] The sensitivity of the effectiveness of this program to various estimated changes in earnings is examined later.

Discounting The total stream of benefits can now be estimated by multiplying the number of man-years of life by the assumed increase in earnings due to the VR program for each type of handicapped client. Given a preference, however, one would prefer earnings this year to the same amount of earnings at some distant time in the future. To account for that preference, future benefits must be discounted. Just what is the proper amount to discount future costs and benefits from government projects has been subject to extensive study and controversy. Rather than choose a single discount rate, we will use 4 percent in our base case analysis and examine some other values in the later section devoted to sensitivity analysis.

Benefit-Cost Analysis: Base Case

For the base case analysis, we will use Conley's methodology and the data on hearing and vision handicapped youth derived from the FY 1970 case closures described earlier in this chapter. The next section will test the sensitivity of the analysis to various other assumptions.

The relative costs of services per rehabilitant are shown in Table 13.13 by the type and degree of hearing and vision handicap and by race and sex. The corresponding benefit/cost ratios are shown in Table 13.14.

Looking at the relative cost for the different types of handicaps, note that the legally blind youth have relatively high costs compared with those for the less severely visually handicapped and the hearing handicapped. Because earnings at referral and closure are fairly similar for youth with each of these types of handicaps, cost differences account primarily for differences in the benefit/cost ratios by type of sensorial handicap. The average benefit/cost ratio for all these youth is 10.8, using Conley's methodology. The benefits returned per dollar of cost go up as severity of handicap goes down: from 11.0 for deaf youth unable to talk to 12.3 for hard of hearing youth, and from 4.3 for totally blind youth to 13.6 for youth with one good eye. Thus, using Conley's methodology for this base case analysis, the VR pro-

[53]National Analysts, Inc., op. cit., p. 194.

Table 13.13
RELATIVE COST OF SERVICES PER REHABILITANT BY TYPE OF HEARING AND VISION HANDICAPPED YOUTH

Type and Degree of Sensorial Handicap	Cost as Percentage of the Average for All Types of Sensorially Handicapped Youth		
	Total Youth	Female Only	Nonwhite Only
Blind	293%	358%	253%
Partially sighted—legally blind	204	213	176
Partially sighted—20/70 up to 20/200 acuity	109	102	91
One good eye	80	88	67
Other visual impairment	65	54	82
Deaf, unable to talk	98	99	100
Deaf, able to talk	92	95	81
Other hearing impairment	80	79	78
All types combined	100%	102%	81%

gram appears to yield high economic benefits to society in relation to the cost of the services.

The cost per rehabilitant is about the same for the entire group of hearing and vision handicapped youth and for females only. Thus, the lower benefit/cost ratios shown for females are due to a lower average improvement in earnings from time of referral to closure. Much of this discrepancy can be explained by the facts that a lower percentage of women who are rehabilitated enter the paid labor force, as compared with the total population, and those who do earn less than the total population, on the average. Over 87 percent of rehabilitants of both sexes were working in the competitive labor market at the time of closure, but only 78 percent of the female successes were classified as working in that market. The estimated average weekly earnings of female successes at closure was $13.70 less than the average for all hearing and vision handicapped youth rehabilitants.

It is seen that the average benefit/cost ratio for nonwhite youth is slightly higher than that for the total population. However, the costs of service to nonwhite youth were significantly lower, and average weekly earnings of nonwhite youth at the time of closure were also lower by $7.30.

In summary, although it is clear that some types of handicapped youth do better than others in a benefit/cost sense, the program ap-

Table 13.14
VR BENEFIT/COST RATIO BY TYPE OF HEARING AND VISION
HANDICAPPED YOUTH: BASE CASE METHODOLOGY

Type and Degree of Sensorial Handicap	Benefit/Cost Ratio for		
	Total Youth	Female Only	Nonwhite Only
Blind	4.3	3.2	4.6
Partially sighted-legally blind	5.5	4.2	5.5
Partially sighted—20/70 up to 20/200 acuity	10.4	8.7	10.9
One good eye	13.6	11.0	17.8
Other visual impairment	13.5	12.7	17.8
Deaf, unable to talk	11.0	9.8	10.2
Deaf, able to talk	11.4	9.9	11.3
Other hearing impairment	12.3	10.8	10.7
All types combined	10.8	9.0	11.2

pears to offer society a handsome return on investment regardless of the type or degree of hearing or vision handicapped youth. This is in line with previous findings. As we vary some of Conley's assumptions, however, the success of the program appears to be somewhat less than the base case analysis indicates. We now turn to sensitivity analysis.

Benefit-Cost Analysis: Sensitivity to Data and Assumptions

This section explores the sensitivity of the conclusion that the VR program is highly cost-beneficial to those data and assumptions. Many different combinations of data and assumptions are possible. Our tactic here is to vary the most significant of them one at a time to isolate and study their influence, and then to make what appears to be a realistic set of changes of more than one type of data and assumption.

Discount Rate   The base case analysis used a discount rate of 4 percent. Its use assumes that the government or private enterprise does not have an investment opportunity that yields over 4 percent. While it is impossible to say what the correct discount rate is, since conditions in the future will change that rate, we can measure the effects of various discount rates on our conclusions. Table 13.15 presents the benefit/cost ratio associated with various discount rates from 4 to 10 percent. It is seen that even for the relatively high discount rate of 10 percent, the program is still returning positive benefits relative to its cost (i.e., the benefit/cost ratio is greater than one) for all eight categories of handicapped youth studied.

Cost Several of the data and assumptions about cost can be debated. However, for any reasonable changes in the cost used, the conclusion that the program is cost-beneficial does not change. For example, if the cost goes down, the benefit/cost ratio goes up. On the other hand, if the cost goes up by, say, 25 percent, the benefit/cost ratio is reduced by only 20 percent and is still high.

Number of Rehabilitants Who Continue to Work The base case analysis assumes an extremely high mortality rate for these youth and still shows the program to be cost-beneficial. We will not use a still higher mortality rate because it appears perhaps unreasonably high already. The base case analysis also assumes that 80 percent of those with earnings at closure have earnings 5 years from closure, and later earnings increases from employed rehabilitants offset later increases in unemployment. If no change is made in the assumptions about the earnings of those who remain employed, total benefits decline as the 80 percent employment figure is lowered; the benefit/cost ratios in Table 13.16 are obtained for various assumptions about the percentage that stays in the labor force after five years. As the table indicates, the benefits exceed the cost (ratio exceeds 1.0) for even the most severely handicapped youth, even if only 20 percent retain full-time employment. Since no follow-up study on rehabilitants we are aware of has concluded that the rate of employment after successful rehabilitation is that low, the VR program for sensorially handicapped youth appears to be cost-beneficial for all reasonable values of employment rate, if all other assumptions remain unchanged.

Earnings Gain Due to VR Services A major assumption in the base case analysis was that the earnings gain due to VR services was equal to the difference between reported earnings at time of referral and at closure. However, the assumption that earnings at referral were a good indication of what the client would continue to earn in the absence of the VR program is open to serious question. It is difficult to get an accurate estimate of what would happen to those clients if the VR program did not exist since accurate data on earnings of hearing and vision handicapped persons in the general population do not exist and because the VR program clients probably are not typical of that population.

Rather than trying to get a more accurate estimate of earnings without VR services, we use several different earnings assumptions to get an idea of their effects on the base case analysis benefits. Table 13.17 shows the benefit/cost ratio of the VR program under four different assumptions about earnings without services. It is assumed that 25, 50, 75, and 100 percent of those cases closed as successes would have been employed, with the average earnings equal to the 1970 minimum wage, in the absence of VR services (i.e., a minimal $64 a week on the average).

According to the table, even if 100 percent of the rehabilitants could obtain minimum wage jobs on the average without training, the program would be slightly cost-beneficial for the entire client population of hearing and vision handicapped youth, but would not be cost-beneficial for profoundly deaf or legally blind youth. (Where the benefit/cost ratio shown is negative, the VR program is less effec-

Table 13.15
VR BENEFIT/COST RATIO BY TYPE OF HEARING AND VISION HANDICAPPED YOUTH: SENSITIVITY TO DISCOUNT RATE

Type and Degree of Sensorial Handicap	Benefit/Cost Ratio with Discount Rate of:			
	4%	6%	8%	10%
Blind	4.3	3.5	2.8	2.4
Partially sighted—legally blind	5.5	4.4	3.6	3.1
Partially sighted—20/70 up to 20/200 acuity	10.5	8.3	6.8	5.8
One good eye	13.6	10.8	8.9	7.5
Other visual impairment	13.5	10.7	8.8	7.4
Deaf, unable to talk	11.0	8.7	7.2	6.1
Deaf, able to talk	11.4	9.1	7.5	6.3
Other hearing impairment	12.3	9.8	8.1	6.8
All types combined	10.8	8.6	7.1	6.0

Table 13.16
VR BENEFIT/COST RATIO BY TYPE OF HEARING AND VISION HANDICAPPED YOUTH: SENSITIVITY TO RATE OF EMPLOYMENT

Type and Degree of Sensorial Handicap	Benefit/Cost Ratio with Employment Rate After 5 Years of:			
	80%	60%	40%	20%
Blind	4.3	3.2	2.2	1.1
Partially sighted—legally blind	5.5	4.1	2.8	1.4
Partially sighted—20/70 up to 20/200 acuity	10.4	7.8	5.2	2.6
One good eye	13.6	10.2	6.8	3.4
Other visual impairment	13.5	10.1	6.8	3.4
Deaf, unable to talk	11.0	8.3	5.5	2.8
Deaf, able to talk	11.4	8.6	5.7	2.9
Other hearing impairment	12.3	9.3	6.2	3.1
All types combined	10.8	8.1	5.4	2.7

Table 13.17
**VR BENEFIT/COST RATIO BY TYPE OF HEARING AND VISION HANDICAPPED
YOUTH: SENSITIVITY TO ASSUMPTIONS ABOUT EARNINGS WITHOUT VR SERVICE**

Type and Degree of Sensorial Handicap	*Benefit/Cost Ratio with Indicated Percentage Employed at an Average of the Minimum Wage Without VR Services*			
	25%	*50%*	*75%*	*100%*
Blind	3.6	2.6	1.5	0.5
Partially sighted—legally blind	4.6	3.2	1.8	0.3
Partially sighted—20/70 up to 20/200 acuity	9.2	6.9	4.6	2.4
One good eye	12.8	9.8	7.2	4.6
Other visual impairment	12.2	9.0	5.8	2.6
Deaf, unable to talk	8.8	5.7	2.6	−0.5
Deaf, able to talk	9.7	6.8	3.8	0.9
Other hearing impairment	10.7	7.5	4.3	1.1
All types combined	9.4	6.9	4.3	1.8

tive in earnings terms than a program that puts 100 percent of the rehabilitants in minimum wage jobs.)

Within all the categories from the more severely to the less severely disabled, the VR program has economic benefits that exceed its costs even if 75 percent or less earn the minimum wage in the absence of the program.

In the base case analysis that took earnings at time of acceptance as a measure of income in the absence of the program, the benefit/cost ratio for the category of youth with one good eye was some 3 times larger than that for totally blind youth, for example. The practice of "creaming" and serving the least handicapped youth under the base case analysis assumptions would lead to the largest *economic* return. More realistic assumptions about the inherent earning capacity of each type of handicapped youth, however, calls into question whether emphasizing service to less handicapped clients is in fact a rational, to say nothing about equitable, policy from the standpoint of economic return.

Benefit/Cost Analysis: Conservative Assumptions Case

In the preceding section, several of the base case analysis assumptions were varied individually and the conclusion that the program is cost-beneficial in an economic sense did not change. In this section, we shall change three of the most significant base case assumptions and recalculate the benefit/cost ratios for this new set of data and assumptions, which we consider to be more conservative than the base case data and assumptions. If the VR program still appears cost-beneficial even under these rather conservative assumptions that should show the program in the worst reasonable light, we will conclude that the program is effective in a social cost-benefit sense.

In calculating the benefit-cost ratios shown in Table 13.18, we assume the following:

- The discount rate is 8 percent.
- Only 50 percent of the legally blind and deaf youth, and only 70 percent of the less severely handicapped youth, are employed five years after closure.
- In the absence of the VR program, 50 percent of both the legally blind and the deaf rehabilitants, and 75 percent of the less severely handicapped youth rehabilitants, could have been employed earning the minimum wage on the average.

We emphasize that the true value of the above figures is not known. The values shown are not our best estimates of what those true values are, but rather are conservative estimates made to put the VR program to a hard test. Rather than assume, as in the base case analysis, that without the VR program nearly all of these youth would be unemployed throughout their lives, we assume a majority of them would be employed. And rather than assume a 20 percent unemployment rate for successful rehabilitants after five years, we assume a 30 to 50 percent unemployment rate.

Under these much less favorable assumptions, the program still appears to have economic benefits that exceed its costs to society for all eight categories of hearing and vision handicapped youth. Although these benefit/cost ratios are all greater than one, they are close to one for the legally blind.

Many questions about the proper allocation of resources among handicaps remain unanswered. However, the positive quality-of-life

Table 13.18
VR BENEFIT/COST RATIO BY TYPE OF VISION AND HEARING HANDICAPPED YOUTH: CONSERVATIVE ASSUMPTIONS CASE

Type and Degree of Sensorial Handicap	*Benefit/Cost Ratio for Total Youth*
Blind	1.1
Partially sighted—legally blind	1.4
Partially sighted—20/70 up to 20/200 acuity	2.7
One good eye	4.4
Other visual impairment	3.5
Deaf, unable to talk	2.5
Deaf, able to talk	3.0
Other hearing impairment	2.6

benefits of the program coupled with favorable average economic benefits in relation to cost, imply that expansion of the VR program *could* have very desirable effects. If the program were expanded, however, it should be carefully and periodically reevaluated, because diminishing returns on investment can be anticipated as a larger fraction of the handicapped population is served, and because our calculations have been of average costs and benefits, not the marginal costs and benefits of program expansion, for which data are not available.

Benefits and Costs to the Taxpayers

The previous analysis examined the VR program from the standpoint of society as a whole. The question of just who received the benefits and who paid the costs within society was not considered. In this section we view the VR program from the perspective of an investment decision for the taxpaying segment of society.

The costs borne and benefits captured by the taxpayer are different from those discussed in the previous sections. On the cost side, income maintenance payments during rehabilitation are a real cost to the taxpayer while the opportunity cost of withdrawing the client from the labor force, and other-party payments, are not. On the benefit side, only the increment in taxes paid by the employed handicapped youth, rather than the total increase in income, is counted as a benefit to the taxpayer. An additional benefit is the reduction in future welfare payments that is attributable to the VR program. The costs can be calculated from information presented previously; they are $29.5 million for VR clients whose cases were closed in FY 1970.

To estimate the increase in taxes paid by rehabilitants, it is necessary to estimate their income distribution. From the RSA-300 forms, the number of persons in weekly income ranges from $0 to $20, $21 to $40, $41 to $60, $61 to $100, $101 to $150, and over $150 was calculated for each type of sensorially handicapped youth. It was assumed that each person earned the average salary within his weekly income range except for the over $150 category, where average earnings were taken to be $160. The estimated tax was calculated assuming that the young handicapped taxpayer had no other dependents than himself. This may introduce a small upward bias in the benefits that are captured by the general taxpaying population. The estimated federal income taxes paid by rehabilitants in 1970 and the discounted (4 percent) federal tax payments over the lives of the rehabilitants are estimated to be $4.7 million and $57.1 million, respectively, assuming the total federal tax payments will be the same each year for the whole group of rehabilitants.

Table 13.19
NET INCREASE IN FEDERAL TAXES PAID BY REHABILITANTS
(In $ million)

Assumed Percentage Employed Earning Minimum Wage in Absence of VR Program	Net Increase in Federal Taxes
0%	$57.1
25	46.3
50	35.5
75	24.8
100	14.0

We are now faced with the problem of estimating the taxes paid in the absence of the VR program. If earnings at acceptance are used as the tax base, the taxes paid would be negligible. If different assumptions about the percentage that could earn the minimum wage were made, the net increase in taxes paid by the rehabilitants would be substantially different, as shown in Table 13.19.

These estimates of tax benefits are lower than Conley's. The major reason for the difference is that Conley assumes that federal tax payments account for only half of the tax liability of the handicapped person. It is difficult to estimate the incidence of the sales tax and property tax on the poor and handicapped. If the client were truly impoverished, he would probably qualify for public assistance and might receive an income comparable to what many of the successful rehabilitants earn. Thus the property tax and sales tax payments could be approximately the same with or without the VR program for some, but not all, youth. By not counting sales and property tax benefits, we will be underestimating total tax benefits. However, the state income tax should be added into the benefits. Revenue from state income tax was 10 percent of federal revenues from the personal income tax.[54]

By placing clients in jobs, the VR program reduces the number of handicapped youth who need to rely on public welfare and thus benefits the general taxpayer population. The problems in estimating this reduction are as difficult as estimating increases in earnings. Conley uses welfare payments at acceptance and at closure as a measure of the difference in the amount of welfare payments over the life of the client. This methodology is not directly applicable to youth because many of the handicapped youth are supported by their parents at referral but would have needed welfare later. Therefore, before-

---

[54]*Statistical Abstract of the United States: 1971,* U.S. Department of Commerce, Washington, D.C.: federal, p. 385; state and local, p. 398.

Table 13.20
BENEFIT/COST RATIO FOR TAXPAYERS

	Assumed Percent Employed Earning the Minimum Wage in Absence of VR Program				
	0%	*25%*	*50%*	*75%*	*100%*
Benefit/cost ratio	2.4	1.9	1.5	1.0	0.5

and-after welfare payments may not accurately reflect what the client would cost the taxpayer. In the absence of better data, our approach here is to take the average reduction in welfare payments per rehabilitant of any age and assume it is applicable to the youth population under study.

In 1970 there were 266,975 rehabilitants. At referral only 28,308 were receiving public assistance. At closure, this number was reduced to 16,589. The average monthly amount of public assistance dropped from $3.53 million to $1.87 million, or a net reduction of $1.66 million. This works out to a reduction of about $70 per rehabilitant per year in the aggregate amount of welfare payments. Discounting this reduction over the life of the rehabilitants, the lifetime benefit for hearing and vision handicapped youth would be $8.4 million.

The benefit/cost ratios for the general taxpayer population are shown in Table 13.20 for several different assumptions about what the client could earn in the absence of the VR program. The welfare reduction benefit has been decreased in proportion to the increase in the percentage employed.

Note that from the viewpoint of the general taxpaying population, the VR program for hearing and vision handicapped youth has benefits that exceed its costs if we assume that 75 percent or less of these rehabilitants are employed at the minimum wage, on the average, in the absence of the VR program. Because we have excluded all sales and property tax benefits, and thus the benefits were underestimated, the program appears cost-beneficial as a taxpayer "investment," just as it was shown to be cost-beneficial from the viewpoint of society as a whole and is cost-beneficial from the viewpoint of the individual VR client.

NEEDED IMPROVEMENTS IN VOCATIONAL SERVICE PROGRAMS

Improvements needed in the delivery of vocational services to handicapped youth are discussed here; our recommendations appear in italics.

Expand the Vocational Rehabilitation program to serve a larger fraction of the handicapped youth population. This program not only improves the quality of life of youth served by increasing their ability to function more independently, to obtain employment, and to work at higher quality employment, but it also appears to yield economic benefits (reduced service cost later in life, reduced welfare, increased taxes paid, and increased earnings) that exceed the costs of the program.

Insufficiency of funds was the problem most often cited by VR agency administrators we surveyed in the 50 states.[55] A General Accounting Office report on the VR program indicated that "the number of persons needing vocational rehabilitation services has far exceeded the number of persons that have been served under the program" and that "the number of persons rehabilitated annually, although increasing, is still not as great as RSA's estimates of the number becoming eligible each year."[56] The need for additional facilities is also large.[57]

Establish clear guidelines on the categories of handicapped persons to be given priority in the receipt of Vocational Rehabilitation services, and restructure existing incentives so that those categories are given priority, including abolition of the simplistic use and reporting of successful case closures. One might assign highest value to serving those with the severest handicaps (as the "Rehabilitation Act of 1973" does), or to young persons, unemployed persons, persons who show promise of yielding high economic benefits in relation to cost, etc. One might take a dynamic and flexible approach depending on the level of vocational impairment. For example, "normal" youth might receive no special vocational services unless they are unemployed after leaving school, in which case the State Employment Service could give them job information. All handicapped youth might be screened before leaving school, and mildly handicapped youth might automatically be given both job information and placement assistance upon leaving school, and then if they are not vocationally successful, full VR services could be given. And severely handicapped youth could be automatically offered VR services beginning well before their scheduled departure from school. Whatever the priorities assigned, the program will come closer to meeting its goals with its available resources if effort is concentrated on finding, accepting, and

[55]See R-1220-HEW, p. 82.

[56]U.S. General Accounting Office, *Effectiveness of Vocational Rehabilitation in Helping the Handicapped,* Report to Congress by the Comptroller General of the United States, Number B-164031 (3), Washington, D.C., April 3, 1973.

[57]R-1220-HEW, p. 85.

serving clients in priority categories. For example, even before passage of the new Act, we seriously question whether the VR program legislators and administrators really intended that 69 percent of the young visually impaired clients should be drawn from the categories "one good eye" and "other visual impairment" rather than from the more severely handicapped "partially sighted" and "blind" categories. For visual types of impairment, the charge that some VR counselors inflate their success statistics by "creaming" and selecting easy-to-serve clients appears to be true. To best satisfy the intent of the "Rehabilitation Act of 1973"—that the most severely handicapped persons be served first—much better definitions and reporting, including disaggregation within each type of handicap by degree of severity, are needed.

At present, one major way in which the system judges and reportedly rewards its personnel is based on total successful closures and the percentage of successful closures in relation to clients served. The use of gross numbers of successful closures provides disincentives to serving hard-to-rehabilitate clients, disincentives to an individual VR counselor's conserving on program costs, disincentives to offering a wide choice of occupations to clients, and disincentives to train for more than minimal pay and skill occupations. The much discussed, but as yet unimplemented, concept of disaggregating the clients served by degree of difficulty of rehabilitation and type or quality of "gainful employment" obtained is a good one. Either a set of measures of "effect" of each counselor and VR agency, or a weighted measure giving higher value to higher priority types of results, would be a major improvement over the present simplistic measure with its inherent disincentives to desired performance.[58]

Conduct thorough evaluations of state programs that have significantly better than average gainful employment, occupational, and earnings results for handicapped youth, to determine desirable characteristics of those programs that may be exportable to other states. The reasons for low average earnings of successful VR clients, despite extensive and costly services, and the often-heard complaint about the narrow range of occupational choices offered clients, should be

---

[58]For a discussion of these issues, see Ronald W. Conley, "Weighted Case Closures: Concepts, Problems," *Rehabilitation Record,* September-October 1973; J. H. Noble, "A Simple System for Weighting Case Closures," Rehabilitation Services Administration, Office of Planning and Policy Development, Washington, D.C., 1973; K. W. Reagles, G. N. Wright, and A. J. Butler, "Toward a New Criterion of Vocational Rehabilitation Success," *Rehabilitation Counseling Bulletin,* June 1972; and A. Hawryluk, "Rehabilitation Gain: A Better Indicator Needed," *Journal of Rehabilitation,* September-October 1972.

investigated more vigorously than they are now so that this dual problem at least can be alleviated. The current programs in the 50 states are natural "experiments" in alternative methods of serving these youth; they represent a wealth of relatively untapped data that should shed light on program effectiveness as a function of the type and quantity of services provided, expenditures, means of providing the service, type of handicapped youth, and so forth. The current system of reporting on individual clients is the most comprehensive of any we observed in federal programs, but it still has some deficiencies. For example, some of its categories of reasons for rejection or failure to rehabilitate a client are not very illuminating, and it does not adequately mine the wealth of its own data as a means of discovering and evaluating problems and options for program improvement.

Increase the number and improve the geographic distribution of specialists in vocational services to specific types of handicapped persons. Special expertise is needed in serving certain categories of handicapped persons; the need is especially critical for profoundly deaf clients with little or no oral communication skill.[59] Most states now have such specialists, but care should be taken that they are available at least in every major metropolitan region. This holds for both the Vocational Rehabilitation program and the State Employment Service program.

Increase the coordination between Vocational Education, Vocational Rehabilitation, and State Employment Service programs, and establish a mechanism for outreach to all handicapped youth in their latter school years, with follow-up after the time of leaving school. In our interviews with various of these agencies in five states, coordination varied from excellent to practically nonexistent. By and large, however, it appeared that these three programs operate fairly independently of one another at the client level, although they have very closely related purposes and often have "coordinating committees" at the agency management level.[60] They also tend to serve clients that come to them, rather than setting out well-defined priority

[59]S. P. Quigley (ed.), *The Vocational Rehabilitation of Deaf People,* U.S. Department of Health, Education, and Welfare, Publication (SRS) 72-25037, Washington, D.C., 1972; and N. Tully, "Trends in the Professional Preparation of Rehabilitation Workers with the Deaf," *Deafness Annual,* Vol. 3, Professional Rehabilitation Workers with the Adult Deaf, Inc., Silver Spring, Maryland, 1973.

[60]The "Vocational Education Act Amendments of 1968" require cooperative arrangements between Vocational Rehabilitation and Vocational Education agencies, and the "Rehabilitation Act of 1973" (P.L. 93-112) requires that state VR annual plans provide for intergovernmental cooperative arrangements.

categories of youth who need service and then reaching out to find those youth. It would be inexpensive to arrange for automatic referral to or outreach by VR, for example, for all handicapped youth, both in school and applying for State Employment Service assistance. Such a stratagem would provide VR with fairly comprehensive rolls of potential clients from which they could select high-priority types of youth. The precedent is the referral program for disabled welfare clients.

One possible follow-up mechanism not now used is to monitor former clients' earnings through Social Security records.

Modify the State Employment Service program to provide more trained specialists in the placement of handicapped persons, and give those specialists a caseload well below that of current SES personnel. The current workload of SES personnel is so heavy that it appears very difficult for them to provide meaningful job information to handicapped persons, let alone placement service. In addition, the current information systems used in the states are improving but still leave much to be desired in matching handicapped clients with available jobs.

Chapter 14

INCOME MAINTENANCE

OVERVIEW

This chapter discusses programs that provide direct financial aid to a handicapped youth or his family, principally in the form of cash transfers rather than in-kind aid such as in the Food Stamp program. The chapter briefly summarizes current financial assistance programs, describes the nature of expenditures for various types of services needed by handicapped youth, and presents recommendations for improvement. Earlier chapters have discussed human resources development programs that contribute to economic security, such as education and vocational rehabilitation, and programs that provide services to the family instead of cash transfers.

In 1970, welfare agencies spent some $635 million to aid about one million physically and mentally handicapped youth. Of this amount, about $18 million and $25 million, respectively, went for assistance to vision and hearing handicapped youth. The federal, state, and local shares were 54.6, 34.6, and 10.8 percent. (See Tables 14.1 and 14.2.)

The four primary programs serving physically and mentally handicapped youth are Social Security Disability Insurance (SSDI); Supplemental Security Income (SSI), providing aid to the aged, blind, and disabled;[1] Aid to Families with Dependent Children (AFDC); and Income Tax Exemption for the Blind (ITEB). The estimated numbers of physically and mentally handicapped youth served by these programs in 1970 were SSDI, 14,700; AB, 4000; APTD, 29,000; AFDC, 976,000; and ITEB, 9000. The average yearly expenditure per youth served was about $635.

Prior to the Social Security Amendments of 1972, most youth given aid were eligible *not* because of their handicaps, but because they

---

[1]SSI replaces two programs that provided financial aid to handicapped youth: Aid to the Blind (AB) and Aid to the Permanently and Totally Disabled (APTD).

were part of a family receiving Aid to Families with Dependent Children, and the AFDC program does not make allowance for the added expense of the handicapped child. The 1972 amendments permit youth from needy families to draw significantly increased aid based on the existence of a handicap, under the new combined Supplemental Security Income program providing aid to the aged, blind, and disabled. The SSI does not have the age restrictions of the former Aid to the Blind (which in most states did not serve persons less than 16 or 18 years old) and Aid to the Permanently and Totally Disabled programs (which did not serve anyone less than 18 years old).

Table 14.1
ESTIMATED FINANCIAL ASSISTANCE AND SOCIAL SERVICE EXPENDITURES FOR HANDICAPPED YOUTH, 1970

Program	Financial Assistance			
	Federal	*State*	*Local*	*Total*
SSDI	$ 10,936,000	$ 0	$ 0	$ 10,936,000
AB	3,190,000	1,940,000	420,000	5,550,000
APTD	20,110,000	12,750,000	3,330,000	36,190,000
AFDC[b]	311,346,000	205,046,000	64,476,000	580,868,000
GA	0	NE[a]	NE	NE
ITEB	1,000,000	NE	0	1,000,000
Total	$346,582,000	$219,736,000	$68,226,000	$634,544,000

SOURCE: See section "Current Financial Assistance Programs" in this chapter for data sources and estimation methods.

[a] Not estimated, but assumed to be a small portion of total expenditures for financial assistance to handicapped youth.

[b] 1971.

Table 14.2
ESTIMATED FINANCIAL ASSISTANCE TO YOUTH BY TYPE OF HANDICAP, 1970

Handicap	Estimated Expenditures
Visual impairment	$ 18,276,000
Hearing impairment	24,902,000
Speech impairment	203,993,000
Crippling and other health impairments	95,620,000
Mental retardation	160,532,000
Emotional disturbance	88,027,000
Learning disability	43,194,000
Total	$634,544,000

SOURCE: See section "Current Financial Assistance Programs" in this chapter for data sources and estimation methods.

The federal government uses two primary functional mechanisms in this program area: direct provision of assistance in the SSDI and SSI programs, and funding of assistance through state and local agencies in the large AFDC program. Federal involvement in financial assistance has grown to the point where the majority of the funds expended on needy handicapped youth are federal, and three of the five major programs are federally operated. This dominant federal role apparently evolved for two main reasons: (1) state, local, and private sources have had insufficient financial resources to provide socially desirable minimum income levels to an acceptable fraction of the needy population; and (2) under state and locally operated programs, there has been a socially undesirable inequity in the distribution of funds across states. While authorities disagree on what level of financial aid is adequate, and what distribution of funds is equitable, the President's Commission on Income Maintenance Programs concluded that existing aid levels were inadequate and that the distribution of aid was inequitable.[2] In brief, the federal government acquired its present role because it had both the funds and the inclination to distribute them to the needy population across states more equitably and to raise the payments to a more nearly adequate level. Although their roles have gradually diminished, both state and local governments are still very much involved; they supply nearly half the funds expended for needy handicapped youth and operate the AFDC program.

The Federal Social Security Insurance Program is based on a social insurance model wherein an employee and his employer, and self-employed persons, contribute to the system to provide coverage against disruption or reduction of the worker's income due to disability, death, or retirement. Payment levels are not based primarily on need, but on the rate and number of quarter-years of previous contribution to the system, subject to maximums and minimums. Under the Childhood Disability provisions of this program, a person aged 18 or older who has been disabled prior to his twenty-second birthday, and who is the child or grandchild of a retired or disabled worker, could receive payments of up to $166 a month beginning September 1972, while the disabled child or grandchild of a deceased worker could receive up to $256.90 beginning September 1972 if he earns $125 or less per month. Because most handicapped youth under 22 have neither accumulated the required previous earnings record, nor have a retired, disabled, or deceased parent, only a small

---

[2] *The President's Commission on Income Maintenance Programs, Background Papers,* U.S. Government Printing Office, Washington, D.C., November 1969.

fraction actually receive benefits, averaging about $62 a month, from this program. The breakdown by type of handicap is approximately 1 percent visual and 2 percent hearing impaired.

Prior to 1972, the AB and APTD public assistance programs were operated within the states and jointly funded by federal and state governments. The "Social Security Act of 1972" combined these two programs with Old Age Assistance (OAA); the new combined program is federally funded and operated. The new program, called Supplemental Security Income (SSI), established uniform basic payment levels for recipients in all 50 states and the District of Columbia. (Individual states may supplement these federal payments, which could take into account the variations from state to state in the cost of living.) Eligibility requirements, which previously varied from state to state, are also uniform for new applicants. Persons of any age can be eligible, and those 65 years or older need not be blind or disabled. Thus, the new SSI program alleviates many past inequities in payment levels and eligibility requirements which varied from state to state.

Under a state plan in effect as of October 1972, people on the APTD rolls for December 1973 and for at least one month prior to July of 1973 were considered disabled for purposes of the new program, and were considered to meet the resource requirements of the new program. These same provisions apply to people on AB, except that they need not have been on the rolls for at least one month prior to July 1973. These persons were transferred to the SSI rolls on January 1, 1974, if they also met the other requirements of Title XVI, such as income, age, relationship, and the like. A "blind" applicant, however, who is engaged in employment may exclude his working expenses from his earned income. New applicants must meet all requirements of the new program. For a disabled applicant to qualify for payments under the new program, based upon a disability other than visual, he must meet the income and resources test and be unable to engage in any substantial gainful activity by reason of a medically determinable physical or mental impairment that either can be expected to result in death or has lasted (or can be expected to last) for a continuous period of not less than 12 months. A child's income and resources include those of his parents or his parent's spouse, if his parent or parent's spouse lives with him, whether or not they are available to him, except to the extent "determined to be inequitable." "Blind" applicants must meet the income and resources test and must have central visual acuity of $20/200$ or less in the better eye with the use of a correcting lens, or restriction of visual field to 20° or less. Ability to engage in a substantial gainful activity is not a factor in determining eligibility for the blind. One question to be asked is why, if blind, one must be blind and needy to qualify, whereas, if disabled, one must be disabled, needy, *and* unable to work.

As amended by P.L. 93-233, payments for an eligible person who does not have an eligible spouse were set at the rate of $140 per month beginning in January 1974, reduced by the amount of the individual's countable income. Payments for an eligible person who has an eligible spouse were at the rate of $210 per month in January 1974, reduced by the amount of the person's countable income (combined with that of his or her spouse). P.L. 93-233 also raised these figures to $146 and $219, respectively, effective July 1974. These payment levels are higher than the old program payment levels in most states, and any state may supplement the federal payment level if it wishes to. However, the level of payment above the federal minimum to people on the state rolls in December 1973 must be maintained in order to get matching federal funds for Medicaid.

Under the pre-1972 AB program, the average monthly grant ranged from $59 in one state to $177 in another, with a United States average of $104. Coupled with varying payment levels were varying AB eligibility standards by age (5 years in one state, 18 years in many others), by whether or not property liens were required, and by the allowable value of home and personal possessions. Five percent of all AB clients were under 22. We estimated that in 1970, there were 4076 recipients under 22, upon whom a total of $5.55 million was expended. The annualized expenditures per recipient varied across the states from $714 to $2058 and averaged $1372. The number of recipients per 100,000 state population aged 0 to 21 varied from 0.5 to 19. The fraction of total program expenses devoted to administration, service, and training rather than financial assistance varied across states from 5 to 32 percent.

The APTD program had a U.S. average monthly recipient grant of $97 in 1970. Total annual expenditures per recipient averaged $1229, but varied across states from $724 to $1837. A total of 29,000 physically and mentally handicapped persons aged 22 or less that year received APTD, or 3.4 percent of all APTD recipients. Age requirements were uniform across states at 18 years, but other eligibility requirements varied markedly. The number of recipients aged 18 to 21 per 100,000 state population averaged 205, but ranged from 27 to 625. Perhaps the most graphic example of the inequity of the payments distribution is the fact that nearly half of all APTD payments to recipients under 22 in 1970 were paid in California.

The AFDC program provides financial assistance to needy families with children, but to handicapped children only if they belong to families receiving AFDC. In March 1971, the average monthly payment was only $49.60 per recipient person. However, the program is so large that an estimated $580.868 million was expended on 975,920 handicapped youth in 1970. This is by far the most massive financial assistance program serving handicapped youth, and an excellent contact point for identifying those who need nonfinancial types of assistance. As we indicated in Chap. 7, progress in AFDC in implementing a mandated screening program has been slow.

The legally blind are the only handicapped persons allowed to claim an additional exemption from federal income taxes. The exemption may be claimed for a taxpayer or for his spouse but not for other dependents; parents cannot claim an extra exemption for handicapped children. At a marginal tax rate of 20 percent in 1972,[3] the $750 exemption means a tax reduction of $150 per person. This is, in effect, a financial assistance payment to the legally blind person.

General Assistance is a state-local program with eligibility based on financial need. Although information is not readily available, we suspect very few handicapped youth receive long-term GA because of the incentive for states to place such youth on SSI or AFDC where federal funding can be obtained.

In a survey of state welfare agencies, problems cited in the present system included lack of financial support for the programs and inadequate coordination of services.

In summary, we have six principal observations on financial assistance programs for handicapped youth.

1. There was no financial assistance program for handicapped youth prior to the Social Security Amendments of 1972 that removed age restrictions on Aid to the Blind and Disabled. Those prior assistance programs aimed at the handicapped did not serve persons less than 16 or 18 in most states. The AFDC assistance program for needy families with children is designed for the needy and not the handicapped, so allowance is not made for the added expense of the handicapped child for those families who do receive AFDC. The individual payment level of the new Supplemental Security Income program providing aid to the aged, blind, and disabled is significantly higher than the AFDC average payment.

2. The fact that the AFDC and other programs annually contact approximately one million handicapped children represents a great opportunity to screen and identify handicapping conditions in that population and to determine whether nonfinancial assistance needs are being met. Early medical intervention, provision

---

[3]The 1972 marginal tax rate for a married person filing jointly with a taxable income of $4000 to $8000 was 19 percent, while the comparable rate for a single person earning $4000 to $6000 was 21 percent.

of sensory aids, or assistance with language development for deaf children may be especially important.

3. Financial assistance programs do not reach out to find handicapped people. Financial aid is given to needy families with handicapped youth who ask for aid, not necessarily to those with the greatest need.

4. Inequity in payment levels and eligibility requirements exists across states. The new federally administered and combined Supplemental Security Income program corrects many of the former inequities.

5. Although many authorities feel the present payment levels are inadequate, they have neither agreed upon definitions of adequacy and payment levels necessary to provide a socially acceptable standard of living nor studied them in the depth warranted by the importance of the topic.

6. Program evaluation data are woefully inadequate. The estimates of handicapped or other subpopulations reached must be based on rather tenuous assumptions; knowledge of social and other services delivered is scant; and knowledge of the actual effects that the financial assistance program has on the recipients is a small fraction of what it should be.

ROLES AND GOALS

The Federal Role and Objectives

Through a history of legislation which began in 1935, the federal government has accepted partial responsibility for assuring Americans some measure of economic security. One means is through programs affecting individual income levels. Such programs include those aimed at human resources development, such as adult basic education; social insurance, in particular Old Age, Survivors, Disability, and Health Insurance (OASDHI); cash transfer programs, which include public assistance and veterans' pensions; and income-in-kind transfer programs, two well known ones being the Food Stamp Program and Medicare. In addressing income maintenance, we look principally in this section at programs involving cash transfers, as these specifically affect the handicapped.

Originally, the "Social Security Act" provided for federal funds to assist states in providing income to the needy aged, the blind, and families with dependent children. In 1950, permanently and totally disabled persons were added to the federally supported program.[4] In the late 1950s, the federal government began using funds for administration and social service expenses associated with income maintenance programs. The "1972 Social Security Act" Amendments repre-

---

[4]For a more detailed picture, see *The President's Commission on Income Maintenance Programs.*

sent a significant change in role in that the federal government took over operation of Aid to the Aged, Blind, and Disabled programs from the states and established uniform payment levels and eligibility standards across states under the Supplemental Security Income program. It also removed the minimum age restrictions on recipients. Thus, in 37 years the federal government has taken the dominant role in financing and operating income maintenance programs for needy handicapped persons; i.e., it finances and delivers income payments to (1) needy physically and mentally impaired persons, and (2) children who incidentally may be handicapped but receive aid because their families qualify for AFDC.

The President's Commission on Income Maintenance Programs presented the following concepts for evaluating transfer programs:[5] clearly defined rights for potential participants; adequate cash payment to achieve socially desired income distributions; equity for both recipients and nonrecipients; minimum adverse incentives; and low administrative costs. These evaluation concepts are consistent with those of this research project.

In evaluating existing programs against these criteria, the Commission concluded that a new income maintenance program was needed because poverty had not been eliminated under the existing three-part system (built on the ideas that employment would provide adequate income to those who worked, social insurance would assist those forced out of jobs, and residual aid would go to those who were unemployable). The Commission called for a new program that the federal government would finance and administer. A start toward this new program were the "Social Security Act Amendments of 1972," which incorporate some (but by no means all) of the Commission's recommendations.

The main problem in dealing with the goals of income maintenance programs is to define "need" and "adequate" income. Most states have a nebulous definition of need that typically includes words like "sufficient income or other resources to provide a reasonable subsistence compatible with decency and health." This general definition is then translated into dollar terms, often without real knowledge of what various income levels mean in terms of the goods and services that can be purchased.

Models, Functions, Rationales, and Processes

Since 1935 the federal government's welfare role has evolved unmistakably toward direct operation. The "1972 Social Security Act Amendments" continue and strengthen that trend by giving opera-

[5]Ibid., pp. 3–6.

tion of the Aid to the Aged, Blind, and Disabled programs to the federal government under the SSI program.

Two dominant rationalizations have operated historically that account for the federal welfare trend toward direct operation. Insufficient state and local resources have certainly been at the root of and have justified many federal policies, but this rationale becomes weaker as revenue sharing redistributes resources back to local authorities. The balance wheel rationale should continue to be valid as more authority and responsibility are shifted back to the states to deliver and account for specific services and programs, because revenue sharing may redistribute funds across the states.

CURRENT FINANCIAL ASSISTANCE PROGRAMS

The Social Security Insurance System

The Social Security Insurance system is based upon a social insurance model of income transfer. The worker, his employer, and self-employed persons are taxed to finance the system of Old Age, Survivors, Disability, and Health Insurance. In return, the worker is covered against certain types of economic risk—disruption or reduction of income due to death, disability, or retirement. If a person covered by Social Security becomes disabled or attains retirement age, he and certain dependent relatives are entitled to benefits, and if he dies, certain surviving relatives are entitled to benefits. Children receive benefits to age 18 (to age 22 if full-time students) regardless of whether or not they are disabled. Need or financial condition is *not* a factor in determining eligibility. The monthly amount of the benefit is based largely on the rate at which contributions were made (a function of earnings) and the number of quarters during which contributions were made, subject to minimums and maximums. The overall benefits for the Social Security system are established and changed by Congressional legislative action.[6]

Under the Childhood Disability Beneficiary Program the "Social Security Act" provides for benefits to handicapped youth who are dependents of the adult worker. To qualify for benefits under this program a person must (1) be the son or daughter of an insured worker who is retired, deceased, or disabled; (2) be at least 18 years

---

[6]U.S. Department of Health, Education, and Welfare, *The Benefit Provisions of the Old Age, Survivors, Disability and Health Insurance System,* Social Security Administration, DHEW Publication No. SSA 72-11500 (8-71), April 1971; and the U.S. Department of Health, Education, and Welfare, *Social Security Programs in the United States,* Social Security Administration, March 1968; and letter from F. L. Lunsford, Chief, Rehabilitation Planning and Coordination Branch, Social Security Administration, to J. S. Kakalik, The Rand Corporation, June 1, 1973.

of age or older; and (3) have been continuously disabled prior to his eighteenth birthday.[7]

The definition of disability for a child is the same as for a disabled worker; i.e., the individual must be unable to engage in any substantial gainful activity by reason of a medically determinable physical or mental impairment that can be expected to result in death or that has lasted or can be expected to last for a continuous period of at least one year. Under the Social Security disability program, earnings exceeding $140 a month have been established as an indication of substantial gainful activity, and an individual who derives such earnings on the basis of his service is usually not considered disabled within the meaning of the "Social Security Act." Under the definition, substantial gainful activity means the performance of significant duties over a reasonable period of time in work for remuneration or profit or in work of a type generally performed for remuneration or profit.

The Social Security Administration has agreements with 54 state agencies to carry out vital functions in the development and evaluation of disability claims. All but six of these state agencies operate under a vocational rehabilitation plan. These six are either independent agencies or operate under umbrella agencies. Whether the disability determination is made by a VR agency or another state agency, every disability determination includes an evaluation of vocational rehabilitation potential, and persons who can reasonably be expected to benefit from vocational rehabilitation are referred for services.

Additionally, Titles XVI and II provide for reimbursement of VR agencies for rehabilitation services rendered for SSI recipients and selected Social Security disability beneficiaries.

Disability determinations are reviewed by the Social Security Administration's national office in Baltimore to assure consistency and conformity with national regulations. Benefits to a childhood disabled beneficiary are paid on the basis of the father's or mother's work record and earnings account. The benefit level varies depending on the parent's work history and also on whether the parent's status is deceased, retired, or disabled. In 1970, for example, the maximum benefit was $125.40 per month if the parent was retired or disabled and $188.10 if the parent was deceased.

The 1966 Social Security Survey of the Disabled[8] revealed that the

---

[7]The "Social Security Amendments of 1972" changed this to 22 years, the change becoming effective in January 1973.

[8]L. D. Haber, "The Disabled Beneficiary—A Comparison of Factors Related to Benefit Entitlements," *Social Security Survey of the Disabled, 1966,* U.S. Department of Health, Education, and Welfare, Social Security Administration, Office of Research and Statistics, Report 7, June 1969.

population of childhood disability beneficiaries had approximately the same distribution with respect to sex as the general population—half were men and half were women. The median age was 37, and more than 75 percent had completed less than 8 years of school. Few had any current employment, and five out of six had never been employed. For most of this group, Social Security benefits were the principal source of income.

We estimate that approximately 14,700 individuals aged 18-21 receive childhood disability benefits in any one year.[9] In 1968, approximately 245,000 childhood disability beneficiaries received $15.1 million in monthly benefits. This is an average of $62 per month per recipient, or $744 annually. Applying this annualized figure to our above estimate gives a conservative estimate of $10.936 million[10] in money payments per year from the childhood disability program to youth aged 18-21. The breakdown by type of handicap[11] is approximately 1 percent visual impairments, 2 percent hearing impairments, 54 percent mental retardation, 15 percent mental illness, 4 percent orthopedic impairments, and 24 percent other health impairments.

Public Assistance

In addition to the OASDHI, the "Social Security Act" also provides for federal funds for money payments, medical care, and social services for persons who are aged, blind, totally and permanently disabled, and for low-income families with dependent children. These public assistance payments are based on financial need and not conditioned on the recipient having worked and paid into the system a certain number of quarters. *Thus, the model is one of "payments to the needy" rather than one of "insurance."*

Supplemental Security Income   Prior to 1972, federal grants for money payments were made available to states on a matching basis under four separate categories of public assistance programs or under a

[9]Approximately 20,000 new childhood disability cases are approved annually. Of these new recipients, 50 percent are aged 18-24. Assuming these to be evenly distributed across ages, on the average 1470 are in each age—18, 19, etc. Accumulating new recipients and those registered in previous years gives the estimate of 14,700 aged 18-21.

[10]It is estimated that 13,000 additional people became eligible for childhood disability benefits as a result of the age change in the "1972 Social Security Amendments." This group has not been included in the above estimates as no information on them is available. U.S. Congress, Joint Committee on Ways and Means, *Summary of Social Security Amendments of 1972 as Approved by the Conferees,* 92d Cong., 2d Sess., H.R. 1, October 17, 1972, p. 3.

[11]*Social Security Disability Applicant Statistics,* Social Security Administration Publication 35-71 (5-71), pp. 80-81.

single combined program depending on the administering state's agency structure. That is, monies were available under Old Age Assistance, AB, APTD, and AFDC.

In the administration, organization, and conduct of the public assistance programs prior to 1972, the federal government established guidelines and requirements within which the states developed and administered their own public assistance programs. The states set varying eligibility requirements as well as amounts of the assistance payments. Each state defined its own minimum standard of living, which was used in determining individual or family need.

Under the new SSI program, an eligible aged, blind, or disabled individual who does not have an eligible spouse may receive up to $130.00 per month in 1974; an eligible individual with an eligible spouse may receive up to $195.00. If they wish, states can provide payments to individuals who, because of income or resource limitations, do not qualify for federal payments. Recipients of federal program assistance will be allowed to have a home, personal property, and life insurance up to a reasonable value, to be determined. In determining a person's eligibility to receive Supplemental Security Income payments, certain income is disregarded. The first $65 of earned income is disregarded as well as an additional $20 of either earned *or* unearned income.

Initial estimates show an additional total caseload of 2.8 million persons on the SSI program in 1973. With the 3.4 million estimated to be eligible in that year under existing state plans, this makes a total of 6.2 million cases. It is estimated that by 1977 these figures will have grown to 7.2 million, just twice the number that would have been served had the old program continued.[12]

Aid to Families with Dependent Children AFDC is basically an income maintenance program. It is not intended to service handicapped youth specifically, but rather is intended for families with children to whom assistance payments are given based on the family's need.

Several studies have been made of AFDC, but only one investigated the incidence of mental or physical impairment among AFDC children. In the AFDC study of 1967, published in 1970, mental and physical impairments are reported for 47 percent of the estimated 3.9 million recipient children in late 1967.[13]

[12]U.S. Senate, Committee on Finance, Russell B. Long, Chairman, Material related to H.R. 1, *Aid to the Aged, Blind and Disabled; Social Services; Fiscal Relief for States,* 92d Cong., 1st Sess., U.S. Government Printing Office, Washington, D.C., 1971.

[13]U.S. Department of Health, Education, and Welfare, *Findings of the 1967 AFDC Study, Part I. Demographic and Program Characteristics,* National Center for Social Statistics, NCSS Report AFDC-3 (67), July 1970.

These figures indicate that approximately 25 percent of AFDC recipient youth have some physical or mental impairment as evaluated by a professional, and an additional 22 percent are cited by nonprofessionals as being impaired. The data are not of high utility to our study because the 1967 survey team did not give a medical exam to each youth in the study and because the data include youth with slight impairments; e.g., the category "visual impairments" is large, loosely defined, and certainly includes more than legally blind youth. In contrast to the 25.3 percent reported by professional opinion as mentally or physically impaired in the 1967 AFDC survey, the percentage of the total population of youth with an impairment of sufficient magnitude to be termed a handicap is only about half that large.

Without better data, we assume that the incidence rate of handicapping conditions in AFDC recipient youth is the same as the incidence rate for the entire U.S. young population.

In March 1971, there were 7.371 million child recipients of AFDC in the United States, and the average monthly payment per recipient was $49.60. In FY 1970 the respective federal, state, and local contributions were 53.6, 35.3, and 11.1 percent of the total.[14] Assuming that the average grant for handicapped youth is the same as that for all AFDC recipients, then we estimate a total of 975,920 handicapped youth received AFDC in March 1971, at a total annual assistance expenditure level of $580.868 million. Of the total, approximately $311.345 million were federal funds, $205.046 million were state funds, and $64.476 million were local funds.

General Assistance

The third aspect of income maintenance in the United States is General Assistance. This is a noncategorical program that provides financial assistance on the basis of need. The programs are financed solely from state and local tax revenues; there is no federal contribution. Consequently, each state is left entirely on its own to decide if there should be a GA program, what purposes it should serve, the eligibility standards, benefit levels, and administrative agencies and procedures.

It is difficult to generalize about the GA programs because of the wide range of differences among the states. *Characteristics of General Assistance in the U.S.,*[15] shows that in many states GA is limited

[14]U.S. Department of Health, Education, and Welfare, *AFDC: Selected Statistical Data on Families Aided and Program Operations,* National Center for Social Statistics Report, NCSS Report H-4(71), June 1971.

[15]U.S. Department of Health, Education, and Welfare, *Characteristics of General Assistance in the U.S.,* 1970 ed., Social and Rehabilitation Service, Public Assistance Report No. 39, December 31, 1969.

to short-term and emergency assistance only. Many states make assistance dependent upon a work test, limiting assistance to unemployable persons or to families without an employable member. None of the requirements relate specifically to a handicap condition; presumably this would be accounted for where a work test is used. In addition, more than half of the states have relatives' financial responsibility laws. In 17 states, GA is financed completely by the local jurisdiction. The number of GA recipients in 1970 was 1.056 million, and the average monthly grant per recipient was $58.[16]

Income Tax Exemptions

Legally blind persons are the only handicapped allowed to claim an additional exemption on federal income taxes. The exemption may be claimed for a taxpayer or for his spouse but not for other dependents; thus, an extra exemption for handicapped youth cannot be claimed on the parents' tax return. At a marginal tax rate of 20 percent,[17] the $750 exemption means a tax reduction of $150 per person. Since Internal Revenue Service data are not disaggregated by age of taxpayer, the number of youth under age 22 claiming the exemption can only be estimated. If we assume that no more than half of the legally blind persons aged 17–21 would be able to claim the extra exemption, then the total income tax reduction for blind youth would be on the order of $1 million a year.

FINANCIAL AID AND THE NATURE OF EXPENDITURES FOR HANDICAPPED YOUTH

In considering an income maintenance program for handicapped persons, and in considering the issue of whether to provide funds directly to the families or indirectly through payments to service providers, one must examine the nature of the services and expenditures needed by the handicapped person. Several types of service expenditures are discussed below.

Prevention

By definition, expenditures for prevention cannot be part of an income maintenance program for handicapped persons. Payments

---

[16]U.S. Department of Health, Education, and Welfare, *Graphic Presentation of Public Assistance and Related Data, Demographic and Program Characteristics, Financial Characteristics of Recipients, 1971,* Social and Rehabilitation Service, DHEW Publication No. (SRS) 73-03101, October 6, 1972, pp. 3, 30.

[17]The 1972 marginal tax rate on a married person filing jointly with a taxable income of $4000 to $8000 was 19 percent, while the comparable rate for a single person earning $4000 to $6000 was 21 percent.

could be provided for preventive medical care in health programs (e.g., as a vaccination program or as a mandatorily covered expense under health insurance), and some small portion of public assistance payments to families about to have a child or that have children who are not physically or mentally handicapped can be considered as prevention expenditures because of known linkage between nutrition, for example, and handicapping conditions.

Identification

Also by definition, identification cannot be funded as income maintenance for handicapped persons, but is a necessary predecessor of that income maintenance.

Direction

Direction is an information-based service that depends on a steady flow of funds to enable the regular collection and updating of information, coordination with other service agencies in providing an appropriate mix of services to a child, and adequate follow-up for the children. Since, in general, this service is not provided well now, since no agency such as the Regional Direction Centers we propose exists in most areas, and since current direction expenditures are a hidden implicit portion of expenditures for other services such as medical care, education, welfare, and rehabilitation, it does not appear practical to provide funds directly to families for purchase of direction services.

Counseling

The need for counseling is highly variable, and counseling is often provided as part of a package of services from a service agency. If funds are provided directly to a family for purchase of counseling, the amount should be determined on an individual need basis and reassessed periodically.

Medical Treatment

With the extremely high variance over time of medical expenditures for a handicapped child, it is highly impractical to expect a family to pay all their medical bills from a fixed level of income maintenance. Some sort of health care program appears essential, although the forms it might take cover a wide range, including the present Crippled Children's Service program and the proposed National Health Insurance. A family in financial need could be given the insurance or other health care program service or, through regulations on the receipt of income maintenance, the family might be required to purchase health insurance of an approved type and be expected to pay for a small portion of the general medical expenses. If an insurance mechanism is adopted, however, we recommend not applying such a "deductible" to insurance payments for services directly related to the handicap, such as screening and diagnostics, medical or surgical treatment of the handicapping condition, and provision of sensory aids. Applying a "deductible" to those types of services could result in the child's being denied essential services, while yielding relatively little monetary savings.

Education

Current practice is to provide funds for special education to the education agency directly rather than to the families. One practice in very limited use is to give the family a special education "voucher," whereby special education services unavailable locally can be obtained from a school in another region or another state.

Vocational and Special Training, and Job Placement

The need for these services is also highly variable among handicapped youth and over time. Consequently, if funds are provided directly to families for purchase of these services, the amount should be determined on an individual need basis.

Sensory Aids

While the need for one or more sensory aids by hearing and vision handicapped youth is nearly universal, the original costs and time intervals between replacement of personal aids is not constant. Consequently, here again, if funds are to be provided directly to the family for purchase of the aids, the amount of those funds should depend upon the individual degree of handicap and expected life of the aid.

Transportation

For handicapped youth and, in certain cases, for the escorting family member, special transportation needs will arise primarily in conjunction with obtaining some other service such as special education, medical treatment, or some types of special training. Since the added costs of transportation depend on how often those other services are needed and how far it is from the child's residence to service facilities, transportation costs are not uniform and are better handled for financially needy families as part of the costs for those other services—that is, as a segment of the special education budget and as a covered expense under a health care funding program, rather than as a fixed income supplement.

These expenses could also be included as a variable component of an income maintenance program, with the payment determined separately for each individual and with required certification of receipt of other services to which the child must travel.

Necessities of Daily Living

Historically, income maintenance of a fixed amount each month has been provided to help financially needy families to purchase housing, clothing, food, and other goods and services needed by both handicapped and nonhandicapped persons in daily living. The amount a family needs for these types of expenditures for their handicapped child may be slightly higher than that needed for a "normal" child. However, reliable data on the degree of additional need are not available.

NEEDED IMPROVEMENT IN INCOME MAINTENANCE PROGRAMS

Improvements needed in the provision of financial assistance to handicapped youth are discussed in this section; our recommendations appear in italics.[18]

Undertake research and evaluation to obtain much better planning information on the financial needs of handicapped persons. Data on what these programs are accomplishing with respect to handicapped persons are woefully inadequate. Decisions on levels of financial assistance to the handicapped person and his family must be based upon very little information in two essential areas: what the extra financial needs of various groups of handicapped persons are, and

[18]For a review of welfare reform efforts over the last decade, see Gilbert Y. Steiner, *The State of Welfare,* The Brookings Institution, Washington, D.C., 1971. An earlier comprehensive study of welfare in general is J. N. Morgan et al., *Income and Welfare in the United States,* McGraw-Hill, New York, 1962. Current issues in welfare are discussed in a series of papers published by the Subcommittee on Fiscal Policy of the Joint Economic Committee of the Congress of the United States, entitled "Studies in Public Welfare," Papers 1 to 12, dated April 10, 1972 through December 3, 1973. Another Rand report provides an extensive bibliography on welfare-related issues; see D. M. de Ferranti, *Basic Research on Welfare Policies: The Welfare and Non-Welfare Poor in New York City,* The Rand Corporation, R-1381-RC, 1974. Finally, several recent Rand Corporation reports have examined fundamental issues concerning assessment of the effects of various income maintenance programs; these reports go into far more detail than is possible in an overview study like ours. See, for example, J. I. DaVanzo, *An Analytical Framework for Studying the Potential Effects of an Income Maintenance Program on U.S. Interregional Migration,* R-1081-EDA, December 1972; and Dennis N. DeTray, *A Conceptual Basis for the Study of Welfare Reform Effects,* R-1066-DOC, September 1972.

what different levels of support to the handicapped person mean in terms of the total quantity and quality of goods and services that can be purchased with the assistance.[19] The lack of data is a severe impediment to making informed decisions on "need" and "adequate" levels of income assistance. Although many authorities believe the present payment levels are inadequate, they have neither agreed upon definitions of adequacy and payment levels necessary to provide a socially acceptable standard of living nor studied them in the depth warranted by the importance of the topic. Further, the newly implemented SSI program, with its new regulations, needs careful evaluation to see if it is functioning as intended, and how well it is functioning.

Limit direct cash transfers to handicapped youth and their families, in lieu of other mechanisms of making service available, to coverage of normal daily living expenses and to relatively minor special service expenses. This chapter earlier covered the point that, with the major exception of expenditures for daily living, such as for food, housing, and clothing, each of the other major services involves either: (1) expenditures before the child is handicapped or known to be handicapped, in which case the family, by definition, cannot be given dollars in lieu of services; or (2) highly variable and often unpredictable levels of expenses that are not uniform over time and that depend upon the specific needs of the individual handicapped child. In the latter case, the financially needy family could be given an income supplement to cover the cost of the special services. It is desirable, however, to avoid expenditures on families who do not need special services in a given time period, to avoid the possibility that the family will not save the extra funds for the child's future needs, and to avoid the possibility that service needs will exceed the amount of money the family could save from an income supplement. We therefore believe that if funds are to be given to a family for purchase of major goods and services other than those that nonhandicapped persons need for daily living, then it is essential to base the amount of those funds on the handicapped child's periodically assessed need for services. Further, since the child is the one who needs the special service, but is not necessarily the one who decides how the family will spend the money, we believe it highly desirable to protect both the child's rights and society's investment by requiring that any major special income supplements, above income maintenance levels for

[19]While this is a major problem for many groups, it was cited as especially critical for handicapped persons by the Commissioner and several other high-level personnel in HEW's Assistance Payments Administration, in our interviews with them in March 1972.

daily living, be expendable only for meeting the child's specific needs.

If these are to be the procedures, however, there appears to be no persuasive reason for funneling the money through the family rather than directly to the service providers; giving the money to the family does little more than add yet another link to the chain of money-handlers.

Either revise the income tax "extra personal exemption" program to include all severely handicapped persons with relatively low incomes, not just legally blind persons who file a tax return, or restructure the entire program concept. The present extra personal exemption program for legally blind persons is clearly discriminatory; if the program is justifiable for them, by the same rationale it is justifiable for other severely handicapped persons. This program can be questioned on the grounds that it provides a "little something extra" for one type of handicap but not for other types with apparently similar needs, for tax-return filers but not for their children, for persons with sufficient income to pay income taxes but not for others with lesser incomes, and equally for both high-income persons and more needy lower-income persons. This program needs to be thoroughly studied and then revised.

One possible option would be to grant an extra one or two personal exemptions to each taxpayer and dependent who is severely handicapped. Another would be to permit deductions of a portion of all necessary extra expenses incurred because of the handicap of the taxpayer and any of his dependents, with the portion dependent upon the taxpayer's income level and with a maximum ceiling on the amount of the deduction; this is implicitly a voluntary identification program, with the incentive being reduced taxes. A third option would be a revised type of income tax program for handicapped persons that provides benefits ranging from nothing for relatively high-income taxpayers to expense deduction for lower-income taxpayers, to an income "supplement" rather than an income "tax" for handicapped persons in the lower income range; clearly, an income supplement for the handicapped is one major and very flexible alternative to the present Supplementary Security Income program of income maintenance for handicapped persons. Annual qualification might be required and would be voluntary, but could be conditioned on a test of employability or on the person's having participated in other programs such as vocational rehabilitation.

Government contact with youth in families receiving income maintenance represents an opportunity for identification of handicapping conditions, for transfer of youth from the AFDC program to the higher payment SSI program, for diagnosis and treatment under Medicaid or some other health program, and for direction to programs that can supply other needed services. This opportunity should be fully exploited. As we indicated in Chaps. 7 and 13 this opportunity is not being fully exploited, despite special provisions in the Medicaid program for identification and treatment of handicapped youth, and special provision for referral of disabled financial assistance recipients to the Vocational Rehabilitation program.

III

EXPERIENCES AND RECOMMENDATIONS OF THE HANDICAPPED POPULATION

Chapter 15

EXPERIENCES AND RECOMMENDATIONS OF THE HANDICAPPED POPULATION

OVERVIEW FROM THE HEARING AND VISION HANDICAPPED POPULATION'S VIEWPOINT

Evaluation of current and future service policies for handicapped youth requires information from both service providers and recipients. The sample of 77 families personally interviewed had received aid from 665 different service providers, and was selected about equally from (1) the three diverse states of California, Massachusetts, and Wyoming; (2) four types of handicapped youth: the totally blind, partially sighted, profoundly deaf, and hard of hearing; and (3) four age groups, 0 to 5, 6 to 12, 13 to 17, and 18 to 21. Although the sample is too small to use for other than heuristic purposes, the results provided useful insights into the needs and experiences of the handicapped, benefits of various services, and problems of the service system. The family survey should therefore be regarded as a supplement and crosscheck on our analyses presented in this book.

When asked to determine the relative importance of various service needs, families overwhelmingly rated education highest. Medical services and sensory aids were also very important. Services considered and rated less important were vocational training, financial aid, transportation, job placement, counseling, and recreation. (We discussed the importance of identification and direction services, but did not ask the families to rate them.)

When asked if the 665 services had benefited their children, 62 percent of the respondents said they were very beneficial, 24 percent said they were somewhat beneficial, and 14 percent felt the services had yielded little or no benefit.

From the thoughtful and often well-informed opinions of the surveyed parents, a picture emerges of a service system that often surpasses the expectations of its users but has some important shortcomings.

Our interviews led us to make the following major observations:

- In general, service recipients appreciate the service system but are not fully satisified with it.
- Initial identification of the handicapping condition is a major problem.
- Information about available services and direction to the appropriate mix of services is severely lacking.
- The range of services available within a reasonable distance of the families' homes is often very incomplete.
- The quantity of service available is insufficient to meet the need.

Lack of Full Satisfaction with the Service System

Families were generally grateful for the available services, but they saw room for significant improvement.

When asked to assess their experiences with all services and rate their satisfaction with the service system as a whole, 40 percent of the families said they were very satisified, about half said they were satisfied but not completely, and only 5 percent said they were definitely not satisified. Parents of younger children and of less severely handicapped children were least likely to be satisfied. When asked individually about each of the 665 services used, dissatisfaction was reported for 13 percent.

The Problem of Identification

The full set of needed services obviously cannot be given to a handicapped child until the handicap has been identified, and at present identification is too often haphazard, catch-as-catch-can. The parents in our sample reported that initial identification of the impairment was too frequently inaccurate (actual errors were reported by over 10 percent of the families interviewed) or was not made early enough to enable preparations for arranging as nearly normal development as possible for their children. Cases in point were profoundly deaf children who needed service during the preschool language development years. Several sets of parents of these children suspected a problem and consulted doctors. One child's pediatrician refused to believe the mother and would not test; four other children's doctors remarked variously that "nothing was seriously wrong," the child would "grow out of" the problem, it was "just a bad cold," or the child was "just fine." Another child was incorrectly labeled autistic, and another was treated by a psychologist for emotional disturbance for two years before his profound deafness was discovered.

The same problems occur with visual handicaps. One nearly blind child reached the first grade before her eyes were tested. Recounting the incident, the mother told us, "The kindergarten teacher just thought she was dumb." Still another partially sighted child was incorrectly called retarded.

Lack of Direction

The most frequently mentioned of all problems was the lack of *direction*—information about the mix of services needed and where to obtain them. Two-thirds of the families had difficulty finding appropriate services. Direction is presently a major problem because in most areas *no one* has all the information needed or the responsibility to coordinate help for families. The result is that there are gaps or delays in the services received, or inappropriate services are delivered.

Less than half the families were fully pleased with the appropriateness of the amount and variety of services received. Initially contacting the service system was typically either a matter of fortunate chance or time-consuming, frustrating search by the parent; once initial contact is made, the search for service is a chain-like process of going from one agency to another, one at a time, rather than a process of sitting down and choosing among an array of alternatives. The parents' feelings about direction were nicely summarized by one of them: "*Someone* should do it!"

Gaps in Available Services

Fully 60 percent of the families reported that needed services were not available within a reasonable distance. For example, local schools may offer services designed for blind youth but none for the more numerous partially sighted; several children had to go to residential schools so far away that their parents found it difficult even to visit them; eight families moved to obtain appropriate educational services; several families could not obtain speech therapy anywhere near their homes; mobility training was seldom available for young children; and vocational training options were said to be very limited.

Insufficient Supply of Service

Even when a service is provided, the supply may be limited. Some parents had trouble getting their children into nearby school programs because the classes were full. And in one state where high-quality counseling and direction are available, the agency is said to be so understaffed it is unable to see each family more than once or twice a year. In total, only 40 percent were fully pleased with the overall *amount* of services received.

Sensitivity of Service Personnel

Most families were pleased with the service personnel, but a small minority (approximately 10 percent) related experiences indicating insensitivity to the feelings or needs of the handicapped child and his family. Perhaps the worst case was the teacher who punished an 8-year-old girl for "disruptive behavior" by placing a paper bag over her head; being deaf, this represented loss of the child's major form of contact with the world, and she was terrified. Some parents complained that doctors would not take the time to explain anything or would treat their children as cases rather than as persons, or that the hearing-aid dealer was unable to work well with their young children. For example, one woman, suspecting deafness, had taken her child to a clinic for evaluation. After a long series of tests, they were sent home with instructions to call later in the afternoon for the results. Shortly before 5 p.m., the woman finally reached her doctor; sounding rushed and a bit annoyed at being interrupted, he told her, "Your child is fine, fine—oh, except that he's deaf." Later the mother realized that, after dealing with very severely and multiply handicapped children, the doctor might indeed have thought her son to be relatively lucky. But she, though not easily upset, was near hysteria when her husband came home. Another form of insensitivity is illustrated by the family whose child "wasted nine years" in a school that taught only oral communication for deaf youth, before they were told he was not progressing and should go to a school that used manual communication.

Parental Views of Government Roles

To find out what parents thought of various ways in which the government could help them meet their children's special service needs, we questioned parents about a few alternative possibilities.

Asked whether they preferred private to governmental service sources, about half the respondents said they did not care. As one said, "As long as help is there, I don't care *where* it comes from." Of those expressing a preference, equal proportions said "yes" and "no" (about 23 percent in each group). However, only 5 percent of the sample thought that any service role now being undertaken by any government agency was inappropriate. Most parents could not conceive of an "inappropriate" role.

A government role to provide information about available services was enthusiastically endorsed by over three-quarters of the families surveyed. Several also suggested, without being asked, that the government should supply more information to the public so as to "make it acceptable to have a handicap."

We asked if the parents would like to get financial vouchers with which they could obtain services from private sources of their choice, rather than directly from a government agency. We had a hard time explaining this possible government role to the families, and most were at best lukewarm toward the concept, remarking that they would not know where to spend the voucher or that unscrupulous service providers would abuse the system and take advantage of them. In other words, they would still need a direction service.

We also asked their views about a national insurance program whose benefits would include payments for the added service needs of handicapped youth. About half the parents liked the idea; 25 percent did not; and the remainder thought maybe they would be interested. Several also noted that families without handicapped children probably would not like to pay for the insurance.

DESCRIPTION OF THE SURVEY

Survey Design

This survey involved personal interviews with a sample of 77 families of youth with impaired vision or hearing. The sample size was dictated by the need to have a reasonable number of youth in each subclassification (state, age, handicap) consistent with budget and time constraints on this research. We selected three states—California, Massachusetts, and Wyoming—from the five in which members of the project had extensively interviewed personnel in various state agencies, because the states had diverse types of service systems about which we were knowledgeable, because the states were different in size, population, region, and extent of urbanization, and because the contacts we had made provided a basis for requesting a wide variety of referrals.

Families were interviewed, rather than the handicapped children themselves, because we felt that youth, especially very young persons, might react unfavorably to being singled out as handicapped, impaired, or "different" in any fashion, or to the implied criticism of those providing service. In the case of youth over age 17, especially those living away from home, interviews were sometimes conducted with the handicapped person rather than the family, but these were the exceptions.

As one source of families, we contacted staff members of agencies with whom the project staff had dealt in the earlier phase of the study. Although this approach excludes respondents who are not being served by some agency, this is not a severe drawback. The survey is designed to tap attitudes and opinions concerning the system of services presently offered, and those currently in contact with the system are more likely to have accurate memory and detailed opinion about it. We also attempted to reach persons not served by the government programs by requesting referrals from private clinics and physicians, as well as from associations of the handicapped and from an assortment of *types* of agencies serving the handicapped. We also requested referrals from certain schools (both those serving the handicapped exclusively and regular schools with programs for the vision or hearing impaired), welfare agencies, and rehabilitation programs. This provided a wider range of responses and helped prevent the distorted patterns that would occur if agencies referred us only to their "star clients." We explicitly requested names of parents whose children were representative of the handicapped youth served, and requested *three* names for each interview to be conducted, thus making it more difficult for the agencies to select their "stars."

Other strategies designed to ensure a fairly wide range of responses to the survey include a threefold breakdown of the sample—by age, handicap, and geographic location. Four age groups are separated (0 to 5 years old, 6 to 12, 13 to 17, and 18 to 21). The divisions correspond roughly to life stages: preschool, elementary school, intermediate school, and young adulthood.

The sample is also broken down by handicap: blind and partially sighted for the visually handicapped; deaf and hard of hearing for the auditorially handicapped.

In seeking referrals, we tried to obtain equal numbers of families in each of the four age groups, four handicap categories, and the three states. When the interviews were completed, we found that 19 percent of the youth were under 6 years of age, 31 percent were 6 to 12, 25 percent were 13 to 17, and 25 percent were 18 to 21. Of the 77 families surveyed, 22 percent included a blind child, 26 percent a partially sighted one, 27 percent a deaf child, and 25 percent a hard of hearing child. We conducted 26 interviews in California, 25 in Massachusetts, and 26 in Wyoming.

We developed the questionnaire after examining, as models, several other instruments for assessing the service needs of handicapped persons and the effects of programs serving them. Using many open-ended questions, it attempts to elicit the past, present, and projected future needs of the respondents as well as their experiences with and evaluations of specific agencies' services. One section of the interview asks how the client sees the service system as a whole—what unmet needs he perceives, what difficulties he has had in getting information or assistance. Attitudes toward alternative roles for government as a purveyor of services are also explored. The questionnaire attempts to get the "target population's viewpoint" in a number of topical areas, for example:

- Needs for services
- Deficiencies in single services or in the mix of services offered
- Problems with the agency, mechanism, or personnel providing services
- Goals and objectives of parents of handicapped youth
- Importance of each type of service in relation to the others
- Past, present, and projected future effect of various services on the quality of life of handicapped children
- Effect of various services on physical skills, social skills, psychological states, financial states, etc.
- Suggestions for services and program improvement

A word of caution: the findings of the survey are based solely on the perceptions of service users, which may sometimes be inaccurate. Parents' attitudes color and may distort their memories of services received. Some parents are grateful for any help that is offered, while others are perennially dissatisfied. In the latter case, for example, a parent may "forget" offers of services if they do not jibe with his or her own version of the child's needs. Despite these problems, we feel that the views of clients are absolutely necessary in a comprehensive study of the service system, because they are the population the system should serve, and because the agency viewpoint itself is not free of distortions.

The Families

Both parents were present in 69 percent of the families; while only one parent was present in another 21 percent. Grandparents and guardians cared for the other 10 percent of the children.

Most of the children had brothers or sisters. Only 8 percent of them had none, while 18 percent had three or more siblings; in most cases, too, the handicapped child was the only impaired child in the family. The sample was about equally divided between males and females. In two-thirds of the cases, the child's handicapping condition appeared to be stabilized. In 15 percent there appeared to be a possibility that it would become worse, and in 12 percent there appeared to be a chance that it would improve.

Most families were long-term residents of the state in which they were interviewed, four-fifths of them having lived there for at least 10 years.

The particular states chosen provide some variation along an urban-rural dimension. Overall, 25 percent of the surveyed families lived in a rural area and 72 percent were urban or suburban; the remaining 3 percent were persons interviewed in an institutional setting rather than at their homes.

We interviewed approximately equal numbers of families with vision-handicapped children in each state, but the distribution over age categories was uneven (only four such children were under five years of age). The same was true for the hearing impaired, who were mostly in the age groups 6 to 12 and 13 to 17. The replies to a series of questions designed to estimate the functional degree of hearing or vision impairment indicate that we interviewed approximately equal numbers of families with totally blind and partially sighted, and profoundly deaf and hard of hearing children.

Parents' Objectives

Some definable types of parental goals for their handicapped children have emerged. The most ambitious is the wish to help the child "live up to his fullest potential." In this view, expressed by 27 percent of the surveyed parents, the handicap is an obstacle to be overcome—not an insurmountable problem. One mother of a 19-year-old high school senior with very little residual vision remarked that he was able to "make up in intelligence what he lacked in vision." The boy intended to become a scientist and was trying to choose between Berkeley, Caltech, and the Northrop Institute of Technology.

A second parental goal is to help the child "be as much like normal children as possible." Normality is seen as the upper bound of the child's possibilities. One mother of two deaf boys had made a particularly thorough attempt to compare her boys to normal children and to duplicate for them all the experiences of the others. She bought them hearing aids and Vibra-alarm clocks to increase their sensory independence; she encouraged them to have paper routes and other money-making projects; a physical education teacher herself, she enrolled them in an ice-hockey league and helped them engage in other sporting activities. She was eager to have them transferred from a special school for the hearing handicapped into regular schools, and liked the special school they attended because transfer was its goal, too. Thirty-eight percent of the families interviewed indicated that they hoped their children could become as close to normal as possible; this was the most frequently mentioned goal across all disability categories.

A third type of parent seems to have more limited goals for the child. Rather than normality, the parent hopes the child can achieve

enough independence—financial and personal—to be a "functioning, if handicapped, member of society." Such parents, 18 percent of
our sample, seem to be particularly concerned with instrumentalities
like special education and training that they see as a means to the
end—independence.

Finally, the least ambitious goal is the wish to help the child "adjust
to his handicap," to come to terms with it in the sense of learning to
live with it rather than overcome it. Only 8 percent of the parents we
talked with seemed to take this view.

One factor that undoubtedly influences parental attitudes is the
severity of the handicap. Most adjustment-oriented parents had blind
children, while most "full-potential" parents and independence-oriented ones had partially sighted children. Another factor may be socioeconomic status. Upper-middle-class parents emphasized full potential, while most middle-class parents hoped their children could
be normal. Lower-class parents also hoped for normality, but a size-
able minority were independence-oriented.

INFORMATION ON INDIVIDUAL SERVICES

The families' experiences with and views on individual types of services are discussed next, followed by a digest of their comparisons
across the various types of services. The data presented are derived
from analysis of the 665 services used by the families interviewed.
The types of services discussed are: identification; direction; counseling; medical services; sensory aids and other special equipment; education and special training; vocational training; job placement; transportation; personal care; recreation; and financial assistance.

Identification

The search for needed services for handicapped youth begins with
identification of the handicapping impairment. Of the families with
older handicapped youth, the age at time of diagnosis was 0 to 5 in
two-thirds of the cases, and about 40 percent were diagnosed before
the age of one. Of the four categories of handicaps we use, blind
youth were identified the earliest: a majority before the age of one,
and nearly 90 percent before entering school, probably because the
condition is often more obvious than partial sightedness or loss of
hearing ability. In contrast, less than one-fourth of the hard of hearing were identified by the age of one, and only about half by the age
of five.

Usually the parent was first to notice the impairment. The most
frequent sources of initial awareness of the handicap were: nonre-
sponse to aural or visual stimuli (33 percent); unusual behavior, such

as repeatedly falling down or inability to speak at a normal age (20 percent); visible impairment (17 percent); and a medical examination (14 percent). Vision impairment was most often readily apparent (35 percent) or physician-detected (22 percent), while hearing impairment was most often detected as a result of nonresponsiveness (45 percent) and only seldom by physicians (8 percent). As mentioned above, several parents of profoundly deaf children were much distressed by their pediatricians' reluctance even to test for deafness, and other children were wrongly diagnosed. Inaction or erroneous action is very serious. Diminished hearing ability during the preschool years can inhibit the development of language and communication skills to such an extent that the child may be unable to overcome the resultant handicap even if services are given later.

Late or improper identification was also apparent in the interviews with families of partially sighted and hard of hearing youth. For example, one girl with a 60 decibel (dB) bilateral hearing loss was not identified until she was seven and went for a tonsillectomy, and a partially sighted child was incorrectly labeled retarded.

Pediatricians knowledgeable about hearing problems are especially important because parents turn to them most frequently for advice when an impairment is suspected. General practitioners also serve as initial advisors, as do medical specialists in vision or hearing problems. According to our survey, medical professionals were chosen as initial advisors by almost 60 percent of the families; relatives and friends were chosen by about 30 percent.

To sum up our observations: (1) Identification is haphazard—too often a matter of chance, not an organized routine that would give all handicapped youth an early start on the road to needed services. (2) Very significant numbers of the handicapped, particularly the deaf, are either not identified at an early age or are misidentified as having some other impairment. (3) Physicians, to whom families most often turn when they suspect their child has a problem, are not as well trained or as sensitive to potential handicaps as they might be.

Counseling

Parents expressed their need for four kinds of information and counseling. First, they want to know about the handicap itself: what it is, what causes it, and how it will affect the child's development. Second, they need counseling concerning their children's needs and abilities and what they can do to help; even parents who have already reared several children feel they have to "start all over" with the impaired one, and they need advice on how to go about it. Third, parents and their handicapped children may *both* require psychological counseling. And finally, parents need information about available services. Direction, the fourth information need, is discussed elsewhere in this book.

One-fourth of the families surveyed had used counseling services for their children, and about one-half had received parent counseling. These figures are probably higher than the national average, since in both Massachusetts and Wyoming, agencies providing counseling services actively seek out the visually handicapped; however, comparable service is not provided to the hearing impaired.

Only one parent thought that counseling was a major unmet need for the child; eight others would have used counseling had they known where to ask for it. Only two interviewees thought parental counseling had been a major unmet need; fourteen others would have used it had it been available. About one-third of the families thought they could benefit from counseling in the future.

About half of those counseled thought that the service was *very* beneficial—a high rate, indicating the strong need for advice (especially at the beginning of the child's life). Only 3 percent felt it had no effect.

The families used 78 separate counseling services, about evenly distributed among the states and handicaps. Of these, 18 were offered by private organizations (a notable example is the John Tracy Clinic and its correspondence course for families with hearing handicapped youth), 41 were state services, 4 were from private professionals, and 9 were from associations of the handicapped or their parents. Referrals to counselors came from doctors in about one-third of the cases surveyed; about one-fifth were recommendations from schools; about one-tenth came from welfare agencies; and about one-tenth resulted from the parents' own research or the recommendations of other individuals.

Although most of the families that used counseling services found them satisfactory, 10 percent (a rather high rate compared with most other services) were not satisfied. A major criticism was that counseling services were not appropriate to the problems of the child or family. For example, a local PTA had obtained and paid for a psychologist's services for a high-school-age deaf girl. Rightly or wrongly, she was mildly annoyed by his "psychologizing," preferring that he offer her more practical guidance in the choice of a vocational objective. Since a counselor must often deal with the very personal problems of his clients, it is not surprising that he sometimes is perceived as intruding on the privacy of the client. Several persons expressed resentment at "personal questions," and one young divorced mother of a partially sighted and hyperactive boy refused to go back to her counselor because "He told me I was a bad mother." (The families' criticisms, while they deserve to be noted, tabulated, and respected, should sometimes be taken with a grain of salt. Every counselor is familiar with client resistance, the anger that unpleasant truths can arouse, and the frequent distortion of the counselor's remarks. This is not to deny, of course, that some counselors are inept and that even the good ones can make serious mistakes.) On the other hand, many counselors received rave notices from families that had benefited from their support and advice. A third problem is that the counseling agencies are so understaffed that most families that are served are contacted only once or twice a year.

Medical Services

All but one of the families surveyed used at least one medical server, and 60 percent used two or more. This high usage rate is reasonable since each hearing or vision handicapped youth needs at least to be examined by a physician, probably a specialist, to ascertain if anything can be done to correct or alleviate the impairment, or to prevent further deterioration of sensory ability. In many cases, however, the parents were simply double-checking because they were reluctant to accept one man's diagnosis of a severe and uncorrectable hearing or vision impairment.

Upper-income families used more medical service than did other groups, but lower-income parents used more than middle-class ones did, perhaps because they had better access to public financial aid to pay for treatment.

Of the 131 different medical servers used by families in our sample, 86 percent were "private professionals," while 7 percent were obtained through state agencies (such as the Crippled Children's Service) and 2 percent through charitable sources. About half the doctors were located less than ten miles from the respondents' homes, but more families are willing to travel long distances for this service than for any other: a dozen traveled over 100 miles each way for the service. Medical care is sought more intensively than other services. Although most parents seldom considered more than one source for any other service, fully 25 percent of them considered more than one doctor before making an initial choice. If refused service, respondents almost always continued their search elsewhere.

Eleven families wanted additional services, but many of them admitted they were hoping for "a miracle," rather than needing a specific service. However, lower-income families expressed unmet medical needs more often than other income groups and generally cited expense as the reason.

Satisfaction with medical services was lower than for any other service area. Families indicated that 12 percent of the doctors were "not competent" and 11 percent were "not courteous." The commonest complaint was that medical personnel were "impersonal." In several instances university-affiliated hospitals were cited for treating children as cases rather than persons. As discussed above under "Identification," parents complained that pediatricians sometimes disregarded their insistence that something was wrong with their children, especially in the cases of the hearing impaired. Several other parents complained that physicians diagnosed the problem correctly but were unable to advise the families what to expect of the child or where to go for services to meet his special needs. Of course, comprehensive, nonmedical guidance is neither the doctor's nor anyone else's responsibility in most states. However, when a doctor or another member of a hospital or clinic staff was well informed and offered nonmedical guidance, a much-needed service was performed which the parents later remembered with gratitude. Another problem cited with medical treatment services included transportation to a distant service location (mentioned in one-fourth of the cases of service use).

Financial problems plagued some families, though most regarded the burden as a "necessary evil." More than half the respondents paid at least part of the cost of the medical care they received (most other services were provided at little or no cost). Forty-two percent of the families received financial assistance from a source other than their own resources or personal insurance to help pay medical expenses. For two-thirds of those who received no such aid, however, medical care was cited as a financial hardship.

Another problem cited was doctors' failure to appreciate the possibility of multiple impairments, a potential difficulty with highly specialized physicians. One mother, whose daughter is a national hula-hoop champion despite being aphasic and visually and auditorially handicapped, did not learn about the aphasia until a school psychologist amassed all the medical reports concerning the girl and tried to take an overview of the girl's problems. He was the first to suggest aphasia. Later, the same child was also found to have an allergy that affected her hearing. Shots to combat the allergy have made a significant improvement in her hearing.

All in all, the major problem with medical services does not appear to be in the quantity or quality of the treatment given after diagnosis, but in the diagnosis itself.

Despite these deficiencies, the families regarded 35 percent of the medical services as very beneficial, and about 36 percent as beneficial to a lesser degree. Only 18 percent of the medical services were said to have had no effect on the child, and only 6 percent were thought to have had detrimental effects.

Suggestions for improving medical services included the following: Some medical agency or some one doctor in a group practice should take the responsibility for collecting and evaluating all of each child's medical records. Doctors—especially pediatricians, who are usually the initial advisors of parents with handicapped children—should be sensitized to the possibility of handicapping conditions and to the need for early diagnosis of handicaps such as deafness, and should possess information concerning available services. Doctors should be encouraged, even required, to report impaired children's names to state agencies or associations of the handicapped so that service personnel can get in touch with families. Doctors should be given special training in testing children for handicapping conditions. Finally, several parents stressed their wish that the government would sponsor further research into handicapping conditions. They feared they were "hoping for miracles," but with characteristically American faith in technology, they thought concerted efforts could produce better results, if not cures.

Sensory Aids and Other Special Equipment

All but five families had used at least one sensory aid or equipment service; these included hearing aids and lenses as well as aids for mobility (canes and guide dogs), for reading (braille and talking books), and other equipment (special watches, alarm clocks, tape recorders, slates, toys, etc.). Service use was directly related to income, which accounts for the fact that 30 percent of the low-income families claimed they needed additional equipment, while only 12 percent of the upper-middle-class group expressed similar needs. The expense of equipment was cited by ten parents who thought their needs were not fully met. For essential equipment, such as a hearing aid, parents typically settled for less than the best. Another eight families said that the service or equipment they needed did not exist (they mentioned such things as special amplifiers for TV sets and books for blind toddlers).

Of the sensory aids or special equipment services discussed, 43 percent were hearing aids, 25 percent were reading aids (e.g., braille books and tapes), and 16 percent were lenses or magnification aids. In one-third of the cases families were referred to the service by their doctor or audiologist. School personnel recommended sensory aids or special equipment in 13 percent of the cases, and state agencies for the visually handicapped accounted for 11 percent of the referrals.

Although commercial dealers were frequently used, parents did little comparison-shopping for either cost or quality. Two-thirds of the time they considered no alternatives, usually selecting a dealer or agency because someone had recommended it, but the next-most-frequent reason was that it was cheaper. In two-thirds of the cases, all or part of the cost of the aid was paid by someone other than the parents themselves.

One-third of the service purveyors were rated very satisfactory, another half were said to be satisfactory, and only one in ten caused dissatisfaction. The aids themselves were rated very beneficial by about two-thirds of the families with partially sighted or deaf children, and by about half the families with blind or hard of hearing children. The most dramatic and glowing praise was given to the change resulting from a hearing aid: one child began to talk for the first time soon after receiving the aid, and another, a 12-year-old, markedly improved his grades after he received his first hearing aid. Only one in ten service users said the sensory aid or other equipment had no beneficial effect.

Several problems were mentioned by the families using sensory aids or other special equipment services. Fourteen percent said they had to wait much too long for service—usually while the bureaucracy processed the request or while hearing aids or braille books were mailed from out-of-town sources. A Wyoming junior-high-schooler did not receive materials for one course until a week before the final test.

A second problem was noted by parents buying hearing aids and corrective lenses. They usually were given insufficient advice about motivating the child to use the aid and for using and maintaining it. Hence, several cases were found of children not benefiting because the aid was in poor repair or because the child refused to wear it. Another problem was selecting an aid and a dealer. Sometimes audiologists would recommend a special brand, but only one dealer specializing in that brand served the area where the family lived. A few respondents felt "at the mercy" of the audiologist's expertise. When a specific type of aid was *not* recommended, however, several parents said they were at a loss to choose. One family applauded their audiologist for recommending a type of aid and discussing with them the dealers in their area who sold various brands. He would not recommend a specific dealer, but he told them which aids were most expensive and which dealers had been criticized by other parents. One parent also noted price-quotations ranging from $200 to $385 for precisely the same make and model of hearing aid.

Finally, dealers were occasionally criticized for what parents felt was poor service or improper conduct. Some did not inform parents that state services were available to pay part or all of the cost of the lenses or other aid; others seemed too "commercial," e.g., trying to push the more expensive models of hearing aids. Hearing aid dealers were also criticized for their inability to work well with young children. Aside from the parents' opinions, several cases of poor initial selection of an aid or incorrect fitting of an ear mold attest to the presence of a problem.

Suggestions for improvement included special training or licensing of dealers and the provision of information to parents on the merits and costs of different aids. Parents also advocated wider availability of information on use of the aids and programs to pay for them. Finally, parents hoped for the development of new kinds of equipment, such as individualized amplifiers for the television so that a deaf child could have a higher volume of sound while the rest of the family preserved the integrity of their eardrums, and a quieter braille writer so blind students could take notes without disturbing classmates; and for a wider variety of existing equipment, such as more braille and talking books for each age and type of child.

The major message about sensory aids, however, was that they can be extremely beneficial. Consequently, while a few hundred dollars for a pair of glasses or a hearing aid may seem like a great deal, parents believe the cost is reasonable enough in view of the effects they can have on a child's life.

Education and Special Training

Educational and special training services had been used by 69 of 77 families we surveyed. Services included both preschool and regular academic education and the special training needed by impaired children. For the hearing impaired, this usually meant speech therapy, and for the visually impaired, mobility training. As with medical treatment, both upper-middle-class and lower-income families used more services than did middle-class parents. All children who had not been served in any educational program were less than 5 years old.

Although these handicapped youth went to school, *many received no special education services.* The breakdown by type of educational program was: nursery or preschool, 9 percent; regular class only, in public school, 26 percent; regular class with special equipment, in public school, 4 percent; regular class supplemented by special program for the handicapped, 21 percent; special class for the handicapped only, in public school, 12 percent; residential school, 8 percent; and private school, 7 percent. Deaf youth were most often served in special classes for the handicapped only, or in a regular class only; while hard of hearing youth were most often served in a regular class supplemented by a special program or in a special class for the handicapped only. Blind youth were most often served in a regular class only, or in a residential school; while partially sighted youth were most often served in a regular class only or in a regular class supplemented by a special program.

About one-third of the referrals to educational services came from within the educational system. Another fifth came from doctors, and about 30 percent were from counselors, such as those affiliated with state agencies for the visually handicapped, who helped the parents of the more severely handicapped find the right special schools for their children and who were also instrumental, for example, in helping older children find the right vocational training for a post-high-school education.

Most educational services were provided out of public funds, but some—especially preschool or special training—were funded from other sources. Parents themselves paid for 13 percent of the services received, and 7 percent were paid by charitable organizations.

In general, educational services were deemed important and highly satisfactory. Service was typically felt to be sufficient, individualized, offered by competent and courteous personnel, and very beneficial to the youth. The parents of more severely handicapped children tended to give "very beneficial" ratings more often than those of less-impaired youth (80 percent versus 60 percent). Only three families felt the schools were "slightly beneficial," and none said the schools had "no effect."

Several problems were mentioned. One common cause of dissatisfaction was the lack of school programs in the immediate geographic area and the need to send the child to a faraway residential school for most of the year. One result was that parents found it difficult even to visit the child. Another result was that eight families, six of whom had deaf children, had moved expressly to be near a good school for their children.

Another problem related to distance occurred when children had to be transported daily to special schools; only 61 percent of the students went to school within 10 miles of home. Though they lived at home, they could not participate in after-school activities because transportation consumed so much of their free time. One in five students attended a school (including residential schools) more than 50 miles from home.

Parents' views on the curriculum were also noted. One-third of the parents, especially those of blind children and parents of children in residential schools, felt that schools should place more emphasis on the "3Rs." One-fifth of the parents, usually of the more severely impaired children, thought there should be more attention given to training for activities of daily living. Parents with children in special classes typically thought they were getting enough development of social skills, but only half the parents whose children were in regular classes or residential schools agreed. One blind young man argued that residential schools should do more to encourage a spirit of independence in their students.

Occasionally, educators showed insensitivity to the needs and feelings of impaired children. One girl was, in the opinion of her mother, subjected to subtle ridicule by a teacher who continually pointed out her handicap during classes. We have mentioned the 8-year-old girl who was punished for "disruptive behavior" by having a paper bag placed over her head. Other teachers were said to be too willing to keep the child dependent, or to interpret as misbehavior what was really the result of an impairment—for example, the inattention of a deaf child.

Finally, parents sometimes felt that no available program was exactly right for their children's needs. Some parents of deaf children, for example, found that schools emphasized either the oral or the manual method of teaching to the exclusion of the other. They had to send their children to distant or expensive private schools to get the training the parents felt they needed. Several parents with partially sighted or hard of hearing youth mentioned that the only available programs were designed primarily for blind or deaf youth. In two cases, hard of hearing youth were forced to use sign language instead of talk because they were in a school for the deaf. Two other partially sighted youth were taught to read braille instead of printed type because they were in a class for the blind.

Most parents were satisfied with the amount of education received. Six families were not, all of them families with visually handicapped children; 13 others said they would have used more service had it been available. Because of crowding, 11 families had been refused service at the school of first choice. In Wyoming, some parents said their needs were unmet because the services were unavailable in the geographic area; and in Massachusetts, some parents complained because there was no high school for the deaf in their area. One parent suggested that, at the very least, every state and every major metropolitan area should offer a complete range of educational services for handicapped youth.

Two particular kinds of special training were explicitly considered in the survey: speech training for auditorially handicapped youth and mobility training for the visually impaired. Thirty-four of the 40 families with hearing handicapped youth had used speech therapy services. Nine families were dissatisfied with speech therapy as a service, usually because it was *not available in the interviewee's area*. With adequate hearing aids and speech training, many hard of hearing youth can be educated in the regular classroom, instead of needing more expensive, specialized education programs. Thirteen parents had sought and used mobility training services; most of the recipients were blind, not partially sighted, and most were older children. Unmet needs were felt by four parents of totally blind youth. They were unable to obtain service either because it was not locally available or because the children were too young to be eligible. Some parents noted, however, that the services really should be offered earlier than they typically are; as one blind girl in California explained, by the time she was given mobility training in high school, her fears and inhibitions had become so ingrained that she was unable to profit fully by it.

Providing relevant information to the parent was another suggested improvement: information on what training programs are available and how to choose among them, and information on how the parent can help in the child's training at home.

Vocational Training

Four of our respondents had received vocational training: two from a public rehabilitation agency and two from private, commercial training schools. Two of them had used vocational training services only, and two others had been placed in jobs by the schools they attended. Vocational training was not regarded as one of the more important service needs. Most families would not even travel to obtain the service.

Unmet needs were expressed by 12 families, who said that services did not exist as far as they knew, or were not available in the area. Thirteen others thought they might need vocational training in the future. Of these, eight planned to seek help from state or local public agencies; however, most said they thought the service would make some difference but not a great one in their children's lives.

Overall ratings of those receiving vocational training included one family that was very satisfied, two who thought the service was satisfactory, and one young blind woman who was not satisfied. She felt that the service was not helpful because little imagination was shown in choosing jobs for which to train blind youth. She had learned to be a darkroom technician but did not like the work, even when she could find it. Of families that had investigated but not requested service, it was thought that the vocational rehabilitation agency's occupational training choices were limited in both number and desirability. One said he had heard the agency would reject deaf persons with poor speech; another said friends had told him "not to use VR" because of the low occupational expectations the counselors have for deaf people.

Job Placement

Only five of the older youth whose families we interviewed had held a regular part-time or full-time job for more than a year. About three-quarters of the 28 youth who had worked at all had had problems; and the majority of those felt their handicap was the major reason.

Despite these problems, only eleven sets of parents in our sample had any contact with placement services. In four of these cases, the service was limited to the provision of information about available jobs, although in one other case the counselor applied in the youth's name. Three of the youth served were offered only counseling or vocational guidance, not actual job placement services. Placement services were not regarded as critically important by any of the families; only one parent would pay for the service if necessary, and only one would travel to obtain it. Three parents who had been unable to find placement assistance felt that it was a "great need," however, and six others would have used the service had it been available. Most who were unhappy with placement services explained that they did not know where to go or said the services did not exist in their area. Of those using placement services, five rated them "very beneficial," while two each thought they were of "some," "slight," or "no effect."

The only suggested improvement was that rehabilitation personnel should act as advocates for the youth or should try to persuade businesses to consider the applications of impaired youth, and then inform the young people of those who were willing.

Personal Care

Only ten families in our sample had used personal care services: four had hired a day nurse at some time or another, and the rest used full-time but temporary babysitters or relatives. Only five families said they had ever wished for help in caring for their children but were unable to find it. A few parents thought they might possibly require personal care services in the future, but only one of them thought getting the service would make a "great difference." In brief, the families felt that they were capable of meeting the personal care needs of their visually or aurally handicapped youth.

Recreation

One-third of the families surveyed had used recreation services of some sort, usually parties, summer camps, and field trips. Almost two-thirds of the blind children had used at least one recreational service, but only 40 percent of the partially sighted, 24 percent of the deaf, and 10 percent of the hard of hearing had done so. This was partly the result of service availability; although 68 percent of the blind children had been offered recreational services, only 45 percent of the partially sighted, 38 percent of the deaf, and 26 percent of the hard of hearing had received offers.

A significant minority of the parents felt that their children needed more opportunities to interact with peers. Recreational service users were mostly from this group; perhaps these services are sought to fill in perceived gaps left by schools and neighborhood activities. About half the families said they would use more recreational services if they were available. Two-thirds of the rural residents cited unmet recreational needs, mostly because the services were not offered in their area. Urban and suburban respondents thought the services were probably available, but they did not know where to ask about them.

Of the 26 recreation services used, about half were provided by charitable organizations, with associations of the handicapped the next largest source. Most of the families did not regard recreation as a critical need, but those who used services were well satisfied with them. They praised two results of the services: their children learned to be more independent, and they met new friends.

Two problems with recreational services were noted. For children who attend residential schools or special programs in public schools, organized recreation cuts into their time with their families. Parents whose children are away in school all year are loath to part with them in the summer. Second, participation in recreational programs tends to decrease opportunities for play with normal children in the neighborhood. (On the other hand, for children in public schools, recreational programs for handicapped youth provided needed opportunities to interact with other children like themselves.) Some parents felt that programs should be devised to provide a mixture of handicapped and normal children.

Transportation

Thirty-five of the families surveyed had used some sort of transportation service, mostly school bussing. Only one-third of rural residents were getting transportation service, compared with about half of those living in urban or suburban areas. Of the 48 separate transportation services used, one-third were offered by state agencies and one-third by local school districts. Charitable organizations, such as the Foundation for the Junior Blind in California, supplied 16 percent. As with information about many other services, knowledge of programs supplying transportation was more often a matter of luck than routine dissemination of the information. One Massachusetts mother walked a mile with her 5-year-old blind daughter to school each day because she did not have a car and no bus service was available. Pregnant and near the end of her term, she began to worry that she would have to send the little girl to school alone. Finally, she asked a teacher at the school what to do, and the teacher offhandedly replied that she should "use the taxis." The mother knew she could not afford that; so she worried for a few more days. At last she mentioned her problem to another mother, who informed her that the state provided free taxi service to school for handicapped children. She thought the school should make a systematic effort to inform parents of handicapped children about the range of services available to them.

Quite a few families were willing to fight for transportation service if refused it. Not long before the interviews were conducted, a new director of educational services for the handicapped was appointed in Massachusetts. One of his first acts in office was to cut back transportation services, whereupon an army of enraged parents camped on the Capitol steps. As a result the level of service to many was reinstated.

One-third of the sample said they had experienced unmet needs for transportation. About 60 percent of the rural families had had transportation problems; urban and suburban families also cited problems in about a third of the cases. Transportation difficulties resulted in a general reduction in the use of other services for 10 percent of the families surveyed.

Although most families managed to find transportation to other needed services, many of them faced problems in doing so. Since the handicapped population is widely distributed geographically, many of them must travel long distances for services, and this imposes numerous costs. Often parents must pay for the service itself; they must also pay their own transportation and living costs if, say, medical care is offered in a distant city; and they sacrifice time that could be spent with other children or even at work. Several fathers had to arrange days off to drive their children to hospitals.

Transportation to the point at which other services are provided has been a problem cited many times before in our discussion; the reason it is such a problem is that the handicapped population is dispersed widely, while service agencies often are not. That is, transportation is not a problem primarily because the youth are handicapped, but because the service agencies are located as they are.

Financial Assistance

Of the families surveyed, 56 percent had received financial aid either directly or to purchase other specific services.

A total of 51 financial services were used, of which 10 percent were private charities and the rest were public assistance of some sort, split about equally between hearing and vision impaired youth. The volume of funds expended is not known. In 6 percent of the cases, the aid was an income supplement, 8 percent of the time it represented full or partial payment of school tuition, 28 percent of the cases were for medical bills, 14 percent paid for special equipment, and 28 percent of the cases were for more than one of these purposes. In addition to funds, some counseling was provided in about one-third of the cases. These figures do not include cases of the direct provision of service such as schooling, when no financial reimbursement is involved.

Almost one-third of the respondents said they would have liked more financial assistance, and in 9 percent of the cases it was expressed as a major need. One-third of those who expressed needs said they did not know where to ask for help, and another third had been refused financial aid.

About half the sample thought their children might need financial assistance in the future—10 percent were fairly certain they would.

A few problems with financial aid services were cited. A few people had experienced difficulty or delay in arranging payment of medical or special equipment services through state agencies. A few wished that a wider range of services could be provided—such as transportation to a medical or educational service facility, or additional equipment. But most users of financial assistance were delighted to have it, and three-quarters of them thought it sufficient for their needs. Two families charged discrimination in that the blind get an extra income tax deduction while the deaf do not. One family did not take full advantage of needed speech therapy service because they couldn't afford it and did not know the state would assist them.

Several families expressed displeasure at having to accept funds labeled as "welfare," and were displeased with the quality of welfare agency personnel.

One suggestion for improving the financial aid service was to develop a special definition of indigency for parents with handicapped children, much as the Medicaid program has a "medically indigent" classification that includes more persons than the "indigent" classification does.

DIFFICULTIES WITH INFORMATION ON THE SERVICE SYSTEM

Once a handicapped child has been identified, the child or the family needs to know what mix of other services is needed and where to obtain them. The determination of the appropriate mix of services and service providers is what we call *direction*. Only one-third of the families said they had experienced no difficulties in finding appropriate services; another third reported some problems, and another third had had many problems. Parents of hard of hearing and partially sighted children were far more likely to have experienced "many problems" than were parents of blind or deaf children. Gaps in the services available were reported by 60 percent of the families. Only 40 percent were fully pleased with the sufficiency or overall amount of services received, and families with preschool handicapped children or less severely handicapped children felt the least satisfied. Slightly less than half the families interviewed were fully pleased with the appropriateness of the package of services delivered to them; that is, they felt they were "offered the right kinds of services." The families with less severely handicapped youth, or preschool handicapped youth, or hearing handicapped youth were least likely to be fully pleased with the appropriateness of services. Thus, more than half the families reported problems with direction to various services: most reported gaps in the services provided, lack of full satisfaction with the sufficiency of the services provided, and lack of full satisfaction with the appropriateness of the mix of services. Direction is clearly a major problem.

Parents generally reported lack of information about what services are available, and where to obtain them. As one parent put it, "There are so many government agencies, the people don't know *where* to go." Another frustrated parent made an excellent point: "I don't even know what questions to ask." Many reported a "chain of talking and talking and talking" and of referrals "from place to place to place" until, with persistence and much "stumbling around," they found someone who could tell them where to get the needed services. Others were simply lucky, as when a speech therapist accidentally met a deaf child in need of help in a furniture store. In general, however, no one had either the information or the responsibility to help the parents plan an appropriate mix of services and direct them to the service providers. Two notable exceptions are the Division of Services to the Visually Handicapped in Wyoming and the Commission for the Blind in Massachusetts. A good direction program could also eliminate much unnecessary retesting of children by various service providers who presently do not have easy access to each other's test results.

Parental persistence and tediously acquired knowledge of available services clearly made a difference in what the child received. For example, the most services we observed being received by a single family went to a deaf child who lived in a foster home with 11 other children (8 of them multihandicapped) and with two very experienced, savvy, and persistent foster parents.

PARENTAL SATISFACTION WITH THE SYSTEM AND INDIVIDUAL SERVICES

Overall Satisfaction with and Benefits of the Service System

Finally, parents were asked to give their views on their general satisfaction with the service system, and their general assessment of how much their child had benefited from the package of services received.

Forty percent of the families said they were very satisfied with the overall system; about half said they were satisfied, but not completely; and 5 percent said they were definitely not satisfied. Parents of younger children and of less severely handicapped children were least likely to be satisfied.

In assessing the degree to which the service system benefits handicapped youth, 62 percent of the respondents thought the services had been very beneficial on the whole, 24 percent thought they were somewhat beneficial, and 14 percent were convinced the service system had had little or no benefits. Within the majority of parents who felt the overall service effects were very beneficial, however, there were significant variations by type of handicap (67 percent for the hearing impaired versus 57 percent for the vision impaired), and by age (70 percent for 18- to 21-year olds versus 54 percent for children 0 to 5 years old).

Relative Importance of Individual Services

As we have seen, the parents rated both individual services and the system as a whole as to their overall satisfaction, the competence and courtesy of the personnel, and each service's benefit to the youth. A summary look across the services is presented here.

Parents were fully satisfied with 38 percent of the individual services delivered, partially satisfied with 49 percent, and dissatisfied with 13 percent. The three services they considered most important were education, sensory aids, and medical treatment. Of these, educational services received the most "very satisfied" ratings, and medical services the fewest. Similar findings characterized personnel ratings: though very few service agencies of any sort were said to have discourteous or incompetent staff, medical servers and special equipment dealers received more uncomplimentary ratings than did other servers, while medical servers and educators received more "very good" ratings than did other servers. Educational services were given the most "very beneficial to the youth" ratings, with sensory aids and medical treatment following.

Several questions were asked to determine the relative importance of various services to parents. One question was what they thought to be their preeminent service need at the time of the survey. Education was the overwhelming first choice across all categories of parents, followed by special equipment and medical service. We emphasize that these rankings are of *current* need, not of needs throughout the child's lifetime. The remaining services were, in decreasing order of rated importance, vocational education, financial aid, transportation, job placement, counseling, and recreation. We did not ask the interviewees to rate the identification or direction services.

As another measure of importance, we asked parents if they had undergone financial hardship to obtain any services. Two-thirds of those who said yes had done so for medical treatment, about one-fifth for sensory aids, and one-tenth for education. When asked what services they would pay more for if necessary, the three mentioned the most often were education, medical service, and sensory aids. Parents were also asked whether they would be willing to relocate to obtain any particular service. Nearly all of those who *would* move would do so for medical treatment or education; three families *did* move to obtain better medical service, and eight moved to obtain medical treatment or sensory aids, and to obtain education (although they strongly preferred to have their children attend schools near home). They said they would not, and did not, travel far to obtain the other services.

Finally, we asked what strategies parents would use if refused a specific service. Summing the responses for all types of services, 85 percent would "continue the search," 9 percent would "fight," and 7 percent would "forget it." Most of those who would "fight" would do so for educational services; those who would "continue the search" would seek medical treatment, sensory aids, or education; and those who would "forget it" were speaking of transportation and recreation services.

EPILOGUE:
WHAT HAPPENED AFTER THE
RESEARCH REPORTS WERE FILED?

This research project started out like dozens of others: A client was confronted with a problem that was somewhat more complex or time consuming than he or his available staff could handle on their own. After a series of preliminary discussions between the client and several analysts, in which the problem was carefully framed, proposals were written. In time a decision was reached to hire a research firm to wrestle with the problem, to devise and analyze options and alternatives that the client could consider implementing, and to publish research reports documenting the entire experience. All of this is routine enough and generally characterizes the practice of policy research as it exists today. However, for a variety of reasons, some intended, many not, this project has extended beyond the simple publication and filing of reports and has carried over into the decision making and implementation phases of the policy process in several interesting ways.[1] In what follows, we share the highlights of these experiences.

The public focus of attention is one of the most elusive and sought after commodities in our complex society, and the presentation of policy research results that capture and galvanize that attention remains one of the most challenging and formidable tasks imaginable. We have used two different strategies to disseminate our results. With respect to what we call the "Direction Service," where we made our most novel recommendations, a direct, intense, and highly personalized collection of activities was undertaken to call attention to the needs of handicapped children for this "missing" service, to encourage responsible officials and others to take and use our results and ideas, and then to directly assist those given the responsibility for the implementation of the recommendations. This intense effort was

[1]A description of various phases of the "policy process" has been developed in Chap. 4.

made possible by the financial support of the Russell Sage Foundation. For the remainder of the recommendations, an active but more conventional approach to the dissemination of results and recommendations was used; i.e., we issued a press release, we sent copies of the reports to several hundred people we thought might be able to use them, we gave briefings, we wrote this book, and we responded to all inquiries and requests for assistance in using our findings and recommendations.

The general question of research utilization is neither very well understood nor is it appreciated. Folklore has it that "good ideas" will in time surface by virtue of their "correctness," "appropriateness," "timeliness," etc. A corollary myth is that one needs only circulate research containing such "good ideas" to a relative handful of influential and powerful authorities, who, in their own time, guided by their own wisdom, will respond positively and constructively. We seriously doubt this elite model of the research dissemination process. Indeed, the burgeoning number and complexity of issues clamoring for recognition and action by powerful authorities increasingly belie this style of research use. \Opening alternative channels of communication and creating expectations that "good ideas" can in fact be presented by a wide variety of methods are much needed improvements in prevalent practice.

If our experiences with dissemination of results from the handicapped children's project suggest anything, it is that nearly as much time, effort, and resources need to be expended in the research utilization and policy implementation phases as in the conduct of the research itself.

IN THE BEGINNING

In late 1971, Roger Levien (then a Deputy Vice President for Domestic Programs in The Rand Corporation's Washington office) learned that then Secretary of Health, Education, and Welfare Elliot L. Richardson, his Assistant Secretary for Planning and Evaluation, Laurence E. Lynn, Jr., and several members of their respective staffs were concerned that the sheer number and magnitude of programs and services for handicapped children being provided through public resources were outstripping anyone's ability to understand or manage those resources effectively. They knew that there were millions of handicapped children "out there," but how many, and what were the kinds and degrees of their handicaps? What services did they need? What services were being provided at what cost and with what effects? No one was very clear about the answers to these fundamental questions, and, beyond fragments of basic data, no one had attempted to piece together an overall picture of the services to the "target population." They also knew that the federal government alone probably was spending hundreds of millions of dollars to serve this population, but how many dollars, and how were these dollars allocated to the population in need? Again, no one could do much more than provide partial answers to these elemental questions, and a comprehensive accounting had eluded top-level HEW management. Finally, they were keenly aware that the "service system" was not really a system at all, but rather it was a collection of highly specialized, frequently politicized, and traditionally independent agencies, bureaus, and departments, whose aggregate performance often left much to be desired. Richardson, as Secretary of Health, Education, and Welfare, summed it all up well in terming the system to be in the throes of a performance and control crisis.[2]

We are not claiming that our work on handicapped children "solves" the problems responsible for this "crisis of performance and control"; however, we were reasonably certain, as we struck out on our odyssey that spring in 1972, that our clients were genuinely concerned about the crisis—at least as it related to the important population of handicapped children. We are also confident that our efforts resulted in many fresh insights, the generation and assembly of prodigious amounts of data, and an honest confrontation of these data in the light of what our client could do—with varying degrees of effort, commitment, and time.

What we did not fully appreciate at the beginning is that even with the best of clients, adequate time and budget, and a fair share of good fortune, the filing of reports is itself a mere signal that the real work of disseminating research has just begun.

Establishing a Dialogue

Efforts to communicate what we were discovering started very early. In mid-1972, we gave formal briefings to Assistant Secretary Lynn, about twenty of his staff, and personnel of the Bureau of Education for the Handicapped. In those first official briefings, we indicated that data were available to help pin down the characteristics of the handicapped child population and the service system. These data were not highly reliable, some were out of date, and others were at best educated guesses. Even as our project began, we quickly went to the field to examine California's handicapped child service system to get a

---

[2]Elliot L. Richardson, "Responsibility and Responsiveness (II)," *A Report on the HEW Potential for the Seventies,* Washington, D.C.: U.S. Department of Health, Education, and Welfare, January 18, 1973. See p. 1 for the full statement on these matters.

rough, preliminary sense of systemic problems. From this initial foray we learned of gaps, overlaps, redundancies, and other undesirable features—many of which proved later to be chronic and others endemic. These we called to the client's attention in this first briefing. We also learned about many interesting and beneficial programs and, in the process, started meeting the first of the hundreds of dedicated professionals, parents, and public servants who made our research both possible and enjoyable. We relayed these positive impressions as well.

Keeping Their Attention

The first year's effort was filled with repeated trips to Washington, and various states, to talk with most of the key federal officials and their staffs who were in the business of serving handicapped children, with similar and concentrated interviews with officials and other concerned individuals in five target states (California, Massachusetts, Illinois, Arkansas, and Wyoming), and with massive data gathering and assembly efforts, e.g., a lengthy questionnaire to all major service agencies in all 50 states, an extensive literature review, and the acquisition of existing computer records, tapes, and programs from individuals and institutions discovered in the course of the research. During this intense ten or eleven month search and acquisition period, there were plenty of informal contacts with the client—telephone calls to the project monitor, courtesy and informational visits during Washington sojourns, and other routine contacts to get data, find out about personnel to contact, or to clarify program structures and operations. We did not, however, hold any more formal briefings, nor did we publish any reports until the end of the first year of work. The data collection and digestion problems were immense. Rather than having the client begin work on some partial or ill-conceived option, we decided to wait until we had assembled as much of the whole picture as possible so that all options could be considered not only on their own merits, but with respect to other plausible options bearing on the total system's operation.

By May 1973, we completed the first year of work by publishing our "base case analysis," our best assessment of what the current service system looked like, how it was structured, what it did for and to whom, and what some of its major problems were.[3] To facilitate dissemination of our findings, we circulated a press release and a 40-page executive summary of the report to the media and to numerous

[3]*Serving Handicapped Children: A Program Overview,* The Rand Corporation Report, R-1220-HEW, Santa Monica, California, May 1973.

influential individuals. We sent copies of the report to everyone who had been interviewed, answered a questionnaire, or otherwise contributed to the work. We also sent copies to all major federal personnel (including both the executive and legislative branches of government) who were concerned with handicapped children, to all major state agencies responsible for serving these children, and to organizations concerned about them. We sent the report to various journal editors and had it abstracted in information systems such as ERIC in the education area. Several hundred copies of the hefty, 340-page report were circulated in this initial dissemination effort.

With excitement running high, clippings from the press began to find their way to Rand from all over the country; the Associated Press, the *Los Angeles Times,* and *The New York Times,* all picked up on the release and accurately reported the key facts about numbers and dollars and nicely highlighted our list of system problems, e.g., inequities, gaps in service, knowledge lags, lapses of management control, and insufficient resource allocations.

Although our first report contained no recommendations, it contained much new descriptive data and hence was potentially useful to HEW and other federal officials. We began to see our numbers and some of our ideas show up in policy deliberations. For example, the Council for Exceptional Children made sure congressmen deliberating an early version of the "Education for All Handicapped Children Act of 1975" had copies of special education data we had compiled, and HEW officials quoted from our report in their testimony at Congressional hearings on special education legislation.

During the middle and late 1973 periods, Watergate emerged in the public consciousness and began to distract official Washington even more than usual. Secretary Richardson left; Assistant Secretary Lynn left; Deputy Assistant Secretary P. Michael Timpane left; Project Monitor Corinne Rieder transferred to another government agency. The normal game of top-level musical chairs was being played at a faster tempo than usual, with the result that our project monitor and all major federal officials above her who had commissioned and been highly interested in the study were gone.

A new project monitor was assigned, but she was extremely busy with other matters, and our work did not appear to align very well with the collection of professional and policy activities that held her attention most. However, as long as there were no negative signals from us or about us, the research would be allowed to proceed and play out its own course.

The problem confronting us was not unique. The flow of Washington personnel had outpaced the time requirements of a very complex research endeavor. The people who were our major client had changed before our research was completed, and the new people had different interests and priorities.

Given these "facts of research life" and the intellectual and personal investment that had been made, we recognized what had always been true—the *real* clients for this work were handicapped children and their families. This recognition meant that rather than just talking to a handful of top decision makers within the Department of Health, Education, and Welfare, we were now confronting a much more formidable task of communicating our findings and recommendations to many concerned groups of citizens, public and private decision makers, and analysts. With this realization, it became apparent that we would have to cultivate more contacts than we had, to become more visible, and to begin thinking about various forms and media that dissemination of the research results might take—especially in the post-contract stage of the effort.

In August 1973 and again in January 1974, we were invited to make formal presentations to the Education Staff Seminar,[4] many of whose members work on legislative staffs preparing and analyzing policy alternatives that find their ways into laws affecting handicapped children. These informational sessions were productive and resulted in requests to supply several Congressional committees with copies of the first year's report. We began contacting influential members of the service and research communities to press our case and to report on the initial findings of the research. For instance, Mr. Edgar Lowell, the Director of the John Tracy Clinic in Los Angeles, heard of our work and invited us to prepare a paper on the likely future of the existing deaf-blind population of children, which we gladly did.[5] Because of a chance meeting between Brewer and Ms. Elizabeth Berger, a child advocate in California, an invitation was extended to speak to the Annual Meeting of the Child Welfare League of America—another opportunity gladly accepted.[6] Both of these public-professional encounters resulted in additional requests for the source document and for specific information about handicapped programs—informa-

[4]The Education Staff Seminar has over three hundred members of the policy-making community listed on its rolls, and it pursues a vigorous information and educational course of activities throughout the year.

[5]Garry D. Brewer and James S. Kakalik, "Serving the Deaf-Blind Population: Planning for 1980," in Carl E. Sherrick (ed.), *1980 is Now,* Los Angeles: The John Tracy Clinic, 1974, pp. 19–23.

[6]Garry D. Brewer and James S. Kakalik, *Serving Handicapped Children: The Road Ahead,* Santa Monica, California: The Rand Corporation, P-5304, August 1974; later republished under the same title in *Child Welfare,* Vol. 54, No. 4, April 1975, pp. 257–267.

tion that was provided as long as it did not detract from the still demanding chores of completing the formal research project.[7] Numerous invitations were received to speak with various policy research and university groups, and to the greatest extent practicable, most of these were honored. We also eagerly added our executive summary to the pages of a well-respected education handbook, in the hopes that our findings would be more widely known.[8]

Finally, a chance meeting set the stage for most of the dissemination activities reported later in this epilogue related to the direction service. Brewer met Hugh F. Cline, then the President of Russell Sage Foundation, on the Metroliner from Washington to New York. In that meeting not only were research findings spelled out, but our dissemination problems were directly addressed. Cline listened and encouraged us to talk with him and his staff about possible follow-on dissemination efforts. At that time, Cline was trying to create a media program in his foundation, he was concerned about problems of social science research dissemination, and, as the father of a learning disabled child, he empathized. The fortuitous invitation was acknowledged and filed away for future use.

Reestablishing Contact

The last 7 months of the project, roughly extending from Thanksgiving 1973 to May 1974, can only be described as punishing. Working days of 14 to 16 hours were commonplace as maximum effort was expended to carry out all the necessary analyses and to get the final document written, edited, reviewed, and published within the contractual deadlines. At the same time, standards had to be maintained to ensure that our recommendations would not be dismissed out of hand on technical or methodological grounds. As draft chapters were completed, we forwarded them for review to the personnel responsible for the programs and services discussed, and to outside expert consultants. In the former case, we were not only attempting to enhance the quality of our study by having service program people comment on early drafts, but we were also attempting to regain policy makers' attention and to telegraph our assessments about current operations. In the latter case, we were trying to "buy some insur-

[7]Over 100 copies of the Rand reports were distributed as a result of the Child Welfare League contact; many of these came from on the spot requests, but most followed the publication of an article in the journal *Child Welfare*, noted earlier. As with all such broadcast dissemination one seldom knows which ideas will take root and be harvested.

[8]James S. Kakalik and Garry D. Brewer, "Services for Handicapped Youth: A Program Overview," in B. Famighetti et al. (eds.), *Education Yearbook 1974–1975*, New York: Macmillan Educational Corporation, 1975, pp. 174–188.

ance," doing all that we could to avoid technical or substantive errors and oversights, and to let the research and analysis community know that we were about to make some serious recommendations for change.

In the spring of 1974, officials of the Bureau of Education for the Handicapped within the Office of Education of the Department of Health, Education, and Welfare asked us to present an informal briefing for their staff. We did this, outlining most of the recommendations that were beginning to take shape in the final analyses and writing. This was an interesting meeting, and our work was received very well.

AFTER THE REPORTS WERE SUBMITTED

We were very much concerned with the dissemination issue as we struggled to finish the report within the contractual deadlines. We once again tried to mobilize the news media by preparing a press release and by making telephone calls to several of the specialty editors concerned with education, health, and children's affairs—primarily those who had been interested in the first year's work enough to cover it in their papers and journals. An executive summary was prepared highlighting the key points of the two reports. We thought that busy decision makers would read the summary quickly, but that their staffs and subordinates would then at leisure dig deeply into the analytic backup provided in the full reports. We gave this second report the same nationwide distribution, sending several hundred copies to both public and private officials and analysts who we thought might be able to use our findings and recommendations.

Our best laid plans went awry. Official Washington was at a near standstill as Watergate raged on. Despite the fact that our draft and then finished reports had been circulated early and often to the client in the Department of Health, Education, and Welfare, there was little or no follow-up by HEW personnel, e.g., requests for additional information, clarification, briefings. It was not until the Associated Press, taking materials provided in our routine press release, put some of the key recommendations out on its wire service that we heard from Washington, and what we heard was not entirely expected. The Under Secretary of HEW telephoned Rand management and requested explanations for the news stories that were breaking out all over the country. The key message was that they were not entirely prepared to respond to the many inquiries that they were receiving and that they did not appreciate this additional mini-crisis on top of all the other crises then dominating their lives.

Our client, the Assistant Secretary for Planning and Evaluation, requested a briefing and a project "wrap-up." We prepared carefully and departed for Washington not knowing exactly what kind of reception would be waiting for us. It was polite . . . and brief. In the thirty minutes we had, we tried to summarize two and a half years' work, some fifty recommendations, and the key features of the analytic approach that we had developed to do the job. To both the Assistant Secretary and his staff, we strongly emphasized the facts that we had probably assembled more detailed and comprehensive information about the entire service system than had ever been done before; that the service system had some very major problems; that our recommendations would help alleviate those problems; and that we would be willing to follow-up and assist them in using any aspect of the work that was of interest to them. Our arguments were not persuasive enough. They thanked us, and we departed.

We received very positive responses throughout the nation, however. Subsequent to our initial distribution, a total of about 1000 people have requested copies of our first report, and about 1900 people have requested copies of our full second report (as of July 1977). In addition, the abridged summary versions were requested by 2700 people. We have received and approved numerous requests to quote or use various data from our study in publications others were preparing. We have received and responded to numerous requests from various service and program personnel for information and assistance in planning and improving programs—these requests came from such diverse organizations as the U.S. Congressional Budget Office, the Office of the Assistant Secretary for Education of the Department of Health, Education, and Welfare, the Bureau of Education for the Handicapped, the Council for Exceptional Children, the Ford Foundation, and numerous state and local programs. University-based colleagues have been uniformly impressed with the methodological approach and have invited project members to come and discuss the project with their own staffs and researchers. And finally, there were letters from parents—poignant, touching, and reassuring in the sense that we had tried hard to make our messages understandable to this "client" group, and had apparently succeeded.

Were this the "normal" policy research project, that probably would have been the end of the matter. We who in a real sense knew most about the problems, and had some ideas about what might be done to improve the existing state of affairs, would have been detached from our work at just the point when our recommendations were being considered and remedial policies and programs were being thought through. The reports would have been dutifully filed away, and the research cycle would have proceeded pretty much as before. However, this has not been a "normal" project.

The Max C. Fleischmann Foundation

At about this time the Chairman of the Board of the Max C. Fleischmann Foundation asked us to use our research approach to study the mental health and mental retardation service system of the State of Nevada. The study was funded by the Foundation at the request of a committee of the Nevada Legislature. Work began on that project during the summer of 1974 and was completed in April 1976.[9] This work not only gave us more in-depth knowledge about services to mentally handicapped people, which helped us in generalizing our recommendations, but it also reaffirmed to us that our basic methodological approach was an acceptable way to understand and evaluate large-scale, complex systems.

During the same 1974–1976 time period, we also were able to do various things to further disseminate our earlier work for HEW and handicapped children.

The Rand Corporation

Besides the excellent support and working environment that Rand had provided us throughout the life of the official handicapped children's study, Rand management responded nicely to our request for corporate support to produce this book. We argued that a book would serve as a more permanent and accessible record of the entire project; that it would be distributed to broader and different audiences than the reports; that our earlier findings and recommendations could and should be generalized; and, furthermore, that publication of a book would, because of the elapsed time since the formal end of the project, hopefully rekindle interest and support for the many recommendations that had been made. Rand management agreed, and work was begun in the summer of 1975 on revisions, updates, and generalizations of the research reported in the two earlier reports. This book is, of course, the result.

The Center for Advanced Study in the Behavioral Sciences

Brewer had the extraordinary good fortune of being invited to spend the academic year 1974–1975 as a Fellow of the Center for Advanced

---

[9]James S. Kakalik, Garry D. Brewer, Linda L. Prusoff et al., *Mental Health and Mental Retardation Services in Nevada,* The Rand Corporation, R-1800-FLF, Santa Monica, California, April 1976.

Study in the Behavioral Sciences at Stanford, California. This remarkable institution prides itself on assembling forty or fifty scholars in a variety of disciplines for a one-year period, and then not demanding or programming a single feature of their existence. With fine administrative and research support, each fellow is allowed the ultimate luxury of doing whatever he chooses for an entire year—no questions asked and no strings attached.[10]

Besides the intellectual support and stimulation provided by several physicians and other professionals who shared in the year's experience,[11] Brewer was freed to puzzle over the dissemination questions posed by the handicapped children's project and then to do whatever could be done within a year to forward the recommendations and to recapture the elusive foci of public and official attention.

In August 1974, extensive discussions with Hugh F. Cline and his staff at the Russell Sage Foundation were reopened. They wanted to explore the general question of "increasing the use of social science research." They also were interested in the handicapped children's project and were concerned that the dissemination had not proceeded as well as it might have, given the importance of the problem and the directness of the recommendations that had been advanced. No one knew what exactly could be done, but all left those meetings feeling that this was an important opportunity requiring more attention and effort. By October, the rough outlines of an intense dissemination strategy began to take shape. (The results of these meetings are discussed subsequently in the section on dissemination of our direction service ideas.)

Elizabeth Berger, noted earlier as a contact we had made and a friend of children, also reappeared on the scene in 1974. California was well along in the creation of a mass identification program having many of the requisite properties outlined in our basic Rand research on identification. In this case, the political choice to move forward was being made in the 1973–1974 period in the form of the "Child Health and Disability Prevention Act" (CHDP), a state law requiring that all preschool children, somewhere between the ages of 3 and 5, be examined to determine whether or not they were either suffering from a possibly debilitating disorder or were at risk of becoming handicapped in the absence of prompt and appropriate remedial treatment services. Berger introduced people who were revising drafts of the Act to Brewer, who provided them with comments

---

[10]Particular gratitude is owed the Program on Science, Technology, and Society (POSTS), a special category of fellowship supported by the National Science Foundation's Research Applied to the Nation's Needs program, that made this year possible.

[11]Drs. Robert Haggerty, Osler Peterson, and Joe Wray were steadfast colleagues during this period.

on the draft legislation. From the beginning, however, those responsible for the drafting and successful passage of this California Act
knew that proper implementation would be a great hurdle.[12] The
basic problem was, having gotten a significant provision on the
books, to ensure that the legislation did not languish or suffer from
poor implementation. Monitoring the law's implementation was the
key, and indeed the *only,* insurance that the law's supporters could
conceive of to head off this unwanted eventuality. Berger and her
colleagues were in the process of creating an independent, nonprofit
research institution, the Children's Research Institute of California
(CRIC), whose initial responsibility would be to evaluate and monitor the about-to-be implemented California mass screening program.
Brewer joined the Board of CRIC and enlisted the support of David
Mechanic, also a Fellow at the Center, in formulating a research proposal that would accomplish the evaluation and monitoring tasks. In
January 1975, Brewer served as an *amicus curia* on CRIC's behalf for
the research proposal submitted by them to the Robert Wood Johnson Foundation, the nation's largest private source of research funds
in the health policy area.[13] By the summer of 1975, the Johnson Foundation awarded a substantial grant to CRIC, which then staffed and
set out to evaluate California's identification program.

In a world where one seldom receives something for nothing, the
"something" rendered was basic information developed in the Rand
research dealing with identification services and some slight help in
guiding one promising research-implementation effort for identification of handicapped children in California. In return, Berger and
CRIC made available a host of contacts, any one of whom could have
taken and used some portion of the Rand research. It was Berger, for
instance, who suggested that we use the staff and facilities of the
Golden Gate Regional Center in San Francisco as one primary site for
our documentary film on direction services, which we did (this activity will be discussed in detail momentarily).[14] It was Berger who

[12]Professor Randall McCathren, currently of Vanderbilt's Law Faculty and the Center
for the Study of Children and Families, was a key drafter and supporter of the law and
produced this insight in conversation.

[13]Beyond information contained in the Rand research reports and efforts to connect
the CRIC group with Mechanic and Dr. Robert Haggerty (another Fellow at the Center
for Advanced Study), Brewer did not have any direct hand in the drafting or staffing of
the CRIC project.

[14]This contact in turn led to contacts with Drs. Abraham and Rona Rudolph, the
latter being featured in the film and both of whom are interested in the issue of
professional sensitization for those dealing with handicapped children. It also led to
other contacts with the pediatric community nationwide.

made the initial connection to the Ford Foundation-sponsored "Children and Government" project at Berkeley's Law School.[15]

During his year at Stanford, Brewer also made several trips to New York and Washington to follow up on other promising leads for disseminating the results of the handicapped children's project.

The important message contained in all of this is that dissemination is a demanding calling. In this case, nearly a man-year was devoted in various ways to dissemination activities.

Looking back over our recommendations, by far the most significant potential change in services for handicapped children since 1974 has been in the area of special education, where a new era is beginning. Court rulings and legislative mandates have been issued promising appropriate education for all handicapped children. Potentially the most significant piece of legislation, *if it is fully funded,* is the "Education for All Handicapped Children Act of 1975," P.L. 94-142. This Act not only mandates an appropriate education for all handicapped children, but it requires identification of all school-age handicapped children, and authorizes appropriations of up to 40 percent of the excess cost of all special education. Our work may have contributed to passage of P.L. 94-142 in some small measure—primarily by arming advocates of the Act with evidence and ideas they could use to support their positions. However, as with most major policies, change is brought about by the fortuitous and timely combination of many different factors.

As indicated earlier, two different types of dissemination strategies followed the filing of the formal reports. First, we pursued a relatively conventional strategy of issuing a press release, giving briefings, mailing hundreds of copies of the reports, writing this book, and responding to requests for assistance. Second, with financial support from the Russell Sage Foundation, we were able to pursue an intense dissemination strategy with respect to our direction service recommendations. That intense dissemination strategy was successful; our proposed Regional Direction Centers are being demonstrated and evaluated throughout the nation.

INTENSE DISSEMINATION STRATEGY

The Russell Sage Foundation

By October 1974, staff members at the Russell Sage Foundation had decided and then convinced the Foundation's President, Hugh F.

---

[15]One of whose participants, David Kirp, had been instrumental in our thinking about labeling and stigmatization as they relate to the identification service and who later reappeared (1976) with Brewer and others as a member of the National Advisory Board to Nicholas Hobbs' Center for the Study of Children and Families at Vanderbilt University.

Cline, that the direction service was one suitable vehicle for a concerted dissemination effort. There were several reasons for this
choice.

It was a relatively new idea for matching handicapped children
with the various other service programs. There was no established
constituency within the service system responsible for providing direction. A need and a huge potential market for the service existed. If
people could be shown what direction was and how it might benefi-
cially affect the lives of handicapped children, then—or so the argument went—interest and discussion could be generated that would
in time lead to the acceptance of the direction service recommendations advanced in the second Rand Report. All best estimates indicated that direction could be provided relatively inexpensively, and
whatever the costs, benefits accruing from improved system operation and from improved measures of the individual's quality of life
(humane returns) would be high.

Having thus decided on direction as a focus for our intense dissemination strategy, and having obtained a promise of financial assistance from the Russell Sage Foundation, the next question was
how one should make the message more widely known—how to
market this social idea?[16]

The Status of Knowledge: The Media, the Message, and Policy

The amount and quality of research devoted to understanding and
improving the link between the communication media and those
who make and are responsible for policy are, respectively, small and
uneven. Assisted by a bibliography of over 400 books, articles, and
papers prepared by George Comstock and his associates,[17] we found
that little has been done on the impact of media on attitudes and
almost nothing on its impact on policy. Anthologies still republish
studies done thirty years ago on the success and failure of attempts to
change public opinion or attitudes, which are for the most part studies of the effects of propaganda efforts of World War II. Beginning in
1947 with Hyman and Sheatsley's "Some Reasons Why Information
Campaigns Fail," the fund of data collected over the years indicates

[16]This concept of social marketing is beginning to catch on. The Robert Wood
Johnson Foundation, for instance, has begun a modest "social marketing" program. A
Council on Applied Social Science Research has recently been instituted in Washing-
ton to address the more general research use questions. And a Dissemination and
Resource Group within the National Institute of Education is now in operation. There
may be others as well; the topic is ripe.

[17]George Comstock, *Television in Human Behavior: The Key Studies,* The Rand Corporation, R-1747, Santa Monica, California, June 1975.

that the publics most apt to respond to mass-media information messages have a prior interest in the subject areas presented. This finding was encouraging as we intended to induce an already concerned segment of the population to better define their direction problems and consider new solutions in the coordinated delivery of services.

Robert Merton, who gave wise counsel during this phase of the extended project, reminded us of his earlier work with Paul Lazarsfeld that pointed out that the mass media confer status on public issues, persons, organizations, and social movements and that handicapped children were in need of just this kind of status boost. He also noted that mass media campaigns force deviations from a societal norm into view, and that once in view, politicians, bureaucrats, and other authorities are often forced to do something—to take some action.

Evidence of a distinct gap between those who possess the requisite substantive and research skills and those having presentational and promotional skills startled us. Those who know how to communicate seldom have the time, training, or budget to do the research required to inform and guide the production of films or other mass media where the subject matter is complex; and those who possess research skills seldom have the time, training, budget, or inclination to produce understandable segments of their work in forms that can be widely shared and understood. Clearly, an integration of presentational and research skills and proficiencies is called for; however, such an integration rarely exists in practice. We explored this gap with media professionals.

Media men, such as Fred Friendly and Av Westin, an ABC Vice President and Executive Producer of the ABC Evening News, are convinced of the direct impact of television on policy. In fact, the research division of ABC has published a monograph which details the impact of the ABC News *Closeup* programs. From this publication and from interviews with television news and documentary personnel, one might conclude that *Closeup* alone is responsible for changes in law or policy concerning the subjects its programs explored. Regrettably, the total picture, including the political framework, were not explained in the publication and were not discernible in interviews with those in the media business.[18]

Discussions with other leading journalists, documentary film makers, and critics in the field of television news and documentaries

[18]Among those interviewed at this stage were Harrison Salisbury of *The New York Times* and WNET, Joseph Klapper, Director of Research at CBS, William Greeley, Television Editor of *Variety*, Steven Schuer of *TV Key*, and Marcia Leslie and Thomas Bywaters, producers of ABC news and documentary segments.

point up the fact that no one really knows what the role of television and other mass media is in the formulation of policy. From all of this, we realized that whatever mass media efforts we would expend, promoting direction services would be risky and speculative.

A Cautious Approach

Rather than plunging headlong into unchartered territory, it was decided to proceed in stages. The first stage was a feasibility study of some six months duration that was meant to answer a few general questions: How can the direction service be brought into the public consciousness? Who could help with this effort? What media should be relied on to communicate the message?

We decided to try a documentary film, the first step of which was the identification of the general problem of direction—or rather the lack of direction. Our intention was to show that direction was a needed service that probably did not exist because those not having handicapped children assume that finding all needed services is simply a question of going to a pediatrician, the public health department, or the school for assistance; in fact, it is a far more complicated matter than this since no single source has information on the entire service system. We also reasoned that direction probably did not exist because most people within the service system are concerned primarily with their own organization, do not have time to look far beyond it, and do not usually think of the child as a whole person needing other services they do not provide. Both of these lines of thought became central themes of the film.

We went into the field to find families who had had difficulty in locating proper services for their child; we wanted real people to tell their stories. Due to the sensitive nature of this issue, and the pain that many families have suffered in their quest for needed services, our efforts during the pre-interview phase were somewhat circumspect. We talked with provider agencies mainly, trying to locate families who might be interested in the project and willing to be filmed—to share their own experiences.

A choice was made very early in this project not to slant the message in sensational or lurid ways. We wanted to stress the positive to the greatest extent possible: direction often does exist in some form or another, and when it exists, the kinds of benefits postulated in the original research do in fact accrue. This choice led us very quickly to California and the system of regional centers for mentally retarded children that had been highlighted in our Rand research report. These centers are not ideal examples of the direction service, as conceived in the research, but they provide many "direction-like" services among an array of other things that they try to do for handicapped children. We zeroed in on the Golden Gate Regional Center in San Francisco as being a positive example of what we thought the direction service should be.

It was important to show how this center works, to let the people responsible for it talk about themselves and their jobs. In our preliminary perusal of the scanty research on media and policy we did learn that bureaucrats and service personnel are far more likely to implement a new idea that they can see has worked and is actually demonstrated as successful than they are to move forward with the same information delivered at a seminar or conference, but not concretely demonstrated.

The Film: "What Do We Do Now?"

Between July 1975 and February 1976, nearly full time efforts were expended in the production of a thirty-minute film about direction: "What Do We Do Now?"[19] To ensure that the technical quality of the film would not be impeded and hence degrade the promotional messages that it contained, a highly respected documentary film production company was hired. Drew Associates of New York City have been in the documentary business for over a decade, are responsible for many award winning films, and specialize in many of the techniques we wanted to employ, e.g., real people "telling their own stories," synchronous sound, and other specialized procedures and processes. Russell Sage Foundation provided a full-time project leader who had worked in publishing, educational film, and commercial television, e.g., she produced a local Emmy-winning television news and documentary show in New York. She was also genuinely interested in the issues of serving handicapped children and using the media to translate and disseminate social science research results. The Russell Sage Foundation also allowed one of the original researchers from the Rand project to participate in all aspects of the film's production. (For instance, before filming families, the crew was briefed on what the particular family had experienced and how this experience fit into the general themes being developed in the film; the researcher also assisted in most phases of editing and assembly at the conclusion of shooting, and most of the sequences were filmed with the researcher doing the off-camera interviewing.)

[19]This film is being distributed through the National Media Center, funded by the U.S. Bureau of Education for the Handicapped at the University of Indiana, and is available to any interested individual or group for a modest rental fee. It is also available from Modern Talking Pictures, the largest commercial film distributor in America.

The coincidence of the film product with the findings of the research was the result of this collaboration which bridged the gap of
specialization between media practitioners and social scientists.

Dissemination

The third and final phase of the Russell Sage Foundation project was
designated for dissemination. We planned on showing the film in
those settings where it was made: San Francisco, where the Golden
Gate Regional Center's operations and selected clients were filmed;
San Diego, where Dr. Frederick Frye, a pediatrician who provides a
one-man direction service and a patient were filmed; and in Washington, D.C., where Congressman Clare Burgener, the father of a
handicapped child, was filmed. Our intention was to involve these
most highly interested and involved publics in our preliminary dissemination efforts and to see how the film communicated the direction idea. Such information would prove useful, so went our thinking
on the matter, in guiding more widespread and general distribution
efforts.

We also contacted program directors of television stations in these
three cities and elicited firm interest in seeing the film and then determining whether or not to show it to their own audiences and/or to
sponsor the film for broadcast over the entire Public Broadcasting
Service network. Involvement of the local television stations was
judged to be critical not only for their potential sponsorship of a
national feed for the film but more important for the local support
that they might be able to bring to on-the-air discussions between
service providers and the families of the handicapped.[20] We planned
on working with these selected television stations to provide for effective discussion and follow-up, both of which were meant to improve public understanding of the complex needs of serving handicapped children and to demonstrate how direction centers could
help meet those needs.

Other dissemination plans included the preparation of an information brochure for use by families and servers, a brochure that could
supplement the film, but go beyond the more general messages it
contained to describe how one might go about getting a direction
center started. This pamphlet was also designed to encourage the
reader to refer back to the original Rand documentation for more
carefully laid out procedures and practices. To ensure that the information brochure did not overreach our intended audience, plans

---

[20]Merton pointed out the importance of such supplementary, face-to-face discussion in improving the effectiveness of mass communication.

were made to enlist the assistance of those families and professionals who had been of major help in the production of the film to prepare the textual materials.

We began making arrangements with the Golden Gate Regional Center and others in the California system to serve as points of contact for inquiries generated by the film. They were routinely receiving requests for information and briefings about their operations, and we felt that the film and brochure would go a long way toward relieving operational personnel from this important, but often burdensome, requirement.

Official channels of communication were not ignored in our promotional strategizing. A public information center operated by the Department of Health, Education, and Welfare, "Closer Look," is in contact with a great number of organizations serving handicapped children and with many families of handicapped children (see Chap. 10 for details). News of the film's existence and availability were scheduled for publication in a newsletter produced at "Closer Look"; this appeared to be an important outlet to a concerned public.

Private agencies serving handicapped children were another potential resource, and meetings were planned for showings of the film and discussions with the Council for Exceptional Children, a national organization concerned with handicapped children, the National Easter Seal Society, and other such organizations.

Pediatricians are an important source of information for the families of handicapped children, but many of them are not as aware as they might be of the multiple needs of their handicapped charges, and fewer still have the time to be as knowledgeable as they might be about the full range of programs and services that exist especially for these children. Working through the good offices of Dr. Robert Haggerty, who was also a Fellow at the Center for Advanced Study during Brewer's tenure and who is himself a pediatrician of national stature, arrangements were made to have the film shown to national and regional meetings of the American Academy of Pediatrics. Other service-providing professional groups were likewise identified, and plans were drawn to involve them in the dissemination process.

All of these initiatives were, to varying degrees, pursued in the period from mid-1975 to the end of 1976, when the Russell Sage Foundation portion of our dissemination efforts terminated. However, from the standpoint of capturing the attention of key decision makers and encouraging them to consider and then act on the recommendations for the direction service, a main objective of the film exercise, it was a succession of contacts and connections with officials of the U.S. Bureau of Education for the Handicapped (within HEW) that very rapidly paid off.

Action: The Bureau of Education for the Handicapped

The Bureau of Education for the Handicapped (BEH) is one of the most critical governmental organizations for social policy affecting the lives of handicapped children. It is responsible for implementing the provisions of several key pieces of federal legislation for handicapped children (see Chap. 10). This agency was one sponsor of the original Rand Corporation handicapped children's study, although the project itself was officially done for the office of the Assistant Secretary for Planning and Evaluation of the U.S. Department of Health, Education, and Welfare.

The direction center idea was favorably noted by BEH personnel in response to briefings and written drafts of the Rand reports in the 1973–74 period, but apparently nothing tangible was done to follow up on these favorable beginnings.

The first stirrings of major BEH interest came during the feasibility phase of the Russell Sage Foundation project ("A Cautious Approach," above). Shelley Marshall, the principal investigator and film producer from the Foundation, learned about Dr. Harvey Liebergott, who had been in charge of a BEH-sponsored television show featuring public reaction and response to the landmark Pennsylvania Association for Retarded Children legal case mandating schools to provide an appropriate education for every retarded child. Liebergott, who works out of the Boston regional office of the Department of Health, Education, and Welfare, turned out to be an enthusiastic and relentless aid to communication between the Russell Sage personnel and the BEH leadership. When contacted, he was in the process of setting up a type of direction center staffed by volunteer parents from the Special Education Coalition in Massachusetts. Ironically, he was not aware of the Rand reports or the analysis and recommendations about direction they contained. Rather, he was developing a direction concept because he saw the need for it in his practical work in the field.

After extensive correspondence (and sending him copies of the basic research documents) Marshall and Brewer had a fruitful meeting with Liebergott in Boston in January 1975. Not only was he a strong ally and constructive aid in making contact with several television stations, but he suggested that we film Congressman Burgener and Ed Martin, the Head of BEH, which we did. Before filming them in October 1975, however, this contact led to an invitation from Martin and his deputy, Robert Herman, to Brewer to address all thirteen special education Regional Resource Center directors (a program run under BEH auspices) at a special session of the meeting of the Council on Exceptional Children. Details of the direction center concept were spelled out, and a summary of the Russell Sage and Rand Corporation projects on handicapped children was given.

Informal discussions continued with BEH personnel during the summer of 1975, and by November a clear decision had been reached to follow through with the Rand direction center service recommendations. Some $7 million dollars of BEH funds were earmarked for use in the development of several prototype direction centers around the country; furthermore, these centers were to be tried out for a three-year period and, if successful, the final replication and diffusion of the idea and service were to follow on a nationwide basis.

This happy result requires some additional comment to put it into perspective. Regional Resource Centers (RRCs) could be turned into direction-like activities without changing their basic enabling legislation; they are an important institution-in-being. Adjustments in operation would be mostly procedural and depend upon the directors' understanding of the direction concept and their desire to make the recommended changes. While the Rand report noted that the newly created Office for Handicapped Individuals (OHI) would be an ideal federal focus for direction center activities, OHI does not have a sufficient budget to fund even a demonstration of the concept. Implementation by BEH-controlled RRCs is judged to be better than no implementation at all. With appropriate care and a great deal of on-site attention, this less-than-ideal alternative was selected to be the policy instrument to try out the direction idea.

BEH has gone several steps beyond making this one decision and has used the film, "What Do We Do Now?" to instruct those charged with creating direction services in the demonstration sites and to make the film available through its own extensive National Media Center to anyone else interested in the service.

Implementation

Using verbatim segments of the Rand report related to direction services, BEH circulated a request-for-proposal to all the Regional Resource Centers in December 1975. From all the proposals that this elicited, a number of demonstration sites were selected around the country. Such sites were intended to try the idea out in a variety of social and geographical settings and to do so with varying levels of financial support. For instance, Independence, Missouri, was known to have ample services available in the Kansas City area, but such services were not always as well used as they might be with some additional direction assistance; Portland, Oregon, and Vancouver, Washington—just across the river—provided different settings, although the general need for direction was also evident; Price, Utah, located in a relatively remote section of the country, offered different challenges and opportunities; and so forth for the whole range of sites selected for the demonstration. Brewer was invited and agreed to serve as an advisor to BEH for the first year of the direction demonstrations.

At the moment (early 1977), the demonstrations have been in operation for less than a year, but several of them have already established their credibility and usefulness. While it is too early—and probably not appropriate—to judge the viability and success of these demonstrations, early returns have been encouraging. Direction is a needed service, and the demonstration centers as conceived have the potential for providing this service at bearable costs. Consumer reactions have been uniformly satisfying; many have remarked that they really did not know what they had been missing in the pre-direction years and that the service was greatly appreciated. Physicians and other key professionals are beginning to understand what the service is (and is not) and to make full and appropriate use of it for their handicapped clientele. Questions about funding beyond the three-year demonstration period and replication are being raised, and rightly so. With continuing good luck and several valid success stories, many of us who have been involved are optimistic that the necessary and appropriate "next steps" will be discovered and taken to ensure the continuance and spread of this service. All are mindful, however, that there is no such thing as a sure thing in the public policy arena.

THE POLICY PROCESS

This case is an interesting example of the policy process in operation. Beginning with an early sensing of a problem, i.e., families needed information and support in their quest for needed services for their handicapped children, the process next moved into an analytic or estimation stage where various alternative ways that this problem might be overcome were explored. These explorations are documented in Chap. 8 of this book. The process appeared to have stopped at that point, the development of the analyses and attendant recommendations, but because of a rare convergence of chance and opportunity, additional promotional efforts were allowed under the auspices of a private foundation. Because of these private initiatives, public sector decision makers were encouraged to reexamine the options and to decide on a course of action, the selection phase of the policy process. Implementation followed rather quickly after the choice was made, and preliminary evaluations of that partial implementation are now underway. At every phase of the process there was continuity of personnel. At every phase of the process there was continuity of the idea. At every phase of the process many different people worked hard to make an idea come to life in just the ways intended.

It has been a rare and extraordinarily rewarding experience.

A POST SCRIPT

As a courtesy to then-Secretary of Health, Education, and Welfare, F. David Mathews, the President of Russell Sage Foundation sent him a letter outlining the Foundation's efforts and inviting Mathews to view the film, "What Do We Do Now?" In July 1976, Mathews and nine or ten members of his staff and those of the Under Secretary and the Assistant Secretary for Planning and Evaluation spent more than an hour watching the film and learning about direction, the BEH initiatives, and more about the original Rand research.[21] It is our view that as important as the original research reports had been, it was the dramatic, visual presentation of one set of messages from those reports that enabled us to regain the attention of top officials and to redirect public efforts in ways indicated and hoped for earlier. The film had, in effect, accomplished what we had dreamed it would.

In the spring of 1977, the film and its producers were awarded a CINÉ "Golden Eagle," a highly respected national achievement, in the category of documentaries stressing social responsibility. This award came as an unexpected bonus and reassurance that the film had maintained high technical and professional standards.[22] We have shared this experience with colleagues in a variety of fields. Presentations of the film and a version of this tale have been given to the President's Committee on Mental Retardation, to the staff of the President's Commission on Mental Health, to the Policy Committee of the Ford Foundation, to Dr. David Rogers and his staff at the Robert Wood Johnson Foundation, to Dr. Roger Levien and others at the International Institute for Applied Systems Analysis, and to numerous other professional colleagues and associations concerned about applied social research, the use of media, and handicapped children—

---

[21]Another 15 sets of the Rand reports were sent as a result: none of them was aware of the work.

[22]CINÉ is the Council on International Nontheatrical Events. The "Golden Eagle" award is much sought after and confers status on its recipients; e.g., winning films are presented in foreign film contests and festivals as official United States entries in their respective categories.

most of all to those concerned about handicapped children. It is to this latter group that our efforts have always been directed, and it is for this group that the film will serve as a continuing reminder of their needs and possibilities.

NEXT STEPS AND NEW CHALLENGES

A great deal of positive activity exists and has been reported through-out this book. Hundreds of thousands of dedicated professionals are daily laboring on behalf of handicapped children, and to them go our highest accolades—they have earned them. What concerns us is that so very much more is needed and can be accomplished—much of it without enormous expenditures of additional money.

We wish to leave the reader with several "big" questions and issues that hold the keys to making some of this long-overdue progress.

- How can the responsible government officials be better served in the tasks of managing and creating programs and services for handicapped children? What role does analysis have to play in this regard?
- How can comprehensive research strategies, such as that demonstrated in this book, be improved on and exemplified in other policy settings?
- How is the nation to create the improved service institutions that are going to be needed to address the old, emerging, and changing problems of this nation's handicapped people? Who will take the initiatives? Who is to share the responsibility?
- What can be done to reduce the gaps that exist between those specialized to the research task and those vested with authority for decision making? How can specialized knowledge be made more generally available and understandable to the public, to those most directly affected by the research, and to those who must act?
- With what mechanisms and procedures should the nation provide services at reasonable costs for the benefit of our vast unserved and inadequately served handicapped population? What talents are needed? How shall personnel be trained? And with what programmatic responsibilities should various types of person-nel, various types of agencies, and various different levels of government be entrusted?

We dedicate this book to a proposition nearly as old as civilization "The blessing is not in living, but in living well."[23] We hope for noth-ing less.

[23]Seneca, 63 A.D.

INDEX

LIST OF SELECTED RAND BOOKS

Averch, Harvey A., et al., *How Effective Is Schooling? A Critical Review of Research*, Educational Technology Publications, Englewood Cliffs, N.J., 1974.

Dalkey, Norman C., *Studies in the Quality of Life: Delphi and Decisionmaking*, D. C. Heath and Company, Lexington, Mass., 1972.

Fisher, Gene H., *Cost Considerations in Systems Analysis*, Elsevier Publishing Company, Amsterdam, distributed by American Elsevier Publishing Company of New York, 1971.

Greenwood, Peter W., Jan Chaiken, and Joan Petersilia, *The Criminal Investigation Process*, D. C. Heath and Company, Lexington, Mass., 1977.

Kakalik, James S., and Sorrel Wildhorn, *The Private Police: Security and Danger*, Crane, Russak and Company, New York, 1977.

Quade, E. S., *Analysis for Public Decisions*, Elsevier Publishing Company, Amsterdam, distributed by American Elsevier Publishing Company of New York, 1975.

Quade, E. S., and W. I. Boucher, *Systems Analysis and Policy Planning: Applications in Defense*, Elsevier Publishing Company, Amsterdam, distributed by American Elsevier Publishing Company of New York, 1968.

Wildhorn, Sorrel, Marvin Lavin, and Anthony Pascal, *Indicators of Justice: Measuring the Performance of Prosecution, Defense, and Court Agencies Involved in Felony Proceedings*, D. C. Heath and Company, Lexington, Mass., 1977.

Williams, John D., *The Compleat Strategyst: Being a Primer on the Theory of Games of Strategy*, McGraw-Hill Book Company, New York, 1954.

Wirt, John G., Arnold J. Lieberman, and Roger E. Levien, *R&D Management: Methods Used by Federal Agencies,* D. C. Heath and Company, Lexington, Mass., 1975.

Yin, Robert K., Karen A. Heald, and Mary E. Vogel, *Tinkering with the System: Technological Innovations in State and Local Services,* D. C. Heath and Company, Lexington, Mass., 1977.